A COMPARATIVE ANALYSIS OF Complex Organizations

A Comparative Analysis of Complex Organizations

On Power, Involvement, and Their Correlates

BY AMITAI ETZIONI

Revised and Enlarged Edition

THE FREE PRESS
A Division of Macmillan Publishing Co., Inc.
NEW YORK

Collier Macmillan Publishers
LONDON

The Free Press
A Division of Macmillan Publishing Co., Inc.
866 Third Avenue, New York, N.Y. 10022

Collier Macmillan Canada, Ltd.

Library of Congress Catalog Card Number: 74-21488

Printed in the United States of America

First Free Press Paperback Edition 1971

printing number

5 6 7 8 9 10

Library of Congress Cataloging in Publication Data

Etzioni, Amitai.
    A comparative analysis of complex organizations.

    Bibliography: p.
    Includes index.
    1. Organization. I. Title. II. Title:
Complex organizations.
HM131.E78 1975   301.18'32   74-21488
ISBN 0-02-909650-2
ISBN 0-02-909620-0 pbk.

The author gratefully acknowledges permission to reprint the following material:
    Table III-1, page 45. Reprinted by permission of the publisher from Nellie M. Campbell, *The Elementary School Teacher's Treatment of Classroom Behavior Problems* (New York: Teachers College Press, 1935), pp. 22–23.
    Table, page 53. From L. H. Orzack, "Work as a Central Life Interest of Professionals," *Social Problems,* Vol. 7, No. 2 (1959), p. 127. Reprinted by permission of The Society for the Study of Social Problems and the author.
    Table XI-1, page 289. Reprinted by permission of the publisher from *The Dock Worker,* by Members of the Staff of the Industrial Research Section, Department of Sociology, University of Liverpool (Liverpool, Eng.: Liverpool University Press, 1954), p. 82.
    Table XI-2, page 295. Reprinted by permission of the publisher from Stanley E. Seashore, *Group Cohesiveness in the Industrial Work Group* (Ann Arbor: Institute for Social Research of The University of Michigan, 1954), p. 67.

*For the investigators
of compliance*

CONTENTS

ACKNOWLEDGMENTS   *ix*

INTRODUCTION TO THE FIRST EDITION   *xi*

INTRODUCTION TO THE REVISED AND ENLARGED EDITION   *xxi*

Part One: TOWARD AN ANALYTICAL TYPOLOGY

  I.   Compliance as a Comparative Base   *3*

 II.   An Analytical Classification: Coercive and Utilitarian
     Organizations   *23*

III.   An Analytical Classification: Normative and Dual
     Organizations   *40*

 IV.   The Compliance Thesis Revisited   *68*

Part Two: CORRELATES OF COMPLIANCE: GOALS,
EFFECTIVENESS, AND ELITES

  V.   Compliance, Goals, and Effectiveness   *103*

 VI.   Goals and Effectiveness Revisited   *121*

VII.   Compliance and Organizational Elites   153
VIII.   Compliance and Elites Revisited   191

        Part Three: OTHER CORRELATES OF COMPLIANCE

IX.   Compliance and Cultural Integration: Consensus,
        Communication, and Socialization   231
X.   Compliance and Organizational Environment: Recruitment,
        Scope, and Pervasiveness   255
XI.   Cohesion and Compliance   279
XII.   Compliance and the Distribution of Charisma   303
XIII.   Organizational Controls of Charisma   335
XIV.   Other Correlates Revisited   365
XV.   Other Correlates Revisited: A Causal Analysis   392

        Part Four: COMPLIANCE IN A DYNAMIC PERSPECTIVE

XVI.   Concomitant and Successive Division of Compliance   421
XVII.   New Directions   453

        LIST OF NEW COMPLIANCE STUDIES CITED   506

        SELECTED BIBLIOGRAPHY   511

        NAME INDEX   557

        SUBJECT INDEX   572

ACKNOWLEDGMENTS

TO THE FIRST EDITION

This book gives me the first opportunity to acknowledge my debts to my teachers. My first sociology teachers included Martin Buber, Joseph Ben-David and Jacob Katz; in particular I am indebted to the teaching of S. N. Eisenstadt and Yonina Garber-Talmon, all at the Hebrew University in Jerusalem. Work in the *kibbutzim* project directed by Yonina was the source of much of my research training. Nathan Rotenstreich, Yehoshua Bar-Hillel, Hugo S. Bergman, and Edward Poznanski were my teachers in philosophy. Don Patinkin and the late Alfred Bonne introduced me to economics.

The foundation for this endeavor was laid at the University of California at Berkeley, during my study with Reinhard Bendix, Philip Selznick, and Seymour Martin Lipset. The highly stimulating work with Marty Lipset, more than with any other teacher or colleague, guided my efforts.

I am indebted at least as much to my colleagues at Columbia University. Paul F. Lazarsfeld's way of looking at and analyzing data has a salutory effect on my own, particularly with respect to historical documents. William J. Goode's room at the top (of the Alumni House) was a place where more than one theoretical dilemma which blocked the author was solved. Comments by Herbert H. Hyman and Leo A. Goodman improved the methodological sections of this book.

The scope of my indebtedness to Talcott Parsons' analytical framework is best judged by the frequency with which his work and that of his associates is referred to in the text. The paradigm for functional analysis of Robert K. Merton and his conception of middle range theory were guide posts of this endeavor.

Participation in an informal seminar on complex organization at Columbia supplied an opportunity to mold, test, and, hopefully, to improve some of the ideas which are included in this volume. Members of the seminar who commented on parts of the manuscript were: Mary Jean Cornish, William Glaser, Terrence K. Hopkins, Renate Mayntz, Immanuel Wallerstein, Morris Zelditch, Jr., and in particular, David Caplovitz and William Martin. William Taber, John Meyer, and Candace Rogers served as research assistants. Miss Rogers worked with me on improving the manuscript in the long year between the second draft and publication.

I am especially indebted to Arthur L. Stinchcombe, who read each chapter as the work progressed and raised many critical questions. Without the significant comments, patience, and support of Eva Etzioni, this book would never have been written.

The comments of the students in my classes on complex organizations over the last three years were a major source of the kind of stimuli and response an author finds helpful in developing his ideas.

The Columbia University Council for Social Research supplied me with the facilities to prepare this work; a Social Science Research Faculty Fellowship enabled me to complete it. Their assistance is hereby gratefully acknowledged.

TO THE REVISED AND ENLARGED EDITION

In preparing this edition I benefited from the research assistance of Steven Crawford, Pamela Doty, Wolfgang Streeck, and Carol Morrow. In addition, Wolfgang Streeck critically reviewed all my interpretations of the data included here and helped me immensely in my effort to do justice to the authors reviewed. I am particularly indebted to the authors of most of the newly cited works for comments on my discussion of their work. Trish McKeon meticulously typed and retyped the manuscripts and supervised the burgeoning compliance file system, in a most normative manner.

A. E.

INTRODUCTION TO THE
FIRST EDITION

The comparative study of organization[1] is a much neglected field. Its development requires "middle range" organizational theory, falling between high-level abstractions about the characteristics of organizations in general and detailed observations about single cases. Models for the analysis of various organizational types must be constructed. In this book an effort is made to contribute to the formulation of such models through the study of organizational

1. By *organization* we mean, following Parsons (1960, p. 17), social units devoted primarily to attainment of specific goals. Organizations discussed in this volume are complex and have many of the characteristics Weber specified as "bureaucratic." Thus in this volume *organization* stands for "complex bureaucratic organization." Some writers have used *establishment* or *social establishment* to refer to the same phenomenon (Goffman, 1957, p. 43; Janowitz, 1959, p. 7). The term *institution* is sometimes used to refer to organizations and sometimes to designate a normative principle which organizes behavior from the viewpoint of some social function (Hughes, 1942; Ellsworth, 1952, pp. 263-68). Because of this ambiguity, the term will be avoided here. *Formal organization* refers to only one segment of organizational activities, such as regulations and formal communications, and hence should not be equated with the organization as a whole. *Social organization* refers to a different class of sociological phenomena, encompassing all human behavior that is socially regulated (Cooley, 1915; Greer, 1955, p. 6). Thus, social organization is a characteristic of social units; organizations are a type of social unit.

Complete bibliographical details for the references cited in the text appear in the Bibliography.

control and related variables. Numerous published and unpublished studies are drawn on for the development and illustration of propositions.

COMPARATIVE RESEARCH: TOWARD MIDDLE-RANGE ORGANIZATIONAL THEORY

Until recently, the yield of most organizational research has fallen into one of two categories: (*a*) statements on one organization or organizational unit, based chiefly on case studies; this approach has yielded insights and information on which much of the following discussion is based; (*b*) statements concerning general characteristics of organizations. These statements constitute the "upper" level of organizational theory, which this study seeks to supplement with middle-range theoretical statements. Organizational analysis has reached the stage where it becomes crucial to study systematic differences among the various social units classed as organizations. At the same time, the large number of empirical studies now available makes such a comparative examination possible.

The comparative analysis of organizations will lead to a richer and more precise organizational theory. It will be richer because, to the statements on "universal" characteristics of organization, many new statements concerning "specifics" will be added.[2] It will be more precise because many of the propositions which make up general organizational theory are not yet validated. One aspect of validation is to test for the extent of applicability. If we take, for example, the hundreds of propositions which have been examined, codified, or formulated by March and Simon (1958), we see that so far the extent of applicability of very few statements has been tested. Do all the propositions presented apply to the same universe of organizations? The same question must be asked about most general statements about organizations.

The Weberian model, for example, applies particularly to business and governmental bureaucracies, and in part to hierarchical churches

2. Linton (1936, p. 272) distinguished between universal and special cultural elements. The first are shared by "all sane, adult members" of a society; the latter, by subgroups. It might be helpful to apply these terms to theoretical discourse, by distinguishing between universal statements, which apply to all members of a category, and specific statements, which apply only to members of subcategories. On universal (or general) and specific propositions in administrative theory see also Litchfield (1956).

and some military organizations as well. But when we consider prisons, universities, hospitals, research organizations, egalitarian churches, schools, political parties, and labor unions, many propositions must be modified or specified considerably before they hold true. Most of this book supplies evidence to that effect, but the chapters dealing with charisma and with organizational elites are particularly relevant.

Many case studies of organizations close with some universal statements about organizational variables "based" on the study of one organization. Researchers are often lured into such overgeneralization for lack of a middle-range theory which would allow the formulation of specific statements—that is, statements concerning subcategories of organizations. The researcher has no choice but to see his findings as idiosyncratic or else to show their relation to general organizational theory. Thus the lack of comparative models leads not only to overgeneralization but also to undergeneralization. Findings which cannot be related to the highest level of abstraction are left on the lowest level, their relevance for middle-range statements unobserved.

Since there is only one model of bureaucracy, the tendency is to emphasize similarities, while the differences are seen as "exceptions." On the one hand, organizations are reported, again and again, to have regulations, hierarchies, centers of command, and so on. On the other hand, the fact that "the organization studied here does not . . ." have this or that element of the general model is usually recorded with surprise and as an isolated fact, though several authors have pointed out that the Weberian model does not "fit" the organization they studied. D. Granick (1954, pp. 262 ff.), for example, in his study of industrial management in Soviet Russia, shows that Soviet administration does not follow Weber's model, and that in fact it might be dysfunctional for it to do so; that is, another model is required. Fallers (1956, pp. 238-50) reached the same conclusion in his analysis of Bantu bureaucracy, as did Caplow (1953, p. 9) in his discussion of the Navy and Janowitz (1959, p. 36) in his study of combat armies.

Policy recommendations based on such a "universal" model can lead to ill-advised action. Consultants working with one of the universal models, such as the Weberian model or that of the human relations school, tend to recommend changes designed to bring the organization into line with the model. Since the general models as a rule include some specific statements which appear as universals, the consequences may be regrettable. A typical example is supplied by the recommendations given to the Catholic Church by a management consultant firm. The model used is obviously based on the study of large business corporations such as General Motors, and the major recommendations are that the Church maintain depreciation reserves and delegate part of the Pope's authority to his staff and subordinates (*Management Audit*, 1956). Such an approach overlooks features peculiar to the Church which may make recommendations of this kind inappropriate.

Eventually, the comparative study of organizations will:

1. Establish the truly universal propositions of organizational theory.
2. Reduce overgeneralized propositions to middle-range (specific) statements, specifying the categories of organizations for which they hold.
3. Develop new middle-range propositions, so that knowledge of universals will be supplemented with statements about analytical types of organization. Studies in the near future will probably contribute more directly to the development of such submodels than to the general model, since the former have been most neglected.

An extra bonus offered by the comparative approach has long been recognized, in particular by anthropologists. As Ruth Benedict pointed out in *Patterns of Culure*, comparative studies release us from the boundaries of our habits of thought, and show us the wide gamut of patterns possible in human interaction. This applies to the comparative analysis of organizations as well as to the comparative study of other social units.

COMPLIANCE AS A BASE FOR COMPARISON

The value of a comparison depends on the nature of its base; that is, on the nature of the variable or variables chosen to classify the units into subcategories for comparison. Such a variable must be selected on two criteria: It should be one of a set of related variables —that is, part of a theory; and it should lead to statements which are significant for the problems of the researcher. The significance of the variable used here lies, we shall see, in its relevance to the problem of social order.

We have chosen the nature of compliance in the organization as the basis for classification. Compliance is a relationship consisting of the power employed by superiors to control subordinates and the orientation of the subordinates to this power. Thus, the study combines a structural and a motivational aspect: structural, since we are concerned with the kinds and distribution of power in organizations; motivational, since we are concerned with the differential commitments of actors to organizations (as units which exercise power over them). It seems to us that the articulation of the social system and the personality system reflected in this combination is one element essential to organizational analysis.

Compliance, we intend to show, is related to many other organizational variables. Organizations which differ in their compliance structure tend also to differ in the goals they pursue; in the kind, location, power, and interaction of their elites; in the level and kinds of consensus attained and in the communications and socialization employed to attain it; in recruitment, scope, and pervasiveness; and in the distribution and control of charismatic participants. Moreover, organizations which differ in their compliance structure tend also to differ in the way they allocate tasks and power over time.

COMPLIANCE AND THE PROBLEM OF SOCIAL ORDER

We accede here to the professional norm which urges an author to show in his introduction the wider context in which his work may be placed. Broadly interpreted, the study of compliance may contribute to the study of social order.

Sociology was born out of the intellectual search for a secular and empirical explanation of social order. Three major sociological approaches emerged, each locating the source of social order in a different factor. The elite approach has focused on the hierarchical distribution of force.[3] The Marxian approach emphasizes property relations, seeing the organs of violence (the state) and normative elements (ideology) as secondary powers, dependent on the distribution of ownership. The normative approach emerges primarily

---

3. E.g., Pareto (1960, pp. 269-81).

from a synthesis of Weber's study of the role of ideas in social action and Durkheim's study of shared sentiments.[4]

Modern sociology has drawn on all three sources in the study of social order, which continues to be one of its cardinal themes (e.g., MacIver and Page, 1949; Bierstedt, 1957). But, as has often been pointed out, the relative weight given to the three elements has not been equal (Coser, 1956, pp. 15-31; Dahrendorf, 1959, p. 159; Aron, 1957, pp. 118-35).[5] The normative elements of social behavior have been given much attention in both research and theoretical writing. Varying degrees of attention have been given to the market and other economic regulating factors. Paraphrasing Durkheim, we might say that the emphasis on precontractual relations has led to the neglect of contractual relations. Force is usually considered an environmental or residual factor, a source of disruption. Only rarely do contemporary sociologists consider the distribution of force as a major source of social order.[6]

The assumption underlying the present study is that there are three major sources of control, whose allocation and manipulation account to a great extent for the foundations of social order. These control sources are coercion, economic assets, and normative values. Social relationships differ in the relative predominance of this or that kind of control; but none has an a priori superiority, nor is there one which, as a rule, is the most powerful.[7] Accordingly, three types of compliance serve as the basis for our comparisons between organizations: coercive, utilitarian, and normative compliance, each representing one type of social order. All three enjoy equal status. No assumption is made that force is necessarily disruptive, or that

---

4. For the analysis of these schools which has had the largest impact on sociology in the last two decades, see Parsons (1937). Dahrendorf (1959, pp. 157 ff.), discussing the emphasis given to different factors in the study of social order, distinguishes between a Utopian and a Rationalist approach. The first emphasizes "general agreement of values"; the other "holds that coherence and order in society are founded on force and restraint."

5. The differences in emphasis have been explained in part by ideological associations which the three approaches and some of their exponents have acquired. The stress on force is associated with fascist ideologies; the focus on economic relations with Marxian and hence Communist ideology; the emphasis on normative controls is often associated with a conservative approach to society (Coser, 1956; Dahrendorf, 1959; Birnbaum, 1960, pp. 466-67; Nisbet, 1952). Of course, there is no necessary ideological intent in the writings of every, or even many, exponents of the three approaches.

6. Cf. on this point Mills (1956), Parsons (1957), and Bell (1958).

7. The three kinds of social control seem to be universals, since they regulate behavior with regard to three universal potential dysfunctions: interaction among actors who do not share ultimate values and solidary ties; the scarcity of means; and the imperfectibility of socialization.

economic factors ultimately determine the distribution and dynamics of the others, or that an organization is one integrated collectivity.

Organizations serve as collectivities within which the general problem of social order may be studied empirically. They constitute a "strategic site" [8] for such a study because social order in modern society is based to a great extent upon interaction in and among organizations.

Our approach differs from Weber's "class, status, and power" approach (Gerth and Mills, 1946, pp. 180-95) in three ways. First, we see all three as powers, not just one. Class is one expression of economic power; status is an expression of normative power. Our more inclusive treatment of power permits us to engage in a more extensive analysis of the correlates and effects of power than many studies conducted in the Weberian and related sociological traditions. Second, force is a power central to our schema, but it is not a part of Weber's typology of the foundations of social order. Finally, Weber does not apply his threefold typology to the study of bureaucracies but uses instead the distinction between legitimate and illegitimate power. This is probably the point where the present undertaking differs most from the Weberian tradition. We do not focus on the individual's moral judgments about the source and nature of the directives he receives; other factors are examined for the impact they have on the orientation of participants to the organization, their acceptance of its directives, their response to its power—in short, for their impact on the degree to which the organization's mode of social control is effective.

THE PLAN OF THE BOOK

The plan of this book may be visualized as a wheel. Compliance —the organizational equivalent of social order—is our core variable or hub. It is related to other variables which make up the rim. Each chapter or section constitutes a spoke.

We are concerned primarily with the relationship between compliance and each variable introduced, and only in a limited way with the relationship among these variables. For example, we explore the relationship between compliance and cohesion, and between compliance and leadership, but not between cohesion and leadership. Given this limited focus, the book can supply at best only a cornerstone for the comparative analysis of organizations.

8. On strategic research sites, see Merton (in Merton, Broom, and Cottrell, 1959, pp. xxvi-xxix; and 1959, pp. 21-27).

Part One introduces our concepts and classification scheme. In Chapter I the concepts essential to the study of social order—power, involvement, and compliance—are defined and their interrelations specified. In Chapters II and III various kinds of organizations are briefly reviewed and then classified according to the way they typically control lower participants and the typical response of lower participants to such controls.

Part Two, the main part of the volume, relates the comparative base presented in Part I to a large number of variables widely considered central to organizational analysis. It should be pointed out that since most relationships reported in this book are reversible, no causal assumptions are made. Our choice of compliance as the independent variable is dictated by our interest in the social order, in power and its effect. But most other variables—for example, goals—could be treated as independent.

In Chapter V we examine the different forms of compliance associated with different types of organizational goals and the different levels of effectiveness attained by various combinations of compliance and goals. Chapter VII examines the relationship between the kind of compliance the organization typically exhibits and the nature of its power structure. The distribution of power among various formal and informal elites, the typical relationships among various elites, and the degree to which the organizational polity is integrated in both instrumental and expressive spheres, are all related to different types of compliance structure. Chapter IX focuses on the cultural integration of the organization. The relationship between compliance and consensus, a measure of cultural integration, is dealt with first. Then two processes—communication and socialization—which modify the level of consensus are examined. The relationship between cultural integration and organizational effectiveness is studied. Chapter X explores two ways in which the social environment is related to organizational compliance structures. First, the effect of compliance on the recruitment process is discussed; then, the structural articulation of the organization with its environment is analyzed. The degree to which different types of organization penetrate the extra-organizational life of participants, and the degree to which the environment permeates their intra-organization life, are considered. Chapter XI differs from the four preceding chapters by suggesting that a relationship which has often been claimed to exist between compliance and another variable does not in fact exist. A close examination of the relationship between cohesion and compliance makes it clear that the degree to which lower participants constitute a cohesive group is not a determinant of their orientation to the organization and hence not a factor in compliance.

All the chapters included in Part Two relate differences in the variables listed above to differences in the compliance structure of lower participants, our independent variable. In this sense the present endeavor is simply a segment of theory. The comparative perspective is introduced in the following manner: Three analytical profiles are generated by the tendency of the "values" of our variables to form three clusters. These profiles are used to classify concrete organizations as more or less "typical"; that is, as resembling the profiles more or less. Comparative statements are then made about systematic differences among the three types. This approach differs from the ideal-type tradition in that the *same* variables are used to construct all three types, and these types consist only of specified combinations of the variables.

Whereas the first and second parts of this book focus on the compliance of lower participants, the third part examines the compliance of higher participants. The discussion focuses on charisma, at once the most potent and potentially the most dysfunctional source of social control. Chapter XII specifies the advantages and potential dangers of various distributions of charismatic power for the compliance structure of various organizations; Chapter XIII outlines control mechanisms which minimize the potential and actual dysfunctions of charisma in organizations. Religious, political, educational, military, and professional organizations, in which the role of charisma is particularly important, are examined.

Part Four is devoted to two dynamic aspects of our topic: the development of compliance structures over time, and suggested lines for the development of the *study* of compliance. Chapter XVI examines two ways in which different compliance patterns, dictated by different organizational tasks, can occur in a single organizational unit: structural segregation versus temporal segregation. The concluding chapter suggests some directions in which the study of compliance might be extended. Ways of specifying the propositions presented and some methodological problems in subjecting these propositions to primary empirical research are discussed.

Interest in dynamic aspects of our subject is not limited to the concluding part. Theorems about changing relationships between power and involvement are presented in Chapter I; the relationship between compliance and goals over time is explored in Chapter V;

and a flow model relating communication, socialization, and involvement in the organization is presented in Chapter X.

METHOD AND PROCEDURES

The major task of this study is to formulate new propositions, report existing ones, and relate propositions to each other. In general, no concepts are examined unless their use in developing webs of propositions is demonstrated. The same holds for taxonomies.

No attempt is made to test propositions. This is not a validating study, but an exploratory attempt to construct one segment of a theory. Obviously, propositions invalidated by available data are not included. But almost no new data are presented to support propositions. Examples drawn from published or unpublished research are supplied in order to illustrate somewhat abstract statements, to point to empirical indicators which have been used to measure the variables discussed, and to suggest how some of the propositions might be tested. Since our purpose is to advance propositions rather than test their validity, no attempt has been made to evaluate the quality of the data presented, or to represent all the relevant data available.

Many statements presented here are formulated on a lower level of abstraction than is common in theoretical writing. This approach has two consequences. On the one hand, we gain the benefit of propositions which can be tested empirically without much reinterpretation or specification. On the other hand, we pay the price of leaving the relative safety of high abstraction and exposing our statements to direct and unequivocal test. No doubt some, perhaps many, of the propositions advanced will prove false; others will have to be respecified before they are accepted as valid. If the propositions validated outnumber those rejected, we shall consider the effort well spent.

Finally, unless otherwise specified, each statement should be read as if preceded by "assuming all other conditions are equal." These conditions include the socio-cultural context. With the exception of a few paragraphs devoted to concentration camps and a few other illustrative examples drawn from earlier periods, our statements refer to organizations in modern democratic societies, mainly—because of the nature of the material available—to the contemporary United States. Their application to the study of organizations in newly developed countries or totalitarian societies will require considerable respecification.

INTRODUCTION TO THE
REVISED AND ENLARGED
EDITION

Social science research is often criticized for its lack of continuity. Different studies, it is pointed out, employ different concepts and inconsistent measures. As a result, it is often difficult, if not impossible, to piece together the findings of various researchers which hobbles the essential processes of replication and accumulation. The knowledge gained remains poorly substantiated and fragmented.

The few instances of continuity in sociological research are generally of two kinds. One is the loose chain of several studies, not closely related, all relevant to the same original statement, and invited to test or extend it. Notable here are the two volumes focused on Stouffer's *The American Soldier* and Riesman's *The Lonely Crowd,* edited respectively by Merton and Lazarsfeld (1950) and by Lipset and Lowenthal (1961). More familiar is the even more disparate effort of hypothesis testing and retesting, illustrated by the occasional efforts to generate empirical data relevant to Durkheim's suicide hypotheses. Only rarely do such tests accumulate sufficient evidence to allow one to securely accept or reject a proposition. Even less often are the tests of several hypotheses derived from the same general theory undertaken, by which in accumulation one can gain a sense of the strength of a theory, not just of its building-stones.

Since the original publication of the compliance theory in 1961, more than sixty studies have been undertaken to test one or another part of the compliance theory or to contribute to it by extending its scope. In this revised publication, I seek to collect, evaluate, and synthesize these various studies. Because they were designed and conducted individually, without the guidance of a master plan, in aggregate they do not represent a neat and balanced test of all parts of the theory. For instance, more studies deal with normative organizations than with the other two major types. Similarly, very few deal with cohesion and its relationship to compliance; many more deal with other compliance "correlates." Nevertheless, as we shall see, when reviewed together the studies do throw fresh light on all the elements of the theory. Although a few of these studies cast doubt on the validity or usefulness of some of the original propositions and although the studies vary considerably in their own methodological strength and data bases, the general picture that emerges is one of substantial and specific support. On balance, the evidence seems to strengthen the theory. Chapters IV, VI, VIII, XIV, XV, and XVII, published here for the first time, are devoted to the review of these studies.

Aside from reviewing here studies aimed at testing various compliance hypotheses, I also review works which extend the theory itself. As we shall see, these efforts have rendered the theory more dynamic and applied it to systems it previously was not applied to, including total societies, developing nations, and international systems. These efforts are also summarized and evaluated in this edition, especially in Chapter XVII.

Those who have an interest in methodology may find this edition of interest in three main ways: (a) as a comparative review of efforts by different investigators to operationalize the same set of variables; (b) as a review of efforts to operationalize organizational properties, e.g., organizational goals, as distinct from individual ones; and (c) more generally, as highlighting the problems of continuity of work, of codifying findings, of relating them to a theory. These problems are severe when different theories, hence different concepts, and often different variables are utilized. One would expect, however, that when a single set of variables—those of compliance and its correlates—is used, the codification essential for continuity would be much easier. The following pages suggest that it is easier, but not very much so. The reasons and problems and partial solutions of such efforts at cumulative work should prove to be of interest to whomever is interested in the development of social science.

The procedures I followed in reviewing the sizeable body of studies are as follows:

1. Only works which explicitly and substantially deal with the compliance theory are covered. There is a many-times larger body of studies published since 1961 whose findings are relevant to the compliance variables but which did not explicitly set out to test the theory or tie their findings to its variables. This material is not reviewed here, chiefly in order to limit the present project to manageable size. (See the list of new compliance studies which precedes the bibliographies.)

2. All the studies I could locate relevant to the compliance theory, published or not, are included, whether their findings support or conflict with the theory. Most are quantitative; few rely on qualitative data. Relatively little attention is devoted to sheerly conceptual elaborations not backed by data.

3. A fair number of new studies present data relevant to more than one proposition of the compliance theory. Their findings are reported in the relevant sections, which deal with (a) compliance thesis (Ch. IV); (b) compliance correlates, goals, and effectiveness (Ch. VI); (c) compliance and elites (Ch. VIII); (d) other compliance correlates (Ch. XIV and XV); and (e) new directions (Ch. XVII). However, in whatever section the study is first introduced, its basic design is also reported. In later mentions these details are not repeated.

4. In each case the researchers' original presentation is provided. Needless to say, findings are not simply reported but also evaluated and interpreted.

5. To minimize the repetition of propositions and arguments from the original theory, cross-references to the relevant pages in earlier chapters are provided. The concluding chapter in the original edition, entitled "Dynamic Perspective on the Study of Compliance," has been dropped, and a new final chapter written.

Numerous publications summarize the compliance theory. Several attempts were made, by me (1964, pp. 58-74, available in several languages; 1965, pp. 650-677; 1967, pp. 369-402; 1968, pp. 94-

109) and by others. Four summaries are particularly economical and effective: Schein (1965, pp. 44-47); Pugh, Hickson, and Hinings (1971, pp. 30-35); Hall (1972, pp. 209-212); and Mackenzie (1967, pp. 259-262). In other languages, extensive treatments include, in Portuguese, Caetana Cavalcante (1966); in Italian, Vianello (1964), and in Swedish, Johansson (1965, pp. 157-163).

There is a tendency among sociologists of organization to move on to other fields. I myself have devoted a good part of the years since the first publication of the compliance theory to macrosociology, the "organization" of societies and international systems. Returning here to my original area of interest (my Ph.D. dissertation as well as my M.A. thesis dealt with the organizational structure of *kibbutzim*), I find that there is considerable unity between the theory which underlies the sociology of organizations and that of macrosystems. (More about this later.) However, one perspective has changed: I have grown, I believe, more aware of the normative implications of sociological work. I was less aware when the compliance book was first written that I was comparing three types of human existence: the deep alienation of coercive institutional domination; the instrumental existence based on exchange of one's work for the coins of the marketplace, and the commitment to life in an organization which is also a community. Similarly, I was less inclined to explicitly state the policy directions of the theory. I feel no need to retract or modify what I wrote half a generation ago about compliance trends, but I do see more room for further elaboration. I did not say much on the subject then, but I believe I did better in dealing with this topic in *The Active Society* (1968, pp. 1-16 and Ch. 21) and, I hope, here.

PART ONE

TOWARD AN ANALYTICAL TYPOLOGY

COMPLIANCE AS A COMPARATIVE BASE

I

A DEFINITION OF COMPLIANCE

Compliance is universal, existing in all social units. It is a major element of the relationship between those who have power and those over whom they exercise it (Simmel, 1896). Despite its universality, it has been chosen as a base for this comparative study because it is a central element of organizational structure. The emphasis on compliance within the organization differentiates the latter from other types of social units. Characteristics of organizations such as their specificity, size, complexity and effectiveness each enhances the need for compliance. And in turn, compliance is systematically related to many central organizational variables.

Compliance refers both to a relation in which an actor behaves in accordance with a directive supported by another actor's power, and to the orientation of the subordinated actor to the power applied.[1]

By *supported* we mean that those who have power manipulate means which they command in such a manner that certain other actors find following the directive rewarding, while not following it

1. For other usages of the term see Bendix (1947, pp. 502-7) and Zetterberg (1957).

3

incurs deprivations. In this sense, compliance relations are asymmetric (or "vertical"). But it is not assumed that the subordinates have no power, only that they have less.[2]

The power-*means,* manipulated to support the directives, include physical, material, and symbolic rewards and deprivations. Organizations tend to allocate these means systematically and strive to ensure that they will be used in conformity with the organizational norms.

The *orientation of the subordinated actor* can be characterized as positive (commitment) or negative (alienation). It is determined in part by the degree to which the power applied is considered legitimate by the subordinated actor, and in part by its congruence with the line of action he would desire. We refer to this orientation, whether positive or negative, as *involvement* in the organization. In sum, there are two parties to a compliance relationship: an actor who exercises power, and an actor, subject to this power, who responds to this subjection with either more or less alienation or more or less commitment.

The next task is to use compliance as here defined to develop an analytical base for the classification of organizations. This is done in three steps. First, three kinds of *power* are differentiated; then, three kinds of *involvement* are specified; and finally, the associations of kinds of power with kinds of involvement are indicated. These associations—which constitute *compliance relationships*—then serve as the basis of our classification of organizations.

THREE KINDS OF POWER: A COMPARATIVE DIMENSION

A Classification of Power

Power is an actor's ability to induce or influence another actor to carry out his directives or any other norms he supports.[3] Goldhamer and Shils state that "a person may be said to have power to the extent that he influences the behavior of others in accordance with his own intentions." (p. 171). Of course, "his own intentions" might be to influence a person to follow others' "intentions" or those of a

2. See Parsons (1957, p. 139); cf. Dahrendorf (1954, p. 169).
3. See Parsons (1951, p. 121). See also Lasswell and Kaplan (1950, pp. 74-102); Easton (1952, p. 116); Dahl (1957); and Cartwright (1959).

collectivity. In organizations, enforcing the collectivity norms is likely to be a condition determining the power-holder's access to the means of power.

Power positions are positions whose incumbents regularly have access to means of power. Statements about power positions imply a particular group (or groups) who are subject to this power. For instance, to state that prison guards have a power position implies the subordination of inmates. In the following analysis we focus on power relations in organizations between those higher and those lower in rank. We refer to those in power positions, who are higher in rank, as *elites* or as organizational *representatives*. We refer to those in subject positions, who are lower in rank, as *lower participants*.

Power differs according to the *means* employed to make the subjects comply. These means may be physical, material, or symbolic.[4]

Coercive power rests on the application, or the threat of application, of physical sanctions such as infliction of pain, deformity, or death; generation of frustration through restriction of movement; or controlling through force the satisfaction of needs such as those for food, sex, comfort, and the like.

Remunerative power is based on control over material resources and rewards through allocation of salaries and wages, commissions and contributions, "fringe benefits," services and commodities.

Normative power rests on the allocation and manipulation of symbolic rewards and deprivations through employment of leaders, manipulation of mass media, allocation of esteem and prestige symbols, administration of ritual, and influence over the distribution of "acceptance" and "positive response." (A more eloquent name for this power would be persuasive, or manipulative, or suggestive power.

4. We suggest that this typology is exhaustive, although the only way we can demonstrate this is by pointing out that every type of power we have encountered so far can be classified as belonging to one of the categories or a combination of them.

Boulding, Neuman, and Commons have suggested similar typologies. Boulding has developed a typology of "willingness" of persons to serve organizational ends which includes identification, economic means, and coercion. He suggests, however, that identification should be seen as an "economic" way of inducing willingness, a position which we believe is unacceptable to most sociologists (see Boulding, 1953, p. xxxi; and Niebuhr, "Coercion, Self-Interest, and Love," *ibid.,* pp. 228-44). Neuman has suggested that "three basic methods are at the disposal of the power group: persuasion, material benefits, violence" (1950, p. 168). Commons distinguishes among physical, economic, and moral power (1957, pp. 47-64). Janowitz analyzes international relations using the concepts of "economic resources, violence, and persuasion" (1960, p. 258). See also Deutsch (1953, pp. 218 ff.).

But all these terms have negative value connotations which we wish to avoid.)

There are two kinds of normative power. One is based on the manipulation of esteem, prestige, and ritualistic symbols (such as a flag or a benediction); the other, on allocation and manipulation of acceptance and positive response (Parsons, 1951, p. 108). Although both powers are found both in vertical and in horizontal relationships, the first is more frequent in vertical relations, between actors who have different ranks, while the second is more common in horizontal relations, among actors equal in rank—in particular, in the power of an "informal" or primary group over its members. Lacking better terms, we refer to the first kind as *pure normative power,* and to the second as *social power.*[5] Social power could be treated as a distinct kind of power. But since powers are here classed according to the means of control employed, and since both social and pure normative power rest on the same set of means—manipulation of symbolic rewards—we treat these two powers as belonging to the same category.

From the viewpoint of the organization, pure normative power is more useful, since it can be exercised directly down the hierarchy. Social power becomes organizational power only when the organization can influence the group's powers, as when a teacher uses the class climate to control a deviant child, or a union steward agitates the members to use their informal power to bring a deviant into line.

Organizations can be ordered according to their power structure, taking into account which power is predominant, how strongly it is stressed compared with other organizations in which the same power is predominant, and which power constitutes the secondary source of control.

Neutralization of Power

Most organizations employ all three kinds of power, but the degree to which they rely on each differs from organization to organization. Most organizations tend to emphasize only one means

---

5. This distinction draws on the difference between social and normative integration, referred to by Parsons, Bales, and Shils (1953, p. 182) as the distinction between the "integrative" and the "latent pattern maintenance" phases. In a volume in progress, Shils distinguishes between social and ideological primary groups (private communication). Coleman (1957, p. 255) has pointed to the difference between group-oriented and idea-oriented attachments.

of power, relying less on the other two.[6] Evidence to this effect is presented below in the analysis of the compliance structures of various organizations. The major reason for power specialization seems to be that when two kinds of power are emphasized at the same time, over the same subject group, they tend to neutralize each other.

Applying force, for instance, usually creates such a high degree of alienation that it becomes impossible to apply normative power successfully. This is one of the reasons why rehabilitation is rarely achieved in traditional prisons, why custodial measures are considered as blocking therapy in mental hospitals, and why teachers in progressive schools tend to oppose corporal punishment.

Similarly, the application of renumerative powers makes appeal to "idealistic" (pure normative) motives less fruitful. In a study of the motives which lead to purchase of war bonds, Merton pointed out that in one particularly effective drive (the campaign of Kate Smith), all "secular" topics were omitted and the appeal was centered on patriotic, "sacred" themes. Merton asked a sample of 978 people: "Do you think that it is a good idea to give things to people who buy bonds?"

Fifty per cent were definitely opposed in principle to premiums, bonuses and other such inducements, and many of the remainder thought it a good idea only for "other people" who might not buy otherwise. (1946, p. 47)

By omitting this [secular] argument, the authors of her scripts were able to avoid the strain and incompatibility between the two main lines of motivation: unselfish, sacrificing love of country and economic motives of sound investment. (*Ibid.,* p. 45)

It is possible to make an argument for the opposite position. It might be claimed that the larger the number of personal needs whose satisfaction the organization controls, the more power it has over the participants. For example, labor unions that cater to and have control over the social as well as the economic needs of their

6. In more technical language, one can say that the three continua of power constitute a three-dimensional property space. If we collapse each dimension into high, medium, and low segments, there are 27 possible combinations or cells. Our hypothesis reads that most organizations fall into cells which are high on one dimension and low or medium on the others; this excludes 18 cells (not counting three types of dual structures discussed below). On multi-dimensional property space, see Barton (1955, pp. 40-52).

members have more power over those members than do unions that focus only on economic needs. There may be some tension between the two modes of control, some ambivalence and uneasy feeling among members about the combination, but undoubtedly the total control is larger. Similarly, it is obvious that the church has more power over the priest than over the average parishioner. The parishioner is exposed to normative power, whereas the priest is controlled by both normative and remunerative powers.

The issue is complicated by the fact that the *amount* of each kind of power applied must be taken into account. If a labor union with social powers has economic power which is much greater than that of another union, this fact may explain why the first union has greater power in sum, despite some "waste" due to neutralization. A further complication follows from the fact that neutralization may also occur through application of the "wrong" power in terms of the cultural definition of what is appropriate to the particular organization and activity. For example, application of economic power in religious organizations may be less effective than in industries, not because two kinds of power are mixed, but because it is considered illegitimate to use economic pressures to attain religious goals. Finally, some organizations manage to apply two kinds of power abundantly and without much waste through neutralization, because they segregate the application of one power from that of the other. The examination below of combat armies and labor unions supplies an illustration of this point.

We have discussed some of the factors related to the tendency of organizations to specialize their power application. In conclusion, it seems that although there can be little doubt that such a tendency exists, its scope and a satisfactory explanation for it have yet to be established.

THREE KINDS OF INVOLVEMENT: A COMPARATIVE DIMENSION

Involvement, Commitment, and Alienation

Organizations must continually recruit means if they are to realize their goals. One of the most important of these means is the positive orientation of the participants to the organizational power. *Involve-*

ment [7] refers to the cathectic-evaluative orientation of an actor to an object, characterized in terms of intensity and direction.

The intensity of involvement ranges from high to low. The direction is either positive or negative. We refer to positive involvement as *commitment* [8] and to negative involvement as *alienation.*[9] (The advantage of having a third term, *involvement,* is that it enables us to refer to the continuum in a neutral way.[10]) Actors can accordingly be placed on an involvement continuum which ranges from a highly intense negative zone through mild negative and mild positive zones to a highly positive zone.[11]

Three Kinds of Involvement

We have found it helpful to name three zones of the involvement continuum, as follows: *alienative,* for the high alienation zone; *moral,*

7. *Involvement* has been used in a similar manner by Morse (1953, pp. 76-96). The term is used in a somewhat different way by students of voting, who refer by it to the psychological investment in the outcome of an election rather than in the party, which would be parallel to Morse's usage and ours. See, for example, Campbell, Gurin, and Miller (1954, pp. 33-40).

8. Mishler defined *commitment* in a similar though more psychological way: "An individual is committed to an organization to the extent that central tensions are integrated through organizationally relevant instrumental acts." Cited by Argyris (1957, p. 202). See also Mishler (1953); Abramson, Cutler, Kautz, and Mendelson (1958), p. 16); H. P. Gouldner (1960, p. 469); and Becker (1960, pp. 35ff.).

9. We draw deliberately on the associations this term has acquired from its usage by Marx and others. For a good analysis of the idea of alienation in Marxism, and of its more recent development, see Bell (1959 and 1960, pp. 335-68). See also D. G. Dean (1960, pp. 185-89).

10. An example of empirical indicators which can be used to translate the involvement continuum into directly observable terms is offered by Shils and Janowitz (1948, pp. 282-83). They classify "modes of social disintegration" in the armed forces as follows: desertion; active surrender; passive surrender; routine resistance; "last-ditch" resistance. In the terms used here, these measures indicate varying degrees of involvement, from highest alienation (desertion) to highest commitment (last-ditch resistance).

Nettler (1958) has developed a 17-item unidimensional scale which measures alienation from society. It seems that a similar scale could be constructed for measuring alienation from or commitment to organizational power without undue difficulties. Kornhauser, Sheppard, and Mayer (1956, pp. 147-48) have developed a 6-item scale, measuring the orientation of union members to their organization, which supplies another illustration of the wide use and measurability of these concepts, which are central to our analysis.

11. Several sociologists have pointed out that the relationship between intensity and direction of involvement is a curvilinear one: the more positive or negative the orientation, the more intensely it is held (Guttman, 1947, 1950, 1954, pp. 229-30; Suchman, 1950; McDill, 1959).

for the high commitment zone; and *calculative,* for the two mild zones. This classification of involvement can be applied to the orientations of actors in all social units and to all kinds of objects. Hence the definitions and illustrations presented below are not limited to organizations, but are applicable to orientations in general.

ALIENATIVE INVOLVEMENT—Alienative involvement designates an intense negative orientation; it is predominant in relations among hostile foreigners. Similar orientations exist among merchants in "adventure" capitalism, where trade is built on isolated acts of exchange, each side trying to maximize immediate profit (Gerth and Mills, 1946, p. 67). Such an orientation seems to dominate the approach of prostitutes to transient clients (K. Davis, 1937, pp. 748-49). Some slaves seem to have held similar attitudes to their masters and to their work. Inmates in prisons, prisoners of war, people in concentration camps, enlisted men in basic training, all tend to be alienated from their respective organizations.[12]

CALCULATIVE INVOLVEMENT—Calculative involvement designates either a negative or a positive orientation of low intensity. Calculative orientations are predominant in relationships of merchants who have continuous business contacts. Attitudes of (and toward) permanent customers are often predominantly calculative, as are relationships among entrepreneurs in modern (rational) capitalism. Inmates in prisons who have established contact with prison authorities, such as "rats" and "peddlers," often have predominantly calculative attitudes toward those in power (Sykes, 1958, pp 87-95).

MORAL [13] INVOLVEMENT—Moral involvement designates a positive orientation of high intensity. The involvement of the parishioner in his church, the devoted member in his party, and the loyal follower in his leader are all "moral."

There are two kinds of moral involvement, pure and social. They differ in the same way pure normative power differs from social power. Both are intensive modes of commitment, but they differ in their foci of orientation and in the structural conditions under which they develop. Pure moral commitments are based on internalization

---

12. For a description of this orientation in prisons see Clemmer (1958, pp. 152ff.). Attitudes toward the police, particularly on the part of members of the lower classes, are often strictly alienative. See, for example, Banfield (1958). Illustrations of alienative orientations to armies are found in Norman Mailer, *The Naked and the Dead,* and Erich Maria Remarque, *All Quiet on the Western Front.*

13. The term moral is used here and in the rest of the volume to refer to an orientation of the actor; it does not involve a value-position of the observer (see Parsons and Shils, 1952, pp. 170ff.).

of norms and identification with authority (like Riesman's inner-directed "mode of conformity"); social commitment rests on sensitivity to pressures of primary groups and their members (Riesman's "other-directed"). Pure moral involvement tends to develop in vertical relationships, such as those between teachers and students, priests and parishioners, leaders and followers. Social involvement tends to develop in horizontal relationships like those in various types of primary groups. Both pure moral and social orientations might be found in the same relationships, but, as a rule, one orientation predominates.

Actors are means to each other in alienative and in calculative relations; but they are ends to each other in "social" relationships. In pure moral relationships the means-orientation tends to predominate. Hence, for example, the willingness of devoted members of totalitarian parties or religious orders to use each other. But unlike the means-orientation of calculative relationships, the means-orientation here is expected to be geared to needs of the collectivity in serving its goals, and not to those of an individual.

As has been stated, the preceding classification of involvement can be applied to the orientations of actors in all social units and to all kinds of objects. The analysis in this book applies the scheme to orientations of lower participants in organizations to various organizational objects, in particular to the organizational power system. The latter includes (1) the directives the organization issues, (2) the sanctions by which it supports its directives, and (3) the persons who are in power positions. The choice of organizational power as the prime object of involvement to be examined here follows from a widely held conception of organization as an administrative system or control structure. To save breath, the orientation of lower participants to the organization as a power (or control) system is referred to subsequently as *involvement in the organization*. When other involvements are discussed, the object of orientation—for example, organizational goals—is specified.

Organizations are placed on the involvement continuum according to the modal involvement pattern of their lower participants. The placing of organizations in which the participants exhibit more than one mode of involvement is discussed in a later chapter.

COMPLIANCE AS A COMPARATIVE BASE

A Typology of Compliance

Taken together, the two elements—that is, the power applied by the organization *to* lower participants, and the involvement in the organization developed *by* lower participants—constitute the compliance relationship. Combining three kinds of power with three kinds of involvement produces nine types of compliance, as shown in the accompanying table.[14]

A Typology of Compliance Relations

KINDS OF POWER	KINDS OF INVOLVEMENT		
	Alienative	Calculative	Moral
Coercive	1	2	3
Remunerative	4	5	6
Normative	7	8	9

The nine types are not equally likely to occur empirically. *Three* —the diagonal cases, 1, 5, and 9—*are found more frequently than the other six types.* This seems to be true because these three types constitute *congruent* relationships, whereas the other six do not.

THE CONGRUENT TYPES—The involvement of lower participants is determined by many factors, such as their personality structure, secondary socialization, memberships in other collectivities, and so on. At the same time, organizational powers differ in the kind of involvement they tend to generate. When the kind of involvement that lower participants have because of other factors [15] and the kind of involvement that tends to be generated by the predominant form of organizational power are the same, we refer to the relationship as *congruent.* For instance, inmates are highly alienated from prisons; coercive power tends to alienate; hence this is a case of a congruent compliance relationship.

Congruent cases are more frequent than noncongruent ones primarily because congruence is more effective, and organizations are

14. A formalization of the relationship between rewards-allocation (which comes close to the concept of power as used here) and participation (which, as defined, is similar to the concept of involvement) has been suggested by Breton (1960).

15. "Other factors" might include previous applications of the power.

social units under external and internal pressure to be effective. The effective application of normative powers, for example, requires that lower participants be highly committed. If lower participants are only mildly committed to the organization, and particularly if they are alienated from it, the application of normative power is likely to be ineffective. Hence the association of normative power with moral commitment.

Remuneration is at least partially wasted when actors are highly alienated, and therefore inclined to disobey despite material sanctions; it is also wasted when actors are highly committed, so that they would maintain an effective level of performance for symbolic, normative rewards only. Hence the association of remuneration with calculative involvement.

Coercive power is probably the only effective power when the organization is confronted with highly alienated lower participants. If, on the other hand, it is applied to committed or only mildly alienated lower participants, it is likely to affect adversely such matters as morale, recruitment, socialization, and communication, and thus to reduce effectiveness. (It is likely, though, to create high alienation, and in this way to create a congruent state.)

THE INCONGRUENT TYPES—Since organizations are under pressure to be effective, the suggestion that the six less effective incongruent types are not just theoretical possibilities but are found empirically calls for an explanation. The major reason for this occurrence is that organizations have only limited control over the powers they apply and the involvement of lower participants. The exercise of power depends on the resources the organization can recruit and the license it is allowed in utilizing them. Involvement depends in part on external factors, such as membership of the participants in other collectivities (e.g., membership in labor unions [16]); basic value commitments (e.g., Catholic versus Protestant religious commitments [17]); and the personality structure of the participants (e.g., authoritarian [18]). All

16. On the effect of membership in labor unions on involvement in the corporation, see Willerman (1949, p. 4); L. R. Dean (1954); Jacobson (1951); and Purcell (1953, pp. 79, 146).

17. See W. F. Whyte et al. (1955, pp. 45-46). Protestants are reported to be more committed to the values of saving and productivity, whereas Catholics are more concerned with their social standing in the work group. This makes for differences in compliance: Protestants are reported to be more committed to the corporation's norms than Catholics.

18. For instance, authoritarian personality structure is associated with a "custodial" orientation to mental patients (Gilbert and Levinson, 1957, pp. 26-27).

these factors may reduce the expected congruence of power and involvement.

A DYNAMIC HYPOTHESIS—Congruent types are more effective than incongruent types. Organizations are under pressure to be effective. Hence, to the degree that the environment of the organization allows, *organizations tend to shift their compliance structure from incongruent to congruent types* and *organizations which have congruent compliance structures tend to resist factors pushing them toward incongruent compliance structures.*

Congruence is attained by a change in either the power applied by the organization or the involvement of lower participants. Change of power takes place when, for instance, a school shifts from the use of corporal punishment to stress on the "leadership" of the teachers. The involvement of lower participants may be changed through socialization, changes in recruitment criteria, and the like.[19]

Because the large majority of cases falls into the three categories representing congruent compliance, these three types form the basis for subsequent analysis. We refer to the coercive-alienative type as *coercive compliance;* to the remunerative-calculative type as *utilitarian compliance;* and to the normative-moral type as *normative compliance.* Students of organizational change, conflict, strain, and similar topics may find the six incongruent types more relevant to their work.

Compliance and Authority

The typology of compliance relationships presented above highlights some differences between the present approach to the study of organizational control and that of studies conducted in the tradition of Weber. These studies tend to focus on authority, or legitimate power, as this concept is defined.[20] The significance of authority has been emphasized in modern sociology in the past, in order to overcome earlier biases that overemphasized force and economic power as the sources of social order. This emphasis, in turn, has led to an overemphasis on legitimate power. True, some authority can be found

19. We return to this dynamic perspective in Chapter V, after introducing the concepts of goal and effectiveness.

20. For various definitions and usages of the concept see Friedrich (1958). For a formalization of the concept in relation to power and to leadership, see Barton (1958). For a psychological discussion of legitimate power see French and Raven (1959, pp. 158-61).

in the control structure of lower participants in most organizations. True, authority plays a role in maintaining the long-run operations of the organization. But so does nonlegitimated power. Since the significance of legitimate power has been fully recognized, it is time to lay the ghost of Marx and the old controversy, and to give full status to both legitimate and nonlegitimate sources of control.

Moreover, the concept of authority does not take into account differences among powers other than their legitimacy, in particular the nature of the sanctions (physical, material, or symbolic) on which power is based. All three types of power may be regarded as legitimate by lower participants: thus there is normative,[21] remunerative, and coercive authority (differentiated by the kind of power employed, for instance, by a leader, a contractor, and a policeman.) [22] But these powers differ in the likelihood that they will be considered legitimate by those subjected to them. Normative power is most likely to be considered legitimate; coercive, least likely; and remunerative is intermediate.

Finally, it is important to emphasize that involvement in the organization is affected both by the legitimacy of a directive and by the degree to which it frustrates the subordinate's need-dispositions. Alienation is produced not only by illegitimate exercise of power, but

21. The concept of "normative authority" raises the question of the difference between this kind of authority and normative power. There is clearly a high *tendency* for normative power to be considered legitimate and thus to form an authority relationship. The reason for this tendency is that the motivational significance of rewards and deprivations depends not only on the objective nature of the power applied, but also on the meaning attached to it by the subject. Coercive and remunerative means of control are considerably less dependent on such interpretations than normative ones. Most actors in most situations will see a fine as a deprivation and confinement as a punishment. On the other hand, if the subject does not accept as legitimate the power of a teacher, a priest, or a party official, he is not likely to feel their condemnation or censure as depriving. Since normative power depends on manipulation of symbols, it is much more dependent on "meanings," and, in this sense, on the subordinate, than other powers. But it is by no means necessary that the application of normative power always be regarded as legitimate.

A person may, for example, be aware that another person has influenced his behavior by manipulation of symbolic rewards, but feel that he had no right to do so, that he ought not to have such power, or that a social structure in which normative powers are concentrated (e.g., partisan control over mass media; extensive advertising) is unjustified. A Catholic worker who feels that his priest has no right to condemn him because of his vote for the "wrong" candidate may still fear the priest's condemnation and be affected by it.

22. For another classification of authority, which includes authority of confidence, of identification, of sanctions, and of legitimacy, see Simon, Smithburg, and Thompson (1959, p. 189).

also by power which frustrates needs, wishes, desires. Commitment is generated not merely by directives which are considered legitimate but also by those which are in line with internalized needs of the subordinate. Involvement is positive if the line of action directed is conceived by the subordinate as both legitimate and gratifying. It is negative when the power is not granted legitimacy and when it frustrates the subordinate. Involvement is intermediate when either legitimation or gratification is lacking. Thus the study of involvement, and hence that of compliance, differs from the study of authority by taking into account the effects of the cathectic as well as the evaluative impact of directives on the orientation of lower participants.

LOWER PARTICIPANTS AND ORGANIZATIONAL BOUNDARIES

Before we can begin our comparisons, the following questions still remain to be answered. Why do we make compliance of lower participants the focus of the comparison? Who exactly are "lower participants"? What are the lower boundaries of an organization? In answering these questions, we employ part of the analytical scheme suggested above, and thus supply the first test of its fruitfulness.

Why Lower Participants?

Compliance of lower participants is made the focus of this analysis for several reasons. First, the control of lower participants is more problematic than that of higher participants because, as a rule, the lower an actor is in the organizational hierarchy, the fewer rewards he obtains. His position is more deprived; organizational activities are less meaningful to him because he is less "in the know," and because often, from his position, only segments of the organization and its activities are visible.[23] Second, since we are concerned with systematic differences among organizations (the similarities having been more often explored), we focus on the ranks in which the largest differences in compliance can be found. An inter-organizational comparison of middle and higher ranks would show that their compliance structures differ much less than those of the lower ranks (see Chapter XII).

23. The term *visible* is used here and throughout this book as defined by Merton: "the extent to which the norms and the role-performances within a group are readily open to observation by others." (1957, pp. 319 ff.)

Who Are Lower Participants?

Organizational studies have used a large number of concrete terms to refer to lower participants: employees, rank-and-file, members, clients, customers, inmates.[24] These terms are rarely defined. They are customarily used to designate lower participants in more than one organization, but none can be used for all.

Actually, these terms can be seen as reflecting different positions on at least three analytical dimensions.[25] One is the *nature* (direction and intensity) of the actors' *involvement* in the organization. Unless some qualifying adjectives such as "cooperative" or "good" are introduced, *inmates* implies alienative involvement. *Clients* designates people with alienative or calculative involvement. *Customers* refers to people who have a relatively more alienative orientation than clients; one speaks of the clients of professionals but not ordinarily of their customers. *Member* is reserved for those who have at least some, usually quite strong, moral commitment to their organization. *Employee* is used for people with various degrees of calculative involvement.

A second dimension underlying these concrete terms is the degree to which lower participants are *subordinated* to organizational powers. Inmates, it seems, are more subordinated than employees, employees more than members, and members more than clients. A study in which subordination is a central variable would take into account that it includes at least two subvariables: the extent of control in each area (e.g., "tight" versus remote control); and the scope of control, measured by the number of areas in which the subject is subordinated. Such refinement is not required for our limited use of this dimension.

A third dimension is the amount of *performance* required from the participants by the organization: it is high for employees, low for inmates, and lowest for clients and customers.[26]

24. For one of the best discussions of the concept of participation, its definition and dimensions, see Fichter (1954, Part I, *passim*).
25. The difference between concrete and analytic membership in corporations has been pointed out by Feldman (1959).
26. Participants of a social unit might also be defined as all those who share an institutionalized set of role-expectations. We shall not employ this criterion since it blurs a major distinction, that between the organization as such and its social environment. Members of most groups share such role-expectations with outsiders.

A criterion of participation which is significant for other purposes than ours is whether lower participants have formal or actual powers, such as those reflected in the right to vote, submit grievances, or strike.

Using concrete terms to designate groups of participants without specifying the underlying dimensions creates several difficulties. First of all, the terms cannot be systematically applied. Although "members" are in general positively involved, sometimes the term is used to designate lower participants with an alienative orientation. Archibald, for instance, uses this term to refer to members of labor unions who are members only *pro forma* and who see in the union simply another environmental constraint, to which they adjust by paying dues.

Most workers entered the yards not merely ignorant of unions, but distrustful of them. . . . They nonetheless joined the unions, as they were compelled to do, with little protest. They paid the initiation fees, averaging not more than twenty dollars, much as they would have bought a ticket to the county fair: it cost money, but maybe the show would be worth the outlay. As for dues, they paid them with resignation to the principle that all joys of life are balanced by a measure of pain. (1947, pp. 131-32)

The term *customers* suggests that the actors have no moral commitments to their sources of products and services. But sometimes it is used to refer to people who buy from cooperatives, frequent only unionized barbers, and remain loyal to one newspaper—that is, to people who are willing to suffer some economic loss because they see in these sources of service something which is "good in itself"— people who, in short, have some moral commitments.

Any moral commitment on the part of mental patients, designated as *inmates,* is viewed either with surprise or as a special achievement of the particular mental hospital; on the other hand, members of labor unions are "expected" to show moral commitment and are labeled "apathetic" if they do not. The fact that some mental patients view their hospital as their home, and thus are positively involved, whereas labor union members may see their organization as a secondary group only, is hidden by the terminology employed. The same point could be made for differences in performance and in subordination.

Although the use of such concrete terms leads to overgeneralization, by implying that all lower participants of an organization have the characteristics usually associated with the label, they can also impede generalization. An illustration is supplied by studies of parishioners. Many of these studies focus on problems of participation, such as "apathy," high turnover, and declining commitment. But rarely are comparisons drawn, or insights transferred, from the study of members of voluntary associations and political organizations. Actually, all these organizations are concerned with the moral commitment of lower participants who have few performance obligations and little subordination to the organization.

Another advantage of specifying the analytical dimensions underlying these concepts is that the number of dimensions is limited, whereas the number of concrete terms grows continuously with the number of organizations studied. Thus the study of hospitals introduces patients; the analysis of churches brings up parishioners; and the examination of armies adds soldiers. Following the present procedure, we can proceed to characterize the lower participants of additional organizations by the use of the same three dimensions.

Specifying the underlying dimensions enables us not only to formulate analytical profiles of a large variety of lower participants, but also to compare them systematically with each other on these three dimensions. For instance, "soldiers" (in combat) are high on all three dimensions, whereas inmates are high on subordination and alienation but low on performance; employees are medium in involvement and subordination, but high on performance obligations. The import of such comparisons will become evident later.

Finally, whereas concrete terms tend to limit analysis to participants at particular levels, analytical terms such as alienative, calculative, and moral can be applied equally well to participants at all levels of the organizational hierarchy.

Ideally, in a book such as this, we should refer to lower participants in analytical terms, those of various degrees of involvement, subordination, and performance obligations. Since this would make the discussion awkward, the concrete terms are used, but only to refer to *typical* analytical constellations. *Inmates* are lower participants with high alienation, low performance obligations, and high subordination. The term will not be used to refer to other combinations which are sometimes found among lower participants in prisons. *Members* is used to refer only to lower participants who are highly committed, medium on subordination, and low on performance obligations; it is not used to refer to alienated lower participants in voluntary associations. Similarly, other terms are used as specified below.

Analytical Specifications of Some Concepts
Referring to Lower Participants *

Lower Participants	Nature of Involvement (Intensity and Direction)	Subordination	Performance Obligations
Inmates	High, negative	High	Low
Employees	Low, negative or positive	Medium	High
Customers	Low, negative or positive	None	Low
Parishioners	High, positive	Low	Low
Members	High, positive	Medium to Low	Low
Devoted Adherents	High, positive	High	High

* This table contains a set of definitions to be used. It is not exhaustive, either in concepts referring to lower participants or in possible combinations of "scores" on the various dimensions.

Lower versus Higher Participants

Higher participants have a "permanent" power advantage over lower participants because of their organizational position. Thus, by definition, higher participants as a group are less *subordinated* than lower participants. Often, though not in all organizational types, they are also more *committed,* and have more *performance obligations* (if we see decision making and other mental activities as performances). Thus the three dimensions which serve to distinguish among various types of lower participants also mark the dividing line between lower and higher participants. These very dimensions also enable us to suggest a way to delineate the organizational boundaries—that is, to distinguish between participants and nonparticipants.

Organizational Boundaries

Students of organizations must often make decisions about the boundaries of the unit they are studying: who is a participant, who an outsider. March and Simon, for example, take a broad view of organizational boundaries: "When we describe the chief participants of most business organizations, we generally limit our attention to the following five major classes: employees, investors, suppliers, distributers, and consumers." (1958, p. 89)

We follow a narrower definition and see as participants all actors who are high on at least one of the three dimensions of participation: involvement, subordination, and performance. Thus, students, inmates, soldiers, workers, and many others are included. Customers and clients, on the other hand, who score low on all three criteria, are considered "outsiders."

We should like to underscore the importance of this way of delineating the organizational boundaries. It draws the line much "lower" than most studies of bureaucracies, which tend to include only persons who are part of a formal hierarchy: priests, but not parishioners; stewards, but not union members; guards, but not inmates; nurses, but not patients. We treat organizations as collectivities of which the lower participants are an important segment. To exclude them from the analysis would be like studying colonial structures without the natives, stratification without the lower classes, or a political regime without the citizens or voters.

It seems to us especially misleading to include the lower participants in organizational charts when they have a formal role, as privates in armies or workers in factories, and to exclude them when they have no such status, as is true for parishioners or members. This practice leads to such misleading comparisons as seeing the priests as the privates of the church and teachers as the lowest-ranking participants of schools, in both cases ignoring the psychological import of having "subordinates." One should not let legal or administrative characteristics stand in the way of a sociological analysis. However, the main test of the decision to delineate the organization as we have chosen follows: it lies in the scope, interest, and validity of the propositions this approach yields.

SUMMARY

Compliance patterns were chosen as the basis for our comparative study of organizations because compliance relations are a central element of organizational structure. It distinguishes organizations from other collectivities because organizations require more compliance than other collectivities do, and it is systematically related to many other organizational variables.

Compliance refers both to a relation in which an actor behaves in accordance with a directive supported by another person's power and to the orientation of the subject to the power applied. There are three kinds of power: coercive, remunerative, and normative; and three kinds of involvement: alienative, calculative, and moral. There are, therefore, nine possible types of compliance. Three of these types (congruent types) are more effective than the other six; they are also empirically much more frequent. These three types form the basis of our comparative study.

Each organizational rank has its own compliance structure. We focus on the compliance structure of lower participants, first because their compliance is more problematic than that of higher participants, and second because organizations can be most fruitfully distinguished from each other at this level.

Lower participants are actors who are high on at least one of the three dimensions of participation: involvement, performance obligations, and subordination. An examination of concrete terms often used to refer to different groups of lower participants shows that they can be seen as positions on these three analytical dimensions, which also enable us also to delineate systematically the boundaries of organizations. We are now ready to engage in the first major substantive step: classification of organizations according to their compliance structures.

II

AN ANALYTICAL CLASSIFICATION
Coercive and Utilitarian Organizations

All patterns of compliance exist in most organizations, but most organizations rely much more on one pattern than on on the other two. Hence organizations are classified in this and the subsequent chapter according to their *predominant* compliance pattern as coercive, utilitarian, or normative. Within each category, organizations are ordered according to the *relative* emphasis given to the predominant pattern: thus some coercive organizations are found to rely heavily upon coercive compliance, whereas others, though also predominantly coercive, place considerably less stress on this pattern.[1] When relevant, the secondary compliance pattern is also specified. The composite compliance distribution, of predominant and secondary patterns, is referred to as the *compliance structure* of the particular organizational rank (e.g., lower participants).

The categories for classification have been established in the preceding chapter. Before we can begin the classification, however, we must specify the units to be classified.

THE UNITS OF CLASSIFICATION

When comparative statements about organizations are made, concrete organizations are usually cited as instances of some common-

1. For a discussion of possible measures see Ch. XIV.

sense "category." The United Automobile Workers is an instance of "trade unions," General Motors an instance of "corporations." Compartive statements are then formulated using these categories: for example, it is suggested that the members of the UAW have more power over their representatives than most stockholders of GM have over theirs, since in general union members are more involved in the union than stockholders are in the company.

The use of such common-sense categories as labor unions and corporations to isolate the units of comparison creates considerable difficulty. This method of classification tends to attach the same label to organizations which differ considerably, and to assign differ-ent names to organizations which are analytically similar in many significant ways, particularly in their compliance structure.

Army, armed forces, and *military organization,* for example, are labels in common use. Actually, they refer to a highly heterogeneous group. The terms comprise, for instance, both peacetime and combat units, which differ in their goals, social composition, training, dis-ciplinary methods, socialization, communication networks, and com-pliance structure. Similarly, General Motors, restaurants (W. F. Whyte, 1948), and newspapers (Kreps, 1954) are all referred to as "industries"; [2] the Communists as well as the Democrats and Republi-cans come under the heading of "political parties"; the term trade union is applied to both Soviet and American workers' organizations.

Again, it is generally assumed that the term *voluntary association* refers to a homogeneous category and that one may therefore gener-alize from findings concerning one voluntary association to the whole category. Actually, the category includes at least two distinct types. In one type, active participation and high commitment are conditions for the functioning of the association; fund-raising organizations such as the March of Dimes, religious orders, and political parties with strong ideological commitments fall into this subcategory. The other type—which also makes strong public claims for participation and commitment—can function effectively only so long as these claims are *not* met, or are met only on some occasions. Most labor unions, most political parties, stockholders' groups, and interest groups are

2. On the problem involved in the use of common-sense classifications, especially with regard to the category "industry" as defined by dictionaries and by the Census Bureau, see Etzioni (1958c, p. 307). Part of the difficulty arises from the use of *industry* to designate any permanent investment of capital and labor, as well as a subcategory of this class—namely, the mechanical and manufacturing branches of producing activities as distinguished from agriculture, mining, and services.

of this type. Apathy, or lack of involvement—the central issue of many studies of voluntary associations—has thus a very different meaning for these two organizational types. For the first type, it means that a basic functional requirement is not fulfilled; for the second, it means that the organization is operating smoothly, and possibly that one of the conditions necessary for its effective functioning is fulfilled.[3]

Some organizations covered by different names reveal more similarity than those grouped together under one name. Selznick (1952) has shown that the power structure, goals, means of communication, and role of primary groups of Communist parties resemble those of combat armies more than they do those of ordinary political parties. From some points of view, the quartermaster services of peacetime armies—classified as "military" organizations—have more in common with large-scale insurance offices and department stores, classified as "industry," than with other military units. Conversely, large insurance offices resemble peacetime armies more than they do mines, shipyards, and most factories, with which they are frequently grouped.

In our discussion, analytic attributes of organizations distinguish the units of classification. Unfortunately, we cannot follow the ideal procedure and classify each organization, because there are many hundreds of thousands of them. On the other hand, we have seen that common-sense classifications are of little use. We therefore take the middle way, breaking up the broad common-sense categories into subcategories. We shall not, for example, talk about military organizations, but about combat units and peacetime units. Similarly, we shall not classify all mental hospitals together, but distinguish between custodial hospitals and therapeutic hospitals. The differentiating criterion is the compliance structure of the various subcategories of organizations.

If all the organizations normally included in one common-sense category fall into the same compliance category, organizations are ordered within the category according to the relative stress on the predominant pattern. For example, many industries fall into the

3. A revised theory of apathy would have to be much more specific than can be suggested here in passing. It is vital, for instance, to distinguish between complete and partial apathy and to determine the type of members who are apathetic (e.g., elites as against rank and file). Some apathy is functional for almost all organizations, although they differ in the degree to which this is true. For a discussion of the functions of apathy, see W. H. M. Jones (1954).

remunerative category, but differ according to how much stress they put on remuneration; blue-collar and white-collar industries, for example, differ in this respect.

The present classification is only a first approximation. As systematic information on organizations increases, new divisions in the categories and units of classification will have to be introduced, and some organizations will probably require reclassification. The present endeavor therefore should be viewed as a beginning, not an end. It should also be taken into account that this classification is designed to serve the study of compliance and its correlates. In all likelihood, other classifications are more useful for some other purpose.[4]

It should be emphasized that in the following pages we can devote only brief, schematic treatment to the examples discussed. There is an entire literature devoted to organizations; our task here is not to deal with all of it, but to place an organization in our scheme and to clarify certain problems which emerge from this classificatory endeavor. Occasionally, a somewhat more extensive discussion is needed to explore the difficulties a researcher might encounter in determining the nature of the compliance structure. In general, however, the reader must be referred to cited sources for a fuller treatment of the organizations briefly reviewed here.

Finally, a comment on indicators is necessary. We cannot hope to overcome the limitations of every secondary analysis: we are introducing *post hoc* concepts into studies conducted by other researchers with other concepts and procedures. We shall have to take whatever measures the study has used as our guide. Indicators of involvement illustrate the point. Sometimes these are holistic measures of the participants' general orientation to organizational power; sometimes they are more specific, as when attitudes toward only one aspect of power —for example, sanctions—are studied; and in still other cases, the

---

4. It is more common to classify organizations according to the functions they fulfill for society. Parsons classifies organizations as: (1) oriented to economic production, (2) oriented to political goals, (3) integrative organizations, and (4) pattern-maintenance organizations (Parsons, 1956, pp. 228-29). This typology has been applied and elaborated by Eisenstadt (1958, pp. 116-17), Etzioni (1958c, pp. 208-10), Scott (1959, pp. 386-88), and Gordon and Babchuk (1959). Differentiation of organizations by goal or function is also used in a study of the technology and organizational structure of factories, mines, hospitals, and universities (Thompson and Bates, 1957); and in a study of "management of conflict" in "ideological organizations," "giant enterprises," and "local enterprises" (Thompson, 1960). Cf. the structural approach used by Moore (1957) in his comparative examination of management and unions, and by Stinchcombe (1959) in his comparison of bureaucratic and craft administration of production.

only information available on involvement encompasses more than orientation to the control structure alone—for example, level of job satisfaction.[5] In those few cases where the indicator is broader than the concept we are interested in, we are forced to use it nevertheless as a tentative clue to the nature of involvement in the organization. This kind of indicator is used only when the control structure constitutes the most salient of the involvement objects reported. Because the present study is an exploratory, proposition-formulating endeavor, this problem is not a crucial one. The material supplied illustrates the propositions; it does not, of course, validate them.[6]

COERCIVE ORGANIZATIONS

Coercive organizations are organizations in which coercion is the major means of control over lower participants and high alienation characterizes the orientation of most lower participants to the organization. Typical cases are concentration camps, prisoner-of-war camps, the large majority of prisons, traditional "correctional institutions," and custodial mental hospitals. Forced-labor camps [7] and relocation centers [8] are also coercive organizations.

Force is the major means of control applied in these organizations to assure fulfillment of the major organizational task: keeping inmates in. Obviously, should the restraints on movement be lifted, hardly any inmate would stay inside. The accomplishment of all other tasks depends on the effective performance of this custodial task. The second major task of these organizations, keeping the inmates disciplined, is also attained through the potential or actual use of force, although here differences among various types of organization are greater.

Even when control relies directly on other means, indirectly it is based on force. An inmate may do many services for a guard in exchange for a cigarette, but this cannot be considered remunerative

5. See Chapter XI, pages 301-302, on this indicator.
6. Naturally the data collected since the publication of the first edition modifies this statement.
7. For a personal account see Parvilahti (1960). There are several reports on such camps in a number of Soviet countries by the Mid-European Law Project, under the general title *Forced Labor and Confinement without Trial* (1952).
8. Leighton (1945, esp. chs. 6-10) deals with the relatively unsuccessful attempts to reduce coercion, develop self-government, and avoid general social disorganization by means other than coercion in these camps. For another study of such camps see LaViolette (1948).

control since the special value of the cigarette and other such objects of satisfaction is derived from the segregation of the inmate from regular markets. This segregation is in turn based on force.

Organizations included in the coercive category may be arranged according to the relative weight of the coercive pattern. Concentration camps apply more coercion than regular prisons; [9] prisons apply more than "correctional institutions" for juvenile offenders, the latter being frequently the first to introduce various reforms (Ohlin, 1956, p. 13). Prisoner-of-war camps in modern democracies frequently apply only as much coercion as correctional institutions, or less.[10] It is reported that some North Korean prisoners of war were kept in a United Nations camp which did not have barbed wire (W. L. White, 1957, p. 8), and that "we had taken about 60,000 prisoners, so gentle that they could be marched to the rear in almost unguarded regiments" (*ibid.*, p. 34).

Assuming that we could control the effect of other factors, such as the degree of initial alienation the inmates bring with them to the various types of coercive organizations, we should expect to find higher alienation in those organizations that apply more coercion.[11] This seems indeed to be the case with one possible exception, that of concentration camps. Here, where the application of coercion reaches the highest level, instances of "utter indifference" and even commitment to the guards and wardens are reported (Bettelheim, 1943, pp. 448-51; Bloch, 1947, esp. p. 338; Kogon, 1950, pp. 274-77). Prolonged and extreme exposure to coercion may lead men to accept some of the power-holders' norms, to identify with them, and to deflect their alienation onto scapegoats. New inmates in concentration camps appeared to serve as such scapegoats, as did groups low in status by external stratification criteria (Cohen, 1953, 26-28).

9. For studies of concentration camps see E. A. Cohen (1953, esp. ch. 1 and ch. 3) and Kogon (1950). Vaughan reports on the informal organization of the "Internees" in "Japanese camps in the Philippine Islands" and on the formal organization (1949, chs. 4 and 10, and ch. 7); for a report from the organizational viewpoint see the autobiography of Hoess (1960). See also Bondy (1943); Abel (1951); Adler (1958); and Jackman (1958).

10. For two of the few studies of POW camps which have sociological relevance, see I. Cohen (1917) and W. L. White (1957).

11. For an experimental study of the effects of mild versus severe punishment, and short versus prolonged and repeated punishment, as well as the effect of various combinations of these types on extinction of the punished behavior, see Estes (1944, esp. pp. 37-38). The severe and prolonged punishment generated more alienating effects than the mild and short. Note, however, that all the subjects of the experiment were "albino rats from the Minnesota laboratory stock."

Thus, in this extreme situation, the relationship between coercion and alienation seems to be reversed.

In all other coercive organizations the relationship seems to hold. If, for instance, one controls the degree of initial alienation, it seems that the alienation produced in the typical correctional institution is less than in the typical prison. Since the application of coercion for purposes of internal control (other than preventing escapes) is particularly small in POW camps administered by modern democracies, we would expect that the alienation produced in these camps is smaller than that produced in prisons.

Comparatively low alienation is reported by Leighton (1945) in his study of American "relocation centers" of civilians of Japanese ancestry. Control was exercised in part by recognizing strikes and grievances and by bargaining through mutual concessions. Force, the coercive organization's typical approach to inmate strikes, was not used. Other parts of Leighton's study also demonstrate the comparatively limited use of coercion for purposes of internal control.[12]

One way to determine empirically the place of an organization on the coercive continuum is to establish the typical punishment for the same kind of offense in various organizations. For instance, the punishment for attempting to escape from a concentration camp was often death or torture; from prisons, the extension of sentence, often by as much as a year; in "correctional institutions," an extension usually much shorter in duration. In American camps of German prisoners of war, the punishment was usually not more than two weeks on bread and water.[13] Similar comparisons can be made for other offenses.

Custodial mental hospitals are difficult to place in this manner, since in these organizations a different interpretation is given to the same offense, and since other forms of punishment—some seen by the staff as therapeutic measures—are available, such as electric shock, insulin injections, and the strait jacket.[14] To the degree that a comparison can be made, we suggest that custodial mental hospitals resemble correctional institutions for youthful offenders rather than

12. Leighton (1945). On means of control see especially pp. 43, 155, 179; on the strike settlement, pp. 208-9. But compare the settlement of another strike, p. 244.

13. Private communication from two wardens of such camps.

14. For a discussion of the punitive use of electrical shock, see Belknap (1956, pp. 164, 191-94, 248).

prisons, to which they are often compared. It seems that youth and insanity mitigate the punitive orientation. People are committed to both organizations against their will, but the same deviant act brings shorter confinement when the offender is either young or legally defined as mentally ill. There is no capital punishment in either organization. Rehabilitation and therapy, limited as they may be, appear more often in these two organizational types than in prisons. Both fall in the relatively less coercive part of the coercive category.

The amount of relevant information on various types of coercive organization varies greatly. Prisons and mental hospitals, the two more common types, are studied rather frequently, and therefore the discussion of coercive organizations in subsequent chapters will focus on them. Information about compliance in concentration camps is very limited. For prisoners of war, we have some data on the compliance of soldiers from democratic societies in the camps of the enemy,[15] but little information about prisoners from totalitarian societies in the camps of democracies. More information on the latter would be required for a fuller analysis of variations in the exercise of coercion in modern democratic societies, the subject of our analysis.

If inquiry into concentration camps, POW camps, forced-labor camps, and similar coercive organizations is to be extended, special attention must be paid to the pitfalls of value-laden labels. The Germans, for example, referred to Dachau and similar camps as "Arbeitslager," that is, work camps (E. A. Cohen, 1953, p. 19). The Japanese camp described in the Vaughan report is usually referred to as a concentration camp, although no violence was exercised except to keep "internees" in the camp.[16] Similar camps in the United States are referred to as relocation centers. On the other hand, the American Andersonville is described as a camp for prisoners of war, although 14,000 soldiers died there from starvation or disease, were maimed by bloodhounds, or were eaten by their crazed fellow prisoners.[17]

The following distinctions of usage may prove helpful: Organizations that serve as tools of mass murder should be called *concentration camps,* including some formally defined as camps for prisoners

15. For a report of the army studies of American prisoners of war in Korea, see Kinkead (1959). See also *The New Yorker* (Oct. 26, 1957, pp. 114-69); W. L. White (1957).

16. "A woman was slapped across the face, another upon her back before a sober guard ordered the drunken ones away. In the history of the camp this was the only one of physical abuse by the Japanese." (Vaughan, 1949, p. 80)

17. For an early report close to the event see Roach (1865); for a recent publication see McElroy (1957).

of war; organizations that serve merely to detain persons are *prisons,* including some so-called mental hospitals, "homes for the aged," and "intern" camps. Relocation centers in which people are involuntarily detained are a kind of prison; so are camps of forced labor, which have production as a secondary goal. Organizations that combine a strong emphasis on detention with some rehabilitation are *correctional institutions.*

UTILITARIAN ORGANIZATIONS

Utilitarian organizations are organizations in which remuneration is the major means of control over lower participants and calculative involvement (i.e., mild alienation to mild commitment) characterizes the orientation of the large majority of lower participants. Utilitarian organzations are commonly referred to as industries. But as we have seen, *industries* is one of those misleading common-sense labels. Although many industries are utilitarian organizations, some important subcategories have normative compliance structures. Thus, for our purposes, industries and divisions of industrial organizations can be classified into three main categories: those whose lower participants are predominantly *blue-collar* workers, such as most factories and mines; those whose lower participants are predominantly *white-collar* employees, such as offices, whether private (insurance companies and banks) or public (various governmental agencies); and those whose lower participants are *professionals,* such as research organizations, planning organizations, and law firms (these, as we will see, are normative organizations).

Statements made about one category of industry also hold, though to a lesser degree, for employees of the same type in subdivisions of other categories of organizations. Thus, statements about white-collar industries apply to office employees in factories; statements about professional organizations are also true for professional divisions in blue-collar industries, as in research and development divisions; and statements about blue-collar industries hold for janitors in a university. The statements hold "to a lesser degree" because the compliance of an organizational subdivision is affected not only by the type of work —manual, clerical, or professional—done by the subunit's employees, but also by the compliance pattern in the rest of the organization. Hospital attendants, who are doing blue-collar work in a normative organization, illustrate this point. We would expect them to be, as indeed they are, the most remunerative, least normative group of the hospital staff, but they are more normatively controlled than blue-collar workers in blue-collar industries. This fact is reflected in their moral commitment to the health of patients, in efforts to develop their professional self-image, in their comparatively high job satisfaction, and, of course, in their lower wages.[18]

Remunerative power—such as the manipulation of wages, salaries, commissions, fringe benefits, working conditions, and similar rewards—constitutes the predominant source of control in blue-collar industries. These sanctions also constitute the predominant means of control in white-collar industries, but they are less pronounced there than in blue-collar industries; and they constitute an important though secondary power in professional organizations. Normative controls play a relatively limited role in blue-collar industries; an important though secondary role in white-collar industries; and they constitute the predominant means of control in professional organizations. In other words, professional oragnizations are not a remunerative but a normative "industry." Hence their compliance structure is examined in the subsequent chapter, with other normative organizations.

The preceding statements can be specified further by differentiating within each of the major categories of industry. Blue-collar workers can be broken into unskilled, semiskilled, and skilled workers, or into industrial workers and craft workers. We would expect the unskilled industrial workers to be the most subject to remunerative controls, and the skilled or craft-oriented ones to be relatively more affected by normative controls.[19]

Similarly, white-collar employees can be divided into subgroups which consist, on the one hand, of lower-ranking personnel such as salesgirls, clerks, and tellers, and, on the other, somewhat higher-ranking personnel such as supervisory clerks or private secretaries, who have closer contact with management. The first are controlled by relatively more utilitarian means than the latter.[20] A comparison of

18. On the professional self-image and intrinsic job satisfaction, see Simpson and Simpson (1959, p. 391).
19. The differences between the two types of workers are aptly described and analyzed by Warner and Low (1947, chs. 4 and 5).
20. For a discussion of the various types of white-collar employees, differences in their reward-structures, and differences in the degree of alienation generated, see Mills (1951, chs. 8 and 10).

typists in a large "pool" and single secretaries attached to "their" executive may illustrate the difference. Female workers, who constitute a large proportion of the lower-ranking white-collar employees, seem to be relatively more given to normative compliance than male white-collar employees.[21]

Finally, semi-professionals, such as engineers and laboratory technicians, seem to be less normatively controlled than full-fledged professionals.

Data on differences in alienation among these groups parallel those on differences in modes of control. Blauner (1960, pp. 342-43) has summarized a large number of studies which suggest that those who would choose the same kind of work if beginning their career again constitute about 20 per cent of the unskilled workers, about 30 to 40 per cent of the service employees, and 65 per cent or more of the professionals. Similar findings have been reported by Moore (1953) and by Morse and Weiss (1955, p. 197).[22]

Blue-Collar Workers

Remuneration is the predominant means of control of blue-collar workers. Its allocation and manipulation make these employees conform to regulations governing the required level and quality of production, the use and treatment of organizational property, tardiness, absenteeism, and the like. It may not be the central factor determining their orientation to work in general, or their choice of a particular line of work, but it seems to be central in affecting their orientation to particular jobs and many job-norms, and to the organization as a control structure.

It is true that other factors, including their basic values, degree of unionization, intrinsic satisfaction from work, prestige and esteem derived from it, and, to some degree, social relations on the job, also influence the job orientation and performance of workers. We suggest, however, that when the relative weight of these various factors is established, remunerative rewards and sanctions will turn

21. Morse (1953, pp. 77ff.) studied involvement of white-collar workers in a company. She found the highest degree of involvement (53 per cent high) among semi-supervisory personnel, who are mostly women. This association holds when other factors, such as salaries, length of service, age, and education, are controlled.
22. See Chapter XI, pages 301-2, on the problems involved in using job satisfaction as an indicator of involvement in the organization.

out to play a more important part in control of blue-collar workers than other factors.

Some relevant material is supplied in a study of the method of control preferred by workers in an electric power company, and the method of control considered effective by their supervisors (Mann and Dent, 1954). Workers rated recommending an increase in pay as the preferred method of control; supervisors rated this as the most effective method. Table II-1 indicates the relative significance of other means of control compared with "recommend pay increase." [23]

Table II-1—"Method of Recognition" Preferred by Workers and Supervisors

METHOD OF RECOGNITION	RANK ORDER	
	Workers Like	Supervisors Find Effective
Recommend pay increase	1	1
Train employees for better jobs	2	6
Recommend promotions	3	3
Give more responsibility	4	4
Praise sincerely and thoroughly	5	5
Give more interesting work	6	9
Tell superiors	7	7
Give privileges	8	8
Give pat on the back	9	2
Make notes of it in ratings and reports	10	10

Source: Mann and Dent (1954, p. 25).

Further evidence is supplied by a study of workers who chose to work on an assembly line in the automotive industry (Walker and Guest, 1952). An examination of their previous jobs indicates that by six criteria of job satisfaction, the workers were much better off on their previous job; 87.4 per cent had formerly held a job where pace was determined individually; 72 per cent had had nonrepetitive jobs; about 60 per cent had had jobs requiring some skills and training; and 62.7 per cent had been entirely or partly free to determine

23. This table is interesting for another reason: there are three discrepancies in the ranking. Workers give "train employees for better jobs" second rank, whereas supervisors rank it sixth—this is a facet of remunerative control; and supervisors give "pat on the back" second place, whereas employees give it ninth—this is a normative control. Supervisors, being higher in rank appear to give more weight to normative controls than employees do. This point was suggested to the author by Candace Rogers. The meaning of the third discrepancy, on "Give more interesting work," is not clear.

how their jobs ought to be done (*ibid., pp.* 34ff.). They chose to leave these jobs and take the frustrating assembly-line jobs basically because the new jobs offered a higher and more secure income. Three quarters of the workers reported that the reasons bringing them to the new plant were primarily economic. Wage differences were about 30 per cent—$1.51 per hour compared with $1.05 (*ibid.,* p. 91).[24]

Social scientists studying industries have emphasized that the earlier image of the worker as a rational machine, from whom greater effort can be elicited when more incentives are introduced, is not valid. By now this point is widely accepted; indeed, it seems at times to be overstressed. Students of industries should be reminded that attempts to increase the normative elements of supervision are in some cases reported to lead only to small increases in productivity; whereas in other cases they cause an increase in "morale" (i.e., job satisfaction) but none in productivity. On the other hand, reports from industry and surveys by government bureaus generally attest to the effectiveness of wage-incentive plans in increasing productivity and achieving other objectives. A government survey of 514 wage-incentive plans in the United States reported in 1945 that, under such plans, production increases averaged 38.99 per cent; unit labor costs were decreased on the average by 11.58 per cent (Viteles, 1953, p. 27). Argyris reviews a large number of studies, all supporting the same point:

[F. H.] Blum (1953, pp. 94-99) gives evidence of the desire to get away from work and "live" outside. He finds that workers are anxious to leave their work. . . . Most employees report that they work in the plant in order to make money "to live" outside. An unusual experimental study that taps factors in "depth" with a relatively large sample (219 women in seven factories in Sweden) provides more evidence for the increasing importance of money (Smith and Lund, 1954). . . . Chinoy (1955) concludes that automobile workers by the time they reach middle age realize that their jobs are not and never will be satisfying, and that advancement for them will be difficult. They adapt, he reports, by placing an even greater empha-

24. A study of workers transferred from nonautomated departments to automated departments shows that they liked their previous jobs better on every single dimension which was examined, including number of friends and closeness of supervision. Since almost all the workers transferred voluntarily, it seems reasonable to suppose this was because of differences in wages. The average wages in the automated departments were higher because of both differences in the composition of the work force and up-grading. See Faunce (1958, pp. 401-7, and 1959, pp. 44-53, esp. 45-46). Information on voluntary transfer and wage differences is based on private communication with Faunce.

sis on employment, security, constant increases in wages, and the increased consumption of material goods. . . . Reigel, in a study of employee interest in company success in eight corporations, notes that half of the respondents report economic incentive as the best means to increase their interest in the company, while less than one third report human incentives. (1957, pp. 107-9)[25]

Manipulation of esteem and prestige symbols is an important source of normative control. To what degree can management rely on these means to control blue-collar workers? It is important to note that the use of esteem and prestige for control purposes requires that management control their allocation. This in turn requires that workers and their superiors share a basic set of values and that the superiors constitute "significant others" for the workers. Otherwise, praise from the superior not only may have little positive effect but may actually have a negative effect. Being reported in a factory publication as the most productive worker of the year may be a source of deprivation rather than gratification. The same holds for other esteem and prestige symbols manipulable by management. We shall see below that blue-collar workers share only a few of the relevant values of management, and that when foremen and workers share such values, it is often because foremen accept the workers' outlook, and not the other way around. Hence, prestige symbols are unlikely to be an effective or important means of control of blue-collar workers (R. R. Myers, 1948, p. 335). That the size of the office, the number of telephones, the place in the parking lot, and similar prestige symbols are highly gratifying to higher ranks of white-collar employees and executives does not necessarily mean that they are effective means of control for all employees. The central means for control of blue-collar workers are remunerative.

White-Collar Employees

White-collar employees are predominantly controlled by remunerative means, but less so than blue-collar workers. Normative controls, though secondary, seem to play a more important role among white-collar employees, and commitment to the organization is higher.

---

25. See also Whyte, "Money Still Vital" (1956).

Table II-2—Best Liked about Company

Remunerative

Hours	28%
Benefits	12
Security	11
Working conditions	8
Lunches	4
Salaries	3*
Advancement opportunities	2
Total	68%

Other

Kind of people	22%
Fairness of treatment	5
Kind of work	4
Not ascertained	1
Total	32%

* Salaries are mentioned infrequently here because employees were dissatisfied with the level of their salaries; infrequent mention does not reflect their lack of saliency. Sixteen per cent of the employees mentioned salaries as the least liked feature of their jobs.
Source: Morse (1953, p. 103).

Morse's meticulous study (1953) of white-collar employees supplies information on what 742 employees "like best about working in the company" studied, and thus casts some light on the relative importance of various rewards and sanctions. Morse's findings suggest the overriding importance of remunerative rewards for white-collar employees, and support our suggestion that the compliance of lower-ranking white-collar employees is predominantly remunerative.

A study of salesgirls by Lombard (1955, esp. pp. 124-30) points out many of the phenomena usually considered typical of manual workers. He reports, for instance, that the work group restricts "output," limits competition among the girls, and enforces other norms which are in direct contrast to those supported by management.

At the same time the manipulation of esteem and prestige symbols, which as a rule has a limited effect on blue-collar workers, seems to be more effective among white-collar employees (Homans, 1953). This point is illustrated in a study of salesgirls which emphasized the role of nonremunerative "symbolic" controls. Salesgirls who made mistakes in writing out sales slips had the slips returned to them, marked with a red rubber band, to be opened and corrected in the presence of the section manager and other salesgirls. These red bands "do not result in fines or punishments of any sort, and yet the clerks feel that to get one is a disgrace" (Donovan, 1929, p. 64). Similarly, "all sorts of honors are bestowed upon the capable and efficient. These have small monetary value, but money is secondary to honor. To be ace—the best saleswoman in your department—is a compensation enough in itself" (*ibid.*, p. 192).

The material available on involvement suggests that, in general, white-collar employees are less alienated than blue-collar workers, though not much less so. Most measures show differences of less than twenty percentage points between the two groups.[26] The data in Table II-3 are not typical, since they are taken from companies whose proportion of satisfied workers is higher than average, but it is of interest that even here the relative position of blue- versus white-collar employees is maintained (this study controlled for rank).

Table II-3—Alienation of Nonsupervisory Male White-Collar Employees and Blue-Collar Employees

Attitude	White Collar (1792)	Blue Collar (4788)
I like my job as a whole	70%	57%
Satisfied with working conditions in general	75	47
Satisfied with company and job as a whole	60	51
Satisfied with present wages	39	28
Satisfied with progress in company up to now	65	64

Source: Katz and Kahn (1952, p. 655).

Several facts may account for the relatively greater importance of normative powers for white-collar employees and for their higher commitment to the organization. First, although income differences between the two groups have declined considerably over the last three decades, the over-all rewards of white-collar employees are still greater because of the prestige attached to their jobs and the larger intrinsic satisfactions involved.[27] Higher rewards tend to be associated with higher commitment to the organization, and hence to

26. See the following review studies of the large literature on the subject: Herzberg, Mausner, Peterson, and Capwell (1957); Herzberg, Mausner, and Synderman (1959); Blauner (1960).

27. The greater amount of reward and, hence, vested interest in the existing social structure extends beyond the organization to the general social structure. It has been demonstrated that white-collar employees systematically vote conservative more often than blue-collar workers (Lipset and Linz, 1956, ch. 4). Differences in the degree of unionization, pointed out by Mills, support the same point (1956, p. 302).

allow for greater application of normative controls. Closer and more personal contact with management also tends to increase involvement; again, commitment is generated when clients of white-collar employees grant them deference because of the power of the organization they represent (Mills, 1945, pp. 242-49). Blue-collar workers as a rule have little personal contact with management and no client contacts, and hence lack these sources of commitment.

In short, it seems that white-collar industries—though exhibiting many borderline cases—should be classified as predominately utilitarian organizations. Normative compliance has a role more important than in blue-collar industries, but still secondary. Professional organizations are discussed in Chapter III as a type of normative organization.[28]

28. The summary for this chapter appears at the end of Chapter III.

AN ANALYTICAL
CLASSIFICATION
Normative and Dual
Organizations

III

NORMATIVE ORGANIZATIONS

Normative organizations are organizations in which normative power is the major source of control over most lower participants, whose orientation to the organization is characterized by high commitment. Compliance in normative organizations rests principally on internalization of directives accepted as legitimate. Leadership, rituals, manipulation of social and prestige symbols, and resocialization are among the more important techniques of control used.

Although there are only two common types of coercive organizations (prisons and custodial mental hospitals), and two common types of utilitarian organizations (blue-collar and white-collar industries), there are at least nine frequently found types of normative organizations. In five of these the normative pattern is highly pronounced and other patterns are relatively minor. These are *religious* organizations, including churches, orders, and monasteries; a subcategory of *political* organizations, those which have a strong ideological program; *general hospitals; universities;* and *voluntary associations,* which, as we shall see, rely mainly on social powers and commitments. Less typical, in the sense that coercion plays an important secondary role,[1] are *schools* and *therapeutic mental hospitals*. Also less typical are *professional* organizations, in which remuneration plays an important part. Finally, *"core"* organizations of social movements tend to have a normative compliance structure, though it is difficult to assess its exact nature.

The greater variety of normative organizations, and the fact that their compliance structure is less often discussed in professional literature, requires that we devote more space to them than to the other two types.

Typical Normative Organizations

Religious organizations must rely predominantly on normative powers to attain both acceptance of their directives and the means required for their operation.[2] No coercion is applied to a Mormon who does not pay his tithe (Webb, 1916, p. 116); he is punished by denial of access to religious services in the Temple.[3] Similarly, police will not arrest, nor will a court fine, a Catholic who is divorced or a nun who breaks her vows and leaves her order.[4] These and other breaches of discipline are major transgressions in the eyes of the various religions, but the impact of such a view depends on the ability of the church to influence the normative orientation of the parishioners. If the typical normative means of socialization in religious schools [5]—participation in religious rituals, sermons, and manipulation of various symbols—fail, there is little else the church

1. For a discussion of methodological aspects of statements on predominant and secondary powers, see pages 78ff.

2. This might be an appropriate place to point out once more that our discussion centers on organizations in modern democratic societies.

3. Private communication with Ivan A. Vallier. For a theoretical discussion as well as a case analysis of the problems involved in the fulfillment of the "adaptive" (in Parsons' terminology) needs of systems emphasizing moral values, such as communes and religious organizations, see Vallier (1959). For another study of this problem see Doll (1951).

4. There are no sociological studies of convents. We do have the sober and authentic autobiographical account of Baldwin (1957) and the fictional account of Hulme (1956). Both books allow some insight into the compliance structure of nunneries. Note that in both cases, when it became evident that no normative power would hold the deviant nun, permission to leave was granted. See also Charques (1960).

5. For a report of socialization in these schools by an "insider," see Fichter (1958).

can do.[6] Needless to say, remunerative powers cannot serve as the basis of religious compliance. Hence heavy reliance on normative means of control and moral commitments is mandatory for religious organizations.

The compliance structure of *political organizations,* such as political parties and labor unions, varies considerably. Some parties, especially on the local level and in particular among marginal groups such as farm hands and new immigrants, rely for the most part on patronage, allocation of spoils, and other nonsymbolic rewards ranging from distribution of coal to cancellation of parking tickets. But the majority of parties, in particular on the national level, have to rely predominantly on normative compliance. This is because no modern party can recruit the material means required to control a large and affluent electorate, and because normative appeals are more effective in maintaining party loyalties.

Labor unions in general are less normative than parties. As we shall see subsequently, business unions emphasize utilitarian compliance in "normal" (nonstrike) periods. Other unions make wide use of coercion for internal control purposes. Yet at least two kinds of unions are typical normative organizations: ideological unions, such as the Socialist and Communist unions in democratic societies, and social unions, which to a great extent rely for compliance on the social power of their *gemeinschaft* life.

General hospitals are tentatively classified as normative organizations, although there is little information concerning the ways in which patients are controlled.[7] A few unsystematic observations and interviews with physicians and hospital administrators suggest that the question of discipline comes up rarely, since the patient's need to comply is highly internalized. When doctors or nurses are asked, "What happens when a patient does not follow orders?" their immediate reply is typical of all contexts where only normative controls operate: "Nothing happens." Further probing shows that disobedience actually triggers a normative campaign whose scope and intensity depend on the seriousness of the consequences for the patient's

6. This is particularly true when the deviant is not an individual but a social group. It has been demonstrated, for example, that no one of the major religious organizations in the South—notwithstanding differences in hierarchical organizational controls—could overcome the resistance of its parishoners and part of the lower clergy to desegregation. See Campbell and Pettigrew (1959) and Zewe (1959).

7. For a descriptive report on the patients' involvement and perspective, see John (1935). See also H. L. Smith (1949) and Wessen (1951).

health, as well as on the prestige of the professional who has been disobeyed and the degree to which the breach of discipline is visible to the various subgroups in the hospital community.

The following techniques of control are applied: (1) Informal talks with the patient by other staff members. A doctor may reinforce a nurse's orders, a chief surgeon those of his intern, a nurse may coax a patient to follow the doctor's orders. (2) The use of the hospital hierarchy to settle "disciplinary" problems of patients. Burling, Lentz, and Wilson report: "The point is that the nurse must now adjust to him [the patient] almost as much as he is required to adjust to her and to hospital rules. When he becomes difficult to handle, the general duty nurse calls upon the authority of the head nurse to bring about more cooperative relations. . . . Serious problems still go to the top [hospital administrator] but others are left to the head nurse for solution." (1956, p. 112) (3) Activation of relatives and friends to convince the patient, for example, to undergo an operation. (4) A visit by an outsider whom the patient respects, such as a pastor. (5) Asking the patient to sign a document releasing the hospital from responsibility for the consequences of his disobedience. This is usually seen as a legal act, which protects the hospital from possible damage suits. In addition, it frequently serves as part of the normative campaign, impressing the patient with the seriousness of his disobedience. Typically, it is used long before the hospital has really given up trying to convince the patient to follow orders. In general, only persons who do not have full legal rights, such as minors, inmates, and the mentally deficient, are treated through coercion.[8]

The diversity of *voluntary associations* is enormous. There is hardly a goal, from watching birds (the Audubon Society) to spacing births (the Planned Parenthood Federation of America) which has not been pursued by some association. It is not our task here to classify this large group according to goals, functions, or any aspect other than compliance.[9] From this viewpoint all voluntary associations have a similar structure: they are primarily social, using in addition

8. There are also some relevant differences in the treatment of paying patients and ward patients which have yet to be explored. Burling *et al.* (1956, p. 112) report that the insured patients have a "more independent spirit."

9. Some of the best analyses of the functions of voluntary associations are unpublished Ph.D. dissertations. See Barber (1948); Axelrod (1953); S. D. Fox (1953); Goldsmer (1943). See the review of various approaches to the subject by Warner (1953, ch. 9); Chapple and Coon (1941, pp. 416-23); Rose (1954, pp. 72-115); Bottomore (1954); Chambers (1954); Henderson (1895). For an interesting classification see Gordon and Babchuk (1959, pp. 22-29).

varying degrees of pure normative power.[10] But the use of normative power rarely has the same significance as it does in religious, political, and educational organizations.

Fraternal associations, such as the Lions, Elks, Masons, Rotary, or Greek letter societies on college campuses, which satisfy their members' gregarious needs through social activities, constitute a subcategory of voluntary associations which apply social power almost exclusively, building up social rather than moral commitments. In this type of organization, membership and degree of activity are so closely related to involvement [11]—while regulations and directives are so limited and open to individual interpretation—that disciplinary problems rarely arise. Social power is exercised mainly through informal sanctions (e.g., withdrawal of approval) and only infrequently through suspension or expulsion. Disapproval is either potent enough to generate conformity or abolishes the very motivation for belonging, since the gregarious needs remain unsatisfied.

Among the voluntary associations which build up moral as well as social commitments are fund-raising organizations such as the American Cancer Society, American Heart Association, United Cerebral Palsy, National Tuberculosis, the National Foundation, and the Community Chest.[12] These organizations tend to develop ideologies which build up the commitment of members and volunteer workers to the organization, and compensate them through symbolic rewards for their work and monetary contributions. It is probable that the feuds among some of these organizations have the latent function of building up such ideologies and membership commitments.[13]

10. Seventy per cent of the volunteers studied by Sills (1957, pp. 99-101) were either "Good Citizens" or "Joiners," both persons who join the Polio Foundation mainly for "social" reasons.

11. This is demonstrated for participation in a labor union by L. R. Dean (1954); for a fund-raising organization by Cornish (1960). For reviews of the research on determinants of participation see Barber (1950, pp. 481-84); and Komarovsky (1946, pp. 686-98). For two effective reviews and analysis of available evidence see Wright and Hyman (1958, pp. 284-94) and J. C. Scott, Jr. (1957, pp. 317-26).

12. For case studies of two of these associations, see Seeley, Junkers, Wallace *et al.* (1957) and Sills (1957).

13. For an account of the public aspect of such an inter-organizational feud, see *The New York Times* (June 15-17, 1959). See also a study by Wiggins (1960); and Kohn, Tannenbaum, Weiss, *et al.* (1956). Rose (1955) studied the impact of inter-organizational conflict on the structure of voluntary associations. For an analysis of a large number of voluntary associations, other than fund-raising organizations, which have normative programs, see Hero (1960).

Coercive Compliance as Secondary Pattern

Educational organizations characteristically employ normative controls, with coercion as a secondary source of compliance. Normative controls in schools include manipulation of prestige symbols, such as honors, grades, and citations; personal influence of the teacher; [14] "talks" with the principal; scolding and sarcasm, demanding "apologies," and similar means which are based on appeals to the student's moral commitments and on manipulation of the class or peer group's climate of opinion. [15] Coercion has declined in significance over the last decades, for modern education de-emphasizes "discipline" as a goal and stresses internalization of norms.

Tables III-1 and III-2, taken from surveys of the means of control used in elementary and in high schools, suggest that normative compliance is indeed the predominant type.

Table III-1—Number of Treatments Used by "Experienced" Teachers in Grades I through VI

	I	II	III	IV	V	VI	Total	Percent of Grand Total
Physical Force	4	4	14	2	0	2	26	0.8
Censure	121	238	435	251	88	109	1,242	46.0
Overtime or extra work	25	43	87	56	12	25	240	9.0
Deprivation	80	116	156	96	30	24	502	19.0
Ignoring	3	8	1	9	5	7	33	1.0
Verbal appeal	49	55	77	41	10	25	257	10.0
Social approval	23	31	25	30	7	6	122	4.0
Explanation	45	46	62	44	24	28	249	9.0
Reward through privilege	10	6	4	10	5	1	36	1.0
Total	360	547	861	539	181	227	2,715	100.0

Source: Campbell (1935, pp. 22-23).

14. To "encourage leadership" and to "use the democratic group process" are the first two "guiding principles" for teachers listed by Parody (1958, p. 63). See also Redl (1944, pp. 58-62).

15. Those who exercise normative controls in schools often assume that the peers of the sanctioned student support the sanctioning agent or his norm, or that the social power of the students does not nullify the normative power of teacher and principal. Recent studies have demonstrated that at least in high schools, behavior is determined to a considerable degree by the values of the students, not the teachers, in cases where there is a conflict. See the outstanding study of ten high schools by J. S. Coleman (1961). See also Gordon (1957).

*Table III-2—The Use of Certain Disciplinary Measures
as Reported by Principals*

DISCIPLINARY MEASURES EMPLOYED	NUMBER EMPLOYING		
	Never	Seldom	Often
Detention after school	23	90	196
Requiring parent to come	3	130	176
Sending pupil to office	1	147	162
Withdrawal of privileges	28	190	90
Reprimand	36	179	86
Suspension of individual	9	260	39
Special tasks	70	162	68
Demanding an apology	101	167	39
Forcing pupil to drop course	95	191	19
Expulsion	136	161	......
Giving demerits	230	27	43
Lowering mark of pupil	212	83	13
Imposition of a fine	215	79	13
Corporal punishment	240	67	1
Group suspension	276	25	2

Source: Garinger (1936, p. 25).

Normative controls are, by far, the most frequently reported in both elementary and high schools. About half (46 per cent) of the "treatments" reported for elementary schools are in the category of "censure," which includes scolding, sarcasm, demanding apology, ridicule, and similar forms of discipline. Deprivation, the next largest item (19 per cent), is normative insofar as it consists mainly of symbolic punishments such as "sending the child to another seat" and "sending into corner." Verbal appeal and explanation make up another 14 per cent. Coercion is used in less than one per cent of the cases.

The report on disciplinary measures in high schools is essentially the same. Most schools never use corporal punishment, and imposition of fines is rare. Sending pupils to the principal's office, withdrawal of privileges, reprimands, demerits, and the like make up the large majority of the punishments.[16]

16. It is of interest to note that in normative organizations, wide application of sanctions, even mild ones, is considered an indication of the elite's ineffectiveness. Hence, it often leads to preventive measures. The following "remedial" activities in schools are listed by Garinger (in rank order): Persuasion and suggestion; trying to improve health of student (poor hearing or eye-sight are sources of some disciplinary troubles); frequent report to parents; assigning one teacher for guidance, and others. (1936, p. 35)

The relevance of these kinds of control to the study of compliance lies in the degree of alienation they create in the student. Schools are not voluntary organizations. A gap exists between the activities which would fulfill the actor's internalized need-dispositions and the activities in which he must participate.[17] Parents, truant officers, police departments, and others coerce children to attend schools.[18] Schools make participation in desired activities contingent upon adequate performance in others. Hence we would expect to find in general a higher degree of alienation in schools than in typical normative organizations.[19]

Despite the relatively high level of alienation and the relatively wide use of extra-organizational coercive enforcement (compared with most other normative organizations), however, only a small minority (estimates vary from one to five per cent) of the students in most schools require and are affected by the large majority of the coercive measures used. Sixty per cent of 4,270 teachers queried by Cutts and Moseley (1957, p. 15) stated that less than one per cent of their students were troublemakers. Vredevoe (n.d., p. 5) reports that 3 to 5 per cent of the students account for 95 per cent of the application of severe sanctions.

Vocational schools have developed in part as an answer to the disciplinary problem created by students who, because of their social background and career prospects, are alienated from the regular high school program. But since even these schools are rarely accommodated to their students' needs, and since their function is often more custodial (keeping teenagers off the streets and out of the labor mar-

17. Stinchcombe (1960) analyzes extensively the sources, patterns, consequences, and some expressions of alienation in a high school.

18. Schools, in particular the more modern ones, tend to externalize the application of coercion by delegating it to parents, courts, police, and other authorities. This enables the school to initiate and partially direct the use of coercion without suffering the full impact of the resulting alienation. Moreover, coercion and other negative sanctions applied in the school, especially the more powerful ones, are not applied by the teacher who has to build up the commitment of the students to himself in order to carry out his educational role effectively. Teachers tend to send their students to the principal for severe sanctioning (Reavins and Woellner, 1930). Garinger (1936, pp. 16ff.) supplies a detailed analysis of the kind of offense and the persons to whom the student is sent for discipline. These persons include principals, assistant principals, deans, "homeroom" teachers, and others. Comparatively few punishments are administered by the regular teacher of the class. See also Douglass (1945, pp. 265-85).

19. From this point of view, schools are comparable to labor unions with a closed or union shop, rather than to political parties, religious organizations, and other normative organizations in which participation is voluntary.

ket) than educational, alienation is in general higher here than in regular schools.[20] Compliance differs accordingly, with considerably more emphasis on internal and external coercive enforcement.[21]

Special schools, like the "600's" in New York City, are schools in which a large number of disciplinary cases are concentrated.[22] Coercion plays a more important (though still secondary) role here than in other schools. Some of these schools regularly have a policeman on the premises.

On the other hand, disciplinary measures disappear almost completely in undergraduate colleges and are practically nonexistent on the graduate level. With some exceptions, for example in military academies, corporal punishment is unknown. Eviction from classes is very rare. Graduates are treated as junior members of the profession; the few instances of misbehavior which are controlled on the undergraduate level are, on the graduate level, considered "private"—that is, outside the University's jurisdiction. Changes in commitment to the organization parallel changes in control: commitment increases steadily as students become better trained and educated.[23] Self- and enforced selection eliminate those who are less involved. Hence, unlike other educational organizations, colleges are treated as a separate class, within the category of typical normative organizations.

To summarize the discussion of educational organizations: In general, normative compliance prevails and coercion plays a secondary role. In ordinary primary and secondary schools, internal coercion plays a rather small role, though there is somewhat more external coercion; internal coercion has more weight in vocational schools, and even more in "special" schools. In colleges and universities, on the other hand, coercion in general is so limited that these schools con-

20. The situation is complicated further because even when the "terminal" training is geared to the student's abilities, background, and future, as well as to the demand of the local market, prestige factors and social pressures push the students to the more academic programs. This has been shown by Clark (1960 and 1960*a*).

21. Evan Hunter's novel *The Blackboard Jungle* (1954) supplies a vivid illustration of the atmosphere and "means of control" used in vocational schools.

22. *America* (December 21, 1957); Samuels (1958); and Brim (1958, p. 52).

23. Newcomb's well-known study (1943) of the acceptance of liberal faculty values by college students from conservative backgrounds, an acceptance which increases and intensifies with the move from freshman to senior year, testifies to the high positive involvement of these students in at least one major aspect of the organizational normative system. Cf. Jacob's review study (1957) of students' tendencies to accept college values.

stitute typical normative organizations. Levels of alienation are closely associated with the degree of coercion applied.[24]

Therapeutic mental hospitals, like schools, apply predominantly normative means of control, making secondary use of coercion. Those which apply predominantly coercive means are classified as custodial mental hospitals, among the coercive organizations.

The shift of mental hospitals from the coercive to the normative category—or, as it is more commonly put, from custodial to thera-peutic (Greenblatt, York, and Brown, 1955)—is much emphasized in the professional and popular literature. Still, it should be pointed out that therapeutic hospitals constitute only a small minority. A study by Tuma and Ozarin, which covered 94 per cent of all public mental hospitals in the United States, Canada, Hawaii, and Puerto Rico, reports that 12.8 per cent of all patients are in open wards, 22.3 per cent are privileged, 45.8 per cent are semi-privileged, and 31.9 per cent have no privileges (1958, pp. 1109-10).[25] Private mental hospitals are more open and have more privileged patients, but they house only a fraction of the total patient population.[26]

A mental hospital which relies on patients' normative compliance is conceived to be a kind of "therapeutic community" (Jones, 1953) in which all personnel, not just the professionals, have a treatment orientation to the patients, and participate in the "other twenty-three hours" (other than the psychoanalytic hour) of treatment. The pa-tient in the hospital is supposedly treated like the patient in private practice. His presence should be voluntary. An open ward is hence ideally one in which there are no locks, no bars, and no guards, so that the patient can walk away whenever he likes, after some formali-

24. In addition to studies cited above, the following analyses of the organiza-tional structure of schools are especially relevant to the study of compliance: Davies and Iannaccone supply a programmatic review of organizational studies of schools (1958); see Sayre's "reply" to this article (1958). See also Campbell and Gregg (1957); Griffiths (1959, pp. 1-7, 47-55); and a special issue of the *Harvard Educational Review* devoted to the subject (1959). For a study of discipline based on life histories see Waller (1932).

25. Tuma and Ozarin use the following categories: "Open Ward: A ward where the doors of the nursing unit and to the outside are unlocked during part or all of the day. Privileged Patient: A patient who is permitted to leave the ward un-accompanied by staff, visitor, or volunteer. . . . Non-Privileged Patient: A patient who is not permitted to leave the ward at any time, except to obtain medical or psychiatric diagnostic or treatment care." (1958, p. 1104)

26. By the end of 1956 there were 166,304 mental patients in public mental hospitals, as compared to 15,773 in private ones (*Patients in Mental Institutions* 1956, Vol. I, p. 14; and Vol. III, p. 13).

ties. Similarly, the acceptance of treatment has to be voluntary. This acceptance is considered mandatory to create the conditions for therapy—in particular, rapport with the analyst. Typically normative means of control are applied: informal talk, the personalities of the analyst and other personnel, and social pressures of the hospital "community," including those of other patients (Rapoport and Rapoport, 1957).

Almost all therapeutic hospitals fall short of this ideal. Although they try to approach it by emphasizing normative compliance, some coercion is frequently used, in at least one of the following ways. (1) There is a closed ward in the open hospital to which disobedient patients are returned or transferred (Tuma and Ozarin, 1958, pp. 1106-17). (2) Patients may be transferred from open to closed hospitals, and from hospitals which have a "good" reputation among the patients to those of which they are more frightened. For many patients in private hospitals in New York, for example, transfer to Bellevue would have such a meaning. (3) The transfer from a closed to an open ward is broken up into many stages of more and fewer "privileges," such as walking on the premises with and without escort, leaving the hospital for short periods of time, and the like (Wilmer, 1958, p. 20). This reward "ladder" is used both to encourage progress and to punish lack of compliance by returning the patient to a less privileged, more coercive state (Curran, 1939, pp. 1382-83; Parker, 1958). (4) "Unruly" patients are kept under heavy sedation, a control which is physical, hence similar to the use of coercion.[27] It is certainly not part of a normative control system and it does not build up commitment. Thus even relatively open hospitals combine their normative power with some coercive controls.

Similar statements can be made about the few open "prisons," or rehabilitation centers.[28] Inmates can usually be returned to closed prisons. Often there are closed wards and solitary confinement in the midst of the "open" prisons. The superintendent of Chino, a California prison known as one of the most "progressive" and open, reports that 25 per cent of his inmates have to be confined to a maximum-security section; and others are sent to solitary confinement when required, though only for short periods (Scudder, 1954, p. 83).

27. On the use of "large" amounts of sedation as a regular means of control see Wilmer (1958, p. 17).
28. Sweden is known as a country in which such centers are highly developed. See Sellin (1947, 1948) and Erikson (1954, pp. 152-62).

In short, although therapeutic mental hospitals and rehabilitation centers (or open prisons) are predominantly normative organizations, they obviously are less normative than religious organizations, general hospitals, or universities. Here, as in schools, coercion, at least latently, reinforces normative powers.

Utilitarian Compliance as Secondary Pattern

Professional organizations utilize mainly normative controls, though utilitarian compliance occurs here to a greater extent than in any other normative organization. In this sense professional organizations resemble white-collar industries as borderline cases, though it seems they fall on the other side of the border: Whereas in professional organizations normative compliance predominates, with utilitarian compliance a close second, in white-collar industries the reverse is true.

Professional organizations are defined according to two characteristics: their goals, and the rank at which professionals are employed. Their chief goals are professional goals, such as therapy, research, and teaching, and most of their performers are professionals.[29] The rank at which professionals are employed differentiates two major types of professional organizations. In one, professionals constitute the *middle* ranks of the organization, as in the general and mental hospitals, universities, and schools which have been discussed. These have been placed above, according to the compliance structure of the lower participants. A second type, to be dealt with here, includes organizations which serve professional goals and whose *lower* participants are professionals. Of this type are research organizations,[30] such as the Stanford Research Institute, the Bureau of Applied Social Research, the Mellon Institute, the Battele Memorial Institute, and the Rand Corporation (Marine, 1959), whose lower participants are research workers and assistants; planning organiza-

---

29. We apply here a procedure developed by Melman (1958, pp. 69-94), who classifies industries according to the ratio of one type of personnel to another—for example, administrative to production personnel. Evan (1959, p. 5) has showed the usefulness of this indicator for the study of authority in a cross-cultural context. Stinchcombe (1959, pp. 172-73) classified industries by proportion of administrative personnel who are clerks, and by proportion of top administrators who are professionals.

30. For six papers on research administration and references to other studies of research organizations, see *Administrative Science Quarterly,* Vol. 1 (1956). For studies of compliance of researchers see Pelz, Mellinger, and Davis (1953); Baumgartel (1955); Meltzer (1956); Shepard (1955, 1956).

tions,[31] such as the private Kaiser engineering corporation and the planning offices of large city administrations, whose lower participants are engineers (Barnes, 1960), architects, city planners, and related professionals, including an increasing number of social scientists; law firms [32] (Dodge, 1955; Smigel, 1960); architectural firms; and some divisions of advertising (Mayer, 1958), public relations, and broadcasting corporations, as well as the editorial wings of newspapers.

Newspapers typically have a dual organizational structure, with a highly utilitarian wing in which the newspaper is actually produced, and a normative editorial wing in which it is written and edited.[33] The cleavage between the "production" and "creative" wings of other communications industries, such as radio and television networks and advertising agencies, is often smaller, since the "creators" participate more in the "production," but the basic dual structure exists there too.[34]

The major means of control in professional organizations are based on prolonged and careful selection, and socialization in universities and professional schools or on the job precedes recruitment to autonomous performance positions. As a consequence, norms are as a rule highly internalized, so that informal controls and symbolic sanctions are highly effective. Social powers, formalized in the professional code of ethics and the professional association and supported by the social bonds of the professional community and professional elites, carry great weight. The use of economic sanctions such as fines, expulsion from the profession, or cancellation of license is extremely rare. The percentage of lawyers disbarred in the United States was 0.0027 in 1956, 0.0030 in 1957, and 0.0022 in 1958 (*American Bar News,* Vol. 14, February 2, 1959, p. 2).

---

31. Homans (1951, chs. 14 and 15) has analyzed a change in the control structure of an electrical equipment company which designed and manufactured costly instruments, in which most of the owners, officers, and salaried employees were engineers. The analysis is based on a case study by Arensberg and Macgregor (1942). The change concentrated more control in the hands of less professionally-oriented officers, which made for less normative and more utilitarian compliance.
32. Considerable information on these firms and their compliance structure is included in a forthcoming study of the Bureau of Applied Social Research, Columbia University, conducted by Jerome E. Carlin and Allen H. Barton.
33. For a fine study of the compliance of newspapermen which demonstrates the stress on normative controls, see Breed (1952, esp. pp. 135ff.; 1955).
34. There are several reports of the Broadcasting Committee which cast much light on these problems in the British Broadcasting Corporation. See esp. the report of 1949.

High intrinsic satisfaction from work, positively associated with positive involvement, characterizes the work of professionals,[35] although this commitment is sometimes dissociated from the organization and the job and vested in the work itself, for which the profession —not the organization—serves as a reference group and object of involvement (Baumgartel, 1955; Meltzer, 1956). As one would expect from the comparatively extensive use of remunerative rewards, despite the importance of intrinsic satisfaction and other symbolic gratifications, commitment to professional organizations is not as high as it is in typical normative organizations.

Secondary Pattern Unclassified

Social movements are not organizations. They are not oriented to specific goals; their dominant subsystems are expressive and not instrumental; there is little segregation between the various institutional spheres; and there is no systematic division of labor, power, and communication (Cantril, 1941; Heberle, 1951; W. King, 1956). Nevertheless, most movements have an organizational core which does have all these characteristics of a typical organizational structure.

The organizational core is the skeleton of the movement's body. It consists of employed personnel (such as party functionaries), who make the organization their career or primary occupation; volunteers; and members who are not only highly involved but who also feel they have high performance obligations to the movement and are

---

35. This point is well demonstrated in several studies. See, for example, Weiss (1956), who shows that 81 per cent of the professional employees are "highly satisfied" or "satisfied" with their work, compared with 10-20 per cent of blue-collar workers usually so reported. See also Roe (1953); Rettig, Jacobson, and Pasamanick (1958); and Marvick (1959).

Professionals not only gain more satisfaction from their work, but their work also plays a more important role in their life than it does in that of other groups of employees. This has been demonstrated by Orzack (1959), who compared the "central life interests" of professional nurses with those established earlier by Dubin for industrial workers. The main finding was as follows:

DISTRIBUTION OF CENTRAL LIFE INTERESTS (PER CENT)

	Professional Nurses (Orzack)	*Industrial Workers* (Dubin)
Work	79	24
Non-work	21	76

SOURCE: Orzack (1959, p. 127).

willing to be highly subordinated to its leadership in the performance of various tasks. The rest of the movement consists of members and sympathizers who are less committed, who have only limited performance obligations and a narrow scope of subordination-acceptance.

For the National Socialist movement in Germany, the core organization was the National Socialist party; for the labor movement in Western European countries it is often a web of organizations which includes one or more parties and one or more labor unions. However, the organizational core need not be a party or union. Many movements have organizations specifically their own.[36] The Townsend movement has its own organization (Messinger, 1955); so does the temperance movement (Gusfield, 1955), the Zionist movement, and the German, Soviet, and Israeli youth movements (Lewin, 1947; Gould, 1951; Eisenstadt, 1956, pp. 33, 101ff.; Ben-David, 1954).

To the degree that core organizations of social movements consist of one of the better-known types of organization, such as political parties or labor unions, their compliance structure is highly normative. Little is known about the nature of compliance of other core organizations, especially with respect to the relative weight of remunerative and normative powers. Even a tentative placement of these organizations according to the relative importance of normative controls must be delayed until more information is available.[37]

This concludes our discussion of nine types of normative organization. Five of these types have highly pronounced normative patterns. Less pronounced normative compliance patterns are coupled in two types with secondary coercive powers, in one with secondary utilitarian patterns. The place of "core" organizations in the normative category is difficult to assess.

36. For an intriguing report on a social movement, some information on its composition, and the role newspapers played in its "core" organization, see H. M. Hughes (1947, pp. 504-7). The significance of the core organization in maintaining a social movement in crisis comes into sharp relief in a study by Messinger (1955).

37. The study of core organizations of social movements is of interest for another reason. It points to the limitations of the bureaucracy-charisma dichotomy. It is probable that a division of labor between a bureaucratic core and a charismatic movement allows for a long-lived, stable charismatic movement. Billy Graham's movement, for instance, has a highly organized core (see also Poinsett, 1960, pp. 25-34). The protest against segregated buses in Montgomery, Alabama, illustrates a similarly effective combination of charismatic movement and highly rational organizational core (see M. L. King, Jr., 1958). See also Hoffer (1951, pp. 112-41).

DUAL COMPLIANCE STRUCTURES

So far we have examined organizations in which one compliance pattern is predominant. Some organizations, however, develop compliance structures in which two patterns occur with the same or similar frequency. We refer to these as *dual compliance structures*.

Earlier we presented some reasons why such a compliance structure would result in some waste of power resources through neutralization, and some loss of involvement because of the ambivalence of lower participants exposed to conflicting expectations (concerning their involvement) associated with the various types of power. Such ambivalence is generated, for example, when lower participants are expected to be calculatively and morally committed at the same time. We would therefore expect organizations with dual compliance structures either to be ineffective or to develop special mechanisms for reducing waste of power resources. The following examination of two dual types illustrates one major mechanism permitting the effective combination of two compliance structures. (A fuller analysis of such mechanisms is one of the subjects of Chapter XVI.)

In the remainder of this chapter, two dual structures are briefly examined: the balanced combination of normative and coercive compliance patterns in combat organizations, and the balanced combination of normative and utilitarian compliance patterns found in some labor unions. Since these organizations have not yet been examined, other problems involved in determining their compliance classification are also discussed here.

There is relatively little information on a third dual type, the utilitarian-coercive combination. This seems to have existed in some of the earlier factories, especially in company towns where management had a private police force, or could use public enforcement agencies for disciplinary action such as strikebreaking and collecting forced debts (to the company store, company housing facilities, etc.). For example, Cash describes the impact of federal relief programs on cotton-growers in South Carolina during the Depression: Workers received more money on relief than they could earn picking cotton; so, to avoid losing their crops, landowners had recourse to the vagrancy laws "and the chief of police issued an ultimatum to the effect that anybody who could not satisfy him as to his means of support would have to accept a job picking cotton or go to jail and be farmed out to the landowners to pay his board bill. . . . In many districts threatened with the migration of labor to other places where higher wages were offered, armed patrols began to ride the roads to head off those who were leaving and drive them back to work at the prevailing wage." (1954, p. 407) [38] Compliance on ships in earlier centuries seems to have had such a compound structure, as evidenced, for example, in the formal right of the captain to arrest a disobediant sailor and the informal but well-established "right" of those higher in rank to beat those lower in rank—particularly that of the boatswain to flog young seamen. Since there is no systematic information on this type and an analysis of the two others will suffice to illustrate our main point, the utilitarian-coercive type will not be further discussed.

Normative-Coercive Structure: The Case of Combat Units

SEGREGATION IN TIME—In order to command the commitments required for effective realization of combat goals, modern combat units have to rely heavily on both normative and coercive powers. Peacetime armies rely on remunerative powers (secure salaries, fringe benefits, fines) and some coercion to control career soldiers; [39] they rely more exclusively on coercion to control draftees. These means would prove unsatisfactory as dominant mechanisms of control on the front lines.

Combat units must to some extent rely on normative powers because the deprivations inflicted by combat are such that no calculative involvement of the kind created by remuneration can compensate for them. No modern army can supply remuneration high enough to induce most lower participants to risk life and limb. [40] Even an

38. For a description of the ways in which municipal police have been mobilized to prevent union organization of workers, see R. S. Lynd and H. M. Lynd (1937, p. 37 and ch. 2, *passim*). On the use of weapons, company police, and intimidation by corporations as well as close cooperation with local police forces to control labor, see Sutherland (1949, p. 141).

39. Janowitz supplies some information on the motivation of 113 military leaders in 1958. He shows that "those who see the military profession as a calling or a unique profession are outnumbered by a greater concentration of individuals for whom the military is just another job." (1960, p. 117) Uyeki supplies some information on the orientation of peacetime soldiers to their "job" (1958, pp. 7-8; 12). The calculative elements are stressed.

40. There were of course mercenary armies in earlier periods. But since they were much smaller, they could recruit their soldiers from the small groups of people whose relative attachment to life, money, and risk is quite different from the "normal."

attempt to compensate for other deprivations, such as separation from family and home, interruption of a career pattern, lack of amenities, and so on, would call for more funds than any modern organization could recruit.

Human beings can be made to follow highly depriving directives in two ways. They may come to believe it necessary to endure them, a feeling created when combat goals are internalized; or they may anticipate even worse deprivations if they seek to escape those of the front line.[41] Intensive moral involvement is created by officers who are leaders; by resocialization in basic training; in military schools; by educational or political officers; and through the influence of chaplains. Other expressive media and situations, such as the prayer before battle, heroes' funerals, and medals, have the same function (Marshall, 1947, pp. 138-56). Coercion is applied through confinement to the base, including the withdrawal of furlough privileges; the imprisonment or execution of deserters; and firing at retreating troops.

The application of the two powers, normative and coercive, is segregated in time in such a manner that the two powers conflict as little as possible. Normative power is applied first; only when this is or seems to be ineffective is there a resort to coercive power.[42]

It is of interest to note that separation in time does not completely solve the problem created by two different types of control. Officers are often censured for misjudging the time for transition. They are considered poor officers (leaders) when they rely too much, and especially too soon, on coercion. On the other hand, if they become too involved with their men, or for some other reason continue to rely on normative powers when things get out of hand, they are considered "soft" and are subject to reprimands. Moreover, it is likely that the use of coercion at any time has some neutralizing effects on normative power and moral involvement even during the period in which coercion is not applied, despite the segregation in time.

SOCIAL OR PURE NORMATIVE COMPLIANCE?—The significance of normative compliance in combat units is widely acknowledged, but it is less clear what kind of normative power plays the main role.

41. ". . . the Nazis sought to counteract the fear of personal physical destruction in battle by telling the men that accurate records were kept on deserters and that not only would their families and property be made to suffer in the event of their desertion, but that after the war, upon their return to Germany, they, too, would be very severely punished." (Shils and Janowitz, 1948, p. 291)

42. Various "rounds" of sanctions are discussed in pages 00-00.

Two well-known and often cited studies—one of the German *Wehrmacht* (Shils and Janowitz, 1948) and the other of American soldiers (Stouffer *et al.*, 1949; Merton and Lazarsfeld, 1950)—both conducted during World War II, raised the question of the relative importance of what, in our terms, are pure normative compliance and social compliance.[43] Several conclusions emerge from these studies. First, formal ideological communications (e.g., leaflet propaganda), when not absorbed and transmitted by leaders,[44] had little effect on the behavior of combat soldiers. However, more internalized values were very significant. The ideal of a "good soldier," of military honor, was one such factor. Shils and Janowitz report: "The code of soldierly honor and its ramifications took a deep root in the personality of the German soldiers of the line—even those who were totally apolitical. . . . For these people a military career was a good and noble one, enjoying high intrinsic ethical value." (1948, p. 296) Second, the importance of group solidarity or cohesiveness in controlling participants' behavior has been stressed in these studies; in fact, later interpretations of wartime studies have tended to overemphasize the role of cohesion in combat compliance. Both Shils and Janowitz have, in later writings, warned against such a tendency. Janowitz states: "Strategic issues and ideological images are elements of combat effectiveness and organizational control. The findings of sociologists on the crucial importance of primary group cohesion in military morale do not overlook or eliminate the role of secondary identifications, although some of the enthusiasts of small group research seem to arrive at such a conclusion." (1959, p. 44) Shils has pointed out that "these data [supplied in *The American Soldier*] support the more complex hypothesis that primary group solidarity functions in the corporate body to strengthen the motivation for the fulfillment of substantive prescriptions and commands issued by the official agents of the corporate body, within the context of *a set of generalized moral predispositions or sense of obligation.*" (1950, p. 22) Third, the various studies of combat behavior leave little doubt that the nature of the group's leadership determined to a considerable degree the combat commitment of

43. For a bibliography and discussion of other studies see Janowitz (1959, pp. 64-82).

44. The significance of such "opinion leaders" for the "translation" of formal into informal communication, and hence for the effectiveness of formal communication, has been demonstrated in spheres other than combat. See Lazarsfeld, Berelson, and Gaudet (1948, second edition, esp. p. xxiii); Katz and Lazarsfeld (1955, ch. 2); and Katz (1957, pp. 61-78).

soldiers (Grinker and Spiegel, 1945, pp. 46-48). When the enlisted men in the *Wehrmacht* accepted the leadership of officers and non-commissioned officers, and when the leaders were devoted Nazis, the units were highly committed to combat goals as reflected in their combat effectiveness. When the leaders were not Nazis, or were rejected, the units were less effective. Furthermore, the higher the proportion of devoted Nazis in a given unit, the greater its combat effectiveness (Shils and Janowitz, pp. 286-88).

Thus two dimensions emerge from these studies which have to be carefully separated: the effect of leadership, and the effect of peer cohesion. In two subsequent chapters we shall examine closely the relationship of both factors to compliance.

To summarize, compliance in combat units rests on a balanced combination of two powers: normative and coercive. Neutralization or waste of those powers is minimized by temporal separation: Normative means are applied first, and only when these fail is coercion employed. Normative power may be either "pure" or "social." Many interpretations of studies describing combat units appear to have overemphasized the role of social power, or cohesion; obviously pure normative commitments, such as honor, prestige, and the leadership ideology, are also potent.

A Classification of Labor Unions

The compliance structures of labor unions constitute a very heterogeneous category. Although some unions are predominantly coercive, some utilitarian, and some normative, other unions appear to have a dual structure of the normative-utilitarian type. The ensuing discussion concerns first those unions in which one pattern of compliance is clearly predominant, then those with varying combinations of patterns, including a dual (balanced) type. The present approach differs from that in much of the literature on labor unions. First, statements are formulated for specific types of unions; we would be reluctant, at this stage of knowledge, to make generalizations about all unions. Second, whereas most classifications of unions rest on their goals, functions, or structure,[45] the present one is based on the compliance relations typical of a particular union's members. The two approaches are closely related—for example, business unions,

45. For a bibliography and a brief discussion of studies following these approaches, see Wilensky (1954, ch. 5). See also Brooks, Darber, McCabe, Taft (1952), esp. the article by Stephansky.

whose goal is to improve their members' standard of living, tend to have a utilitarian compliance structure. But this is not a one-to-one relationship; some unions which have a "business" goal but little economic power, for example, draw on normative compliance.

COERCIVE UNIONS—Coercion as the major means of control seems to be an infrequent compliance pattern. A number of unions may turn to coercion in crisis situations, when all other means of keeping marginal members from strikebreaking or cooperation with management have failed. For example, starting a fight in a bar in order to beat up a disloyal member is a practice followed by members of some of the maritime unions.[46] But there are only a few unions, such as the New York Longshoremen and some Teamster locals (as the McClellan hearings have shown), in which coercion is highly institutionalized;[47] in some cases it even seems to be the predominant compliance factor. In extreme situations, murder occurs.[48]

Bell vividly describes a major source of compliance among New York longshoremen:

Cross the shadow line and you are in a rough racket-ridden frontier domain ruled by the bull-like figure of the "shaping boss." Here brawn and muscle, sustained where necessary by bailing hook and knife, enforce discipline among a motley group of Italian immigrants, Slavic and Negro workers and a restless and grumbling group of Irish. (1954, p. 298)

It is difficult to determine the degree to which coercion is the dominant means of control in these unions. It seems that many members quite willingly accept the "boss" and everything that goes with the regime of a boss (Seidman, London, and Karsh, 1951, p. 82). Hence the actual exercise of force may not be very frequent. But

46. Private communication with two leaders of the Seafarers International Union.

47. It is institutionalized in the sense that it is a stable part of the members' expectations. But the fact that society at large does not consider it legitimate imposes considerable limitations on its application and the institutionalization of the application. On the decline of public tolerance of unions' use of coercion, and its effect on control of members, see Slichter (1959, p. 29).

48. Bell reports: "Waterfront gossip insists, for example, that Cock-eye Dunn, head of three federal A. F. of L. locals before his execution in Sing-Sing in 1949 for killing a recalcitrant hiring boss, was responsible for thirty-seven murders. 'We should be careful,' states Bill Keating, onetime assistant district attorney and former counsel of the New York City Anti-Crime Committee, 'and put the figure at thirteen.' " (1954, p. 298)

A member of the Chicago Moving Picture Operators Union Local 110 was stabbed to death the day before he had been scheduled to produce evidence of racketeer control of his union before a Senate committee; there is a remote chance that this was a coincidence (*The New York Times*, March 3, 1960; see also *ibid.*, March 12, 1958).

it is clear that in some unions, which border on underworld organizations, the use of coercion is rather extensive (Romer, 1959; Loftus,
1959). Sondern (1960, pp. 209-10) supplies a list of the "business"
interests of thirty-one crime leaders who participated in the 1957
Apalachin meeting; "Union, labor" is listed for twenty of the group.
Such unions obviously belong in our coercive category.

Although in some locals coercion is widely applied as the "ultimate" sanction and its potential use supports other sanctions, such
as verbal censure, it is often coupled with other powers. Coercion is
hence not as dominant here as it is in prisons, for example. The
secondary powers differ according to the environment. In industries
where the unions are relatively powerful, the secondary power tends
to be remunerative. In others, where the union is weak but can draw
on ethnic or racial bonds outside the union, the secondary power
is social. To the degree that these secondary powers gain in scope
and function so that they become similar in weight to the coercive,
we class these unions as dual types, as coercive-utilitarian or coercive-
social, respectively.

PURE NORMATIVE UNIONS—Pure normative power is developed
by unions which have strong ideological platforms and which have
succeeded in building up commitments to such platforms in their
members.[49] Unions employing pure normative power as their greatest
source of compliance were much more common in the earlier days
of industrialization than they are now. They characteristically have
political aims, such as changing the social structure drastically, rather
than merely reallocating corporate profits; their major orientation is
to centers of societal, not managerial, power; and typically they are
committed to ideologies such as communism or anarchism.

These unions command little remunerative power, since as a
rule they have little influence over management's allocation of jobs
and rewards, and since they tend not to provide members with
services (in order not to dissipate their revolutionary fervor by
improving their lot in the existing social order).[50] Since belief in the
educability of workers and in the power of indoctrination is high,

49. See Tagliacozzo and Seidman (1956, p. 547) for a characterization of the
"ideological" unionist.
50. Hoxie describes in similar terms the "revolutionary union," the major subcategory of ideological unions: "It is distinctly class-conscious rather than trade-
conscious. . . . It repudiates, or tends to repudiate, the existing institutional order.
. . . In method, it looks askance at collective bargaining and mutual insurance as
making for conservatism and hampering the free and united action of the workers."
(1923, p. 48; see also ch. 6)

coercion rarely figures in these unions. We refer to them as "ideological unions." The Western Federation of Miners (Saposs, 1926) and the Industrial Workers of the World (Brissenden, 1919) were typical examples. Many characteristics of this type still appear in contemporary radical unions, such as the General Confederation of Italian Labor, the Confédération Générale du Travail in France, and some unions in newly independent countries, such as the All-India Trade Unions Federation.

SOCIAL UNIONS—Another source of union control is social compliance, derived from the fraternal relations of its members and channeled by the union's elites. Deviants are punished, as in other cohesive groups, by withdrawal of approval, social censure, ostracism, and the like (Allen, 1954, pp. 32-33). When other groups to which workers belong—such as communities and ethnic groups—support the norms and policies of the union, its social power may be extended to areas of life other than the job. The smaller the union local, the greater its social power seems to be. Technological factors, as well as the way work is organized, are important determinants of the cohesion of work groups, and hence of their social power (Etzioni, 1957a, pp. 3-6). The effectiveness of this power for the organization depends on the degree to which the rank and file support the union, its leaders, goal, and policies.

UTILITARIAN UNIONS—Unions have several sources of utilitarian control. First, they obviously affect the allocation of economic rewards by management, though there are differences of opinion on the scope of this effect (Ross, 1948; Kerr, 1954). Second, collective bargaining almost always brings more benefits to some subgroups than to others (Sayles and Strauss, 1953, pp. 43ff.). This distribution can be used to reward loyal members and punish deviants, as well as to "pay off" a vocal or powerful opposition. Furthermore, whenever the union has influence not only over wages and benefits but also over allocation of jobs, this influence tends to be used for control purposes. The union affects management's job allocation, or the union itself functions as a labor exchange (Strauss, 1956). Legislation against the "closed shop" has somewhat curtailed this source of union power, but the "union shop" and the permit and apprentice systems allow it to persist in many industries (Barbash, 1948, pp. 84, 88-89).

There are many other ways in which the union recruits remunerative power. In the International Typographical Union, for example, printers, not management, determine who will substitute for them, get overtime, or be hired temporarily when work is extended (Lipset, Trow, and Coleman, 1956, pp. 127-35).

In many cases, universalistic mechanisms have been developed to reduce favoritism and thus the control power of these allocations. Lists posted in the union's hiring hall, numbers assigned to members, and allocation by lot are among the more commonly used techniques. But there is little room for doubt that this control power has at best been curtailed, not eliminated (Barbash, 1956, pp. 69ff).

The services unions supply directly to members are another major source of remunerative control. These include health services, various forms of social insurance, and entertainment.[51] Raskin reports, for example, that the I.L.G.W.U. and its affiliated locals have $250,000,-000 in pension, welfare, and treasury resources (1959, p. 77). Expulsion frequently means loss of access to these services, which may themselves be a source of calculative involvement in the union.

Union members have at their command a larger number of small-scale remunerative sanctions with which to penalize a disloyal member; the use of these sanctions depends on the degree to which members are willing to enforce the union's policies. The income of a disloyal member may suffer because other workers refuse to lend him their tools, withhold information about jobs in general or the task at hand, disarrange the machine set-up (when shifts are changed), or leave difficult, low-paying jobs for him (A. N. Turner, 1957). Similarly, the union may give differential treatment to personal grievances, which may be neglected or strongly pushed, with or without exposing the source of the complaint to management (Strauss and Sayles, 1952, pp. 143ff.). Fines are another remunerative sanction used, particularly to increase attendance at union meetings.

NORMATIVE-UTILITARIAN CONTINUUM—Unions may be arranged along a continuum according to the relative degree of remunerative compared with normative (pure or social) compliance, the middle section of the continuum constituting a balanced (dual) type. Some unions, especially large industrial ones such as the United Steel Workers and the United Rubber Workers, fall closer to the remunerative end. Some unions, such as the United Automobile Workers and the International Brotherhood of Electrical Workers, combine predominantly remunerative controls with some normative powers.

---

51. These and many other services supplied by unions are extensively discussed by various authors in Part Five of Hardman (1951).

Others fall close to the center of the continuum and give normative and remunerative compliance similar weight—that is, they exhibit a *dual structure*. The International Ladies' Garment Workers Union (Shepard, 1949, p. 315), the United Mine Workers (Seidman, London, Karsh, and Tagliacozzo, 1958, pp. 18-23), the International Alliance of Theatrical and Stage Employees and Moving Picture Machine Operators, and several of the construction unions seem to have such a dual structure.[52] Finally, some unions fall close to the highly normative end of the continuum. Most of those are of the ideological type. Only a few, such as the nineteenth-century shoe-makers, are predominantly social in their compliance structure (Commons, 1909).

The main difference between dual and other types of compliance in unions is that in dual structures increased deviation from organizational norms and directives is followed by activation of a *different* type of power, while in the other types it tends to activate *more* power of the *same* type. Thus, in a coercive union, if a slap does not serve as a warning, a load dropped on the uncooperative worker's feet may come next. If this is of no avail, the coercive union may turn to acid, the knife, or dynamite. Similarly, a remunerative union will start with a fine, then keep the worker unemployed for a few days (if it controls employment), and finally expel the worker from the union, which often means that he will find it difficult to gain employment in his present occupation. On the other hand, in the dual normative (social)-utilitarian type, two powers are applied, usually not at the same time but alternately, depending on the specific kind or degree of offense. For example, a worker who is "rate-busting" will first be censured by the steward in an informal friendly chat; if this is ineffective, his workmates will stop cooperating with him, to his economic loss; if this does not produce the desired results, extreme

---

52. Consumers leagues are another type of organization which tends to have a utilitarian-normative dual structure, as Kelley has pointed out (1899, p. 289). One would expect consumer organizations to be purely utilitarian, but actually consumption in itself does not command sufficient involvement to serve as a stable source of membership participation and loyalty—a point elaborated elsewhere (Etzioni, 1958, pp. 261-62). Hence consumer movements develop mainly when a moral issue is added to the economic one, so that a foundation for normative compliance is added (e.g., Donald, 1942). Consumer cooperatives in England and the Continent, for instance, draw on Socialist ideology. The lack of such a foundation in the United States explains their general failure there; where it does exist we find the few cases of success (Lipset, 1960, p. 315). This argument also explains the success of consumer strikes in the South against segregated buses and lunch counters.

curtailment of social interaction (e.g., "sending to Coventry") is likely to follow. Finally, efforts may be made to make the company fire the worker. Thus, both kinds of power are successively applied. Again, we find controls segregated in time, although temporal segregation in unions differs from that in combat organizations. At the front, one is subjected first to normative controls and then to coercive ones, but there is little alternation between the two. In unions, shifting back and forth between the two modes of compliance seems to be rather common.[53]

SUMMARY

In this and the preceding chapter an analytical classification of organizations, based on the characteristic compliance of lower participants, was presented. Organizations were classified into three major categories of compliance relations and ordered within each category according to the emphasis given the predominant pattern. It was impossible to classify each single organization because of the enormous number of organizations. Instead, we attempted to characterize subcategories of larger common-sense types. Thus, we did not attempt to characterize all military forces as such, but distinguished between combat units and peacetime armies; labor unions were found to have a large variety of compliance structures, from pure normative to predominantly coercive.

Many other organizations doubtless remain to be characterized by their compliance structure. Some have not been classified because information about them was too limited to permit even a tentative judgment (courts, for example [54]). But we did not encounter organizations which could not be placed when information about their compliance structure was available. The extension of this exploratory classification requires collection of more relevant information, addi-

---

53. Segregation in time, as an adjustive device in dual compliance structures, operates when two types of compliance occur in the same organizational unit. We discuss below the structural segregation of compliance relationships which is found in organizations stressing one type of compliance in one subunit and another in a different subunit (see Ch. XVI).

54. If we consider citizens as the lower participants of the courts, we find that all three kinds of power are exerted: prison sentences, fines, and exhortation by the judge. We find also the full range of involvement modes. A central question for the sociology of law is to determine empirically the most effective power applications by type of offense and offender. There is, however, almost no relevant data on the relationship between lower and higher participants in the hierarchy of judges and court administration.

tional analysis of information which is at hand, and further differentiation of the categories suggested. New evidence might relegate various organizations to different categories or different places within categories. For the present, however, the main task is to show the fruitfulness of this approach and classification for organizational analysis. This is the subject of the following twelve chapters.

SUMMARY OF CLASSIFICATION

Organizations in each category are listed according to the relative weight of the predominant compliance pattern in their compliance structure. Those giving the predominant pattern greatest weight are listed first.

1. *Predominantly coercive*
   Concentration camps
   Prisons (most)
   Correctional "institutions" (large majority)
   Custodial mental hospitals
   Prisoner-of-war camps
   Relocation centers
   Coercive unions

   Place in category undetermined: Forced-labor camps

2. *Predominantly utilitarian*
   Blue-collar industries and blue-collar divisions in other industries
   White-collar industries and white-collar divisions in other industries (normative compliance is a secondary pattern)
   Business unions (normative compliance is a secondary pattern)
   Farmers' organizations (normative compliance is a secondary pattern)
   Peacetime military organizations (coercive compliance is a secondary pattern)

3. *Predominantly normative*
   Religious organizations (including churches, orders, monasteries, convents)
   Ideological political organizations (for classification of other political organizations see pp. 107-109)
   General hospitals
   Colleges and universities
   Social unions
   Voluntary associations
      a) fraternal associations (high social compliance)
      b) fund-raising and action associations (high social plus secondary emphasis on pure normative compliance)

Schools (coercion in varying degrees is the secondary pattern)

Therapeutic mental hospitals (coercion is the secondary pattern)

Professional organizations (including research organizations, law firms, newspapers, planning firms, etc.; utilitarian compliance is the secondary pattern)

Place in category undetermined: "Core" organizations of social movements

4. *Dual structures*

Normative-coercive: Combat units

Utilitarian-normative: Majority of unions

Utilitarian-coercive: Some early industries, some farms, company towns, and ships

IV

THE COMPLIANCE
THESIS REVISITED

Practically all the studies conducted since the original publication of the compliance theory reflect in one way or another on the basic thesis that organizations which differ along the suggested dimensions in the means of control they apply will also differ systematically in the involvement of their lower participants and that "deviations" from the predicted congruent patterns will be unstable. However, only the findings of those studies which deal chiefly or primarily with this thesis, rather than with other elements of the compliance theory, are reviewed in this chapter. The question to be addressed is as basic as it is often left unanswered in the history of the social science theories: Did data collected after the formulation of a theory support or refute its core hypothesis?

THE RELATIONSHIPS BETWEEN POWER AND INVOLVEMENT[1]

In Normative Organizations: A Study of Five Hospitals

Research conducted by Joseph Julian provides a good example of both the approach and the findings of studies which directly test the

1. Three important, extensive discussions of the concept of power, including detailed and in part critical discussion of its status in compliance theory, are to be found in Dahlstrom (1966), pp. 263ff.; Warren (1968), pp. 951-970; and Lehman (1969), pp. 453-465. For a more recent statement of the author's views than the compliance publication, see Etzioni (1968), chs. 13 and 14.

compliance thesis. Julian (1966, 1968) studied the compliance structure of five hospitals: a university hospital, a medium-size general hospital, a large general hospital, a tuberculosis sanatorium, and a veterans' hospital. All are located in the same part of the country, a large Western city. Data were collected from a sample of 183 lower participants (patients) through a combination of interviews and questionnaires. Patients' involvement was measured on the basis of responses indicating perception of and orientation toward staff sanctions.

Beginning with the involvement component of the compliance relationship, Julian found that the dominant mode of the patients was positive, as expected in organizations whose compliance structure is predominantly normative. In all five hospitals, the majority of the patients indicated approval of the sanctions that they perceived the staff to be employing. The proportions ranged from .54 to .77 (see Table IV-1).

Table IV-1—Patient Involvement in Terms of Proportional Endorsement of Specific Sanctions*

| | INVOLVEMENT | | | | | |
| | Positive | | Neutral | | Negative | |
Hospitals	Proportion	Rank	Proportion	Rank	Proportion	Rank
A (university)	.64	3	.14	3	.21	4
B (medium general)	.77	1	.08	5	.15	5
C (large general)	.65	2	.11	4	.23	2
D (TB sanatorium)	.54	5	.16	1	.30	1
E (veterans')	.63	4	.15	2	.22	3

* The higher the proportion, the more frequent the occurrence.
Source: Julian (1968), p. 13. Reprinted with permission of University of North Carolina Press.

Julian's data also support the proposition that organizations tend to have one dominant involvement type, while the other types tend to occupy clearly secondary or tertiary positions. (A more or less proportional distribution is expected to be an exception and not a stable condition, pp. 6-8.) Thus, even the hospital with the lowest positive involvement (the sanitorium), at .54 of one mode, in this case positive involvement, rated .30 in the secondary category of negative involvement and .16 in the tertiary category of neutral involvement. (The null hypothesis would be a distribution of .33, .33, .33.) The other four hospitals are also clearly "typed." Moreover, the differences between the second and third modes of involvement are quite sizeable in all the cases.

Next, Julian studied the power element of compliance structure of the five hospitals. He used a 36-item scale based on patients' statements about the staff's conduct; a panel of judges evaluated and ordered these items as being from "very coercive" to "very persuasive" (1966, p. 386). He found that "in all five hospitals normative sanctions are applied in well over half of the possible reported occurrences, suggesting that in those hospitals the utilization of normative power prevails" (*ibid.*). As in two of the five, however, hospitals *D* and *E*, coercive sanctions scored more than .50, Julian (following, p. 55) refers to these hospitals as dual compliance structures.

Table IV-2—Rate of Reported Occurrence of Three Types of Sanctions Based on Patient Perception

SANCTIONS

Hospitals†	Normative Proportion	Rank	Coercive Proportion	Rank	Neither Proportion	Rank	Total Amount of Control*	Rank
A (40)	.67	4	.34	5	.39	4	.47	4
B (30)	.58	5	.35	4	.32	5	.43	5
C (39)	.72	3	.46	3	.42	3	.55	3
D (39)	.76	2	.54	1.5	.45	2	.60	2
E (35)	.79	1	.54	1.5	.49	1	.62	1

* This index of amount of control is determined in the following manner: (1) multiply the ratio of reported occurrence of the three types of sanctions by the number of indicators of each type of sanction, (2) total the multiplied ratios, and (3) divide by the total number of sanction indicators.
† Figures in parentheses represent the number of patients in each hospital.
The ranks indicate the proportions of the patients questioned reporting the incidence of a particular type of sanction.
Source: Julian (1968), p. 14. Reprinted with permission of University of North Carolina Press.

Finally, Julian tested the congruency thesis. In part, the results follow directly from the data already presented: In all five hospitals involvement is more positive than negative, and power more normative than either coercive or utilitarian. Moreover, the strength of the theory lies in predicting a much more precise relationship: Differences in *degree* of one kind of power used (as compared to the others) are expected to correlate with differences in *degree* of positive (or negative) involvement. The strength of Julian's study is that it allows this much more specific test. As Julian puts it:

Hospital *D* has the highest rank in terms of the frequency of reported coercive sanctions and ranks highest on negative involvement. Hospital *A* (the university hospital) and Hospital *B* both rank the lowest on number of coercive sanctions and are also ranked the lowest on the extent of negative involvement.

Table [IV-2] further reveals that there is an inverse relationship between the frequency of coercive sanctions and positive involvement. Hospital *D* and Hospital *E* (the veterans' hospital) report the highest proportion of coercive sanctions and the lowest degree of positive involvement. Moreover, Hospital *B* is low on coercive sanctions and high on positive involvement (Julian, 1968, p. 14).

Julian made one finding which, on the face of it, deviates from the theory's expectation: The reported frequency of the use of normative means of control and the extent of positive involvement did not relate so closely as one might expect. He suggested that this can be accounted for when the total amount of control exercised, not just the type, is taken into account: All said and done, is the quantity of power of all the kinds employed large or small? Thus, for instance, in a contemporary *kibbutz,* no coercion is exercised, and almost no utilitarian controls; normative power, when used, is often rather mild. It follows that the total amount of control is low, which will enhance positive involvement. In contrast, in a mental hospital where frequent and encompassing controls are in effect, even if many of the regulatory acts are normative in nature, the high amount of control may dampen the positive involvement.

Julian adds:

There is other evidence which tends to support this proposition. Smith and Brown's study of the League of Women Voters (which would be classified as a normative organization) indicates that decentralized control is directly related to member loyalty and that total amount of control is inversely related to member loyalty (Smith and Brown, 1964; and Tannenbaum, 1962). Further support is furnished by research in blue- and white-collar industries which are typically utilitarian organizations. Gouldner, for example, found that increased control through bureaucratization led to an increased alienation on the part of subordinates in a gypsum plant (Gouldner, 1955). While on the other hand, Guest discovered that the relaxation of bureaucratic rules promoted the approval of employees (Guest, 1960). Additional data presented in Table [IV-2] also support this hypothesis. It will be observed that there is an inverse relationship between the hospital ranks on total amount of control exercised and the ranks on the degrees of positive involvement. Hospitals *D* and *E* are high on total control and low on positive involvement (Julian, 1968, p. 15).

Thus, Julian's data suggest that if we take into account differences in total amount of control, we shall be able to predict how positive a positive involvement will be and how negative alienation will be. This finding further specifies the basic thesis but does not modify it; whether the total amount of control is low or high, the basic congruent relationship between control and involvement, Julian's data indicate, remains the same.

In a Variety of Utilitarian Organizations

Jack L. Franklin (1972a, 1972b, 1972c) carries the test of the core compliance proposition into a utilitarian context. He studied the compliance structure of six organizations in the same Midwestern area. These included two newspapers, a general hospital, a small manufacturing plant, a creamery, and a public service company. From complete lists of nonsupervisory employees, random samples of 40 employees were chosen and interviewed in each of five of the organizations, and 65 in the sixth.

Franklin found that all six organizations relied more on utilitarian than on normative power. Power scores were calculated based on the degree to which the employees' supervisors indicated preference for either utilitarian or normative means of control. These values were standardized for all organizations under study, and for each organization an overall "power-mix" score was arrived at by subtracting the utilitarian power score from the normative power score. As all organizations were more utilitarian than normative, all power-mix scores were negative. The three organizations with the smallest such scores (−.68, −.71, −1.69) were then classified as "less utilitarian," and the other three (−2.80, −2.86, −3.06) formed a second, "more utilitarian" group of organizations.

This classification, which put the manufacturing plant, the general hospital, and one newspaper in the more utilitarian category and the creamery, the public service company, and the other newspaper in the less utilitarian category, was reinforced by rankings on a Perceived Closeness of Supervision scale that rendered the same categorization. (In the more utilitarian organizations, the closeness of supervision scores were 14.35, 13.4, and 12.17; in the less utilitarian they were 11.81, 11.80, and 11.67).

Franklin notes in passing that this classification appears to be at odds with the original prediction that hospitals and newspapers would reveal less utilitarian and more normative compliance structures than blue-collar industries. However, there are two explanations for this apparent anomaly. Firstly, for all the organizations, Franklin defined lower participants as "employees who are in nonsupervisory positions" (Franklin, 1972c, p. 9). This definition, which excludes lower participants who are not employees, gives a utilitarian slant to the operationalization that the findings reveal, especially with respect to the organizations labelled "normative" in Franklin's original classification. Thus, although the compliance relationship between nonsupervisory hospital employees and their organization is clearly utilitarian, this is not characteristic of the relationship between the hospital and its other lower participants, the patients. With regard to the newspapers, my classification of papers as relatively normative was based on the predicted compliance pattern for the reporters. If all nonsupervisory personnel are included, a more utilitarian profile is to be expected. Even more to the point, great pains were taken in the original compliance theory publication to stress that an organization's name is a poor indicator of its mission or compliance structure (pp. 23ff.) Thus, a labor union may be a coercive, utilitarian, or normative organization, depending on the means of control actually used and the involvement elicited. The point is, once the power structure is empirically established, it and not the organization's title "predicts" the involvement of the participants and, vice-versa, involvement and not titles "predicts" power. The organization's name or "category" is only useful as a shorthand. Many prisons are coercive; many factories are utilitarian; and so on. Although we can thereby classify them on a statistical basis as tending to be of one compliance type or the other, one cannot predict where a specific organization will fall. Actually, one of the claims of the compliance theory was that it replaced a bewilderment of concrete types and labels with an analytic typology, based on variables which are members of a theory.

Among those who missed this point is Charles Perrow. Having set out to write a free-for-all "critical essay," he charges Etzioni with ". . . the neglect of wide ranges of differences with the types. Some churches and schools, for example, are run like factories; some like prisons" (1972, p. 165). This is the point I made in 1961, which now appears on pages 23-27 of this book.

Next, Perrow sees the typology as tautological: Prisons are coercive because coercive power is used and members feel coerced (1972, p. 164). But, as he himself points out a page later, not all organizations of the same title use the same control means with the same results. Second, although the analytic classification of an organization is indeed tautological with its specific compliance base (e.g., a coercive organization relies predominantly on coercive power, associated with alienated involvement) in that names of analytic variables and what they denote must be parallel, the consequences of such a compliance base for other variables are not "derivable" from the compliance characterization. Indeed, he who sees tautologies here should try to derive the correlations reported in the following discussions from the degree of reliance on coercive, utilitarian, or normative compliance, to see how often the data can thus be anticipated.

To return to Franklin: Once he classified organizations not by their names but by their actual power scores, the more utilitarian

Table IV-3—Commitments of Lower Participants to Support Goals and Norms and to Remain, in Less and More Utilitarian Organizations (in percentages)

	LESS UTILITARIAN (N = 120)			MORE UTILITARIAN (N = 145)		
Indicator	Not Committed %	Moderately Committed %	Highly Committed %	Not Committed %	Moderately Committed %	Highly Committed %
CO1(Norms)*	5.0	15.8	79.2	13.8	11.7	74.5
CO2(Goals)†	27.5	44.2	28.3	49.7	31.7	18.6
CO3(Remain)‡	10.0	45.0	45.0	28.2	42.8	29.0

* The difference between levels of commitment in more and less utilitarian organizations is significant at a probability greater than .02, less than .05.
† The difference is significant at a probability greater than .001, less than .01.
‡ The difference is significant at a probability greater than .001, less than .01.
Source: Franklin (1972c), Table 3.

organizations had less committed workers than the less utilitarian (and relatively more normative) organizations. Four indicators support this conclusion:

1. Turnover rates, an indicator of negative involvement, were higher in the more utilitarian organizations. In the less utilitarian organizations the turnover scores were 4.1, 8.5, and 4.7; in the more utilitarian they measured 19.2, 61.9, and 67.2.
2. Willingness to uphold the norms of the organization was significantly lower in the more utilitarian organizations and higher in the less utilitarian ones (as represented in Table IV-3 by indicator CO1).
3. Similarly, more participants in the less utilitarian organizations

indicated a willingness to support the organizational goals than in the more utilitarian ones (see Table IV-3, indicator CO2).

4. Finally, more participants in the less utilitarian organizations showed a desire to remain in their organizations as compared to those in the more utilitarian ones (see Table IV-3, indicator CO3).

The differences in commitment of blue-collar workers between less and more utilitarian organizations (reported in Table IV-4) are

Table IV-4—Commitments of Blue-Collar Workers to Support Goals and Norms and to Remain in Less and More Utilitarian Organizations (in percentages)

	LESS UTILITARIAN (N = 60)			MORE UTILITARIAN (N = 70)		
Indicator	Not Committed %	Moderately Committed %	Highly Committed %	Not Committed %	Moderately Committed %	Highly Committed %
CO1(Norms)*	6.7	20.0	73.3	8.6	14.3	77.1
CO2(Goals)†	23.3	41.7	35.0	37.1	37.1	25.8
CO3(Remain)‡	11.7	36.7	51.6	22.9	42.8	34.3

* The difference between levels of commitment in less and more utilitarian organizations is significant at a probability greater than .50, less than .70.
† The difference is significant at a probability greater than .20, less than .30.
‡ The difference is significant at a probability greater than .05, less than .10.
Source: Franklin (1972c), Table 4.

small but in the predicted direction. Moreover, by controlling for occupational type (blue-collar versus white-collar), Franklin found that there is a greater difference between the percentage of white-collar employees positively involved in less utilitarian organizations and in more utilitarian organizations than there is between the percentages of blue-collar workers in the two categories or organizations. As he notes himself, "these findings support the argument that less utilitarian, more normative power has very little positive effect on blue-collar workers but more positive effect on the commitment of white-collar workers" (see pp. 36-37). (Franklin, 1972c, p. 13).

In Coercive Organizations: Prison and Army

Douglas A. Bigelow and Richard H. Driscoll (1973) studied the compliance relationship in a federal correction center. Fifty-nine inmates detained in dormitories were compared to 38 involved in workshops, because preliminary informal discussions with the staff and inmates suggested that the first organizational unit was more

coercive than the latter. Both a coercive power scale and a cooperative attitude scale were devised on the basis of inmate reports. The
discriminatory validity of the scales was tested and confirmed. Next,
the informal designations of the organizational units as differing in
their control structure were tested. It was shown that workshop inmates were indeed subject to less coercive supervision than were the
dormitory inmates (see Table IV-5, first row).

**Table IV-5—Involvement Differences Between Coerced (Dormitory) and
Less-Coerced (Workshop) Groups (mean scores)**

Scale	Dormitory Group	Workshop Group	Level of Significance
Coercive power	2.84	1.26	.001
Cooperative attitudes	4.26	5.53	.001
Cooperative norms	3.79	4.47	.025

Source: Bigelow and Driscoll (1973), p. 13. Reprinted with the permission of the American Psychological Association. Copyright, 1973.

Now Bigelow and Driscoll were ready to test the core thesis: Do
groups subject to more coercion exhibit higher degrees of alienation?
Six agree–disagree questions, including such items as "If the shop
foreman asked me to clean up the shop right away, I would do it, even
if he wasn't around to see that I did," were combined in a six-point
"cooperative attitudes" scale. Similarly, six items such as "If you
want to get along well with the guys in this group, you can't be too
friendly with the shop foreman" were combined in a six-point "cooperative norms" scale. Table IV-5 shows that the less coerced inmates in the workshop group averaged higher scores on both measures
of involvement than the dormitory group. That is, they were less
alienated, as the power–involvement hypothesis predicts.[2]

Seppo Randell (1968) studied a rather different organization, the
Finnish armed forces, focusing on the compliance of draftees (not
regulars). Randel did not study the means of control, either as used
by the military or as perceived by the draftees. Instead, he compared
a sample of draftees to a sample of seniors in high schools. If one
grants that being in an army involuntarily, especially in the absence of
a morale-building war, is a more coercive condition than being in
school (also involuntary but a relatively more meaningful activity),
one is prepared to see the effect of coercion in a comparison of the

2. For a similar finding see Thomas and Miller (n.d., a).

organizational orientations of draftees to those of the high school seniors.

The study was conducted in 1962. A self-administered questionnaire was used for both the draftees and the seniors. The high school students were drawn from a nationwide random sample, of which 1044 returned the questionnaire, making for an 82% return rate. Of the army sample, 1040 draftees (an 88% return rate) completed the questionnaire. Randel refers to the army group as his "experimental" group and to the students as his "control" group.

As expected, the draftees were significantly more alienated than the seniors, on two measurements. They were much less inclined to choose being a military officer as a career: 53% of the draftees responded negatively (compared to 22% of the seniors); 19% answered postively (compared to 36%); and 28% were neutral (compared to 42%) (Randell, 1968, p. 65).

Also, the attitudes of the draftees toward military officers were much more negative than those of the seniors, as measured by the Semantic Differential Method developed by Charles Osgood. 16% of draftee responses were positive (compared to 51% of the seniors); 54% negative (compared to 16%); and 30% neutral (compared to 16%) (*ibid.,* p. 67).

However, when their feelings about national defense were tapped, the draftees were found to be significantly more committed to it than the seniors (by a difference of 20 percentage points). Randel's explanation for this difference is that the Finnish military is not a purely coercive organization, but rather one that combines normative controls (e.g., effort to gain the draftee's acceptance of national goals) with coercion (the induction). The draftees work out this conflict by accepting the goals of the military while being alienated from its organization and its representatives (*ibid.,* pp. 66ff.). Also, although the draft is coercive by definition, servicemen in the peacetime Finnish army are not found to be subject to much day-to-day coercion. Last but not least, Randel found the draftees he studied in a reserve officers' school, and they are probably less alienated than an average draftee.

We were alert from the beginning to the fact that, because lower participants react differently to different facets of the organization, we needed to work out an index or some other way to deal with this phenomenon to allow for meaningful comparisons (pp. 10-11ff.). Suffice it to say here that (a) attitudes toward abstract values or goals of an organization often deviate from most attitudes toward other facets of the organization (as though the former had an unreal or idealized nature) and that (b) Randel's draftees fall where predicted on two out of three indicators.

In a Dual Organization

Infantry basic-training units, which combine normative and coercive compliance (see p. 55, on dual structures) are the subject of Robert B. Smith's fascinating secondary analysis of a survey of 1155 recruits, conducted by Hanan Selvin in 1952. Two of Smith's numerous findings seem to be particularly relevant in the present context.

First, Smith investigated the type and incidence of controls employed by the officers. To measure coercive control, Smith used the soldiers' answers to questions about whether there were, among their superiors, men who "seem never to let any opportunity go by to punish the trainees in some way" and who "treat the trainees 'like dirt.' " The use of utilitarian power was determined by questions concerning the officers' decisions on the assignment of unattractive work and the allocation of favor. These two types of control correlated highly, and Smith decided to combine them into a single variable he called "domination" (1973, ch. 3, p. 5). The contrasting power type, normative power, was then assessed by the trainees' reports on whether their superiors showed "real interest" in them and generated a feeling of confidence.

How do the two kinds of power relate to each other? Smith's data allow us to establish to what degree they tend to separate within the organization. Looking at Table IV-6, we find that normative

Table IV-6—The Relationship Between Normative Power and Domination

NORMATIVE POWER	DOMINATION		
	Low	Medium	High
High	48%	41%	34%
Medium	26%	32%	33%
Low	26%	27%	33%
(N)	(259)	(404)	(492)

$\chi^2 = 4.333$, $df = 4$; not significant at .10.
Source: Smith (1973), ch. 3, p. 7 (table edited).

power tends to be slightly stronger when domination is low than under high domination: The difference between high and low normative power is 22% under low domination, 14% under medium domination, and only 1% under high domination. However, this relationship is not statistically significant. That is, in this dual organization the two powers do not segregate.

The same result is found when we look at the distribution of the study's population over the various "power mixes" in Table IV-7.

Table IV-7—Distribution of Power Mixes in Infantry Basic-Training Units

POWER MIX	INCIDENCE		
	%		N
Pure normative power	17		191
Primarily normative power	14		166
Dual power	32		368
Low power		6	68
Medium power		11	129
High power		15	171
Primarily domination	14		163
Pure domination	23		272
	100.0		1160

The categories in Table IV-7 are based on the principle underlying Table IV-6. "Pure normative" includes cells 1 and 4 of Table IV-6, "Primarily normative"—cell 2; the dual patterns are represented by cells 3, 5, and 7, respectively; "Primarily domination" is cell 6, and "Pure domination" comprises cells 8 and 9.
Source: Table provided by Robert B. Smith.

Across the board, more members are subject to domination than to normative power (23% are under the influence of pure domination, 17% of pure normative power). But taking everything together, the distribution is remarkably balanced. Those subject "primarily" to domination or to primarily normative power (as distinct from "pure") are almost the same. 14% and 14% respectively. The dual power patterns, comprising 32% of the subjects, form the mode of the distribution, in accordance with the compliance theory.

Finally, Smith's data allow us to examine the effect of different power mixes on the involvement of those subject to power (Table IV-8).[3] Involvement is measured by two items: the respect soldiers award their officers and the willingness of soldiers to follow their

3. For important discussion, see Almond (1974), esp. p. 32. See also Kern and Bahr (1974).

Table IV-8—Power Mix and Involvement in Infantry Basic-Training Units

POWER MIX	HIGH INVOLVEMENT	
	%	N
Pure normative power	73.3	140
Primarily normative power	68.7	114
Dual power	54.3	200
Low power	23.5	16
Medium power	51.9	67
High power	68.4	117
Primarily domination	44.8	73
Pure domination	23.5	64
		1160

Source: Table provided by Robert B. Smith.

superiors into combat (*ibid.*, ch. 5, p. 6). In line with the compliance theory, involvement steadily increases to the degree that the proportion of domination in the power mix used by the officers declines. The difference between involvement under pure normative power and under pure domination amounts to no less than 50% (73% versus 24%). As expected, the dual power falls in between normative and coercive in the involvement effect.

Looking at the three dual patterns (equal amounts of normative and dominative power), we find that where only a low overall amount of power is applied, involvement is much lower than under high power. This effect may be due partly to the fact that in the high dual pattern, there is as much normative power present as in the purely normative category, athough it is combined with an equal amount of domination. Another explanation might be derived from the assumption that where there is no power at all, involvement cannot be generated because without power there would be no organization to be involved in. However, this proposition is almost impossible to test, as our present capacities to measure and to compare total amounts of power are limited.

An Indirect Test of 52 Organizations

Morris Mitzner (1968) provides a more indirect test of the core compliance thesis than those reported so far, but he covers 52 different organizations, a much larger number than represented by the previous studies combined. Mitzner uses an interesting measurement he designed: He compares the prestige scores that employees grant various organizational roles with the official prestige rankings given to the same roles in the organizational chart of their organizations, which include all three compliance types (*ibid.*, p. 198). Mitzner theorizes that the strength of the correlation between employee prestige scores and organizational role demands (operationalized as indicated by formal specifications—in particular, by the organizational rank) is a measure of organizational effectiveness in gaining acceptance of its intended distribution of authority. Stated another way, the strength of the correlation within one organization, Mitzner suggests, indicates the degree to which employees have internalized organizational values. As such, the measure also indicates the employees' involvement. It therefore follows that a high positive correlation indicates, according to Mitzner, a prevalence of "moral commitment"; a moderate proportion of significant positive correlations would signify "mild calculative commitment"; and a low proportion of significant positive correlations would point to a general pattern of "alienation" (*ibid.*, p. 198).

Mitzner's data were collected by means of questionnaires administered to 589 respondents in 63 distinct units of 52 organizations. Of the 63 organizational units the compliance patterns of 29 were predominantly utilitarian, of 22 predominantly normative, and of 12 predominantly coercive (*ibid.*, p. 96).

The results of the correlation of employees' prestige scores and official ranking of organizational roles, given in Table IV-9, support

Table IV-9—The Distribution Among Compliance Patterns of Significant Correlations Between Group Prestige Scores for Each Position and the Organizations' Intended Ranking of These Positions

Compliance Pattern	Total Number of Groups	Number of Groups with Significant Correlations	Proportion of Groups in Each Category with Significant Correlations
Utilitarian	29	21	.724
Normative	22	19	.864
Coercive	12	6	.500

Source: Mitzner (1968), p. 107.

the compliance thesis. Groups of employees in coercive organizations have the smallest proportions of significant positive correlations, employee groups in utilitarian organizations have a higher proportion, and those in normative organizations have the highest proportion of positive correlations (*ibid.*, pp. 107-108).

One suspects that the differences in proportion of significant positive correlations might well have been even greater if Mitzner had administered the questionnaire only to low-level organizational participants and if, in the case of normative and coercive groups, he had focused on those whom we defined as the "lower participants," such as patients in hospitals and inmates in prisons, rather than defining the lower participants as the lowest-ranking paid employees. Because relations between an organization and its paid workers contain a significant utilitarian element by definition, Mitzner's definition of the lower participants means that the compliance patterns in the organizations he classified "normative" are actually normative-utilitarian and those he classified as "coercive" are actually coercive-utilitarian. Thus, his findings seem to support the core thesis somewhat more strongly than may be indicated on the face of it.

Differences in Sub-Organizations: Production versus Laboratory

The significance of the relationship between means of controls used and the participants' orientation to the organization is high-lighted when different divisions of the same organization are compared. In the original text, care was taken to point out that different sub-units of the same organization—General Motors, the Catholic Church, or whatever—may display quite different patterns of behavior, as measured by numerous indicators, if their compliance bases are different—if, for example, one section is more alienating or committing than another (see p. 426).

In a directly relevant study, though one less tied to the compliance theory than many of the others cited, George A. Miller (1967) studied two organizational units of the same aerospace corporation, one of the largest in the country. Data were collected in 1965, in two divisions: a Basic Science Laboratory with an atmosphere "more like that of a university" and an aerospace group, "more representative of traditional research and development work" (*ibid.*, p. 758). Miller measured the attitudes of scientists and engineers in both divisions by means of mailed questionnaires and achieved an 80% completion rate (419 out of 523 potential subjects). All "nonsupervisor" personnel were regarded as lower participants.

Involvement was measured with questionnaire items, focusing mainly on negative involvement or alienation. Organizational control was classified as directive, participatory, and *laissez faire*. Miller also assessed the extent to which the division relied on what he calls "professional" incentives (e.g., helping scientists get recognition in their fields), which are normative means, and on what Miller refers to as "organizational" means (e.g., differentiation in salaries), which are utilitarian rewards.

Miller found, in line with the compliance theory, that:

1. The more utilitarian the incentives and the more directive the control, the more negative was the involvement. Correspondingly, the more normative the incentives and more participatory or *laissez*

Table IV-10—Degree of Work Alienation in Aerospace and Basic Laboratory Organizational Units, by Type of Control and Incentive

CONTROL-INCENTIVE STRUCTURE	WORK ALIENATION				
	Low	Medium	High	N	
Supervisor type					
Directive	.10	.33	.57	63	
Participatory	.32	.42	.26	158	
Laissez faire	.35	.42	.23	176	Gamma = —.30
Company encouragement					
Low	.20	.39	.41	142	
Medium	.26	.38	.36	107	
High	.42	.44	.14	144	Gamma = —.35

Source: Miller (1967), p. 762 (table slightly edited). Reprinted with the permission of the American Sociological Association.

faire the control, the more positive the involvement. Alienation was at .57 under directive supervision, compared to .26 under the more participatory form and .23 for *laissez faire* supervision. The alienation percentage was .41 for those under low normative and high utilitarian control; .14 for those under high normative and low utilitarian control.

2. Alienation was much higher in the aerospace group than in the basic laboratory. In the latter only 4% were highly alienated, as compared to 34% in the former. 63% in the laboratory displayed low alienation, compared to 25% in the aerospace unit. Thus, the general thesis "works" for subdivisions within an organization as well as it does for differences among them.[4]

4. Brager's study (1969), discussed in detail later, also found a systematic difference when he compared sub-organizations or divisions within a normative organization, the Mobilization For Youth, a politically active welfare agency. The core staff was significantly more committed to the organizational goals than the administrative unit, composed of accountants, public relations staff, and the like.

Table IV-11—Degree of Work Alienation in Aerospace and Basic Laboratory Organizational Units, by Type of Professional Training

					Work Alienation				
ORGANIZATIONAL UNIT	*ENGINEERS*					*SCIENTISTS*			
	Low	Med.	High	N		Low	Med.	High	N
Aerospace group	.21	.43	.36	199		.31	.38	.31	147
Basic laboratory	.58	.42	.00	12		.65	.30	.05	37
		Gamma = −.75					Gamma = −.62		

Source: Miller (1967), p. 767. Reprinted with the permission of the American Sociological Association.

A "Hostile" Test of the Thesis

Walter W. Hudson (1973) did more than test the relationship between power and involvement in a public welfare agency; he also checked to see whether an alternative theorem could better predict his findings in what he himself refers to as a hostile test of the compliance theory. The results are quite friendly, as we shall see shortly.

Hudson's research took place in the Cook County Department of Public Aid in Chicago, Illinois, where he studied 482 persons who terminated their employment in a one-year period from March 1967 to February 1968. Interviews were the main instrument; if a person could not be interviewed, a questionnaire was mailed to him.

The measurement of power was based on supervisors' conduct as reported by the former employees. Involvement was measured by a five-item scale derived from the same data base.

In line with what the theory would lead one to expect, Hudson found that utilitarian power was much more prevalent here than either normative or coercive power. Specifically, utilitarian power accounted for 28.20% of the variance in involvement scores, normative for 7.34%, and coercive for 2.25% (*ibid.*, p. 55).

Hudson next used a multiple-regression analysis in which all three types of power ($r = .54$) were found to jointly account for 28.63% of the involvement variance. Examination of the beta coefficients shows that the coercive power effect is not significant when the effects of the other two are held constant. (This is particularly reassuring as Hudson's definition of coercive power is psychological rather than physical: no violence or threat of violence is involved, but supervisors are reported to be aggressive or domineering, better scored as negative normative power).

Table IV-12—Summary Statistics for Multiple-Regression Model Which Regressed Organizational Involvement on Three Types of Power

Type of Power	B	Beta	F-ratio	p less than
Utilitarian	.251	.504	136.45	.001
Normative	.055	.105	3.10	.05
Coercive	.080	.065	1.34	.30
Constant	3.504			

$R = .535$; $R^2 = .2863$; F-ratio for full model $= 62.33$ with 3 and 466 degrees of freedom; $SE = 5.16$; twelve degrees of freedom were lost because of missing data.
Source: Hudson (1973), p. 56.

Hudson says he would have expected such findings in a business organization, but not in a government agency. But not only are these white-collar employees expected to be more utilitarianly controlled than normatively (p. 36), but Hudson studied only employees who for one reason or another were leaving the agency. Hence, Hudson submitted the data to two additional tests: one holding constant for various background factors (age, sex, and so on) and one of statistical rigor. In both cases the basic finding remained unchanged.

Finally, Hudson tried to develop an alternative typology, i.e., to predict the involvement scores (his dependent variables) from a set of independent variables other than power. Rather than derive those from a theory, he drew them out of a factor analysis of his own data (using a principal-axis factor solution with an oblique rotation, p. 81). This provides tough competition to any theory because the analysis is *post hoc* and completely tailored to the particular body of data.

Four factors emerged in what Hudson calls an influence typology. These include peer relations, relation to supervisor, training and work volume, and physical environment. When related to involvement, the influence model consistently displayed less explanatory power than did the power typology. The unique contribution of the power model in terms of the total commitment variance is 18.86%; the influence model accounted for 15.58% ("unique" refers to the part of the variance accounted for after the effect of the control variables has been removed). If the part of the variance that is confounded between the model and the control variables is added, the models explain 30.79% and 23.41%, respectively (*ibid.*, pp. 110, 167).[5]

5. The second set of values for the power model differ slightly from the R^2 given in Figure IV-I because, in the comparison with the influence model, Hudson eliminates those control variables that have proven to be without significant contribution.

Hudson tackles one more question of great interest: Is the relationship between the means of control applied and the involvement generated unilinear or curvilinear? The question is far from a merely technical one. The substantive issue is: Does the control power of ever-higher utilitarian rewards have a declining marginal utility, so that as people get sated, their desire for other rewards increases, especially normative ones, or—at least under the given conditions of our society—do people have a practically unlimited appetite for utilitarian rewards? Regarding normative power, will movement from very little to "somewhat" yield as much involvement as movement from "somewhat" to higher values, despite the fact that the basic positive relation is lacking? And, once force is used, will more force generate a declining or a rising effect?

Hudson's findings are summarized in the following chart:

Figure IV-1 — *The Conditional Relationships between Involvement and Three Forms of Power with Seven Control Variables Held Constant*

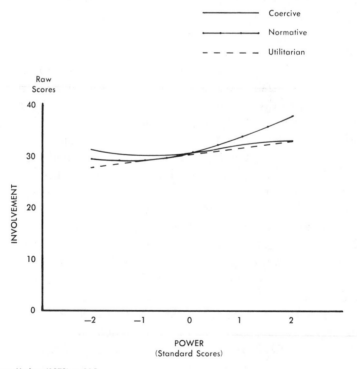

Source: Hudson (1973), p. 115.

1. Units of normative power, the data show, have greater effect when they are added to an existing pile than when there are few. Thus, a change from -1 to 0 in normative power produces a gain of about 1.32 points on involvement, while a change from 0 to $+1$ produces 2.84 points (*ibid.*, p. 117). This suggests that, at least before very high scores are reached, the marginal utility of normative power is not declining but rising, a finding not heretofore reported but wholly plausible.

2. Utilitarian power, unlike normative, relates in a unilinear manner. As its range in the present study, of course, is rather limited, this finding cannot be taken as disproving the more general theory of declining marginal utility for larger amounts. To put it simply, even the most rewarded welfare workers are not so highly rewarded that an increase will have less effect on them than on the less well-paid ones.

Although the finding regarding the curvilinear effects of coercive power is in line with the theory, we ignore it here because of the way coercive power was operationalized in this study. All said and done, Hudson's study provides a rigorous test of the compliance thesis; his findings support it and at the same time elaborate it beyond the original formulation.

Charles N. Greene and Dennis W. Organ (1973) focus on the question of what factors mediate the often-observed relationship between "role accuracy"—the degree to which an organizational participant correctly perceives what others expect of him—and role satisfaction. Data were collected on the relations between 142 first-line supervisors and their immediate superiors in the financial and research and development divisions of four large industrial organizations.

The authors hypothesized that two variables may play a role in linking role accuracy and satisfaction: the degree to which an actor complies with the expectations directed at him ("compliance") and the evaluation of his performance by other actors who can reward or punish him ("performance evaluation"). Role accuracy was measured by asking the first-line supervisor how frequently his superior expected him to perform 34 specified tasks. The responses were compared to the superior's actual expectations, as indicated by himself on a similar questionnaire. Compliance was seen as the reversed value of the difference between the superior's expectations and the supervisor's report on how frequently he in fact performed each of the 34 activities.

(Note that this operational definition of compliance leaves out half of the concept, the lower participant's involvement, and focuses on the other half, that of control). Performance evaluation was ascertained through the assessment of the supervisor's work by his superior, again on all 34 dimensions. Satisfaction was measured by administering Bullock's Job Satisfaction Scale.

Table IV-13 gives the zero-order correlation coefficients. It shows that by far the highest correlation exists between role accuracy and compliance.

Table IV-13—Zero-Order Correlations

	Role Accuracy	Compliance	Performance Evaluation	Job Satisfaction
Accuracy	1.00			
Compliance	.79	1.00		
Evaluation	.35	.45	1.00	
Satisfaction	.38	.50	.58	1.00

Source: Greene and Organ (1973), p. 97. Reprinted with the permission of *Administrative Science Quarterly*.

In their next step, the authors constructed a series of four different causal models, linking role accuracy and satisfaction. In order to find out which of the models fitted the data best, partial correlation coefficients were computed for those relationships predicted to be zero (see Table IV-14). As it turned out, model C was the only one whose predictions were met by the data. In other words, role accuracy was found to be unrelated to satisfaction when compliance was controlled (−.028), while compliance had both a direct influence on satisfaction and an indirect one, through the superior's evaluation of the supervisor's work. (The size of positive partial correlation coefficients between compliance and satisfaction, as reported by the authors in a personal communication, is .33, significant at the .01 level).

The authors then proceed to explain their findings. Referring to the compliance typology, Greene and Organ suggest that "Etzioni's theory provides a means for extending implications of the findings to organizations." As the study focuses on finance and R&D departments of industrial organizations, the authors base their interpretation of their data on the compliance theory's assumption "that compliance in white-collar industries is predominantly utilitarian in nature, with normative compliance a secondary pattern; that compliance in research organizations is primarily normative and secondarily utilitar-

Table IV-14—Four Causal Models of Role Accuracy and Satisfaction

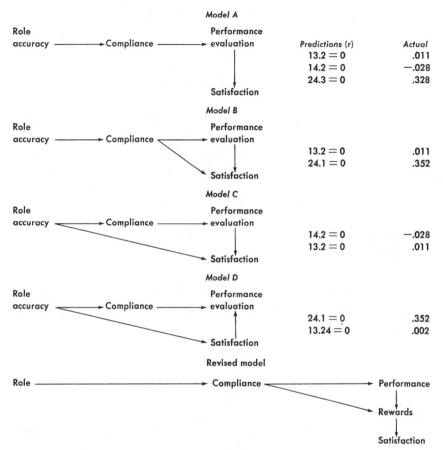

	Predictions (r)	Actual
Model A	13.2 = 0	.011
	14.2 = 0	—.028
	24.3 = 0	.328
Model B	13.2 = 0	.011
	24.1 = 0	.352
Model C	14.2 = 0	—.028
	13.2 = 0	.011
Model D	24.1 = 0	.352
	13.24 = 0	.002

Actual partial correlation coefficients are given only for those relationships which are predicted, by the particular model, to be zero. Predicted relationships are expressed in terms of the order of antecedence of the variables involved; thus, 13.2 = 0 means that the relationship between the first variable in the model (role accuracy) and the third variable (performance evaluation), controlled for the second variable (compliance), is predicted to be zero.

Source: Greene and Organ (1973), p. 98. Reprinted with the permission of *Administrative Science Quarterly*.

ian." This, as the authors see it, may serve as a starting point for a theoretical explanation: "If normative compliance is interpreted as intrinsically satisfying, and utilitarian compliance as being satisfying indirectly through its connection with performance evaluation and other rewards, then the findings here seem quite consistent with his predictions—especially since the sample here was composed of both white-collar semiprofessional employees and professionals.

Brief Encounters

A NORMATIVE PARALLEL—John Andes (1968) analyzed universities in terms of compliance "subsystems," pointing out that different university divisions differ rather substantially in their modes of control and involvement. He distinguishes among technical, managerial, service, and "institutional" subsystems, under the influence of Parsons' four phases. He sees the participants in these subsystems as differing according to Robert K. Merton's classification of locals versus cosmopolitans and Robert Presthus' categories of upward mobile, indifferent, and ambivalent. The result is chiefly a multidimensional chart, as Andes' work is basically classificatory in nature, although he does here and there draw upon his experience.

AN INADVERTENT TEST—Geoffrey K. Ingham's (1967) secondary analysis of data on workers' compliance in factories is of interest because he did not set out to test the compliance thesis, but the data led him to do so anyway. Ingham was interested in explaining the often-reported inverse relationship between organizational size and involvement, the latter as measured by rates of absenteeism and workers' turnover. As intervening variables, Ingham introduced functional specialization and bureaucratization, assuming them to be positively associated with size and at the same time causing negative involvement.

Ingham found, however, that functional specialization did not covary with size and hence "should therefore be excluded from consideration in any attempt to provide an explanation of the size effect" (*ibid.,* p. 239). Bureaucratization was found to be associated with size, but, Ingham argues, its effect on the workers depends on their general orientation to the organization, which in turn depends on whether a *congruence* exists between orientation to work and orientation to organizational control structure (*ibid.,* pp. 248-251). Thus, Ingham's analysis led him to find compliance of more interpretative power than the variables he had set out to study.

BRIEF REFERENCE—Much briefer applications of the basic compliance frame of reference are listed here, for completeness' sake. These include a discussion of the Peace Corps as a normative organization (Rourke, 1969, pp. 73-74); several discussions of voluntary associations as normative organizations (Palisi, 1972, pp. 40-41); Warner (1972), pp. 73-75, 78); Scherer (1972, p. 90), and Smith,

Reddy, and Baldwin (1972, p. 195). For a discussion of the Church as a normative organization, see Rudge (1968, pp. 11, 12, 21) Snook (1974) and Takayama (1974); of a therapeutic mental hospital as a normative organization, Stotland and Kobler (1965, pp. 238ff.); of a social welfare agency, Miller and Fry (1973, p. 307) and Toren (1972, *passim*); of professional organizations, Quarantelli (1970, p. 381), Glaser (1963, p. 50, note 15), and cf. Ference, Goldner, and Ritti (1971, pp. 174-175); of semiprofessional organizations, Simpson and Simpson (1969, p. 231); of a British union which is highly utilitarian, Ashdown (n.d.); of unions in general Hall (1972, p. 162) and DeFleur, D'Antonio, and DeFleur (1973, p. 486); on military organizations see Lang (1965, p. 863); universities—Pashley (1974); and on prisons, Cressey (1965, pp. 1061-1). See also Aage (1974), Balog (1974), Cherkaoui and Lindsey (1974), Franklyn (1974), Hanson (1974), Krause (1974), Reddy (1974), Weber and Polm (1974), and Wright (1974).

For a detailed conceptualization of the social structure of a welfare agency, including lower and higher participants as well as "audience participants," in terms of the compliance theory, see Levinson and Schiller (1966, pp. 97-98), and Levinson (1964, p. 373ff.). For additional discussion of the relationships between administrators and professionals in a social welfare agency, from a compliance viewpoint, see Leonard (1966, pp. 12-13).

James Q. Wilson (1973) has an excellent book-length analysis of political organizations, which "parallels" the compliance theory, according to the author (*ibid.,* p. 52). (The parallelism was also noted by Heydebrand, 1973, p. 91). He also finds some subtle differences, which lead him to use different labels for the same variables we covered. As he barely hints at his reasons for doing so, there is no way to deal with them.

COMPLIANCE AND OTHER THEORIES

The Relative Weight of Compliance

Clagett G. Smith and Michael E. Brown (n.d.) tried to weigh the relative explanatory power of three approaches to organizational analysis. The first, the structural one, is characterized as locating the main interpretative force in "the social structure of the organization operating as a manifestation of rationality in goal-setting and goal-seeking" (*ibid.*, p. 4). The second approach sees the elite or leadership as the prime forces. Finally, the normative approach views consensus and shared values as all-important.

The authors characterized the compliance theory as a prime example of the elite approach. Such a characterization is correct in one sense, as compliance theory does focus on the means of control and the orientation of the lower participants to the organization, but it is not valid if it suggests that the elites determine, or even largely shape, the resulting pattern. The compliance relationship, I hold, is a good place to start the analysis because it tends to correlate highly with other variables; it is a good indicator as to the whole organizational pattern, described by many other variables (the "correlates"). However, this is not to suggest that the compliance relation determines the others, nor that the elites determine the compliance relationship itself; the pattern is codetermined by the lower participants.

A more precise placing of the compliance theory would be in a structural approach—not of the formalist kind which Smith and Brown study, but one which encompasses formal and informal variables and their interaction (Etzioni, 1965, p. 688). In the terms used by the authors, all three approaches touch on compliance variables: the second, by their definition; the first, by its treatment of the formal aspect of power relations; the third, by its focus on involvement and consensus, which the authors themselves refer to as dealing with the "normativeness" of the organization in Etzioni's terms.

What can we learn from Smith and Brown's data? They studied seven populations, including those of four union locals, a sample of 112 locals of a voluntary association, 26 branches of a government utility, 32 stations of a delivery company, 36 local branches of a national sales organization, 40 offices of an insurance company, and 36 branches of a brokerage firm. The authors decided to use as dependent variables, in testing the explanatory power of the three approaches, the total *amount* of control exercised and its *slope,* defined as the extent to which rank-and-file members share in the control as opposed to its monopolization by the upper echelons. These concepts have been previously defined and used by Tannenbaum and others (Tannenbaum, 1962, and Julian, 1968).

The authors' main finding is that all three approaches made a contribution, all correlated significantly with the two dependent variables (see Table IV-15). Thus, no one approach prevails. As I see it, this actually shows that all these variables must be included in a

Table IV-15—The Correlates of Control

CONTROL STRUCTURE

PREDICTOR VARIABLES	Unions N=4		Voluntary Associations N=112		Government Utility Steam Plants N=12		Government Utility Engineering Plants N=14		Delivery Company N=32		Sales Organization N=33		Insurance Company N=40		Brokerage Firm OFFICE A N=18		Brokerage Firm OFFICE B N=18	
	Slope	Total Control	Slope	Total Control	Slope	Total Control	Slope	Total Control	Slope	Total Control	Slope	Total Control	Slope	Total Control	Slope	Total Control	Slope	Total Control
I. Social Structure																		
Bureaucratization	-1.00*	-.40	-.45§	.14	.24	-.44*	.35	-.38	.14	.03	.00	-.17	-.12	-.46‡	-.35*	.16	-.22	.06
Size	.00	.80	.31§	.00	-.03	.03	-.43*	-.41	-.08	-.30†	-.03	.32†	.05	.34†	-.13	.37†	-.29	.13
Complexity	.00	.80	—	—	-.02	.23	-.50†	-.34	-.05	-.27*	-.09	.24*	-.20	.40‡	.17	.18	.14	.22
Differentiation	-.95*	-.15	.23‡	.14	-.04	-.01	.04	-.59†	.11	-.26*	.15	-.23	-.45‡	.14	—	—	—	—
II. Leadership																		
Initiation of structure	1.00*	.40	.06	.08	.09	-.32	.09	-.71‡	-.41‡	.62§	.20	-.08	-.07	.59‡	-.15	.76§	-.33*	.32*
Supportiveness	1.00*	.40	.13	.12	-.28	.62‡	.29	.63†	-.27*	.52§	.32†	-.07	-.03	.76§	.02	.68§	.16	.82§
III. Normative system																		
Cohesiveness	—	—	—	—	.04	.45*	-.29	-.19	.31†	.27*	.25*	.19	.21	.53§	-.07	.71§	.29	.54§
Consensus	.40	1.00*	.24‡	.15†	-.14	-.30	.50†	.40	-.57§	.63§	.22	.15	.09	.18	.17	-.03	-.43†	-.03

* Significant at .10 level, two-tailed test
† Significant at .05 level, two-tailed test
‡ Significant at .01 level, two-tailed test
§ Significant at .001 level, two-tailed test
Source: Smith and Brown (n.d.), pp. 36–37.

viable organizational theory, a requirement which, as I have suggested, compliance theory lives up to.

Next, Smith and Brown consider differences among organizations. In the union locals and the chapters of the voluntary association, the authors found low amounts of control and relatively high levels of democratization (positive slope), associated with relatively high normativeness of these organizations.

The government utility plants combine a stress on efficiency with placing "a premium on the joint participation of workers and management, and have many formal (and legal) means of assuring a representative form of decision-making ultimately under public control" (*ibid.,* p. 20). No wonder, the authors say, that here bureaucratization and elitism are negatively associated with total amount of control and with democratization (slope). In my terms, this utility is a less normative organization than the union or voluntary association but not as utilitarian as those to follow.

Differences among the remaining utilitarian organizations are explained by differences in the amount of control the task requires, in terms of either the technology used or the skills the workers need. Presumably the higher the need is for control technically, the greater its acceptance by the workers as legitimate rather than as alienating; and the greater are the skills workers must command, the less controllable they are by utilitarian means. Roughly as expected, consensus is relatively higher and other indirect indications of positive involvement are somewhat higher, when the task is highly technical and requires skill than when it is not. Thus, the compliance theory is supported, as other organizational theories are also reported as valid.

The reason the preceding observations rely on comments by the authors rather than refer to their data (summarized in Table IV-15) is that Smith and Brown present their data in the form of correlations between compliance variables and amount of control and slope, but do not give the data on each variable which went into the correlations. It is hence not possible to determine if, for instance, involvement in the average utilitarian organization was lower than in the more normative ones. Moreover, the independent variables by which the authors test the validity of the "leadership approach"—as can be seen from Table IV-15—are not quite identical with those included in the compliance theory. "Initiation of structure" includes the elite's "planning, providing information, clarifying roles, instigating formal procedures, and coordinating efforts" (*ibid.,* p. 5). Supportiveness, on the other hand, is the degree to which the leadership understands the needs and interests of the lower participants and guides them by giving or withholding support (*ibid.*). To gain the original data and work with it proved not practical. Hence, relying on the way the data are reported, we can tell only that the compliance variables correlated positively or negatively with amount of control and slope, but not whether both were high or low or which were high and which low. It is chiefly the authors' discussion that provides the comments which have some bearing on the compliance thesis.

The main contribution of the authors' study, aside from showing that compliance variables "work," is to return to the concept of the total amount of control and introduce the concept of "slope" into the compliance family of correlates. Also, they suggest that the technology and skills required are background factors that must be taken into account. This idea is supported by other studies cited later (especially Rossel).

Intratheoretical Consistency

A quite different approach to confirming the fruitfulness of a typology is to assess its relationship to other typologies which have proven fruitful. If a combination of theoretical reasoning and empirical research has established the value of a given theory and if we can show that another theory relates to but does not duplicate the first theory, their similarity supports the second theory (and strengthens the position of the first one, too). In this way, *theoretical continuity* is advanced. If it is possible to move from the concepts of one theory to those of another, on the basis of empirically verified steps, fragmentation is reduced and the integration of the discipline at hand is advanced.

Richard H. Hall, J. Eugene Haas, and Norman J. Johnson (1967) undertook such an exercise in intertheory bridge-building, using data from 75 organizations. These organizations do not constitute a random sample because, as the authors point out, there is no defined universe of organizations one can sample. Rather, the organizations to be studied were selected to represent the main institutional sectors of society, such as the economic, political, religious, and other sectors. A further effort was made to balance governmental and nongovernmental organizations. Size was also varied, with the organizations covering a range of 6 to 9,000 participants. Data about the organizations were obtained through interviews with their top executives and examination of records. The authors divided the organizations into four classes on the basis of the Blau-Scott typology (1962) and into three classes based on the compliance theory.[6] The first classification is based on who is the main beneficiary of the organization.[7] It allows assessment of the central problem the organization is preoccupied with and the nature of the members' commitment to the organization. The main classes are organizations who benefit, primarily (a) the membership, "mutual benefit associations," (b) the owners, "business concerns," (c) the clients, "service organizations," and (d) the public at large, the "commonweal" organizations.

Hall, Haas, and Johnson assigned "mixed" organizations (e.g., schools serving both the clients and the public at large) in line with the way Blau and Scott assigned them and found the following distribution:

Mutual benefit: 14, including labor unions, a farm federation, a political party, and so on; *Service:* 18, including universities, schools, hospitals, and so on; *Business:* 27, including banks, hotels, factories, restaurants, and the like; and *Commonweal:* 16, including a city recreation department, an educational television corporation, a post office, a state penal institution, and so on.

Problems were also encountered with placing these organizations in the compliance typology, relying on the lower participants' involvement and control. "The final placement of these organizations," the authors say, "was based on the collective judgment of the research workers" (1967, p. 122). The 75 organizations included:

Coercive: 11, including prisons, a state hospital, and a state school; *Utilitarian:* 35, including banks, plants, restaurants, stores, and so on; and *Normative:* 29, including a church, city recreation department, a political party, a public school system, and the like.

The relationships among the typologies are reflected in Table IV-16. Obviously the typologies were found correlated on a highly significant statistical level (.001). Some of the bunching is quite obvious—for example, many business organizations are also utilitarian—and some are less so. On the face of it, one might not expect there to be twice as many coercive commonweal organizations as either

6. These are the two "most widely used typologies of organizations," according to Price (1972, p. 12 and also p. 145) and March (1965, p. x).

7. For another dicussion of the use of typologies in organizational theory see Burns (1967).

Table IV-16—Interrelationships Between Blau-Scott and Etzioni Typologies*

	Mutual Benefit (N = 14) %	Service (N = 18) %	Business (N = 27) %	Commonweal (N = 16) %
Coercive (N = 11)	0	17	0	50
Utilitarian (N = 35)	43	6	89	25
Normative (N = 29)	57	77	11	25

* $\chi^2 = 52.25$; 6 df; $p > .001$
Source: Hall, Haas, and Johnson (1967), p. 123. Reprinted with the permission of *Administrative Science Quarterly*.

normative or utilitarian ones, which suggests that the public relies heavily on the government for its well-being, and that the government relies more on coercion than on other means. It is also not obvious that mutual benefit organizations rely as often (even slightly more) on normative means as on utilitarian ones. That service organizations rely heavily (77%) on normative means is surprising and certainly deserves to be re-checked. By reversing the direction in which the percentages were computed (see Table IV-17), we are able to move

Table IV-17—Interrelationships Between Blau-Scott and Etzioni Typologies*

	Coercive (N = 11) %	Utilitarian (N = 35) %	Normative (N = 29) %
Mutual benefit (N = 14)	0	17	28
Service (N = 18)	27	3	48
Business (N = 28)	0	69	10
Commonweal (N = 16)	73	11	14

* $\chi^2 = 52.25$; 6df; $p > .001$
Source: Hall, Haas, and Johnson (1967), p. 123 (table has been reversed).

from compliance types to those of beneficiaries, which highlights that most coercive organizations are commonweal (73%) and most utilitarian organizations are businesses (69%), although there are utilitarian organizations of all four types; and normative organizations are most dispersed, from this viewpoint. Most important for our purposes here, though, is the basic finding: The compliance typology has been supported by this intratheoretical consistency test.

The Logical-Empirical Status of the Compliance Theory

Ikka Heiskanen (1967) critically examined four theories, those of Weber, Simon, and Parsons and the compliance theory, from chiefly two viewpoints: (a) are the propositions tautological, or are they subject, in principle, to refutation by empirical test? (b) is the theory "open" to unification with other bodies of knowledge, so that science may be integrated? To put it first briefly, none of the four theories survives either test; and Heiskanen is bound to form her own theory, which, she points out, draws liberally on these four.

We review and discuss here only the main points made in reference to the compliance theory. First, Heiskanen holds that the compliance core thesis is logical and hence untestable. The theory, she correctly reports, holds that there are congruent and incongruent compliance types and that organizations are expected to strive toward congruence and, once they approximate it, to resist leaving it, because congruence is more effective than noncongruence and organizations are under external and internal pressure to be effective. Heiskanen next points out that this position is logically derived and normative, as the theory suggests that the six incongruent types are "possible" but not effective (Heiskanen, 1967, p. 87-88).

"Well," says the critic, "are organizations really social units under pressure to be effective? Is the direction of 'internal' and 'external' pressure toward effectiveness the same, so that they do not cancel each other?" My answer is straightforward: These are empirical questions, to be answered through research, not by arguments. These questions, by implication, also specify under which conditions the core thesis (in its dynamic formulation) can be rejected. That the thesis was deduced rather than induced does not make it less subject to such a test. The way a theory is derived has nothing to do with its empirical status or falsifiability.

Heiskanen further holds that the correlates of the basic compliance variables, to which we shall turn shortly, are derived from the compliance thesis. This, again, is correct only in the sense that the theory predicts that if an organization is scored in reference to its position on the compliance continuum, this score will "predict" its score on other variables (such as consensus, elite structure, and scope). If an actual organization's observed score differs from the predicted (or expected) score, the nature of the strains such differences will cause are predicted. If those are consistently not evident, the theory is wrong.

In short, Heiskanen has built her case on a confusion between two meanings of derivation: the procedure through which a proposition has been reached and the way it is validated. The compliance propositions were indeed in part logically developed, but they are not logically true, like mathematical formulae; their truth value must be assessed through the kind of empirical studies reported in the preceding and following pages.

Stanley J. Udy, Jr. (1965) characterized this aspect of the theory extremely clearly. He compares the compliance theory with that of Blau-Scott. The latter "essentially conceives an organization as a complex of interrelated, yet discrete elements. Changes in the state of one element produce changes in one or more of the other elements, and so forth. The theoretical result is a series of interrelated propositions . . ." (*ibid.*, p. 681).

Compliance theory presents "a basically organic view of organization, which stresses the containment of less general by more general original elements, and in which a unified system emerges as a cumulative result of successive adaptations" (*ibid.*).

While I would not use the term "organic," because it implies a greater degree of interconnectedness of the parts than I suggest is fruitful to assume, it is basically helpful to view organizations as social units which do have a fair measure of internal structure, cohesion, and as we shall see, guidability. Hence the effects of changing the value of one variable on other variables will depend on the general pattern of the organization, whether it is coercive, utilitarian, or normative. This general pattern "slants" the interaction effects among the other variables, although it, in turn, registers the effects of all the other variables on the pattern.

Second, Heiskanen argues that "because of the lack of independent testability of the deductions, no new concepts are generated and no new interpretations of the basic model can be attempted" (*ibid.*, p. 94). The theory is said to fail the second test, openness to unification. Above all, Heiskanen argues, Etzioni points out that both the powers which elites employ and the lower participants' involvement are in part determined by extra-organizational variables. As the compliance theory "cannot" encompass those, it is not unifiable. Heiskanen is of course correct that the compliance does not comprise extra-organizational variables; that would move it toward a total social theory—ultimately, toward a global theory, a unity of all science, an ambitious task, best not attempted as a side-trip for an organizational theory-building. In this sense, then, compliance—and all other theories—are subtheories of a larger, nonexisting utopian entity. But this is not proof at all that compliance theory cannot be integrated into other more comprehensive theories. Actually, as the discussion in Chapter XVII suggests, a fair amount of progress in this direction has been made.

Barney G. Glaser and Anselm L. Strauss (1967) also assessed theories; they ask how "grounded" they are. To put it briefly, the authors hold that theory induced from data is superior to theory logically deduced from *a priori* assumptions (*ibid.*, pp. 2-6). The authors find compliance theory more "grounded" than several other theories, but not grounded enough (*ibid.*, pp. 142-144). They summarize our enterprise as one which "makes comparisons of an array (of diverse phenomena) to generate theory, principally using categories derived from existing theory" (*ibid.*, p. 144).

Glaser and Strauss quite accurately report the way the theory was arrived at: by an interaction of theoretical concepts and the analysis of hundreds of empirical studies, i.e., neither derived nor induced but formed out of an interaction of both approaches. This, I believe, does make for better theories than either sheer deduction from theoretical premises or sheer induction from empirical data. This statement is of course itself subject to verification. One of the purposes of this volume is precisely to show that such an approach works.

PART TWO

CORRELATES OF COMPLIANCE
Goals, Effectiveness, and Elites

V

COMPLIANCE, GOALS, AND EFFECTIVENESS

The second and major part of this volume is devoted to an examination of the relationship between compliance and other organizational variables. The association between compliance and organizational goals is explored first.

Organizations that have similar compliance structures tend to have similar goals, and organizations that have similar goals tend to have similar compliance structures. The second proposition obviously does not "follow" from the first, and each must be validated in its own right. But the arguments in favor of both are similar: Certain *combinations* of compliance and goals are more effective than others. Hence we present arguments and some illustrative materials that indicate an association between compliance and goals without making any inferences about the direction of the relationship.

ORGANIZATIONAL GOALS

A Classification of Goals

By *organizational goals* we mean a state of affairs which the organization is attempting to realize. A goal is an image of a future state, which may or may not be brought about (Parsons, 1937, p. 44). Once it is realized it becomes part of the organization or its environment, but it ceases to be an image that guides organizational activities and hence ceases to be a goal. The goal of an organization can be determined in the same way other sociological characteristics of organizations are established. It can be determined by an examination of organizational processes, such as the flow of work in a factory, and attributes of its structure, such as priorities in the allocation of means (reflected in a balance sheet or budget) or the assignment of personnel.

The *stated* goals of an organization can serve as a clue to the actual goals of the organization. But a researcher cannot uncritically accept the stated goals of the organization as its actual sociological goals, since organizations tend to hold "public" goals for "front" purposes.[1] Nor can he elicit this information from the top elites of the organization since they may not be free to communicate these goals to the researcher. Hence the need to draw on an examination and extrapolation of on-going organizational processes, especially "production," in the study of organizational goals.

Organizational goals can be classified in many ways. The present classification is oriented toward examination of the relationship between compliance and goals. From this viewpoint, three types of organizational goals can be distinguished: order, economic, and cultural goals.[2]

Organizations with *order* goals attempt to control actors who are deviants in the eyes of some social unit the organization is serving (frequently society) by segregating them from society and by blocking them from further deviant activities. This is a negative goal in the

1. These goals are referred to as "public" since they have the same function for the organization as public attitudes have for individuals. For a study which relates empirically private and public attitudes of individuals to those of organizations (churches), see Schank (1932). Sociologists who focus on the legitimating rather than the directing functions of goals tend to study public rather than real organizational goals. The distinction between public and private goals and its consequences for organizational operation and effectiveness, for organizational structure, and for interchange with the organization's environment are the subject of a number of recent studies: Cicourel (1958); Frank (1958-59, 1959); Ohlin (1958); and Perrow (1959, 1960).

2. The classification of goals may seem similar to that of compliance and the association therefore expectable. Goals and compliance, however, are independently defined, both conceptually and operationally, and are hence separate variables. Moreover, we shall see, there is no one-to-one relationship between the two variables. The association may not be surprising, but it is not self-evident in the logical sense of the term.

Eisenstadt's classification of goals of bureaucratic organizations includes economic, socio-political, and cultural goals (1958, p. 116). The first and last types parallel those defined here. See below for the discussion of political goals.

sense that such organizations attempt to prevent the occurrence of certain events rather than producing an object or a service. Order-centered organizations differ according to the techniques and means they use to attain their goals. Some merely segregate deviants; others segregate and punish; and still others eliminate deviants altogether. But all are predominantly order-oriented.[3]

Organizations with *economic* goals produce commodities and services supplied to outsiders. These include not only the manufacturing industries but also various service organizations, from the post office and insurance companies to movie theaters, Chinese laundries, banks, and brokerage firms.

Organizations that have *culture* goals institutionalize conditions needed for the creation and preservation of symbolic objects, their application, and the creation or reinforcement of commitments to such objects.[3a]

Most culture-oriented organizations specialize in the service of one or two culture goals. Research organizations, for example, specialize in the *creation* of new culture (science is a subsystem of culture). Research-oriented universities emphasize creation of culture, although, like all educational organizations, they also contribute to the *preservation* of the cultural heritage by transferring it from generation to generation, mainly through teaching. Professional organizations specialize in the *application* of culture, mainly science and art. Churches strive to build in and to reinforce certain commitments to cultural objects.

The goal of therapeutic mental hospitals is classified as cultural since the application of science is the central activity of these organizations. Moreover, if we see in the mental patient a deviant whose commitment to social norms and beliefs must be restored, it is clear why therapeutic goals have to be classified as culture goals (Parsons, in Greenblatt, Levinson, and Williams, 1957, p. 111).

Organizations that have *social* goals are classified, following our earlier argument, as a subtype of those oriented to culture goals. Social goals are served by organizations that satisfy the gregarious needs of their members—for example, social clubs, fraternities, sororities, and the like.

3. The order goal of (custodial) mental hospitals was pointed out by Demerath (1942, p. 67), who expressed his indebtedness to Merton on this point. Goals of concentration camps are analyzed by E. A. Cohen (1953, pp. 7-18).

3a. *Culture* is used here as defined by Parsons (1951, pp. 15ff.). It includes the belief systems and the value orientations of society.

Compliance and Organizational Goals

What is the relationship between organizational goals and compliance? We would expect that organizations serving order goals will tend to have a coercive compliance structure; organizations serving economic goals will tend to have a utilitarian compliance structure; and organizations serving culture goals will tend to have a normative compliance structure.

A Typology of Goals and Compliance

	Order	Economic	Culture
Coercive	1	2	3
Utilitarian	4	5	6
Normative	7	8	9

That is, of the nine possible combinations of goals and compliance shown in the accompanying table, we would expect most organizations to reveal one of three combinations (Nos. 1, 5, 9); there are, however, cases in the other six categories. For example, some deviants are segregated and controlled (but not "cured") by the use of normative compliance in rehabilitation centers ("open" prisons). This would be a case in cell No. 7. In the same cell are homes for the aged which house those senile persons who earlier were committed (and to some degree still are) to closed mental hospitals (Colb, 1956; Drake, 1960, pp. 309-11). Their goal is order since they control actors who otherwise cannot or will not conform to social norms and folkways (Tec and Granick, 1960; Granick and Nahemow, 1960). These persons are controlled by normative means and a minimum of coercion because of their general physical and mental state and, in particular, because of their emotional dependence on the home (Granick, unpublished; Herz and Zelditch, 1952). Camps for conscientious objectors established during World War II in the United States also segregated deviants by predominantly normative means (Dahlke, 1945). Some production is conducted in most coercive organizations, especially in camps of forced labor (No. 2), and in some religious orders (No. 8). Some learning is carried out in strictly utilitarian organizations, such as typing schools and some institutes for the study of foreign languages, where instructors have little if any normative power over students and the student's orienta·· tion is calculative (No. 6).

Thus there are some cases in cells other than the three cardinal ones (Nos. 1, 5, 9), but these appear to be few and limited in significance. The large majority of organizations reveal one of the three central combinations. Prisons and custodial mental hospitals fall in the first cell; blue- and white-collar industries fall in the fifth cell; religious organizations, universities and colleges, general hospitals, voluntary associations, schools, therapeutic mental hospitals, and professional organizations fall in the ninth cell.

Many organizations serve more than one goal. Sometimes these goals fall in the same general category, as in the case of universities which conduct both teaching and research, two culture goals. Sometimes the same organization serves goals of two different categories, as do forced-labor camps, which are both order- and economic-oriented. Usually, however, there is one predominant goal. The main point for us is that in organizations that serve dual or multiple goals, we would expect to find a parallel "combination" in the compliance structure. For example, the more production-oriented a prison or a forced-labor camp becomes, the more utilitarian (hence, closer to the coercive-utilitarian dual type) we would expect its compliance structure to be.[4] Thus the association between compliance and goals is maintained.

Political Goals and Compliance

Political goals at first glance seem impossible to place in our typology. It is often suggested that political goals, in particular those of parties, are to attain and maintain power. This is not an order, economic, or culture goal, but in a sense comprehends all three. Nevertheless, if we are to pursue our original objectives we must ask: Granted that all political organizations are power-oriented, how do they differ?

Descriptions of political organizations as oriented to power alone result in part from not observing carefully the distinction between elite goals and organizational goals. The leadership of political organizations may, as Michels suggests, have one predominant interest, to gain and retain power (1959, p. 205). Power is a universal key to all three ends; it may be pursued in order to control or change the allocation of coercion, to affect the allotment of material resources, or to change a normative pattern, as well as to serve various com-

4. On regulations aimed at keeping the level of coercion low in Soviet Hungary's forced-labor camps see Fischer, Kalnoky, and LeNard (1952, p. 9).

binations of these goals. However, realization of the power goal requires that it be related to organizational goals which are more acceptable to the rank and file and more legitimate in the eyes of the public (Selznick, 1952, pp. 2-4). Political organizations can be fruitfully classified according to the direction taken by this transformation of power goals into organizational goals.

Some political organizations, such as business unions, "tariff" parties, and the "Greenback" party, and much political activity on the municipal level, are predominantly concerned with allocation or reallocation of material resources and services. These organizations can be seen as oriented to economic goals.

Other political organizations are predominantly concerned with gaining control of command positions over legitimate means of coercion, such as the armed forces and the police. This seems to be the central goals of revolutionary organizations, whatever their ideological orientation, especially shortly before and during the revolutionary episode itself (Brinton, 1938, pp. 405-6), and of groups such as the Latin-American juntas (Christensen, 1951). These organizations can be seen as pursuing an order goal.

Finally, some social movements and radical parties focus on the dissemination of a new ideology. These are often revolutionary parties which are relatively unsuccessful in recruiting members and gaining power, which operate in societies where the existing political structure is well established. Typical examples are Communist parties in Sweden, Norway, and Israel in the fifties (Lipset, 1960, pp. 124 ff.), "long-run" small parties which realize that gaining control of the state or influencing significantly the national allocation of resources is beyond them, and hence devote their limited means to indoctrination of their rank and file, hoping that a change in the situation will open the power structure to them. These political organizations, at this stage, can be perceived as pursuing a culture goal: that of creating and reinforcing commitments to specific ideologies.

In short, the organizational goals of political organizations may be economic, order, or culture goals—or, quite frequently, some combination of these. Thus political goals do not fall in one cell of our classification; instead, we find some type of political goals in all of them. The main point is that *differences in political goals,* as we have defined them, *are associated with differences in the compliance structures* of the organizations serving them.

Political organizations whose goal is the allocation of material resources tend to emphasize, as the means of maintaining the commitment of their members and supporters, continuous allocation of products and services, referred to as "sharing the spoils," "pork-barreling," patronage, and the like. Some such practices are found in most political organizations, but this type tends to use allocation as its central control mechanism (Steffens, 1957; Cook and Cleason, 1959).

Political organizations whose goal is control over the legitimate means of violence are more likely than other political organizations to apply coercion in the control of their members. Revolutionary parties in the revolutionary stage are a well-known illustration (Brinton, 1938, pp. 105 ff.), as are the groups that initiate various coups in Latin America and the Caribbean.

Finally, political organizations with a culture goal, such as indoctrination, tend to emphasize normative compliance and to minimize both the use of coercion and remunerative allocation for internal control purposes (Duverger, 1954, pp. 154 ff.; Lenin, 1952). The major American parties are often contrasted with their European counterparts as being less ideological in their goals and more oriented to the allocation of resources. Similar differences, we would expect, would be found if the involvement of members were compared. For example, one would on the average expect commitment to parties in Western Europe to be higher than in the United States, as reflected, for example, in the proportion of members changing their party affiliation. Thus, if the goals of political organizations are specified, the general proposition concerning relationships between the nature of the goal and the nature of the compliance structure seems to hold.

ORGANIZATIONAL EFFECTIVENESS

The preceding discussion raises the problem of accounting for the fact that certain types of goals and certain types of compliance structures tend to be associated. Are they functional requirements for each other? Could we go so far as to say that one *cannot* rehabilitate in a traditional prison, produce in a religious order, segregate deviants by normative means? The answer seems to be, in one sentence: It is feasible but not effective. The three congruent types of goals and compliance are more effective than the other six combinations, although all nine types are "possible."

Survival versus Effectiveness Models

It is often suggested in sociological literature that a specific relationship is "functional." Thus one might say that it is functional to employ coercive compliance if one is pursuing order goals, or to employ utilitarian compliance in pursuing economic goals, or to employ normative compliance in serving culture goals. But there are two types of functional models that can be used in making such statements, and it is vital to know which one is being used. One is a *survival* (or feasibility) model; the other, an *effectiveness* model. Briefly, the two models differ as follows: A *survival* model specifies a set of requirements which, if fulfilled, allow a system to "exist." All conditions specified are necessary prerequisites for the functioning of the system; remove one of them, and the system will disintegrate. The *effectiveness* model defines a pattern of interrelations among the elements of the system which make it most effective in the service of a given goal (cf. Barnard, 1938, pp. 43, 55).[5]

The difference between the two models is considerable. Sets of functional alternatives which are equally satisfactory from the viewpoint of the first model have a different value from the viewpoint of the second. The survival model gives a yes or no answer to the question: Is a specific relationship functional? The effectiveness model tells us that although several functional alternatives satisfy a requirement (or a "need") some are more effective in doing so than others. There are first, second, third, and *n*th choices. Only rarely are two patterns full alternatives in this sense; only rarely do they have the same effectiveness value.[6]

The majority of functionalists work with survival models.[7] This has left them open to the criticism that although societies or other

5. The same point holds for social units which are not goal-oriented. Here we have to distinguish between a model which determines the survival of the unit and a model which determines the "survival" of a particular structure and level of processes. A model of organizational effectiveness encompasses both. It is for social systems what Lazarsfeld's and Rosenberg's accounting scheme (1955, pp. 387-491) is for the study of action.

6. Merton's concepts of functional alternatives and functional equivalents effectively express this distinction (1957a, p. 52). See also Nagel (1957, pp. 276-8).

7. One of the few areas in which sociologists have worked with both models is the study of stratification. Some ask whether stratification is a necessary condition for the existence of society. This is obviously a question posed by a survival model of societies. Others ask which form of stratification will make for the best allocation of talents among the various social positions, will maximize training and minimize social strains. These are typical questions of an effectiveness model. Both

social units have changed considerably, the functionalists still see them as the same unit. Very rarely does a society, for example, lose its ability to fulfill the "basic" (i.e., survival) functional prerequisites (Myrdal, 1944, pp. 1051-56). This is one of the reasons why it has been claimed that the functional model does not alert the researcher to the dynamics of existing social units.

March and Simon have pointed out explicitly, in their valuable analysis of organizational theories, that the Barnard-Simon analysis of organizations is based on a survival model:

The Barnard-Simon theory of organizational equilibrium is essentially a theory of motivation—a statement of the conditions under which an organization can induce its members to continue participation, and hence assure organizational *survival*. . . . Hence, an organization is "solvent"— and will continue in *existence*—only so long as the contributions are sufficient to provide inducements in large enough measure to draw forth these contributions. (1958, p. 84, italics supplied)[8]

If, on the other hand, one accepts the definition that organizations are social units oriented to the realization of specific goals, it follows that the application of an effectiveness model is especially appropriate for the study of this type of social unit.[9] It is utilized throughout this volume.[10]

Compliance, Goals, and Effectiveness

Let us assume that a wide range of empirical studies has supported our hypothesis about the association between compliance and goals,

---

models have been applied in enlightening debate over the functions of stratification. See Davis (1942), Davis and Moore (1945), Tumin (1953), Davis (1953), W. E. Moore (1953). See also Barber (1957, pp. 1-18), Buckley (1958), and Simpson (1958). The study of stratification in *kibbutzim* has contributed some empirical evidence to the question. See Rosenfeld (1951), Talmon-Garber (1952), and Schwartz (1955).

8. Caplow has developed an objective model to determine the survival potential of a social unit. He states: "Whatever may be said of the logical origins of these criteria it is a reasonable assertion that no organization can continue to *exist* unless it reaches a minimal level in the performance of its objective functions, reduces spontaneous conflict below the level which is disruptive, and provides sufficient satisfaction to individual members so that membership will be continued." (1953, p. 4)

9. For a discussion of effectiveness which treats it in a manner similar to ours, see Kahn, Mann, and Seashore (1956, p. 2). For a fine empirical study of the correlates of effectiveness, see Georgepoulos and Tannenbaum (1957). Lucci developed an index for measuring tthe effectiveness of a voluntary association (1960, pp. 9-10). See also Steward (1950, pp. 202-8).

10. The points made in the text have been elaborated, and some of the normative as well as methodological problems involved in applying the effectiveness model have been discussed, in Etzioni (1960b).

and has demonstrated that in fact organizations that serve order goals do tend to have a coercive compliance structure; that those serving economic goals tend to have a utilitarian compliance structure; and that those serving culture goals tend to have a normative compliance structure. We have then to explain this association. The first step has been taken above, when we suggested that these three associations are more effective than the other possible six. In other words, effectiveness is our central explanatory intervening variable. In the following paragraphs we attempt to show in some detail why each of the three congruent relationships is more effective than the other two combinations that might be associated with the same goal. In other words, additional intervening variables are introduced. Since these variables account for one relationship at a time, they are naturally on a less abstract and general level than the central intervening variable, that of effectiveness.

ECONOMIC GOALS AND EFFECTIVE COMPLIANCE—There are several reasons why organizations that have economic goals function more effectively when they employ remuneration than when they employ coercion or normative power as their predominant means of control. Production is a rational activity, which requires systematic division of labor, power, and communication, as well as a high level of coordination. It therefore requires also a highly systematic and precise control of performance. This can be attained only when sanctions and rewards can be readily measured and allocated in close relation to performance. Remunerative sanctions and rewards are the only ones that can be so applied, because money differentials are far more precisely measurable than force, prestige, or any other power differentials.

Much production requires some initiative, interest, "care," responsibility, and similar attributes of the lower participants. Engineers and personnel people frequently describe the great damage caused when workers carry out orders to the letter but ignore the spirit of the directive, in order to "get even" with a supervisor. Effective performance requires some degree of voluntary cooperation, which is almost unattainable under coercion. Only the limited types of work that can be effectively controlled through close supervision (e.g., carrying stones to build a pyramid, rowing in the galleys) can be controlled by coercion without great loss of effectiveness. We would therefore expect production in coercive organizations to be of this kind, or to be ineffective. The following statement by work supervisors in a prison may therefore reflect not the inmates' "inherent" inability to work, but their alienation from work under coercion:

The total result of the prevalence of these attitudes has been to reduce "imprisonment at hard labor" to a euphemism existing chiefly in the rhetoric of sentencing judges and in the minds of the uninformed public. The inmate social system not only has succeeded in neutralizing the laboriousness of prison labor in fact, but also has more or less succeeded in convincing prison authorities of the futility of expecting any improvement in output . . . the prevalent attitudes of work supervisors toward convict labor: "Convicts are inherently unindustrious, unintelligent, unresourceful, and uninterested in honest work." (McCorkle and Korn, 1954, p. 92)

We would also expect either that forced-labor camps will be predominantly punitive, and productivity—that is, *effectiveness*—low; or, that chiefly manual work, of the type described above, will be carried out.

Forced labor in Soviet countries during the Stalin period seems to have been mainly of the highly punitive, relatively ineffective type (Parvilahti, 1960). Moreover, work in these camps consisted typically of building barracks, felling trees, excavation, or performing duties of an orderly in the camp (Rosada and Gwozdz, 1952, p. 26). These jobs, to the degree that their description allows us to judge, are of the routine, simple, easily supervised type, as specified above. The Japanese relocation camps in the United States during World War II were not highly coercive but at the same time did not develop a utilitarian system. Workers were paid 50 cents a day. The consequence was that some work was conducted, but the level of productivity was very low (Leighton, 1945, pp. 72, 86-87, 108, 242-43).

Weber pointed out the advantages of remunerative over coercive control of modern work when he showed that slaves cannot serve as the basis of a rational economy (of the bourgeois capitalist type) whereas free wage labor can. He lists eight reasons, most of them resting on differences in mobility between the two groups. But he also notes that "it has in general been impossible to use slave labour in the operation of tools and apparatus, the efficiency of which required a high level of responsibility and of involvement of the operator's self interest." (1947, p. 253) J. N. Blum (1948) compared the productivity of servile agricultural labor with that of wage labor during the first part of the nineteenth century in Austria-Hungary. He found that wage labor was from two to two and a half times as effective as servile labor (*ibid.,* pp. 192-202).

The use of normative power in organizations serving economic goals may lead to highly effective performance, but in general only for work of a particularly gratifying nature, such as research and artistic performance, or for limited periods of time, particularly in crises. Thus, for example, the work of transferring the defeated British army home from Dunkirk, under the pressure of the approaching German army, was conducted by a fleet of volunteers under normative command. Similar efforts on the industrial front take place in the early stages of war.

Normative compliance can be used to conduct "services" of a dramatic nature (in the sense that they have a direct relation to ultimate values), such as fighting fires, helping flood victims, searching for lost children, or collecting money for the March of Dimes and similar causes. But production engaged in by lower participants in typical blue-collar or white-collar industries lacks such qualities. Its relation to ultimate goals is indirect; it is slow to come to fruition; the worker is segregated from the fruits; and activities are highly routinized, spread over long periods of time, and evoke little public interest. Hence production as a rule cannot rely on the moral commitments of lower participants and the normative power of organizational representatives; for example, when a relatively "dramatic" service such as searching for lost children requires continued, routinized activity, the number of volunteers and the level of normative compliance tend to decline rapidly.[11] This is one of the reasons such activities are often delegated to permanent utilitarian organizations, such as the fire department and "professional" fund raisers. In summary, effective production of commodities and services is carried out almost exclusively by utilitarian organizations.

CULTURE GOALS AND EFFECTIVE COMPLIANCE—Organizations that serve culture goals have to rely on normative powers because the realization of their goals requires positive and intense commitments of lower participants to the organization—at least to its representatives, and such commitments cannot be effectively attained by other powers.

---

11. The shift from wartime to peacetime is therefore the period when military organizations have to shift from more normative to more remunerative controls. Large raises in salaries of N.C.O.'s and officers, as well as of enlisted men where there is no conscription, usually come some time after the war, especially when chance of "action" seems remote (*New York Times,* May 31, 1960). It is typical that the Womble Committee of the Department of Defense found in 1953, after the Korean War, that the pay of military personnel "had not kept pace with changes in civilian society." (Janowitz, 1960, p. 50)

Studies of charisma, persuasion and influence show that commitment (or identification) of followers to their leaders is the major lever by which the followers' commitments to values are created, transmitted, or extended (Parsons and Shils, 1952, p. 17 ff.). Communication studies demonstrate the low effectiveness of formal communication not supported by informal leaders, and the importance of positive affective interpersonal relations between the priest and the parishioner, the teacher and the student, the political leader and his followers, for effective operation of their respective organizations (Karsh, Seidman, Lilienthal, 1953; Härnqvist, 1956, pp. 88-113). In short, the attainment of culture goals such as the creation, application, or transmission of values requires the development of identification with the organizational representatives.

When participants are alienated from the organization they are less likely to identify with its representatives than if they are committed to it. However, even when commitment to the organization is high, identification with its representatives need not occur. But since normative power is the least alienating and the most committing kind of power, it is the most conducive to the development of identification with representatives and hence to effective service of cultural goals. We shall see below that in organizations that serve economic or order goals rather than culture goals, identification of followers with organizational representatives is indeed a far less common component of the elite-lower participant relationship (see Chapter VII).

Coercion makes identification with organizational representatives very unlikely. This is one of the major reasons rehabilitation work is unsuccessful in prisons and also a reason for the strong objections of progressive educational philosophy to the use of corporal punishment.[12]

12. It is often pointed out that traditional European schools were rather coercive but also quite effective. But the comparison implicit in this statement is misleading, since some important differentiating conditons are not controlled; for one, the European schools were highly selective. This fact may partially account not only for the compliance attained, but also for the high effectiveness. Second, these schools were effective, despite an extensive use of coercion, in part because their students came from families, social classes, and a general socio-cultural environment in which the "tolerance for coercion" was considerably higher than it is in modern democratic societies. Hence the alienation produced by coercion was less and the negative effect on discipline, smaller. For studies of Prussian schools which support these points see Arnold (1892), F. E. Keller (1873), and Kerschensteiner (1909). For background of students see *Statistik der Preussischen Volksschule*, published every five years since 1901. The same points hold for English public schools, whose compliance structure is well depicted in Hughes' *Tom Brown's School Days* and in Hilton's *Good-bye, Mr. Chips*. For a general discussion of continental schools from this viewpoint see Arnold (1868).

In order to build up patients' motivation to be cured, doctors have to attain their nonrational commitment—to achieve normative power over them—since patients do not have the knowledge required to accept the doctors' directions on rational grounds. A similar relationship exists between teacher and students, and other professionals and their clients.

Remuneration cannot serve as the major means of control in organizations serving culture goals because the commitments it tends to build are too mild and rational. Manipulation of pay, fines, and bonuses does not lead to internalization of values. At best it produces superficial, expedient, overt commitment.

In summary, organizations that serve culture goals must, for effective service of these goals, rely predominantly on normative compliance and not on other means of control.

ORDER GOALS AND EFFECTIVE COMPLIANCE—Effective service of order goals requires that coercive rather than remunerative or normative power be the predominant means of control of the organization serving this goal.

Remunerative powers as means of control can augment but not replace coercion as the central means of control in serving order goals. Fines, for instance, can be used to a limited degree to punish minor violations of the code in prisons. But in general the income of inmates is too small and violations are too frequent and, in the eyes of the prison, too severe, to be controlled by remuneration. Moreover, control of deviance, the order goal of these organizations, requires that a depriving situation be maintained. Coercive control is typically negative, inflicting deprivations but granting few gratifications. Other types of control tend to balance reward and punishment, if not to stress reward.

Normative compliance is ineffective in the service of order goals since it is, to all intents and purposes, impossible to maintain normative compliance in order-oriented organizations for the large majority of inmates. A small minority of inmates, usually rather atypical—such as middle-class executives committed to open prisons in Sweden for driving while intoxicated, or conscientious objectors—might be controlled by normative means. But most inmates do not allow their behavior to be significantly affected by prison representatives. The social and cultural background, reinforced by inmate social groups, and the prison situation, which is inevitably depriving because of its segregative nature, generate high alienation which does not allow the normative power of the prison to develop. The inmates "oppose, negate and even nullify the ideology and symbols used by the officials." (Weinberg, 1942, p. 720) In short, control by the use of normative power in the prison is in general neither effective nor feasible.

Coercion is common even in custodial mental hospitals, where confinement of deviants and not their punishment is the order goal. One reason for the prevalence of coercion seems to lie in the level of effectiveness demanded by society or by the community in which the organization is situated. These external collectivities tend to ask both of prisons and of custodial mental hospitals one hundred per cent effectiveness in controlling escapes and suicides. This requirement leads to the need to apply coercion, and to apply more coercion than would otherwise be necessary. Lindsay (1947, p. 92) has pointed out that mores, which in other circumstances can rest on what we have referred to here as moral commitments and normative powers, require the support of coercion (their transformation into laws) when they are expected to hold for *all* people *all* the time. Even when the large majority of people are willing to comply, there are some people all the time, and most people sometimes, who are not willing to comply. Hence even when in general normative compliance would do, the expectation of "one hundred per cent" performance increases the use of coercion, since the deviating minority can rarely be specified with complete assurance. Sykes makes this point in his study of a prison:

One escape from the maximum security prison is sufficient to arouse public opinion to a fever pitch and an organization which stands or falls on a single case moves with understandable caution. The officials, in short, know on which side their bread is buttered. Their continued employment is tied up with the successful performance of custody. . . . In the light of the public uproar which follows close on the heels of an escape from prison, it is not surprising that the prison officials have chosen the course of treating all inmates as if they were equally serious threats to the task of custody. (1958, pp. 18 and 20)

Grusky showed that basically the same situation exists in a minimum-security prison (1959, p. 458). The same point is true for custodial mental hospitals as well, and is one of the reasons why "opening" them has proceeded so slowly.

This association between order goals and coercive compliance illustrates a general point: The specification of an effectiveness model —for example, effective compliance-goal pairs—is influenced by socio-cultural environmental factors. This is true because the social groups that set organizational goals tend also to set limits on the means that the organization can legitimately use to attain these goals, including the means that can be used for control purposes. For example, to the degree that the public becomes more tolerant of inmates' escapes, in particular those of mental patients who are a nuisance but do not endanger the public safety (e.g., some types of exhibitionists), less coercion can be applied without loss of effectiveness.[13] Thus for each socio-cultural state, the concrete combination of compliance and goals which creates the highest degree of effectiveness differs; but the basic relationship between the type of goal and the type of compliance—as specified in our hypothesis—does not differ. In some cultures, for example, the most effective attainment of order goals requires much coercion; in others, less; but in all cultures in which complex organizations operate, we would expect effective attainment of order goals to require more use of coercion than economic or culture goals; economic goals to be most effectively served by utilitarian structures; and culture goals by normative ones.

Dual compliance structures are found in organizations that serve goals differing in their compliance requirements either because they fall in different categories or because effective attainment of one goal requires development of supplementary tasks belonging to different goal categories. A business union, for example, has to maintain calculative involvement of the members in "normal" periods and to build up their moral involvement in pre-strike and strike days. A full examination of the relationship between compound goals and compliance structures is deferred to Chapter XVI, since in order to handle the issue additional variables, to be examined in the following chapters, have to be drawn into the analysis.

13. In Britain almost all mental hospitals are state hospitals. They draw their inmates from adjacent areas with only very limited possibilities of transfer from one hospital to another (like the public schools in most American cities). Hence one can more readily observe the effect of community tolerance. It is therefore of interest to note that the three most "open" mental hospitals in Britain seem to be located in or close to upper-middle-class communities, which properly are more tolerant of mental patients than the neighborhoods in which the other mental hospitals are located (private communication with John Wing, M.D., and Elizabeth Monck). For a study of community attitude to mental patients in the United States see Cumming and Cumming (1957). See also Aberle (1950).

A Dynamic Perspective

There are three major effective combinations of goals and compliance: order goals and coercive compliance, economic goals and utilitarian compliance, and culture goals and normative compliance. The other six combinations are less effective than these three, although organizations having such combinations may "survive" and even to some degree realize their goals. In the six ineffective types we would expect to find not only wasted means, psychological and social tension, lack of coordination, and other signs of ineffectiveness, but also *a strain toward an effective type.* We would expect to find some indication of pressure on goals, compliance, or both, to bring about an effective combination. Thus, for example, some contemporary mental hospitals have incongruent goal-compliance structures. They are expected to maintain "order" (i.e., inmates should not be able to escape or commit suicide), but to do so by predominantly normative means (cell No. 7, p. 106). This incongruity creates pressure to regain or extend the social license to use coercion (movement toward No. 1), or to educate the public so that these hospitals will be allowed to measure their success not by lack of escapes but by rehabilitation rates—that is, to "adjust" the goals to their compliance structure (movement toward No. 9).[14]

The tendency toward an effective compliance-goal combination may be blocked by environmental factors affecting any one of the three major variables making up the relationship: involvement, power, and goals. Involvement, as we have seen, is determined in part by such external factors as membership in other systems, previous value commitments of the participants, and basic personality structure. The kinds of power an organization can employ depend, among other things, on the resources it can command and the social license it can attain. Organizational goals are determined in part by the values of the social environment, and changes in the goals which the organization can initiate or introduce are limited by constraints set by this environment. Agents of such constraints include boards of directors or trustees (in cases where these represent external financial interests or various community elites and are not used as "fronts" by the organization); control organizations (e.g., regulatory com-

---

14. For a keen analysis of the structural factors involved in such a change from a custodial to a more therapeutic mental hospital see Cumming, Clancey, and Cumming (1956).

missions, grand juries, and congressional committees); in addition to less institutionalized forms of social control, such as the voting public, the press, and various voluntary associations supporting one value or another (such as the Anti-Defamation League of B'nai B'rith, or the N.A.A.C.P.).[15] These constraints explain the lack of congruence between goals and compliance, despite the loss of effectiveness generated by such states, and despite the strain toward effectiveness which characterizes organizations. Our dynamic hypothesis should be considered valid if, when these constraints are removed or reduced, the organizational compliance-goal structure changes in the direction of one of the effective types.

SUMMARY

This chapter was the first to examine the relationship between compliance and other organizational variables. The association studied was that of compliance and goals. By goals we mean future states of affairs to which the organization is oriented. There are three major types of goals: *order, economic,* and *culture.* Political goals, we saw, may fall in all three categories. Organizations that have order goals tend to have a coercive compliance structure; those that have economic goals tend to have a utilitarian compliance structure; and those that serve culture goals tend to have a normative compliance structure. Other combinations of compliance and goals are feasible and sometimes found, but they are less effective.

The functional model used throughout this book is one that determines which functional alternatives are more effective in attaining specified goals, rather than one that specifies which items of behavior or cultural patterns allow the system to continue to operate. We examined briefly the reasons leading us to believe that coercion is a functional requirement of effective service of order goals, utilitarian compliance of economic goals, and normative compliance of culture goals. The chapter concluded with a dynamic statement similar to that relating power and involvement. It was suggested that when environmental constraints allow, organizations move from incongruent goal-compliance combinations to congruent (effective) ones.

15. The problems of external (or environmental) controls over organizations have been analyzed from this viewpoint in some detail in Etzioni (1958).

VI   GOALS AND
EFFECTIVENESS REVISITED

Organizations can be characterized as artificial beings. Unlike tribes, communities, or societies, they are not naturally occurring but deliberately constituted and often deliberately restructured. They are created, at least in part, to advance specific goals, i.e., to bring about a desired change in the state of affairs. Depending on the kind of change sought—more order, increased production, or higher cultural achievement—there is a corresponding type of compliance structure that will be most effective in attaining the goal in a congruent manner (pp. 103ff.). A large variety of factors, however, ranging from poor understanding of administrative processes to the pull of vested interests, may cause the formation or development of organizational structures and processes incongruent with their goals. Compliance theory specifies which combinations of compliance structures and goals are expected to be congruent and which are not, as well as the consequences of incongruence for effectiveness. A fair number of new studies have cast direct light on this set of hypotheses.[1] First, however, we review two which have confirmed the empirical status of the concepts used.

1. See Scott (1964), pp. 505-506; Elling (1963), p. 104 and note 21; Warriner (1965), pp. 139-140; cf. Silverman (1971), p. 10ff; and Gross (1968), p. 519.

THE CORE CONCEPT

Goals: Stated Versus Actual

Organizations have been defined as social units specializing in the service of goals. But which goals? Many organizations deliberately or unwittingly come to pursue goals other than their official, *stated* goals. (On stated goal, see pp. 103-104 and Etzioni, 1964, p. 7.) We have discussed already, for example, the case of a prison assumed to be committed to rehabilitation (i.e., an educational goal), but which was actually in the law-and-order custodial business. As stated goals command few resources and little psychic energy, they cannot serve as the starting point for most directions of organizational analysis, including compliance studies. In fact, they are expected to be poor explanatory variables of anything but issues which arise directly from their very inauthentic existence (Etzioni, 1968, Ch. 21; Price, 1968, pp. 3-4).

But can we find empirical indicators for the distinction between stated and real goals, arrived at conceptually? Or in reality, do actual goals and stated goals "mesh" into each other? Are there significant differences in the amount of resources and degree of psychic energy mobilized by various goals?

Jack L. Franklin, Lee D. Kittredge, and Jean H. Thrasher (1973) studied the relationship between stated and actual goals of seven units of a mental health complex. Stated goals were easy to find: They were posted in the units involved. Sample: our purpose is to "provide the best possible environment conducive to good care, treatment, and rehabilitation to maximize the human potentials of patients and employees alike" (*ibid.,* p. 7). Each unit displayed several such goal statements.

Next the aides and the professional staff were asked how much importance was actually given and how much should be given to these statements. In addition, the directors of the units were asked what the unit's actual goals were.

The data that resulted are shown in Table VI-1. All reflect the capacity to make the distinction. The measurement differentiated among seven units. By and large, units the aides perceive as pursuing goals more distant from the stated ones are also viewed as experiencing a higher goal-discrepancy by the staff (e.g., both are relatively more

Table VI-1—Ratings of Stated Goals on Appropriateness and on Congruence with Practice, by Aides and by Professional Staff of Mental Health Complex

Unit	N	AIDES 1	2	3	4	5	N	PROFESSIONAL STAFF 1	2	3	4	5
A	22	50	50	68	50	50	7	29	29	57	29	14
B	20	45	35	45	40	50	7	14	71	57	43	29
C	13	31	15	69	23	31	9	11	67	44	44	22
D	4	100	75	50	75	75	5	40	60	80	40	60
E	12	75	67	75	75	58	6	100	67	67	50	50
F	17	29	53	53	29	41	9	11	22	33	11	22
G	16	63	38	69	50	63	12	33	50	67	42	42

Ranking by Aides of Goal Congruence of Seven Units:

Highest	E	+5	(all goals meet expectations)
	D	+4	
	G	+2	
	A	+1	
	F	−1	
	C	−3	
Lowest	B	−4	(four goals do not meet expectations)

Ranking by Professional Staff of Goal Congruence of Seven Units:

Highest	E	+3	(three goals meet expectations)
	D	+1	
	B	−1	
	G	−2	
	C	−3	
	A	−3	
	F	−5	(five goals do not meet expectations)

Source: Franklin, Kittredge, and Thrasher (1973), pp. 10–11 (table slightly edited). Reprinted with permission.

critical of units *C* and *F* than of *E*). Also, the rank ordering of the units as to the relative neglect of stated goals, by aides and by staff, were rather similar (Table VI-1), although the staff was more aware of a lack of congruence (and was in this sense more critical) than the aides. Using the 50% congruence point, staff gave a total of 11 positive (above 50%) evaluations, while the aides gave 16. Negative scores by the staff were 21; by aides, 12.

The authors proceed to show that these differences are related to patients' satisfaction, but—as one would expect from the limited importance of stated goals—many other variables intercede. The main significance of the data for our purpose is to indicate that the difference between stated and actual goals is a valid operational concept and to reiterate that for the purposes of compliance analysis, actual goals, not stated ones, must be studied.

The Typology of Goals Revisited

In his study on "Planned Organizational Change" (1969), Garth N. Jones analyzed data on 190 cases of developmental strategies— their carriers ("change agents"), recipients ("client systems"), goals, and means. A more comprehensive discussion is provided in Chapter XVII. In the present context, we are merely concerned with the way Jones determined what the goals of his 190 strategies were, how he classified them, and what relationships he found among them.

Based on his knowledge of the cases under study and following his judgment, Jones first decided according to the compliance typology whether a strategy pursued order goals, economic goals, or cultural goals. Being aware of the possibility that multiple goals may be involved, Jones allowed for a strategy to have all three types of goals at once. As 190 cases were studied, this procedure allowed for a maximum of 570 goals, but only 391 actual goals were established. Each goal found was then rated as to its relative salience for the "change agent" and for the "client system." The results of this rating are displayed in Table VI-2.

Table VI-2—Salience of Order Goals, Economic Goals, and Sociocultural Goals for Change Agents and Client Systems

Change Agent	Order Goal	Economic Goal	Sociocultural Goal	Total
Not present	126	39	33	198
Marginally present	39	23	22	84
Present	11	27	34	72
Quite important	7	39	53	99
Paramount importance	7	62	47	116
Insufficient information	—	—	1	1
Total	190	190	190	570
Client System				
Not present	126	30	29	185
Marginally present	40	33	20	93
Present	10	33	59	102
Quite important	8	50	45	103
Paramount importance	3	41	37	81
Insufficient information	3	3	—	6
Total	190	190	190	570

Source: Jones (1969), p. 143. Reprinted with the permission of Praeger Publishers, copyright, 1969.

Of the 391 goals Jones studied, 18% were found to be order goals, 40% economic, and 42% cultural. As to their relative degree of salience, the data in Table VI-2 suggests not only that order goals were the least frequent category in the sample but also that where order goals appeared, they tended to be of marginal salience. On the other hand, the degree of salience of the economic and cultural goals seemed to be quite similar. In other words, the majority of the organizations studied fell in the category of having weak order goals and strong economic or cultural goals.

Unfortunately, the data do not allow us to establish how the various types of goals, when present in the same organization, related to each other. For instance, we would be interested in the extent to which there is a clear difference in salience between simultaneously pursued goals. According to the theory, we would expect that equal significance of two goals would require either adaptive structures (p. 119) or cause losses in effectiveness (pp. 109, 120). The only hint Jones provides as to the "clustering" of goals concerns an interesting difference between order goals on the one hand and economic and cultural ones on the other: "Cases which placed high on the scale of significance order goals usually included one or both of the other types of goals. This was not the case for either economic or sociocultural goals. Where these goals are of primary significance, order goals are usually not present or are of low significance" (*ibid.*, p. 142).

On a more basic level, Jones' study shows that not just the concept of actual goals but the compliance typology itself can be utilized in empirical research.

INCONGRUENT STRUCTURES: TESTS OF THE LINKS AMONG GOALS, COMPLIANCE, AND EFFECTIVENESS

The theory suggested that when goals and compliance are incongruent, effectiveness will be lower than when they are congruent. The first study to be reviewed deals directly with this thesis. The results of trying to rehabilitate inmates (an educational-cultural goal) in a coercive organization are reviewed. The next two studies provide a sense of the effectiveness of less-congruent versus more-congruent conditions in the same organization, although the basic research designs are "static" in the sense that they explore a relationship at only one point in time. One study focuses on the pattern in an organization that forms "layers" through which many lower participants pass sequentially (the educational system). A comparison of these layers, whose compliance mix differs, provides a dynamic dimension, although no actual flow-throughs are studied. The second study, which deals with a normative organization, gives a "before-and-after" picture, describing a shift of the relations between goals and compliance, although only the "after" condition was directly studied; the analysis of the antecedent state is based on recollection and interpretation.

Rehabilitation in a Coercive Organization: An Incongruent Structure

Charles W. Thomas and Michael Miller (n.d.) provide no data to prove that the prison they studied is committed to rehabilitational goals, but they assume that objective from the prison's definition of its mission. They proceed to show that its compliance structure is unsuited to such an objective. Of course, if one were to assume the prison to be in the "ordering-keeping" (or custodial) business, that is, seeking to confine people rather than to change them, its compliance structure would be evaluated quite differently.

Miller and Thomas collected their data from a systematic random sample of 401 inmates, all in a maximum security prison for male felons, with sentences considerably longer than the national average. The prison is situated in a southeastern state; data were collected in 1970. A high questionnaire-completion rate of 84% was achieved. Miller and Thomas first scored inmates as to how alienated they were from the prison, using a scale measuring sense of powerlessness. In line with their expectations, the more alienated an inmate was from the prison, the more likely he was to adopt the anti-prison inmate code (gamma coefficient = .47. For additional background on the measurement, see Thomas and Zingraff (1974), Thomas and Poole (1974), and Davis (1967). The scale used to measure adherence to this code included statements indicative of such "unrehabilitated" values as stress on physical toughness and pride in exploitative sex relations.

Adoption of this code, in turn, correlated highly with criminal identification ($\gamma = .50$), measured by the inmates' willingness to associate with criminals in the outside society as well as identify positively with the criminal label rather than seek to avoid it. Code adoption also correlated highly ($\gamma = .54$) with opposition to the prison as a formal organization and with opposition to the legal system ($\gamma = .70$). This attitudinal cluster of opposition to the organization and agreement with a pro-criminal and pro-inmate code suggests that, as expected (p. 108), a coercive organization which alienates cannot effectively resocialize and rehabilitate its inmates.

Bigelow and Driscoll's (1973) findings closely parallel that of Miller and Thomas. As we have seen, the more strongly coerced inmates revealed a less cooperative orientation to the prison (Chapter IV, p. 76). Also, these inmates were less accepting of the prison's work values promoted as part of the prison's rehabilitation program, although the difference was statistically very weak. The "work value" mean score of coerced subjects was 5.35, that of the less coerced was 5.74 ($t = 1.17; p \leqq .150$) (1973, p. 13).

Education: From Moral to Technical, from Normative to Utilitarian, a Congruent Relation

Schools were classified according to the congruence hypothesis as requiring normative compliance by their lower participants—their students—if effective education was to take place (pp. 45-6, 48). The compliance structure of the teachers, as middle participants, was not specified; nevertheless, one would expect, because of their status as "paid professionals," that normative and utilitarian elements would combine, with the composition of the mix varying according to the nature of the schools. For example, large bureaucratic schools would tend to be more utilitarian than "quality" private schools.

Benjamin J. Hodgkins and Robert E. Herriott (1970) studied a national sample of 3,039 teachers. The authors hypothesized that the organizational objectives of schools evolve from primarily moral goals for primary grades (building character, transmitting values) to relatively more production-oriented goals at higher levels (intermediate, junior high, senior high)—a development which reaches a peak in college (as the stress on transmitting instrumental skill and knowledge rises). They also assumed that although utilitarian compliance on the part of the teacher would predominate at all age-grade levels, the emphasis on utilitarian compliance would increase with increasing age-grade levels, and that normative compliance, characterized by moral commitment of the teachers, would be greatest at the lower age-grade levels. As the authors put it:

Organizational emphasis upon transmitting an orientation, as opposed to a specific skill, presupposes a greater degree of moral involvement on the part of the teacher than would otherwise be the case. Similarly role expectations of teachers are much more diffuse in the elementary than in the secondary school, requiring a greater sensitivity on the part of the teacher to organizational norms, as well as a higher degree of moral commitment. (*ibid.,* pp. 96-97)

Differences in teacher compliance, aside from being related to differences in school goals, were also expected to correlate with differences in student compliance. Pupils were also expected to be more committed in lower grades and less committed in higher grades. It was theorized that as the student body develops an appropriate orientation and internalizes the school's norms, the teachers can devote less time to the inculcation of values and more to the teaching of skills.

The data supported the core hypotheses of Hodgkins and Herriott: The age-grade structure was shown to be related to goal emphasis, which in turn was related in the predicted manner to the teachers' compliance structure.

Teachers' compliance structure was measured by the degree to which teachers had an opportunity to influence the school's policy-making. Hodgkins and Herriott asked how frequently principals submitted teachers' suggestions regarding changes in school policy to a vote of the faculty. "A high frequency of such organizational behavior would be indicative of a normative compliance structure, for by drawing teachers into the organizational decision process their identification with organizational authority would be increased" (*ibid.,* p. 99).

The data in Table VI-3 show (a) a high level of consultation in all schools (61% to 75% of the teachers report being consulted "frequently" or more often) and (b) a higher frequency of consultation in the lower age-grades, a lower rate in the higher age-grades.

Hodgkins and Herriott used 13 other items to test the same hypotheses. Four indicators concern staff participation in decision-making, and nine concern the extent of supervision. Closer supervision of teachers by principals was said by the authors to indicate a more normative structure, both because "the more diffuse role expectation associated with the transmission of an orientation . . . necessitate greater concern in schools at these levels with supervision" and because close supervisory control allows the school to "enforce normative standards of teacher conduct" (*ibid.,* p. 100). The finding:

Table VI-3—Cumulative Percentage of Teachers' Reports of the
Frequency with Which Their Principal Submits
Teachers' Suggestions Regarding Changes in
School Policy to a Vote of the Faculty,
by Age-Grade Level **(N = 3039)**

FREQUENCY WITH WHICH PRINCIPAL PUTS TEACHER SUGGESTIONS TO A FACULTY VOTE	AGE-GRADE LEVEL			
	Primary (K–3)	Intermediate (4–6)	Junior High (7–9)	Senior High (10–12)
Always	25%	19%	15%	13%
Almost always	60	51	46	39
Frequently	75	73	67	61
Occasionally	88	85	83	77
Almost never	95	94	93	91
Never	100	100	100	100
Mean normative compliance score*	4.43	4.22	4.04	3.81
Number of teachers reporting	626	506	1058	849

* Computed using weights of: Always = 6, Almost always = 5 . . . Never = 1. Exact probability of the four mean scores being ordered as predicted is .041.
Source: Hodgkins and Herriott (1970), p. 99. Reprinted with the permission of the American Sociological Association.

"For all 13 items, the difference between the mean scores at the primary and senior high levels is as predicted; for all but two items the means fall monotonically as the grade-age level of the school rises" (*ibid.,* p. 100).

The authors took pains to check their findings for possible "spurious" associations. For instance, it might be suggested that the size of the school or the principal's sex might explain the variance in teacher's compliance patterns, rather than differences among the age-grades and student compliance. In the higher grades teachers are more likely to be male and classes to be smaller. The class and school size might also affect the intimacy of teacher-principal relationships and teachers' identification with the school. Finally, female principals, in the days the data were collected (1960-1961), might perhaps have been less "authoritative and hence less utilitarian" than male ones. Female principals were more common in lower grade schools. Hodgkins and Herriott found that the relationships already reported still stood when these variables were controlled (*ibid.,* pp. 102-103).

Hodgkins and Herriott showed that the particular compliance mix of a school (its degrees of the utilitarian and the normative) is associated with the school's age-grade level and thus with the school's goals.

A Dynamic Situation: Goals and Compliance Grow Incongruent

In the work of Hodgkins and Herriott (1970) and in that of Randell (1968), the dynamic relationships are analytic, not observed. By comparing the orientations of different age-grades we gain an understanding of what it means for a child to move up the age-grade structure, or for teachers to be transferred to higher grades, or for seniors in high school to be drafted. But no actual cohort is traced. A study by George Brager (1969) provides an insight into an actual dynamic situation, although the data is, in part, retrospective. We see the goals of a normative organization at one stage; the main staff is highly committed to them; the "functional" staff (accounting and public relations) and the governing board, less so. Under environmental pressures the board forces a change of goals toward the much more utilitarian definition discussed hereafter. The main body of the staff, for the transformative period studied, remains committed to the old "cultural" goals. As the incongruent situation (incompatibility between present utilitarian goals and normative compliance) develops, the result, Brager reports, is as expected: a significant decline in staff commitment.

Brager studied the Mobilization For Youth (MFY), a comprehensive delinquency-prevention and antipoverty project in New York's Lower East Side, in the early and middle sixties. It was a nonprofit corporation, akin to "a philanthropic service agency" (*ibid.*, p. 483). Drawing more than $12 million dollars in foundation and federal funds, the project was aimed at combatting delinquency and poverty in New York's Lower East Side. Its goal is characterized as cultural rather than utilitarian because it sought to change people's orientation, attitudes, and above all, political beliefs rather than to directly change their income or wealth.

In 1964, the MFY came under powerful attack from the press, Congressmen, and city, state, and federal investigators, ostensibly for using its facilities, funds, and manpower to foment rent strikes and racial disorders and for "harboring Reds." The organization's board, faced with a dilemma between standing up for its values and members at the price of risking its survival or compromising its goals (e.g., ceasing many of its mobilizing activities) and firing its radical members, chose basically the second course. Brager, by collecting data on members' orientation both to MFY's original goals and to its "crisis strategy," i.e., the new focus on survival, allows one to gain a dynamic insight, even though, in strict temporal terms, no "before-and-after" data were collected.

Brager gathered his data by questionnaires completed by 76% of the board and 74% of the staff (see Brager, 1967, for more details). To measure orientation to the "pre-crisis" "cultural" goals, Brager relied on two main documents: the original founding papers and a major progress report. These were prepared by the staff and thoroughly "processed" by it just before the crisis. Out of these he culled 20 items, arranged in a Likert scale. A panel of judges which checked the discriminative validity of the scale found it to be significant at the .01 level. A 15-item measure was used to study staff and board reactions to the crisis. It was reliable, as measured by the split-half method with correction, at .948.

Brager found that although numerical scores on strength of commitment to the original goals could range from 20 to 100, the members (staff and board) were sharply skewed in the positive direction, as one would expect in a normative organization: 53.1% (121) scored 80 or higher; 25.9% (59) had scores falling between 70 to 79. Only 4.8% (11) scored between 50 and 59, and none less than 50. (In addition, the staff scored very high on job satisfaction. Only 2% reported their job very or mildly unsatisfying).

The situation was quite different with regard to the new goal, stressing survival at the price of principle: 35% (73) disapproved; 33% (68) took a middle position, and 32% (66) an approving one. Although the approving group is in a minority, it is sizable, and its strength and the size of the middle group seem to weaken the notion that the new goal was "incongruent." Brager shows, however, that many in the approving camp were not "the" staff of the organization, nor the "Program Core staff," but people in supportive functions, such as accounting and public relations, and board members who, he further shows, were actually outsiders (for data, see p. 488).

Moreover, those approving of the new goal were much less approving of the old one! Thus, only 13.1% (8) of those highly committed to the old goals approved of the new ones, versus 57.4% (35) of those less committed to the old goals. And, conversely, of those disapproving of the new goal, 54.1% (33) were highly committed to the old goals, and only 4.9% (3) less committed (p. 488).

In short, most of those who were organizational members according to our sociological definition (as distinct from a legalistic or formal one), especially the core staff, had been strongly committed to the former "cultural" goals and possessed a congruent normative compliance orientation, as expected. When this pattern was broken by the crisis, most of these persons remained normatively involved with the organization, and hence, as expected, were alienated by the new utilitarian goal. For those whose profile was the reverse, the proposition held as well: They were more committed to the organization once the new utilitarian goal suited to their utilitarian compliance orientations was introduced.

Thus, Brager, carefully weaving together quantitative with qualitative data, provides a fine illustration of the dynamic relations between goals and compliance and the "need" for congruence (Table VI-4).

Table VI-4—Reaction to Crisis Strategy by Commitment to Values (N = 207*; Board of Directors and All Program Staff)

COMMITMENT TO VALUES INDEX	REACTION TO CRISIS STRATEGY				
	Approval	Mid-Position	Disapproval	Total	%
Low	57.4%	37.7%	4.9%	—	—
	(35)	(23)	(3)	61	29.5
Medium	27.1%	29.4%	43.5%	—	—
	(23)	(25)	(37)	85	41.1
High	13.1%	32.8%	54.1%	—	—
	(8)	(20)	(33)	61	29.5
Total	66	68	73	207	100.0

* Excludes managerial staff and 9 "no response."
Source: Brager (1969), p. 488. Reprinted with the permission of the American Sociological Association.

EFFECTIVENESS, GOAL MODELS, AND SYSTEM MODELS

A Return to the Basic Assumptions

Compliance theory hypothesized that if an organization's actual goals are incongruent with its compliance structure, either the means of control will be changed to become compatible or the organization's goals will not be realized, i.e., the organization will be ineffective (pp. 103-10). Effectiveness is defined as the extent to which a goal is realized, to be distinguished from efficiency, the cost per unit of "output" (or realization). Hence, effectiveness may be low, but efficiency high, and vice versa.

Basically, effectiveness is what organization is all about: An organization is an artificial social unit whose inner logic and manifest purpose call for greater effectiveness than found in natural units. In some cases, an effort to attain high effectiveness may undermine an organization and prevent it from being effective in the longer run. For instance, a high level of success may be attained temporarily by violating the laws of congruence between the compliance structure and the organizational goals. Thus, reliance on coercion to get "more out of" a labor force heretofore decently paid may increase output for a while but soon lead to lower production, especially in terms of quality (which is less supervisable than quantity).

It seems wiser, then, to define organizational effectiveness not merely as a level of goal realization but as a pattern of relationships among the elements of an organizational system which enhances its service of one or more goals (p. 110). ("In the longer run" is implied, because an exclusive, or supreme, focus on activities directly relevant to the goal will show a strain on other activities even in the short run, although it will often tax effectiveness, as measured by the traditional standards, only in the longer run.) The suggested definition of effectiveness allows taking into account system needs which ensure effectiveness beyond the short—often the very short—run. Because of the importance of this point, both for organizational analysis in general and our present review of the new compliance studies in particular, we elaborate in the following pages on the differences among goal models, system models, and mobilized system models. (For a previous discussion, see Etzioni, 1960, pp. 257-278.) It should be stressed from the outset that, although goal models are without a concept of system, system models *of organizations* include the concept of goals as an integral part.)

GOAL MODEL—The literature on organizations is rich in studies in which the criterion for assessing the effectiveness of the organizational efforts is derived from the organization's goals. This goal-model approach is considered an objective analytic tool because it omits the values of the explorer and applies the values of the subject under study as the criteria of judgment.

Actually, such a model has several limitations. One of the major shortcomings of the goal model is that it frequently makes the study's findings dependent on the model's assumptions. These studies tend to show (a) that the organization which is being investigated does not realize its goals effectively and (b) that the organization has other goals than those it claims to pursue. Both points have been made for political parties (Michels, 1959; Ostrogorski, 1902), trade unions (Michels, 1959; Foster, 1927; Kopald; 1924), voluntary associations (Seeley *et al.*, 1957), schools (Hunter, 1954), mental hospitals (Belknap, 1956), and other organizations. It is not suggested that the characterization of these organizations as ineffective is not valid but rather that this finding is of little value as it can be deduced from the way the object of study is approached.

Goals, as sets of meanings depicting target states, are cultural entities. Organizations, as systems of coordinated activities of more than one actor, are social systems. There is a general tendency for cultural systems to be more consistent than social systems (Parsons, 1951). This has mainly two reasons. First of all, cultural images, to be realized, require investment of means. Because more means are always needed than are available, social units are always less perfect than their cultural anticipations. A comparison of actual Utopian settlements with descriptions of their ideals of such settlements by the leaders of Utopian movements is a clear illustration of this point (Zablocki, 1972; Houriet, 1971).

The second reason for the invariable discrepancy between goals and social units, of special relevance to our discussion, is that all social units, including organizations, are multifunctional. Therefore, while devoting part of their means directly to goal attainment activities, social units have to devote other parts to other functions, such as the creation or recruitment of further means to the goals and the maintenance of those units which serve the goals more directly.

Looking at the same problem from a methodological viewpoint, one sees the mistake as one of comparing objects not on the same level of analysis, namely, when the present state of an organization (a real state) is compared to a goal (an ideal state) as if the goal were also a real state. Measured against the Olympian height of the goal, most organizations score the same: very low effectiveness. Seen in this light, the differences in effectiveness among organizations are of little significance. One who expects a bulb to turn most of its electrical power into light would not be very interested in the differences between a bulb that utilizes 4.5% of its power as compared with one that utilizes 5.5%. Measured against the ideal state of 100% conversion, both are extremely ineffective. A more realistic observer would compare two existing bulbs with each other and find one of them quite superior. The same holds for organizational studies that compare actual states of organization one with another, in terms of achievements, as distinct from comparing an organization to its goal. If organizations, as a rule, do not realize their goals, why spend years proving that this or that organization failed its goals?

SYSTEM MODELS—An alternative model that can be employed for organizational analysis is a particular version of the system model. The starting point for this approach is not the goal itself but a working model of a social unit capable of achieving a goal. Unlike a goal, or a set of goal activities, it is a model of a multifunctional unit. It is assumed *a priori* that some means have to be devoted to such non-goal functions as service and custodial activities, including means employed for the maintenance of the unit itself. From the viewpoint of the system model, such activities are functional and contribute to organizational effectiveness. It follows that a social unit that devotes all it efforts to fulfilling one functional requirement, *even if it is that of performing goal activities,* will undermine the fulfillment of this very functional requirement because the needs of other subsystems will be neglected.[2]

Effectiveness establishes the degree to which an organization realizes its goals under a given set of conditions. But the central question in the study of effectiveness is not "How devoted is the organization to its goal?", but rather "Under the given conditions, how close

2. Gouldner distinguishes between a rational model and a natural-system model of organizational analysis. The rational model (Weber's bureaucracy) is a partial model, as it does not cover all the basic functional requirements of the organization as a social system—a major shortcoming, which was pointed out by Robert K. Merton (1957), pp. 195-206. It differs from the goal model by the type of functions that are included as against those that are neglected. The rational model is concerned almost solely with means activities, while the goal model focuses attention on goal activities. The natural system model has some similarities to our system model, as it studies the organization as a whole and sees in goal realization just one organizational function. It differs from ours in two ways. First, the natural system is an observable, hence "natural," entity, while ours is a functional model, hence a construct. Second, the natural system model makes several assumptions that ours avoids, for example, viewing organizational structure as "spontaneously and homeostatically maintained" (Gouldner, 1959, pp. 404ff.).

does the organizational allocation of resources[3] approach an optimum distribution from the viewpoint of the actual goals the organization seeks to serve?" Thus, goals do re-enter here, but as critical criteria of systems, rather than as isolated, and out of context, sets of activities.

All system models, by definition, deal with relationships among subsystems. But organizational systems differ from others in that they give primacy to goal attainment rather than integration, tension management, or some other subsystem. Organizations, by definition, treat all subsystems other than goal attainment as instrumental to goal attainment. Their model might hence best be referred to as a mobilized system model (for additional discussion see Etzioni, 1968, especially Ch. 15).

It might be thought that we have here reached a tautology: Actual organizational goals are derived from the organizational patterns of mobilization of resources and so is effectiveness. But this is not the case. The actual goal is derived, or extrapolated, from the organizational patterns; effectiveness results from a comparison of the aim to the actual achievements or existing patterns. Thus, if an organizational analysis shows that a political party is indeed gearing itself to gain a larger following among a minority it had previously poorly penetrated—e.g., by increasing the number of the minority's representatives on its boards or delegations, by preparing educational material aimed at this social group, and by changing its platform to appeal to this group—but only little penetration is achieved, we shall not doubt the goal but shall score the campaign as ineffective.

The concept of a mobilized system has another virtue: It calls attention to subtle differences among various systems, which the system model tends to neglect, as the following discussion suggests.

SURVIVAL AND EFFECTIVENESS MODELS—A system model constitutes a statement about relationships which, if actually existing, would allow a given unit to maintain itself and to operate. There are two major types of system models. One depicts a *survival model,* i.e., a set of requirements which, if fulfilled, allows the system to exist. In such a model each relationship specified is a prerequisite for the functioning of the system, i.e., a necessary condition; remove any one of them and the system ceases to operate. The second is an

---

3. "Resources" is used here in the widest sense of the term, including, for example, time and administration as well as the more ordinary resources.

effectiveness model. It defines a pattern of interrelations among the elements of the system which would make it most effective in the service of a given goal.

The difference between the two models is considerable. Sets of functional alternatives which are equally satisfactory from the viewpoint of the survival model have a different value from the viewpoint of the effectiveness model. The survival model gives a "yes" or "no" score when answering the question: Is a specific relationship functional? The effectiveness model tells us that, of several functional alternatives, some are more functional than others in terms of effectiveness. There are first, second, third and *n* choices. Only rarely are two patterns full-fledged alternatives in this sense, i.e., only rarely do they have the same effectiveness value. Merton discussed this point briefly, using the concepts functional alternatives and functional equivalents (Merton, 1957, p. 52).

The majority of functionalists have worked with survival models,[4] which has left them open to the criticism that, although a society or a social unit might change considerably, they would still see it as the same system. Only very rarely, for instance, does a society lose its ability to fulfill the basic functional requirements. This is one of the reasons that it has been claimed that the functional model does not sensitize the researcher to the dynamics of social units.[5]

4. One of the few areas in which sociologists have worked with both models is the study of stratification. Some are concerned with the question: Is stratification a necessary condition for the existence of society? This is obviously a question of the survival model of societies. Others have asked: Which form of stratification will make for the best allocation of talents among the various social positions and will maximize training and minimize social strains? These are typical questions of the effectiveness model. Both models have been applied in enlightening debate over the function of stratification. (Davis, 1954, p. 309-321; Davis and Moore, 1945, p. 242-249; Tumin, 1953, 387-394; Davis, 1953, p. 394-397; Schwartz, 1955, p. 424-430).

5. March and Simon (1958) pointed out explicitly in their outstanding analysis of organizational theories that the Barnard-Simon analysis of organization was based on a survival model: "The Barnard-Simon theory of organizational equilibrium is essentially a theory of motivation—a statement of the conditions under which an organization can induce its members to continue participation, and hence assure organizational *survival*. . . . Hence, an organization is "solvent"—and will continue in *existence*—only so long as the contributions are sufficient to provide inducements in large enough measure to draw forth these conditions" (*ibid,* p. 84) (all italics supplied). For a discussion of "organization strain toward survival" Caplow (1953) developed an objective model to determine the survival potential of a social unit. He states: "Whatever may be said of the logical origins of these criteria, it is a reasonable assertion that no organization can continue to exist unless it reaches a minimal level in the performance of its objective functions, reduces spontaneous conflict below the level which is distributive, and provides sufficient satisfaction to individual members so that membership will be continued" (*ibid.,* p. 4).

If, on the other hand, one accepts the definition that organizations are social units oriented toward the realization of specific goals, the application of the effectiveness model is especially warranted for this type of study.

There is a close relationship between survival models and "sheer" system models; they are too undiscriminating to capture levels of mobilization. Also, there is a close kinship between effectiveness models and mobilization models. The main difference is that the concept mobilization calls attention over and above the sheer system model to the dominance of the goal-attainment subsystem, while the survival-effectiveness model focuses on the extent to which any and all subsystems are serviced. In the study of organizations, we are concerned chiefly with mobilized effectiveness systems. We differ here from James. Q. Wilson (1973, p. 10ff.), who raised the possibility that the organizations pursue goals other than the wants of the members. Some organizations may be that anarchic; most, we suggest, find ways to force or convince their members to advance one or more goals of interest to the organizational collectivity in their efforts to serve themselves.

The Critical Perspective

The various models also make for rather different normative positions on the part of researchers and observers. First, as has been mentioned, the goal model passes for "neutral," as it seems not to take a position; its position is to accept that of those who run, manage, or own the organizations. Pure system models study the organizational community, its level of integration or conflict and internal contradiction, without assuming any purpose or guideability. It is a collectivist, uncybernetic model. (For additional discussion, see Etzioni, 1968, Ch. 4). Mobilized system models call for the observer to judge where the organization, as a system, is headed and how effectively it is progressing toward the realization of its goals.

Second, when the goals-in-themselves (without a related system model) are used as a measure of criticism, the criticism tends to be Utopian and unrealistic and, hence, tends to encourage either simple conclusions in favor of rapid, comprehensive transformation or total despair. The more gradual but cumulative change which builds on broad-based efforts, which draws on a wide variety of groups, whose prime roots may lie in divergent subsystems, is often overlooked. (For additional advantages of this concept, its relationship to functional theory, and its difference from a mere survival model, see pp. 110ff.; Etzioni, 1964, Ch. 2; and Etzioni, 1969).

This idea has triggered a certain amount of dialogue. After all, "perhaps the most popular model of organizational evaluation has been the goal-attainment model" (Baker, 1973, p. 21). Silverman (1971, p. 29ff.) questions our approach as it entails attributing human characteristics to social constructs, regarding organization. In the system approach the organization is said to have needs and to act, which, Silverman says, only persons can have or do. But, on further examination, he too concludes that an act may be explained as a result of a pattern of social relationships and that, hence, the use of the construct is appropriate. Stein warned that the system approach, which he views as "goal-less," is not sufficient, that both stated and actual goals should be considered (1962, p. 22ff.). This is of course in line with our view of the organization as a mobilized system, mobilized to serve its actual goals.

Ephraim Yuchtman and Stanley E. Seashore (1967) come down on the side of the system model. They review the various criticisms of what they call the traditional goal approach and contrast it with two approaches, the functional model and the system one. The functional approach "reports what the goals of an organization are, or should be, as dictated by the logical consistency of [the] theory about the relationships among parts of *larger* social systems" (1967, p. 895, italics provided). Reference is made largely to Parsons (1956).

Effectiveness here is viewed not as a contribution to the organizational goals but rather to the superordinate system. This view is justified because legitimacy of the organization is dependent on the organization's contributions to the society. This position, Yuchtman and Seashore point out, ignores the organizational autonomy, *its* needs and ability to serve the goals of its members. Indeed, this approach does constitute a semi-organistic model, which allows for no conceptualization of conflict or forces of change in terms other than deviance.

The authors next endorse the system model because it:

(1) takes the organization itself as the focal frame of reference, rather than some external entity or some particular set of people; (2) explicitly treats the relations between the organization and its environment as a

central ingredient in the definition of effectiveness; (3) provides a theoretically general framework capable of encompassing different kinds of complex organizations; (4) provides some latitude for uniqueness, variability, and change, with respect to the specific operations for assessing effectiveness applicable to any one organization, while at the same time maintaining the unity of the underlying framework for comparative evaluation; (5) provides some guide to the identification of performance and action variables relevant to organizational effectiveness and to the choice of variables for empirical use. (*ibid.,* p. 897)

Similarly, Basil S. Georgopoulos (1973) defines his "research model" as a system and effectiveness one, which he contrasts with goal and survival models (pp. 102-103). Richard H. Hall (1972, pp. 25, 80, 89-91, and 96ff.) also favors a system approach.[6]

Petro Georgiou (1973) provides probably the most encompassing attack on the goal model to be found in the literature. He sees it as having "retarded analysis by requiring disassociation of conceptual scheme from incompatible empirical findings on organizations" (*ibid.,* p. 291). Chester Barnard's system model is offered as the "counter" model. For reasons at least this author was unable to comprehend, Etzioni's work, as summarized in the preceding pages, is characterized as a goal model (*ibid.,* pp. 295-296). The same fate has befallen Price (1968), who is said to have followed Etzioni (*ibid.*).

Frank Baker and Herbert C. Schulberg (in Baker, 1973) also reject the goal model in favor of the system model. They apply it to the conceptualization of a mental hospital. They state first:

The open systems model is concerned with establishing a working design of a mental hospital which is capable of achieving a variety of goals, such as patient care, research, and training. Unlike the goal-attainment model of evaluation, which limits its assessment to the measurement of specified outcome criteria, the open systems model goes further by seeking to determine the degree to which an organization realizes its goals under a given set of conditions. What counts from this perspective is a balanced distribution of resources among all organizational objectives rather than the maximal attainment of any single goal. Thus a mental hospital would not be considered maximally effective if reorganization were possible that would improve a major part of the organization without damaging any other part. (*ibid.,* pp. 481-482)

They next advance the model by analyzing the system relations of a mental hospital in terms of input, "throughout" structures and

6. See also Price (1968), p. 124; Cressey (1965), p. 1063; Larkin (1974); Osborn and Hunt (1974); Deutscher (1974); Nelson and Johnsen (1974); and Joyner and Joyner (1974), p. 67.

processes, output, and feedback, listing the variables and operational procedures for each. The detailed steps neither can nor need be repeated here. Their work indicates that the system model has gained in following over recent years, as compared to the goal model. The same point will be further illustrated after we digress briefly to ask how, once we accept the desirability of thinking about organizational effectiveness as a system attribute, that system is most effectively conceptualized.

How to Conceptualize the Organizational System

The question of how to conceptualize the organizational system can be answered in more than one way; in my recent work I lean toward more "grounded" or concrete conceptualizations than previously, without questioning the virtue of an abstract overlay. (For the reasons for this position, see Etzioni, 1968, pp. 123-125). Earlier work drawing on the Bales-Parsonian four-phases model—i.e., on highly analytic concepts—provided the overlay. Bales and Parsons view the organizational system as a subcategory of social systems, which in turn are so composed as to provide an "answer" to the functional needs of the system. Every social system is viewed as confronted with four basic functional problems. When simple social systems become more complex, four distinct subsystems emerge, each predominantly devoted to one of the major functions (Parsons, Bales, and Shils, 1953).

The four universal functional problems are (a) the system's need to control the environment; (b) the gratification of the system's goals; (c) the maintenance of solidarity among the system units; and (d) the reinforcement of the integrity of the value system and its institutionalization. The first pair is often referred to jointly as "instrumental," the second as expressive. Singly they are referred to, respectively, as "adaptation," "goal attainment," "integration" or "solidarity," and "latency" or "tension management."

The empirical power of these distinctions has been reported in studies of non-organizations (such as small groups, families, and processes of socialization) as well as organizations. One study found that the elites in communal settlements arranged themselves according to these conceptual divisions (Etzioni, 1963). The Iowa State studies applied them to the study of compliance.

THE SYSTEM MODEL OPERATIONALIZED AND TESTED

The Iowa State Compliance Studies

The label "Iowa State Compliance Studies" is used here to refer to a group of 15 different reports and publications dealing with compliance variables whose authors are or were at Ames, Iowa.[7] The senior members of the group are Charles L. Mulford, Gerald E. Klonglan, and Richard D. Warren. Other project co-directors have included George M. Beal and Joe M. Bohlen. Other members and students include Janet B. Padgitt, Otto F. Sampson, Paul F. Schmitz, Robert Schafer, Dan. L. Tweed, Frederick T. Evers, and Mervin J. Yetley. Their findings are reported here as they relate to the concept of effectiveness. Other findings are reported in subsequent chapters. Taken together these studies constitute the single most systematic effort of a group of scholars and researchers to test and advance the compliance theory.

The steps which we are about to follow are somewhat intricate and hence deserve a brief preview: (a) discussion of the way the four phases were operationalized; (b) the relationship of these concepts to that of effectiveness; (c) the nature of this relationship in two different compliance structures, the utilitarian and the normative; (d) the treatment of environmental factors (which could cloud the internal organizational picture); and (e) the relationship of organizational effectiveness to the individual member's role performance.

The Iowa State Compliance studies use two main sources of data for their analysis.[8] One is a Civil Defense Preparedness Agency

7. The Iowa State Compliance Studies have been the result of a unique research team arrangement continued over a 15-year period. In the late 1950's Drs. George M. Beal and Joe M. Bohlen began assembling a research team to study the interface of individual and organizational phenomena. In 1960 Gerald Klonglan and Richard Warren became team members. And in 1965 Charles Mulford joined the other four as co-principal investigator of several studies. In the early 1960's the research team initiated two major areas of study from which the "Iowa State Compliance Studies" have emerged. These were investigations of: (a) the Civil Defense Preparedness Agency (a normative organization) and (b) farmer cooperatives (a utilitarian organization). Major civil defense organizational field studies were carried out in 1962, 1965, and 1971-72. Major farm cooperative field studies were carried out in 1966 and 1971. Several graduate students have played key roles in the completion of these studies over the years.

8. A more detailed description of the data base used by the Iowa State Compliance studies can be found in Ch. XV, p. 393.

charged with contingency planning for disasters. The agency as a whole is characterized as a normative organization. Local directors are appointed by elected officials and are usually volunteers or, at most, paid part-time workers. They work with local government departments as well as local voluntary associations and constitute the lower participants of this study. There are about 7,000 such directors throughout the U.S. The study is based on a random sample of 90 local jurisdictions in each of three states, in 1965. Both interviews with 240 directors and data from their files were utilized. Also, data were obtained from a national representative sample of coordinators from the same agency in 1971-1972. However, most of the findings cited in this text are from the earlier study.

Adaptation was defined as the ability to secure resources needed by the organization from the outside. It was measured by whether or not the "program paper," a document the local office needed to obtain federal funds, was completed; by the increase in office space and personnel over a year's span; and by whether or not the unit attained a separate budget from that of other local civil services.

Integration was defined as the number of linkages developed with other local government services, local groups, and voluntary associations. (Integration is the relevant measure here rather than cohesion among staff both because there is no "staff," each unit usually having only one member, and because performance of the organizational mission requires these linkages.)

Latency (or tension management) was defined as the degree to which local directors were satisfied with various aspects of their positions on the assumption that the more gratifying the role, the more managed the system's tension.

Goal attainment was defined as the extent to which the official goals are accomplished. Data is presented to show that official goals in this case were rather close to actual goals. Those local units which ranked high on official performance goals also ranked high in subjective performance evaluations. The correlation reported is .474, significant at the .01 level (Mulford, Klonglan, Warren, Padgitt, 1973, p. 10).

Although all conceptualizations and measurements are subject to additional refinements (one may suggest, for instance, that actual and not official goals be used as foci of the analysis when data are available), the Iowa State approach is one of the most successful attempts to operationalize the phase model. One has only to recall how often researchers have asked whether the model can be operationalized at all to realize how much progress the authors have achieved. Also, the Iowa State authors, in line with our system model, define high *effectiveness* as a high reading on all four subsystems, rather than merely as goal attainment. An organization is more effective if several or all of its system needs are fulfilled than if its output is merely maximized. This idea finds here an operational basis. Moreover, the authors show that units which score higher on the three subsystems other than goal attainment are also higher on goal attainment.

Sampson (1973) applies, after some modification, the same basic approach to a utilitarian organization, a group of farm cooperatives, which constitutes the second main site of the Iowa State Compliance studies. The goal of these organizations is to purchase supplies for their members and sell their members goods under advantageous conditions. Sampson's source of data is a 1966 study of Iowa farmer cooperatives, drawing on interviews with 82 managers from a sample of more than 200 farm-supply and grain cooperatives. Also, economic data and documents are studied.

Goal attainment here is defined in terms of the ability of the managers to service the particular economic needs of the co-op members. Six measurements are devised, including average ratio of savings to fixed assets; average ratio of saving to sales, average net saving, and the managers' orientation to profit.

Adaptation is studied in terms of the efforts undertaken to deal with the environment, as measured by steps managers have (or have not) taken to protect the farmers against price changes in products and supplies; relevance of factors relied upon in choosing supplies and outlets, evaluation of managers' market decisions, and the like.

Integration is viewed as the extent to which managers take into account in making their decisions the various departments and functions that are part of the organization, other than their own; the methods used in determining the qualities, numbers, and work loads of employees; rate of employee turnover; and others.

Latency is defined as steps taken to insure commitment and continued participation.

Again, although details deserve deliberation (e.g., one wonders why a measure of managers' satisfaction is included in goal attainment), the study demonstrates the general applicability and operationalization of the basic approaches to a utilitarian organization.

Because Sampson uses several indicators measuring the extent to which each subsystem is served, the resulting tables showing the effectiveness profiles of various units are complex and cannot be reproduced here (see Sampson, 1973, pp. 141-151). The main finding is a positive relationship between some of his subsystem service indicators and the level of goal attainment. The relationship was much stronger with adaptation than with either integration or latency, but all relations were far from strong ones. (For details see Sampson's Table 5.7, pp. 163-164). The weakness of the associations might be due in part to the attempt to apply a detailed statistical analysis, including cross-tabulations of scores of indicators, to a relatively small number of cases, namely, 82 (*ibid.,* p. 120). The main achievement, hence, is the operationalization of the model to a utilitarian organization and not in the strength of the statistical links established.

Sampson's next step, as that of Mulford, Klonglan, and Warren (1973) in a previous publication, is to tie the four phase indicators to compliance variables, to which we return later.

Another way of looking at the four subsystems, or phases, of organizations is to see them as aspects of the organizational efforts. Adaptation, integration, latency, and goal attainment proper are functional requirements that social systems have to meet in order to continue to exist: In order to be met, these functional requirements have to be somehow represented among the objectives the system strives for through its daily actions and decisions.[9] Organizational decision-makers must not focus their attention exclusively on goal attainment; they have to be able to recognize, and to be motivated to pursue, the system's other three needs. But how do adaptation, integration, and latency enter into organizational decision-making? Are decision-makers aware of the various needs of their organization, are they able to distinguish among them, and do they feel pressure to satisfy these needs? These questions are addressed by two of the Iowa State Compliance papers—Warren, Rogers, and Evers (1973), and Evers, Warren and Rogers (1973)—and they are answered in the affirmative.

The articles, drawing on Evers' M.S. thesis, use the responses of

9. In connection with this point and with the study we are going to discuss in the next paragraph, cf. our remarks on the necessity to specify in functional explanations the concrete mechanisms that provide for linking a social system's actual behavior to the functional requirements. This specification is necessary unless one is prepared to assume that the actors under study themselves interpret their "world" in terms of functionalist theory and are willing to abide by its "prescriptions." See **pp. 313-314.**

153 managers of farm cooperatives who ranked the relative importance for a viable cooperative of organizational flexibility (ability to
adjust to changing demands of customers), satisfaction of employees
with jobs and working conditions, efficiency (obtaining a maximum
return), and productivity (obtaining a high volume of business).
Flexibility, satisfaction, efficiency, and productivity were used as
indicators, respectively, of adaptation, tension management, integration, and goal attainment. In a second step, the managers were asked
to indicate to what extent they felt "pressure to achieve one or the
other of these goals."

Using a variety of sophisticated testing procedures, the authors
found significant differences among the four goals. Each goal's mean
relative importance score deviated significantly, at the .01 level, from
the grand mean of all importance scores. In addition, comparing
pairs of goals with each other, the study established that all pairs
except two were significantly different in mean importance. These
results support the authors' hypothesis that managers are able to make
meaningful distinctions among the four aspects of organizational goal
systems.

A similar picture emerged from the analysis of perceived pressure
to achieve the goals. Managers were found to differ significantly as
to the total amount of pressure experienced. The mean pressure score
for each goal was different from the overall mean, and pair comparison showed only one pair to be not significantly different. Turning to
the rank order among the four subsystems, in both cases—in terms
of importance as well as of pressure—two different ordering procedures produced consistent results within each category. The rank
orders established by the study are shown in Table VI-5.

**Table VI-5—Rank Ordering of the Four Subsystems by
Importance and by Pressure**

RANK ORDER

By Importance	By Pressure
Efficiency	Efficiency
Satisfaction	Satisfaction
Flexibility	Productivity
Productivity	Flexibility

Adapted from Evers, Warren, Rogers (1973).

Finally, the authors studied the interrelationships between importance (attributed to each subsystem) and felt pressure and variations within each of these categories. Although the managers' ranking of one goal was not related to their rating of others, there was a significant correlation among pressure scores. As the authors put it, this indicates that "as pressure to achieve one goal increased the pressure to achieve the other goals also increased" (Warren, Rogers, Evers, 1973, p. 15). Except for efficiency, where pressure and importance correlated at .25 (significant at .01), no relationships were found between the relative importance and the relative pressure of a particular goal for the individual manager. As the authors conclude, "apparently the managers were distinguishing between importance and pressure" (ibid.).

Thus these two articles, which cover basically the same ground, support the validity of looking at the goal systems of complex organizations in terms of the AGIL scheme. They also lend plausibility to the suggestion that the four functional prerequisites have a "subjective" dimension, in that they can be experienced by organizational leaders in terms of their relative importance and of the pressure emanating from them.

Individual and Organizational Effectiveness

Sampson's study, as well as earlier Iowa State Compliance studies, in particular Klonglan, Beal, Bohlen, and Mulford's voluminous 1966 report, made great inroads in operationalizing and studying individual "role performance," that is, individual effectiveness, a measure used later in several Iowa State Compliance studies, and correlated the measure with compliance variables (see Chapter XV). The main approach was, in the case of the civil defense organization, to define seven tasks which the "program paper" and central leadership of the organization expected the local directors to carry out. Detailed sophisticated scales were developed to ascertain the extent to which the local directors fulfilled these tasks, relying both on subjective (e.g., asking the directors) and objective data (for example, checking the local documents, how many shelters were prepared, size of budgets, number of volunteers enlisted).

Now it goes without saying that we are ultimately interested in organizational rather than individual effectiveness. It is the organization's success which the "appropriate" congruent compliance structure is expected to help promote, not necessarily individual achievements. One would expect individual and organizational effectiveness to correlate, but certainly not in a one-to-one association. Organizational effectiveness may be higher or lower than an aggregation of all individual efforts.

Each individual may carry out his mission to perfection, but if the organizational coordination patterns and division of labor are not optimal, the collective effectiveness could well be less than the sum total of the effectiveness of individual participants. On the other hand, if resources are available to the collectivity that are not the result of current performance, e.g. large amounts of savings or capital, the organizational achievements may well exceed those of its present participants.

The Iowa State Compliance Studies of the Civil Defense System did not need to face this problem immediately, because they used as their focal point a sub-unit composed of one, the local civil defense director. Here, individual and organizational, at least sub-organizational, effectiveness are coextensive (see Klonglan *et al.*, 1966, p. 45ff; Klonglan, Mulford and Tweed, 1974, p. 6; and Mulford *et al.*, 1972b, p. 11).

However, the Iowa State compliance group, which left undone few steps that could be done, did check the correlation between organizational effectiveness and individual effectiveness (Yetley, 1973). Yetley distinguished between the two by measuring the manager's personality (his suitability to his role, pp. 105-106) separately from the success of his co-op. He found that the relationship between the two variables is not only not tautological, but not even necessarily high. Of four different relationships explored, role performance was significantly related only to economic effectiveness, and that only at 0.18 (F = 3.607) (*ibid.*, p. 144).

Controlling for the Environment

Organizations should never be treated as sociological islands. Even total societies encased in nation-states can be so treated only at the analyst's peril. Certainly organizations, which are much more integrated into their respective social, cultural, political, and economic "environments" than national societies, cannot be fully understood without taking into account their external linkages. These provide the main cause of incongruent compliance patterns: goals are set, in part, under outside pressures (as we saw in the case of the Mobilization For Youth board reported by Brager) and may then not fit the existing compliance structure (as exemplified by attempts to achieve rehabilitation in coercive prisons), or participants are recruited whose predispositions do not fit the organizational goals (e.g., persons with little tolerance for routine become highly alienated assembly-line workers).

Similarly, the organizational environment deeply affects how successful an organization can be in realizing its goals. One may have hardworking members, be well organized, and have the compliance structure its goals demand, and yet achieve little because of depression, war, cuts in federal funds, and so on. Another organization may be quite poorly managed, riddled with a contradictory compliance-goal structure, and still be successful because of market rises, a change in fashion, federal favor, and the like. Hence, for both analytic and practical purposes, it is necessary to try to identify which parts of the achievements of an organization are due to external conditions and which parts to internal factors, the compliance pattern. It should come as no surprise, by now, that the Iowa state group attended to this matter.

Warren, Mulford, and Yetley (1973, p. 19) developed two concepts of effectiveness, the one ("economic effectiveness") being more environmentally determined, the second ("sociological effectiveness") more internally, organizationally determined. This distinction was worked out in the context of the farm co-ops, that is, of a utilitarian organization, and has yet to be applied to the other two types of organizations.

The "economic effectiveness" concept is based on net operating revenue. This variable is measured by taking gross commodity sales, subtracting commodity costs, and adding revenue from services provided (*ibid.,* p. 15). As net operating revenues are determined not only by the actions of the organization's members but also by "the competitive economic situation and the purchasing decisions of customers" (*ibid.,* p. 19), we may view this measure of effectiveness as primarily or at least substantially environmentally determined.

The sociological measure was based on the firm's adaptiveness, i.e., its ability to use a given environment or its changes well, by

(a) capturing resources and (b) manipulating internal and external factors to facilitate goal-attainment activity (*ibid.,* p. 14). These were measured by inquiring about

(a) decision-making steps or processes used, (b) evaluation procedures used, (c) criteria used to organize the business into departments and functions, (d) criteria for the selection of wholesale sources, and (e) procedures used to protect the business against market price changes. The managers' recorded verbal responses to each of these questions were randomly presented to judges for scoring on the basis of performance leading to successful management of retail businesses. For each question, the raw scores of the judges were transformed to normal deviates, and an average score was obtained. The sum of these average scores is the adaptation score. This score has a reliability of .69. (*ibid.,* p. 14)

As expected, the compliance variables accounted for more of the variance of sociological effectiveness than of economic effectiveness among farm co-ops as organizational units. The detailed links are explored in our later discussion. Total variance accounted for was 26% for the economic measure, versus 48% for the sociological one (Warren, Mulford, Yetley, 1973, p. 17ff.). For a similar finding of a weak correlation between task performance and compliance see Franklin (n.d.), Table 6.

No such distinction is employed with regard to the civil defense organization studies, though one could imagine that a similar distinction could be developed for normative organizations. For instance, for a political party, one could compare how successful it is in mobilizing its members (a relatively more internally determined factor) with its success in increasing its proportion of the vote, which is relatively less determined by the party's efforts and more by many environmental factors.

A VARIABLE ADDED: GOAL SPECIFICITY AND COMPLIANCE

Hall, Haas, and Johnson (1967) asked whether the extent to which goals are specified is associated with the kind of compliance structure the organization exhibits. Using the organization's official goal statements, the authors asked a panel of "expert judges" to rank the goals in terms of the ease of determining or measuring goal achievement. This is, of course, of great interest because without an ability to measure the organizational goal, be it "national interest," national security, or salvation, effectiveness will be very difficult to assess not just for the researcher but also for the actor. Under this circumstance one would expect that organizational efforts would tend to be even more likely to become an end in themselves than when there are measurable goals.

How do the three compliance types differ in the specificity of their goals? (See Table VI-6.) Utilitarian organizations are found to have

Table VI-6—Ease of Determining Goal Achievement for the Three Compliance Types

	Compliance Type		
GOAL SPECIFICITY	COERCIVE	UTILITARIAN	NORMATIVE
	(N = 11)	(N = 35)	(N = 29)
	%	%	%
Relative ease	0	34	17
Medium ease	45	40	24
Difficult	55	26	59

$\chi^2 = +10.98$, $df = 4$, $p = .05$
Source: Hall, Haas and Johnson (1967), p. 131. Reprinted with the permission of *Administrative Science Quarterly*.

the most specific goals, normative organizations are second in rank,[10] and coercive organizations have the least specific goals. (Note that if the actual rather than the stated goals had been used, coercive organizations—whose main goals commonly are to keep inmates inside and avoid riots—would almost surely rank much closer to utilitarian organizations in the degree of specificity of their goals). The main interest, though, is not in "placing" organizations, although the ability to do so on yet one more variable supports the general thesis that the typology is productive. The main purpose, to study the tensions and adaptations and the effects on the compliance structure of organizations whose goals are vague or not measurable, largely remains to be done. Such work would be of value not just for those organizations already mentioned whose goal realization is extremely difficult to assess, but also for the much larger number whose goals are vague enough to allow for different interpretations of achieve-

10. For a study of goal specificity in a church, see Scalf, Miller and Thomas (1972). The study is not sufficiently tied to compliance theory to be included in our review.

ments, not just by the researchers but by members and elites. This holds for all organizations where quality of service is at stake (e.g., health, educational, and research professional organizations). Inherently, quantitative goals such as profit or output of discrete commodities of one or few relevant attributes are of course the most specific, but even here there are considerable debates over indicators of achievement (e.g., should one, five, or ten years' profits be used as a yardstick?), making even such organizations subject to some of the tensions and adaptive mechanisms and compliance problems most manifest in organizations that have practically unmeasurable goals.

VII

COMPLIANCE AND
ORGANIZATIONAL ELITES

We saw that organizations which differ in their compliance structures tend also to differ in their goals. This chapter examines the distribution of control among various positions in the organizational structure. We shall see that the *form* of an organization's power structure is correlated with the kinds of power it exerts and the kinds of involvement it commands. Before the relationship can be explored, the attributes characterizing power structures have to be spelled out. The somewhat lengthy conceptual section may be justified by its by-product; it outlines a paradigm for the analysis of power structures, particularly lower-ranking elites, which should be of use for studies other than those whose focus is on compliance.

A PARADIGM FOR THE COMPARATIVE STUDY OF LOWER ELITES

Sources of Power

By *elites* we mean groups of actors who have power. *Lower elites* are groups of actors who have direct power over lower participants.[1] Elites differ according to the *source of their power*, which may

1. Here and throughout this book the term *group* is used to refer to a number of actors larger than one. When assumptions are made about the degree of cohesion of the group, or other characteristics, this is indicated by a qualifying adjective—for example, "cohesive groups."

be derived from the actors' organizational offices, personal character·
istics, or both.

Power derived from the actor's office may be coercive (e.g., the
guard's right to use a gun), remunerative (e.g., the foreman's right
to recommend a pay increase), or normative (e.g., the pastor's right
to administer the sacrament). Actors whose power is derived mainly
from their position in the organization are referred to as *officers.*
Actors whose power is derived from their personal characteristics are
referred to as *leaders* as long as the kind of power involved is normative.[2] Other kinds of personal power—physical or remunerative—
have little organizational significance and are therefore disregarded.

Actors who occupy organizational offices which entail power, and
who also have personal power over their subordinates, are referred
to as *formal leaders.* Thus, in the terms used here, it makes sense to
state that a formal leader leads an informal group. Actors within
the organization who have personal but not official power over lower
participants are referred to as *informal leaders.*

The same person may have official power over some subordinates
and personal influence as well over others. Moreover, he may be an
"officer" to some of his subordinates, a formal leader for some others,
and an informal leader of participants of his own rank over whom he
has no official power. In the following discussion elite members are
classified by their relationship to the majority of their subordinates.

A Typology of Elites

	Power Derived from Office	
Personal Power	+	—
+	Formal Leaders	Informal Leaders
—	Officers	Non-Elite

2. For a rigorous analysis of the various approaches to the concept of leader,
and an outline of a new approach, see Bennis (1959). For a recent publication
reviewing the literature on leadership and a rich bibliography, see Bass (1960). On
the psychological dimensions of leadership and submission to leadership, see Krech
and Crutchfield (1948, pp. 417-40). See also Redl (1942). Hopkins (1958) analyzes
the concept of leadership in terms of rank and influence. Seeman and Morris (1950)
supply a provocative paradigm for the interdisciplinary study of leadership. Bavelas
(1960) underscores the difference between leadership as personal quality and as
function.

We shall, for the sake of convenience, refer here to the formal leaders and officers on the lower organizational level simply as "organizational elites." The informal leaders constitute a nonorganizational elite, since their power is not derived from the organization.[3]

The difference among the three types of elites becomes evident in uninstitutionalized change or crisis situations. Only leaders— formal or informal—succeed in maintaining compliance in such situations, when compliance beyond the boundaries of the bureaucratic "zone of indifference" (Barnard, 1938, p. 167) is required.[4] Informal leaders have only personal power to rely on; hence their power tends to be less stable and their influence less institutionalized than that of officers or formal leaders. Therefore, it is difficult to rely on informal leaders for control of routine and continuous performances, or in any situations in which personal, particularistic bonds are constantly undermined—for example, in a military replacement system with high turnover. In such situations officers are most effective.

Activities Controlled

INSTRUMENTAL AND EXPRESSIVE ACTIVITIES—Parsons (1951, 1953) has pointed out that every collectivity must solve four basic functional problems: It must fulfill two instrumental needs of input and allocation, and two expressive needs of social and normative integration. Collectivities tend to develop differentiated action systems to fulfill the two sets of instrumental and expressive needs. Each system in turn requires control positions for its direction. Bales and his associates have shown in studies of experimental groups that the control positions of the two systems tend to become segregated, in the sense that different actors tend to hold them (1953, pp. 111-61; 1958). This is partly because incompatible role orientations and psychological characteristics are required by these positions (Bales, 1956). It appears, then, that the effective functioning of a collectivity requires the cooperation of both types of elites, although the types of

3. External elites which have power over the participants but do not constitute part of the organization—for example, business agents of labor unions—are not discussed because their examination would require a study of the relationship of the organization to its environment, in itself a major endeavor.

4. An experiment by Hamblin (1958) has shown that leadership is more influential in crisis than in noncrisis situations. See also Hemphill (1950). The role played by leaders rather than officers in maintaining control in crisis situations is a favorite topic of war novels, as in Herman Wouk's *The Caine Mutiny*.

control are segregated from each other (Bales and Slater, 1955; Slater, 1959; Wispé, 1955; Norfleet, 1948).

The authors of the studies on which these theorems are based have pointed out that they should not be treated as universals. Some groups do find leaders who effectively combine both controls; they are referred to as "great men." Empirical studies demonstrating the segregation of control positions have focused primarily on task-oriented groups and families. It is possible that there are other types of groups for which the statements made above do not hold. Until such groups are found, however, and considering the universality of instrumental and expressive needs, it seems justified to assume that these propositions about group structure apply to all collectivities.

The theorems formulated in these studies have been widely applied to small groups, such as families, committees, and experimental groups.[5] Occasionally, suggestions are made that this model could be applied to complex organizations, such as industries or hospitals.[6] We attempt to combine the dual elite model which has emerged from the study of small groups with some propositions about the relationship between informal and formal leaders and to apply the composite model to elite structures in complex organizations. A further extension is undertaken below, when the findings and insights of the Michigan studies of leadership styles in industries are introduced into our model.[7]

ELITES AND THE ACTIVITIES THEY CONTROL—We have distinguished among elites according to their source of power and according to the nature of activities they control. Relating the two dimensions, we now ask which kind of elite controls which kind of activities.

Expressive activities usually require moral involvement of the actor. Hence, they are best supervised by elites having normative power over the performers, for normative power, we have seen, is most supportive to moral involvement. Although this power may be derived from a position, personal characteristic, or both, personal

5. On small groups, see Heinicke and Bales (1953) and Bales and Slater (1955). On families, see Zelditch (1955, pp. 307-51); Bell and Vogel (1960); and Herbst (1960). On committees, see Bales (1954).

6. For an outline applying this model to industrial organizations, see Parsons, Bales, and Shils (1953, pp. 254-64); to mental hospitals, see Caudill (1958).

7. For a more detailed report on the effort to codify the Harvard approach (instrumental-expressive), the Mayo tradition (formal-informal), and the Michigan line of inquiry, see Etzioni (1959*a*).

rather than official normative power tends to be more effective. Hence the elites that are most likely to control expressive activities effectively are informal or formal leaders; officers, who have the power of office but little of their own, are less effective. Informal leaders tend to be more effective than formal ones because, as we see in detail subsequently, they can be more "purely" expressive.

Instrumental activities, we have seen, tend to require calculative involvement. Hence they are best supervised by elites having utilitarian power over the performers. This power is, as a rule, derived from organizational positions. Hence we would expect officers or formal leaders, rather than informal leaders, to exert effective control over instrumental activities. Since normative power, particularly personal influence, is not necessary and under certain conditions can be dysfunctional, officers are more likely to hold control positions over instrumental activities than are formal leaders.

Types of Elites and Activities Controlled

	Informal Leaders	Formal Leaders	Officers
Instrumental Activities	X	XX	XXX
Expressive Activities	XXX	XX	X

X least likely
XX more likely
XXX most likely

Relationships Among Elites

Once the elites are classified and the kind of activities they control are determined, the *relationships* among the various elites must be established. First, the *relative power* of each elite has to be determined. Here we repeat a proposition developed in an earlier publication, namely that the *effective elite hierarchy is one in which the structure of the elites and the hierarchy of goal (or goals and means) are congruent* (Etzioni, 1959a, p. 52). For example, in a factory the elites which embody the production or profit goals must, functionally speaking, be more powerful than those which represent professional or artistic values. When those groups representing the secondary goals (or the means) are more powerful than those representing the prime goals, the organization is likely to be ineffective; for instance, a factory that has such a dysfunctional elite hierarchy may make solid and well-designed products but no profits (Homans, 191, pp. 369-414).[8]

Relationships between elites are also compared according to the *form* their interaction takes, in terms of the degree of antagonism or cooperation.[9] The concrete forms taken by these two general modes of interaction vary a great deal. Cooperation, for instance, may be based on formal co-optation or informal collaboration; antagonism may be accompanied by open or overt conflict, or by none at all. The degree of cooperation between elites, we have seen, is a determinant of the level of effectiveness an organization maintains.

Elites and Subcollectivities

Before we can proceed to analyze the relationships between compliance and elite structures, a comment on the relationships between elites and subcollectivities is required.[10] Subcollectivities may crystallize in organizations, so that there are internal boundaries (or cleavages) in some of the organization's activities. Subcollectivities differ from one another in scope; some penetrate only into one sphere of activity, others encompass several. For example, solidary relations of lower participants may not include higher participants, and vice versa; the two groups of participants may attempt to reduce their economic interdependence and to increase their dependence on members of their own group. Similarly, the polity of the organization may be split so that lower participants direct varying proportions of their activities according to their own standards. Obviously there are always some shared sets of activities; otherwise we would refer to two (or more) collectivities, rather than to subcollectivities of one organization.

There are three major ways in which the boundaries in question can be determined: (1) The degree to which lower participants hold to *standards* of their own defining legitimate and desirable action.

8. Marcus (1960) showed that a hostile environment stimulates expressive elites, and a friendly or bland environment, instrumental elites. For purposes of comparison we assume that the environment is that which is "typical" for the particular organization. Conflict situations, for example, are typical for political parties, as is a "friendly" environment for social clubs.

9. For an outstanding discussion of these patterns of interaction as applied to organizational theory in general and power relations in particular, see Thompson and McEwen (1958, pp. 23-31).

10. This relationship is explored at greater length and from a dynamic perspective in an earlier publication (Etzioni, 1959c).

This problem is the subject of the subsequent chapter. (2) The degree to which the relationships (e.g., economic, solidary) among lower participants are inclusive or exclusive of higher participants and vice versa; in other words, the degree to which relationships are intra- versus inter-rank. In our terms, an organizaional collectivity is *integrated* when the proportion of inter-rank relations is comparatively high; when this proportion is low, lower participants have a sub-collectivity of their own, *segregated* from that of the rest of the organization.[11] The degree to which organizational relations are segregated or integrated must be determined separately for expressive (e.g., solidary) and instrumental (e.g., economic) activities. Organizations may differ in the degree to which their various spheres of activity are integrated. (3) The degree to which subcollectivities have a polity of their own—that is, have a differentiated set of elites, instead of accepting the control of the elites of the organization. We refer to the first state as one in which the elites are *differentiated,* and to the second as one in which they are *amalgamated.* Since this chapter concerns the power structure or polity of the organization, we concentrate on this last indicator of intra-organizational boundaries. We refer to the integration or segregation of relationships between organizational ranks only to the degree that this helps us understand the power structure of the organization and of its subcollectivities.

The degree to which an organizational polity is differentiated or amalgamated must be examined for each sphere of activity, because amalgamation (or differentiation) may be high in one area and not in the other.

To summarize, our question is *who* controls *what,* and what the *relationships* are among those who control. The following outline includes the elements basic to the subsequent comparison of elites in organizations with different types of compliance structures.

1. *Source of power:* personal versus positional
   Three types of elites: officers (positional only), informal leaders (personal only), and formal leaders (positional and personal)

---

11. High integration does not assume that inter-rank relationships occur as frequently as intra-rank relationships; rather, it means that the proportion of inter-rank relationships is higher than in a poorly integrated collectivity. The proportion required to maximize various organizational attributes—for example, *esprit-de-corps*—will have to be established empirically for each type of organization.

2. *Types of elites and kinds of activities controlled*
Type of elite (officers, formal leaders, informal leaders) controlling kind of activities (instrumental, expressive) [12]

3. *Nature of relations among elites*
    a. Relative power: who subordinates whom
    b. Cooperation versus antagonism

4. *Elites and subcollectivities*
For each sphere of activities and type of elite:
    a. Subcollectivities: integrated versus separated
    b. Elites: amalgamated versus differentiated

A COMPARISON OF ELITES IN THREE TYPES OF ORGANIZATIONS

Elite Structure in Coercive Organizations [13]

The most important characteristic of the elite structure of coercive
organizations follows from the sharp segregation of the "inmate social
system," as it is often called, from the rest of the organization. The
staff and the inmates are divided into two camps which share few
values and mores and have few, if any, social bonds.[14] Weinberg
states: "The inmates and officials are two segregated strata whose
relations and attitudes, like those of other castes . . . are impersonal,
and the individual members of the respective groups are considered
as stereotypes. . . . The antagonistic relationships extend the social
distance between the two strata and relatively isolate them." (1942,
p. 718) Interaction between the two camps is minimized to the extent
that talking to a guard, unless required, is often considered a violation

12. The term *instrumental control* (or *expressive control*) will be used to refer
to control over activities that fulfill predominantly instrumental (or expressive)
functions.

13. The following illustrations are drawn mainly from the data on the coercive
organization most often studied, the prison. We expect the same points to apply to
other coercive organizations, with corrections to allow for the greater or lesser
emphasis on coercive compliance.

14. Hayner and Ash distinguish between the "prison community" and the
"prisoner community" (1939, p. 362). See also Sykes and Messinger (1960) and
McCorkle and Korn (1954, pp. 40-42).

of a taboo.[15] If this caste system is broken down to any significant degree by other than isolated individuals (such as "rats" and "stoolies"), we find the power-holders accepting the outlook, values, and norms of their subjects, not the reverse.[16]

Guards as a rule have to rely predominantly on their organizational power, and hence are "officers" and not leaders to the inmates. Leadership over inmates is developed only by inmates—that is, it is informal. It is based on the ideology, symbols, and economic as well as administrative needs of the inmate subcollectivity. The inmate leader with the most prestige and power, the "right guy," is the person who engages in what Cloward calls "conspicuous defiance." The central values he personifies are defiance of the prison's pressures and official values, courage, and—most important of all—adamant refusal to concede the superiority and validity of the prison value system (Cloward, 1959, p. 153).[17]

Both McCleery and Cloward emphasize that the inmate elite supports *some* norms in which the guards are interested—for example, maintaining order, suppressing a potential riot, or not assaulting a guard (McCleery, 1956, p. 718; Cloward, 1959, p. 165). However, support of these norms is based on interests that happen to coincide; they lack the foundations of shared mores and social bonds. Any change in the situation may cause this limited area of concurrent interests to disappear.

The inmates develop a highly autonomous subcollectivity seeking to extend as far as possible the control span of their own elites. Hayner and Ash state: "Closer acquaintance with any American prison reveals a sub-rosa organization composed entirely of inmates."

---

15. Cloward, who studied an army prison, reports on this point: "Although many inmates were permitted to remain aloof from other inmates, they nevertheless had to avoid incurring their emnity. The most severe sanctions were imposed upon informers. Hence conformists feared the possibility that they would be suspected of such treacherous activity. In order to divert suspicion from themselves, they over-conformed to the anti-Army norms. . . . In short, the safeguard against becoming alienated from one's peers was to engage in *ritual defiance*." (1959, p. 138) See also McCleery (1956, p. 376).

16. The process by which this takes place is explored by Sykes (1956). See also McCorkle and Korn (1954, p. 93); and Roucek (1936).

17. "The right guys exert tremendous power and influence over other inmates in enforcing strict observance of the 'Prisoners' Code.'" (Caldwell, 1956, p. 651) The right guy should not be confused with the "hero," who also sets examples in his behavior for counter-prison behavior and norms, but does it in an irrational and "irresponsible" way. The hero plays a central role in periods of instability, especially in riots. The right guy is the central figure of the stable period. On the hero, see Hartung and Floch (1956).

(1939, p. 362) The social and normative bonds of this subcollectivity are obviously limited to inmates, governed by their codes and controlled by their expressive leaders. This is one reason rehabilitation, which requires changes of attitudes and values in the direction favored by the prison staff, is unlikely to succeed.[18]

Inmate control over instrumental activities is more difficult to attain. Work assignments are to a large degree made by the prison staff; food, clothing, and shelter are supplied and allocated by the prison. The inmates strive to overcome this lack of control in several ways. They attempt to reallocate or to influence the allocation of goods and services supplied by the prison. They develop their own commodities and services, from producing weapons to brewing alcohol.[19] Inmates reallocate their goods—cigarettes, food, liquor, narcotics— according to their criteria. These allocations and reallocations serve to reward those who conform to the inmate code and to punish those who deviate—that is, they serve as a means of control peculiar to the inmate subcollectivity and its elites.

There are usually some inmates in particular who control production and allocation of goods, referred to in the prison argot as "merchants" and "peddlers," and some who specialize in influencing the allocation of the prisoners themselves to jobs and living quarters, the "fixers." Both constitute the instrumental ("business") elite of the inmate subcollectivity.

Nevertheless, the inmate subcollectivity never becomes self-sufficient. Although expressive control is almost completely in inmates' hands, control over some instrumental activities, such as work assignments and allocation of some products and services, remains in the hands of the prison officers. The difference in inmate control over expressive and instrumental activities is reflected in the prestige allotted to the various inmate elites. The merchants, promoters, and fixers, who are concerned with instrumental activities, are lower in rank than the expressive leaders, the right guys. According to Cloward:

18. The effect of the inmate collectivity on treatment, especially of the traditional type, is analyzed with great insight by Ohlin and Lawrence (1959, pp. 7-8). See also Ohlin (1956, pp. 18-22). When coercion in a prison is reduced, alienation of the inmates declines, staff-inmate interaction increases, and the chances for rehabilitation are reported to increase (V. Fox, 1954). See also Ohlin (1958, pp. 65-66).

19. Hayner and Ash (1939, p. 366) describe the operations involved in supplying warm coffee to inmates after they have been locked in their cells. Brewing illicit whiskey in the prison kitchen is reported by Cloward (1959, pp. 148-49). On "moonshiners" and weapons production, see Caldwell (1956, p. 652).

The merchant seeks access to and control over the distribution of goods and services. . . . He is held in contempt by the most of his fellows for his "self-seeking attitudes." . . . The politician is a figure of power in the prison, commanding a superior position because he manipulates the transmission of information between the official and the inmate systems. . . . men submit to him because he can reward and punish by giving or withholding vital information. . . . Finally, the right guy, renowned for his unerring loyalty to the inmate code whatever the personal sacrifice or show of official force, occupies a position of immense honor and esteem among his fellows; he is the charismatic leader of the inmate system. (1959, p. 144)[20]

The politicians, according to Hayner and Asch, constitute a middle elite between the two in terms of both function and status:

Inmate "politicians" play a role in prison similar to that of their prototypes in a corrupt city government. As in the outside community, they must grant favors in order to hold their position and yet they are frequently hated for their self-seeking attitude. The "right guys," on the contrary, can always be trusted to remain loyal to their fellow cons. Clemmer found that "being right" was the essential and most admired trait of prison leadership. (1940, p. 579)[21]

Information about interaction among the various types of inmate leaders is limited, but it seems that since a certain stigma is attached to instrumental activities, expressive leaders try to stay clear of instrumental leaders and to control them by indirection. There is one kind of instrumental activity, however, which does not suffer low prestige, and that is the planning, working out, and execution of escapes. Since this activity is directly related to the inmates' ultimate values, symbolized and reinforced by the expressive leaders, it carries high prestige. The "engineers" and "organizers" of escapes seem to work closely with the expressive leaders. But even here, the instrumental leader, as a "means-man," is subordinated to the expressive leader.[22] The latter sets norms, settles conflicts among instrumental

20. See also Sykes (1956, pp. 132-33) and Clemmer (1938, pp. 861-72).

21. Cf. Caldwell (1956, p. 654), who suggests that the politicians constitute the upper class and the right guys the middle class of the prison. Caldwell bases his observation on Caran (1948, p. 590). Merchants are not placed. See also Cressey (1958, p. 628).

22. Lacking better evidence, we turn to a "comedy melodrama" written by two ex-P.O.W.'s, Bevan and Trzinski, *Stalag 17* (1951). Hoffy is the expressive leader, "the barrack's leader chosen by the men. . . . His sincerity, kindness and interest in the welfare of the men have made him the obvious choice." (p. 3) Price (who later turns out to be a German spy) is the accepted instrumental leader. He deals with security arrangements and escape plans. He is second in command to Hoffy (pp. 8-9). Sefton is the "merchant" of the barrack, "not a very likeable guy." Hoffy keeps control over him, but from a distance (pp. 18 ff.).

leaders, approves plans and schedules, and gives the decisive order when the escape route and plans are completed.[23]

In a less coercive organization, such as a relocation camp (Leighton, 1945), we would expect inmate elites to be relatively more amalgamated into the control system of the organization. We would expect this amalgamation to be limited, however, and to occur predominantly in the instrumental sphere. Leighton's study illustrates this kind of "less coercive" structure.

We have already noted that the Japanese relocation camps in the United States were relatively less coercive than the average prison. Force was used to detain the inmates, but almost no coercion was applied to control activities within the camp. When a strike occurred and disorder seemed imminent, the head of the administration resisted suggestions that he use military units attached to the camp to restore order. He negotiated with the internees' representatives, and, by true bargaining, in which real concessions were made by both sides, a settlement acceptable to both sides was reached. Still, it is important to note that the trigger-event of the strike was not economic, but the arrest of two inmate leaders—that is, a coercive act.

The level of alienation in the relocation centers paralleled the level of coercion applied. As one would expect, moral commitment to the camp administration was out of the question. Even the most cooperative internees did not accept the proposition that "the Japanese loyal to America were glad to stay in a Relocation Camp as their contribution to the war." (Leighton, 1945, p. 45). Fear, frustration, and anger are reported to have characterized most internees' attitudes toward the camp. Still, the counter-ideology was less developed than in most prisons. For instance, some limited acceptance of the camp's orders rested on commitment to American ultimate values.

There was a considerable amount of instrumental cooperation with the administration, including areas in which cooperation is rarely gained in prisons. Not only did internee foremen organize and supervise the inmates' work; an internee police force helped to maintain order, and the internees' representatives cooperated with the camp authorities on the allocation of goods and services. But here, as in the prison, efforts were made to influence the allocations controlled by the administration in order to bring them into line with

23. For studies of inmate interaction which indirectly bear on these points, see Moreno (1934) and Jennings (1943).

criteria derived from internees' value and status systems, though the efforts were more open and direct than in prisons. They were expressed as demands by the internees' councils and committees and by delegations to the camp administration.

Efforts at self-control were almost as wide in scope as in prisons. The camps' personnel were as a rule treated as officers whose directives are followed because of their impersonal coercive—and sometimes remunerative—power. Only one or two staff members (mainly the "people-minded" director) had any leadership power, and this was limited to the instrumental sphere (*ibid.*, pp. 226, 241).

Expressive control was in the hands of internee leaders. The most prominent of these had both Japanese and American education and a good command of the English language and was also a Buddhist and a judo expert, so that he expressed the dual or ambivalent value system of the inmates. He led them in settling internal conflicts and acted as a leading member of the Judicial Commission of the internees and as their representative to the administration (*ibid.*, pp. 163 ff.). Other expressive leaders were found among the elders of the camp, many of whom had power in various subgroups of the internees.

In short, the basic similarities to the control structure in prisons are evident. Amalgamation into the control system of the organization is somewhat wider, but still limited to the instrumental sphere.[24]

So far we have sought to determine which elites control which activities of the lower participants and what the relationships are among those in control in coercive organizations. We have seen that there are two sets of highly differentiated elites, each representing one of the two "castes": the organizational officers, who have control over some of the instrumental activities of the inmates, and the inmate elites, composed of informal leaders who control some instrumental and practically all expressive inmate activities. The relationship between organizational elites and inmate elites ranges from open conflict to limited *ad hoc* cooperation. The relationship between

24. Some information on leadership in another "less coercive" organization is supplied by Rowland's study of a custodial mental hospital (1938). Here too we find a larger degree of cooperation with the organization, especially by some inmate leaders to whom Rowland refers as the "ward-bosses" than in prisons. But power seems to be concentrated in the hands of the expressive anti-organization leaders who plan escapes and "make trouble" for the hospital administration. (For descriptions of the leaders, see *ibid.*, pp. 324-31). Rowland comments that such leaders are less frequently found in mental hospitals than in penal organizations (*ibid.*, p. 330).

instrumental and expressive inmate leaders varies according to the nature of instrumental activities in which the inmate elite is involved. When these activities are related to illicit consumption, the inmate instrumental elite ("merchants") is controlled indirectly and remotely by the inmate expressive elite ("right guys"). When the instrumental activities are directly related to inmates' goals (e.g., escapes) which are supported by the expressive inmate elite, contact between the two elites is more direct and intimate. In either case the expressive inmate elite is dominant.

To the degree that the material available allows comparisons between more coercive and less coercive organizations, it seems to be in line with our hypothesis. The less coercive the organization, the higher the degree of amalgamation of organizational and inmate instrumental elites, the greater the acceptance of officers as agents of instrumental control, the less precarious the inmate cooperation, and, under special conditions, the greater the likelihood that organizational elites will exert some limited personal influence over inmates in instrumental matters.

Elite Structure in Normative Organizations [25]

In many ways the elite structure of normative organizations is diametrically opposed to that of coercive organizations. Whereas elites are differentiated in coercive organizations, they are almost completely amalgamated in normative ones. Whereas prison elites exert only partial instrumental control and hardly any expressive control over inmates, organizational elites in normative organizations have wide and effective control over both the expressive and the instrumental activities of participants. In this sense lower participants in normative organizations are much better integrated into the organizational polity than lower participants in coercive organizations, and they are less likely to develop even a partial polity of their own.

ELITE AMALGAMATION AND COOPERATION IN NORMATIVE ORGANIZATIONS—In typical normative organizations, instrumental as well as expressive activities are controlled chiefly by the organizational elites. Although instrumental control positions are in the hands of officers, such as deacons or party treasurers, who as a rule have

25. We focus on the "typical" normative organizations, although we expect that the points made apply, after the necessary adjustments are made, to less normative ones as well.

little personal influence over the rank and file, expressive positions are frequently in the hands of formal leaders, such as ministers or party leaders. In contrast to coercive organizations, the normative organization tends to provide the leadership for the lower participants, thus reducing the likelihood that informal leaders will arise among them.

There are three major mechanisms for keeping the elites of normative organizations amalgamated or cooperative. The first, which might be termed *absorption,* occurs when potential informal leaders are recruited into full-time organizational positions. The most active union members are likely to become stewards, and eventually business agents. Active party members can climb the political ladder from local to district and from district to state or national positions.[26] Churches were channels of mobility for potentially charismatic peasants' sons even in the low-mobility medieval society. Active members of voluntary associations become local officials. Only in schools and therapeutic mental hospitals is the barrier between lower participants and elite positions rarely crossed.

The absorption of lower participants with leadership ability into higher organizational ranks often requires training, education, and the individual's willingness to make the organization his career. Normative organizations have developed another mechanism—which, following Selznick, we refer to as *co-optation* [27]—to recruit lower participants who have leadership ability but lack other necessary characteristics. Special positions and tasks are developed which make it possible for them to contribute to organizational goals and to become committed through participation without special training, education, or full-time devotion to organizational activities. Membership on boards or committees and volunteer work are typical examples of such roles. Fichter (1954) describes the large network of such ancillary positions in athletic, welfare, and social activities which develops around the church as part of the parish structure. Although all these activities are directly or indirectly controlled by the pastor, they supply positions for active and powerful lay leaders (*ibid.,* pp. 3-49). The degree of commitment to the pastor associated with holding such

26. Michels (1959, pp. 164-84) has suggested that this is the major channel for recruitment to top positions in political parties and labor unions.

27. On the concept and a fine case study employing it, see Selznick (1953, and 1948, pp. 33-35).

positions is reflected by the fact that 93.9 per cent of 245 lay leaders studied were willing to accept the pastor's advice, direction, decision, or even complete control. Only 6.1 per cent insisted on sharing power equally with the pastor (*ibid.*, p. 36). The distribution of answers to a similar questionnaire would probably be different in a more equalitarian church. But even there, holding a lay position in the church or an ancillary organization probably increases the tendency of emergent leaders to use their influence in support of the church and its full-time formal elites.

Collaboration is a mode of inter-elite cooperation which occurs when informal elites support organizational values and goals without holding any formal position in the organizational structure itself. In coercive organizations collaboration, as we have seen, is limited to *ad hoc* support of norms that both sides are interested in maintaining. It tends to be withdrawn whenever changes in the situation make it disadvantageous for the inmates.[28]

Absorption, co-optation, and collaboration are also found in utilitarian organizations. Co-optation of workers' leaders through work councils, co-determination and similar mechanisms is rarely effective, however, because of the workers' tendency to lose faith in leaders who participate in such activities.[29] There is some evidence that when leaders are co-opted by management, or appear to workers to be "over-cooperative" even without holding positions in collaborative groups such as work councils, they are likely to face a wildcat strike or the loss of election.[30]

28. Furthermore, in coercive organizations attempts at co-optation of informal leaders are likely to fail: the inmate government, for example, either does not represent the inmates because it is comprised of "stoolies" rather than of inmate elites (Ohlin, 1957, p. 10), or is used by inmates to co-opt the prison management, instead of the other way around. McCleery (1956) describes the various forms inmate governments have taken as a result of changes in the relationship between inmates and various groups of the prison staff. Caudill describes the co-optation efforts of the management of a mental hospital and the "rebellious" behavior of the inmate representatives (1958, pp. 68-86). See E. Katz and Lazarsfeld (1955, pp. 120-24), on communication blocks created by such governments.

29. For an extensive survey of the council movement in England, Germany, Austria, and the United States, as well as an analysis of the issues involved, see E. S. Miller (1922). For more recent studies see Harbison and Coleman (1951, pp. 112-17); Blum (1953, pp. 19-22); and Waris (1959).

30. For a detailed report on an "unofficial" strike which resulted from what workers perceived as over-cooperation of the union with management, see The University of Liverpool (1954). See also Gouldner (1954a, pp. 95-100) and Sayles (1954, pp. 43-44).

In normative organizations even deviant leaders tend to come from those who hold organizational positions; they rarely emerge directly from the ranks of lower participants. In the few cases where informal leaders do not collaborate and are not absorbed or co-opted, they either disappear after a short period of high activity, in which the specific issue they were fighting for is resolved, or they break away and form a new organization in which they compose the organizational elite. Among the three types of organizations, "rebellion" and secession seem to occur most often in normative organizations.

There are several reasons for the instability, in typical normative organizations, of informal leadership which is neither co-opted nor collaborative. First, in normative organizations but not in the other two types, there is usually a high degree of consensus between lower participants and lower elites concerning the ultimate values, mores, and norms governing the behavior of elites, members, and the organization. In addition, there is a strong positive commitment to the organization, and hence serving the organization or cooperating with its elites is not a source of stigma among lower participants. On the contrary, such activity is a source of prestige, esteem, and favorable self-evaluation. Finally, the degree of participation in typical normative organizations is highly associated with the degree of commitment. The most active members, including most informal leaders, also tend to be highly committed to the organization, and hence inclined to support it and its elites; those most alienated from the organization—including those who have leadership potential—tend to be inactive or to drop out.

The elite structure of colleges and graduate schools, another class of typical normative organizations, is like that of religious organizations. As a rule the students accept the expressive leadership of the instructors. One of the best indicators of this is the fact that students tend to change their values in the direction of those held or advocated by the faculty (Newcomb, 1943). As a rule, the instrumental direction of the administration is followed. Student governments or representatives in colleges tend to cooperate with deans, or to be co-opted by them. In schools, which are less typical normative organizations, the tendency for expressive leadership to be informal is considerably higher than in colleges, although some teachers and other staff members usually maintain expressive control of their pupils. It is only in the relatively coercive special and vocational schools that the students tend to have an extensive subcollectivity of their own, controlled by informal student leaders.[31]

ELITE HIERARCHY IN NORMATIVE ORGANIZATIONS—We have suggested which persons control lower participants in normative organizations, and pointed to the high degree to which formal and informal elites are amalgamated. But what is the hierarchy of power among these elites? Our basic assumption is that optimal effectiveness occurs when the elites in control of goal activities subordinate those in control of means activities (*supra,* pp. 157-8). In coercive organizations this question is irrelevant, since the organizational collectivity is almost split in two, and the elites are so differentiated and antagonistic that their relationship often approximates a state of open conflict; it cannot be seen as an established pattern of superordination of one elite by the other. (In the informal subcollectivity, however, expressive elites dominate instrumental ones.) We shall see below that in utilitarian organizations it is functional for economic goals that instrumental elites subordinate expressive elites. For the culture goals of normative organizations, it is functional that expressive elites dominate, since expressive elites initiate and direct goal activities, such as building up and sustaining the required value commitments, whereas the instrumental elites control the recruitment of means and the management of facilities. This pattern seems to be followed in political parties (e.g., treasurers are subordinate to political leaders) and in labor unions, as Wilensky demonstrates in his study of the relationship between leaders and experts (1956, esp. pp. 187-95). Wilensky shows that representatives of the "political-ideological" line—that is, the expressive leaders—subordinate the representatives of the "technical-economic-legal" line—that is, the instrumental elite, on almost all issues.[32] Sayles and Strauss analyze two types of union leaders, administrator and social leader, depicted as typical instrumental and expressive leaders (1953, pp. 123-31). No evidence is presented on the relationships between the two types of leaders and their relative power; we would expect the administrator to be subordinate to the social leader in effective ideological and social unions; and the social leader to be subordinate to the administrator in effective business unions.

---

31. Hunter (1954), in his novel about a vocational school, describes the "right guy" of the classroom, Miller, and its "hero," West.

32. It would be of interest to examine the various types of union discussed above to see what differences exist in the hierarchy of their leadership.

In religious organizations a larger variation can be found in the actual allocation of power between the two types of leaders. Among the religious organizations which fulfill this functional requirement is the Jesuit order, in which the head of a house, a rector in charge of "spiritual matters," is clearly superior to a father-minister, in charge of "temporal and external discipline." [33] The subordination of deacons, an instrumental elite in charge of church administration, to the clergy in the Episcopalian church reflects a similar functional arrangement.

In some of the larger urban Catholic parishes, on the other hand, the pastor who tends the parish frequently devotes much of his time to administrative matters, such as recruiting support for and directing the large web of schools, hospitals, and other enterprises he controls (Fichter, 1954, pp. 154-64). The pressure on top-ranking religious functionaries to neglect their expressive roles and become engrossed in instrumental activities is common to most modern religious organizations. The following information is cited from a forthcoming study by Samuel W. Blizzard:

Pastors spent most time in roles they considered least important. They spent approximately 40% of their ten-hour working day as administrators, about 25% as pastors. Preaching and priestly duties took up almost 20%, organizing took 10%, and teaching the least, 5%. Stenographic tasks consumed more time per day than sermon preparation. (Cited by Chamberlain, 1958, p. 33)

The curates become, to some degree by default, the expressive elite in charge of expressive services, such as most religious rituals. Catholic writers who are aware of the dysfunctional consequences of such a division of labor have suggested the introduction of deacons into the Catholic service, to relieve the pastor of some of the administrative work and to be subordinate to him. Epagneul, for example, writes:

Details of administration accumulate with the building of schools, parish organizations, convert and catechism instruction, and complicated finances. In such a welter of activity the priestly direction of individual souls is all but impossible outside the confessional. Pastors themselves recognize the need of helpers . . . who could gather up the loose ends of parish activities and knit them into a well-organized program. Precisely how would deacons help? With proper training they could, *under the supervision of the priest,* handle ordinary financial details . . . teach catechism, do the spade-work in preparing converts, establish initial contacts with fallen-

33. Private communication with members of the order.

away Catholics, direct lesser parish organizations, organize and take the parish census, and manage the constant stream of secretarial work. (1959, pp. 74-75; italics supplied)

Jenkins emphasies that it is necessary for the minister to be superior to lay (instrumental) representatives in expressive matters:

Some Protestant churches, especially those of comparatively recent origin, need to understand what place office should have in the Church and to make sure that the Church's officers have adequate powers to fulfill their function properly, without being at the mercy of arbitrary and irresponsible action by congregations or trustees. Among these offices, ministers are the chief. (1958, p. 35)

In congregations where much of church financing and administration is in the hands of local laymen, as in the egalitarian Protestant churches and the American Jewish congregations, laymen constitute the instrumental elite, leaving primarily expressive functions to the minister or to the rabbi. Since the lay elite is usually more powerful (e.g., it hires and fires the religious functionaries), this also means that the instrumental elite subordinates the expressive one (Pope, 1942, pp. 143-61; Underwood, 1957, pp. 240-58; R. and H. Lynd, 1956, p. 356; and Churchill, 1959, pp. 89-90). A major dysfunction resulting from such a relationship is overemphasis on the congregation's instrumental activities; for example, facilities such as buildings are expanded, while salvation and other religious goals are relatively neglected (Gustafson, 1954). A similar displacement of goals seems to occur more often in colleges and universities where the board of trustees or the state has extensive control than in those academic organizations in which the faculty has the decisive power (L. Wilson, 1955; Sullivan, 1956).[34]

Sills (1957), in a study of a highly effective fund-raising voluntary association (The National Foundation for Infantile Paralysis), found two committees which constituted the local elite: the executive committee, whose central figure is the chapter chairman, and the medical advisory committee. The first is a typical expressive elite position. Despite the need for administrative skills, which is mentioned in the formal "job description" of the chairman's position (sent by

---

34. An increase in faculty power over the administration in United States colleges and universities is reported for the period from 1939 to 1953; other periods are not studied (A.A.U.P., 1955). Comparative material is included in Lazarsfeld and Thielens (1958, *passim*).

the headquarters of the Foundation to each chapter), other qualities seem to play a major role:

> The Chairman . . . must be . . . a person of poise and administrative ability, with a deep interest in people, public health and human welfare. Try to select an individual who has proved himself interested in civic, philanthropic and health activities. . . . There are no professional qualifications. The Chairman might be a businessman, an attorney, an educator, or a housewife. . . . Physicians and public health officers should not be asked to serve as Chairman. . . . (*Ibid.,* p. 48)

On the other hand, the medical advisory committee, composed of experts, is instrumental. Its role is not to build up or sustain moral commitments, but to perform or direct "technical" staff functions. Typically, it is subordinate to the expressive executive committee:

> Professional training is of course utilized by the Chapter through the establishment of a Medical Advisory Committee, which furnishes professional and technical guidance. But it is of the utmost significance that this is an *advisory* committee; final responsibility rests in the hands of the Chapter Officers and the Executive Committee. (*Ibid.,* p. 50)

Brim analyzes several studies of the relationship between instrumental and expressive elite roles in the school. He shows that the role of the effective leader tends to be an instrumental one; that

> . . . the dominant role prescription for teachers is to be task-oriented, though either role is acceptable; that teachers follow this at the expense of expressive considerations; that they gain respect but lose attraction in doing this; that both teacher and student wish more attention were (or could be) given to expressive or social-emotional matters, and, finally, that if they do, learning (or task accomplishment) suffers. (1958, p. 49)

This raises the question of who supplies the expressive leadership and how he is related to the teacher. Most frequently this leadership is supplied by students. The degree to which they support the school authorities in general and the teacher in particular varies with the degree to which the controls applied by the school are normative rather than coercive. Some expressive leadership is supplied from organizational positions, such as the football coach, youth worker, and some of the teachers. The support of these leaders for academic values is not automatically assured, but it is more likely to be forthcoming than that of informal student leaders.

Brim's analysis suggests that in schools, in contrast to other normative organizations, it is functional for instrumental elites to subordinate expressive ones. It seems to us that this model follows from a view of the school as a training organization, which communicates knowledge and develops skills. The training goal can be served comparatively well in predominantly instrumental relationships, though in order to maintain motivation to acquire training, in the absence of remunerative rewards, a stronger expressive element is required than exists in other predominantly instrumental relationships. Moreover, to the degree that the school, in particular the primary school, educates (communicates values) more than it trains, supremacy of expressive leadership in the classroom in general, and in the teacher's role in particular, seems to us highly functional.[35]

Caudill's monograph on a therapeutic mental hospital shows that patient-leaders have expressive control positions, whereas instrumental activities and some expressive ones are controlled by the hospital (1958, p. 89). Varying degrees of cooperation between the instrumental elite of the hospital and the patient-leaders are reported, but it is not clear which elite has a power advantage. Ohlin reports an experiment in a correctional institution in which effectiveness of rehabilitation was increased by granting professional staff (social workers) authority over the more instrumentally oriented line (lay) personnel in twelve out of sixteen "cottages." Rehabilitation remained low in the four cottages where such reallocation of power did not take place (1958, pp. 67-69). E. and J. Cumming show clearly the dysfunctional effects of a powerful lay administrator on rehabilitation in a mental hospital (1956).

Elites in effective schools and in therapeutic mental hospitals realize that for effective service of culture goals, instrumental control of lower participants is not sufficient; they therefore strive to gain expressive control as well. Efforts to gain such control generally take two forms. First, the major professional groups of the organization (teachers, psychoanalysts) are under pressure to develop expressive leadership.[36] In order to increase their chances of success those instrumental controls over lower participants which are particularly tension-

35. The informal group of the classroom has the same hierarchy of elites as do inmates' subcollectivities. Informal expressive elites subordinate informal instrumental ones (Gold, 1958, pp. 50-60), and for the same reason: these are collectivities which are oriented to "social" and normative rather than to "production" goals.

36. Parsons (1957, pp. 127-28) explored the association between the positions of psychiatrists as superintendents and the supremacy of the therapeutic goal. Caudill (1958, pp. 345-63; see also p. 84) sees the administrator as the main instrumental leader of the therapeutic mental hospital and the therapist as the main expressive leader.

creating are delegated to others: in schools, punishments are handed out by principals, police departments, or parents; in mental hospitals, instrumental controls and punitive measures are administered by nurses, aids, or administrators. But neither teachers nor psychiatrists can escape the necessity of applying instrumental controls because of the very nature of their tasks, and thus they cannot entirely avoid the consequent alienation of lower participants.

A second major way in which these normative organizations try to gain expressive leadership is by creating positions in which relationships with lower participants lack even the limited instrumental strains which exist between teachers and students or between psychiatrists and patients. In schools such positions are held by sports instructors, football coaches, and youth workers—in short, the elite of the highly expressive extracurricular activities. In therapeutic mental hospitals, these positions are held by social workers, entertainment officers, and some occupational therapists (Caudill, 1958, pp. 105-6).[37]

Such formal leaders, to the degree that they succeed in developing expressive leadership, prevent the emergence of a leadership vacuum and thus reduce the probability that informal leaders will develop. At the same time these formal leaders are a source of potential dysfunction to the organization because their activities are marginal to organizational goals; compare, for instance, the work of the football coach

---

37. Military organizations to a greater extent than any other organization invest conscious planning and manpower in the effort to supply both types of leadership, to assure their amalgamation into the military structure and their "coalition." The commanding officer and the N.C.O. in combat units, functionally speaking, supply the two types of leadership, but the division of power between the two positions differs in armies of different tradition. It seems that in the American army the tendency is for the N.C.O. to fulfill the expressive role, and for the officer to fill the instrumental one. This is illustrated in Uris' *Battle Cry*. Huxley, the commanding officer, is the ever-demanding, unmerciful, cool, instrumental leader. Mac, the sergeant, handles the personal and social problems of the men. They come to him for support when their wives betray them; he saves them from the military police; and he helps the newcomers and a soldier named Levin to become accepted by the group. Mac is clearly the expressive leader. The men typically feel closer to Mac but have more respect for Huxley. The unit is effective not only because it has both types of leaders but also because they support each other.

In the Soviet military organization the expressive role is sometimes carried out by a political officer (when he succeeds in building up moral commitments to himself, often by participation in combat). In other situations political officers are themselves a focus of alienation. On the role of such political officers in the Israeli army see Etzioni (1952, pp. 156-62). The relationship between the expressive (civilian, political) and instrumental (military, professional) elite on the highest organizational level is the central subject of Huntington's study (1957). See also Feld (1959, pp. 15-22).

to that of the regular teacher, or of the "group-activity" worker to that of the psychiatrist. Since expressive leaders are more likely to command identification than instrumental ones, because less relationship they develop with the lower participants generates less alienation, they may channel loyalties and attention from the central organizational goals to secondary or marginal activities. The football coach may increase identification with sports and sports idols, and reduce identification with learning and teachers.[38] Social workers may unwittingly reinforce alienation from the relatively remote analyst and gain more commitment to group therapy and occupational therapy than the goals of the organization prescribe.[39]

To summarize: In typical normative organizations, lower participants are highly integrated into the organizational collectivity. They tend to accept the control of organizational elites over expressive matters, which are the major activity of these organizations, and over the limited instrumental activities as well.

High commitment of lower participants to the organization allows the organizational elites to develop leadership over them; consequently, leadership outside the organizational power positions is infrequent. Potential informal leaders are absorbed by upward recruitment to lower organizational power positions and co-opted by recruitment to part-time roles in various auxiliary organizations. Those few leaders who maintain solely informal power tend either to collaborate with organizational elites or to break away from the organization altogether.

In less typical normative organizations, the lower degree of members' integration into the organizational collectivity is paralleled by a higher degree of differentiation in the organizational polity. Organizational elites have less leadership power, and informal leaders play a more central role in the control of lower participants. Special efforts are made in these organizations to encourage formal expressive leaders, in order to reduce the dysfunctional effects of alienated informal leadership.

38. For a rigorous study of the role of sports in the high school culture and its effect on commitments to academic values, as well as other values, see Coleman (1960).

39. There seems to be no evidence on patient-leadership in general hospitals. We would expect to find some at least in hospitals for chronic diseases, such as TB, where patients stay for long periods and develop extensive social relationships. Similarly, the little relevant information which exists about these matters for professional organizations does not allow us to extend these speculations to them.

Elite Structure in Utilitarian Organizations

The compliance structure of utilitarian organizations falls between the coercive and normative types. The elite characteristics of utilitarian organizations also fall in the middle of the various dimensions specified above. We find that although there is great variation in the elite structure of various blue- and white-collar industries, even when workers' commitments are relatively high, their integration into the organizational collectivity and control structure is not so high as that of members of typical normative organizations; and even when their alienation is relatively high, their segregation from the organization and its elites tends to be less extensive than that of inmates in coercive organizations.

Differences among blue-collar and white-collar elite structures follow the line we would predict on the basis of their compliance structures. White-collar industries reveal an elite structure closer to that of normative organizations, whereas the elite structure of blue-collar industries more closely resembles that of coercive organizations.

More specifically, workers in utilitarian organizations tend to develop their own expressive elite (to the degree that there are expressive activities in industrial collectivities). The main difference between alienated workers and committed workers lies in the role the foreman plays.[40] Therefore we focus on this role as we examine the elite structure of industries in which workers are relatively highly alienated, and compare them with those where they are relatively highly committed.

ALIENATED WORKERS AND INSTRUMENTAL ELITES—Alienated workers develop a rather powerful ideology counter to the normative claims of the factory, frequently based on some version of socialism. Alienated workers strive to reduce the organization's control over their work by developing their own control system. The foreman tends to be an instrumental officer, who gains compliance only within the limits of the contractual relationship; even this instrumental control is curtailed by the workers' efforts to make supervision follow their norms. Instrumental leaders among the workers usurp some of the foreman's prerogatives.

40. A detailed typology of worker-foreman relationships is suggested in Etzioni (1958b, pp. 36-38). For a similar typology derived from different theoretical assumptions, see Hopkins (1959, pp. 6-9, 17-18).

The often cited Bank Wiring Observation Room case is a description of an alienated work group (Roethlisberger and Dickson, 1939, chs. 18-21). The workers constituted a cohesive group which had a well-developed normative system of its own. The norms specified, among other things, that a worker was not to work too hard, lest he become a "rate-buster"; nor was he to work too slowly, lest he become a "chiseler" who exploited the group (part of the wages were based on group performance). Under no condition was he to inform or "squeal."[41] By means of informal social control, the group was able to direct the pace of work, the amount of daily and weekly production, the amount of work-stoppage, and allocation of work among members. In short, the workers attained a high degree of self-control on both the expressive (enforcement of their norms) and the instrumental (control of the production process) levels. The management representatives, including the group chief, assistant foreman, and foreman, had little control over the group; the group chief had little power,[42] and the foreman and his assistant did not even have the information required for interference.

Another case reported by Roethlisberger and Dickson illustrates the relationship between alienation and the development of a segregated workers' collectivity and elite, which include both an instrumental and an expressive leader. The group is reported to have revealed

. . . general dissatisfaction or unrest. In some, this was expressed by demands for advancement or transfers; in others, by a complaint about their lot in being kept on the job. . . . I [the observer] then noticed that two of the workers in particular held rather privileged positions in the group and were looked up to by the rest of the members. On these two the group seemed to place considerable responsibility. Of A they said: "He can handle the engineers, inspectors, and the supervisors. . . ." In speaking of B they expressed admiration for his work habits and capacities.

41. It is of interest to note that the strong taboo against squealing, which is often considered peculiar to prison culture, existed here also (Harper, 1952, pp. 56-58). The taboo seems to be caused by the high alienation of lower participants and the high degree of autonomy attained by their collectivities, not by the concrete nature of the organization in which this norm develops. In organizations where commitment is high, upward "reporting" is considered a moral obligation. This is true, for instance, in convents (Hulme, 1956, pp. 44ff.), in colleges where there is an honor system, and in the Communist party.

42. Homans, in his incisive analysis of the case, said of the group chief: "He was perfectly well aware of the devices by which they maintained their production at a constant level. But he was able to do very little to bring about a change." (1952, p. 646)

Although the instrumental capacities of B were respected, his expressive functions were not emphasized:

"So-and-so talked too much a while ago, and B shut him up" . . . all expressed appreciation of his willingness to help them. A, in his interviews, told of fights with supervisors and arguments with engineers and inspectors . . . "I made several machines work after an expert from the East said an adjustment was impossible." B told of helping other adjusters. He said that he threatened to punch one operator in the nose because he had let the supervisor know that he had finished early.

The investigator summarized the situation:

The supervisory control which is set up by management to regulate and govern the workers exercises little authority except to see that they are supplied with work. It is apparent that the group is protected from *without* by A . . . and protected from *within* by one (B) capable of administering punishment for any violation of the group standards (1939, pp. 383-84. Italics supplied)

In our terms, this is a case of an alienated group which dissociated itself from the organization both expressively and, to the greatest possible extent, instrumentally. Informal leaders include an instrumental one (A), mainly concerned with external adaptation, expertise, and production, and an expressive one (B), chiefly concerned with social integration and normative compliance and with some instrumental command. Which—if either—leader was more powerful, and to what degree the two informal leaders cooperated, cannot be ascertained from the information available.

COMMITTED WORKERS AND INSTRUMENTAL ELITES—The more committed the workers, the more they are inclined to accept members of the organizational elite as leaders. But since commitment is rarely so high as in normative organizations, as a rule even highly committed workers accept only instrumental leadership from the organization and develop their own expressive leaders.

Significant material relevant to this point is supplied by the Michigan studies of the relationship between leadership practices and productivity and morale (Katz, Maccoby, and Morse, 1950; and Katz, Maccoby, Gurin, and Floor, 1951). Before this material can be presented, a conceptual note is required. The Michigan studies as well as some other studies use the term *leader* in a general way. Every actor who has influence or power, from whatever source, is referred to as a leader. All foremen, for instance, are seen as leaders by *definition*. A researcher may define his terms in the manner most helpful to his work, and so long as he uses them consistently, as the

Michigan studies certainly do, there is little room for argument. The only question which can be raised concerns the relative fruitfulness of various definitions in use. It seems that using *leaders* as a synonym for elites and for managerial positions results in three names for the same phenomenon, and none for what is referred to here as *leadership*—that is, power based predominantly on personal characteristics, usually normative in nature.[43]

Applying the terms used throughout this book, the Michigan findings seem to suggest that *foremen in low-productivity divisions tend to be instrumental officers, whereas those in high-productivity divisions tend to be instrumental (formal) leaders.*[44] Neither of the two types of foreman controls the expressive activities of the workers; they differ in the degree to which they have power over instrumental activities. The low-productivity foremen, it seems, have to fall back on their official power; the high-productivity foremen have some degree of personal influence over the workers in instrumental matters. Almost all the findings reported in a summary statement of the Michigan studies seem to support our point (Kahn and Katz, 1953, pp. 612-28).

Using the terms applied here, the findings read: Foremen-leaders devote more time to directing their men than foremen-officers, while foremen-officers are more inclined to engage in non-supervisory duties (*ibid.*, p. 614). This may be because foremen whose influence is limited (the officers) attempt to increase productivity by engaging in it themselves. The second set of findings which seems to support

43. Bendix remarks: "The distinction between leadership and authority has been emphasized by Robert Bierstedt. 'A leader can only request, an authority can require. . . . Leadership depends upon the personal qualities of the leader in the situation in which he leads. In the case of authority, however, the relationship ceases to be personal. . . .'" (Bendix, 1960, p. 301). See Bierstedt (1954, pp. 71-72). The distinction between authority and leadership is an analytical one; one person may of course have both.

Bass has pointed out: "One cluster of definitions makes leadership synonymous with the importance of one's position. The concept *status* can be used to refer to the value of one's position and although status may produce leadership, it is distinguishable by observation and measurement from leadership and can be independent of leadership under specified conditions." (1960, p. 87) J. D. Thompson distinguishes between leadership and "headship" (1958, p. 1). This point has also been made by Nisbet, cited by Josephson (1952, p. 113); Gibb (1954, p. 882); and Selvin (1956, p. 12).

44. The difference between instrumental officers and instrumental leaders, which should be kept separate from the distinction between instrumental leaders and expressive leaders, can also be applied to the study by Leighton (1945, esp. pp. 81-89). Leighton distinguishes between two types of *administrative* staff, "stereotype-minded" (officers, in the terms used here) and "people-minded" (instrumental, not expressive, leaders). The expressive leaders are the informal leaders of the camp.

our point is that leaders tend to engage in general rather than in close supervision, whereas among officers the reverse is true. Perhaps this is because leaders, since they command more influence over their subjects, can attain greater internalization of their directives than officers; therefore they can rely more often on general rather than on close supervision.[45] Similarly, the fact that the high-production foremen rely less on punitive measures and more on normative control is an indication of their leadership power (35 per cent of the foremen in high-production sections, as against 50 per cent in low-production sections, were reported as "punitive" by their workers; *ibid.,* p. 621). Perhaps the most important finding, in the light of our earlier discussion of the leader's role in change situations, is that leaders were reported more often than officers as "teaching men *new* techniques and duties" (29 per cent of the foremen in high-production sections "teach the men new techniques and duties," as against 17 per cent in the low-production sections; *ibid.,* p. 621).

As we would have expected, formal leadership is more common and more effective in white-collar industries than in blue-collar industries. We suggested above that time spent on supervisory duties (as against nonsupervisory duties) is an indication of leadership by the foreman. The data for one white-collar and two blue-collar industries are shown in Table VII-1.

Table VII-1—Proportion of Time Spent in Supervision in Relation to Section Productivity

	SECTION PRODUCTIVITY	TIME SPENT IN SUPERVISION	
		50% or More	Less than 50%
Insurance Company:	High	75%	17%
	Low	33	59
Railroad:	High	55	31
	Low	25	61
Tractor Factory:	97-101%	69	31
	91-96	59	41
	86-90	48	52
	80-85	41	59
	50-79	54	46

Source: Kahn and Katz (1953, p. 615).

45. We would expect, according to our hypothesis, to find more remote supervision in white- than in blue-collar industries. This seems indeed to be the case. Argyris' study of supervision of bank employees shows that control is particularly limited in scope and remote (1954, pp. 56-63). Likert showed that close control over white-collar personnel is especially alienative (1958, pp. 41-50).

In all three industries foremen in high-productivity sections spent more time on supervision than those in low-productivity sections—that is, they exercised more power. Since there is no reason to believe that they had more official power, one may assume that they had more personal power or leadership. When highly productive sections are compared, we find that supervision in the white-collar industry occupies more time than in blue-collar industries, which suggests, if our premise is valid, that the foreman exercises more leadership in the white-collar industry.

There seems to be no relevant evidence on differences in the incidence of informal leadership (whether instrumental or expressive) between blue- and white-collar industries.

EXPRESSIVE ELITES IN UTILITARIAN ORGANIZATIONS—Foremen tend to be instrumental officers or leaders, but they are not usually in control of workers' expressive activities. Expressive leaders tend to be informal—usually an older worker, an experienced hand; sometimes a union steward.

The informal leadership of stewards points to a limitation of the widely used informal-formal dichotomy. Participants are often members of more than one organization at the same time, putting claims on them in the same situation. For example, a doctor may be both a member of the American Medical Association and a participant in an army. Workers participate concomitantly in labor unions and in factories. What is *informal* from the viewpoint of one organization may be the *formal* activity of another organization in the *same* interaction context.

As a rule, lower participants who have no concomitant power positions in other organizations are more likely to be informal expressive leaders than those who have such a position. Hence a steward is less likely to be the informal expressive leader of the workers than workers who have leadership potential but no union position. The steward has *some* of the problems of a foreman, since he must occasionally put instrumental pressures on the workers in his role as representative of the union (Sayles and Strauss, 1953, pp. 83-98; Peck, 1960, pp. 3-15). These pressures include demands to pay dues where there is no check-off system, to participate in meetings and other union activities, and the like. An especially powerful strain is put on the worker-steward expressive relationship when the union undertakes to support a productivity drive by management (Whyte *et al.,* 1955, pp. 149-66). But as a rule the steward's role has a smaller instrumental segment [46] than that of the foreman, so that although he is less likely than other workers to be the expressive leader, he is more likely to be one than the foreman (Jacobson, 1951).[47]

The human relations school trains the foreman to become a leader, implicitly following the traditional model of unidimensional leadership, widely accepted in political science and the study of history. It is assumed that there is one leader, and that he fulfills the various elite roles, including those that would be defined as instrumental and as expressive by Parsons, Bales, and their associates. The foreman is trained to direct the production activity of his team, control the pace and quality of its work, advise on technical matters, and represent management in general to the workers. At the same time he is trained to be close to his workers, their friend, a person to whom they can turn for advice and support in personal matters, and so on.

If the propositions presented above concerning the *dual*-elite structure of collectivities are valid, it follows that in order for the human relations line of training to be effective, a foreman would have to be recruited from the limited group of human beings who can effectively fulfill both roles. The rarity of this ability is reflected in the term chosen by Borgatta, Bales, and Couch to refer to such people: "great men" (1954, pp. 755-59). But there is no reason to believe that foremen are really recruited to any significant degree from this rare and highly sought-after group, nor does the human relations tradition recognize the need for such highly selective recruitment.

If the analysis based on the dual-elite model is valid, human relations training is likely to boomerang. Psychological and social tensions in the work situation will increase rather than diminish because the average foreman is encouraged to attempt what is for him the impossible: to wear two hats at the same time.

More specifically, one would expect something like the following to happen: Returning from a training period, finding that his instrumental position is relatively more assured, the foreman struggles to

46. The concept *role-segment* is used here and throughout this book as in Gross, Mason, and McEachern (1958, pp. 138-41).

47. The following agree-disagree statement is probably quite effective in measuring expressive leadership: "I feel free to discuss my personal problems with my union committeeman (or steward)." Seventy-three per cent of rank and file agreed; 17 per cent disagreed; 10 per cent were undecided (N=1251; Uphoff and Dunnette, 1956, p. 20).

gain expressive leadership. This puts him under pressure to grant concessions in the instrumental realm. Emphasizing productivity, reducing tardiness, and improving quality stand in the way of developing expressive relations. But giving unauthorized concessions to the workers tends to generate counterpressures from the line management, which emphasizes the instrumental effectiveness of the foreman.[48] The foreman, expected to please two masters, or rather his masters and his "servants," is caught in the conflicting role-prescriptions.[49] He cannot perform either of the two effectively. His level of dissatisfaction and personal strain increases, as does that of most persons who are in a role-conflict.[50] His relationship with the workers becomes strained both because he cannot be consistently expressive and because he tends to threaten the informal leader of the group (to the degree that one exists) by his endeavors to build up his own expressive leadership. Relations with higher levels of management become strained as the foreman becomes less effective instrumentally. In short, we suggest that it is quite likely that this kind of leadership training leads to results opposite to those expected by its advocates.[51]

48. Pelz (1952, p. 8) showed that foremen who were close to the workers "socially" were more inclined to side with the workers, whereas those who were less close were more likely to side with management.

49. Halpin (1954) showed that the same problem exists when bomber commanders attempt to follow a human relations policy with regard to their men. The subordinates value "consideration," whereas those higher in rank than the commanders emphasize "initiating structure." The terms *consideration* and *initiating structure,* central to the various Ohio leadership studies, come close to the concepts *expressive* and *instrumental* as they are used here.

50. Other sources of this role-conflict have been pointed out (see footnote 52, for references). For an excellent analysis of the relationship between authority and affection, in the father-son relationship as well as in other superior-subordinate relationships, see Homans (1951, pp. 244-48).

51. Argyris showed that the effective foreman limits himself to an instrumental control position, and that interfering with the "informal employee culture" (and, we would add, informal social relationships and expressive leadership) is dysfunctional from the viewpoint of the organization. "When made foremen, they are told by management that they will be considered successful to the extent that they maintain high production, low grievance rate, and low absenteeism. The foremen realize that the way to get the employees to behave in this manner is to maintain the informal employee culture, and not to behave in a way that violates the culture's norms. Thus, eighty-seven per cent of the foremen report that in order to be effective, they must strive hard (1) to keep everyone busy with work that (2) guarantees a fair take-home pay, (3) to distribute the easy and tough jobs fairly, *and (4) to leave the employees alone as much as possible.* In sort, a successful foreman, from the foremen's point of view, is neither directive nor is he the expert in human relations that some imply he ought to be. The employees agree with this logic. Eighty-seven per cent in A and B describe an 'understanding' foreman in terms similar to those above." (1959, p. 141. Italics supplied.)

There are two sets of findings which, if our interpretation of them is validated, support our point. First, there is considerable evidence that foremen are a highly dissatisfied group, under considerable psychological and social strain. This finding is usually interpreted as reflecting a decrease in the functions, rights, and authority of the foreman subsequent to unionization and the simultaneous extensive development of staff functions.[52] There is no doubt that these processes account for a considerable part of the increase in the foreman's role-strain.[53] It would be of interest to hold these conditions constant and compare, let us say in the same factory, the level of strain and the performance of foremen trained in human relations and untrained foremen. We would expect the role-strain of the trained men to be higher, not lower.

That this may be the case is suggested by the well-established "washout" effect that sets in after human relations training. Several evaluation studies have shown an "improvement" when attitudes of foremen at the beginning and at the end of a training course are compared. But when these attitudes are measured after the foremen return to their actual positions, the "improvements" tend to disappear. In some cases, the attitudes become even "worse" (by the criteria of the trainers) than they were when the training was initiated. Fleishman, Harris, and Burtt state:

An obvious discrepancy appeared when the results of this evaluation made in the work situation were compared with those obtained in the limited post-training evaluation made in the School. In spite of the actual increases in Consideration and decreases in Initiating Structure which appeared in the post-training evaluation, the Consideration behavior of the most recently trained group back in the plant was reported significantly lower than that of the untrained control group, and the trends in attitudes were in the same direction. (1955, p. 48; see also p. 92)[54]

This washout effect is usually explained by the fact that the foremen's superiors and subordinates have changed neither their behavior nor

52. See Bendix (1956, pp. 213, 215); Wray (1949, pp. 293-301); Mills (1956, pp. 87, 91); Greer (1955, pp. 1-4); Whyte and Gardner (1945, pp. 1-28); Dalton (1954, pp. 176-85); Slichter *et al.* (1945, pp. 155-61); and Charters (1952).

53. This concept is used here and throughout the book as in Goode (1960).

54. Jennings compared workers' evaluations of 52 foremen before training and six months after their training, and found that "the before and after evaluation recorded little change in relative descriptions of the items for the foremen as a group. Before and after evaluation of what best described the foremen correlated highly (+.62)." (1954, pp. 30-31) The "after" measure appears to have been taken after the washout effect had been completed.

their expectations of him.[55] Hence, when the foreman returns to his position, he is under pressure to return to his old patterns of inter- action. Training down the line or simultaneous training of all ranks is recommended as a solution (Fleishman, 1951, p. 8). The effective- ness of these training procedures has not yet been demonstrated.

It is quite possible, however, that the washout effect is in part a consequence of the role-strains discussed above, generated when a foreman tries to carry out two partially incompatible leadership roles simultaneously. Measuring role-strains before and after a down-the-line human relations training program might shed some light on this alternative hypothesis.

Training which encourages foremen to strive for both instru- mental and expressive leadership generates strains in still another way. The effective operation of a group requires not only the existence of the two types of elites, but a certain amount of cooperation between the two. When the foreman strives to develop expressive leadership, the position of the existing informal expressive leader, if there is one, is threatened, and he will probably fight back. Since he is not required to represent management and since, as a rule, he does not have to put any instrumental pressures on the workers, the informal leader is likely to gain or maintain control of the expressive elite position.[56] Furthermore, it is fair to assume that if he has not been alienated before, such a power struggle is likely to alienate him; if he is already alienated, his alienation will increase. In short, it seems likely that training for foremen would be more effective if it sought only to change foremen from instrumental officers to instrumental leaders, pointing out to them the alienating nature of close super- vision and helping them to recognize and accept the dual leadership structure of collectivities.

Implicit recognition of the difficulties involved in expecting the

55. On the artificial atmosphere of the classroom and its consequences see Haire (1956, pp. 102-22); see also *Leadership and Supervision: A Survey of Research Findings* (1955, p. 4) and Fleishman, Harris, and Burtt (1955, p. 61). Mann and Dent (1954, pp. 28ff.) supplied considerable data to show that the behavior of a supervisor, in particular his approach to his subordinates, is considerably affected by the approach of his superior to him. Cf. Levenson (1961).

56. Leaders who impose tasks on the group are more likely to be deposed than leaders who direct groups toward tasks the group has chosen. This supports an assertion that instrumental formal leaders, who impose the organizational demands, are more likely to lose their leadership status (or not gain it) than informal expressive leaders, who usually lead "self-chosen" activities. The relationship be- tween leadership stability and the imposed versus chosen nature of the task was explored by Katz, Blau, Brown, and Strodtbeck (1957).

foreman to develop expressive leadership can be seen in the effort of some industries to institutionalize the expressive leadership role in positions other than that of foreman—for example, counselor, therapeutic interviewer, social worker, personnel officer, and the like. The development of such positions was both recommended by, and part of, the well-known Hawthorne project reported by Roethlisberger and Dickson (1939). Although such bifurcation of instrumental and expressive roles is undoubtedly functional, it does not follow automatically that expressive officers appointed by management will assume formal expressive leadership. There are at least four factors working against such a development: (1) expressive positions are held by specialists (staff) who are likely to develop specific and not diffuse relationships with the workers; (2) these specialists are thought of as representatives of management, and really are to some degree inhibited in their expressive efforts by the instrumental policy of management; (3) their social background is often too different from that of the workers; (4) they have only limited opportunities for interaction with the workers.

The generalization that foremen can rarely combine expressive with instrumental leadership has one important exception, which occurs among workers on assembly lines (Walker and Guest, 1952). Here the role of instrumental elites has been considerably reduced, because work is highly routinized and hence requires less instrumental control, and the pace of the work is determined by the pace of the line, not the foreman. The foreman becomes, in part, a general assistant and liaison man to the supply department, maintenance men, and repair personnel (Guest, 1960). Blau discussed the role of the foreman at the assembly line in the following terms:

But how could foremen become identified with the workers in their section and still discharge their managerial responsibilities? Walker, Guest, and Turner argue that a successful foreman must play a dual role, representing both his men and the management. It may also be, however, that assembly-line production itself has a bearing on the problem. The unrelenting movement of the conveyor constrains workers to a certain output, relieving the foreman of responsibility for their productivity. But of all his duties, it is only the exercise of control over subordinates that benefits from social distance. Thus, the fact that the conveyor system substitutes in part for the foreman as a mechanism of control makes it possible for him to identify himself with the workers without impeding operations. (1957, pp. 59-60)[57]

57. Cf. Walker, Guest, and Turner (1956, ch. 3). Simpson (1959, pp. 192-96) supplies evidence to support Blau's thesis.

The foreman's opportunity to develop expressive leadership is increased in the new technological situation, although, as Blau continues to point out, he is not relieved completely from other control responsibilities, such as supervising quality and keeping the line manned. He is in a better position to become an expressive leader than a regular foreman is, but in competition with an informal leader he would still be likely to lose.

A foreman can also develop expressive leadership through giving up enforcement of management's regulations and directives. Sykes analyzed this process among prison guards, referring to it as "corruption of authority" (1956, pp. 259-63). He pointed out that the guards, under the pressure of constant and close contact with inmates, may lose much of their commitment to the collective norms of the organization they are expected to represent, and tend to accept many of the values and norms of the inmates. This process is not limited to the prison.[58] Foremen, socially isolated from higher echelons of management, similar in social background to the workers, usually ex-workers themselves—in some cases even members of the same union as the workers—tend to become "corrupted" in the same manner as guards. Sometimes foremen or their assistants even become informal "upward" representatives of the workers rather than formal "downward" representatives of management, using their contacts with management and their inside information to support rather than control their men (see, e.g., Roethlisberger and Dickson, 1939, pp. 38-43). Under such conditions the foreman's acceptance by the workers naturally increases; he may even become their expressive leader.

Finally, expressive leadership, whether formal or informal, may not develop at all in a utilitarian organization. Contrary to the widely accepted image created by some of the literature on industrial relations, solidary relations on the job are found among about a quarter of the workers (for evidence, see below, p. 269). The workers' integration into a utilitarian organization is in many cases only partial, limited to instrumental activities, the "missing" expressive functional requirements being fulfilled in external (off-the-job) collectivities, such as social life in the community or in the union. In terms of leadership, this means that no participant is an expressive leader,

58. Sykes (1956a, fn. to p. 103) pointed out that his analysis of the role of the guard applies to the role of the foreman as well.

that expressive needs of the organization and of the workers are satisfied outside the work situation and are controlled by external expressive leaders.

HIERARCHY OF ELITES—We saw that the hierarchy of elites is most effective when it is congruent with the hierarchy of goals (or goals and means), so that the elite directly serving the highest goal will dominate, and the elites serving the "lower" goals (or means) will be subordinate. In utilitarian organizations it is functional for the instrumental managerial elite to subordinate expressive elites, whether they exist in the various staff positions (e.g., personnel department), as "corrupted" foremen, or in the form of expressive informal elites. The dominance of the instrumental elite assures that "social harmony" will remain a goal secondary to production. What the actual power structure of utilitarian organizations is has yet to be established. Special attention will have to be paid to the expressive-instrumental role segregation of elites, a subject studied mainly in small groups but largely unexplored on the organizational level.

Summarizing this section, we can say that the elite structure of utilitarian organizations falls between that of coercive and normative organizations. Workers are better integrated into the organizational collectivity than inmates are, but less well integrated than "members." Utilitarian organizations tend to control the instrumental activities of the workers, employing instrumental officers or instrumental formal leaders. Expressive leadership tends to be informal, with the exception of situations in which the organizational representative does not have to carry out instrumental supervision or neglects it in order to win expressive leadership away from informal leaders.

SUMMARY

This chapter has examined the relationship between compliance structure and the distribution of power in the organization. This inquiry, in turn, is related to an examination of the degree to which the organization as a collectivity is integrated in the economic, administrative, and solidary spheres.

Coercive organizations have a split collectivity; that is, inmates tend to develop a separate subcollectivity which penetrates into many spheres, though their success in separating themselves from the rest of the organization is much more marked in the expressive sphere than it is in the instrumental one. The distribution of power follows suit. Inmate activities are controlled to a large degree by informal inmate leaders and not by the organizational elites. "Right guys" and "heroes" supply the expressive leadership, while "merchants," "fixers," and escape-"engineers" constitute the inmate instrumental elites.

In normative organizations, on the other hand, there are few boundaries between lower participants and higher ones; the organization is a highly integrated collectivity. The organizational elites lead the lower participants; informal leaders tend to collaborate with these elites, to be co-opted by them, or to be absorbed into organizational positions.

In utilitarian organizations, alienated employees tend to develop a more segregated subcollectivity than do committed employees; but even highly alienated employees are usually less segregated than inmates, and even highly committed employees are less thoroughly integrated than members of normative organizations. The elite structure follows suit. Alienated employees tend to have informal expressive and instrumental leaders, but follow the direction of organizational instrumental officers within the limits of the contractual relationship. Committed employees tend to accept organizational leadership in instrumental matters, but as a rule do not accept organizational direction in expressive matters. The implications of these statements for the human relations approach were exposed.

Relationships among elites and their consequences for organizational effectiveness were examined for each type of compliance structure. In normative organizations it is functional for the expressive elite to subordinate the instrumental one; this seems indeed to be the case in the Jesuit order, the Episcopalian church, and in some labor unions, but not in other normative organizations, particularly egalitarian churches. In utilitarian organizations, high productivity is associated with subordination of the expressive elite by the instrumental elite, and cooperation between the two. In coercive organizations the antagonism between organizational and informal elites makes for an unstable relationship instead of a clear pattern of subordination.

VIII

COMPLIANCE AND ELITES REVISITED

Formally, we are studying the different roles played by organizational elites and the relationships among various elites in organizations which differ in their compliance structures in order to establish the correlates of compliance. That is, we hypothesized that compliance differences correlate with many other significant organizational variables; here we review data on their relationship to one such set, the attributes of the power structure, the leadership, the elites. Substantively, differences among elites closely suggest divergent organizations); another in which the organizational officialdom has neither a chance nor need to lead the lower participants in order to the organization's mission will not be carried out (in normative organization); another in which the organizational officialdom has neither a chance nor need to lead the lower participants in order to effectively discharge its coercive duties; and, finally, one in which organizational leadership is often limited to instrumental matters—an arrangement which may be quite sufficient for most utilitarian goals. In addition, there is a practically unlimited number of intermediate types. (For additional discussion, other than that in the preceding chapter, see Etzioni, 1965, pp. 688-698, and 1959, pp. 476-487; Hall, 1972, pp. 48, 198, 217, and 244; and Schurmann, 1966, pp. 165, 224, 310, and 313).

New studies illustrate how the conceptual distinction between expressive and instrumental elites and their relative positions can be operationalized. We first examine two studies which see each elite as varying in its ratio of instrumental orientation to expressive orientation. One study ties these differences to the degree to which the organization is utilitarian; the other, to religious and administrative effectiveness. A second group of studies deals with the two kinds of leadership in college organizations and tests the hypothesis that expressive leadership is needed for normative education while instrumental leadership suffices for cognitive education. In a third approach, the same question is explored both in a dual (normative-coercive) organization and in a coercive organization.

In common parlance and in social science literature, frequent reference is made to "a" leader or "the" leader, assuming a single top post. Theoretical analysis and some re-examination of data suggest structural pressures to form two separate leadership roles in most organizations and emphasize that it is important that the relationship between these two be compatible with the organizational goals and compliance structure (pp. 157-190, and Etzioni, 1965). Elaboration of this thesis, and some data in its support, is presented later in this chapter. The chapter closes with an extension of our previous discussion of the role of charisma in normative organizations.

INSTRUMENTAL–EXPRESSIVE RATIOS IN VARIOUS ELITE POSITIONS

The Instrumental–Expressive Ratio Varies by Hierarchical Loci and with "Utilitarianness"

Concepts are relatively easy to define. But they gain a value for scientific study only when empirical indicators can be found to test the propositions utilizing the concepts when the differences they designate are intellectually or theoretically significant. The twin concept of instrumental–expressive leadership is central to our analysis. Robert Rossel (and several authors to be reviewed subsequently) both operationalizes this concept and shows its fruitfulness.

Rossel's study of eight business organizations (1970; see also Rossel, 1966, 1971, and n.d.) uses data from the Yale Technology Project files prepared by Charles R. Walker and his associates. In order to determine the leadership styles employed by the organizations' managements, Rossel analyzed the contents of verbatim transcripts of open-ended interviews with 297 top managers, middle managers, top supervisors, and lower supervisors. "The content categories focused on a set of 49 frequently occurring cliches. . . . Examples of categories are such words as red tape, cooperation, hard work, teamwork, practicality, and efficiency" (1970, p. 307).

The patterns of covariation in the use of these cliches were factor-analyzed. This resulted in a reduction of the 49 categories to a "set of independent conceptual variables representing clusters of categories with high common variance" (*ibid*). Two "modal conceptions of leadership" (*ibid., p. 311*) were found; as it turned out, they fitted the expressive-instrumental distinction. At the instrumental pole, Rossel found categories such as "quality of product," "efficiency," "responsibility," "morale"; at the expressive pole, "reasonable expectations," "leadership skills," "getting along," "anti-authoritarian," and the like.

As each respondent received a standardized factor score on each of the factors extracted, Rossel was able to divide the respondents, on the basis of the distinction found by the factor analysis, into two groups, the one more expressively oriented, the other more instrumentally. Sample responses from members of the instrumental group include:

The main thing in this business is production. And the only way you can do production is to have at the helm a production man. Now take our plant manager. He's a good man, but he's not a production man. You must realize that books are all right in their place, but apart from what we learn in books, you never learn production except by producing. (case 055, Rossel (1970), p. 311)

My biggest and most important job is to see that the production schedule is met . . . I have to maintain the discipline of the department, check to see that the efficiency of the men is up. (case 220, Rossel (1970), pp. 311-12)

I have to check my absentees and lateness to make sure that my discipline doesn't fall down. (case 220, Rossel (n.d.), p. 14)

Rossel also scored as instrumental stress on work flow rather than workers' happiness, "pride in work," and the like. Sample instrumental responses follow:

I . . . feel that we built (the organization) up to a point where people were willing to pay a premium price for our produce, and that was because people took pride in their work. Now the foreman's job in production and their responsibility for quality has increased due to the fact that his men have never been implanted with that respect for quality which they had in the old days. (case 125, Rossel (1970) p. 312)

We always get the idea that those guys are sitting up there in the front office with their thinking caps on and everything is going along nice and okay, and they feel that, well, "We've got to get something started up." So there's never a dull moment. If those fellas had more to do, they wouldn't come out with those silly things that they do come out with. But you can't get away from it. Without production we wouldn't have anything in this world. Production is the greatest thing we have. (case 055, Rossel (n.d.), p. 15)

On the expressive side, Rossel included those concerned with avoiding the arbitrary use of authority and with not putting unreasonable demands on people and those anxious about hostilities with or among workers that might slow down production and inhibit achievement of the organization's goals:

As a foreman I'm the one who issues all the orders to the men. It's a funny thing but when I think of those words, "issue orders," I am somewhat amused because I hardly ever issue orders. The more I think of it, I never order anyone to do anything. (case 156, Rossel (1970), p. 312)

W. and D. lack some of the basic traits of good managers. They both issue direct orders, don't take any excuses and don't listen to reason. (case 195, Rossel (1970) p. 312)

I don't enjoy putting that kind of pressure on people and I shouldn't have to. (case 195, Rossel (1970), p. 312)

Reading these quotes helps one to see why some responses were classified as instrumental and some as expressive and to appreciate the likelihood that people who perceive their roles so differently will also act differently, although there is, of course, no simple relationship between people's self-concepts and people's behavior.

After having classified his respondents in this way, Rossel proceeded to ask for the distribution of instrumental and expressive leadership over the different organizational positions. Are those close to the workers more expressive than others? How is one's position in the hierarchy of the business organization related to his style of leadership? Rossel found that, on the average, top management was most strongly instrumentally oriented. (See Table VIII-1. Mean positive scores indicate the presence and the extent of instrumental orientations, negative scores indicate expressive orientations.) Second in instrumental orientation were the immediate supervisors; the two middle layers, however, scored slightly more expressive than instrumental. Differences were significant at the .10 level.

Had Rossel stopped his analysis at this point, he would have established (a) that the twin concepts can be operationalized; (b) that, all four levels taken together, management are more instrumental than expressive in their role conceptions, as one would expect (p. 189); (c) that the immediate supervisors are instrumental, not

Table VIII-1—Instrumental and Expressive Orientations by Position and Required Labor Commitment

REQUIRED LABOR COMMITMENT	TOP MANAGEMENT		MIDDLE MANAGEMENT		TOP SUPERVISION		LOWER SUPERVISION		ROW MEANS
	Mean	N	Mean	N	Mean	N	Mean	N	
High	1.25	9	.09	27	.00	27	−.17	54	.29
Low	−.17	6	−.26	32	−.02	30	.38	54	−.02
Column means	.54		−.09		−.01		.11		

	F-Ratio	Degrees of Freedom	Significance Level	Omega
Position	2.39	3	$p < .10$	.17
Required labor commitment	3.09	1	$p < .10$	.09
Interaction	5.40	3	$p < .01$	.58

Source: Rossel (1970), p. 313. Reprinted with the permission of *Administrative Science Quarterly*.

expressive leaders (pp. 182ff.). However, Rossel took his study a significant step further by introducing another independent variable, the extent to which an organization requires the commitment of its members in order to operate efficiently. This is very much in line with the general idea which underlies the compliance theory: Prisons can keep their inmates locked up, even when the inmates are not very happy about it; but schools cannot, under coercive circumstances, transmit values. Pyramids can be built under relatively alienating labor conditions, because ferrying stones can be readily supervised; but building a computer entails a much higher degree of self-supervision and requires greater internalization of production norms. This, in turn, demands a much less alienating compliance structure (pp. 9ff.). Thus, Rossel hypothesized that management's leadership styles would be more expressive, the more commitment was required on the part of the lower participants (*ibid.*, p. 307).

In order to measure what he calls "Saliency of Labor Commitment" (SLC), Rossel developed a four-item scale, consisting of (a) the extent to which, in the particular organization, the worker controls the quality of his work; (b) the quantity of his production; (c) the degree to which the technical arrangement of the work requires interaction among workers; and (d) the need of the organization to adapt to a changing and uncertain environment. The greater these four factors, Rossel hypothesized, the more important it would be for the organization to keep its workers' commitment at a relatively high level.

All eight organizations were rated on the SLC scale, and an overall "Index of Required Labor Commitment" was computed. As the findings reported in Table VIII-1 show, only on one level, that of lower supervision, did the leadership style and the SLC vary in line with Rossel's hypothesis. The higher the required labor commitment, the more expressive was the lower supervisors' leadership. However, there seems to be no difference for the top management; and middle management and top management, according to Rossel's data, are more instrumentally oriented when high labor commitment is required and less so when the organization's SLC score is low. Furthermore, the row means of Table VIII-1 show that high SLC tends to be associated with a more instrumental leadership style, rather than with expressive.

In conclusion, it is only at the lowest level of the organization's chain of command that a high requirement of labor commitment affects the strategies of leadership in the expected direction. Rossel offers an intricate set of reasons for this finding which cannot be repeated here. One point, however, might be emphasized. The way Rossel derives his SLC index—by adding the scores for the three "technological" items and multiplying them by the score for required adaptiveness to external pressures—assigns much weight to external, extra-organizational factors. These factors are, as a rule, more strongly perceived by the top and middle management than by the supervisory level. Conversely, internal factors—such as the degree of autonomy the worker experiences in the production process—can be expected to affect more the leadership styles of those close to the workers than the leadership strategies of the top managers. It might be better to separate these two indicators in future studies.

However, the data at hand do support the compliance expectation on the single most important point: The expectation was that the immediate supervisors—not higher ranks—would divide clearly between expressive and instrumental leadership (pp. 182). And, indeed, on this level, the SLC did correlate as expected: In high SLC organizations the lower supervisors' mean leadership score was —.17, i.e., expressive, while the score of the low SLC was .38, i.e., instrumental.

The Expressive-Instrumental Ratio in 120 Churches

The study reviewed next shows, as does Rossel's, that elite roles can be characterized as more expressive or more instrumental, a finding of especial interest because the study method is radically different from the one just visited. It also casts further light on a core hypothesis of the compliance theory, namely, that "the effective elite hierarchy" is one in which the structure of the elites and the hierarchy of goals (as goals and means) are congruent" (p. 157). In the case of effective normative organizations this would suggest the superiority of expressive elites, at least in the lower reaches of the hierarchy.

The study, by James B. Ashbrook (1966, 1967), covers 120 Protestant Churches in upstate New York. It is outstanding in that it represents, in dependent samples of both, the elites and the lower participants (rather than relying on questions asked one of the two to characterize the other). 117 ministers and 534 lay people completed three questionnaires in 1963, at 65% and 91% response rates, respectively.

The first measurement, entitled "Experience in the Ministry," is a self-rating questionnaire on a minister's perception of his career. Ashbrook asked ministers about their degree of satisfaction with various tasks such as "preaching," "counseling," "administering," and "ecumenical involvement" (the last defined as "activity related to councils of churches in which most denominations participate" (Ashbrook, 1967, p. 7).

The second measurement, the "Leader Behavior Description Questionnaire" developed at Ohio State (see Stogdill and Coons, 1957), was completed by the lay members. It is designed to measure specific attributes which reveal "how a leader goes about leading." Its items are regarded as descriptive rather than evaluative of leader behavior. This questionnaire consists of 11 subscales such as "tolerance of uncertainty" (10 items indicating ways in which the leader "responds to uncertainty and defeat in relation to group process and decision-making") and "role assumption" (10 items pointing toward "leader competence in taking initiative and necessary action, as well as maintaining his leadership position").

The third measurement, called "organizational criteria" and designed to measure effectiveness, is based on evaluation of the minister by the lay members and on objective measures such as size of church membership and attendance at worship.

Ashbrook classified all questionnaire items on theoretical grounds into expressive and instrumental ones (see Ashbrook 1967, p. 10). Ashbrook then factor-analyzed the responses to all three questionnaires in order to find out if they supported the theoretical classification. His findings reveal that both task satisfactions and leader behaviors could be distinguished as expressive or instrumental. Five factors emerged, two for task satisfactions and three for leader behaviors. On the instrumental side, a minister's satisfaction from "ecumenical involvement" showed a factor loading of .82; its loading on the expressive factor was less than .20. This factor also included "community involvement satisfaction" and "denominational satisfaction." The expressive side dominated a minister's "preaching satisfaction," which showed an expressive factor loading of .79 but less than .20 on the instrumental factor. Similarly, for leader behaviors, "leader role assumption" had a factor loading of .75 on the instrumental factor that also included leader "initiation of structure" (.77) and "leader production emphasis" (.73), though it also included "leader persuasiveness" at .77, contrary to the prediction (see Ashbrook, 1967, p. 14). The items had a loading above .30 on the expressive leadership factor. The latter was dominated by "leader tolerance of uncertainty" (.79) and "leader tolerance of member freedom" (.75), neither of which had a loading of above .20 on the instrumental minister-competence factor. Of the five factors, only one combined instrumental and expressive elements about equally.

Having empirically confirmed the conceptual distinction between instrumental and expressive ministers' behaviors and feelings of satisfaction with their tasks, Ashbrook next averaged the scores for all ministers on each item to determine whether ministers were likely to behave expressively rather than instrumentally, as we would predict for effective churches, and to gain greater satisfaction from expressive rather than instrumental tasks. Table VIII-2 shows the results.

Taking the leader behavior subscales first, the data reveal that where statistically significant differences were found, expressive behavior predominated. "Consideration of persons" was given far more

Table VIII-2—Distribution and Significance of Task Satisfactions and Leader Behavior Descriptions[a]

Task Satisfaction of Ministers

	EXPRESSIVE			INSTRUMENTAL	
	Mean	S.D.		Mean	S.D.
Worship	73.06	18.66**	Calling	61.02	22.37
Preaching	66.92	20.04**	Administration	52.52	19.06
Counseling	64.38	21.75**	Denomination	54.42	21.94
Teaching	65.06	18.56**	Ecumenical	53.58	21.14
			Community	55.92	20.71

Leader Behavior Description (Given by Lay Members)

	Mean	S.D.		Mean	S.D.
Persuasion	39.52	3.75	Initiation of structure	39.77	3.23
Tolerance uncertainty	37.63	3.66	Role assumption	40.13	3.62
Tolerance freedom	39.44	3.07	Representation	39.72	3.04
Consideration	41.30	3.16**	Predictive accuracy	37.40	3.16**
Integration	38.80	4.26	Demand reconciliation	39.98	4.24
			Production emphasis	34.54	3.94**

a ** .01 level of significance.
Source: Ashbrook (1967), p. 16 (table slightly edited).

often as a description of how the leader "goes about leading" than "predictive accuracy" (based on a five-item scale), and "indicating the leader's ability to sense accurately what is happening and what will likely happen," i.e., reality testing versus "production emphasis" (based on 10 items measuring the "pressure of the leader on the group to get work done") (ibid., p. 8).

With regard to task satisfactions, the differences are even more pronounced. Table VIII-2 shows that ministers indicated more satisfaction with the expressive tasks of leading worship, preaching, teaching, and counseling than with the instrumental tasks of calling, administration, and denominational, ecumenical, and community involvement. Only calling, defined as "contacting individuals to relate the church to them and them to the church," is not significantly less satisfying than the expressive tasks. It seems that calling may be as expressive as instrumental; it did not load highly on either of the two factors. Thus, Ashbrook's findings support the empirical status of the distinction between instrumental and expressive leadership roles and strengthen the proposition that in normative organizations expressive leadership and related tasks will take preference over instrumental ones.

Ashbrook did not directly test our proposition that effective normative organizations require a superior expressive elite, apparently because there was only one minister in many of the churches he studied; but he did test it indirectly by comparing the organizational outcomes of churches whose ministers scored differently in their expressive versus instrumental measures. The relationship between various indicators of leadership behavior and various criteria of effectiveness, as far as the relations studied turned out to be significant, are shown in Table VIII-3.

Table VIII-3—Leadership Behavior and Effectiveness of Protestant Ministers*

CRITERION	LOW EFFECTIVENESS			MODERATE EFFECTIVENESS			HIGH EFFECTIVENESS			Total
	L.B. N	Other N	χ^2	L.B. N	Other N	χ^2	L.B. N	Other N	χ^2	χ^2
(1) High Expressive and High Instrumental Behavior										
Effectiveness	0	20	3.33	5	59	2.33	12	21	12.69	18.35
Results	2	20	.79	12	39	3.32	3	41	2.10	6.21
Adequacy	1	19	1.46	7	62	1.06	9	19	6.99	9.51
Achievement	0	26	4.42	5	63	2.82	12	11	26.27	33.51
Benevolence	3	40	1.98	5	37	.20	9	23	4.76	6.94
(2) High Expressive and Low Instrumental Behavior										
Adequacy	3	17	5.68	2	67	.30	0	28	1.25	7.23
Achievement	3	23	3.36	1	67	1.31	1	22	.00	4.67
(3) Low Expressive and High Instrumental Behavior										
Success	4	13	3.97	5	74	.79	2	19	.00	4.76
Achievement	6	20	5.73	2	66	3.33	3	20	.36	9.42
(4) Low Expressive and Low Instrumental Behavior										
Effectiveness	8	12	34.45	0	64	4.70	0	33	2.41	41.56
Results	2	20	.17	6	45	1.93	0	44	3.23	5.33
Adequacy	7	13	34.84	1	68	3.15	0	28	2.05	30.04
Success	6	11	21.67	2	77	2.30	0	21	1.54	25.51

df = 1; χ^2 = 2.706, p < .10; 3.841. p < .05; 6.635, p < .01
* The table shows to what degree the overall distribution of ministers over the various effectiveness criteria deviates from the distribution, over the same criteria, of ministers in the four leadership behavior categories. "L.B.N" refers to the number of ministers in the leadership behavior category under examination, "Other N" to the remaining cases in the respective distribution.
Source: Ashbrook (1967), Tables 2, 7, 8, 5 (tables edited).

Ashbrook examined four different combinations of instrumental and expressive behavior:

1. *High Expressive and High Instrumental Behavior* (*17 cases*): On four of the five criteria of effectiveness, ministers falling into this category ranked significantly higher than their colleagues (the fifth category, "Results," is weakened by its dependence on ministers' self-ranking).

2. *High Expressive and Low Instrumental Behavior* (*5 cases*): Only two criteria yielded significant results; on these, a disproportionate number of the ministers in this category displayed only low effectiveness.

3. *Low Expressive and High Instrumental Behavior* (*11 cases*): On one criterion, these ministers' distribution differed significantly from their colleagues; a disproportionate number fell in the low-effectiveness category.

4. *Low Expressive and Low Instrumental Behavior* (*8 cases*): On three counts, these ministers ranked significantly below average; the weak effect of "Results" may again be attributed to the influence of self-rating.

Comparing these results with our hypothesis, the findings with respect to categories 4 and 1 are in line with our assumption that effectiveness varies with the degree of expressiveness of leader behavior. However, as these cases do not discriminate between expressive and instrumental behavior, these results can only lend plausibility to our elite hierarchy proposition. Category 3 is more important in that it shows that effectiveness tends to be low where expressiveness is low even if a leader ranks high on instrumental behavior. On the other hand, Category 2 does not fit our hypothesis; we would have expected that high expressiveness would compensate, in terms of effectiveness, for low instrumental behavior.

Ashbrook's data, however, are not quite conclusive. First, the fact that there are only five cases in the second category is in itself a significant finding, suggesting that the combination of high expressive and low instrumental behavior is not very likely to occur. Second, Ashbrook's analysis of the effectiveness problem is based on only 48 cases; these represent only the extreme ends of the leadership behavior distributions, leaving out the 69 "moderate" cases. In order to test our hypothesis properly, we would have to establish the overall relationship between the various criteria of effectiveness on the one hand and expressive and instrumental behavior on the other. We assume that expressive behavior would, on the whole, be better able to explain the total variation in the effectiveness scores than instrumental behavior. Unfortunately, the way Ashbrook presents his data precludes any recalculation to this effect.

We turn now to Ashbrook's findings about member involvement. Again, Ashbrook distinguished between instrumental and expressive activities, this time the activities being those of church members rather than ministers. Classifying involvement as "moral commitment" or "calculative involvement," he then tested several hypotheses about the consequences for organizational effectiveness of different types of involvement in the different types of activity, effectiveness again being measured by the same "consequence criteria."

As no known testing instrument dealt with calculative involvement and moral commitment in expressive or instrumental organizational activities, Ashbrook developed a questionnaire entitled *A Picture of Your Local Church*. To do so, he initially postulated two dimensions. One was regarded as reflecting primarily instrumental activity, and "its attributes consisted of items such as constituency support in specific church objectives . . . and building and equipment in reasonably good repair" (Ashbrook, 1966, p. 401). The other was regarded as reflecting primarily expressive activity; "its attributes consisted of items such as closeness of relationship among members, fellowship . . . , and wholehearted participation in the organization." The questionnaire consisted of 32 pre-tested questions, all but two of which were Likert-type items with respondents indicating degree of agreement. For administrative reasons, Ashbrook's findings are based upon a sample analysis of a total of 104 questionnaires from 59 of the 120 churches.

Ashbrook, to adjust for response bias towards the ideal, computed a hierarchical factor solution to extract from the factor dimensions a general factor that "leaves the other factors more independent of each other and therefore more specific" (*ibid.,* p. 402). Eight such specific factor dimensions remained. Four of these Ashbrook classified as expressive activities: "fellowship life" (a group of items reflecting "caring, meaningful interaction of member with member in the church"), "interest in church life," "involvement satisfaction," and "self-involvement" (items about taking part in church life for "moral reasons"). Classified as instrumental activities were the other four: "organizational encouragement" (items indicating member encouragement with organizational developments), "responsibility climate" ("with items describing an atmosphere in which members assume responsibility in the church"), "financial participation," and "property responsibility." These factor dimensions were intercorrelated and themselves factor-analyzed; the three factors that emerged, as shown in Table VIII-4, supported the expressive-instrumental classification in general.

Table VIII-4—Expressive and Instrumental Organizational Activity, Means and Standard Deviations

EXPRESSIVE ACTIVITY	Mean	s.d.[a]
Interested in church	23.56	2.22
Involvement satisfaction	24.46	1.72**
Fellowship life	23.51	1.87
Self-involvement	21.45	1.39**
INSTRUMENTAL ACTIVITY		
Organizational encouragement	19.28	3.20**
Responsibility climate	20.33	2.84**
Financial participation	23.39	3.32
Property responsibility	23.27	1.73

Note.—To determine activity scores, items with the highest loadings on each factor were added. Additional items to be scored were found by subtracting out response set items, which maximized the contribution of the specific factor while minimizing that of others. The total of added and subtracted items represented the separate factor activity scores. By this method factor scores constitute an averaging of different response set patterns so as to reduce bias.

[a] ** .01 level of significance.

Source: Ashbrook (1966), p. 408. Reprinted with the permission of the *Journal for the Scientific Study of Religion.*

Comparisons between antecedent attributes of member involvement and effectiveness-consequence criteria measures were made by using the same cell-square contingency method (of testing contributions to prediction) used in Ashbrook's examination of ministerial leadership. Ashbrook found that the expressive organizational activities scored significantly higher than the instrumental ones. The mean scores for the expressive activity labeled Involvement Satisfaction were significantly higher than the scores for such instrumental activities as Organizational Involvement and Responsibility Climate.

Finally, Ashbrook analyzed the impact of member involvement on the effectiveness of various kinds of organizational activities, using the same method and the same criteria of effectiveness just reviewed. The results can be summarized as follows (see also Table VIII-5):

1. *High member involvement in both expressive and instrumental activities:* No significant predictions were found. As to the number of cases in this category, Ashbrook reports only that it is "small" (1966, p. 412).

2. *High member involvement in expressive activities, low member involvement in instrumental activities (11 cases):* The table shows that effectiveness tends to be lower than on the average, both with respect to expressive and instrumental criteria. This finding parallels

what was found with regard to high expressive and low instrumental leadership behavior (see p. 201).

3. *Low member involvement in expressive activities, high member involvement in instrumental activities (8 cases):* This combination is associated with higher "organizational achievement," "results of ministry," and "benevolence." However, the *chi* squares are significant only at the .10 level.

4. *Low member involvement in both expressive and instrumental activities (13 cases):* On two effectiveness criteria, predictions reached only a .10 level of significance. Moreover, these two predictions were inconsistent, pointing to moderate ministerial effectiveness and low organizational achievement. Furthermore, ministerial effectiveness is an expressive criterion, while organizational achievement is an instrumental one. We would have expected the impact of calculative involvement to be negative on the expressive dimension, not on the instrumental one.

Table VIII-5—Expressive and Instrumental Church Member Involvement and Their Effectiveness

CRITERION	LOW EFFECTIVENESS			MODERATE EFFECTIVENESS			HIGH EFFECTIVENESS			Total
	L.B. N	Other N	χ^2	L.B. N	Other N	χ^2	L.B. N	Other N	χ^2	χ^2
High Involvement in Expressive and Instrumental Activities										
There are no significant predictions.										
High Involvement in Expressive Activities, Low Involvement in Instrumental Activities										
Results	5	17	4.57	4	47	.13	2	42	1.22	5.92
Adequacy	5	15	5.72	4	65	1.06	2	26	.15	6.93
Achievement	6	20	5.73	3	65	2.00	2	21	.13	7.86
Low Involvement in Expressive Activities, High Involvement in Instrumental Activities										
Results	1	21	.17	1	50	1.91	6	38	3.19	5.27
Achievement	2	24	.29	2	66	1.62	4	19	4.04	5.95
Benevolence	1	42	1.38	2	40	.26	5	27	3.88	5.52
Low Involvement in Expressive Activities, Low Involvement in Instrumental Activities										
Effectiveness	0	20	2.50	11	53	2.40	2	31	.86	5.76
Achievement	6	20	3.77	4	64	1.88	3	20	.07	5.72

Source: Ashbrook (1966), pp. 411–2 (table edited).
For note see Table VIII-3.

As Ashbrook himself concludes, "the relationship of intensity of member involvement to consequences was not decisive and appeared more varied than hypothesized" (1966, p. 414). He acknowledges some methodological problems, and we would reiterate the point made earlier about "extreme case" analysis. In this case, the number of members morally committed to expressive activities and calculatively involved in instrumental activities (11) is greater than the number calculatively involved in expressive activities and morally committed to instrumental activities (8), which is consistent with the finding in Table VIII-2 that the expressive organizational activities were scored significantly higher than the instrumental ones. Nevertheless, the methodological criticism remains valid; we simply do not know enough about the large number of middle category cases to be able to determine how reliable our conclusion is. To the extent it is reliable, it further supports the dual-leadership part of the compliance theory.

THE ROLE OF LEADERSHIP IN EFFECTIVE EDUCATION

Thus far we have revisited leadership patterns in eight utilitarian organizations and 120 churches. Next, we explore them in colleges. Again, the factor of effectiveness is not ignored. Although normative education requires, as the hypothesis suggests, expressive faculty and involved students (p. 313), there are clearly faculty who at best are instrumental leaders and students who are alienated. This does not conflict with our position, as long as no effective re-socializing education takes place. Two studies are relevant to this thesis.

Leadership Patterns in Two College Divisions

Zelda Gamson (1966, 1967) studied utilitarian and normative orientations toward education among the faculty of a newly founded small general education college within a state university, which she calls "Hawthorn." Interviews were conducted with 33 faculty and administrators (of whom 3 were former faculty members) during 1962–1963. Hawthorn had three departments—natural sciences, social sciences, and humanities. The interviews revealed that the most important attitudinal differences among the faculty were between the natural and the social scientists; the humanities professors had no clear departmental ethos of their own. Each group of the two departments had an entirely different conception of the relations between students and faculty, the nature of general education, the goals for which Hawthorn should strive and how a college should be organized.

Indeed, recognition of these differences was, according to Gamson, possibly the only area of high consensus across departments (1966, pp. 48-49).

Responding to semistructured interview schedules about the educational objectives they favored, the natural scientists and the social scientists gave markedly different responses indicative of the relatively utilitarian orientation of the former group and the normative orientation of the latter. Gamson characterizes the contrasting goal orientations of the two faculty groups as "performance versus personalism" (1967, p. 297). Among the faculty themselves, the two views were contrasted in the interviews as the "crisp versus limp" approach or as the "curricular versus collegiate" approach (1966, p. 56).

The natural scientists, when discussing the impact they wished to have on students, placed virtually total emphasis on affecting students cognitively. Their prime goal was to "maintain intellectual standards" by extracting maximum performance from students.

The social scientists, on the other hand, although not uninterested in imparting specific knowledge and skills and developing a capacity for analytic thinking, placed much greater emphasis on affecting "the whole person," on changing values on personal relationships and on acculturating students to a whole new world view (*ibid.,* pp. 54-59).

Gamson identifies two major subgroups among the social scientists: the ideologists and the identity-makers (akin to the difference between "L" and "I" in the Bales-Parsons scheme; see p. 155). The *ideologists* wanted to affect students by changing their values, by leading them to be more critical of modern mass society and more politically active. They often referred to themselves in the interviews as "missionaries." The *identity-makers* stressed more personal as opposed to political solutions to alienation. They were concerned with molding better human beings who would not, as one interviewer put it, sell out to a sick society or "join the ranks of the middle classes" (*ibid.,* pp. 58-59). Although these two subgroups of the social scientists differed somewhat as to their goals, the department's overall orientation was clearly normative.

Predictably, the natural scientists did adopt more instrumental leadership strategies than the social scientists and employ less expressive means of controlling students. One of the best indicators of these different leadership patterns is provided by data on the uses of grading by the two faculty groups. To the natural scientists, grading is part of a clear-cut contractual process, in which fairly specific grading units are exchanged for fairly specific student behaviors or attitudes. Standards are predetermined, a student's performance either measures up or falls short, and the grade assigned to him rewards or punishes him accordingly. The natural scientists believed that it was the natural state of a student not to work; therefore, in order to stimulate good performance, the instructor had to appeal to the student's calculative self-interest, not only by rewarding good performance by good grades but in a negative sense by keeping students "a little worried about grades." In the natural scientists' view, no circumstances extraneous to the predetermined standards are allowed to come into the picture to influence the grade. Thus, Gamson points out, the grading process in the natural sciences has such characteristics of instrumental relationships as universalism, specificity, and affective neutrality (1966, p. 72).

By contrast, the social scientists revealed their normative orientation and emphasis on expressive leadership by using grades as rewards and inducements to better performance in the future but not as punishments. They felt that students should be "intrinsically motivated" (1967, p. 284). Nine out of 16 social scientists explicitly stated that they used grades as rewards and avoided using them as punishments. Rather than give low grades, the social scientists preferred to give incompletes (1967, p. 283). Also, the student behaviors and attitudes which justified good grades were much less clearly defined, especially because particularistic criteria, relating to students' personal characteristics, were considered important and necessary tools in evaluating performance.

Social scientists took into account such factors as poor and privileged backgrounds, innate ability and lack of talent, motivation, and hard work. They tended to grade students in terms of the amount of progress they showed in relation to their backgrounds rather than in terms of standardized objective criteria. They said that they frequently graded students higher who worked hard in the course (1967, p. 284). Only two (out of 16) social scientists said they graded strictly on performance, while eight (out of 11) natural scientists claimed to use solely "objective" criteria (*ibid.*, p. 285). The tendency of the social scientists to give higher grades based on personal evaluation than would have been merited on the basis of objective criteria alone is shown in Table VIII-6, in the discrepancy between examination grades and final grades in courses which did not require papers, i.e.,

Table VIII-6—Examinations Versus Final Grades in Social Science Courses with No Papers

		FIRST COURSE, FALL 1959			FIRST COURSE, FALL 1961		
		Total Examination	Final Grades	Final Grades Minus Examination*	Total Examination	Final Grades	Final Grades Minus Examination*
A		2%	15%	+13	11%	20%	+ 9
B		27	35	+ 8	29	39	+10
C		53	40	−13	32	32	0
D		17	8	− 9	23	6	−17
E		1	2	+ 1	5	3	− 2
		100%	100%		100%	100%	
	N	256	292		274	290	

* p of overall difference in grade point average <.001

Source: Gamson (1967), p. 286. Reprinted with the permission of the American Sociological Association.

in which the final grade was based only on the examination and the instructor's evaluation.

Because of the greater weight given by the social scientists to personal characteristics and their tendency to grade higher on the basis of these considerations, social science grades were generally higher than natural science grades. Although both the social and natural scientists reserved A's for outstanding performance, the natural science grades followed a normal distribution and the social sciences grades were skewed in the direction of a greater proportion of B's and C's and fewer D's and E's (see Gamson, 1967, p. 282).

Thus, Gamson's intensive analysis supports the hypotheses that (a) expressive leadership is more relied upon in more normative organizations (or organizational units), while instrumental leadership is more likely to appear in more utilitarian ones and that (b) communication of values, as distinct from mere knowledge or skills, is associated with expressive leadership. The next study casts additional light on these hypotheses.

Faculty Concern and Students' Work

In his study of 174 students at a small east-coast college ("Boro College") in the spring of 1965, William R. Taber (1969) established empirically the importance of expressive leadership for an educational organization. Taber's study focuses on the determinants of faculty authority and its effect on the effectiveness of the educational process.

Faculty authority is seen as having two dimensions, an "attitudinal" and a "behavioral" one—the first being measured in terms of students' respect paid to the faculty, the second in terms of students' self-reported compliance with the work assigned by the faculty. With regard to both dimensions, Taber found—after much careful and detailed analysis for which we refer the reader to the original text—that one variable emerges as being of crucial importance: "attributed concern," the degree to which students assumed that faculty members "are really concerned for their students' welfare." The basic distribution of attributed concern is as follows: Concerned, 31%; Neutral, 19%; Not Concerned, 49%; with an N of 172.

It seems safe to assume that where students attribute to their teachers a concern with their welfare, this constitutes a relationship that has significant positive, committing, expressive elements. At the same time, the attribution of personal concern can be assumed to be not unrelated to the behavior of the faculty. In this sense, the degree to which personal concern is attributed by the students to the faculty can be taken as an indicator of the faculty's expressive leadership.

Measured in terms of attributed concern, expressive leadership was found to be of considerable significance in determining students' perception of the faculty's competence, an essential element of accepting the faculty as legitimate and, hence, as authoritative. Taber had shown previously that "perceived competence" (an index combining the questions, "To what degree do you admire the competence of your instructors?" and "Most faculty members know what they are talking about," agree/disagree) was positively related to and predicted by "attitudinal respect"—a measure of a general preparedness to accept faculty's authority (based on the question, "Most faculty members deserve great respect," agree/disagree). When this relationship was controlled for attributed concern, the picture shown in Table VIII-7 emerged— showing, in Taber's own words, "that pre-existing attitudes of respect, or disrespect, control the legitimating rationale *only* when the students are convinced of the *lack* of faculty concern for their welfare. . . . A lack of faith in faculty concern thus *reverses* the institutionalized rationale for normative faculty authority, insofar as respect is a manifestation of this authority" (*ibid.*, p. 201ff.).

Looking at the table, we see that the presence or absence of respect has a different impact on perceived competence, depending on the attribution of concern. Under high concern, respect accounts for

**Table VIII-7—Attributed-Concern Controls Conditions under
Which Attitudinal Respect Predicts
Perceived Faculty Competence**

PERCEIVED FACULTY COMPETENCE	CONCERN		NON-CONCERN		
	Respect %	Non-Respect %	Respect %	Non-Respect %	
Full	89	73	66	25	
Limited	6	13	14	23	
Doubtful	6	0	16	27	
Denied	0	13	5	25	
N =	36	15	64	44	N = 159

Source: Taber (1969), p. 200 (table edited).

a difference in the number of students perceiving full competence of
16%; where no concern is attributed, however, this difference more
than doubles (41%). Thus, attributed concern significantly affects
the degree to which students perceive faculty as competent and thus
affects the extent to which faculty can rely on their "real" competence
as a "resource" of authority. In this sense, Taber sees attributed
concern—that is, expressive leadership—as a "bulwark against the
dominance of pre-conceptions of respect and non-respect as factors
in judgments of faculty competence" (*ibid.*, p. 209).

As to the *behavioral* aspect of students' acceptance of faculty
authority, Taber measures students compliance by the question: "What
kind of student are you? How thoroughly do you do the assigned work
in your courses?" Table VIII-8 shows the basic distribution of the

**Table VIII-8—Incidence of Pedagogic Compliance in Boro College
"What kind of college student are you? How thoroughly
do you do the assigned work in your courses?"**

Amount of Assigned Work Done	Incidence of Pedagogic Compliance		
100%	16%		
83%	37	High Attempt:	53%
67%	27	Low Attempt:	27
50%	12		
33%	6		
17%	2		
0%	1	Minimal Attempt:	21
	100%		100%
		N =	177

Source: Taber (1969), p. 247 (table edited).

answers. As indicated in the right-hand part of the table, Taber takes the responses not as indicators of the work the students are in fact doing, but rather as the degree to which they attempt to live up to the work norms set for them by their professors. That is why Taber sometimes refers to this variable as "pedagogic compliance *motivation*" rather than as compliance.[1]

Whatever the name of the variable, in his attempt to explain its distribution Taber found that two independent variables accounted for almost 90% of the variance. One of these, again, is "attributed concern"; the other, the student's felt "pedagogic obligation." Pedagogic obligation is measured by the question: "As a student, and regardless of personal preferences, what obligation do you feel that you have to do or not to do the following: Read all the required assignments given by the instructor." Pedagogic obligation differs from pedagogic compliance in that the indicators of "obligation" try to measure the norm, not the actual behavior (or the motivation to live up to the norm, depending on how one views the respondents' understanding of the question). In any case, 78% of the respondents reported that doing the reading assignments was an "absolute must" or "preferable," 19% were undecided ("may or may not"), and 3% held the assignments "preferably" or "absolutely" should not be done (*ibid.*, p. 254).

As with the attitudinal dimension of faculty authority, Taber found that the effect of pedagogic obligation on the dependent variable was mediated by attributed concern (Table VIII-9). (For Taber's reasons, attributed concern has to be seen as an intervening rather than an antecedent variable, as compared to pedagogic obligation. See our further discussion of Taber's work in Chapter XIV.) Where concern was attributed, i.e., where expressive leadership was manifested, obligation contributed no less than 56% to high pedagogic compliance. Under "non-concern," although the direction of the relationship, as indicated by the arrow, is the same, the difference is only 8.47%. On the two other levels of compliance, low and minimal compliance are generally associated with low obligation. However, low obligation predicts low compliance much better under high concern than under "non-concern."

Generally, the overall impact of "concern" is evidenced by the fact that the differences in compliance on the different levels of

1. Cf. the use Taber makes of this same indicator in his discussion of selectivity and socialization, reported in Chapter XIV of this book. The remarks made there apply to the present discussion, too.

Table VIII-9—Effect of Pedagogic Obligation upon Pedagogic Compliance under Varying Conditions of Attributed Concern

COMPLIANCE PEDAGOGIC	UNDER CONCERN PEDAGOGIC OBLIGATION		UNDER NON-CONCERN PEDAGOGIC OBLIGATION	
	Prescriptive, Preferential	Expedient, Rejected	Prescriptive, Preferential	Expedient, Rejected
High Attempt	78%	⟵ 22%	35%	⟵ 27%
		Diff. = 56%		Diff. = 8%
Low Attempt	12%	⟶ 56%	34%	⟵ 46%
		Diff. = 44%		Diff. = 12%
Minimal Attempt	10%	⟶ 22%	31%	⟵ 27%
		Diff. = 12%		Diff. = 4%
	100%	100%	100%	100%
N =	41	9	82	26

Source: Taber (1969), p. 286 (table edited).

obligation are considerably greater where concern is attributed than where it is not. (It should be noted that in one of the columns we are, at this point, down to nine cases.) Thus, Taber's findings support the hypothesis that the achievement of cultural goals, especially when directly related to socialization efforts, presupposes at least a measure of expressive leadership within the socializing institution and that without such leadership cultural goals may not be effectively pursued (p. 174).

EFFECTIVE LEADERSHIP IN DUAL AND COERCIVE ORGANIZATIONS

The following two studies explore the factors conducive to effective leadership in quite a different context than the two preceding ones. The earlier studies focused on normative organizations, colleges; the subjects of the studies to be discussed next are a dual (normative-coercive) and a coercive organization. Smith deals with the role of leadership in basic military training; Bigelow and Driscoll deal with it within a prison.

Expressive Instructors Are More Effective Than "Dominant" Ones

Smith's (1973) analysis supports the hypothesis, of considerable interest in terms of both theory and social consequences, that for a leader to effectively transmit value orientations, he must generate some kind of identification on the part of his subordinates or followers and that this is likely to occur only when the higher in rank relies on normative rather than on coercive or utilitarian power (pp. 59, 60). Smith's study, in other words, shows that this basic principle holds in dual organizations as well as in purely normative organizations; insofar as the organization's effectiveness depends on effective value transmission, expressive leadership has to be provided for or the organization will not be able to achieve its mission.

As an indication of the extent to which officers were able to resocialize the draftees into a military value system, Smith chose the recruits' responses to the question whether they felt that their officers were able "to create in the trainee a real fighting spirit against the enemy" (*ibid.*, p. 9). If we use "fighting spirit" as a measure of effectiveness, we see that the type of power used makes a sizable difference (effectiveness under normative power is 68%, $N = 286$; under dual 48%, $N = 626$; and under domination 27%, $N = 243$). Under normative power, 39% more than those under domination (a combination of coercive and utilitarian power) perceived their officers as effective expressive leaders.

A similar relationship, also in line with the theory, appears when effectiveness is related to the second component of compliance, involvement. In this case, a slightly different indicator of effectiveness was used—the proportion of soldiers reporting that "many of their officers" had "influence" upon them (*ibid.*, Ch. 5, pp. 8ff.). The relationship between involvement and the "influence" measure of effectiveness is as follows: when the degree of involvement is high, effectiveness is 65%, $N = 378$; when medium, 39%, $N = 205$; and when low, 21%, $N = 99$; the difference between high and low involvement, in terms of effectiveness, being no less than 44%.

Prisons Breed "Counter-Elites"

Bigelow and Driscoll (1973) studied the relationships between compliance and leadership in a rehabilitation institution which had a program of academic education, vocational training, and recreation. They found that the inmates, depending on the sub-unit of the institution they were assigned to, were subject to more or less coercion (see p. 75). Bigelow and Driscoll hypothesized "that inmate groups interacting with a less coercive elite would have more cooperative attitudes than would inmate groups interacting with a more coercive elite" (*ibid.*, p. 13).

This expectation was supported by the data. The less coerced inmate group received a higher score on the cooperative attitude scale (5.53; for a description of the scales mentioned in the present context, see our discussion of Bigelow and Driscoll's study in Ch. IV, p. 76) than the more coerced group (4.26). The same relationship appeared when "cooperative norms" were measured. In this case, the groups scored 4.47 and 3.79 respectively.

Bigelow and Driscoll proceeded to test the hypothesis that coerced groups tend to develop counter-elites representing values in conflict with those of the organization's institutionalized leadership (pp. 160ff.). Accordingly, those recognized as leaders in the less coerced group were to be expected to rank higher on the cooperative attitudes scale than the leaders of the more coerced groups. Or, as the authors put it, the theory implied that the correlation between a subject's self-reported cooperative attitudes score and his leadership rank would be positive in the less coerced group and negative in the more coerced one.

The data support this expectation. Measuring leadership position by the frequency of a subject's being named by other inmates as someone to turn to, listen to, and the like, the authors found a correlation between leadership and cooperativeness of $-.20$ for the more coerced and .24 for the less coerced group (difference significant at the .025 level). These findings provide substantively as well as methodologically strong confirmation of our propositions about the "counter-elite" and their compliance effect.

DUAL LEADERSHIP REVISITED

Dual Leadership in a Normative Organization

Amitai Etzioni and Ethna Lehman describe a case of dual leadership at work in a mental patient rehabilitation program (Etzioni and Lehman, 1965). The study focuses on Altro Health and Rehabilitation Services, Inc., an agency known for its effectiveness in assisting recovering patients in their transition from hospital to community.

The theory of dual leadership suggests that rehabilitation is more effective if emotional support and pressures for growth are allocated to different roles, thus separating expressive and instrumental leaders —provided that the leaders support each other's efforts and reinforce each other's authority. The Altro program provided supervised employment in an Altro operated workshop and provided social worker services to oversee a patient's progress. Thus, it offered both instrumental and expressive leadership, work supervisors and case workers, under the same organizational roof but through different roles and hierarchies of authority.

The work supervisors were especially limited to instrumental roles. Recruited through routine employment channels, they were laymen who were often unaware that the position applied for was in a therapeutic workshop. They were further screened against overly amelioristic attitudes. Those hired were charged with the responsibility for Altro's meeting its production commitments to its customers. Nevertheless, Etzioni and Lehman report some deviation towards "expressiveness," which is attributed to the therapeutic environment, the nonprofit situation, the evidence of illness, and the supervisors' exposure to the more expressively oriented social workers.

The social workers, on the other hand, were not restricted to expressive roles, to providing emotional support. Their roles also included the instrumental one of ultimate arbitration in the sanctioning system. But the Altro structure contained several mechanisms for reducing the dysfunctional effects of such instrumentality, including the practices of reassigning patients to easier or more suitable jobs and temporarily withdrawing them from the program.

Almost as important as the division of functions between expressive and instrumental leaders is the level and degree of collaboration between them. Etzioni and Lehman found that Altro policy carefully regulated the contacts between social workers and work supervisors in order to harmonize the two sets of leaders, while guarding against the blurring of the two functions. Normally, the social workers, whose offices were located some distance away, were allowed in the Workshops only twice a week, and even then they were barred from the production floors. Direct contacts between social workers and work supervisors, especially informal ones, were "particularly discouraged"; production reports, requests for advice, and such were made in writing or through some intermediary. This regulation of contact serves several functions. One, stressed by Altro, was to keep the work supervisors at their jobs instead of interacting with the social workers. Another function, also recognized by Altro, was to reduce the exposure of the work supervisor to the social workers' values and norms and the attendant risk that the work supervisors will begin to view themselves more as therapists and less as production officials. The policy of limiting contacts between the two groups to those taking place in the presence of higher-ranking personnel also serves to protect the autonomy of the work process by allowing the work supervisor to bring his difficulties with patients to the attention of higher-ranking staff members who presumably are more committed to Altro's production goal than the rank-and-file social worker and from whom he can expect more support for his position.

The autonomy of the work supervisors, needed to protect the instrumental function, is not to be confused with instrumental dominance. Here the stated goal is the actual goal. The title of the organization (a rehabilitation service), its charter, and the writings and statements of the director and other staff members indicate the superiority of the therapeutic goal. At the Workshop conferences most of the time is devoted to psychiatric rather than production issues, and virtually all final decisions, including those relating to work matters, are made by the social workers and their superiors.

The greatest problem of the leadership structure was found not within Altro but rather between Altro and other organizations that shared the patients. (The patients spent their days at Altro but their nights and weekends in hospitals nearby.) Some coordination was achieved through interagency consultation, but a fair measure of conflict remained, especially concerning what was to be done for a given patient, whether he was ready for discharge from the hospital or the Workshops, what living arrangements were to be made for him, and so forth. As each agency could call on its own psychiatric staff to buttress its position, there was no clear center of interagency power at which disputes could be firmly adjudicated. On the whole, attempts at coordination tended to be *ad hoc* and seemed often inconclusive. Thus, while agency effectiveness did correlate with dual leadership and stress on normative function correlated with expressive superiority (of the therapeutic staff), the problems caused by insufficient coalition-formation of different agencies in charge of the same set of activities curtailed Altro's achievements, as one would expect.

Hierarchy of Elites

Two additional bits of evidence apply to the question of what effect the hierarchical relations between elites, given a specific compliance structure, have on organizational effectiveness. In both cases, the hierarchy puts the instrumental elites at the top, to the detriment of the achievements of normative organizations.

Brager characterizes the top elite of the Mobilization For Youth, the board, in the following manner: "A considerable number of Mobilization board members were involved for utilitarian motives" (1969, p. 490). He goes on to explain that the board members were largely representatives of local institutions in the area, who sought to benefit from Mobilization For Youth for their own purposes. Data cited earlier (p. 130) shows that the board members acted to advance the utilitarian "goals" of the organization, its "maintenance" rather than its "cultural" goals.

Immediately below the board was the expressive elite, also found in organizational positions, the high-ranking staff members. They showed a high commitment to the organizational values and "cultural" goals. Although only 10.7% of the board fell in the upper third of the Brager commitment-to-values scale, 48.1% of the executive staff placed in the upper third. (For the other ranks it ranged from 38.4% to 26.1%).

The theory suggested that the effectiveness of normative organizations will be higher if the expressive elites are superior to the instrumental ones, rather than the other way around, because the expressive elites are closer to the normative purposes and compliance structure (pp. 157-8, 170). In the case at hand, the opposite relationship was in effect: the highly instrumental board was superior to the more expressive staff. The results, as predicted, were detrimental to the organization's compliance structure and effectiveness: a high level of alienation from the crisis strategy formulated by the board and a high level of discord.

Susan Amendola (n.d.) studied the activities of the two elite groups, administration officials and professional staff, of a child guidance clinic. Although this is primarily a normative organization whose goal is to promote health and which is nonprofit, it has utilitarian elements, as it must engage in fund raising to maintain itself and employs paid professionals. Amendola's study focuses on the way the two elite groups allocated their attention to the two groups of tasks the organization had to accomplish.

Data were collected on the number of hours spent by a sample of six administrators and seven clinicians on "normative" activities (clinical service, consultation, training, planning, research) and on "utilitarian" activities (administration). As could be expected, clinicians were found to devote a significantly greater amount of their time to normative activities than administrators. However, not only clinicians but also administrators were found to spend significantly greater amounts of time on normative activities than on utilitarian ones. While 46% of the sample were administrators, only 17% of the total staff working time (hours put in by both administrators and clinicians) was spent on utilitarian activities. Looking at each group separately, the clinicians spent 98% of their collective working time engaged in normative activities, and 2% on utilitarian ones, while the administrators spent 65% of their collective time on normative activities and only 35% on their ostensibly primary function, taking care of utilitarian matters. The reason for this is, according to Amendola, that all but one of the administrators were primarily professional clinicians, who preferred working on professional rather than administrative matters.

This low degree of inter-elite differentiation, Amendola argues, leads to a neglection of the hospital's "utilitarian needs." This, in turn, strengthens the role of the board of directors which, being unchecked by a powerful and energetic administration, tended to fill the power vacuum and to assume leadership in day-to-day affairs and in program decisions. However, this led to conflicts with the staff, which did not recognize the legitimacy of the board's attempted influence on the way the clinic was run. Moreover, lacking support by administrative personnel, the board, according to Amendola, could not but make "ill-advised and arbitrary" decisions (*ibid.,* p. 47). Thus, Amendola makes a case for a stronger differentiation between staff and administration, reducing the board to its real functions, making broad decisions to be "programmed" by the staff, and preserving the normative orientation of the organization. Such changes would also restitute the superiority of the expressive elite (board and staff) over the supporting, instrumental elite (administration).

THE ROLE OF CHARISMA REVISITED

The Model of Protest Absorption

Charisma, in an organizational setting, can be turned to the service of normative compliance or to its distintegration. Charisma is, in a sense, the nuclear energy of normative organizations. The explosive energy created by a nonconformist leader, recruiting followers to a cause at odds with the organization, is highly threatening to the organization's stability and routine, and in some instances to its continued viability. By the same token, the moral involvement sparked by allegiance to a charismatic leader can, when the leader is committed to the organization, provide the strongest possible bond linking lower participants to organizational goals. Ruth Leeds Love (1964), expanding upon an idea briefly discussed by Etzioni (pp. 348-350), developed a theoretical model of the process which seeks to contain the charismatic energy, indeed, to absorb it, once it has turned deviant, and transform it to supportive energy.[2] The process of "protest absorption," as outlined by Love, is a mechanism available to an organization's top leadership for transforming the disruptive type of charisma into the integrative form. The essence of protest absorption entails "integrating the protest of the nonconforming enclave into the organization by converting it into a new legitimate subunit. Through conversion, the nonconforming enclave obtains a legitimate outlet for its nonconformity, and thereby contributes to the attainment of the legitimate goals of the organization" (*ibid.*, p. 116).

The model is illustrated with case histories of two nonconformist enclaves, the Flying Tigers led by General Claire Chenault and the Discalced Carmelites under St. Theresa. Their potentially disruptive charisma was defused and their energies harnessed to serve the parent organizations (the U.S. Army at war and the Roman Catholic Church).

The model contains three parts: the characteristics of the nonconforming enclave, the organizational conditions which provide a situation ripe for nonconformity, and the process of absorbing protest. A potential for the emergence of a nonconformist enclave exists wherever there is an organizational sub-unit which has become ineffectual either through lack of innovation or decline of legitimation of its goals.

Sub-unit ineffectiveness, however, does not necessarily lead to the formation of a nonconformist enclave. Sub-unit members, particularly if the leadership is not innovative, may well respond to the situation with ritualistic conformity to rules and practices which have become

---

2. See also Love (1973). For a relevant discussion of charisma in an Ethiopian tribe, see Knutsson (1967), pp. 197-199.

inappropriate. The emergence of a nonconformist enclave assumes sub-unit members are responding with a search for new rules and procedures which would increase unit (or sub-unit) normative effectiveness. This entails the allegiance of sub-unit participants to a leader, whose "charisma of office" (as incumbent of a particular position) is no longer sufficient. He gains in personal charisma, thus transforming the followers' loyalty from an organizational position to a personal loyalty. This leader also must have tendencies toward nonconformity and a flair for originality which permits him to create new strategies, ideologies, and symbols to replace the withering ones of the organization.

Typically the leader is assisted by lieutenants who are also nonconformists and innovators, though less influential and original than the leaders. The cause espoused by the nonconformist enclave is usually that of developing and propagating means for reviving allegedly neglected organizational goals or for achieving current organizational goals more effectively. Generally a peculiar aura of either asceticism or adventurous romance surrounds the enclave, strengthening its internal cohesion, making it highly visible among the other units, and highlighting its dedication to its cause. (St. Theresa, for example, broke from the Carmel Order of the 16th century by reviving the asceticism of the early Carmelite Sisters.)

Although such a noncomforming unit can develop at any time, given these conditions, it finds its most fertile ground in contexts where one or more of the following varieties of organizational weakness are present: (a) the legitimacy of the total organization, not of just the sub-unit, is eroding; (b) the organization is insensitive to potential nonconformity, often because of an inadequate communication network, and control mechanisms are not activated in time to prevent a nonconforming official from gaining a personal following; (c) internal authority is weak because of the corruption of those responsible for enforcing conformity or lack of (or limited) control over enforcement facilities, making control mechanisms ineffectual, and (d) the diversion of resources to combat an external challenge, or stoppage of inputs, limits the availability of means to curb nonconformity (*ibid.*, p. 123).

Once a nonconforming enclave has been formed, mild checks are no longer sufficient to contain it; and the techniques used to control individual nonconformists, unsuccessful under the conditions just listed, become even more susceptible to failure. Furthermore, the "stakes" which may be lost if such techniques as condemnation, avoidance, and expulsion are used are drastically higher when the organization is confronted with a charismatic leader and his band of followers rather than a lone nonconformist. Use of these techniques can lead to conditions which will threaten the future viability of the organization in its current form such as internal polarization, even wider spread of the nonconformity, a loss of resources which might otherwise be channeled to serve organizational goals, or the creation of a separate rival organization which may destroy its parent.

In contrast, protest absorption, if it is successful, will both reintegrate the pocket of nonconformity into the normative organization and strengthen the organization as a whole, by providing it with the services of an energetic devoted group. This process also allows for the gradual legitimation of innovations which facilitate organizational goal attainment. The chief risk of protest absorption is that during the time the organization seeks to check and reassimilate the enclave, its leaders may gain access to key power positions and assume control of the total structure (*ibid.*, pp. 124-125).[3]

The process of protest absorption typically has several "rounds," each of which is characterized by the granting of a slightly larger modicum of legitimacy and expansion of autonomy by the top echelon. (Theresa, for example, was first given permission to start her own house. Next the "Discalced" became a separate province, then a separate congregation, and finally a separate order.)

Finally, in exchange for autonomy and legitimacy, the enclave must accept certain "stabilizers": (a) it is expected to develop rules to guide its future conduct, subject to external approval; (b) it must agree to accept a regular and approved source of finance, eliminating unauthorized solicitations, which place the unit in direct competition with existing units for resources; and most importantly (c) the unit's activity is limited to one particular field of operation. The introduction of "stabilizers" typically attenuates the leader's personal charisma by reconverting it, in part, to charisma of office; and the more radical members of the enclave (who see their leaders as giving in) become disaffected and leave. Gradually the unit becomes routinized and concerned chiefly with self-maintenance. Yet its history of nonconformity is never wholly forgotten; it always remains somewhat set

3. Love's perspective, which we here report, is obviously from the viewpoint of the total organization. Clearly, what is risky or "functional" from this viewpoint will be quite differently assessed if the perspective of the sub-organization is adopted.

apart from the rest of the organization by the aura of its past and hence it harbors a greater potential for a resurgence of nonconformity and, possibly, another cycle of protest absorption (*ibid.*, pp. 128-131).

Protest absorption, as a mechanism for channeling potentially disruptive charisma, can be either "conservative" or "progressive" in its organizational implications. If the nonconforming enclave, once legitimized, fails to accomplish the task it has set for itself, its strength becomes so sapped that it will be unable to exact or affect organization-wide "reforms." In this case the organization may well return to the pre-protest status quo. On the other hand, if the nonconforming enclave succeeds in attaining its now legitimate goals, the organization as a whole may change. The innovations of the charismatic leader may be institutionalized and, depending on the significance of these innovations for core policies and practices, the organization may emerge strengthened and perhaps even radically restructured; its normative compliance much more effective than before the whole process started.

Charisma at the Top

J. Timothy Sprehe's 1966 analysis of latent protest movements and Vatican II virtually begins where Love's article stops. Indeed much of the article is written in dialogue with the Love-Etzioni model of protest absorption. In examining Vatican II under the leadership of Pope John XXIII, Sprehe concerns himself primarily with how this case study can shed light on the conditions most conducive to thoroughgoing structural change within an organization.

Sprehe also takes issue with the characterization of the Roman Catholic Church as a normative organization, whose priests, bishops, and other officials are expressive leaders (pp. 310-313). He points out that the Church exemplifies in many ways a dual compliance structure, concerned not only with theology and the saving of souls, but also with the administration of a huge international ecclesiastical structure, not to mention the auxiliary organizations such as the schools and social welfare agencies which the Church is responsible for in many countries.

The dual compliance structure, Sprehe says, is found despite the fact that in some cases instrumental and expressive functions are carried out by the same person (e.g., the priest who is both administrator and pastor), while in other cases the functions are performed separately (e.g., the priest serves as administrator while his curate serves as pastor). Sprehe points out that in some countries, such as the U.S., bishops are almost exclusively administrators, while in other countries, such as Belgium and France, their duties are primarily expressive.[4]

The situation is further complicated by the distinction Sprehe draws among expressive leaders, between staff and line officials. The staff officials are those whose chief concern is "theoretical theology," that is, theology as a philosophical and scholarly discipline, "whose task is the examination and explication of the Church's founder and the historical teachings of the Church," (*ibid.*, p. 6). These professional theologians are chiefly to be found on the faculty of seminaries. The line officials, first the Pope, then the bishops and priests, insofar as they are expressive leaders, concern themselves with "prescriptive theology," defined as the "legislative translation of the founder's charisma to Church members at different points" (*ibid.*). If there is any overlap between theoretical and prescriptive theology, it is to be found among the members of the Roman Curia, who try to apply theoretical theology in advising the Pope when he sets down dogma or sends out pastoral directives to the bishops and priests. (This conforms closely to the separation of two expressive elites, the ideologues and the social-integration leaders, discussed in Etzioni, 1959).

This explication of the structure of the Roman Catholic Church has great bearing on the evolution of the theological "protest" movement which came to be championed by John XXIII and crested with the convocation of Vatican II. This theological reform movement began as what seems to the reader of Sprehe as a protesting enclave among the professional theologians in the seminaries, whose research on the scriptures and early Christianity, carried out with the tools of modern ethnology, archeology, linguistic analysis, and literary criticism, led them to basic new insights which they shared with non-Catholic scholars and gave rise to the "ecumenical movement," "the biblical movement," and the "liturgical movements." This "protest

---

4. Another relevant study is by Anna Anfossi (1967), who studied the Catholic Churches in a rural area in Sardinia. Her main observation is that as over the years utilitarian considerations (welfare, jobs) became more paramount in the expectations of the parishioners from the churches, the incongruence between lower participants and priests increased. This was especially so once the lower participants increasingly ceased to view the Church's material contribution as charity (and hence less in conflict with the normative orientation) and more as a service to which they had a right.

enclave," however, differed from the kind of "protest enclave" described in the protest absorption model, in that its members were dispersed internationally among seminary faculties and the movement as a whole was fragmented and leaderless.

Sprehe refers to it therefore as a "latent protest movement," and so it remained for fifty years. As such it appears to be a classic example of a protest movement that for a long period was readily contained by mechanisms other than protest absorption. Sprehe provides only a small amount of data on the mechanisms used to contain the reform movement, but it seems clear that the extreme compartmentalization of "theoretical" and "prescriptive" theology facilitated containment. Because of the rigid separation of the two groups, there were only two routes of passage for ideas from staff (the loci of the reformists) to line: (a) the education of seminary students, most of whom would enter the "line hierarchy" as parish priests and some of whom would gradually move up into positions of greater authority, and (b) the avenue of gaining the Pope's ear and influencing his proclamations and directives sent down through the hierarchy to the faithful. However, in order to gain access to the Pope, the protest had first to pass through the Roman Curia, a highly conservative group which, as will be evident from the following quotation, functioned like the "middle hierarchy" in the protest absorption model, blocking communication with the top (the Pope) and engaging in obstructionist techniques. According to Sprehe, at the time of Vatican II,

slowly and sometimes painfully, the professional theologians who advocated new approaches to the "settled" theological questions, who insisted on the interpretation of Church dogma in the light of its historical circumstances—slowly they had won some recognition from Rome in the form of papal documents. They were not, to say the least, filled with accounts, both before and during Vatican II, of censorship actions on the part of the Roman Curia towards the "new theology", a theology which has not been really new for perhaps fifty years but is only now reaching the public awareness of the Church. (*ibid.,* pp. 9-10)

Up to this point the evolution of the theological reform movement prior to John's accession to the papacy conforms quite well to the part of the model dealing with the early phase of protest absorption— that is, up to the point where an enclave is first accorded a modicum of legitimacy by the top hierarchy. At this point, however, there arrives a yawning gap in the data. A good deal of mystery seems to surround Pope John's decision to recognize and indeed champion the cause of theological reform. Sprehe mentions that before he became Pope, John was considered rather ineffectual and old-fashioned and that his subsequent actions amazed those who had known him intimately (*ibid.,* p. 3). Sprehe also makes it clear that it was not any "gathering force" of the movement which led John to recognize it. (Indeed it was John himself who had to coalesce the dispersed forces and create a following among the bishops at Vatican II). Nor do we have any data on less known protest leaders, or outside intermediaries, who might have been influential in John's apparent conversion.

In any case, the leaderless, fragmented, and semidormant state of the movement, at the time John chose to legitimize it, resulted in his becoming the movement's charismatic champion, a role which fused some of the elements of "enclave leader" with that of "top official granting legitimate status." That is, although John did not initiate the substantive proposals for theological reform, he spread them into the "line" structure of the Church; and, as Pope, he was in the felicitous position of being able to accord considerable institutional legitimation to the innovations he endorsed.

In this regard, Sprehe sees the evolution of Vatican II as departing from the Love-Etzioni model of protest absorption; the personal charisma that spearheaded the reform movement arose not several levels below the top of the hierarchy but at the very pinnacle of authority, in the Pope himself. Furthermore, as Sprehe suggests, the protest or reform movement was legitimized not through the creation of a new sub-unit to be absorbed into the existing administrative machinery of the Church but through the convening of an "extraordinary" council, Vatican II, and the establishment of a new legitimate sub-unit, the Secretariat for Promoting Christian Unity, which operated outside normal channels. Moreover, John's position as official head of the Church enabled him to introduce structural changes much more far-reaching than those accomplished by the charismatic leader of the typical "successful," newly integrated and legitimated protest enclave. John's aims went far beyond the creation of new sub-units; he intended nothing less than a top-to-bottom reorganization of the lines of authority and communication within the Church (*ibid.,* p. 12).

To what extent do Sprehe's findings require a revision of the Love-Etzioni model of protest absorption? As far as the Secretariat for Promoting Christian Unity is concerned, this is clearly a protest-absorption unit. It was made directly responsible to the Pope alone in order to free it from the authority of its enemies, the conservative theologians of the Roman Curia, and to give it enough leeway to accomplish its task. Moreover, Sprehe's account ends in 1966, in midstory, as it were. Since then, the protest-absorbing function of the Secretariat has become increasingly evident. Vatican II was only the first round of a process that is still going on, and although Sprehe covers mainly these highly dramatic initial phases, the overall picture fits well into the model of organizational change devised by Love and Etzioni.

But what about the role of the Pope? Protest absorption, as discussed in compliance theory, is only one way to revive the charisma of an institution and thereby to strengthen normative compliance. Another way to accomplish this end is the revitalization of a compliance relationship from the top, by the developing of personal charisma on the part of the inhabitant of the organization's highest position of formal authority. This kind of replenishment of an institution's stock of routine charisma has been illustrated by the revival of the British monarchy under Queen Victoria (p. 308). It seems that in the case of Vatican II these two ways of organizational rebuilding of normative compliance structures merge, at least to some degree. The outcome, however, remains the same: Normative compliance is strengthened by increasing the charisma the organization has at its disposal.

Charisma in the Ranks

The preceding two studies of attempts to bring about reform through charismatic leadership focused primarily on T-structured and L-structured organizations, in which charisma is either localized at the top, e.g., Henry Ford as head of his corporation, or is present throughout a hierarchy of line positions, e.g. the Catholic Church. The two papers by John M. Dutton and Roger L.M. Dunbar (1973a, 1973b) with which we close this chapter deal with an attempt to bring about change in an R-structured organization. R-structured organizations are ones in which charisma is localized in a rank which is formally subordinate to another rank not possessing charisma.[5]

5. For additional discussion of the relations of professionals and administrators, see Gross (1969), p. 657; Scott (1965), pp. 65ff.; Scott (1969), p. 108; Freidson (1963), p. 50; Goss (1963), pp. 172, 185; Heath (1974); Palumbo and Styskal (1974); Stancato (1974); Tinto (1974); and Warnecke (1974). Role of Charisma— Reiss (1974) and Kaufman (1974).

Thus, in a university, for example, the administrators tend to be the formal heads of the organization, but they possess chiefly utilitarian power, while faculty members, who serve the university's normative goals more directly, tend to possess whatever charisma there is.

The Dutton and Dunbar papers analyze an attempt by a newly appointed chairman of a university department (who as an administrator was a competent noncharismatic) to upgrade departmental standards relating to the competence of the faculty. Not surprisingly, the attempt tended to be seen as threatening by those professors whose competence was lowest according to the new standards. Because they had been hired when standards were lower, they also tended to be senior faculty, who, having tenure, also had the highest rank and commanded the greatest amount of charisma.

Many department members tended to equate resistance to upgrading standards, on the part of many senior professors, with a generational conflict between an old guard of older men and a new guard of young men. Dutton and Dunbar, however, by correlating degree of competence according to the new standards (as evaluated by a panel of judges) with degree of support or resistance to the change, found that the relationship of resistance to age was a spurious correlation masking the true basis of resistance in incompetence by the new, stricter standards. For example, 91.5% of those having high competence by the new standards supported upgrading the department while 60.4% of those with low competence offered moderate or high resistance to the policy (see Table VIII-10). Faculty members could not, of course, use these grounds to oppose the change. Instead, to be able to use their charisma to full effect, they had to fight the battle on normative terrain. Thus, they made the issue the chairman's

Table VIII-10—Faculty Support and Competence (r = .16)

Competence Level	High Support	Neutral	High Resistance
High competence	91.5%	8.5%	0.0%
Medium competence	64.1	6.4	29.5
Low competence	19.0	20.6	60.4

Source: Dutton and Dunbar (1973), p. 8, Table 2 (edited).

use of his utilitarian power in violation of professorial norms; that is, the chairman's use of financial inducements as a control device and to attract competent junior faculty, making the salaries of some assistant professors virtually commensurate with those of some full professors. Though the chairman did not retreat from his policy, he had to proceed in the face of a high level of conflict and dissatisfaction.

The main virtue of these two qualitative studies is to illustrate the fruitfulness of concepts introduced in the chapters dealing with the role of charisma as the source of the expressive leadership and intensive positive involvement that normative compliance requires. Highly normative compliance, in many ways the most attractive of all, is the most difficult to sustain. These studies (like the one by Skinner and Winkler, discussed on pp. 484-494) advance our understanding of the condition under which normative compliance can be maintained or revitalized. That our understanding of this significant issue is far from complete is quite evident.

PART THREE

OTHER CORRELATES OF COMPLIANCE

IX

COMPLIANCE AND
CULTURAL INTEGRATION
Consensus, Communication,
and Socialization

In the two preceding chapters we saw that organizations which differ in their compliance structure tend also to differ in the goals they pursue and in the degree to which lower participants are integrated into the organizational collectivity and controlled by its elites. This chapter examines the relationship between compliance and the cultural integration of lower participants. Each collectivity has a cultural system which includes sets of values and cognitive perspectives (Parsons, 1951, pp. 326 ff.). Participants in a given collectivity differ in their orientation to this cultural system. Some, usually the elites, accept it more fully than do others and tend to represent in interaction with insiders as well as outsiders. Others accept it in part, while still others are opposed to most of its elements and attempt to maintain a subculture of their own. In organizations, the higher ranks tend to support the cultural system; participants lower in rank vary widely in their orientation to it.

The orientations of lower participants to the cultural system of the organization are examined in this chapter from three viewpoints. First we discuss the degree to which lower participants accept the organizational position as theirs; this is the *level of consensus* between organizational representatives and lower participants. Next we examine two processes that modify the position of lower participants. These are *communication processes,* which penetrate all organizational units, and the more intensive and distinct *socialization processes,* focusing on the "acculturation" [1] of new participants. The effectiveness of these processes determines to a high degree the impact of the inevitable turnover of personnel on the organization's cultural integration. Following the general line as in preceding chapters of this volume, differences in the level and the determinants of cultural integration are related to differences in compliance.

COMPLIANCE AND CONSENSUS

Studies of consensus inquire into the degree to which the cultural orientations of various individuals or groups are congruent. Thus, whereas statements about involvement inform us what the orientations of one group of actors are, statements about consensus point out differences and similarities in the orientations of two or more groups. In addition, the following examination of consensus takes into account the major areas in which the organization holds a specific viewpoint, from an opinion on the nature of crime to an opinion concerning the fluoridation of water.

The degree of consensus is a measure of the degree to which the organization is integrated as a collectivity, though no assumption is made that high consensus is generally found in organizations, nor that it is universally required if an organization is to operate effectively. Organizations differ not only in the degree of general consensus they require, but also in the degree of consensus they require in various *consensus-spheres.*

The literature does not offer a list of consensus-spheres that can be used for the study of consensus in all organizations—or, for that matter, for the study of consensus in other collectivities. The list used varies with the problem explored. Interest in the integration of societies often leads to a focus on consensus with respect to ultimate values. In writings on political structures, especially democratic ones, consensus on political procedures (or the rules of the game) is frequently specified as a requirement. In the study of power structures, as in that of complex organizations, shared values concerning the right to exercise power—that is, the bases of authority, are

---

1. *Enculturation* may be a better term to refer to these processes. It has been suggested in this context by P. B. Hammond and applied by Avery (1960, p. 20).

stressed.[2] For studies of compliance the following list seems to cover most relevant spheres:

1. Consensus on *general values;* that is, values that are not peculiar to the organization under study, such as societal or community values, often including ultimate values. When general values are shared, consensus on organizational goals and means is more likely to be attained, but general value consensus is not a necessary condition for consensus on organizational goals or means.

2. Consensus on the *organizational goals;* that is, on the state of affairs the organization endeavors to bring about.

3. Consensus on *means,* policy, or tactics (other than those which concern directives and sanctions).[3] The need for consensus in this sphere requires some explanation. It would seem that once the goals are agreed upon, means would be selected by rational criteria in order to achieve the goals most efficiently. First, however, this assumes consensus on the kinds of issues to be decided by rational standards. Second, the relative efficiency of various means is often difficult to establish ahead of time, and quite often even after the fact (Caplow, 1953, p. 8). Beliefs therefore play an important role in decisions about means, and it is necessary to determine the degree of consensus about what means are to be used.

4. Consensus on *participation* in the organization. Lower participants can be viewed as continuously deciding whether or not to participate in the organization. In organizations where participation is voluntary, this kind of consensus is reflected in agreement about the frequency of participation: how often, for example, the minister thinks a parishioner should come to church, as against how often the parishioner thinks he ought to come. Where participation is coerced, this kind of consensus is obviously close to nonexistent; the organizational representatives demand that all the lower participants stay, whereas almost all of them would prefer not to. Still, even here there are differences in the level of consensus, or rather dissensus, reflected, for example, in the amount of effort invested in attempts at escape.

2. A very useful list of consensus-spheres for organizational studies which focus on subjects other than compliance is supplied by Speier in his examination of the findings of *The American Soldier* (1950, pp. 125-27).

3. Directives and sanctions are excluded because they are part of the definition of involvement in the organization and hence of compliance, which we are about to relate to consensus.

5. Consensus on *performance obligations*. Once lower participants have "decided" to participate, there remains a question of the degree of consensus about the duties they are to carry out.[4] This is a major sphere of potential conflict in factories: how much, for example, is the "day's work" which the worker owes the company for his "day's pay"?

6. Consensus on *cognitive perspectives*. Concurrence about facts, it has often been pointed out, assumes a common language, a shared frame of reference, and an agreed-upon set of canons for empirical test. When lower and higher participants differ in their normative positions on some or all of the five consensus-spheres listed above, it is likely that they will differ also on the sixth—that is, there will be dissensus about what the facts are, and what constitutes relevant and sufficient evidence for determining them.[5] But since this sphere has more empirical anchorage than the others, it may be assumed that consensus will be relatively higher here than in the other five spheres.

Finally, no paradigm for the study of consensus is complete unless it specifies the *status groups* among whom consensus is measured. Marx and Mannheim have pointed out that actors who occupy different social statuses differ more in their perspectives than do those who occupy the same or similar statuses. Hence, the assessment of consensus among actors in *different* statuses is the central problem in the study of normative and social integration. In complex organizations, one of the major cleavages lies between lower and higher participants. Another separates those who serve different funtions, such as staff and line, finance and production, and so on. In the subsequent discussion we follow the same general procedure as heretofore, focusing on consensus between lower and higher participants.[6]

4. The differences between the decision to participate and the decision to perform are spelled out by March and Simon (1958, pp. 84-111).

5. For a study which examines the effect of organizational position on perception (knowing the names of superiors or subordinates in submarines), see Scott (1958). See also Porter and Ghiselli (1957) and Porter (1959). On the effect of differences in "officer" behavior, as perceived by their subordinates, on the subordinates' behavior and hence on organizational effectiveness, see Ohio State Leadership Studies, esp. Hemphill and Coon (1950) and Halpin (1954). The relation of inter-rank perception and morale in the Air Force is explored by F. J. Davis (1954).

6. An important specification of the present model would require that we measure consensus in each rank and among various functional groups (e.g., staff and line), in order to determine to what degree they agree with each other and to what degree the higher ranks represent the organizational position. This raises the question of how to determine organizational values, norms, and perspectives as distinct from those of any specific group of participants, in particular those of higher

Some Illustrative Data

We would expect total consensus to be more frequent in normative than in utilitarian organizations, and to occur more often in utilitarian than in coercive ones. Despite the large number of studies of consensus among participants in various kinds of organizations, there seem to be no *comparative* studies of consensus in different types of organizations. The numerous studies of consensus in one organization or another differ in the instruments used, and in methods of collecting and analyzing data, to a degree that makes comparative statements extremely hazardous. The following findings, taken from studies of consensus in a prison, a factory, and a church are presented strictly for illustrative purposes. They show the severe limitations imposed on secondary analysis by the lack of continuity in social research.

Wheeler (1959) studied consensus on norms governing the behavior of prison inmates (e.g., squealing). Using a five-item, agree-disagree test, he found that statements with which at least 75 per cent of the prison staff agreed were acceptable to only 12 per cent of the inmates. (*ibid.,* p. 17). Of even greater interest to us is that in the same prison there were considerable differences in the degree of consensus among inmates and prison employees in various organizational units, which correlate with differences in the degree of coercion used in these units. "The smallest percentage of high conformity [on five items] is found in the segregation unit (14%), followed by the close custody unit (21%), medium custody unit (34%), honor farm and reception unit (44% and 47%), and the protection unit (83%), where inmates are held for their own protection from other inmates, chiefly because they are defined as 'rats' who have violated norms regarding informing on other inmates." (*Ibid*) Thus, the less coercive an organizational unit, the higher the consensus; or, the higher the consensus, the less the coercion exerted.[7]

Table IX-1 presents data for foremen and workers in four blue-

---

participants. This problem is discussed briefly in Chapter XII, p. 300. For a study of consensus between two higher ranks of management in four companies, see Maier, Read, and Hoover (1959, pp. 19-25); between members of school boards and teachers, see Greenhoe (1941); and between members of school boards and superintendents, see Gross, Mason, and McEachern (1958 esp. pp. 116-37).

7. These relationships between compliance and consensus are probably due in large part to differential recruitment (private communication with S. Wheeler). See Chapter X on this factor.

collar industries. The scores reported are means representing the proportion of positive comments made in answer to a set of open-ended questions. The questions covered attitudes to various levels of management but also to management-union relations and to the job.[8]

Table IX-1—Attitudes of Rank and File, Foremen, in Four Factories

	RANK AND FILE		FOREMEN	
	Mean % Positive	(N)	Mean % Positive	(N)
Metal Products	57.8	(56)	89.1	(15)
Construction A	84.5	(34)	85.4	(12)
Grain Processing	71.7	(59)	75.4	(28)
Construction B	77.8	(13)	61.5	(6)

Source: Chalmers, Chandler, McQuilty, Stagner, Wray, and Derber (1959, pp. 48-51). The study reports on eight cases, but the four in which the attitudes of fewer than five foremen are reported have been omitted from the table.

The differences between workers and foremen in the proportion of positive attitudes expressed are nonexistent in one company, less than five percentage points in another, and more than fifteen percentage points in the other two. But since this study examines a different consensus sphere, with a different instrument, any comparison with the prison study is extremely hazardous.

Leiffer (1947) studied the attitudes of lay leaders in the Methodist church, who constitute an important subgroup of the organization's representatives; the attitudes of a group of women; and those of two youth groups.[9] Answers from approximately one thousand respondents were scored on an approval-disapproval continuum ranging from +10 (maximum approval) to −10 (maximum disapproval). Average scores are reported for about one hundred different attitude items; almost all concern what we have defined as general

8. For other studies reporting similar findings see Fleishman, Harris, and Burtt (1955, esp. p. 59); and Vollmer and Kinney (1956, p. 11). See also Vollmer and Kinney (1959, pp. 431-41, esp. p. 439). For a comparison of the attitudes of non-supervisory personnel, first-line supervisory, and second-line supervisory employees (white- and blue-collar, mixed), see Vollmer (1960, pp. 73 and 80).

9. We ignore the first youth group since these respondents were "nominated" for the study by the lay leaders (Leiffer, 1947, pp. 20-21). Including them might artificially increase the consensus score.

values, goals, or policy. The findings in general are similar to those in Table IX-2, picked arbitrarily from Leiffer's tables.[10]

Table IX-2—Consensus in a Church

	Average Score		
	HIGHER PARTICIPANTS	LOWER PARTICIPANTS	
	Lay Leaders	Women	M.Y.C. Members*
How acceptable will a minister be in your church:			
If he is not effective in winning decisions for Christ?	—5.4	—7.1	—6.5
If he does hold evangelistic meetings	5.8	6.0	3.2
If he holds theological views which are in disagreement with those of the people in the church?	—5.1	—5.3	—3.7
If he preaches against the liquor traffic?	7.6	8.0	7.4
If he and his wife do not get along well?	—8.0	—8.1	—7.2

Source: Leiffer (1947, pp. 153-160).
* Members of Methodist Youth Council.

The data suggest high consensus on most issues. Women are in general somewhat more "conservative" or "orthodox" than lay leaders, and the youth group is systematically more "liberal" or "free," in the sense of expressing less extreme approval (or disapproval). But for all five items the direction of lower participants' responses is the same as that of the leaders, and the differences are small—less than two points on a twenty-point index.

A comparison of the attitudes of workers ($N = 109$) and supervisors ($N = 26$) in a social work agency—that is, a professional organization—shows high consensus. Attitudes concerning seven major policy questions (sphere No. 3) are reported by Thomas (1959, p. 33). The average difference between supervisors and social workers is 14.5 percentage points. High consensus is also reported for faculty and students in college (Goldsen, Rosenberg, Williams, Jr.,

10. This study has several limitations for our purposes. Disregarding questions of method and validity, we would prefer to have data from ministers instead of lay leaders, and information from members of the parish rather than "representative" women and members of youth councils, whose views are more likely to be similar to those of lay leaders and ministers than those of the rank and file. But since we found no other comparable data on consensus in the church, these will supply an illustration of the point. A study of consensus by Glock and Ringer (1956) used an index constructed in such a way that the kind of comparison made here is not possible.

and Suchman, 1960), and in a theological school (Hartshorne and Froyd, 1945, p. 49). Stouffer (1955) compared the attitudes of a sample of selected community leaders with the attitudes of a cross-section of citizens in the same communities. He found a difference larger than we would have expected: On the scale of tolerance of nonconformists, 66 per cent of the leaders, compared with 32 per cent of the cross-section, were scored as "more tolerant" (*ibid.,* p. 51). This "deviant" finding can be explained as follow: The cross-section includes nonmembers—that is, people who are not members of the organizations led by these leaders, which may increase dissensus; and both leaders and members include many participants in other than normative organizations.

The findings presented in the preceding paragraphs illustrate the kind of data available on consensus in various organizations. It is clear that differences in the instruments used, the methods of collecting and analyzing data, and the spheres in which consensus was measured allow us to use these findings only to illustrate the kind of material available and the limitations it imposes on comparative analysis. The steps that would have to be taken in primary research to make comparative statements possible are a complex subject, which, if discussed, would require at least another volume.

Compliance and Consensus-Spheres: A Theoretical Note

We suggested above that the three types of organizations differ systematically in the frequency with which total consensus is likely to be found in them; that is, if we construct a measure of consensus in which all six consensus spheres are represented, we would expect it to be higher for normative organizations than for utilitarian ones, and higher for utilitarian than for coercive ones. We turn now to a more specific question: How do the three organizational types differ in the degree of consensus they require in each of the six spheres for their effective operation? The discussion is limited to a theoretical argument because there are almost no data to illustrate the points made.

For effective operation, typical *normative organizations* require consensus on all norms directly related to expressive activities, though considerably less consensus is required than was long believed. Religious organizations, for example, attempt to maintain high consensus in all six spheres, although, to be sure, varying degrees of importance are assigned to them. But in the last hundred years, while they have not entirely given up attempts to define the cognitive perspectives of their members, religious organizations have learned not to stress their frames of reference for the perception of the empirical world (sphere No. 6). Similarly, modern religious organizations have given up, though reluctantly and incompletely, their influence over the value commitments of their members in such matters as political opinion and economic behavior. Still, high consensus concerning ultimate values (sphere No. 1) may prove to be a requirement of effective operation. Religious organizations have shown great flexibility in modifying participation demands (No. 4) and performance obligations (No. 5). Ministers may still officially be in favor of weekly attendance, but the majority of lower participants obviously think otherwise. Only 12 per cent of Jews, 25 per cent of Protestants, and 62 per cent of Catholics attend religious services every Saturday or Sunday (Hoult, 1958, p. 99).[11] Moreover, many ministers adjust their expectations and informal positions accordingly.

The spheres in which consensus is most emphasized appear to be the special values served by the particular religious organization (No. 2) and the means for attaining them (No. 3). It is the nature of every ritualistic (and for that matter every expressive) activity that the means become sanctioned and gain ritualistic value in themselves (Parsons, 1937, pp. 210-11). In short, out of six spheres, high consensus in three—concerning ultimate values, goals, and means—seems to be essential for highly effective operation of religious organizations, where as high consensus in the other three seems to be desirable but not necessary.

Much of the same analysis holds for core organizations of social movements and for those political organizations with strong ideological platforms. Analysis of the relative importance of consensus-spheres in other normative organizations must be deferred until more information is available. But it seems likely that the cognitive, participation, and performance spheres carry greater weight in the less typical normative organizations, such as educational and professional organizations, whereas the importance of consensus on ultimate values is probably less.

Utilitarian organizations require a high degree of consensus for effective operation mainly in spheres concerning instrumental activi-

11. Similar statistics are supplied for attendance a generation ago by Fry (1924, p. 93).

ties. The basic reason for this is that production is a relatively rational process and hence can rest on contractual relationships of complementary interest, not shared sentiments or values (Durkheim, 1947, p. 6). It is not mandatory for effective operation that management and workers hold congruent views on general values (No. 1), organizational goals (No. 2), or organizational policy (No. 3). On the other hand, consensus in the three remaining spheres is vital for effectiveness. Basic consensus about the scope of performance and participation obligations (Nos. 4 and 5) is functionally required, although the system can operate quite effectively when there are limited differences of opinion. Consensus is vital also in the sphere of cognitive perspectives (No. 6). If the employees do not accept the organization's definition of the technical aspects of production, effective production often becomes impossible.

In *coercive organizations,* both the degree and the range of consensus required are most limited. There is usally high dissensus concerning the general values (e.g., the nature of crime and punishment), the organizational goals (e.g., detention), and the means employed to attain them (e.g., search of inmate cells). Cognitive dissensus does not carry much weight, since such differences of opinion have only limited effects on most organizational activities. Consensus in the two remaining spheres, on the legitimacy of forcing actors to stay in the organization (to "participate") and on the limited performances required by coercive organizations (e.g., work in the prison's gardens), has some impact on organizational effectiveness. But it should be emphazied that coercive organizations can operate quite effectively and for long periods with considerable dissensus even in these three spheres.

Summarizing this comparison of the three types of organization, we can say that normative organizations require both a high degree and a wide range of consensus. Dissensus in any area, in particular with respect to values, goals, and means, is dysfunctional for the achievement of organizational goals. Utilitarian organizations require high consensus mainly with respect to performance obligations, participation, and cognitive perspectives, since these three spheres are directly related to production goals and to the contributions of lower participants. Coercive organizations are so structured that they can operate in the face of widespread or even total dissensus, although consensus regarding participation and performance may increase their effectiveness to some extent. Coercive organizations do not have one cultural system; their participants hold to two sets of evaluative, cognitive, and expressive perspectives while sharing a few norms, such as those defining the substance of the language used for communication between groups.

Since the degree of consensus can be used as one measure of the integration of a collectivity, we find here again that an organization is not necessarily one integrated collectivity. Only normative organizations require consensus across the ranks concerning the core of the cultural systems; utilitarian organizations can manage with what amounts to consensus on procedures; coercive organizations require little consensus.

COMPLIANCE AND COMMUNICATION

The study of communication in organizations is of special import because the large size, high degree of complexity, strain toward effectiveness, and elaborate control structure of organizations all require extensive communication networks and roles and mechanisms especially devoted to the flow of communication.[12] We are interested in the study of communication chiefly as a symbolic process by which the orientations of lower participants to the organization are reinforced or changed.[13]

More than any other section in this book, the analysis of communication is based on a mixture of theoretical considerations and direct observation, rather than on distillation of existing data. Most communication studies are conducted in the human relations or cybernetics tradition, neither of which includes all the variables used by this analysis. There are very few functional-structural studies of communication, in particular of communication in organizations.[14]

12. An examination of the relationships among communication processes, networks, specialized roles and situations, and reference-group behavior constitutes the major subject of an analytical essay by Eisenstadt (n.d.).

13. Communication and consensus are closely related but independent concepts. A measure of consensus supplies a snapshot of the degree to which various groups of participants share cultural orientations. An analysis of communication explores some of the processes affecting this state of consensus.

14. For functional-structural studies of communication in a societal context, see Eisenstadt (1952, 1953); for an organizational context, see Shepard (1954). A number of studies relate the amount and nature of communication flow to the structure of organizational units (e.g., Bavelas, 1950; Leavitt, 1951; Christie, Luce, and Macy, 1952; and Guetzkow and Dill, 1957). Note that these studies use the terms *structure* and *organization* differently from the way they are used here. *Organization* is used in the social organization tradition (*supra*, pp. xi); and *structure* comes close to what we call communication networks.

Organizational communication systems consist of two quite different networks, distinguished by the *substance* of the communication transmitted. One network allocates instrumental communications, the other transmits expressive communications. *Instrumental communication* distributes information and knowledge, and affects cognitive orientations. Blueprints, technical textbooks, and experts' directives are typical examples. *Expressive communication* changes or reinforces attitudes, norms, and values. Preaching, praising, and expressions of acceptance are typical examples.[15] Instrumental communication primarily affects consensus about procedures (or means) and cognitive perspectives, whereas expressive communication is more likely to affect consensus in the other five consensus spheres.

The *direction* of the communications flow is the other dimension by which communication networks are characterized. Communications may flow vertically or horizontally in the rank structure, and vertical communications may flow upward or downward.[16] The amount of communication of each kind (instrumental, expressive) carried by the various networks, and the direction of flow, are central determinants of organizational effectiveness. The amount required for effective operation is directly affected by the scope and effectiveness of the socialization processes which take place in the organization, or as preparation for participation in it. As Simon pointed out in *Administrative Behavior* (1957, pp. 169-71), communication and training can partially substitute for each other. The better trained the person is before he enters a job, the less the need to communicate with him while he is on the job. Not only can technical training substitute to some degree for the flow of information; internalization of criteria for decisions through expressive socialization can also partially replace directives or expressive communication. Finally, examination of the flow of communication is

15. Eisenstadt distinguishes among three types of communication in his study of new immigrants: " 'technical' communications, the main aim of which is to transmit to the new immigrants various technical information which would enable them to orient themselves in the new set-up. . . . The second main type is what may be called general 'cognitive' orientations, which are seemingly without direct reference to any concrete social situation. . . . The third category includes what may be called 'normative' communications, by this we mean communications oriented to the transmittal and upholding of various social norms and to the definition of proper behavior in various roles and social situations." (1955, p. 154)

Expressive communication, as used in this book, refers to approximately the same processes as *normative communication* in Eisenstadt's terms, and *instrumental* includes his *technical* as well as *cognitive* types of communication.

16. For an empirical study applying these concepts in the study of a factory, see Simpson (1959).

not complete unless we locate *communication gaps* or blocks, determine the factors that produce them, and explore their consequences for organizational effectiveness.

Communication in Coercive Organizations

The forms taken by communication networks in the three types of organization are quite similar to their elite structures; hence there is no need to discuss these systems in great detail. Briefly, they seem to be as follows: In coercive organizations instrumental communication with inmates predominates. The elites in charge of this type of communication tend to follow one of two communication policies. One, usually supported by the professional treatment-oriented personnel, is to supply the inmates with as much valid information as possible concerning, for example, prison policy. The alternative, quite common in traditional prisons, is to withhold information from the general inmate population and to allocate it to a selected few in a manner that will turn information into a source of reward and control. McCleery (1957) pointed out that order is maintained in a custodial prison through the exercise of arbitrary power, combined with allocation of valid information to a selected elite of inmates, in tacit exchange for their support of order in the prison.[17] The inmate elite controls other inmates in part because it can anticipate searches of the cells, for example, and thus keep inmates out of trouble or cause trouble for them by planting contraband.

There is little instrumental upward communication in coercive organizations. Almost any information volunteered by an inmate to a guard or other prison employee is considered squealing, and is severly punished by the inmates. Strong taboos ensure that communication with guards will be minimal (McCleery, 1956, p. 375).

Downward expressive communication is rare in coercive organizations because the high alienation of inmates, together with the differentiation of elites, almost completely blocks the acceptance of such communications. On the other hand, horizontal expressive communication in the inmate subcollectivity is a major means of informing new inmates and reinforcing desired attitudes among older ones. The wide scope of the organization cuts inmates off from the

17. The underlying processes which, on the one hand, link exercise of arbitrary power by the prison with effective control of the inmates and, on the other hand, link the supply of valid information to the inmates with a high degree of disorder are the subject of a formalization of McCleery's study by Barton and Anderson (1961).

communication networks or other social units, making them almost entirely dependent upon internal horizontal communication for recognition and acceptance (McCleery, 1956, p. 375).

Communication in Normative Organizations

Expressive communication is essential for the effective performance of normative organizations. In order to attain their goals, they must maintain an intensive flow of downward expressive communication and remove blocks that may develop. Hierarchical religious organizations rely more on direct downward communication to each individual; egalitarian religious organizations tend more often to link their downward communications with the horizontal communication nets existing among members of the congregation, in order to enlist the support of these informal relationships. But all religious organizations emphasize some mode of downward expressive communication. Political parties and ideological labor unions rely relatively more on direct downward communication, whereas social unions and voluntary associations make greater use of supporting horizontal nets. The educational process is a downward communication process, although the role played by interaction and communication among students is important. In typical normative organizations, such as graduate schools and colleges, downward communication is supported by horizontal networks. In relatively less normative organizations, such as some of the special and vocational schools, horizontal nets often transmit communications that reduce the effectiveness of downward communication, and in this sense resemble the prison model.

Upward expressive communication is limited in all organizations, but those normative organizations which have representative structures, such as unions and parties, are usually somewhat more open to it than are appointive structures. However, it has been pointed out by Schumpeter (1950, pp. 269-83) and others that even in highly democratic structures, criteria for decisions tend to be communicated downward more often than upward.

In typical normative organizations instrumental communication is limited because instrumental activities requiring it are few. Much of whatever instrumental communication there is does not flow downward to lower participants but circulates among the staff or among the staff and some outsiders (Chamberlain, 1958, p. 145). One major exception is the downward communication of information and knowledge in educational and professional organizations.

Communication gaps are least frequent in normative organizations, where elites are least differentiated, alienation is lowest, and consensus among lower participants and organizational representatives is high.

Communication in Utilitarian Organizations

Utilitarian organizations emphasize vertical instrumental communication as a condition of effective production. Since this is the most rational type of the three, and since coordination, planning, and centralized decision making are emphasized here more than in the two other types, upward instrumental communication, especially of information, is required almost as much as downward instrumental communication (Read, 1959). If the "center" does not obtain performance reports, or if these are delayed or distorted, the effective operation of the organization is impaired. Much of the so-called red tape, the files and archives Weber saw as a central characteristic of bureaucracies in general, are an indicator of extensive instrumental communication, which exists mainly in utilitarian organizations.

Vertical expressive communication is limited in utilitarian organizations, although less than in coercive ones, because of the calculative orientation of lower participants to the organization and their tendency to develop independent (horizontal) expressive communication networks when on-the-job expressive subcollectivities exist. The scope of horizontal expressive communication depends on the existence of peer relationships within the organization and on the degree to which actors are members of the same external collectivities, such as communities, neighborhoods, and labor unions. These external bonds serve as channels of horizontal communication in themselves and enhance such communication within the organization by supplying a shared frame of reference.

In summary, normative organizations emphasize downward expressive communication; utilitarian organizations emphasize vertical instrumental communication; while in coercive organizations vertical channels tend to be blocked, and there is a great deal of expressive horizontal communication.

COMPLIANCE AND SOCIALIZATION

Socialization refers to "the acquisition of the requisite orientations for satisfactory functioning in a role." (Parsons, 1951, p. 205;

see also Merton, 1957*a,* pp. 287-93). Primary socialization, which determines the form of the basic personality, takes place as a rule in the family and to some degree in various peer groups, such as neighborhood and street gangs of children (Parsons, 1951, pp. 236-48). For most actors the main part of socialization is completed with maturity, but learning of specific skills and role orientations continues with every change of status, in particular with membership in new social units, such as organizations. Thus the study of organizational socialization, like that of communication, is concerned with the processes by which the beliefs, norms, and perspectives of the participants are brought into line with those of the organization. Unlike communication, however, it is concerned with the period before or shortly after new participants join the organization, when efforts to induce consensus between newcomers and the rest of the organization are comparatively intensive.

We are interested in determining, first, the *substance* of socialization—that is, to what degree it prepares for participation in the *instrumental* system (a preparation often referred to as training) or in the *expressive* one (a preparation that might be characterized as education minus training). Weber distinguishes between these two types in his discussion of the education of the gentry and elsewhere in his writings, using the terms *specific* versus *charismatic* education (Bendix, 1960, pp. 138-41). The *amount* of socialization of each type required for effective participation in each type of organization has yet to be determined. One way of measuring this would be to assess the length of education required to prepare for participation.

The fact that a socialization process prepares for participation in an organization does not in itself indicate that the organization can direct it according to its needs. Hence we identify the socializing agents, using the term *formal* socialization to refer to socialization by office holders, as opposed to *informal* socialization by lower participants. For the same reason, we ask whether socialization to organizational roles is carried out within the organization or by outsiders; outsiders are likely to be less subject to control by the organization than office holders and most lower participants are.

Socialization in Coercive Organizations

Formal socialization in coercive organizations is very limited in scope and, for the most part, highly ineffective. Some rather limited instrumental socialization by the organization takes place in the "fish tank," where new inmates are classified and introduced to the formal regulations and procedures of the prison or mental hospital (Wilson, 1953, pp. 57-58; Chessman, 1956, p. 194). But counter-socialization, through informal relations and contact with old-timers, is already highly effective at this initial stage of participation. It increases with the integration of new participants into solidary groups of the inmate subcollectivity. It is a commonplace among professionals familiar with these organizations that "correctional institutions are the schools of crime, and prisons its universities." Young offenders who serve more than a year in a prison often "graduate" as accomplished criminals, both trained in the techniques of crime and indoctrinated with its values.

On the formal level, instrumental socialization such as vocational training is more likely to be effective than expressive socialization, as efforts to rehabilitate inmates in prisons and to cure patients in custodial mental hospitals have shown.[18] Expressive socialization is an exclusive inmate domain.

As we would expect, formal socialization is more effective in less coercive than in more coercive organizations. McCleery examined a prison's socialization techniques in a highly coercive and in a much less coercive period:

In the authoritarian prison, the official process of admission did little more than reduce the new inmate to a condition of helpless dependence. The positive work of orientation, plus a liberal mixture of exploitation, fell to the informal inmate social system. As long as that process resulted in the thorough subordination of the new men, the officials of the old prison seemed to be satisfied. (1956, pp. 631-32)

When the prison goal was changed to emphasize rehabilitation, the exercise of normative power became more pronounced:

One of the first acts of those who represented the new regime in the administration was to make the official program more positive. . . . It consisted of lectures delivered to groups of new men over a period of some weeks after their admission to the prison. . . . (*Ibid.*, p. 632)

At the beginning the new program encountered some difficulties and informal socialization was still more influential, but as the traditional inmate culture started to disintegrate, inmates became more dependent on the formal program and their leaders worked together with the

18. The limitations on expressive socialization or resocialization in prisons have been noted by Reimer (1937); Sykes and Matza (1957); Galtung (1958, p. 138); and Ohlin (1959, p. 2).

prison staff on its extension. "Provision was made for testing, vocational guidance, counseling, character training, and group discussions in addition to the regular lecture series." (*Ibid.,* p. 636)

In short, in typical coercive organizations the socialization of newcomers maintains dissensus between ranks; in less coercive organizations, formal socialization—particularly instrumental socialization —has some effect on inmates.

Socialization in Utilitarian Organizations

Formal socialization in utilitarian organizations is more extensive than it is in coercive organizations. As one would expect, it is mainly instrumental in nature and consists of giving the work force technical training and a few hours of orientation, mainly on safety devices, company regulations, and the like (H. F. Clark and Sloan, 1958, p. 41). Factories rarely train higher-ranking participants. In the United States in 1946, only 5 per cent of the 3,459 corporations studied had an executive training program of their own (*ibid.,* p. 8). Utilitarian organizations rely on comparatively autonomous external social units, such as vocational schools and colleges, for much of their instrumental socialization.

Expressive socialization in utilitarian organizations is limited. Some efforts are made to build up the "morale" or "motivation" of the workers, but utilitarian organizations can rely on participation in external collectivities of the expressive type (family, community, other primary groups) as the chief source of "meaning" for remuneration gained in these organizations. Somewhat more expressive socialization is carried out informally by solidary work groups, especially in introducing workers to production norms and norms of interaction with supervisors and union representatives.

Some corporations engage in more extensive expressive socialization than suggested above, but these are not purely utilitarian organizations. Nor is the goal of such activity production or profit; instead, it serves ideological and political purposes. W. H. Whyte states:

Among other things, the trainees take HOBSO. This is the course in How Our Business System Operates, originally developed by Du Pont to inoculate blue-collar employees against creeping socialism. Though GE has no reason to fear its trainees are ideologically unsound, it explains that the course will help them "detect any bad guidance they receive from union and political leaders, and even from educational and spiritual leaders." (1957, p. 134)

The New York Times noted the political indoctrination activities of big business among its workers under the following title: "Big Corporations Mount Soapboxes: 'Political Awareness' Drive Enters the Stage of Espousing Causes":

In its initial stage this movement spurred the establishment of dozens of "political awareness" programs for employees. The emphasis was on teaching employees the essentials of politics and exhorting them to take an active role in their political parties. Now several important companies are taking this idea a step further. Instead of merely urging employees to take positions on key issues the companies themselves are taking positions. They are circulating these opinions to employees through company magazines, confidential newsletters and other media. (May 24, 1960, 3:1)

Thus, to the degree that there is extensive expressive formal socialization, it is not found in purely utilitarian organizations, nor is such activity directly geared to production goals.

Socialization in Normative Organizations

Normative organizations differ considerably in their socialization processes, although in all of them socialization plays a central role, and is carried out to a considerable degree through formal mechanisms and by holders of organizational offices, such as ministers and teachers.

Normative organizations vary in the degree to which expressive as against instrumental socialization is emphasized, although expressive socialization predominates in most of them. Religious and political organizations as well as mental hospitals stress expressive socialization; training is limited in scope and often directly tied to educational expressive goals rather than instrumental ones. For example, work is used to build up motivation to recuperate or increase identification with values rather than for occupational training.

Educational organizations stress expressive socialization in lower grades; with the movement from grammar school to high school, and from high school to college and graduate school, expressive socialization decreases until, in the graduate school, instrumental socialization is markedly predominant.

Expressive socialization is given strong emphasis in such professional schools as theological seminaries and political schools (Hartshorne and Froyd, 1945, pp. 172-88). It is given somewhat less weight in military academies, and considerably less in law and medical schools,[19] where training predominates and indoctrination plays a minor role. Professional organizations such as universities, hospitals, and research organizations, the least normative of the normative organizations, typically emphasize instrumental socialization. Much of the limited expressive socialization which takes place here is unorganized, and is sometimes an unintended consequence of other processes such as interaction with peers and senior members of the profession. (Merton, in Merton, Reader, and Kendall, 1957, pp. 41-42; Kendall, 1960, pp. 12-14; Nicholls, in progress).

The amount of socialization required by organizations depends, of course, on the degree to which organizational behavior differs from behavior the participants have learned elsewhere. Army life, for example, appears to resemble the traditional authoritarian social life of the rural classes more than it does the life of the urban middle classes; we would therefore expect that in order to attain a given level of effectiveness, draftees with these different social backgrounds would require different amounts of training and indoctrination. This fact has been demonstrated for American soldiers by Stouffer *et al.* (1949, pp. 105-54), for Swedish naval conscripts by Härnqvist (1956, pp. 62-73), and for Dutch naval cadets by Lammers (in progress).[20]

Considerable socialization for organizational roles may be accomplished outside the particular organization in which the actor is to function; when this preparatory socialization is effective, it reduces the amount of socialization the organization itself must undertake. Vocational schools, for example, conduct instrumental socialization for certain industries. Colleges provide future students of medical schools with premedical instrumental training as well as some expressive socialization—for example, by introducing them to some of the professional norms. A study of medical students showed that there was little change in their basic normative orientation during their stay in medical school, a period in which one would expect consider-

19. Increasing stress on instrumental elements as professional training advances is analyzed by Kendall and Selvin (1957).

20. Hollingshead (1946) supplies an analytical model and rich data for the analysis of this adjustment process. The phases of the process are specified and the social and cultural conditions affecting it are spelled out. Coker, Miller, Back, and Donnelly (1960) supply comparative data on the adjustment of medical students of different backgrounds.

able professional socialization to take place.[21] This lack of change is explained, in part, by the fact that when these students entered medical school they were already well socialized to professional values as a consequence of selection (e.g., many were relatives of professionals, especially doctors), premedical education, and other forms of anticipatory socialization.[22]

Theological seminaries that recruit their students from graduates of religious schools can rely on these schools for much of the expressive socialization of their students. Similarly, a study by Greenhoe (1941) of students in training to become teachers showed little change in attitudes during the course of their higher education. For example, asked whether they would approve a "known militarist" as a teacher, 16.3 of freshmen and sophomores approved, compared with 20.3 of juniors and seniors and 27.5 of graduate students. Similarly 70.2, 81.0, and 84.5 would approve an applicant from another state. Of fifteen questions, only two showed differences greater than 15 percentage points between freshmen and graduate students (*ibid.*, p. 37).

Some indirect support for the assumption that professional schools can limit expressive socialization without detriment to the professional quality of their graduates, because earlier socialization has already committed the student to the "necessary" values, is offered by a study of nursing education. Nurses—who come from a lower socioeconomic background, have less previous education and fewer professional relatives than do medical students, and who therefore have less "preparatory" socialization—change their normative orientation in

21. The writing of these paragraphs on the professional school has benefited from discussions of professional socialization with members of the medical project at the Bureau of Applied Social Research, Columbia University. The project is directed by R. K. Merton. For preliminary findings see Merton, Reader, and Kendall (1957). Additional findings are reported in doctoral dissertations by members of the project: Renée Fox (1957); Goss (1959); Caplovitz (1960); May Jean Cornish, T. Falaguerra, W. Martin, E. D. Nasatir, and W. Nicholls (in progress). See also Thielens (1958).

Insights into occupational socialization, particularly the mechanisms by which professionals come to identify with their status and role-image (a central base of normative compliance), are reported in the following articles: Becker and Strauss (1956); Becker and Carper (1956); and Becker and Geer (1958). The first article deals with adult occupational socialization; the second, with professional socialization; the third, with socialization in the medical school.

22. Thielens reports that of the 498 medical students he studied, 281 had a relative who was a professional (private communication). Fifty per cent had a relative who was a doctor; 17 per cent had a doctor as a parent (1958, p. 156). On the increasing emphasis on selection in medical schools, see *ibid.*, p. 165

professional schools more markedly than do medical students (Martin and Katz, 1959, p. 8).

Control Over External Socialization Units

The three types of organization differ considerably in their degree of control over external socialization units. Very little socialization supportive to the organization takes place in coercive organizations or in collectivities external to them. Utilitarian organizations leave much of the instrumental socialization they require to outside units, over which they ordinarily have little direct control. Vocational schools and colleges are typical examples. Industries attain some indirect control over these educational organizations through financial contributions and through representatives on their boards of trustees (W. H. Whyte, 1957, pp. 110-20; McGrath, 1936). Such indirect control serves, for example, to encourage the expansion of those vocational programs which are of service to the industry.

In direct contrast to utilitarian organizations, normative organizations tend either to conduct socialization internally, as one of their major activities, or to delegate it to a social unit over which they have comparatively strong and direct control. The political schools of parties and labor unions and theological seminaries are typical examples. It is interesting, therefore, to note that whereas utilitarian organizations have largely replaced the apprentice system—which allows direct organizational control over socialization—with training in regular and vocational schools, some normative organizations still utilize the apprentice system on a large scale. Internships in medical, judicial, and research organizations are cases in point.

These differences in control over socialization units by organizations recruiting their graduates suggest that the larger the role played by expressive compared with instrumental socialization, the more control over socialization units is sought. The role of expressive socialization is smallest in the highly instrumental industries; larger in professional organizations; and largest in highly expressive religious and political organizations. The reasons for the relationship between type of compliance and the significance of expressive socialization, if it proves to be consistent, have yet to be explored. They may lie in the greater visibility and measurability of instrumental training compared with expressive education. It is relatively easy to identify the potential recruit who has received adequate instrumental training, but since the consequences of expressive socialization are more difficult to assess, control over the socialization process itself becomes necessary. The difference may also be due to the fact that a non-conformist can ordinarily cause more damage to a religious or political organization than a technically incompetent person can do to an industrial organization—a point to which we return below. Hence, the need for control of socialization units becomes greater as the expressive socialization demanded by the organization increases.

In summary, organizational socialization is highly limited in typical coercive organizations; to the degree that it takes place, it is instrumental in nature. Expressive socialization is almost completely the monopoly of the inmate subcollectivity. Utilitarian organizations tend to rely on autonomous external units for both instrumental (e.g., vocational training) and expressive (e.g., motivation to work) socialization. They engage in little intra-organizational expressive socialization, nor do their production goals require it. More expressive socialization is carried out informally by workers' groups. Normative organizations exhibit the greatest amount and scope of organizational socialization. In these organizations socialization varies considerably, not so much in its intensity as in its substance; in some, emphasis falls exclusively on expressive elements, and in others instrumental elements are also stressed. When normative organizations delegate socialization tasks to external social units, they tend to keep comparatively close control over them.

Informal socialization is lowest in typical normative organizations; to the extent that it is operative, it tends to be supportive of the organization. In less typical normative organizations, such as schools and therapeutic mental hospitals, informal socialization resembles that which occurs among employees or even inmates.

SUMMARY

The integration of lower participants into the cultural system of the three types of organization has been examined from three viewpoints: the degree of consensus between lower participants and organizational representatives on cultural orientations in a number of spheres; the symbolic processes reinforcing or modifying these orientations; and the processes introducing new participants to the culture of the organization and that of the lower participants' subcollectivities.

We would expect consensus to be highest in normative, lowest in coercive, and intermediate in utilitarian organizations. Six consensus-spheres were specified, and hypotheses concerning the degree of consensus required in each were suggested. It seems reasonable to suppose that effective operation of coercive organizations can be attained with considerable dissensus in all spheres; that, in contrast, typical normative organizations require high consensus in most spheres, particularly in those directly related to their goals—namely, the goals themselves, ritualistic means for their attainment, and ultimate values; and that the effective operation of utilitarian organizations requires consensus in those spheres which are directly related to instrumental activities—namely, cognitive perspective, participation, and performance obligations.

Communication processes are also linked with organizational type. There are many inter-rank communication blocks in coercive organizations, few in normative organizations, and an intermediate number in utilitarian organizations. Horizontal expressive communication is emphasized in coercive organizations and egalitarian normative organizations. Downward expressive communication is stressed in hierarchical normative organizations. Vertical instrumental communication, both up (information) and down (technical directives), is essential for the effective operation of utilitarian organizations.

Socialization is the mechanism through which the existing consensus structure and communication practices are transferred to new generations of participants. Expressive socialization is usurped by the inmate subcollectivity in coercive organizations. Utilitarian organizations tend to rely on external units to supply them with well-trained and motivated participants. Typical normative organizations carry out more socialization than other organizational types do; much of it is expressive in nature and is supervised by the organization itself.

X

COMPLIANCE
AND ORGANIZATIONAL
ENVIRONMENT
Recruitment, Scope,
and Pervasiveness

In this chapter we discuss the relationship between compliance and three aspects of the organization's articulation with its environment. First we consider the recruitment of organizational participants; then two modes of organizational "penetration" into the environment, its scope and its pervasiveness, are examined.

COMPLIANCE AND RECRUITMENT

Almost all organizations have at least some turnover of personnel, since they tend to outlast the duration of most members' participation, and since they refill at least some of the vacated positions (organizations limited to the veterans of one war are among the few exceptions). Therefore some organizational means must be devoted to the recruitment of new members. This point raises several questions: How are differences in means of recruitment related to the organization's compliance structure? What are the criteria according to which participants are recruited? How selective are the three types of organizations?

Compliance and Means of Recruitment

Means of recruitment differ considerably among the three types of organization. Coercive organizations rely on coercion applied by the police, military forces, or delegates of the courts. Utilitarian organizations compete for potential recruits in a labor market as they compete for other means of production, through a price mechanism. Typical normative organizations have to rely predominantly on expressive communication and socialization for their lower participants. Professional organizations are the only kind of normative organization which recruits lower participants in part through market competition. But even here recruitment is quite different from that of most utilitarian organizations, since prestige and research or training facilities augment or even outweigh remuneration and related rewards. Although these noneconomic rewards and conditions also play a role in utilitarian organizations, they seem to carry more weight in professional organizations.[1]

Our hypothesis—to be modified below—is that the means employed by organizations to acquire participants from the environment resemble those they employ to control participants once they have been acquired. Typical normative organizations tend to rely mainly on normative means of recruitment, which increases the likelihood the members will remain morally involved in the organization. Coercive organizations can force participants to "join" them, since they do not require their cooperation once they are in. Utilitarian organizations have to compete for their participants in a market in which sentiments and beliefs play a relatively small role, and rational-calculative considerations loom comparatively large. This, again, is in line with their compliance structure.

Although the association between the kind of power applied in an organization and the mode of recruitment to the organization seems obvious, it should be pointed out that it is not a necessary relationship. Recruitment affects only *initial* involvement. Organizational socialization, communication, and the experience of participation may change it greatly after recruitment. It is possible, for example, to recruit by means of force and then, after intensive socialization, to rely on normative compliance. The first Janizaries were Christian children kidnapped from their parents and intensively socialized until they became the most loyal bodyguards of the Moslem sultans. Many kindergartens and grammar schools perform a similar feat: they turn "coerced" participants into devoted students. In other

1. The similarities and differences between the regular market and that of academic participants are discussed by Caplow and McGee (1958).

cases, normative recruitment is associated with at least some degree of coercive compliance. Almost all military units which accept volunteers, such as commando units, paratroops, and combat wings, require that the volunteer surrender his right to quit and subordinate himself to the full scope of the military law for some period, after which he can revolunteer or resign (often only after the end of the war). Similar coercive clauses exist for regular army personnel who join the service out of calculative motives. In short, the relationship between recruitment and compliance has to be empirically established; neither can be derived from the other. They tend to be "congruent," but are not necessarily so.

Criteria of Recruitment and Selectivity

A CONCEPTUAL NOTE—Criteria of recruitment may be established by comparing the distribution of some characteristics in the organization's population with the distribution of the same characteristic in the population of the collectivity in which the organization operates. We can safely state that all organizations recruit their participants disproportionately from some social groups (or categories). Rather than merely pointing to over- (or under-) representation, therefore, it is of interest to compare the extent and kind of the "disproportionate" recruitment of the same organization over time, or the recruitment of different organizations, in order to establish which are more selective and in what ways their selection differs.

A major difficulty in establishing the criteria and degree of selectivity is that actual recruitment reflects not only the preferences of the organization but also those of the members of external collectivities, as well as the "market" conditions.[2] Thus one would not conclude that the N.A.A.C.P.'s criteria of recruitment exclude Southerners or that low-quality colleges exclude top-quality students.

As a rule, organizations recruit their participants from a number of potential participants which is larger than that of the actual participants but much smaller than that of all members of all the collectivities the organization is recruiting from. For most organizations the characteristics of potential participants are far from clear, a fact which reduces the effectiveness of recruitment procedures. Consider, for example, the recruitment of students to American

2. The same problems arise in assessing the determinants of voluntary turnover. The effect of various turnover rates on organizational effectiveness has been demonstrated in experiments conducted by Trow (1959).

colleges.[3] There are only a few organizations which have, at least formally, a clearly defined group of potential participants, as military organizations have under a conscript system. Factories can draw their employees from those unemployed, but they can also attempt to attract those employed elsewhere. Many modern religious organizations (other than missions) have a tacit or explicit agreement to concentrate their recruitment efforts on members of their own religion who become inactive, or on agnostics, but they do recruit some members of other religions as well. Moreover, the size of the potential group is often dictated by the resources the organization is willing or able to invest in recruitment.

Keeping all this in mind, there still seems to be some usefulness in the notion of "potential participants," since it serves to remind us that for many organizations the participant market is limited, and that we ought to determine the extent of this group and its effect on organizational activities. The *criteria of recruitment* will thus be defined as the criteria by which an organization selects from its potential participants those which it actually recruits. The *degree of selectivity* is a ratio of actual participants over potential ones—for example, freshmen over applicants.

CRITERIA OF RECRUITMENT AND SELECTIVITY IN COERCIVE ORGANIZATIONS—In principle, coercive organizations have no recruitment criteria of their own. Inmates are "selected" for them by external agencies, and they accept whoever these agencies send them. Effective operation of a typical coercive organization requires comparatively little selectivity; only less coercive organizations, or those which are moving in this direction, emphasize selectivity.

Often what is seen as an achievement of the new, less coercive and more normative compliance structure is actually a consequence— at least in part—of selecting "better" inmates; that is, inmate closer to the "output" state or those who are more amenable to rehabilitation, psychotherapy, and similar normative techniques. There seems to be no direct evidence to support this point, though several sociologists who are studying mental hospitals have confirmed this observation in private communications with the author. Wilmer emphasizes

3. Since many students apply and are admitted to more than one college at a time, a college which is issuing admission letters cannot determine which and how many of the accepted applicants will actually become freshmen. A college which had three times as many applicants as it had vacancies, and accepted half of them, may end up with some of its vacancies unfilled. The college has little control over this stage of the selection process.

that the success of *his* therapeutic community was not dependent on transferring out "unmanageable" patients (1958, p. 20, fn. 4).

Similarly, when rehabilitation is emphasized in a prison and the rate of recidivism decreases, this decrease is often achieved not solely by changes in compliance and a consequent increase in the effectiveness of organizational socialization, but by increased selectivity. The rehabilitating prison transfers the "tougher" inmates to other prisons; or the prison is divided into high and low security divisions, and rehabilitation is concentrated in the minimum-security section, where those inmates most amenable to rehabilitation are located. High selectivity—not just higher rehabilitation efforts—explains, for example, much of the success of the California Institution for Men, an open prison. Inmates were carefully selected when the institution was opened and constantly screened while it was in operation (Scudder, 1954, pp. 80-82). Some of the achievement claimed for particular teaching methods, the curriculum, or local traditions of various colleges and universities can actually be explained by differences in recruitment criteria and degree of selectivity. Holland pointed out that "differential student populations among colleges appear as a more probable explanation of differences in productivity (of scientists and scholars) than the special qualities of individual institutions." (Cited by Clark, 1959, p. 1) Some of the most effective business schools, in terms of income and position of their graduates, recruit a larger proposition of their students from sons of corporation executives and from the executives themselves than do less "effective" business schools. (The relationship is further obscured by the fact that the more promising students are attracted to the more effective schools.) The same point can of course be extended to all studies on the relationship between education and mobility.

In short, typical coercive organizations are low in selectivity, whereas less coercive organizations are more selective. This fact must be kept in mind when one attempts to evaluate the impact of changed compliance structures on organizational output and effectiveness.

CRITERIA OF RECRUITMENT AND SELECTIVITY IN UTILITARIAN ORGANIZATIONS—Utilitarian organizations, compared with typical coercive ones, are highly selective. They often maintain mechanisms especially suited to selection, such as examinations, interviews, and private investigations. Weber emphasized the relationship between these recruitment procedures and bureaucratization (Gerth and Mills, 1946, pp. 240-41, 422-26). Like his discussion of other organizational processes mentioned earlier, Weber's model is particularly applicable to the study of utilitarian organizations.

Selection is of special significance for utilitarian organizations because they tend to rely on external agencies, such as vocational schools and colleges, for the socialization of their lower participants. Once selected, their participants are to a large degree "given"; selectivity and not organizational socialization is the more important determinant of effectiveness. The fact that utilitarian organizations have relatively little control over the substance of socialization in these external units further increases the stress on selectivity. An organization may employ "reverse selectivity" by discharging unwanted participants after they have been recruited. But this tends to be a wasteful process because of training and other investments in each new participant. Furthermore, the ability of organizations to reselect participants by merit is limited by the power of unions, seniority systems, job rights, and concern with morale. In short, selectivity in effective utilitarian organizations is likely to be high.

CRITERIA OF RECRUITMENT AND SELECTIVITY IN NORMATIVE ORGANIZATIONS—Normative organizations differ considerably in their degree of selectivity. As Becker has pointed out, the following continuum of selectivity exists among religious organizations: The cult is most selective, next comes the sect, then the denomination, and finally the church, which is least selective of all.[4] Selectivity seems to be positively associated with the intensity of commitment of the average participant. Commitment is considerably higher for members of cults or sects than for the average member of a demomination or a church. An impressionistic comparison of various religious orders leads to the same conclusion. The more selective ones, notably the Jesuits, seem to command the highest commitment on the part of members.

Similarly, from this viewpoint, there are two kinds of political parties. On the one hand there are the highly selective, "closed" or elite parties, which select new members with great care; the Communists are a typical example. On the other hand there are the mass democratic parties, which accept almost everyone who wishes to join. A comparison of the two shows that the commitment of average members is considerably more intense in the first kind than in the second. Similar differences can be detected among various types of labor union. Probably for quite different reasons, the degree of com-

4. See Becker (1932, pp. 624-28).

mitment—and hence effectiveness—which highly selective educational, professional, and therapeutic organizations command is much higher than that of less selective ones. Exclusive voluntary associations seem to command more of their members' commitment than do less exclusive ones. In each case factors other than selectivity may explain the higher commitment of the average member. In the case of ideological parties, for example, its source may lie in the substance of their beliefs. We suspect, however, that if all these factors were held constant, the degree of selectivity would still be positively related to the level of commitment.

A Flow Model: Recruitment and Socialization

Recruitment is related to compliance in two ways. It affects compliance directly, since the means of recruitment *in part* determine the lower participants' involvement, and hence the kind of power which can be effectively exerted over them; and it affects compliance indirectly, by determining the amount and kind of socialization required for the effective operation of a given compliance structure. A discussion of this indirect effect of recruitment supplies an opportunity to relate some of the variables discussed here and in the preceding chapter in the form of a flow or process model.

The following flow model emerges from our discussion of selectivity and socialization: The criteria of selection and the degree of selectivity affect the initial involvement of new lower participants. Initial involvement may be modified by formal and informal socialization. The state of involvement which stabilizes *after* the operation of these processes, or "established" involvement, is the one affecting the power which can be effectively applied to lower participants; it is this established involvement, then, which in part determines the compliance structure of the organization.

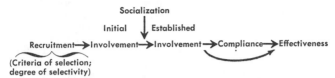

The impact of recruitment on the quality and effectiveness of the organization is examined in the same model. If selection leaves the initial quality of the lower participants "low" (very different from that required by the organizational roles they are expected to carry out, or very different from the end-state the organization is supposed to produce in them), then the effectiveness of the organization tends to be comparatively low, because socialization is not sufficient to modify the undesirable characteristics or because doing so would require diverting considerable resources from other activities. If, on the other hand, the criteria and degree of selectivity ensure that the initial quality of lower participants is "high," effectiveness will be comparatively high, either because resources that would otherwise be required for socialization can be shifted to other tasks, or because the socialization process can carry lower participants closer to the "output" state (if their state is the chief organizational "product," as it is in schools) without increased expenditure of resources.[5]

All other things being equal, socialization and selectivity can frequently substitute for each other, on the simple ground that if the organization can recruit participants who have the characteristics it requires, it does not have to develop these characteristics through training or education. On the other hand, if the organization has to accept every individual who wishes to join, or every member of a specific but large and unselected group, it has to turn to socialization to produce the desired characteristics. Becker (1932, p. 655) has suggested, for example, that the church relies more on socialization, whereas the sect relies more on selectivity. It may well be that modern education takes longer not only because there is more to learn, but also because in the era of compulsory education, schools have become less selective.

The relationship of selectivity and socialization to organizational quality [5a] becomes clearer if we consider the following: Assume there are 100 potential participants, of whom 10 are to become actual participants in an organization. If the organization were to select the 10 best qualified, but not socialize them, or socialize any

5. The relationship is not necessarily linear. A law of marginal utility of a sort applies here; often the last 5 per cent of an accomplishment is disproportionately difficult to attain. Hence the differences between the initial state and the end state are best measured in terms of units of effort and resources required to attain a change, and not in terms of the qualities whose change the organization is striving to bring about.

5a. *Organizational quality* is used here to refer to the worth of the organization in terms of its goals. This judgment is based in part on the various tangible and intangible assets of the organization; and in part on its past performances and potential for future performance (i.e., on its effectiveness). It should be pointed out that quality, as used here, is a concept of the observer. Actors tend to judge the quality of an organization, for example in ranking it according to its more visible assets and performances as well as according to their own values.

10 without selecting them for their qualifications, we would expect their contribution to the organizational quality to be less than if the latter could exercise both selection and socialization. The effect of selectivity and socialization on organizational quality (of course holding constant all other variables), can be represented as follows:

Selection, Socialization, and Organizational Quality

SOCIALIZATION EFFORTS	SELECTIVITY	
	High	Low
High	High Quality	Medium Quality
Low	Medium Quality	Low Quality

The same quality may be achieved by varying combinations of selectivity and socialization. This is not to suggest that there are no constraints on the substitution of selectivity for socialization, or the other way around. If the number of potential participants is close to that of actual participants, the degree to which selectivity can be increased is limited and the organization will have to rely on socialization to attain a given level of quality.

Second, substitution requires a social license which is not always granted. By rejecting 10 per cent of their students, many elementary schools could greatly improve their quality, or produce the same average quality with much less educational effort. But the demand that "everybody" be granted an elementary education does not permit this substitution of selectivity for socialization.

Finally, there are two inherent limitations on the substitution process. On the one hand, a very large number of potential participants and a very high degree of selectivity may be required to recruit participants who do not need any socialization at all in order to fulfill organizational requirements. The size of the group and the degree of selectivity required may often be so high as to be impractical. On the other hand, even very intensive socialization may fail to produce participants with the required characteristics if no selection whatsoever has been exercised in their initial recruitment. Hence it seems safe to say, at least for noncoercive organizations, that all organizations will apply some degree of both selectivity and socialization;

they vary mainly in the relative emphasis they give to the two processes and in their effort to attain a given level of effectiveness and to maintain a given level of organizational quality.[6]

SCOPE, PERVASIVENESS, AND COMPLIANCE

Scope and Pervasiveness

Organizations differ in the degree to which they "embrace" their lower participants. Some organizations serve as the collectivity in which many or most of an individual's activities take place; other organizations serve as a base for one specialized type of activity only. Some organizations attempt to regulate much of the participants' extra-organizational life; in others, behavior of the participants, even while in the organization, is partially controlled by the norms and elites of external collectivities. For example, Warner and Low (1947) showed that the social integration of management and workers in the shoe factories they studied was generated and sustained in expressive relationships outside the factory.[7] The degree to which an organization "embraces" an individual is inversely related to the degree that he participates in other collectivities which constitute the social environment of the organization. Hence the study of organizational scope and pervasiveness—the two components of the organizational "embrace"—deals at the same time with one aspect of the articulation of the organization and its social environment.

SCOPE DEFINED—Organizations differ in their scope, that is, in the number of activities in which their participants are jointly involved. We determine scope by discovering the extent to which activities of the participants of an organization are limited to other participants of the same organization, as against the degree to which activities of participants involve nonparticipants as well. Organiza-

6. Studies of colleges permit documentation of most of the points made here since they supply information about organizational quality, effectiveness, and selection of students. For a fine sample see Berelson (1960, esp. pp. 109-15, and 130-39).

7. Applying Merton's concepts, this statement can be reformulated in more precise terms: Integration in one role-set of a status of an actor may have integrative effects upon another role-set of another status of the same actor if the same persons are in both role-sets. On these concepts, see Merton (1957). On person-set, see Caplovitz (1960, Appendix).

tions whose participants share many activities are *broad* in scope.[8] Organizations which include most or all of participants' activities are referred to—following Goffman's pioneering study of organizational scope—as *total* organizations.[9] *Narrow* organizations are those in which participants share few activities. These may be instrumental activities, as in business unions, or expressive activities, as in social clubs. In broad organizations participants share either both types of activities (as in social labor union) or a wide variety of one type. For example, a church which is a center of both religious and social activities, both expressive, is broader in scope than a church which is a place of worship only.

SCOPE, SALIENCY, AND LEVEL OF TENSION—Scope is related to two major variables which directly affect the compliance of participants: the saliency of the organization and the level of tension. *Saliency* refers to the relative emotional significance of participation in one collectivity compared to that in others. Saliency as a dimension of involvement differs from intensity. It refers not to the intensity of commitment or alienation an individual may feel for the organization, but to the importance of this involvement—whatever its intensity —compared to his involvement in other collectivities.

In general, expressive collectivities, such as families, communities, and nations, have higher saliency than do instrumental ones, such

8. *Broad* and *narrow* scope are not synonyms for *diffuse* and *specific* patterns of interaction, as these terms are defined by Parsons. *Scope* refers to the number of activities into which the relationship among organizational participants penetrates. *Specific* versus *diffuse* refers to the nature of each interaction. Hence, a narrow organization may still be a diffuse one and patterns of interaction in a broad organization may be all diffuse, all specific, or exhibit various combinations of both. Narrow social units tend to sustain specific patterns of interaction and broad units tend to be associated with diffuse ones, but this is an empirical association, not a necessary one. Friendship among neighbors may be diffuse but narrow (limited to social-ecological activities). Relations among members of a labor movement who participate in the same party, union, and several voluntary associations, are broad in scope, since they penetrate into several sets of activities, but may be specific in each one of them.

9. Goffman pointed out four features of total organizations: "First, all aspects of life are conducted in the same place and under the same single authority. Second, each phase of the member's daily activity will be carried out in the immediate company of a large batch of others, all of whom are treated alike and required to do the same thing together. Third, all phases of the day's activities are tightly scheduled. . . . Finally, the contents of the various enforced activities are brought together as parts of a single overall rational plan purportedly designed to fulfill the official aims of the institution." (1957, p. 45) Obviously, an organization may have some of these features and not others, though, as Goffman suggests, they tend to occur together. Our use of *total* most nearly resembles the second feature Goffman lists.

as utilitarian organizations. If this factor is controlled, we suggest that the broader the scope, the greater the saliency of the organization —for example, coercive and some normative organizations tend to be more salient than utilitarian ones. When the scope is broad, actors have fewer alternative opportunities for emotional investment; hence whatever their lot in the organization, it acquires great significance. When the scope is narrow, there are frequently other activities which are more salient. We would expect this to lead to greater "affective neutrality" in participants' orientation to the organization.

The *level of tension* experienced by the average lower participant because of his activities in the organization is also directly affected by the organizational scope. Every social activity leads to emotional strains which have to be "managed"—that is, they have first to be contained, then released (Parsons, Bales and Shils, 1953, pp. 185 ff.). Participation in organizations is likely to create tensions, particularly because of the comparatively high level of rationality, discipline, and affective neutrality it demands. The organization's scope is a major factor in determining the tension level and governs even more closely the opportunities for release of tension.

Narrow organizations can rely on "natural" ventilation; no specialized tension-releasing mechanisms have to be employed. Since the low saliency of the activity keeps tensions down and intermittent participation in other systems (where participants interact with non-participants) allows for tension release, "natural" ventilation is satisfactory. The integrative function of the family for the occupational role of the husband is probably both the most central and the most cited case. Note, however, that the reverse also hold true: leaving the home to work and interacting at work with people other than family members provides a major outlet for the release of family tensions.[10] This is one reason co-employment of husband and wife is considered undesirable, and is formally forbidden in many organizations.

Broad organizations, especially where there are few internal segregating cleavages between higher and lower participants (for

10. This raises the question of the sources and modes of "ventilation" in primitive society and traditional businesses in which the family is the work unit. One might suggest that there were other sources of tension release—for example, segregated leisure activities of husband and wife; and that the level of tension was higher but that the family could stand higher tension because its numerous instrumental functions supplied other than emotional ties between members. Moreover, the tension level seems to be lower to begin with because instrumental values are stressed less; behavior is more institutionalized; and the family is considerably larger.

example, in combat armies) either exhibit a high level of tension or develop more specialized release mechanisms than other organizations do (cf. Selvin, 1960, pp. 67-68).

PERVASIVENESS DEFINED—Before the relationship of scope to compliance can be explored, the difference between scope and a related though analytically independent concept—*pervasiveness*—must be briefly reviewed. The range of pervasiveness is determined by the number of activities in or outside the organization for which the organization sets norms. Pervasiveness is small when such norms cover only activities directly controlled by the organizational elites; it is larger when it extends to other activities carried out in social groups composed of organizational participants; for example, army officers maintain "formalities" in their club. Finally, an organization may pervade other collectivities by setting norms for the behavior of its participants in social units which include nonparticipants and which are, at least in part, governed by nonorganizational "external" elites. Schools define "desirable" leisure-time activities of students; some churches specify the candidates they wish their members to support in the political arena.[11] Pervasiveness differs from consensus since it refers to the range of activities for which the organization sets norms, whereas consensus refers to the degree to which these norms are accepted by lower participants. Thus, high pervasiveness may be associated with low consensus and vice versa.[12]

PERVASIVENESS AND SCOPE INTERRELATED—Pervasiveness may be more or less encompassing than the organizational scope, which is another way of saying that the normative boundaries of a collectivity (as measured by pervasiveness) and its action boundaries (as measured by scope) do not necessarily coincide. A prison is a type of organization whose scope is more extensive than its pervasiveness. Because inmates are segregated from other collectivites, they have to carry out almost all their activities with other participants. On

11. The amount of influence these organizations have on the political behavior of their participants is far from established and varies a great deal from organization to organization, among groups of lower participants, and in different historical periods and cultural environments. Barbash (1959, p. 68), for example, emphasizes the limited influence of labor unions on the political vote of their members. On the other hand, Wilensky (1956a, p. 117) reports a case where the union influence is considerably larger. Whatever the degree, it can hardly be questioned that most normative organizations are pervasive, which is another way of saying that participation in these organizations tends to have a normative halo effect.

12. Although low consensus tends to generate pressure to reduce the range of pervasiveness (i.e., not to maintain, in the long run, unaccepted norms), high consensus may be associated with either low or high pervasiveness.

the other hand, organizational norms govern only a few of these activities. Most are under the control of norms of collectivities other than the prison (as an organization). Thus the prison as an organization is pervaded rather than pervasive. Churches are an example of organizations which have a relatively narrow scope but are highly pervasive; only a few activities are carried out by groups of participants as such, but organizational norms are set for activities in many other collectivities.

There are other organizations which have both low scope and low pervasiveness. Those factories in which workers have few expressive relationships, or none, are typical examples of narrow organizations. We shall see below that, contrary to a widely held impression, the majority of the factories are probably narrow in scope. Both narrow and broad factories tend to be low in pervasiveness, since they tend to limit the norms they set to activities carried out inside the factory.

Finally, there are organizations which are both broad in scope and highly pervasive. Monasteries, nunneries, and religious orders are typical examples. This fact suggests a systematic distinction between two kinds of total organizations: Both are broad in scope (by definition), but one is low and the other high in pervasiveness. Prisons are of the first kind, nunneries of the second; peacetime armies tend to be of the first kind, and combat armies of the second. We expect the two kinds to differ considerably in many ways, including their control and tension-management structure, a subject which cannot be pursued here.

Scope, Pervasiveness, and Compliance

Most coercive organizations tend to be similar in scope and pervasiveness, as do utilitarian organizations. Normative organizations, on the other hand, tend to vary considerably in scope, though their pervasiveness is usually high. The relationships between scope and pervasiveness can be represented schematically as follows:

Scope, Pervasiveness and Compliance

SCOPE	PERVASIVENESS	
	High	Low
Broad	Normative Organization	Coercive Organization*
Narrow	Normative Organization	Utilitarian Organization

* Pervasiveness here is not as low as in utilitarian organizations, though it is much lower than in normative ones.

SCOPE AND PERVASIVENESS IN COERCIVE ORGANIZATIONS—Typical coercive organizations are broad in scope but low in pervasiveness. If emphasis on coercion declines, as when rehabilitation becomes more pronounced in prisons, or therapy in mental hospitals, scope tends to decline and pervasiveness to increase. Visitors are allowed more frequently; there is less restriction on communication with the outside world. In mental hospitals and in the psychiatric wards of general hospitals, daytime, evening or weekend leaves are introduced. These measures increase participation in nonorganizational social groupings and hence reduce the organization's scope. Pervasiveness increases with the recruitment of professional staff and the emergence of a therapeutic orientation. The organization strives now not merely to control public behavior in the compounds of the coercive organization, but also to affect internalized values, and thus to change private behavior as well as future behavior outside the organization.

SCOPE AND PERVASIVENESS IN UTILITARIAN ORGANIZATIONS—Typical utilitarian organizations are narrow in scope and low in pervasiveness; that is, they are mainly instrumental groupings, and have little interest in the norms governing the behavior of their lower participants in noninstrumental matters or outside the organization.

It is often suggested that workers develop solidary relations or groups on the job and thus satisfy an important segment of their gregarious needs in activities shared only by participants. This would suggest that factories, typical utilitarian organizations, are broad in scope. There is mounting evidence, however, that the frequency with which workers are members of solidary work groups has been grossly overstated. The impression has been created that industries are full of primary groups. Actually, we suggest, a comparative study of organizations would show that lower participants of utilitarian organizations are less likely to be members of participant primary groups than those of coercive or normative organizations. Although at least 50 per cent of prison inmates are members of such groups,[13] and the ratio in normative organizations seem to be even higher (see p. 171), studies suggest that on the average no more than 25 per cent of the blue-collar workers are members of primary groups whose recruitment is limited to organizational participants.

13. Clemmer (1958, p. 117) studied the social affiliation of 177 inmates and found that 17.4 per cent were members of primary groups; 40.7 per cent were members of semi-primary groups (which are actually quite similar to what most researchers would refer to as primary groups); and 41.9 per cent were "un-grouped."

Dubin's survey of the "central life interests" of 1200 industrial workers showed that "only 9% of the industrial workers in the sample prefer the informal group life that is centered in the job." (1956, p. 136) "The industrial workers' world is one in which work and the workplace are not central life interests for a vast majority. In particular, work is not a central life interest for industrial workers when we studied the informal group experiences and the general social experiences that have some affective value for them. . . . At the same time it seems evident that primary human relations are much more likely to be located at some place out in the community." (*Ibid.*, p. 140)

A study by Walker and Guest (1952) of 179 assembly-line workers showed that there were virtually no social groups on the job. Workers had some friends working close to them; most preferred to be able to talk on the job if possible; but none were reported to form a cohesive group. Seashore (1954) studied the workers of a midwest machine company, using a measure of group cohesion which was not very stringent. Still, the large majority of workers, 140 groups out of 228, were members of low- rather than high-cohesion groups (*ibid.*, p. 71). Vollmer (1960, p. 75) reports that 71 per cent of female clerical employees, 72 per cent of male specialists, 53 per cent of male semi-skilled, and 63 per cent of male skilled workers, have "no co-workers as close friends outside work."

In earlier periods, factories had a broader scope and higher pervasiveness. Bendix vividly describes tsarist Russia:

It was common practice for employers to build barracks for their workers and to provide facilities for the purchase of necessities on the premises of the factory . . . the employers attempted to control every detail of the worker's life, partly because he lived on the premises of the factory and partly because necessity and tradition gave to labor relations the character of a household discipline. Fines were imposed in case of absence from the factory barracks at certain prohibited hours. Visitors could not be received if their stay exceeded the "length of an ordinary visit." Workers were forbidden to put pictures on the walls of their rooms. (1956, pp. 181-82)

Similar descriptions have been written about life in company towns in earlier generations in the United States (MacDonald, 1928; Rhyne, 1930). The factory controlled much of the economic, religious, educational, and political life of the workers. But this was also a period when factories were less typically utilitarian organizations, when coercion was the secondary compliance source.

With the decline of authoritarianism and paternalism in organizations and the increased emphasis on utilitarian compliance, there has also been a decline in the degree to which organizations seek to dominate their participants' nonproductive activities.[14] Industries build up good will in communities in which they are located by supporting schools, hospitals, swimming pools, public gardens, sport clubs, and charity, but they have become more and more reluctant to own them or control them directly (J. F. Scott and Lynton, 1952, esp. pp. 60, 77-78).

Although in general company towns have declined, a new type has emerged in the government-managed, professional "company" towns such as Oak Ridge, Los Alamos, or Hanford (Vincent and Mayers, 1959, p. 131). Although they are less pervasive and narrower in scope than their predecessors, even these "enlightened" company towns are under pressure to reduce their pervasiveness and scope:

After 15 years as a company town servicing the big-secret plutonium works known as the Hanford Atomic Project, Richland had voted itself out from under the paternalistic wings of the Atomic Energy Commission and General Electric, prime AEC contractor. . . . No family could own its home. Not general necessity but General Electric determined the site of stores and set their rents. Police, firemen, even the city librarian were G.E. employees. More and more, Richland residents began to move out to nearby Pasco and Kenneswick, to own their homes and chat over the fence with non-G.E. neighbors. . . . In 1955 a petition for incorporation as an independent municipality lost 3 to 1. . . . After another petition for incorporation was circulated, Richlanders poured out last July (1958) to approve it, 5 to 1. (*Time,* December 22, 1958, p. 18)

Likert's study (1956), in which participation in company-sponsored recreational activities—an indicator of broad scope—is shown to be negatively related to productivity, suggests that broad scope may be dysfunctional for production goals and utilitarian compliance.

In short, typically utilitarian organizations are narrow in both scope and pervasiveness. The more coercive utilitarian organizations are, the broader their scope and the higher their pervasiveness; and

14. The internal strains of a total organization and the related processes which led to a considerable reduction in organizational scope are analyzed with great insight and effectively documented with historical data by Diamond (1958).

although there is no evidence on this point, we would expect that the more normative utilitarian organizations are, the higher their pervasiveness tends to be. Banks set more norms for employees than factories; and we would expect to find more work-based primary relations among white-collar employees than among blue-collar workers.

SCOPE AND PERVASIVENESS IN NORMATIVE ORGANIZATIONS—Normative organizations are on the average comparatively high in pervasiveness, though they range from narrow to broad in scope. The less typical normative organizations are less pervasive, though more so than coercive or utilitarian types.

The relationship between normative compliance, effectiveness in serving culture goals, and range of scope and pervasiveness is evident in each one of the normative organizations described below, though the intervening variables explaining these relationships differ considerably from one type of normative organization to another.

Although training is usually performed in organizations which have a narrow scope and although it can ordinarily be accomplished effectively there, the effectiveness of education or expressive socialization increases with the scope of the organization (although the optimal point seems to lie short of total scope, which tends to inhibit tension release). One of the functions of extracurricular activities in schools is to extend scope and, with it, the involvement of the student in the school and the school's influence over him. The liberal arts colleges best known for their impact on the values and character of students are residential. Kneller states:

The dire need for new halls of residence is of particular concern to British university authorities because of the intimate way in which corporate life within the two ancient universities has persistently contributed to the essential character and personality of their graduates. The traditional ideals and behavior of academic life, forged in the colleges during the period of free association, become a model for national behavior. (1955, p. 48)

Similar conditions exist in the better known preparatory and "finishing" high schools. The English "public" schools, in which the British elites have been molded for centuries, are boarding schools. When professional schools are compared, those which emphasize training in professional skills tend to have a narrow scope; they see development of the professional personality as a goal of limited importance. On the other hand, almost all professional schools which emphasize character building are total organizations. Compare, for example, medical, law, and engineering schools with theological seminaries, military academies, and political schools. In short, we suggest that the scope of the organization is closely associated with the type and effectiveness of the socialization it employs. The reason for this relationship may be that the more completely students are isolated from other collectivities, the more they must find their "significant others" in the school community. To the degree that these are teachers, guides, or students who share faculty values, organizational socialization is likely to be effective.

Like socialization, resocialization (e.g., rehabilitation) seems to increase in effectiveness as the scope of the organization increases. But for organizations aiming to return lower participants to other collectivities, total scope may not be desirable. Mental hospitals are usually total organizations. But the ability to operate in organizations with a narrow scope, without the warm support of a broader organizational Gemeinschaft, and the ability to participate in several collectivities concomitantly, are essential requirements for the autonomous operation of persons in modern society. Hence, it seems to be functional for mental hospitals to limit their scope somewhat by granting privileges of weekend visits with the family, evenings in town, and the like to as many mental patients as possible (Stanton and Schwartz, 1954, pp. 98-100). On the other hand, if the organization intends to sever the bonds of the actor to the external society and to cut him off from its values, as monasteries do, total scope is obviously most effective.[15]

The effective operation of socializing and resocializing organizations requires high pervasiveness. There is little use for broad scope unless the organization can set the norms controlling behavior in the activities encompassed by it. It is not sufficient to reduce bonds with the outside; in order to create an educative or "therapeutic" milieu, it is also necessary for most shared bonds to be fused with organizational norms. Hence the tendency for these organizations to set norms for almost all activities encompassed by them. Moreover, since the

15. The total nature of "basic training" for new recruits to the army, which segregates them from civilian society and its values and accelerates socialization into the military way of life, has been often pointed out (e.g., Mills, 1959, p. 193). See also Brotz and Wilson (1946, p. 374) and Freeman (1948, p. 79).

prime purpose of these organizations requires the extension of their influence to the behavior of their participants after "graduation," they tend to set norms for extra-organizational behavior as well.

The scope and pervasiveness of political organizations vary with the emphasis they give to normative compliance and "cultural" goals. Radical parties and ideological unions, for example, tend to have both broad scope and high pervasiveness. Segregation of members from external collectivities, particularly competing political organizations, takes several forms. As in other organizations, ecological segregation is the most common means of attaining broad scope, by reducing interaction and communication with outsiders (Kerr and Siegel, 1954; Lipset, 1960, pp. 87ff.). Segregation can take other than ecological forms, however. Unions whose members work at night, such as musicians and printers, tend to have a broader scope than others since the work and leisure schedules of members lead them to limit their social life to co-workers.[16]

High pervasiveness is likely to be attained when the cultural needs of a party's members are satisfied by a party newspaper and publishing house, their educational needs by separate schools, and their social needs by party-affiliated clubs, as was the case in "Red Vienna." Thus, although ecological and temporal segregation are effective in increasing scope (and thereby enhancing pervasiveness), cultural segregation increases the pervasiveness potential of an organization directly, and its scope only indirectly.

Religious organizations vary considerably in scope; the broader the scope, the higher the commitment of the average lower participant tends to be. Monasteries and nunneries command more commitment than do churches; churches which also serve as centers of social activity probably command more devotion than those which are places of worship only.[17] Sects command more commitment than the average church, and seem more likely to isolate their members psychologically from other collectivities—and therefore to have not only a broader scope but also higher pervasiveness potential.

16. For studies of the effect of isolation in time on workers see Blakelock (1960, pp. 446-67), who compares non-shift workers to shift workers. The latter participate less in various social activities of larger units (pp. 455-57). One would expect this lesser participation to lead to higher in-group social activities, cohesion, and communicative isolation. See also P. and Faith Pigors (1944) and McCay (1959, esp. Pt. I). On printers, see Lipset, Trow, Coleman (1956, p. 154 ff.).

17. See Douglass (1926) for what may well be the first sociological study of church scope.

Professional organizations place less emphasis on normative compliance than other normative organizations do. Hence the fact that they have the narrowest scope of all normative organizations is in direct support of our hypothesis. Their scope, however, is not so narrow as that of utilitarian organizations. Hence we expect *occupational communities*—that is, social life on the job and off the job, based on work relations among coworkers—to be more common in professional organizations than in utilitarian ones.[18] In support of this assumption is the finding that while on the average only 25 per cent of blue-collar workers are members of primary work groups, Weiss and Jacobson (1955) report that 82 per cent of employees of a professional organization were members of such groups.[19]

In sum, scope and pervasiveness seem to be closely related to compliance. Coercive organizations tend to be broad in scope and low in pervasiveness; utilitarian organizations tend to be narrow in scope and low in pervasiveness; and normative organizations tend to be high in pervasiveness, but to vary in scope from total to relatively narrow. The relationship holds not only with respect to the three major categories, but also for subcategories. Taking scope first, there seems to be a curvilinear relationship between scope and compliance. It is broad for coercive organizations, narrower for dual coercive-utilitarian organizations, narrowest for typical utilitarian organizations (blue-collar industries), somewhat broader for less typical utilitarian (secondary normative) white-collar industries, still broader for normative (secondary utilitarian) professional organizations, and broad to total for some religious organizations, for therapeutic mental hospitals, and for political organizations with strong ideological commitments. This curvilinear relationship can be explained by the nature

18. Hospitals and universities are not professional organizations by our definition because their lower participants are not professionals. Yet both hospitals and universities approximate professional organizations in serving professional goals. It is therefore of interest to note the broad scope found among the lowest-ranking professionals in these organizations. Mishler and Tropp (1956, p. 195), for example, report that 50 per cent of the nurses and technicians working in a psychiatric hospital have either regular or frequent interaction with one or more persons in nonjob-related situations either during or after the working day, whereas only 19.5 per cent of attendants, who resemble blue-collar workers in their compliance structure, have such contacts.

19. Note that all participants, not just lower participants or just professionals, were included (Weiss and Jacobson, 1955, p. 666). For a general description of this organization see Weiss (1956).

of the goals and the compliance structure of the three types of organization. Coercive organizations require broad scope in order to maintain their segregating control and to realize their order goals. Those normative organizations which have a wide scope use it to build up effective expressive socialization or to increase their psychological grip over their members. Utilitarian compliance can be developed and production goals can be effectively served by an organization which has a narrow scope. Moreover, broad scope, a condition for effective operation for other organizations, may well by dysfunctional for utilitarian organizations.

Pervasiveness is related to compliance in a linear way. It is lowest for the most coercive organizations and highest for the most normative organizations. It increases with the decline in the reliance on coercion (in mental hospitals, correctional institutions, and schools); it increases with the reliance on normative controls, being higher for white-collar than for blue-collar industries, higher for professional organizations than for white-collar industries, and higher for typical normative organizations than for professional ones.

SUMMARY

In this chapter we have explored the ways in which an organization's compliance structure is related to several aspects of its articulation with its environment: the means by which it recruits new participants from outside its boundaries, the degree to which its boundaries are consolidated through the enclosure of its members in relationships of broad or narrow scope, and the degree to which its norms permeate the social relations its participants have with each other and with nonparticipants.

The relationship of recruitment to compliance is quite complicated. An organization may, if the population on which it can draw is large enough and if it is free of other constraints, be highly selective in its choice of members; if it selects participants which match its requirements closely, it need invest relatively few resources in socializing them. If it can impose few selective criteria, it may have to divert a large proportion of its resources to the socialization process and will hence tend to be less effective. Coercive organizations, because their order goals require little commitment or cooperation from inmates, do not need to exercise selectivity or expressive socialization. Utilitarian organizations, because they are under pressure for efficient matching of individual characteristics to role requirements, and because they do not usually control the socialization of potential participants, exercise a great deal of selectivity. Normative organizations, which have to attain particularly high commitments, stress both selectivity and socialization (e.g., Communist party; cults); those which exercise little selectivity must rely mainly on socialization to gain whatever level of commitment they succeed in building up (mass parties; churches).

Depending, then, on the degree of selectivity an organization can employ, and the consequent initial involvement of its new participants, it utilizes various amounts and kinds of socialization. The subsequent "established" involvement then helps to determine which type of compliance the organization can successfully employ. As we noted, although organizations tend to use the same means of recruitment they later employ for control, this relationship is not a necessary one; coercive recruitment, for example, can be linked with later normative commitment, as in the case of schools or the Janizaries.

Organizational *scope* is defined as the number of activities (instrumental or expressive or both) the participants carry out in groups composed of participants. *Pervasiveness* is defined as the number of activities inside or outside the organization for which the organization sets norms. Scope and pervasiveness are not necessarily co-extensive. Prisons are organizations with high scope and low pervasiveness; churches exemplify low scope, high pervasiveness.

The relationship of scope and pervasiveness to compliance seems to be as follows: Utilitarian organizations tend to be narrow in scope, low in pervasiveness; coercive organizations are likely to be broad in scope, low in pervasiveness; high pervasiveness combined with narrow or broad scope is likely to appear in normative organizations. The relationship holds also for intermediate compliance patterns; for example, the less coercive among coercive organizations are narrower in scope and higher in pervasiveness than the highly coercive ones; less utilitarian white-collar organizations are broader in scope and in pervasiveness than the typical utilitarian blue-collar industries.

This discussion of the relationship between compliance and some aspects of the organization's articulation with its social environment concludes the main part of the study of correlates of lower participants' compliance. The next chapter examines a variable which is a noncorrelate. The rest of the book is devoted primarily to the compliance of higher participants and to the dynamic aspects of compliance structures.[20]

20. There are probably many other correlates of compliance which we have not examined. Arthur L. Stinchcombe has pointed out to the author that organizations which differ in their compliance structure also seem to differ in their stratification. Coercive organizations have a caste structure, which rigidly separates lower from higher ranks and allows no mobility across the caste bar. Utilitarian organizations tend to have a multi-level, highly differentiated rank structure (more than fifteen in many government agencies; not much less in big corporations). Normative organizations tend not only to be comparatively egalitarian, but also to stress the distinction between members and nonmembers, insiders ("believers") versus outsiders ("heretics"), as the central status criterion, over any internal differentiations.

XI | COHESION AND COMPLIANCE

It is the central thesis of this chapter that cohesion is not a factor which determines the direction of involvement of lower participants in the organization—that is, it does not determine whether that involvement is positive or negative.[1] This approach differs from that which asserts that cohesion has a positive or negative effect, sometimes both, upon the participants' involvement, as indicated by effects on productivity, attitudes toward the company, combat discipline, and similar criteria.

The second assertion to be examined is that cohesion reduces the variation in group members' behavior. Applied to the study of involvement in the organization, this thesis suggests that the more cohesive a group of participants, the less the variation in the direction of their involvement. For example, if workers are highly alienated, and express this alienation by restricting output, the more cohesive the group, the more likely members will be to adhere to the restricting norm. As far as the behavior of small groups is concerned, this thesis is probably valid. When mechanically transferred to the study

1. An almost complete lack of information about the relationship between cohesion and the exercise of various kinds of power does not allow us to examine the relationship between cohesion and the other element of compliance, the kind of power applied.

of organizations, however, it does not hold. If it is restated to take the distinct nature of organizations into account, it appears to be true.

PEER COHESION AND DIRECTION OF INVOLVEMENT

A Conceptual Note

By *cohesion* we mean *a positive expressive relationship among two or more actors*. A comparison of this definition with the many different definitions used in the field would constitute a major digression.[1a] However, two characteristics of the definition as used here should be noted. First it avoids the term *group,* because this term is itself often defined as a number of actors who have a cohesive relationship; thus the use of this term in defining cohesion leaves both terms undefined. Second, we assume that a cohesive relationship is one in which the actors have positive emotional investment in each other and that these investments are not "wild" but are governed by norms. On the other hand, we do not assume that cohesion requires sharing any norms other than those defining the relationship (and those few norms required for any process of interaction). Hence by this definition cohesion does not imply shared goals or values. To define cohesion as referring both to social integration or solidarity and to consensus or normative integration blurs a valuable distinction. This broader usage turns the concept from a definition into a proposition which is *assumed* to be valid [2]—that is, that solidarity and normative integration are positively associated and change in an associated way. We prefer to keep cohesion and consensus strictly apart.

Cohesion is an abstract concept; its application requires specification of the actors among whom this relationship is expected to exist. Much confusion has been created by using cohesion to refer to a relationship between actors who have different organizational ranks as well as between those who have the same or similar ranks. For the study of almost all problems in organizational theory in which cohe-

---

1a. For various approaches to the study of cohesion see Cartwright and Zander (1953, esp. Pt. II); Festinger, Schachter, and Back (1950); Israel (1956, pp. 20-42); and Libo (1953).

2. This logical fallacy is discussed by Zetterberg (1954, p. 261).

sion is a variable, the rank distribution of the actors united by cohesion is of great importance. Is cohesion limited only to workers, or does it also include foremen? Is it limited to enlisted men or does it include N.C.O.'s and officers as well? These are central questions which must be answered through empirical investigation, and should not be blurred by the term used. In order to avoid this confusion, we employ the cumbersome procedure of adding a qualifier to designate the group of actors among whom the relationship is presumed to exist. Lacking better terms, then, we refer to *peer cohesion* whenever the cohesive bond links actors of the same rank; to *hierarchical cohesion* when the bond links actors of different ranks.[3] *Cohesion* without a qualifier is used only to designate an abstract relationship in which the rank of the actors is not relevant.[4]

The distinction between peer cohesion and hierarchical cohesion has not been developed in past organizational research, apparently because concepts, propositions, and findings from small-group studies have been transferred to the study of complex organizations without due adjustment. In small-group studies the distinction between the two types of cohesion is not pertinent, since all members usually have similar social rank. This is of course not the case in complex organizations.

Positive, Negative, or Both?

Three different statements about the relationship between cohesion and the direction of involvement are frequently made in the extensive theoretical and interpretive literature on the subject: Cohe-

3. Additional specifications can, of course, be introduced. Sometimes, for example, it is important to distinguish between cases where cohesion extends across all organizational ranks and those where it links only two or three. But these additional specifications are only elaborations of the basic distinction between peer cohesion and hierarchical cohesion. Another major dimension of cohesion—its *extent* among people of similar rank—is discussed below, when group cohesion is differentiated from rank cohesion. A third dimension has been emphasized by Gross and Martin (1952). The authors point to the difference between interpersonal cohesion (for instance, between two friends) and unit cohesion (e.g., among all the members of a peer group). On this point see also Schachter (1952); Albert (1953); and Blau (1957). For a methodological analysis of this problem see Lazarsfeld (1959, pp. 55-59). For purposes of the present discussion, this distinction is less important then it is for most studies of cohesion. Unless otherwise specified, the statements in the text hold for both interpersonal cohesion and unit cohesion.

4. In reporting findings of studies, "cohesion" is used as defined by the researchers who conducted them. We then proceed to indicate its relation to the terms used here.

sion makes for positive involvement or commitment—for example, it increases the fighting spirit of combat units;[5] cohesion makes for negative involvement or alienation—for example, it is associated with restriction of productivity;[6] under some (unspecified) conditions cohesion may increase either commitment or alienation—for example, in some cases it is associated with "academic" commitments of students, and in others it is associated with anti-school ideology and behavior, for example, among gang members.[7]

Many of these statements represent the empirical observation that in a particular organization a high degree of cohesion was observed, and at the same time this or that form of involvement in the organization was also observed; or that in the same organization members of more cohesive groups tended to be committed to the organization whereas those in less cohesive groups tended to be alienated. There can be no argument with such observations. But when a causal relationship is attributed to this correlation, as when cohesion is believed to be a cause of the direction of involvement, then—it seems to us—the statements have no validity.

5. "During World War II many sociologists in the armed forces were impressed with the crucial contribution of cohesive primary group relations to morale . . . the psychiatrists Roy R. Grinker and John P. Spiegel summarized their work in the Air Force with this statement: 'The men seem to be fighting more for someone than against somebody.'" (Janowitz, 1959, p. 64). Cartwright and Zander summarized the approach of industrial sociologists in their excellent review and analysis of cohesion studies: "Pride or involvement in the work group and productivity are interacting variables . . . an increase in either one tends to bring about an increase in the other . . . the relationships in the primary group are also important among the determinants of morale, especially satisfaction with the job *and with the larger organization.*" (1953, pp. 624-25; italics supplied.)

6. "The most commonly held view of the function of informal groups is that they are subversive of the purposes of the formal organization. They come into being in order effectively to oppose demands coming from higher authority and work counter to the purposes set by management." (Dubin, 1951, pp. 47-48; see also Matthewson, 1931)

7. E. Gross showed that "the degree of small-group cohesion in an Air Force unit was related to the attitudes of members to certain aspects of Air Force life. Highly cohesive groups tend to be satisfied with the Air Force and with its group goals but dissatisfied with the air site and their jobs." (1954, p. 24) "Some groups support the goals and norms of the school, others are indifferent but may place competing demands upon their members and others openly rebel against the school. A Rutgers study of 2500 high school students in eight middle-class communities indicates that the great majority of students are being influenced by their peers to perform well as students and to look forward to an adult role of success and achievement." (Riley, Riley, and Moore, in press.)

A Theoretical Point

An examination of the process through which cohesion presumably affects the direction of involvement shows that higher or lower degrees of peer cohesion cannot determine the direction of members' involvement.[8] Studies of cohesion make the valid point that once a group takes a position toward the organization, the more peer-cohesive it is the more powerful it is likely to be in inducing individual members to take this position. But the real question is: Under what conditions does a group of lower participants take a positive, negative, or neutral position toward the organization? There is nothing in peer cohesion, or in the degree of peer cohesion, which can answer this question. A highly peer-cohesive group (under the same conditions) can be equally effective in building up either commitment or alienation in the lower participant. Cohesion is like a pipe through which any kind of normative content may flow. The higher the peer cohesion, the better the flow, but the substance communicated is not determined thereby. This fact is not immediately apparent because we tend to think in terms of the influence of cohesion on individual members, and then to generalize to a group of members. Certainly, if a member holding position A joins a group holding position B, then the more cohesive the group, the more likely he is, all other things being equal, to change to position B. But this assumes that the group already *has* a position. To conclude that the degree of cohesion in a group determines *its* position is unwarranted.

Peer Cohesion and Coincidentally Related Norms

Some organizational norms seem to gain support from, or to be undermined by, high peer cohesion not because it reinforces (or undermines) these norms, but because cohesion itself is what the organizational norms prescribe or because peer cohesion requires the existence of conditions which are also functional (or dysfunctional) for one or more of the organization's prescriptions. We now

8. Evidence in support of this point is supplied by Schachter, Ellertson, McBride, and Gregory (1953). It is also corroborated by Berkowitz (1954). The former study did not gain the attention it deserves, and did not have the effect one would expect it to have, perhaps because the authors represented as an empirical finding what is actually a theoretical, logical problem, and because they did not differentiate clearly enough between group norms and directives of the experimenter. Actually, one can see the experimental setting as a formal organization, with the experimenter representing the organization and the experimental group as an informal group in the organization.

turn to the examination of some norms that seem to be related to cohesion in this way.

ABSENTEEISM—Many organizations are interested in reducing absenteeism, a source of concern not only for production organizations but for religious, political, educational, and other organizations as well. Since most studies of absenteeism concern themselves with workers, we draw our illustrations from industrial studies, although the point to be made applies to all organizations which seek to combat absenteeism.

Belonging to a highly peer-cohesive group, it has often been argued, leads workers to enjoy their stay on the job more, and hence makes them more willing to show up for work (Mayo and Lombard, 1944, pp. 211-13; J. B. Fox and Scott, 1943; Mann and Baumgartel, 1953). Gouldner, however, makes the opposite point: "As our comments about the traditionalism of miners' absenteeism underscore, a high absentee rate may go together with high informal social cohesion when absenteeism is a group value." (1954, p. 151, fn. 5). Management decreed "that those who were absent without premission, or a 'good excuse,' would be laid off for the same number of days that they had taken. Far from inhibiting absenteeism, this rule actually encouraged it in the mine, for the miners took the regulation as a direct challenge. When several miners had been penalized in the specific way, others would deliberately take off without excuses." (*Ibid.*, p. 151) Since both a high level and a low level of absenteeism can be supported by a high degree of peer cohesion, it is apparent that no intrinsic relationship exists between peer cohesion and an organizational norm.

INSTRUMENTAL COOPERATION—One of the organizational norms most frequently studied in its relation to cohesion is the organizational demand for intra-team cooperation as a condition of high productivity. Empirical evidence concerning this relationship, quite characteristically, points in all three directions. Some studies show that the greater the peer cohesion, the greater the instrumental cooperation (Gardner and Thompson, 1956, pp. 264-68; and Blau, 1954, pp. 531-33); some show that the greater the peer cohesion, the less the instrumental cooperation (Horsfall and Arensberg, 1949, p. 21; Fiedler, 1954, 1955); and some show a positive relationship for some groups and a negative relationship for others (Seashore, 1954, pp. 49-51, 69ff.) This diversity of evidence can be readily understood if we apply our major point here too—that is, that the *substance* of the norm supported by a peer-cohesive group affects the nature of the instrumental cooperation. A highly peer-cohesive group may support a norm of instrumental cooperation; such support is likely if the group accepts the organizational definition of goals, tasks, and means. But a highly peer-cohesive group may just as well support a norm of sabotaging the organization by inhibiting instrumental cooperation.

In addition, a peer-cohesive group may not be coextensive with the instrumental team; there may be team members who are not group members and conversely. The accompanying chart illustrates our point. Assume that instrumental cooperation is required in team X and in team Y but not among the teams. The cohesive bonds include some members of team X and some of team Y. Does cohesion enhance or reduce instrumental cooperation? There is no way of answering this question unless we know what attitudes team members who belong to the cohesive group hold toward members of their team who are not part of this cohesive grouping. Thus, again, the relevant factor is the substance of the orientation, not the degree of cohesion.

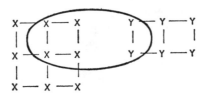

Another way in which peer cohesion supposedly affects instrumental cooperation is by its impact on communication processes; the higher the degree of peer cohesion, the fewer the communication blocks.[9] But again, increased communication makes the norm more

9. We would like to note in passing that the relationship between peer cohesion and the flow of communication is curvilinear, and not simply positive, as is often suggested. Groups with very low peer cohesion seem to be ineffective because of the large number of communication gaps, for example, "misunderstandings." Groups with a high degree of peer cohesion tend to be ineffective because members suppress instrumental communication in order not to endanger intensive expressive bonds. Medium peer cohesion, limited in scope, may be the optimal level from the viewpoint of organizational needs. Blau has shown that employees developed limited primary relationship in order not to block their instrumental relationships: "The coexistence of these two contradictory requirements has given rise to a form of social relationship in bureaucratic work groups that resolves the contradiction. The associations between particular individuals are valued, as in the case of friendships . . . but mutual obligations are definitely circumscribed. . . ." (1955, p. 143) A curvilinear relationship between cohesion and performance is reported by Goodacre (1951). Adams (1954) reports that bomber crews which had higher "equalitarian" scores tended to have a higher performance rating, but the correlation did not hold for the crews which had the highest performance rating. This finding indicates a curvilinear relationship in the direction we suggested.

visible and more potent; it does not affect the substance of the norm, which may support or hinder instrumental cooperation.

TURNOVER—Most organizations try to keep turnover down because of the cost involved in recruiting and socialization, in the loss of experienced personnel, and in the disruption of routine. High cohesion requires a certain amount of stability in the membership of the group, since too much turnover prevents the growth of mutual emotional investment. Hence a low turnover rate is functional both for highly cohesive groups and for most organizations. For example, when other rewards are unsatisfactory, workers who do derive satisfaction from membership in highly cohesive groups may be less inclined to leave the organization. An increase in peer cohesion may thus cut down turnover, not because the group supports the organizational norm, but because this norm happens to be coincidentally related to the intrinsic needs of the cohesive group. It should also be pointed out that when there is high peer cohesion and low turnover, the coincidental benefit to the organization engendered by cohesion is highly specific and limited in scope. It is limited to maintaining a low turnover rate and covers, as a calculative commitment, only the norms which must be obeyed in order to avoid being fired or expelled. All other organizational norms, which often constitute the large majority, remain unaffected by the degree of peer cohesion.

In summary, then, no necessary relationship exists between low absenteeism and peer cohesion, or between instrumental cooperation and peer cohesion. These are norms like other norms, whose acceptance or rejection is not determined by peer cohesion as such. The anti-turnover norm of the organization is the only exception, since it tends to gain support from cohesion—not because the directive of the organization is accepted as such, but because cohesive groups themselves require low turnover.

SOME DETERMINANTS OF INVOLVEMENT AND OF COHESION

"Background" Factors

Correlations reported between peer cohesion and direction of involvement frequently appear to be spurious.[10] Some other factors

10. On the problem of testing for the presence of spurious relationships, see Kendall and Lazarsfeld (1950, pp. 137-41 *et passim*) and Hyman (1955, esp. ch. 6; see also ch. 7).

determine both the degree of peer cohesion and the direction of involvement, creating the impression that the two are causally related. It is important to note that many of these factors temporally precede organizational participation, and hence precede both peer cohesion and involvement in the organization. Such factors include the socioeconomic status of the participants, the nature of their early socialization, their basic personality structures, and some of their religious and political beliefs.

Dalton (in W. F. Whyte *et al.*, 1955, pp. 39-49), for example, compares rate-busters with workers who restrict output. The rate-busters are more highly committed to the organization; they accept its demands for more production, its methods of inducement, and even seem to be devoted to it in a diffuse way. As one worker put it, "I'm always on time. I never lay off an' I don't sneak out early. *The company can count on me.*" (*Ibid.*, p. 41) The restricters are peer-oriented rather than factory-oriented. They do not trust the factory. Their attitude to it is calculative and mildly negative. In the words of one restricter, "Don't misunderstand me. I'd like a little bonus. But they don't give it away, and I won't pay the price they want, be a ———." (*Ibid.*) The rate-busters are social isolates; the restricters are members of a peer-cohesive group. But it would be misleading to attribute the difference in involvement to these differences in patterns of association. There are many other differences between the two types, which precede both peer cohesion and involvement in time; it is among them that the determinants of both cohesion and involvement are likely to be found.

The restricters, Dalton reports, come from urban working-class families. The rate-busters come from farms and lower-middle-class families. An urban working-class background may tend to generate an alienative attitude and to develop predispositions to peer solidarity; boys who grow up in the urban slums tend to be "active in boys' gangs. Such activity tends to build loyalty to one's own group *and* opposition to authority." (*Ibid.*, pp. 41-42) Rate-busters presumably grew up with fewer opportunities to learn patterns of peer solidarity and tend to accept closer paternal supervision. Patterns of interaction learned during early socialization affect later interaction; hence these differences in background between restricters and rate-busters in part explain differences in peer relations and in acceptance of authority and organizational norms.

Restricters in Dalton's study were Catholics; rate-busters were

Protestants. Durkheim has already shown that these differences in religious affiliation are related to differences in patterns of association. Groups of Catholics tend to be more cohesive than groups of Protestants. Weber's well-known thesis is that these religious differences are also associated with differences in orientation to output, that Protestants are more committed to productivity values. Again, "background" factors explain differences in both peer cohesion and involvement in the organization, without assuming a direct link between the two variables.[11]

Rowland's study (1938) of interaction among mental patients supplies another illustration for our contention. In this case differences in personality structure seem to be the "hidden" factor. Rowland distinguished three categories of mental patients according to their level of social interaction. Interaction among patients in the first category "produces in-group and out-group identifications. The typical picture is one of small, closed friendship groups." [12] Among patients in the second category outbursts of affection and hostility are so common that very little regulated group interaction and cohesion is possible. Members of the third category are typically highly withdrawn; there are practically no social relationships among them. Rowland refers to these as the isolates.

The orientation of these patients to the hospital varies with their interaction type. Patients in the first category are "adjusted to the hospital" as an organization; they accept discipline. Those in the second are only somewhat disciplined. The third category has, so to speak, no discipline, since it has little or no social orientation in general.

It seems obvious that although orientation to the hospital seems to be associated with peer cohesion, actually both are determined to a considerable degree by the nature of the patient's illness and his stage in treatment. We are not surprised to learn that the first category included patients who were not very ill to begin with and patients in an advanced stage of treatment, both relatively well adjusted to the hospital authorities and to each other. The second category included primarily less advanced patients in the "treatment" wards and the "continued care" wards. The third category consisted of deteriorated patients and catatonics. In short, differences in the

11. In another report Dalton (1947, p. 324) emphasizes the relationship between higher productivity and higher education, and between productivity and political beliefs: Republicans are reported to be more productive than Democrats.
12. *Ibid.*, p. 327. For a description of the three types, see pp. 327-35.

personality state of the patients seem to account, at least in part, for their orientation both to each other and to the hospital.

Differences in personality characteristics may be the hidden factor accounting in part for many of the relationships reported in industrial studies between an actor's integration into a social group and his positive attitude toward the company and toward management. It may simply be that people who get along well with each other are more likely to get along well with those higher in rank, and to have a more positive orientation to the company and to their jobs (and, for that matter, to many other things) than people who get along less easily with others—for example, who are of the "aggressive" type.

Kornhauser cites a study of workers in which personality seems to play a similar role: "A high proportion of the socially alienated workers also express self-alienation in their low sense of personal accomplishments, their low estimate of chances for personal improvement, and other indications of personal dissatisfactions." (1959, p. 109). Such reports suggest that personality characteristics should be added to the list of factors which are likely to cause both certain forms of involvement and a high or low tendency to become a member of peer-cohesive groups.

A comparison of "gang" members and isolates among dock workers in England further supports our contention that the relationship between peer cohesion and involvement is spurious. The relation between peer cohesion and job satisfaction is shown in Table XI-1.

Table XI-1—Satisfaction of Members of Gangs and Other Dock Workers

	GANG MEMBERS		FLOATERS		DRIFTERS		TOTAL	
	%	N	%	N	%	N	%	N
Completely satisfied with job	55	(62)	47	(43)	33	(15)	48	(120)
Not completely satisfied with job	45	(52)	53	(49)	67	(31)	52	(132)
Total	100	(114)	100	(92)	100	(46)	100	(252)

Source: University of Liverpool (1954, p. 82).

The first group "consists of the men who have . . . been able to establish harmonious and stable relationships with colleagues and superiors. The men in the second group prefer to move around. . . . The third group . . . consists in the unfortunate men with poor reputations as workers who cannot get themselves accepted as permanent members of any gang." (University of Liverpool, 1954, p. 61)

As can be seen from Table XI-1, there is a relationship between cohesion and job satisfaction, an indicator of involvement in the organization.[13] The most cohesive workers are the most satisfied (55 per cent); the next level of cohesion is linked to a lower proportion of satisfied workers (47 per cent); and the least cohesive workers are least satisfied (33 per cent).

A comparison of the three types of workers shows that they differ in the jobs they obtain, so that income, economic security, working conditions, closeness of supervision, prestige, and other rewards are affected. The gangs (highly cohesive) get the best jobs, are first to get work when jobs are scarce, have higher average earnings, higher prestige, and are less closely supervised. The "drifters" (least cohesive workers) are on the oposite end of the scale on each of these items, while the floaters, who exhibit an intermediate degree of cohesion, are in the middle. Thus it seems likely that differences in job satisfaction can here be better explained by differences in rewards than by cohesion.

The duration of the foreman-worker relationship is the "hidden" factor in this relationship. It explains both the different levels of peer cohesion and the differing rewards of the three categories of workers. The gangs are built on permanent relations between workers and their foreman. Gang members follow their foreman from job to job even if this sometimes requires accepting less pleasant jobs (*ibid.*, p. 63). The foreman, in turn, takes first and best care of his own gang members. The drifters and floaters, on the other hand, are free to choose their own jobs and turn down unpleasant ones, to pick their foremen and change them with each new assignment. They have more freedom but less income, prestige, security, and other rewards. Thus the greater degree of permanence in foreman-worker relationships explains the better reward-balance of gang members compared to other workers.

It has been suggested that the more frequent (Homans, 1951, p. 133) and enduring [14] the interaction in a group, the more cohesive it becomes. This relationship should be enhanced among the dock

13. On the problems involved in the use of this indicator, see below pages 197-198.

14. Lipset, Trow, and Coleman (1956, pp. 159-60) show that the number of friends a printer has in his shop increases with the length of time he is in a particular shop. The first eight years are particularly important.

workers, since undesirable or incompatible members—who reduce peer cohesion in other work situations—can be excluded; members can put pressure on their foreman not to accept unwanted workers; and foremen are not motivated to recruit them. Thus the relationship to the foreman, which we saw above, explains differences in rewards and hence in job satisfaction; it explains also the differences in peer cohesion. The more positive the relationship with the foreman, the longer workers stay with him; the longer they stay with him, the greater their material and to some degree their symbolic rewards, *and* the more likely they are to develop a cohesive peer group. The accompanying chart indicates, in a schematic way, the possible effect of the "hidden" factor, and how it may render spurious the relationship between peer cohesion and job satisfaction.

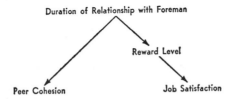

Duration of Relationship with Foreman

Reward Level

Peer Cohesion   Job Satisfaction

Hierarchical Cohesion as a Factor

The study of dock workers supplies a good example of why it is vital to distinguish between peer cohesion and hierarchical cohesion. Since workers were free to choose their foreman and to leave and choose another if the supervisory relationship became strained, we suspect that in those cases where a long-standing relationship between foremen and gang members arose, it was based at least in part on a positive expressive relationship—in other words, there was a hierarchical-cohesive relationship linking two different organizational ranks. That workers seem to exercise this freedom as individuals and not as groups suggests that hierarchical-expressive bonds existed first, and that in the course of working together on the same job with the same well-liked foreman, workers developed peer cohesion.[15] Thus, the stable and satisfactory relationship with the foreman was not only a source of commitment but also a determinant of peer cohesion (See also Blau, 1960, p. 188).

This is by no means an isolated case. The leaders of a group, formal or informal, are often a powerful factor in determining the direction of the group's involvement; commitment to the leaders

15. There is no directly relevant evidence in the study with which to check the *sequence* of events.

often means commitment to their norms or the norms they represent
—that is, those of the organization. We saw earlier, in the study by
Shils and Janowitz (1948), that, regardless of what we call peer
cohesion, the combat effectiveness (i.e., commitment to organizational
goals) of *Wehrmacht* units was determined by the degree of commitment to officers and by their political orientation. When the
officers and the N.C.O.'s were Nazis and their enlisted men included
them in their primary relations—that is, when there was hierarchical
cohesion—the military units were highly committed to combat goals.
When the leaders were excluded from the men's groups, or when
these leaders were not themselves highly committed to combat goals,
high peer cohesion was not associated with high commitment to
combat goals. The findings of the various Michigan studies, discussed
earlier, indicate the significance of hierarchical rather than peer
cohesion in affecting productivity. Similarly, the often cited studies
by Lewin, Lippitt, and White (1939) and by Coch and French
(1952) all deal with the effect of hierarchical cohesion ("leadership-
style")—not peer cohesion—on morale and productivity.

The conclusion seems warranted, then, that at least in these cases,
what looks like a correlation between peer cohesion and involvement
is actually a spurious relationship. Background factors such as social
origin, early socialization, and extra-organizational membership,[15a]
many of which precede participation in the organization, influence
both the degree of cohesion [16] and the direction of involvement in the
organization. Since there is usually more than one "hidden" (or
"real") factor, introducing any one of them will not show the
spuriousness of the relationship between peer cohesion and involvement because it will only reduce the relationship, not eliminate it.
We suggest that when all the real factors are introduced, the relationship will disappear. It should be pointed out, however, that here
these factors have been introduced in a *post hoc* interpretation. It
remains to be demonstrated, through primary empirical research or

15a. Mumford showed that the norms enforced by a group of canteen workers
are simply those of the community from which they are recruited (1959, pp.
149-51).

16. We are concerned in this chapter with peer cohesion as an independent
variable supposedly affecting involvement. Many of the findings in the cohesion
literature point out factors which determine the degree of peer cohesion. For
example, danger (in mines), tension in contact with clients (in a bank, in employment agencies), pride in the work group, and other factors are all reported to
affect the degree of peer cohesion. On mines, see Gouldner (1954, pp. 134-36); on
tensions with clients, Blau (1955, p. 204) and Argyris (1954, p. 129 ff.); on pride
in the work group see Cartwright and Zander (1953, p. 624).

secondary analysis of statistical data, that the contention of spuriousness is valid.

COHESION AND VARIABILITY OF INVOLVEMENT

Group Cohesion and Rank Cohesion

It has often been demonstrated that cohesion is associated with similarity among group members with respect to a variety of characteristics, including status characteristics and attitudes. The relationship holds both ways: The more nearly homogeneous a group, the more likely it is to develop peer cohesion; and the more peer-cohesive the group, the more likely it is to become homogeneous.[17] Since we are concerned with peer cohesion as an independent variable only, as it affects involvement, we examine only the second part of this proposition. One can hardly overestimate its significance. It is the basis for the prediction by Lazarsfeld and his associates about the direction in which cross-pressures in primary groups are resolved.[18] It is the basis for the explanation of how nonconformists' attitudes change (Asch, 1951) and of what happens to the attitudes of new members who join an established social group,[19] for example, replacements who join veteran combat units (Stouffer *et al.*, 1949, Vol. II, pp. 265-72).

Not only is this theorem well established through research findings; the social-psychological mechanisms through which it operates are among the best known and most often discussed processes in social science.[20] Briefly, the individual has a need for approval and recognition. This need is satisfied on condition that he conform to the group's norms. Hence he is under pressure to change his behavior to conform to norms the group enforces.

As we noted earlier, this formulation assumes that the group has a norm. It can explain why individual nonconformists change their behavior or orientation—for example, their involvement in the organization—to conform to that of the group; but it does not explain how the group's norms are established. In a highly peer-cohesive group

17. On the appropriate measure this statement requires, see Hemphill and Westie (1950, p. 340).

18. Lazarsfeld, Berelson, and Gaudet (1948, pp. 141-45); and Berelson, Lazarsfeld, and McPhee (1954, pp. 94-101, 120-22). See also Festinger (1947, pp. 154-80), Riecken (1959) and Baur (1960).

19. For a number of relevant studies see Part IV of Swanson, Newcomb, and Hartley (1952); Back (1951); Gerard (1954); and Homans (1958, p. 602).

20. For an effective analysis see Simon and Guetzkow (1955).

the lack of consensus on norms other than those defining the expressive relationship may be a source of frustration, and pressure may develop to establish *some* shared norms and to increase consensus. But *which* norm is chosen depends on prior characteristics of the members as well as external conditions, not upon the degree of peer cohesion. However, in studying the effect of cohesion on conformity, these norms can be taken as given.

We have no argument with this theorem. The problem arises only when it is transferred from the study of small (simple) groups to the study of large (complex) social units,[21] such as organizations, without due adjustment. It is valid, to the best of our knowledge, to say that the more peer cohesive a small group, the more uniform[22] the behavior of its members. But *it does not follow* that the more peer-cohesive an organizational rank,[23] the more uniform the behavior of the rank members. What does follow depends on the way we specify "more peer-cohesive" in the organizational context. This specification is one of the major adjustments required when the cohesion theorem is transferred from the study of small groups to that of ranks, organizations, and other complex social units.

The statement that the lower participants of organization X are more peer-cohesive than those of organization Y may mean: (a) that when the cohesion of various *groups* of lower participants is measured in the two organizations, the average peer cohesion of a group in organization X is higher than that of organization Y, or (b) that the peer cohesion of the whole *rank* in organization X is higher than in organization Y.[24] Statements of the second type require a measurement of cohesion among all the various groups which make up a rank, not only within each group.

21. On the relationship between complexity and size, see Zelditch and Hopkins (1961, p. 470).

22. In order not to complicate the argument unnecessarily, we assume here and in the following paragraphs that the norm at hand prescribes the same behavior for all members; hence greater conformity is, by definition, greater uniformity. Actually, since peer groups are much more likely than ranks to enforce norms prescribing uniform behavior, the difference between the two, with respect to the cohesion-uniformity propositions, is even more marked than is suggested in the text.

23. By *rank* we mean all the actors in an organization who have the same or similar formal status: privates in an army, for instance. Most status groups, such as nurses, doctors, army officers, include more than one rank. For our purpose here it suffices to treat all lower participants as one rank.

24. For the terms used by Lazarsfeld and Menzel to conceptualize the difference between group and rank characteristics, see (1961, p. 430).

Group Cohesion and Rank Variability

When "more cohesive" is interpreted to mean more peer cohesion *within groups* of lower participants, as is the case in most studies of cohesion in organizations, the presumed association between high peer cohesion and uniformity of involvement among all lower participants does not hold. It does seem to hold when cohesion throughout the entire rank is high. In order to avoid confusion between the two interpretations, we refer to the first as *group cohesion* and to the second as *rank cohesion*.[25]

When groups of lower participants become more cohesive, without an independent increase in rank cohesion, uniformity within each group increases, but differences between groups in the same rank *vary independently*.

Seashore (1954) conducted one of the few studies which both show an awareness of the issue and investigate it empirically. He found that low group cohesion is associated with high group variability in actual production (Table XI-2).

Table XI-2—Group Cohesiveness and Within-Group Variance

	1-4 (Low)	5-7 (High)
Number of Groups	140	88
Within-Group Variance	1.89	1.55

Source: Seashore (1954, p. 67).

He found also that highly cohesive groups differ *more from each other* than less cohesive groups do. Variability in production among noncohesive groups was 16.66; among highly cohesive groups, 25.77 (*ibid.*, p. 71). This finding suggests that variability among lower participants as a rank may increase, not decrease, as a consequence of high or increased group cohesion.

It should be pointed out, however, that high group cohesion could have the opposite effect. Imagine that the majority of members in each of *n* low cohesive groups support the same involvement norms, but because cohesion is low, little pressure is exerted on nonconform-

25. Solidarity might be reserved as a synonym for rank cohesion, as in "the solidarity of the working classes."

ing members; hence the over-all rank variability is relatively high. Then suppose that by some means group cohesion in each one of the *n* groups is increased, with a consequent increase in uniformity within each group. This will lead to a *decrease* in rank variability.[26] In short, group cohesion and variations in the involvement of rank members may be related positively or negatively, depending on differences in the norms supported by the groups.

Rank Cohesion and Rank Variability

The preceding discussion suggests that the proposition about the relationship between cohesion and uniformity of involvement should be revised, to state: The higher the rank cohesion, the less the variability in attitudes and behavior of rank members. For example, the higher the *rank* cohesion of workers, the more likely they are to join the same union, to strike together, or to vote for the same resolution.

It is important to remember that the mechanisms by which high cohesion and low variability are obtained throughout a rank are quite different from those which produce such results in a small group. Members of a rank often include thousands, sometimes hundreds of thousands, of individuals. To see them as a kind of large "small group," in which the majority of members exert direct psychological pressure on the nonconforming minority, is to overlook the most important aspect of rank cohesion—namely, that ranks often include cohesive subunits (groups). Rank members who hold nonconformist opinions are likely to form groups in which they constitute the majority and in which they use the group's power to enforce a group conformity which deviates from the rank's position.

Moreover, to the degree that rank cohesion or rank conformity exists, it is unlikely to result from a direct relationship between each individual and all or most other rank members. Cohesion tends to be built up in small groups of rank members and to be extended from these groups to the rank. The groups are intermediary bodies between the actor and the rank as a social unit. The rank in this sense is a reference group, not a primary membership group.

26. Note that a measure of rank variability different from Seashore's would have to be used to test this hypothesis. He measured differences in the orientation of groups within a rank. We suggest measuring differences among all members of a rank taken as a collectivity.

The mechanisms through which cohesion extends from small groups to larger units, and the conditions under which this extension is enhanced, inhibited, or blocked, are of major interest to the student of complex organizations and complex social units in general. These mechanisms include formal organizations, such as patient government in mental hospitals and unions in factories; voluntary associations in which the rank as a reference unit is activated, such as servicemen's clubs; rituals reinforcing solidarity; and horizontal communication systems, such as newsletters to members.

Janowitz is one of the few sociologists who have analyzed the difference between group cohesion and cohesion of larger social units. He points out that a military replacement system which permits "buddies" rather than single individuals to be transferred is not an effective way to maintain the cohesion of a larger military unit.[27] In this context he also identifies a major source of cohesion in the recruitment of all soldiers in a division from the same community—that is, from a large social unit which is itself cohesive. In World War I the American military unit was still composed of residents of one locality, a source of unit pride and identification (Janowitz, 1959, p. 68). Thus homogeneity of social background, an important correlate of cohesion in small groups, is also a source of cohesion in larger units. But the reasons for the association differ: In small groups, background homogeneity increases the chances that the members will reach consensus and hence exert social power to generate conformity; in large social units, it increases the probability that participants will share external loyalties which can be extended to the organizational unit.

A major difference, then, between group cohesion and rank cohesion is that in order to attain the latter, cohesion which is generated in small groups, subunits of the rank, or external units has to be extended to the larger unit.[28] The mechanisms through which such extension takes place, briefly indicated above, also apply in extending cohesion from one rank to another or from one rank to the whole

27. Janowitz (1959, p. 69) cites a study by Chesler, Van Steenber, and Brueckel (1955) which documents the point.
28. The difference between group (subunit) cohesion, which is often intense, and unit cohesion, which is in many cases less intense, is reflected in the following distribution of answers to the question of where Negro soldiers should be placed in white military units: 1 per cent of the enlisted men said "in same platoon with white soldiers," 85 per cent said "in a (Negro) platoon within the company." (Star, Williams, and Stouffer, 1958, p. 599).

organizational unit, and, for that matter, to a larger social unit as well, even to society as a whole. The study of these mechanisms seems to be one major direction in which sociology must develop if it is to become less a study of small groups and more a study of society.

COHESION AND INTENSITY OF INVOLVEMENT

One might agree that the degree of cohesion does not affect the direction of actors' involvement, but suggest that it intensifies whatever feelings, attitudes, or inclinations they have. Assume that five workers, previously unacquainted, have some grievances about the way they are treated by management. They come to know each other, exchange views, and find that their co-workers are supportive of their initial viewpoint. This may affect their feelings in several ways.

First, it may be postulated that actors will hold to substantially the same positions, but feel more strongly about them. We refer to this change as *intensification of involvement*. Second, they may change to more extreme positions on a substantive scale. At first, let us say, each thought management unfair. Once all five workers support each other, and see that "everybody else" thinks the same, they may all feel that management is flagrantly exploitative. We refer to this effect as *radicalization*. Finally, there may be no change in intensity or in the substance of the position, but actors will hold to their position more tenaciously. We refer to this as the *anchorage* effect.

With respect to *intensification,* we suggest that social groups define not only the substance of their norms but also the intensity with which they should be held. It is commonly believed that the British culture prescribes low intensity for many norms, while more expressive nations, such as Italian or Latin American societies, allow intensive support of a wider range of norms. Education seems to be associated with tolerance and with "seeing both sides of an issue," which may suggest that intensity is lower. Similar distinctions are often made among social classes, various ethnic groups, and other social groups, though there is little valid information on the cultural distribution of intensity. We would expect cohesion to affect the degree to which norms prescribing intensity (like all others) are enforced, but not to determine their "substance"—that is, the level of intensity they define as proper.

Radicalization is expected to occur because the discovery that an opinion is shared by others makes actors more secure and therefore inclined to assume a more extreme position. Coch and French state: "Strong cohesiveness provides strength so that members dare to express aggression which would otherwise be suppressed." (1952, p. 479). The opposite hypothesis would be that since higher cohesion makes actors more secure, they have less need to take extreme positions. For example, they would be less aggressive. A third hypothesis would be that once the various actors find their opinions shared by others, they will be less inclined to modify their opinions in any way. If the amount of reward obtained for an opinion already held is increased, there is no motivation to become more or less radical.

These alternative hypotheses appear equally plausible. If there is empirical evidence which makes it possible to determine which is valid and which is false, we are not aware of it. In any event, although cohesion may well determine the level of emotional security an actor feels (although the cohesiveness of all the groups in which he interacts has to be taken into account, as well as the congruence of their norms), there is no clearly established association between emotional security and a specific form of behavior or involvement. A secure person may be secure in rejecting, accepting, or being indifferent to an organization. Hence it cannot be claimed that cohesion, via security, modifies the direction of involvement.

We have suggested that the relationship between cohesion and involvement is spurious; that it will completely disappear once the real determinants are accounted for. On the other hand, cohesion is related to intensity; but intensity is also affected by many other variables, both intervening (e.g., security) and independent (e.g., level of education). Cohesion, we suggest, does not determine the substance of an intensely held norm but does influence intensity—for example, through its effect on the actor's security—although indirectly, to a limited degree, and in ways not clearly established.[29]

Finally, it is correct to say that it is more difficult to change an individual's behavior if he belongs to a highly cohesive group than if he belongs to a less cohesive one (Coch and French, 1952, p. 479),

29. Experimental studies which effectively "hold constant all other factors" tend to prove that X, let us say cohesion, is a factor, but rarely tell us how much of the variability of the dependent variable is accounted for by the factor. It may be rather small, as it seems to be in this case.

though it is easier to change the behavior of an entire group when the group is highly cohesive than when it is not. The main point is that cohesion will anchor any norm—that is, resist its change regardless of its substance.

SUMMARY

There is no necessary correlation between peer cohesion on the one hand and direction of involvement in the organization on the other, because there is no way in which peer cohesion can determine the norm specifying what members' involvement shall be. Peer cohesion affects the orientation of nonconforming individuals by enforcing whatever norms the majority of the group, or its more powerful members, subscribe to.

In contrast to peer cohesion, hierarchical cohesion (across organizational ranks, as between officers and men) may, if the high-ranking personnel are committed to organizational norms, be directly related to lower participants' positive involvement in the organization. This difference is one reason for emphasizing the distinction between hierarchical and peer cohesion.

Higher cohesiveness within groups of lower participants tends to reduce the variability in members' involvement within each group, but not necessarily throughout the rank, across groups. Rank cohesiveness varies independently of group cohesion. The mechanisms by which rank cohesion is generated and sustained, and through which it exerts power over members, are different from those involved in the formation and influence of group cohesion.

Intensity of involvement, like its direction, is prescribed by the substance of social norms independent of the degree of peer cohesion; there is no reason to believe nor evidence to suggest that peer cohesion leads systematically to either radicalization of positions or its opposite. Cohesion has an anchorage effect, but since it will "anchor" both alienation and commitment, our assertion that there is no correlation between peer cohesion and direction of involvement still holds.

APPENDIX: COHESION AND JOB SATISFACTION

Studies of cohesion, especially of work groups, frequently use job satisfaction as an indicator of the orientation of lower participants to the organization. This is not a very effective indicator for two reasons: because it correlates less well with other indicators than they correlate with each other (for some evidence see below, page 304); and because it refers to variables other than orientation to the organization alone (regardless of how "organization" is defined). For example, it reflects the degree of satisfaction one has with one's line of work, or occupation, not just with the particular job in the particular organization. The value of this indicator for our purposes is particularly limited because aspects of the organization other than its directives, sanctions, and representatives affect job satisfaction, and it is these three aspects which have been defined as the object of involvement in the organization. We use job satisfaction only when no other information on involvement as here defined is available in the studies from which illustrations are drawn.

Many statements about the relationship between high cohesion and job satisfaction suffer from a much more serious flaw than the use of a comparatively poor indicator. They are frequently *logically* true. These statements are actually based on one of the two following mathematical theorems: (*a*) if you increase a subtotal, the total increases; or (*b*) if you add to a sum, the sum increases.

The first theorem applies when job satisfaction is defined as including all the satisfactions derived from a job (as it usually is defined.) *Cohesion* then refers to social relations on the job as a source of satisfaction.[30] The more cohesion, the more satisfaction from this source. If other satisfactions have not decreased, then, logically, the total amount of satisfaction is larger.

The second theorem applies if job satisfaction is defined to include all satisfactions other than those derived from cohesion. It then means that if satisfaction derived from cohesion is added, the total amount is larger.[31]

The proposition about high cohesion and job satisfaction can be made testable by reading it to imply that there is a "halo" effect—that is, if actors gain more satisfaction from cohesion, they will also gain more satisfaction (or less frustration) from other elements of

30. The statement that social relations are a source of satisfaction is assumed to be valid. But the same criticism applies, with reversed signs, if the statement is invalid.
31. For an outstanding study of the determinants of job satisfactions, which avoids both flaws, focusing on factors other than cohesion, see Zaleznik, Christensen, Roethlisberger (1958).

the job situation, assuming that those other elements have not changed. It seems fair to suggest that the proposition is rarely given this interpretation, one which requires the development of psychological theories and research techniques for the study of "halo" effects— an area of much interest, but one not particularly related to the study of cohesion or complex social units.

XII

COMPLIANCE AND THE DISTRIBUTION OF CHARISMA

In the preceding chapters relationships between compliance structure and other organization variables were examined. For the purpose of this examination, organizations were classified according to the compliance structure of their lower participants. The next step is to analyze the compliance structure of higher participants or elites. Elites were studied in Chapter VII as power-holders over lower participants, and as recruiters of their involvement. This chapter examines the elites themselves to discover the nature of their involvement in the organization and the kinds of control the organization has over them.

Three general observations can be made about the organizational control of elites:

1. The control of lower elites by higher elites is affected by the control higher elites exercise over lower participants. We shall see, for example, that higher elites can use lower participants to control lower elites, so long as lower participants are not more committed to the middle ranks than to the higher ones.

2. The compliance structure of elites or higher participants varies much less from one type of organization to another than the compliance structure of lower participants. The basic differences between the compliance of higher and lower participants are as follows: Coercive power is rarely applied to higher participants; their involve-

ment is usually moral or calculative, and only rarely alienative. Second, pure moral involvement is relatively rare because higher participants are more likely than lower participants to have career or. economic interests in the organization. This means that the higher ranks exhibit a more limited range of compliance patterns than lower ranks do. The compliance structure of guards in a prison is quite similar to that of foremen in a factory, and, since the clergy too is a vocation, with income, promotions, and prestige differentials, the compliance structure of ministers does not differ as much from the foreman's pattern as his parishioners differ from workers in compliance.

3. Finally, in most organizations, the higher the rank, the more normative the control exerted on it (though exclusive normative control is found mainly in the control of lower participants in typical normative organizations). Coercion is not, as a rule, applied to higher participants. Remunerative deprivations are relatively rare. Informal talks, subtle warnings, and transfer to less important positions—in short, normative deprivations—are the typical sanctions.[1] Moral involvement in one's duties is expected, as well as the ability to gain satisfaction from the intrinsic nature of the work and from prestige, esteem, and similar symbolic rewards.[2] This holds for the prison's warden, the corporation executive, and the bishop. The higher the rank, the greater we would expect the average commitment to be (Argyris, 1957, pp. 94-95). Although there are systematic differences among organizations, and much of the following discussion is devoted to these differences, they should be seen as specifications of a basically similar pattern.

In Part Three we focus on normative power and moral involvement because these factors are central to our preliminary study of the compliance of higher participants. The study is limited to an examination of diffuse and intense normative power, or charisma. This

1. The great pains taken to "cool the mark out" when deprivations such as demotion are applied to those higher in rank are indicative of the organizational effort to sustain their moral commitment to the organization. Goffman (1952) has trenchantly analyzed the "cooling out" mechanisms. We would expect to find them operating more systematically and deliberately the higher the rank of the deprived person (cf. Garfinkel, 1956, esp. p. 423). Davis (1948) emphasizes the reluctance of military organizations to punish their officers.

2. "The opportunities for personal power and for creative work are, if not limitless, certainly very great. In this respect, non-financial rewards may provide a more powerful stimulus than monetary compensation to the business executive of a large corporation." (Gordon, 1945, p. 314; see also Newcomer (1955, pp. 121-31) and Copeland (1952).

limitation is justified on two grounds. First, statements about charisma hold, with some modifications, for other, less intense normative power; and second, as both Weber and Parsons have pointed out, all normative power is derived originally from charisma. The differential distribution of charisma among the ranks of various organizational types is studied first. Then we consider the ways in which the distribution patterns are related to differences in compliance structure, and to the functional needs the various distributions fulfill. In the following chapter, the potential dysfunctions of charisma in higher ranks are examined, along with the control mechanisms that operate to minimize these dysfunctions.

THE PLACE OF CHARISMA IN ORGANIZATIONS

A Conceptual Note: Charisma as a Type of Normative Power

Charisma has been studied from many viewpoints. It has been examined as a major factor in historical change; its role in the religious and political spheres has been explored; and its psychological nature has been discussed. We follow those who study the function of charisma in organizations.

Charisma is usually defined as "an extraordinary quality of a person" (Gerth and Mills, 1946, p. 295; Gerth, 1940, p. 517, fn. 2). It seems to us to be preferable to define the concept as *the ability of an actor to exercise diffuse and intense influence over the normative orientations of other actors*. This suggests that charisma is a form of normative power which ultimately depends on the power of a person (Parsons, 1937, p. 665). Specific influence—for example, influencing the choice of a movie, or a dress, or a drug—is therefore not charismatic; [3] similarly, instrumental influence—for example, influencing the choice of tools on the job—is not indicative of charisma. Political and religious leaders, on the other hand, have charisma because they typically exert diffuse influence upon the normative orientation of their followers.

As defined above, charisma, like authority, is a relational property. But whereas authority, as usually understood, implies only that the subject holds in abeyance his own criteria for decision and action, and accepts as legitimate the directives of his superiors, charisma

3. For an extensive review of the literature and an empirical study of non-charismatic, specific leaders or communicators, see Katz and Lazarsfeld (1955).

implies that the subject has been influenced to modify some of his own criteria (Simon, 1957, p. 127). For this reason Bendix prefers the term "charismatic leadership" over "charismatic authority" (1960, p. 304).

Weber distinguished between two types of charisma, *pure* and *routinized* (1947, *passim;* Gerth and Mills, 1946, esp. pp. 52-53). One is the charisma of a "natural" leader; the other is the charisma of such a leader which becomes invested in an office or transferred to future generations along a hereditary line.

Two dimensions seem to underlie Weber's concept. One is the intensity of the influence the charismatic leader has over the person subject to his power. It is high for pure charisma and lower for routinized charisma.[4] The second dimension is the manner in which charisma is acquired, through *achievement* or through *ascription*. Pure charisma is achieved not just once but again and again. Its holder is frequently called upon to redemonstrate his power. Routinized charisma comes with the attainment of charismatic office. Although the office itself frequently has to be achieved, office charisma is ascribed. Every incumbent, regardless of his ability or performance, obtains it with the office.

The idea that the ascribed nature of charisma is the significant characteristic of routinized charisma, and not its investment in a particular office, leads us to suspect that there may be statuses other than organizational offices in which charisma may be invested. Actually, ascribed (routinized) charisma may be found in any social status. "Familial charisma is present in some form in all aristocracies and finds its most intensive development in the Indian caste system." (Bendix, 1960, p. 314, fn. 13)[5] It may be found in the status of membership in an order such as the Jesuits, and in the status of a qualified professional, such as a doctor or a professor. When we examine the influence of persons carrying titles such as S.J., or M.D., or Professor, especially in European societies, their charismatic nature is quite evident.[6] Again, each of these positions has to be attained,

4. The term *charisma* was used by Weber to refer mainly to the "quality" of leaders who influenced the process of history and changes of major social structures. But sociologists have often extended its use to "lesser" leaders, those who have less influence (Harrison, 1959, p. 5).

5. Hereditary charisma is disregarded in the following discussion, which is limited to organizations where this type is rare.

6. The function of titles and other status symbols in maintaining status charisma is a topic of much interest, which has not been explored empirically. For pertinent analytical observations see Parsons (1951, pp. 399-407).

but every incumbent, once he has achieved the status, automatically has the status charisma. The significance of this will become evident below.

Sources of Routinized Charisma

According to Weber, routinized charisma develops as follows: First, pure charisma is generated outside structural positions by "natural" leaders; then it becomes invested in offices—that is, routinized. Future incumbents of these offices borrow their charisma from the stock supplied by the founder, the pure charismatic leader. The stock tends to diminish over time, and the only way to replenish it is by recruiting new (pure) charismatic leaders to the office from outside the organization. These usually emerge when the structure is in a crisis, and are more likely to build a new structure on the ruins of the old than to supply the existing structure with a new stock of routinized charisma. The establishment of the Fifth Republic by De Gaulle supplies a recent illustration.

We would like to suggest that *personal (or pure) charisma may be originally achieved in organizational offices.*[7] There are several ways of demonstrating that this in fact occurs. First, incumbents of the same office reveal considerable difference in the degree of their charisma. Compare, for example, George V with George IV,[8] Franklin Roosevelt with Harding,[9] or Churchill with Baldwin. All these examples satisfy two conditions: (1) actors who exhibited high personal charisma fulfilled the same office *after* those who had low charisma. (If only the reverse sequence had occurred, it could be suggested that the differences were due to the general trend suggested by Weber, that of the decline of office charisma with time.) (2) The actors de-

7. We equate here the "pure" or "genuine" charisma of natural leaders, with the personal charisma developed above and beyond office charisma by leaders in organizational positions. To those who suggest that personal charisma developed within an organization is not "genuine" we must counter by saying that we are not aware of an empirical indicator that would allow us to establish the difference. Certainly there is no systematic difference in the intensity of the power or in the ways it is attained, the two criteria Weber used to distinguish genuine from routinized charisma.

8. George IV is depicted as "disreputable and somewhat ludicrous," as one during whose life the "kingship of Britain was at a very low ebb." (Thomson 1950, p. 21; see also pp. 169-70). On George V, the same source (p. 174) states: "The combination of dignity and popularity, of respect and affection, which he achieved won him a personal esteem which produced extraordinary scenes of genuine popular emotion during his illness, on the occasion of his Jubilee, and at his death."

9. For an analysis of changes in the status of the Presidency under the impact of the personal power of various presidents, see Rossiter (1956, esp. p. 62ff.)

veloped at least an important part of their charisma while already in office.

Second, some actors who enter office without revealing much personal charisma, and find that the stock of office (routinized) charisma has been considerably reduced, develop so much personal charisma while in office that when they leave it, its stock of routinized charisma is replenished. This was the case, for example, with Victoria. She had little, if any, personal charisma in the first decades of her reign. After the death of her husband, the gap separating her from the people widened, and the legitimation of the monarchy continued to decline. Only in her later days, under the influence of Disraeli, did she become closer to the people and considerably more popular and influential. By the time she died, the Republican movement to abolish the monarchy in England had lost its impetus.

Queen Victoria left the British monarchy in a vastly stronger position than she found it. In 1837 when she came to the throne it had sunk low in popular esteem because of the character of her predecessors, George IV and William IV. . . . It was clear enough, by 1837 . . . , that the monarchy was surviving in spite of the monarchs. During the reign of Victoria it can be said that it survived only because of the monarch. (Thomson, 1950, pp. 169-70)

Note also that Victoria's charisma is reported to have increased mainly from 1871 on (*ibid,* pp. 171ff.).

It therefore seems that a modification of a widely accepted theorem is called for: *Personal charisma may be achieved in an office.* Actors may have only personal charisma (natural leaders, or informal leaders in organizations) or only office charisma ("unimpressive" kings, presidents, doctors, or professors), but they also may have both office *and* personal charisma ("outstanding," personally influential, officeholders).[10] This means that Weber's evolutionary assumption is unnecessary; a charismatic movement may develop into a bureaucratic structure, but a bureaucracy may also become highly charismatic. This occurs, for example, whenever a peacetime army enters combat. Katz and Eisenstadt (1960, pp. 128-30) showed that

10. Some confusion is created in the literature because the term *charisma* is sometimes used to refer only to personal charisma, and sometimes to both personal and office charisma. It seems to us that the safer approach is to treat charisma as a general category and to add qualifying adjectives whenever necessary.

Persons who have charisma, regardless of its source, will be referred to as charismatics. A person may have charisma over some individuals but not over others. We see a person as charismatic if he has charisma over the majority of the lower participants he is expected to control.

sometimes bureaucrats become the charismatic leaders of their clients; nurses in a well-baby clinic initiated a "suffragette" movement among the mothers who came to be served by the clinic.[11]

Still another departure from the Weberian approach is implied. Weber saw the charismatic and the bureaucratic authority structures as two distinct types. Constas (1958, esp. pp. 401-2) has made explicit two conceptions of bureaucracy she finds implicit in Weber, one rational-legal and one charismatic. Still, she views these as two distinct types.

In contrast, we follow Parsons (1937, p. 716), who has suggested that Weber's ideal types should be analyzed so that their elements can be treated as variables of an analytical system, and Wolpert (1950, pp. 690-93), who has suggested that the concepts of bureaucracy and charisma be so treated. Charisma and bureaucracy can be combined to varying degrees; as Bendix has said, "It should be remembered that genuine charisma also recurs in combination with other types of domination." (1960, pp. 305-6).[12] A structure might be purely bureaucratic, or have some charismatic positions, or have a large number of such positions, or be almost completely staffed by charismatics and governed by the patterns of behavior typical to charismatic movements.

Three Types of Charisma Distribution

When pure charisma becomes routinized, according to Weber, it is concentrated in top positions, in nonbureaucratic heads of bureaucracies, such as popes or kings.[13] Other positions borrow its light, but, like the moon, have no light of their own.

Actually, we suggest, charisma may be functionally required and actually developed in a large variety of organizational positions, not just the top ones. If we classify organizations according to the posi-

11. The place and role of "irrational" leaders in formal organizations was also analyzed from this viewpoint by Josephson (1952).

12. Lawrence Krader has pointed out (personal communication) that in some tribes, shamanism is strictly hereditary, while in others it is "personal" (i.e., any member of the tribe who behaves in certain "unusual" ways may become a shaman after some testing and/or socialization). There are also tribes in which the two forms of recruitment are combined: Shamans are chosen from certain hereditary kinship groups; but only members of these groups who show certain peculiarities in their behavior are selected to be "trained" for the position of shaman. The latter case would be one in which personal charisma develops later, superimposed on status charisma.

13. Hence, the succession crisis is usually studied on this level. Levenson (1961) suggests that many of the problems of succesion exist in all organizational positions. This, we would suggest, is especially true whenever the superiors have personal charisma over the subordinates; for example, when influential teachers are replaced.

tions in which charisma is functional, we find that there are at least three major forms of distribution, each related to a distinct type (or subtype) of compliance. In one form of distribution, charisma is concentrated in *top* positions; this is referred to as a *T-Structure* (e.g., Ford Motor Company under the direction of Henry Ford). In a second, all *line* positions are filled by charismatics; this is referred to as an *L-Structure* (e.g., the hierarchy of the Roman Catholic Church). In a third, charisma is limited to one or more *ranks* other than the top one; this is referred to as an *R-Structure* (e.g., doctors in hospitals). Finally, in some organizations (e.g., a prison) there is no organizational position in which charisma is required. (Organizations which have L-, R-, or T-Structures will be referred to as L, R, or T organizations.)

Like many of the generalizations which constitute contemporary organizational theory, Weber's model of bureaucracy, although touching briefly on other organizations, is based primarily on insights into the operation of governmental and business bureaucracies. Therefore, it is not astonishing to find that what Weber considered to be true of bureaucratic organizations in general holds only for a subcategory: only utilitarian organizations tend to limit charisma to their top positions. Typically, the only charismatics in these organizations are their heads, such as kings, presidents, prime ministers, and top executives ("the old man").

Other types of organization, we suggest, require other distributions of charisma. Normative organizations which emphasize pure normative compliance (for higher as well as lower participants) tend to require an L-Structure of charisma. Hierarchical religious organizations, especially the Roman Catholic Church, the Mormon Church, and the Church of England;[14] ideological political parties and labor unions, and military combat organizations [15] all require charisma in

14. For a discussion of less well-known hierarchical religious organizations, such as the Aztec and Maya priesthoods, the Peruvian hierarchy and others, as well as an extensive bibliography, see Wach (1958, pp. 385-89). Nonhierarchical churches exhibit neither L- nor R-Structures but a "middle" type, ranging from an R-Structure to a state approaching an L-Structure. They are discussed in the last section of this chapter.

15. Combat units are not normative organizations; they have a compound normative-coercive compliance structure. But since the normative element of their structure requires the development of charisma, we must ask of them, as we ask of organizations in which normative compliance predominates, what the nature of the charisma distribution is. We suggest that in combat units it takes an L form. Hence combat units are discussed in this and the following chapter together with other normative organizations.

all their positions. Moreover, office charisma alone is not considered satisfactory. A priest who says mass and hears confession but does not "have the spirit," a party or union secretary who only "does his job," an army officer who relies on his rank and does not "show leadership," are all illustrations to this effect.

Normative organizations which emphasize social compliance (among higher but not lower participants) [16] tend to require an R-Structure of charisma. In universities, colleges, general hospitals, therapeutic mental hospitals, and research organizations, charisma is restricted mainly to professionals, such as doctors, professors, and researchers.

Professionals draw their ascribed charisma from their special knowledge or skill and from their organizational rank. In addition, there are well-known differences in personal charisma. Every profession has its national or international charismatic leaders, and each campus or hospital its local ones. A comparative study of various professions would probably show that there are systematic differences in the proportion of their members who are charismatics. One would expect to find fewer persons (or positions) exercising charismatic influence over students in "technical" professions, such as engineering and statistics, and more in "normative" disciplines such as literature and philosophy. This proposition is based on the assumption that the diffuse normative influence which charismatics exercise is less relevant for the more "technical"—that is, specific-instrumental—disciplines.

Whether they are lay administrators or nonpracticing professionals, top executives of these professional organizations as a rule have little, if any, personal charisma, and considerably less office charisma than professionals.[17] Only rarely are personal charismatics recruited to these positions.[18] Finally, coercive organizations tend not to have any charismatics in organizational positions, and are therefore ignored in the subsequent discussion.[19]

16. There is relatively more stress on social, less on pure normative compliance in these organizations than in the L type, though the more normative pattern is predominant.

17. These types should be considered "ideal types." See below, pp. 328-333.

18. We refer to the top power positions of these organizations. For public relations purposes, some organizations appoint charismatic figureheads to positions which formally outrank the top power position of the organization (e.g., presidents above general directors, chairman of the board above the top administrator).

19. The present discussion is devoted to charisma in organizational positions only. The effect of charismatics without such positions is not studied regardless of the effect they may have on the organization.

THE FUNCTIONS OF CHARISMA IN THREE STRUCTURES

In the following sections, the functions and then the dysfunctions of charisma in various types of organization are discussed. The discussion is comparative: functions and dysfunctions are examined in organizations which differ in their compliance structure. Unless otherwise specified, the following propositions are expected to hold both for positions whose holders command only office charisma and for positions whose holders command both office and personal charisma. But we expect the statements to be more strongly supported when the two sources of charisma are combined, because this suggests, other things being equal, that the level of charisma is higher.

One generic function of charisma for organizations is well known: It serves as a major source of legitimation. In addition, it influences the need-dispositions of the participants in such a manner that their participation in the organization, in particular in its symbolic activities (e.g., rituals), will increase their gratification and hence their positive orientation. It therefore builds up commitment.

Weber tended to emphasize the dysfunctional or destructive role of pure charisma, as exemplified by the true prophet's "anti-system" preaching. Similarly, Constas (1958, 1958a) pointed to the dysfunctions of charisma in bureaucracy, both for science and for rational administration. Charisma is explicitly depicted as an evil—a source of irresponsible government, a temptation to turn the bureaucracy from a tool in to an end in itself. We, on the other hand, wish to emphasize that charisma—pure as well as routinized—if developed in or recruited to the right organizational positions, may be highly functional for the organization.

Although all organizations would benefit from some amount of commitment, the main point of our discussion is that the amount required can vary immensely. The nature of an organization's compliance structure is an important determinant of the amount of charisma required. Obviously, the more normative power is relied upon, the greater the need for moral involvement, and the greater the need for charisma. The more the organization relies on remuneration or coercion, the less charisma is required. But the compliance structure is not the only factor to be considered. The pervasiveness of the organization must be taken into account as well. Are lower participants expected to accept only organizational decisions about means, or also decision about ends? Decisions about ends require more legitimation and commitment than decisions about means because they are based on value judgments, while decisions about means are based on factual information and rational knowledge and hence can draw, in Western societies, on the actors' general commitment to such value judgments.[20] For similar reasons, inducing participants to accept guidance in expressive matters requires more legitimation and thus more charisma than does acceptance of instrumental guidance. In summary, the kind of involvement required, the extent of organizational pervasiveness, and the nature of activities controlled are three central determinants of the amount of charisma required.

Normative organizations require a higher degree of moral involvement and expressive performance than the other two types of organization. This explains why coercive and utilitarian organizations can operate effectively with no charismatic positions [21] or only a few, at the top, whereas normative organizations require more such positions (all line positions or a relatively large group of professional middle-rank positions). There is thus a difference in the *amount* of charisma required, in the number of positions in which charisma is functional. Even more important, these differences among the various types of organizations explain the different *form* taken by the distribution of charisma in these organizations. We suggest that the kind of involvement required, the distribution of means and ends decisions, and the ratio of instrumental to expressive performances, all are associated with the distribution of charisma in the organizational structure. Positions in which decisions about ends are made, expressive performances are controlled, and moral involvement of subordinates is necessary, require charismatics. For positions in which decisions about means are made, from which instrumental activities are controlled, and in which moral involvement of subordinates is not necessary, charismatics are not required for effective performance; their presence may even be dysfunctional.

Since the actual distribution of charisma in organizations often

20. On the difference between ends-decisions and means-decisions see Simon (1957, ch. 1, ch. 3, and p. 98).

21. *Charismatic position* refers to an organizational position in which office charisma or personal charisma is functionally required.

comes close to that which is functionally required, a question arises about the mechanisms which assure the desired distribution. A full analysis requires not only that we establish the functions of an existing item but also that we indicate the processes which brought about its existence and sustain it. This part of the analysis is often overlooked. Some of those who use functional models write as if the actors were sophisticated functional analysts. For example, it is suggested that primitives observe the incest taboo "because" they would otherwise deteriorate biologically or destroy the integration of family into society. This assumes that primitives are members of a sophisticated school of biological or sociological functionalists. The Darwinist "solution" to this dilemma is to suggest that one can explain actual behavior by demonstrating its function, since when functions are not fulfilled, the unit will sooner or later disappear. But, as Merton has pointed out, not all behavior is functional; furthermore, there are functional alternatives, requiring an explanation of why this and not that alternative was chosen. This latter fact is of special importance, since, as was suggested above, the alternatives do not have, as a rule, equal "value." In short, a full analysis would require a study of the processes bringing about a particular state of affairs.[22]

Two sets of factors are examined here in order to explain in part why the actual distribution of charisma is often close to the functional one. One set includes the personality characteristics of the actors; the other, the interaction between elites and lower participants.

People recruited to positions in which decisions about means are made and/or instrumental activities are directly controlled tend to be either *specialists* (people in charge of one kind of activity) or *segmentalists* (people in charge of a multi-functional subunit). People recruited to positions in which decisions about ends are made (e.g., top executives), or to positions from which expressive activities are directly controlled, tend to be *generalists*. We treat specialists, segmentalists, and generalists as personality types, meaning the types of persons typically found in such position. No assumption is made about a one-to-one relationship between a personality type and a role. We assume only that the people typically found in each type of role differ systematically from those in others. We would expect this to be

22. See Nagel (1957). For a discussion of the problem of causation in functional analysis see Homans and Schneider (1955, pp. 57-60). See also Gouldner (1959, pp. 259-61).

the case because in most roles only a limited range of personality types would find their need-dispositions best satisfied and would function most effectively. Hence self-selection, organizational selection, and psychological adjustment after recruitment (role adaptation) create an association between personality and role. Since organizations are rational social units in which selection is legitimate and systematically planned, we expect this association to be relatively high compared with other social units.

The psychological syndromes of specialists and generalists have often been discussed, especially in the literature of industrial sociology, the psychology of occupations, and administration, and therefore do not need to be discussed here.[23] Segmentalists are persons whose outlook is limited not to one function but to one multi-functional division of the unit in which they operate. Their limited outlook is often not just a matter of adjustment to their contemporary role but is deeply rooted in their personality. Such an orientation is the widest scope they are capable of encompassing, and it may best meet their psychological dispositions. Middle-ranking executives who "do not have what it takes" to become top executives are often of this type. We expect segmentalists to fall between specialists and generalists on various psychological scales, such as scope of the field of perception, time orientation, orientation to means, flexibility, and others.

Although the following proposition cannot be demonstrated here, we suggest that *people who have the psychological syndromes of generalists are more likely to be charismatics than segmentalists or specialists.* The discussion which follows assumes that this proposition is valid.

A second factor related to the actual distribution of charisma is the nature of the interaction between elites and participants. We suggest that *the more continuous and the closer the control elites have over their subordinates, the less likely they are to have charismatic power over them; the more intermittent and distant or lax the control, the more likely charisma is to develop and to be sustained.*

Two dimensions underlie this proposition. One is the amount of interaction between the ranks; the other, the "tightness" of the con-

23. See, for example, Gerver and Bensman (1954, pp. 228-30); the section on "The Executive" and "The Specialist" in Dubin (1951), and the sources cited there; the literature on staff and line often follows these assumptions. See for example, Danielson (1957). The concepts of expert and generalist are central to the analysis of Ahmad (1959).

trol. Moreover, it is assumed that in most cases close control and high interaction are associated.[24]

In the following paragraphs we examine the various determinants of the distribution of charisma in three types of organization. More specifically, our comparative paradigm covers the following dimensions:

Determinants of the Distribution of Charisma

1. Nature of involvement required (moral versus calculative or coercive).
2. The distribution of means-ends decisions among various organizational positions.
3. The distribution of control over instrumental and expressive activities among various organizational positions.
4. The psychological characteristics of actors typically recruited to various organizational positions.
5. The frequency of interaction between elites and lower participants and the closeness of control over lower participants.

In T-Structures

Utilitarian organizations have the means-ends structure often considered typical for organizations in general. The lower ranks are instrumental performers; decisions about means are made by middle ranks of the line personnel and by the middle-ranking staff; decisions about ends are concentrated at the top (cf. Parsons, 1959, pp. 11-13). This division suggests that the highest need for legitimation occurs at the top, where indeed charisma is concentrated.

Middle ranks are entrusted both with decisions about means and also with direct control over lower participants. But, as we have seen above, the compliance of lower participants in utilitarian organizations does not require charismatic elites. "Officers" can control them rather effectively, predominantly through means of remunerative control. Since utilitarian organizations are, as a rule, highly routinized, involvement which is specific and of low intensity is satisfactory. The

24. It is of interest to note, as indirect support for this proposition, that top executives, heads of state, and kings, who have charisma in the eyes of the public and lower participants, have little or no charisma in the eyes of those with whom they are in daily and routinized contact, or of those whom they control directly—for example, private secretaries, valets, and cabinet ministers.

kind of diffuse and intense involvement generated by charisma is in general not required.[25]

Development of charisma on levels other than the top is not only unnecessary but is likely to undermine the rational processes required to maximize organizational effectiveness. A charismatic expert, for example, is dysfunctioinal in utilitarian organizations because his counsel is accepted on grounds other than his ability to demonstrate the validity of his observations and advice.

Production requires that lower elites maintain constant and relatively close control over lower participants. As a consequence, alienation of lower participants tends to focus on these elites, which reduces the ability of the latter groups to develop and sustain charismatic power over lower participants. Therefore, to the degree that the organization succeeds in building up some moral commitment to its goals and to itself as a unit, this commitment tends to develop through identification with the top elite, not with lower elites. Occupants of top positions rarely come in direct contact with lower participants, and when they do it is in expressive or ritualistic situations such as a Christmas party, the opening of a new plant, or escorting a distinguished visitor. They rarely initiate instrumental orders directly to the lower participants. Such differences in orientation to top and to lower elites is reported for state bureaucracies as well as industries, both utilitarian organizations.

Many citizens in totalitarian societies—who are often compared with lower-ranking employees in a bureaucracy [26]—identify with the head of the administration while they reject or resent lower elites and local directives and practices. There is a wide belief that the leader does not know of these objectionable practices, that if he did know he would abolish them, and that his personnel gives him bad counsel and hides the real situation from him:

". . . and now they have no use for the Communist Party, but all of them are for President Tito. In fact, everybody is." This, I believe, is almost literally true. While there appears to be little sympathy for the men around him, and hardly any for his Communist Party, the whole country seems to like Josip Broz (Tito). . . . They say they wish he would travel less and devote more time to looking after the nation's problems himself.

25. Limited involvement seems to be one of the reasons why these organizations are less effective in crisis situations, such as fires or hurricanes. See Killian (1953); Rosow (in press).
26. For a review and analysis of pertinent literature see W. Kornhauser (1959).

There is a widespread belief that his underlings do not keep him fully informed. "If only Tito knew about this, he would surely do something about it," people say. (*The New Yorker,* October 17, 1959, pp. 184-85)

Similar differences in involvement were found in a study of a dock company. Management is spoken of as "robbers," "twisters," and "slavedrivers." But the managing director is exempt:

. . . it is particularly interesting that the attitude of the dock workers to the Managing Director of the Ship Canal Company was very different from their attitude to top management as a whole; . . . The Managing Director, who was always referred to either by his full Christian name and surname, or as the "Head of the Canal," appeared to be immune from direct criticism. There were occasions when the dock workers disliked an instruction coming from Head Office and each time they blamed the Managing Director's immediate subordinates, who, they said, had given him bad advice. But he himself was referred to in intimate terms by men who had probably never spoken to him and could have had no knowledge of his character. Endowed with pleasant personal qualities, he was identified with the dock workers' own point of view; and, according to a widespread myth, would immediately have righted all their wrongs, had he known what was really happening. (The University of Liverpool, 1954, pp. 95-96)

To the degree that top elites develop charisma not only over lower participants but also over lower elites, this influence has a special function in settling conflicts, especially those involving sharp differences of interest or belief. It is a common practice in newly independent societies to settle conflict in or among governmental agencies and other utilitarian organizations by referring the issue for "ultimate verdict" to the head of state, who in these societies has especially high charisma as a state-founder. I. Wallerstein, for example, notes (in private communication) that in Accra, Ghana, a new sanitary law (passed under the pressure of the larger and more modern bakeries, which were represented in the Accra Municipal Council), threatened to put the small, street-corner women bakers out of business. In reaction, the Accra Women Bakers Association was founded. When the conflict between the two groups deepened and no solution was in sight, the two organizations—both composed of supporters of the party in office, the Convention People's Party—decided to let the highly charismatic Nkrumah settle the case. He ordered a compromise change in the law, which settled the conflict like magic.

A clear indication that charisma in governmental bureaucracies is required only in top positions is the fact that potential recruits for top positions must continually put their charisma to the test by winning elections, whereas occupants of middle and lower positions are, as a rule, appointed. In corporations fictional elections are held for top executives, who are "elected" by the stockholders. Election is not considered necessary for other positions.[27]

Thus, in utilitarian organizations the ends-means structure coincides with the distribution of charisma, which takes the form of a T-Structure. Ends-decisions and charismatics are concentrated at the top. Development of charisma in other positions is not only unlikely but also dysfunctional.

In L-Structures

Whereas in T-Structures the nonrational elements are concentrated at the top and superimposed on a rational body, in L-Structures such nonrational elements compose not merely the top, but a good part of the whole structure. The rational segment is a subordinated subunit, limited in scope and in significance. True, churches and political organizations have administrative (instrumental) units and activities, but they constitute the means-structures which, in effective organizations, are subordinated to those sections of the organizations which serve the organizational goals more directly. Whereas the activities directly related to goals in T-Structures are instrumental, in L-Structures they are expressive. It follows, we have seen, that it is functional for expressive elites to subordinate instrumental ones. The line personnel sees its main tasks as directing and participating in expressive activities. A bishop, a leader of an "ideological" union or party, or a combat officer [28] who spends a large part of his time on instrumental duties feels that "I am not doing *my* job." Fichter states:

Many a priest has been dismayed by the inroads which the business role has made on the spiritually more important priestly roles. Not only is it

27. We do not wish to imply that heads of business corporations are necessarily charismatic. The holders of top positions in utilitarian organizations are more likely to be charismatic than others, but they may not have much charisma, or they may have office but not personal charisma. Larrabee and Riesman emphasized that charismatic business leaders are found more often in novels about business than in the business world (1957, pp. 325-28). On heroes in "business" novels, see also Friedsman (1954). For a case study of lower-executive leadership and reliance on the power of office, see Argyris (1953).

28. Armies are not normative organizations but organizations which have a compound structure of normative and coercive compliance; thus, fittingly, they have only some but not all of the characteristics of a normative organization and L-Structure. Charisma is functionally required in all line positions, and increases with rank. Line officers are generalists. On the other hand, there is considerable task performance on the lowest level, and control is relatively close and constant.

time-consuming but it is worrisome and, worst of all, it obtrudes on the spiritual values. . . . As one priest has remarked, "Matthew may be the businessman's saint, but he became a saint only after he stopped collecting money." (1954, p. 131)

It is not functional for the direction of instrumental activities to be the predominant role segment of the priest's role.

The organization's goals require that normative compliance be maximized. In order to build up intensive commitments to themselves, which they then extend to the organization and its goals, line elites have to avoid instrumental activities and positions from which such activities are directed. It is also functional for all the line elites, not just the higher ones, to maintain only intermittent and comparatively lax control over lower participants, which is what they actually tend to do. Their control is, as a rule, limited to lower participants' expressive performances (e.g., attendance at prayers) and to expressive aspects of lower participants' instrumental activities in collectivities other than the organization (e.g., ban on work on Saturday or Sunday).

Lower elites in this type of organization have many of the psychological characteristics of generalists and in this sense differ considerably from lower elites in utilitarian organizations. There are relatively few specialists in these organizations, and they are recruited predominantly to staff positions. Wilensky (1956) has shown that in labor unions, one type of L organization, bureaucratic features and personalities are rare.

Thus, in this subtype of normative organization, charisma is required and tends to develop for the most part in line positions. It is not required and, for the reasons discussed above, is unlikely to develop, in staff positions, Again, the distribution of charisma parallels the distribution of rational and nonrational elements in the organization.

In R-Structures

In normative organizations which have an R-Structure, the locations of means- and ends-decisions differs most from the one usually depicted. In effective R organizations the top ranks, which consist mainly of either lay administrators or nonpracticing professionals, are primarily concerned with means-decisions and instrumental activities, such as controlling services in a hospital or the administration of a university. The middle ranks, in which professionals are concentrated, are the ones in which ends-decisions are made and activities directly related to the organizational goals take place. Diagnosis and treatment, what to teach, and which research to conduct are three major types of decisions made by professionals. It is one of the peculiar characteristics of these organizations that those who make the decisions also carry out an important part of the task-performances they control.

A major difference between the two subtypes of normative organization is that L organizations are primarily concerned with the institutionalization of ultimate values, whereas R organizations, which are also concerned with this institutionalization, in addition create and apply other subsystems of culture, especially science. But in professional organizations even those decisions and activities which are most directly concerned with science are not free from nonrational considerations—for example, decisions concerning what research problem to study (Merton, 1946, esp. pp. 186-93). What is more important for the present discussion is that even when these decisions are based on rational grounds, their acceptance by lower participants is, as a rule, mainly nonrational. Usually a layman has little rational basis for accepting professional advice, guidance, or teaching. He lacks the knowledge and competence necessary to judge the activity of the professional,[29] and must accept it on the basis of his general belief in science or education, the reputation of the professionals in the lay community, and, finally, the charisma of the professional.

To some degree, office charisma carries the load. Patients are

29. Peterson, Andrews, Spain, and Greenberg state: ". . . there is no linear correlation between the quality of medical care provided by a physician and his net income. Actually this is hardly surprising in view of the fact that the lay public has few valid criteria for assessing a physician's competence. Indeed, it is part of folklore that a layman values a physician's personality or 'bedside manner' more highly than his professional knowledge which may be less tangible or evident." (1956, p. 130)

RELATIONSHIP BETWEEN QUALITY OF PRACTICE AND NET INCOME

Qualitative Rank	Mean Net Income
V	$14,500
IV	18,900
III	17,300
II	14,600
I	13,400

SOURCE: Peterson, Andrews, Spain, Greenberg (1956, p. 130). Lowest qualitative rank is number I.

more impressed by the pronouncements of a chief surgeon than by those of an assistant surgeon, and students give more *a priori* weight to statements of senior professors than to those of junior instructors. But to a considerable degree, personal charisma is the decisive power. The highly charismatic doctor not only has a larger practice but also is more effective in building up and sustaining the motivation of the patient to be cured and in curing the more psychosomatic aspects of illness; the highly charismatic teacher more effectively communicates his teaching to his students and maintains a higher level of motivation to study; and the charismatic researcher inspires more students to work out his theory and to apply his method; he is more likely to generate a new "school." [30]

In direct contrast to utilitarian organizations, the development of charisma in top administrative positions is dysfunctional for R-Structures. It gives the administrator additional power, which may be used to overemphasize values such as economy, efficiency, and instrumental expansion, while direct service of the professional goals of the organization is neglected. It tends to introduce lay interference with professional decisions and goal-related activities—for example, in the recruitment and promotion of personnel—which is likely to inhibit the organization's pursuit of its dominant goals.[31]

The interaction of professionals with patients, students, or research assistants is intermittent, and supervision is, as a rule, not close. Often close supervision is delegated to semi-professionals, such as nurses, teaching or research assistants, and others. This, we have seen, is functional for maintaining charisma.[32]

30. The second volume of Jones' biography of Freud supplies a powerful illustration.

31. The goals of professional organizations and some values of professionals are the same: therapy, education, establishment of scientific truth, etc. But this does not mean that in all cases professionals will be the best representatives or guardians of these values. In organizations owned and managed by public representatives in which professionals enter as private entrepreneurs, the administrators may have to force some professional norms on the professionals. But, in general, professionals are the organization group closest to the goals of these organizations, while administrators are closer to values such as economy, balanced budget, efficiency—what can be referred to as instrumental values. For a fuller discussion of the relationship between professionals, administrators, and organizational goals, see Etzioni (1959a).

32. Teachers have less charisma, on the average, than professors and doctors not only because they have less professional training, their knowledge is considered less forbidding, and their roles involve communication of knowledge rather than its creation or application, but also because they are in more frequent, continuous, and close contact with their "subordinates." Teachers who, because of the nature of their vocation or other reasons, interact less frequently and less closely with their students are likely to be relatively more charismatic.

Top positions in R organizations do not require generalists as much as do top positions in T or L organizations, since, functionally speaking, decisions about ends and control of expressive activities are left in the hands of the professionals. In other words, although a top position always requires some degree of "generalization," the administrative position in R organizations requires more of the characteristics of a segmentalist or specialist, less of a generalist, than in other organizations. This may be one of the reasons training courses for hospital, school, and college administrators seem to be relatively more successful than parallel courses for corporation executives. People can be more readily trained for segmentalist positions than for generalist positions. Preparation for the latter type of position is gained through experience and depends more on personality and less on knowledge and technical skills.

On the other hand, professionals working in a professional organization are not typical specialists. Although they are specialists in their field, they must have a comparatively more "generalist" personality in order to gain the moral involvement of lower participants (this is left predominantly to nonprofessionals in T organizations), and in order to make ends-decisions.[33] It would follow from this that professionals in utilitarian organizations play a role quite different from that of professionals in professional organizations and, within the same profession, are likely to have different personalities. For one thing, we would expect professionals in R-Structures to be more charismatic. This corresponds with the earlier observation that while it is dysfunctional for an expert to be charismatic in T organizations, it is functional for R organizations.

To sum up, charisma is functional in positions which require moral involvement of subordinates. These are positions in which decisions about ends are made, and from which expressive activities

33. The intermediary position of professionals can be more readily characterized if we apply to personality systems the concepts used in Chapter X (page 265) to characterize social systems. Specialists are "specific"-oriented actors, *and* their orientation is limited to that of one system. Generalists are actors whose orientation is "diffuse" *and* wide in scope; note, for example, the tendency of charismatic leaders to affect their followers not only diffusely, but in many spheres of their life as well. Professionals' orientation varies on both dimensions. Some wish to affect the life of their clients diffusely, but in one sphere (as doctors want to increase their patients' motivation to be cured); others wish to extend their influence to many spheres (as teachers desire to affect the character of the student). Still others see their task as mainly specific and limited to one system; they exert influence (in one system) only in order to sustain motivation to accept their authority and communication (e.g., dermatologists, grammar teachers).

are controlled. In other positions, charisma is not required or is dysfunctional. Positions which require charisma are concentrated in the top echelon of utilitarian organizations, in the line structure of one subtype of normative organization, and in the middle rank of a second subtype of normative organization—namely, professional organizations. We shall see below that these two subtypes differ in their compliance structure; one relies more on pure normative compliance, the other on social compliance.

Some of the reasons why the actual distribution of charisma seems to approximate the functional one have been discussed. They lie mainly in the different types of personalities which various organizations and organizational positions attract, and in the kind of controls required for their effective performance.

DYSFUNCTIONS OF CHARISMA IN THREE STRUCTURES

When used as a means of fostering commitment, charisma is highly effective so long as it is harnessed. If it occurs in positions in which it is dysfunctional, or if it becomes "hot," as when a charismatic deviates, charisma has effects more dysfunctional than those caused by the malfunctioning of other means of attaining compliance.

Charisma may emerge in the wrong place, from the viewpoint of the organization, either outside the organization or in an organizational position. To discuss the effect of external charisma, such as that of labor leaders on factory workers, would require an extensive analysis of the relationship between organizations and their environment. Such an analysis exceeds the scope of this volume. However, it should be pointed out that the less the commitment of lower participants to an organization, the more susceptible they are to external charisma. Participants in utilitarian organizations are therefore more susceptible than participants in normative ones, and a labor union—an external organization—frequently succeeds in enlisting their prime loyalty and moral involvement. Unions have developed most often in organizations or organizational division where utilitarian compliance is most pronounced, and less often where it is less pronounced. Blue-collar industries are most heavily unionized; 48.1 per cent of blue-collar workers were unionized in the United States in 1958. The less utilitarian white-collar industries are considerably less unionized; only about 10 per cent of white-collar workers were unionized in 1958.

Obstacles to unionization seem to be greater in utilitarian divisions of universities—than in utilitarian divisions of utilitarian organizations.[34] Normative divisions or normative organizations exhibit least unionization.

The dysfunctions of charisma in "wrong" organizational positions were discussed above; the main examples are the charismatic expert in T organizations, charismatic executives in R-Structures, and some types of informal leaders discussed in Chapter VII. The present discussion focuses on a second kind of dysfunction: charisma which is in the "right" place, but which is not fulfilling its role and is serving as a source or center of deviant activity. A charismatic who commands the personal loyalty of lower participants may extend this commitment to values or norms other than those of the organization in which he operates and which he supposedly represents, or transfer them to a collectivity (often an organization) other than the one in which he participates.

Basically, the problem is one of conflict between two functional requirements. On the one hand, charisma is a potent source of commitment to a person. On the other hand, organizations rely on loyalty to the unit, acceptance of general norms, and commitment to the collective orientation of the organization, so that any commitment to a person is a potential danger. A charismatic may use his power for functional purposes, but he may also employ it as a threat to the integration of the organization, or to distort its allocation of resources and rewards—for example, by using his extra power to gain for himself or for his subunit more resources than the functional needs of the organization prescribe or allow. From the viewpoint of the organization, personal power is therefore a constant threat; the conditions which breed it are allowed to exist only because such power is highly effective when supportive of the organization.

Organizations differ in the degree to which charisma is a potential problem because they differ in the extent and location of charisma. The following table presents a summary of the distribution of charisma in the three types of organization discussed above, suggesting differences in potential conflict between personal and organizational loyalties.

34. Factors other than differences in compliance, of course, affect the degree of unionization (Mills, 1956). Statistics are cited from the *Monthly Labor Review*, 83 (1960), pp. 79-82.

Distribution of Charisma and Compliance Structures

ORGANIZATIONAL HIERARCHY	TYPE OF COMPLIANCE			
	Coercive	Utilitarian	Normative: Sub type L	Normative: Sub type R
Highest Ranks	−	+	+	−
Middle Ranks	−	−	+	+

+ Charismatics
− "Officers"

The potential conflict between charisma and organizational discipline is not built into the structure of coercive organizations, since their charisma (over inmates) does not usually develop in formal power positions. Among the three types of organization in which charisma does develop, its potential dysfunction is smallest in utilitarian organizations which exhibit a T-Structure—that is, charisma concentrated at the top. If the head of an organization sets rules, he cannot, by definition, break them. His "deviation" is the establishment of a new rule. If the organization is part of a larger organizational network, or subordinated to another social unit such as a community or a nation, we come back to the question of interaction between the organization and its environment, which cannot be discussed here. But insubordination of top personnel is unlikely. Their position fosters commitment to the organization, and their power is such that they can change rules set by their predecessors or, previously, by themselves, to suit their anticipated course of action (or even to legitimate action that has already taken place). In short, the charisma-discipline conflict is minimal in a T-Structure.

It is in L-Structures that the potential strain between charisma and discipline is greatest, since here lower elites command charisma and can therefore threaten the allocation system and the integration of the organization. The mechanisms devoted to control these potential dysfunctions are a subject of the next chapter.

One would expect the strain between discipline and charisma to be greatest in R-Structures, where the middle ranks have charisma but higher ones do not. This means that R-Structures lack two important sources of control which exist in L-Structures, where lower participants are often more committed to the top elites than they are to lower elites, and lower elites tend to be committed to those above them. But actually the amount of strain is much less in R- than in L-structures.[35]

Two major factors explain the low level of strain in R-Structures. First, professional organizations are so structured that these potential dysfunctions are in part avoided. This is achieved not so much by controlling charisma as by not demanding discipline, in many spheres, to begin with.[36] In effective professional organizations control over ends-decisions and expressive activities is delegated to the charismatic professionals themselves, either as individuals or as groups. The top elites control means or service activities, which are largely carried out by nonprofessionals and noncharismatics such as clerks, aides, janitors, and other service personnel.

To put it another way, R organizations are split into two substructures, one in which the charismatics are actually at the top, making ends-decisions and performing the work or delegating it to their subordinates; and another, the service structure, which is like a utilitarian organization and is run by administrators.[37] Considerable strain appears at points of articulation between the two, as in those personnel groups which perform services for both substructures (e.g., nurses in hospitals), but this strain is not of the charisma-discipline type. Thus, although at first it would seem that the charisma-discipline conflict would be greatest in R organizations, it is actually smaller than in L-Structures (cf. Deutsch, 1957, pp. 29 ff.). Giving charismatics a large degree of autonomy reduces the strain between charisma and organizational control. On the other hand, this delegation of control entails giving up some of the virtues of monocratic organizations, such as systematic division of labor, high coordination, and centralized communication.

The second major reason for a lower-than-expected charisma-discipline strain in R-Structures is that a deviant charismatic can do

35. The present discussion concerns "ideal types." See below on deviations from these types.

36. This is one of the most important ways in which social structures adjust to potential deviance. Behavior which is generally regarded as deviant is declared legitimate when the norm is very likely to be violated. The areas are carefully specified so that the "concession" is isolated and limited and saves the system the strains of an unsuppressed or recurrent deviance. Typical examples are the right of a wife not to testify against her husband, and the exemption of some religious groups and *bona fide* conscientious objectors from military service.

37. Several writers have pointed out this "dual" nature of the structure of one professional organization or another. See, for example, J. Henry (1954, pp. 139-51); and H. L. Smith (1958).

little collective damage. Because decisions about ends are dispersed, because of the lack of a power center, "taking over the organization" has limited significance. As a rule, only control over the service structure can be attained (Etzioni and Lazarsfeld, forthcoming).

In summary, the charisma-discipline strain built into the structure of organizations which employ charismatics, is smallest in T-Structures and greatest in L-Structures. Strain in R-Structures is closer in degree to T-Structures than to L-Structures.

THE DISTRIBUTION OF CHARISMA AS A CONTINUUM

We have discussed three forms of distribution of charisma in organizational structures as three discrete "ideal types." More specific statements can be made if we see the types as representing analytical components; different combinations of these components supply continua along which many subtypes of charismatic distribution can be arranged.

For one continuum the T distribution constitutes one pole and the L distribution the other; in between we find organizations in which more than just the top position, or some but not all line positions, are charismatic. Those organizations in which only the top and a few of the highest positions are charismatic fall close to the T pole; those in which almost all the line positions are charismatic, except some of the lower ones, fall close to the L pole. Another continuum seems to exist in which L-Structures constitute one pole and R-Structures the other. In the middle we find organizations in which some of the higher positions have charisma, but where the middle ranks have less than in the pure R-Structure.

"Across-the-Board" Comparisons

We expect organizations falling at different points on these continua to score differently on other dimensions which, as suggested above, are related to the distribution of charisma. For example, distribution of charisma is related to the amount of moral involvement required, the place of ends-decisions, and the scope of expressive activities to be controlled. In short, viewing the distribution of charisma in an organization as located on a continuum allows us to formulate more specific propositions than the relatively elementary statements permitted by ideal types.

Professional organizations, for example, can be compared according to the degree of charisma achieved by their top executives and the functions—decision-making, for example—the executives perform. In addition to personal differences, the factors that seem particularly to affect the charisma achieved by executive roles in professional organizations include the following: the professional training of the head executive, the size of the organization, and its financial resources. In general, professionally trained directors seem to have more charisma over participants than lay administrators;[38] heads of large organizations seem to be less charismatic than heads of small ones; heads of rich and well-financed organizations are more charismatic (over participants) than heads who have to devote most of their time and energy to raising funds (though this may require more charisma over the general public).

When these factors are controlled, various types of professional organizations still seem to show systematic differences in their charismatic structures. For example, principals in grammar and high schools appear to acquire more charisma over students than do university presidents over their students or heads of hospitals over patients. This difference may be explained in part by differences in function, background, and power. In terms of function, the average principal is less of an administrator and more of an educator than the average university president, and less of an administrator than the head of the average hospital. Unlike the others, he can delegate many of his administrative duties to control agents outside the school, such as the parents, the police, the PTA, and the superintendent. The principal is ordinarily less concerned with fund raising and construction than the average university president, and has far fewer instrumental services to direct than a hospital administrator, who is running a "hotel" in addition to a professional service. Thus the role-structure of the school principal is the most expressive and least instrumental of the three. Charisma is again found to be more common in the more expressive positions.

Research institutes are difficult to place as a type because of

38. More than 90 per cent of principals have been teachers (Farmer, 1948, p. 32). The proportion of university presidents who have been professors seems to be smaller (Cf. Wilson, 1942, p. 85). Only a minority of the administrators of general hospitals, about 22 per cent, have an M.D. (Block, 1956, pp. 121, 136). Thus the principal has the highest degree of legitimation for interference in ends-decisions made by the professionals of his organization. The average principal has more power over his teachers than the average head of other professional organizations has over the professionals employed by or associated with his organization (Becker, 1952, p. 476; 1953)

the great differences in the degree to which they are incorporated into other organizations, such as industries, military establishments, and universities. In general, the less autonomous they are—that is, the less internal administration is required—the more "professional" and expressive direction the head can give, and the more likely he is to be charismatic.

A Dynamic Perspective

So much for the static comparison of several organizations at one point in time. The continua may also be used to characterize one organization at different points in time, to see whether changes in the amount and distribution of charisma are related to other structural changes along the dimensions specified above. For example, organizations change their charismatic structure at different stages in their natural history. Many organizations are more charismatic in the first period of their existence than at later times. This change expresses itself both in the number of charismatic positions and in their distribution. In other words, routinization means a decline not only in the *intensity* of charisma, as Weber pointed out, but also in the *number* of positions in which it is found, and a change in the form of its distribution as well. Many R-Structures, for example, start as L-Structures; that is, they have in their initial period highly charismatic top executives who are later replaced by more "routine" administrators, while the middle-ranking professionals maintain their charisma. Many top American universities were established in such a way. Learned and Wood state: "It was no accident that men of the quality of Gilman, Hall, and Harper headed these institutions; they were selected for the tasks because in every case those behind the new enterprise could not conceive of its succeeding without leadership of a high order." (1938, pp. 144-45) White had the same charismatic role in the history of Cornell University.

All this is not to suggest that an established university, or any other R organization, may not have a highly charismatic top executive. It does suggest that in normal routinized periods such executives will be less functional and less likely to emerge; and that after long periods of routinization, especially of conservatism or deterioration, an organization, like a society, may need a charismatic leader to revitalize it by introducing major innovations (Etzioni and Lazarsfeld, forthcoming) Eliot played such a role at Harvard, and Burgess at Columbia University. But soon after such a charismatic fulfills his innovating function, the structure returns to its "normal" state, where there is no functional role for a highly charismatic head.[39]

But if we compare organizations at the same stage in their natural history—for example, in the routinized period, we find that corporations tend to be T-Structures, professional organizations to be R-Structures, and religious and political organizations to be L-Structures, for reasons that have been explored above.

Obviously not all religious and political organizations are L-Structures. Yet it should be pointed out that *religious and political organizations which begin as R-Structures tend to change in the direction of an L distribution.*[40] One important form of this change occurs when previously independent units, each with a charismatic leader of its own, band together to form one "federal" organization. At first each unit is expected to maintain expressive self-control. The larger unit is to concentrate and coordinate only some of the instrumental activities. Charismatics are expected to continue heading local units, while the heads of the larger structure are noncharismatic administrators in charge of means-decisions and instrumental activities. Thus at first a typical R-Structure is formed. But with the passage of time, the larger "federal" unit frequently acquires more and more expressive functions and meaning for the members; it commands more and more moral involvement; the national center of the organization

39. Note that we are examining the functions of charisma for the control of participants only. Even when no charismatic is needed for this purpose, a charismatic top executive may be required and functional for external purposes, such as recruiting funds for the organization or defending it from outside pressures, such as political and ideological interference. To the degree that such an executive is oriented to the organizational environment, his charisma is not dysfunctional for the R-Structure and does not turn it into an L-Structure.

40. We refer here to a secular trend. Obviously there are ups and downs in the movement of each single organization; various reforms often temporarily reverse the trend (Hagstrom, 1957). Note also that organizations which were founded as L-Structures show some inclination to become less so, and to move in the direction of an R-Structure, but such movement seems to be much less common and much more limited than the opposite discussed in the text. This fact suggests that organizations whose goal is to build up and sustain beliefs, and which have a purely normative compliance structure, may require an L-Structure for their effective operation. This point is, of course, a central issue in religious dogma as well as in the study of religious organizations. One would hardly be inclined to accept even tentatively generalizations about such an inherent "inclination" without thorough historical and sociological research. The preceding statements should therefore be treated strictly as an hypothesis.

accumulates more and more power; and the occupants of top positions gain more and more charisma.[41] In short, the R-Structure comes closer and closer to an L-Structure, although it rarely becomes as centralized as structures which were founded as L-Structures to begin with, or which developed not upward, but downward, from their national power centers to the local units.[42]

Harrison (1959) supplies a fine illustration of the change from an R-Structure toward an L-Structure in his study of the American Baptist Convention. The Northern Baptist Convention was first organized in 1907 as an administrative roof organization of various Baptist societies. Harrison states: "The new organization was primarily designed to augment the promotional and budgetary affairs of the societies . . . to coordinate the missionary and evangelistic activities." (pp. 42-43)

Both the value system of the Baptists and the special pains taken by the founding convention to restrict the power of the central body were strong forces against change from an R- to an L-Structure. The religious beliefs were, briefly, that "no church leader could legitimately claim special access to the divine power, and since God is the only absolute sovereign it follows that all religious authority must be penultimate and limited. . . . The local church was the ultimate authority." (*Ibid.*, pp. 53, 55)[43] Powerful administrative devices were deliberately introduced in order to limit and control the central power and to restrict it to instrumental activities. "The founders of the Convention attempted to limit executive power in three ways. First, they stated that executives could make no policies for the missionary organizations. . . . Second, the delegates to the annual meetings of the Convention would be sent directly from the local churches. . . . Finally, it was stated that no ecclesiastical organization . . . could promulgate legislation which would be binding upon the local churches. (*Ibid.*, p. 13; see ch. 3 for an analysis of these mechanisms.)

41. The history of the United States supplies ample illustration of the relationship between the locus of power and charisma. Seligman (1955) showed that there is a secular trend for both the power and the charisma of the president to increase.

42. On these two forms of organizational development and the related consequences, see Sills (1957, pp. 9-12).

43. Harrison supplies a full analysis of the theological issues involved and shows that several approaches to this issue can be found in the Baptist tradition. See especially Chapter 3, "The Freedom of Man and God," and Chapter 4, "Authority and Power in the Baptist Tradition."

Analyzing the situation fifty years later, Harrison found that what had begun as an administrative arrangement had gained expressive functions, that the central headquarters and its personnel had increased their power considerably, and that the executives had become leaders with considerable charisma. One respondent interviewed by Harrison went so far as to refer to a "Baptist Pope." [44] ". . . The executives, even though their official position is tenuous, exercise a tremendous control over the policies of the denomination and the activities of the local churches. . . . They have been accepted as legitimate authorities on the basis of their charismatic qualities." (Ibid., p. 14; see also ch. 6) They had been executives; now they were leaders. Moreover, reflecting a true L-Structure even though working not by direct order but through manipulation of the "federal" structure, the higher authorities replaced lower leaders who were either incompetent or deviant (ibid., pp. 76, 93-94, 103, 195-96).

Obviously, although the normative and organizational constraints on higher authority levels have weakened, the constraints have not disappeared. The American Baptist Convention does not take the form of an outright L-Structure, but it has lost many of its R characteristics, moving in the L direction.[45]

Thus a dynamic examination of changes in the distribution of expressive and instrumental activities in one organization suggests the same conclusion as that supported by a static comparison of various organizations. The distribution of charisma is closely related to the locus of means- and ends-decisions, to the positions from which instrumental and expressive activities are controlled, and to the kind of involvement required by the effective operation of the organization and its various subunits.

44. Ibid., p. 74. Wilensky (1954, p. 90) has suggested that the rise of a central charismatic figure was associated with the centralization of control and transfer of loyalties from the local to the larger unit in a labor union (that of miners in the United States).

45. Using material drawn mainly from Burton (1953), Dulchin (1960) has analyzed a rather similar development among the Congregationalists. At first the Secretary of the National Council of the Congregational Christian Church, like other National Council officers, had almost solely advisory functions on various instrumental problems of local churches and various associations and societies. With time he increased his power and became an official in charge of many instrumental activities. By the end of the thirties he was given the additional charismatic title of "minister," and he became to some degree also the spiritual, expressive leader of the organization (Burton, 1953, pp. 14f.).

SUMMARY

This chapter has initiated the study of compliance among higher participants, a study in which normative power, charisma in particular, is central. Charisma is the ability of an actor to exercise diffuse influence over the normative orientations of other actors. Personal charisma differs from office charisma in intensity, and it is achieved and not ascribed; but—modifying a well-known Weberian theorem—we suggest that personal charisma may originate in organizational positions, and that personal charisma is not incompatible with established organizational structures.

A second Weberian theorem modified here is that charisma is concentrated at the top of the organizational structure. Actually, it seems to be distributed in three major forms: at the top only; in all line positions; or in one or more ranks other than the top. These distributions are associated with the compliance structure of the organization: coercive organizations have no charismatic organizational positions; utilitarian organizations tend to have charisma concentrated in top positions only; pure normative organizations are likely to have a line concentration; and social-normative organizations usually have a rank concentration.

The functions and dysfunctions of charisma in each one of these types of organization were analyzed. It was suggested that the organizational locus of ends- versus means-decisions, and the positions from which expressive activities are controlled, are directly associated with the locus of charisma, as are the proportion of expressive to instrumental activities, the personal characteristics of higher participants, the frequency of their interaction with lower participants, and the tightness of control they exercise.

The concluding section compared different types of organizations, then different temporal stages of one organization, in order to indicate ways in which the general statements made earlier in the chapter can be made more specific.

XIII

ORGANIZATIONAL
CONTROLS OF CHARISMA

The use of charisma as a source of compliance imposes certain strains on organizational discipline because it grants members a highly personalized power. This chapter compares the control mechanisms employed by two types of organization, those which emphasize pure normative compliance and tend to exhibit a line distribution of charisma, and those which emphasize social compliance and tend to exhibit a rank distribution of charisma. As we would expect from the preceding analysis, mechanisms focused specifically on the control of charisma are considerably more extensive in L- than in R-Structures. Actually, we shall see that in R organizations, most of the controls over charisma are exerted by mechanisms which are designed to check many other forms of deviance as well. Hence the analysis of control of charisma in R organizations inevitably leads to a general analysis of control and compliance in R organizations. The last section of this chapter examines critically the frequent assertion that the behavior of professionals in R organizations is predominantly controlled through social power and commitments, and not through charisma and other, more "hierarchical," powers.

MECHANISMS OF CONTROL

Control mechanisms are social processes which prevent or reduce deviance. We are concerned here with those control mechanisms which assure that charisma is associated with positions requiring it and which confine its use to activities functional for the organization.

We distinguish between two types of control mechanism: preventive and post-factum. *Preventive* mechanisms protect positions which require charisma from being occupied by either (a) persons with little or no potential for personal charisma (e.g., keep "unimpressive" novices from becoming ministers), or (b) potentially deviant charismatics (e.g., keep Stalinists from central party positions in contemporary Russia). The two control functions are discussed concomitantly because frequently the same control mechanism serves both. *Post-factum* mechanisms handle dysfunctions which occur despite preventive measures.

Control mechanisms differ according to the kind of structure in which they are instituted. Some mechanisms are built into existing structures, whereas others are segregated. A mechanism is *built in* if a social unit or activity which primarily serves other functions is also used for control purposes (e.g., a school admissions test which weeds out deviants). A control mechanism is *segregated* when a social unit or activity primarily serves control functions (e.g., customs officers). It is segregated because the control function is separated from other functions by having its own unit or set of activities. As will become evident below, preventive mechanisms are typically built in, whereas most post-factum mechanisms are segregated.

We turn now to examine these control mechanisms in L- and in R-Structures. Control mechanisms in T-Structures are not discussed because, as we have seen in the preceding chapter, the limited amount and the relatively "safe" place of charisma in these organizations do not create enough potential deviance to require control structures especially devoted to harnessing charisma.

CONTROL IN L-STRUCTURES

Since the problem of control in L-Structures is by far the largest, for reasons spelled out in the preceding chapter, one would expect organizations which have this type of charismatic structure to have the most elaborate preventive and post-factum mechanisms of control. This is indeed the case.

Preventive Mechanisms

Candidates for line positions are carefully *selected* so that potential deviants and persons who seem to have no charisma potential are left out. Candidates who pass the selection tests are sent to training organizations which combine technical vocational education with training designed to develop personal charisma and to weed out potential heretics (Ettisch, 1960). The importance of socialization for charismatic positions in L organizations is so great that, unlike other organizations, they employ their *own educational units* and do not rely on those supplied by society. Religious organizations have theological seminaries; parties and labor unions with strong ideological commitments have political schools, such as the Jefferson School in New York, Brookwood Labor College, the Rand School, and Commonwealth College (Wilensky, 1956, p. 253; Field, 1950). Military organizations use their academies and officer schools for the same purpose (Dornbusch, 1955; Janowitz, 1960, pp. 127-45).

These schools differ from most others in two ways. First, they are under the direct control of the organizations which recruit their graduates. This assures conformity. Second, unlike other schools, they are usually "total" organizations, encompassing virtually all areas of the neophyte's life. The broader the scope of an organization, as we have seen, the more likely is it to have diffuse effects on the normative characteristics of its participants. Therefore L organizations, in order to prevent deviant tendencies and assure the development of potential charisma, turn to total organizations for socialization of recruits.

In order to assure effective prevention of deviance, lower participants are under constant *observation*. The staff of these schools is often required to live on the premises in order to maintain personal contact with the participants, both to increase the effectiveness of socialization and for purposes of observation.

The effective operation of these schools as agencies for the development of potential charismatics supports our earlier statement that personal charisma can be achieved.[1] It is not "God-given" nor is it an innate personal characteristic, as those subject to this power often believe. There is some reason to believe that in ancient Israel there were schools where the archetype of the charismatic—the prophet—attained his charisma. Saul joined in his youth a "company of prophets." It is reported that when they were prophesying, "the Spirit of God came also to him, and he too began to prophesy." (Samuel I, 10:5-11)

The training period is followed by *practice and test assignments,* such as giving a service in the chapel of the theological seminary, agitating among the workers in the neighborhood of a political school, or recruiting members for a labor union among new immigrants.[2] These functions are carried out under supervision so that they can be used as training situations.[3] They also serve as test situations, to examine both charisma and devotion.

The need for *testing grounds* creates some difficulties. Members of normative organizations tend to become alienated when used for instrumental purposes such as training. They are irritated by mistakes the novice makes in sacred matters, such as administering a ritual, and because the novice, whose assignment is temporary, is not genuinely interested in them. Two common adaptations are employed. The functionary on trial is closely supervised by an experienced superior so that annoying mistakes are minimized. The superior at

1. Some of the organizational conditions under which personal charisma tends to emerge are discussed in the text. A more nearly complete study of the determinants of charisma would have to compare the subject groups also. Obviously, the same person has more charisma for some groups, less for others, and none for still others. The lower the socio-economic status of a subject group, for example, the more open it appears to be to charisma. The same holds for females as against males, for young and old compared to adults, and for unemployed compared to employed workers. There also seem to be systematic differences by national character and by stage of acculturation. For a review of the literature on factors which open subjects to political charismatics in modern societies, and an analytical model for the study of this issue, see Kornhauser (1959); for a recent case study of a social-political movement of elderly persons focused on a charismatic leader, see Pinner, Jacobs, and Selznick (1959).

2. "While at [political party] school, students participate in the life of the party. They are sent as delegates to party conferences and speak at public meetings. They address workers at the gates of a factory." (Micaud, 1952, p. 344)

3. The Union Theological Seminary in New York, for instance, gives a course in "Practice Preaching" at James Chapel, which is described in the 1959-60 catalogue as devoted to "Regular preaching of full-length sermons with criticisms by instructor, class, and if desired by consultants from the departments of Speech, Bible, and Theology." (p. 95)

least formally maintains the charismatic office so that it is not "secularized" by the novice. Young seminarians, for example, are assigned to assist in but not to conduct religious services (though in some churches, seminarians take over all religious responsibilities while the minister is away for the summer). Novices may also be assigned to work with a "captive audience" which the organization is unlikely to lose.[4] Young priests are sent to serve for a short period in Retreat Houses; young politicians in England often make their first public speeches before tourists and bums in Hyde Park. This has the additional function of staffing less rewarding positions.[5]

The first "real" or *field assignment* serves functions similar to those of practice or test assignments. Actually, the testing of loyalty and charisma never stops. Politicians and union representatives have to be reelected, priests have to draw a congregation to the church, agitators have to gain a following. But after the first assignments have been successfully performed, testing is less frequent and less intensive.

Often those who have completed their training but have not shown a satisfactory amount of charisma in their early assignments are *sidetracked* to staff positions, such as clerical, administrative, or editorial jobs.[6] Sidetracking for the very same reasons may take place at any stage in the career sequence, but it is used more frequently

4. I am indebted for this point to Edward Lehman.

5. These arrangements raise a point of general interest. Parsons called attention to the operation of "adaptive structures" in social units. These are structures which reduce potential dysfunctions, in particular social and psychological tensions which would have been generated by attempts to apply the dominant values consistently (1959, pp. 168-69). For example, total competition would have a disruptive effect; therefore seniority is introduced as an "adaptive structure" (Moore, 1951, pp. 91-92). Similarly, test situations are an "adaptive structure" for normative organizations. But these structures, although reducing some major actual or potential dysfunctions, frequently cause some of their own. In our case, training through practice generates alienation. Hence we expect adaptive structures frequently to call for *second-level adaptive structures*. Close supervision of the novice, not granting him the official responsibility and assigning him to a "captive audience" fills such a functional need.

6. Micaud reports that Communists in political schools are sent to speak at public meetings and address workers at gates of factories: "In this way good agitators can be selected, while those who prove incapable are directed to other kinds of work." (1952, p. 344) The hero of Sartre's *The Crime of Passion,* who as a son of a bourgeois family intellectual and has no charisma over the working-class members of the Communist party, is assigned to various desk jobs. On the other hand, sidetracking from low-ranking line to staff positions may bring about upward mobility. This leads to upward mobility because for some organizations the qualities required by high positions are close to those required by low line positions. This seems to be the case in peacetime military organizations, in schools, and in churches. It has been demonstrated for monsignors in the Church of New York (Bosse, O'Flannery, and Macisco) and for military organizations (Janowitz, 1960, p. 166).

in this initial placement and evaluation period, and again close to the end of the career.

The Catholic Church, for historical reasons which are far from clear, has partially given up these mechanisms of control by granting life tenure not only to cardinals and bishops but also to a large number of priests. Permanent pastors can be removed or reassigned to other positions only by a judicial process (*Management Audit,* 1956, p. 7). Pastors who are senile or incapacitated through illness or accident, or who simply lack charisma, cannot be removed or transferred to positions in which they would be less dysfunctional.[7]

The potential dysfunctions of giving up the right to reassign are reduced in several ways. First, efforts are made to grant tenure only when competence, loyalty, and charisma have been demonstrated, though seniority plays an important role in promotion. Younger priests and curates are moved around freely. They tend to be trained in the city, then sent for a tour in the country; those who do well are then recalled to the city.[8] Thus again, prolonged socialization and selection are used to assure that at least the more important and powerful positions will be filled by loyal charismatics. Other ways of overcoming possible dysfunctions of tenure include promotion of bishops or cardinals to titular positions "without authority" (*Promoveatur ut amoveatur*), and ordering them to Rome, which takes them out of line positions and brings them closer to papal supervision (*Management Audit,* 1956, p. 20). Also, although it is difficult to remove some church officers from their position, any or all of their duties may be removed (*ibid.* p. 7).

Other L organizations tend to preserve their right to transfer officials, even high-ranking ones. Most parties reserve at least the formal right to reassign full-time personnel, as do labor unions, combat organizations, and some hierarchical religious organizations. Orders are free to reassign their members and frequently do.

It is of interest to note that a special safety device has been developed in many normative organizations of this type to keep

7. Rodehaver and Smith (1951, p. 420) report that the average stay of pastors in a Roman Catholic parish was twice as long as that of pastors in parishes of the egalitarian religious groups studied. Mean number of years for pastors in 79 localities in New York (1924-29) was 18.8 for Catholics but 7.4 for Universalists. see Stanton and Schwartz (1954, pp. 234 ff.).

8. Interview with two officials of the Church, January 1960. Success is associated with movement to the city, "as in other professions" (Rodehaver and Smith, 1951, p. 416). See also Chapman (1944, p. 203).

lower participants from becoming disaffected until replacement occurs. *Organizations deny lower participants the right to decide that their superiors are deviant or lack charisma.* The organization may replace them, but until they are replaced, lower participants are required to treat them as effective and conforming charismatics. The Catholic Church has a special taboo, established as early as the fourth century, which fulfills this function. The prohibition of the Donatist Heresy denies the right of parishioners to judge that their priest has lost his right to say mass, hear confessions, and carry out other religious duties even though he may be in a state of sin.[9] Armies, radical political parties, and ideological labor unions similarly insist on "discipline." Orders must be obeyed, regardless of the leadership shown by the commander or local secretary.

Accelerated promotion of those who reveal a high level of personal charisma increases the probability that they will remain loyal to the organization. In organizations as in society, blocked mobility channels lead to deviant behavior, and upward mobility increases one's stake in the status quo. Upward mobility means that a person is allocated an increase in material or symbolic rewards, that he comes into personal contact with top leaders more frequently, and that he is closer to the informal channels of communication of the organization and therefore knows better "what's going on." [10] Organizational activities are likely to appear more meaningful from higher positions, since they are seen from a broader perspective. The increased share of responsibility which often accompanies promotion makes clear the need for compromise, a frequent source of frustration and rebellion for those lower in rank.[11] It is therefore functional for organizations to keep the rank of participants in balance with their personal charisma. Cripps, who was later expelled from the British Labor party because of his support for a Popular Front with the Communists—which was against the declared policy of his party—was first promoted. *The New York Times* noted: "Sir Stafford, who is

9. "If anyone says that a minister in the state of mortal sin, though he observes all the essentials that belong to effecting and conferring the sacrament, does not effect or confer the sacrament; let him be anathema." Canon 12, Session VII, Council of Trent. In Clarkson *et al.* (1955, p. 264). The phrase, "let him be anathema," means that the proposition is condemned as heretical.

10. On the effects on morale of knowing and not knowing "what's going on," see Stanton and Schwartz (1954, pp. 234 ff.).

11. On the frustrations generated and on the functional needs for compromise, see Barnard (1938, pp. 200-11).

one of the ablest men in the party, a year ago received a place in the high command in hopes that he would quiet down." (May 29, 1939, 4:7)

In some military organizations the occurrence of a high degree of charisma in the lowest rank is formally acknowledged as grounds for accelerated promotion. Every soldier who obtains a medal for heroic performance, a frequent source of charisma, is automatically promoted. Similarly, potential saints are not allowed to remain "privates." Bernadette Soubirous, better known as St. Bernadette (of Lourdes), was a French peasant girl (1844-1879) when she was reported to have had eighteen "visions." After she had been acknowledged by the bishop of her diocese (in 1862), she wanted to return to her village, marry, and live a "normal life." But she was persuaded to join the "higher ranks" by joining an order. In 1866 she became a novice at the house of the Sisters of Charity. Thus, charisma and rank were kept in equilibrium.

For normative organizations of this type it is functional for *the higher ranks to have charisma, not only over lower participants, but also over the middle ranks;* and for the charisma which higher ranks have over lower participants to be greater than the charisma which middle ranks have over lower participants.[11a] This arrangement serves both as a preventive and as a post-factum control. It serves as a preventive device because lower elites are likely to accept the direction and guidance of higher elites when the latter have charismatic influence over them. It is a post-factum device because the higher charismatics serve as a "retreat line." When lower participants become disillusioned with their immediate superiors, they are not lost to the organization. The higher ranks may still tie them both to the organization and to its goals, replace uncharismatic "officers" and soothe complaints about lower elites. When in Guareschi's novel Don Camillo, the village pastor, became too violent in his treatment of deviant parishioners, the bishop interfered.

The higher elite's charismatic power over lower participants may be used to dethrone lower-ranking deviant charismatics. Even when this power advantage is not activated, its very existence has a preventive effect. Finally, as in T-Structures, higher charismatics may

---

11a. We have seen above the far-reaching structural adjustments which are required when superiors of charismatics are not charismatics themselves, as is the case in R-Structures.

use their power to settle both administrative and normative conflicts among lower elites.

It should be pointed out that all the preventive mechanisms discussed above are built-in mechanisms. For example, control is sought through organizational units whose primary function is to train, or through regular organizational processes such as replacement and promotion. Post-factum mechanisms, on the other hand, usually have segregated structures.

Post-Factum Mechanisms

Once deviant charisma has manifested itself, despite the elaborate preventive mechanisms, counterprocesses are set into motion. These are of two major kinds: those which attempt to eliminate the deviant charisma; and those which seek to limit its effect.

The first sanctioning round is usually highly informal and private. To acknowledge a deviant charismatic by formal or public action may increase his influence. When friendly warnings of peers and conferences with superiors fail, more powerful and public means are activated. Churches, political parties, and labor unions *suspend* members and leaders for a limited period of time, during which they are given a taste of the full consequences which may follow if deviance is continued. After the suspension is terminated, an institutionalized opportunity to repent is often provided. If suspension is of no avail, deviant charismatics are *excommunicated* (in religious organizations), *expelled* (in political organizations), or *discharged* (in military organizations).

A point of general interest here is that in contrast to what one might expect, removal of deviant charismatics from the organization is frequently not abrupt but is a process with several stages. Dismissal from office comes before membership is withdrawn. Often the process of removal has even more than two steps, distributed over a period of time. Trotsky, for example, was divested of his military post in January 1925, dropped from the Politburo in October 1926, expelled from the party in October 1927, exiled to Alma Ata in 1928, and expelled from the Soviet Union in 1929 (Fainsod, 1954). Elias, a deviant leader of the Franciscan order, was similarly removed, step by step: "His unbridled ambition and his violent exercise of power led to his eventual *dismissal* from office, and finally to his *expulsion* from the order. Subsequently he incurred *excommunication* on account of his association with Frederick II." (Nigg, 1959, p. 230; italics supplied.)

This form of removal has several functions. It gives the deviant leader an opportunity to repent and eventually to return to good standing and even to office. The political career of Bevin supplies a typical example. Gradual removal also allows testing of the deviant's power before risking a complete break. Moreover, if the deviant leader does not want to risk expulsion because he hopes for a "comeback," this procedure puts some restraint on him. He cannot, for instance, give open support to competitive organizations or build one of his own. In addition, the gradual removal makes expulsion more legitimate in the eyes of lower participants ("they gave him another chance"). In the period of membership without office, the deviant leader is likely to lose support, since he has lost access to the means available only to those in office [12] without gaining access to opportunities available to outsiders. Final expulsion usually comes if the leader continues deviant activities after he has been expelled from his office, but is weakened enough so that the organization is not afraid to risk a complete break; or if he uses the limited legitimation membership gives him to further extend his deviant activities.

Expulsion is often not enough to eliminate the influence of a deviant charismatic. Organizations throughout history and in many societies have therefore turned to *execution* and *assassination* of deviant leaders. But often even physical elimination has not proved completely satisfactory to the ruling elite. Deviant charisma may continue to lead as an example and a symbol of identification long after its original carrier is dead. This is referred to, in the language of the political organizations, as "the danger of creating martyrs." *Character assassination* is employed to counteract it. The Communists struggled for more than ten years with the public image of Trotsky before he was assassinated in 1940. The frequently revised entries on celebrities in the Soviet Encyclopedia are another example.

Even physical elimination combined with character assassination may not obliterate deviant charisma. In such cases, both the Catholic

12. These include, in addition to patronage and "inside" information, access to formal communication channels of the organization, access usually reserved for leaders who hold office. On the significance of this power see Michels (1959, pp. 130-36), and Lipset, Trow, and Coleman (1956, pp. 260-61).

Church and the Communist Party have employed a mechanism which allows them to turn deviant charismatic symbols into a focus of conforming identification. In the Church, canonization has sometimes played this role; by reinterpreting the image of the deviant leader, devotion to the charismatic symbol is rechanneled to the organization and its goals. The canonization of Joan of Arc is probably the best-known example. Similarly, the Red Army revalorized Ivan the Terrible during the revival of national commitments in World War II.[13]

Character assassination and canonization are similar processes but they work in opposite directions. Both manipulate the public image of a charismatic, both reinterpret the meaning of symbols. In the first case, symbols of positive identification are redefined as representing negative values (from the viewpoint of the organization). In the second case symbols of negative values are reinterpreted as a legitimate focus of identification.

Canonization is a dangerous mechanism. If used widely and freely, it may encourage deviance because it grants the deviant hope of becoming a saint. The Church has special safety devices against this possibility: No one may become a saint until fifty years after death, and extensive tests are required before a person is recognized as a saint. Very few deviant charismatics pass the tests. A deviant can hardly count on sainthood.

When organizational weakness or the deviant leader's power make elimination or expulsion a risky procedure, mechanisms aimed at *isolation* of the leader are activated. Pains are taken to stop the spread of deviance to others, and to prevent the deviant leader from accumulating power. Isolation may be achieved by transferring the deviant leader to a solitary and distant district such as Outer Mongolia, or to a foreign capital. General Robert Lee Scott, Jr. supplies the following example of this widely used technique of control. He was trying to regain a combat assignment in China: "When I walked dejectedly in to Colonel Blain I quickly discovered what these conformists did to odd-ball nonconformists like me, who didn't have sense enough to leave their way of running the war alone. My orders

---

13. This procedure is, of course, not limited to organizations. Wallerstein states: "The developing nationalist movements see the political value inherent in the revalorization of heroes and empires. Samory, whom the French saw as a rapacious and cruel warrior finally subdued, was presented for West African nationalists as the noble and heroic chieftain finally repressed by the invader." (1960, p. 6)

said I was going to La Paz, Bolivia. Assignment—air attaché." (1959, p. 251)

Isolating transfers can be used only when the leader has not yet acquired a wide following. If he refuses to go, he is rebelling prematurely and thus supplies a legitimate excuse for his expulsion or elimination. If he agrees to go, he will be separated from his constituents and sent to a place where new accumulation of power and a following will be difficult, if not impossible.[14]

If, on the other hand, the deviant leader has gained wide or strategic support, the "Outer Mongolia" device becomes dangerous for the organization. It may supply legitimate excuse for an incipient rebellion; it may induce some groups which had been hedging to join the rebels or support them. Therefore, different mechanisms are employed to handle a powerful deviant. An effort is made to *compartmentalize* the deviation, to stop its spread and eventually overcome it. On ships and submarines, when a compartment is damaged it is temporarily abandoned; the bulkhead doors are locked, separating these units from others. Organizations have an analogous device. In the Catholic Church compartmentalization can be attained through regulation of the right to serve as a priest. An ordained priest has the "power of orders" to hear confession, say mass, and fulfill other religious functions, but in order to exercise it in a particular parish he needs the permission of the bishop of the diocese in which the parish lies. This is technically referred to as "faculties" or "power of jurisdiction." When a pastor or member of an order wants to preach or carry out other religious functions in a parish which is not in the territory for which he has "faculties," he has to gain the permission of the bishop.[15] Usually this is a mere formality, but when deviance occurs, this formality can be used to block its spread to other dioceses.

---

14. "The new foundation had hardly survived its initial difficulties when an unexpected tragedy came upon it. . . . Suddenly he [Bruno] was called by the Pope 'to the service of the Holy See.' The summons . . . faced Bruno with a well-nigh insoluble dilemma. As a monk, he knew the duty he owed to the Pope, yet at the same time this meant that he had to renounce his own mission. . . . The sacrifice required of him was all the greater because the young foundation threatened to collapse without him. After mature deliberation, Bruno decided to obey the Pope, and left his monastery, which he was never to see again. Bruno's departure had catastrophic consequences. His brethren . . . abandoned their retreat and scattered far and wide." (Nigg, 1959, pp. 162-63)

15. "Bulkhead doors" in organizations, as in ships, are used sparingly because they make movement awkward. Therefore, power of jurisdiction is usually granted for a diocese, not just for one parish.

It is quite clear, for example, that Father Feeney, who was excommunicated in 1949, would have been denied such a permit in the period preceding his excommunication.[16]

There are no parallel formal rules in political organizations, but there are parallel mores. In many political organizations, a local leader's visits to other districts are expected to occur only with the approval of the leaders in those districts. Repeated visits to distant districts and "tours" of the country, unless organized or approved by the national machine, are seen as attempts to build up national power in order to sieze the center of the organization or some national position, such as the presidential candidacy. Such moves are frequently criticized as "undermining the unity of the party" or "building a faction." Pressure is put on local leaders to close the door to such visitors.

A closely related device, which anticipates the need to limit the spread of deviance, is the *taboo against formalization of factions*. In some parties there is a formal rule which calls for automatic expulsion of every member who attempts it. Mapai (Israeli Labor Party) introduced such a regulation after a national faction (known as Faction B), under the highly charismatic leadership of Tabenkin, broke away from it and formed what has been ever since a strongly competitive left-wing party, Ahdut HaAvodah.[17]

Organizations are especially careful to *protect strategic positions* from the penetration of deviant charismatics. Such positions include the national headquarters, communication centers, and socialization units. Hence the jealous control over the party's school and newspapers, and the assignment of top positions in political schools and media to the "safest," but often not the ablest, leaders. This practice may partly account for the often observed dullness of radical and

16. Father Feeney was the head of the Catholic Youth Center (St. Benedict's Center) at Harvard. He and his associates and students developed a dogma which is, from the viewpoint of the Church, a deviation. Feeney was advocating that Catholic students be educated only in Catholic schools and universities, and that inter-faith cooperation and contact be reduced. His "faculties" were withdrawn by the Archbishop J. Cushing of Boston after Feeney refused to obey the orders of his superiors on January 1, 1949. He was excommunicated on April 19, 1949, after he supported publicly four teachers who were discharged from Boston College High School because they supported his viewpoint. On this case see O'Dea (1949, ch. 9). See also the newspaper clippings from Boston newspapers attached to the essay.

17. For a study of the role of these two parties in the Israeli political system, and statistics concerning the effect of the split on the power of Mapai, see Etzioni (1959, p. 200).

religious newspapers. It is also one reason such decisive action was taken against Father Feeney, who occupied a strategic position by virtue of his post as director of the Catholic Youth Center at Harvard.

Another mechanism by which strategic positions are protected from deviant leaders is found mainly in countries where there is proportional representation. Party representatives in parliament are required to sign an undated resignation letter, before the elections, so that the party can force a representative to resign if he does not follow its orders. (McKenzie, 1955, pp. 598-99).

When deviant tendencies are strong, the organization weak, or control mechanisms activated too late, the deviant charismatic accumulates power, recruits a following, and initiates a movement. In the Church such a movement has often taken the form of a sect. Such sects may split the organization, or break away from it and from society,[18] or gain control over the organization as a whole.[19] Each of these outcomes is highly dysfunctional from the viewpoint of the organization or its commanding elite. Hence, when the deviant charismatic has accumulated enough power to be a major threat to the organization or its elite, a last-resort control device is activated which gives the organizational elite one more chance to contain the deviating charismatic power. The organization *creates a new division,* into which the deviant power is channeled. This "protest-absorbing" unit often succeeds not only in containing the potential or actual deviant force but also in turning it into a conforming, sometimes even conformist, force, while the formerly deviant charismatic remains its leader. Historically, orders have served as such protest-absorbing units in the Church; marauder armies have had such functions in combat organizations; and some factions in political organizations have played similar roles. The history of the labor

18. This double withdrawal requires development of a "total organization"—a social unit which is both an organization and a community. The Mormons' withdrawal into the West is a case in point (O'Dea, 1957, pp. 41ff.). Another illustration is supplied by a Jewish sect, the Essenes, which withdrew into the desert in the second century B.C. The same holds for many of the Utopian settlements (Buber, 1949).

19. The Cluny movement, for example, was a small order in France at the beginning of the tenth century. It continued to accumulate power and influence; its members were elected to strategic positions as abbots, papal counselors, and delegates, so that for the two hundred and fifty years which followed (till the middle of the twelfth century), it had decisive influence over religious, ecclesiastical, and political policies of the Church. The suppression of simony is attributed to this movement. Another such movement, the Company of the Holy Sacrament, in the seventeenth century, is analyzed by Chill (1960).

movement, especially since the first split between Socialists and Communists, supplies numerous instances of this development. The development of youth factions is probably the best-known example.

How do protest-absorbers function? Why are they frequently effective when other mechanisms of control fail? The answer seems to lie in the following characteristics of these units: First, they give the potentially deviant leaders and followers a new, legitimate area of activity. Second, this area of activity is usually specifically delineated. A religious order, for example, is usually a teaching order, a preaching order, or a nursing order, but in most cases not a multipurpose unit like the parent organization. The same is true of military units which have a protest-absorbing function. They are normally restricted to one rather special type of warfare at one front. This sets limits to the power of the deviant force.

In addition, the activity assigned to the protest-absorbing unit is frequently a new one, or it tests a new means of effecting an older task. This satisfies, in part, both the innovating spirit of the deviants and the needs of the organization. Transforming a deviant group into a conforming unit is an important tool for innovation or renovation in organizations. The Flying Tigers, for example, tested and later introduced new equipment and methods of air warfare (Scott, 1954).

The Jesuits strengethened the front against the Protestant movement and answered the increased need for learning and teaching in modern societies. Political factions control new groups which come to power, such as members of labor unions or newly enfranchised voters.

Michels (1959) has pointed out that organizing protest mitigates it. This holds not only for labor unions and radical parties but also for orders, factions, and military units. The potential deviants invest their means, energy, and time in organizing the new unit, expanding it, and making it a success. As a result, these resources are not available for nonconforming activities. Once the unit is established, the leaders have acquired so many "secondary gains" from conformity that they hesitate to risk the tool they have created and the personal satisfaction they draw from it.

Whereas achievement in most subunits tends to be credited to the head of the more encompassing unit—a frequent source of frustration for lower leaders, especially the more ambitious—leaders of protest-absorbing subunits tend to receive more recognition for their efforts.

Being head of such a unit makes the leader more visible, which may satisfy his ambition and reduce his motives for breaking away from the organization.[20]

It should be pointed out that all these mechanisms and devices, both preventive and post-factum, often fail. Actors in lower elite positions develop "hot" charisma, and all efforts to cool it off are of no avail; organizations are split and new ones, usually competitive, are created. Luther and Tito supply perhaps the best-known examples. John L. Lewis played a similar role in 1935 when he and other members of his faction took their unions out of the AFL to form the CIO. Mrs. Ballington Booth, a commander in the Salvation Army, left in 1896 and created the Volunteers of America, drawing heavily on former members of the Salvation Army. She is typical of the myriad lesser-known leaders who have split organizations and created new ones. History tends to play up the deviant who succeeds in establishing a new organization, or at least in breaking up the old one. Actually the effectiveness of control mechanisms in L-Structures is best demonstrated by the fact that for every deviant charismatic who succeeds, many others are at one stage or another kept from splitting or weakening the organization.

CONTROL MECHANISMS IN R-STRUCTURES

Charisma, Competence, and Control

The structure of R organizations must be briefly reviewed before we can explore their distinctive control mechanisms. In R organizations, ends-decisions and charisma are concentrated in one or more organizational ranks other than the top one. The charismatic rank is usually composed of professionals.

---

20. William A. Glaser pointed out to the author that "protest absorbers" are also found in philanthropic foundations and in the United States Congress. Foundations have established "sub"-foundations for highly charismatic leaders with deviant tendencies. These subfoundations have limited, specialized goals, often somewhat deviant from the predominant tradition of the foundation, and directing them has mellowing effects on the rebellious spirits of their leaders.

One way of dealing with charismatic deviant leaders in the Congress has been to give them a specially created investigating committee and staff to pursue a limited topic of their choice. Creating the apparatus, planning and executing the hearings, and so on often preoccupies these leaders sufficiently to prevent them from directly threatening central party leadership.

Professionals have two sources of "office" charisma. One follows from their status as accredited professionals. (It is *ascribed* in the sense that although the status has to be achieved, charisma follows automatically once it is attained. It is not based on continual demonstration of the power.) Professional knowledge is charismatic because the typical layman cannot understand it and thus finds it "extraordinary" (Wilson, 1954, pp. 9-14); because the layman has to accept directives on nonrational grounds (hence the more educated a person is, the less charismatic professionals are in his eyes); and because professionals deal with problems of the meaning of man, nature, and God (Naegele, 1955, esp. pp. 13-20).[22]

A second source of ascribed charisma is the professional's organizational position. Full professors have more charisma than assistant professors, head surgeons more than interns, and senior researchers more than junior researchers.

Professionals may also vary in personal charisma. One source of such charisma is an extraordinary talent, skill, knowledge, or competence. Many academic professions have their "great teachers" with numerous disciples. Interns and residents come from all over the world to participate in "rounds" conducted by outstanding surgeons or physicians. Some leaders of research bureaus have similar international influences in their fields. In addition to the few great charismatics, there are numerous lesser ones at most campuses, schools, and hospitals.

Personal charisma may be derived in part from sources such as persuasive powers and eccentric behavior. When this kind of charisma is associated with competence, it may still be functional. No matter what the source of charismatic power, a persuasive teacher gets his material across more effectively than a less persuasive one, a persuasive researcher may inspire students to develop a neglected field, and a persuasive doctor may have unusually therapeutic effects on his patient, especially when the illness has psychosomatic aspects.

But personal charisma may not always be associated with sound knowledge, true skill, and professional integrity. There is the ignorant

22. Rieff pointed out that Freud was aware of the psychoanalyst's office charisma: "The analyst, too, must keep in mind the formal character of Eros. In his esoteric papers Freud took care to instruct psychoanalysts that theirs was an office charisma, not a personal one. The analyst 'must recognize that the patient's falling in love is induced by the analytic situation and is not to be ascribed to the charms of his person.'" (1959, p. 171).

and shallow teacher who fascinates undergraduates with his colorful language, imagery, and "charm." There is the "Park Avenue" doctor whose reputation and authority over his patients derive from the way he is dressed, the locale of his practice, his manner of speech, even his physical bearing, and not from professional competence and integrity, two qualities he often lacks. In short, personal charisma and competence [23] may be combined in any one of the following ways:

	Personal Charisma	
Competence	$+$	$-$
$+$	1	2
$-$	3	4

The first of the four possible combinations is of no concern to the control mechanisms because it is the most desired. The fourth, one may assume, is usually kept to a minimum through selection and reselection, at least in effective training organizations. The major concern of the control mechanisms seems to be the *incompetent charismatic* (3), and the *competent noncharismatic* (2).

The primary function of control mechanisms in R-Structures is to maintain the association of charisma (over laymen) with professional knowledge and skill. Just as churches cannot allow pastors to use their charisma to lead parishioners away from "the truth," it is dysfunctional for professions to allow their members to use charisma to spread or apply unsound knowledge, or to conceal a faulty performance. The church must activate its controls in order to keep members and to retain their commitments. The professions must control charisma if they are not to lose their potential clientele, the trust of clients who continue to consume their services, and their right to self-control.

Control mechanisms in R organizations also assure that those who have the required competence will also have at least the minimum of personal charisma required; this amount varies considerably in different professional organizations. Research organizations are the haven of noncharismatic professionals because effective performance

23. To save space, the term *competence* will represent "competence, skill, knowledge, and integrity." Obviously, an actor may have some of these qualities and not others, but we are concerned here only with the relationship between charisma and the professional qualifications for which competence serves as a generic term.

here does not require intensive personal influence. Schools fall at the other end of the scale, for here personal charisma is a central requirement. The more effective schools rarely employ teachers who lack normative influence over their students.

Other organizations fall between these two poles in the amount of personal charisma they require for effective performance. Universities resemble schools in this respect. Although the role of professor is viewed very differently in various colleges (Barzun, 1946; Caplow and McGee, 1955), covering almost the full range from teacher (in many liberal arts colleges) to researcher (in top universities), tenure appointments are rarely granted to professors who are known to be really poor teachers.

Similarly, although competence is emphasized in the selection of medical students, they are also screened to see whether they have the potentials of a "doctor's personality," often described as the ability to "impose one's will on the patient." The relative weight of this factor is difficult to establish, but it seems to be underestimated more often than overestimated. It is widely accepted that "personality" is more important for lawyers than doctors, but future doctors do not think so. Thielens (1958) shows that 40 per cent of the medical students he studied consider "pleasing personality" to be the second most important factor making for a good doctor; "high intelligence" was listed as the first factor by 73 per cent. Law students, asked a parallel question about factors making for a good lawyer, gave the attributes virtually identical weight: 73 per cent listed intelligence first and 44 per cent put "pleasing personality" second (*ibid.*, p. 148). Doctors and lawyers, therefore, like professors, appear to fall between teachers and researchers in the amount of charisma required for effective performance of their roles.

Control Mechanisms in R Organizations

Control mechanisms in R organizations are similar in form to those in L organizations, but their functions are quite different. Mechanisms whose major function in L organizations is to control charisma operate here to control various kinds of deviance (e.g., from the professional code of ethics); two among many forms of behavior which are controlled are the maintenance of a satisfactory level of charisma and its association with competence. The fact that R organizations do not find it necessary to establish special control mechanisms for charisma, but deal with it as merely one of many potential spheres of deviant behavior, indirectly supports our earlier point that lack of charisma and deviant (incompetent) charisma are relatively less dysfunctional in R than in L organizations. This is true because they cause relatively less potential damage to the organization and because there are other forms of deviance which are more common and more threatening to R organizations.

We therefore review these control mechanisms only briefly and focus the rest of the discussion on the main difference between control structures in L and R organizations—the exercise of pure normative power versus social power.

PREVENTIVE MECHANISMS—Many of the major control mechanisms of R organizations, as in L organizations, are preventive and built in, and fill two functions at the same time: They screen both noncharismatics and potential deviants. Control begins with careful *selection* of candidates, starting early in the undergraduate school and continuing through all the successive stages of training. This mechanism is built in, since selection is carried out mainly in order to recruit students who have the potential professional *competence;* checking for potential charisma is at most a secondary selective criterion. Actually, all the mechanisms which assure competence also act as preventive controls over charisma, since they guarantee that the charismatic will have at least the basic minimum of competence, although they cannot guarantee that the more charismatic will be more competent.

The same statements can be made about *socialization* in R organizations, which assures competence (instrumental socialization) and acceptance of professional values (expressive socialization). Indirectly, socialization affects charisma; increasing competence reduces the possibility of an incompetent charismatic and indoctrination increases the charismatic potential. In contrast to L organizations, the emphasis here is more on instrumental and less on expressive socialization. This difference in emphasis follows from the basic differences between the two types of organization. In L organizations, the elites "work" more with their personalities and command of knowledge is relatively less important; in R organizations, specific skills and knowledge count as much as personality. Hence, in R organizations, less stress need be put on personality and charisma, in selection of participants and in their socialization. (Note that training for positions in R organizations is, on the average, much longer than in L organizations.)

The statements made about selection and socialization also apply to other preventive mechanisms, such as *examination, practice period* (e.g., internship), and *observation* during first assignments. The parallels hold not only in general but also in detail. Thus, for example, paralleling the "captive audience" used in L organizations for training and testing, we have the ward (nonpaying) patients in hospitals, and introductory courses, "sections," night classes, and summer schools in colleges and universities.

Transfer of potential or actual deviant charismatics by order of a higher-ranking participant, practiced widely by many L organizations, is a device rarely used in R organizations. Universities, hospitals, and research organizations usually cannot reassign their professionals. Several features of the structure of R organizations explain this difference. First, it is functional for superiors to have only limited power over the professional, for reasons discussed above (see pp. 320-24). Hence such a powerful sanction as forced transfer is excluded. Second, unlike L organizations, which have many branches in many localities linked to one center of authority, R organizations are usually limited to one or very few localities. Therefore, there are considerably fewer opportunities for involuntary transfer. But even transfer to different divisions in the same organization cannot usually be ordered (even when the difference in skill required is small, as in assigning a teacher of graduate students to undergraduates). All these statements hold not only for professional organizations but also for religious organizations such as the various egalitarian churches, which also have an R-Structure.

Finally, whereas L organizations tend to see their higher participants as permanent staff who can be reassigned but who must, as a rule, be retained, R organizations tend to fire deviants rather than reassign them. Actually, deviants are reassigned through the labor market to lower positions, but this process is not under the direct control of any one organization or power center.

Sidetracking in R-Structures occurs frequently, as it does in L-Structures, and in a way which enhances organizational control, but it is less planned and less controlled by superiors than in L-Structures. Certain features in the reward system of R-Structures make for functional sidetracking. Individuals who pass through the various selection and socialization stages but lack some of the qualities needed for a successful professional career are attracted by the rewards of other roles. (It should be noted, in passing, that when these rewards greatly exceed those supplied by the organization, dysfunctional sidetracking may occur as actors who are well qualified to serve the organization's main activities are attracted to secondary or marginal positions, often positions for which they are less well qualified.)

Professional organizations even have their equivalent of the Donatist Heresy. According to the professional norms of R organizations, no layman is "allowed" to determine that an accredited professional does not have the required skills and knowledge, since this would undermine the office-charisma of the profession. Hence a professional is expected to defend his colleagues before laymen, even when he is aware that the lay criticisms have some validity. This does not mean that no action will be taken against a deviant professional. But action, it is usually felt, ought not to be initiated by the layman, and preferably should not be known to him. This limitation offers to the professional's performance immunity from particularistic pressures, assures his ability to take risks, and defends the autonomy of professional controls.

Suspension and *expulsion* are used in R organizations as rarely as in L organizations. Expulsion from office (withdrawing attending privileges in a hospital, nonrenewal of an appointment to a university) may precede expulsion from the profession. This two-step mechanism has functions similar to those in L organizations, discussed above. Expulsion in both types of organization means a very considerable loss of prestige, income, and social reward. It is therefore a very strong means of control as a threat, even when used very sparingly.

POST-FACTUM MECHANISMS—There are considerably fewer post-factum mechanisms in R organizations than in L organizations; those which do exist are less powerful and, in part, independent of the organization's power structure. Execution, assassination, canonization, compartmentalization and similar powerful post-factum mechanisms are almost never employed in R organizations, either because these organizations do not have the social license required for such controls,[24] or because deviance here is usually individualistic or

---

24. The differences in social license are, of course, due in large degree to historical factors; R organizations, unlike L organizations, exist chiefly in modern societies, where social license to apply coercion is highly restricted.

isolated and relatively powerless. R organizations have only limited power over professionals; therefore the latter have little to gain from a coup, and the organization needs fewer defenses.

Peer and Superior Control in R Organizations

There is one major difference in the control of higher participants in L and in R organizations: R organizations tend to rely on social power and commitments whereas L organizations utilize pure normative powers and moral involvement. As we have seen, in the exercise of pure normative power the control agent tends to be higher in status than the subject; in the case of social power, groups of actors similar in status and power control each other (Bierstedt, 1950, p. 730). Charisma—intense, pure normative power—is more likely to develop when there are already some status differences than when there are none. Moreover, charisma by its very nature is a vertical relationship. A person subject to charisma sees himself as lower in status than the charismatic even when there are no other status differences. In short, charisma is more likely to emerge where rank differences already exist; if there are none, it creates them. On the other hand, peer relations are by definition relations among equals, actors of the same or similar status. Hence peer relations and charismatic relations are incompatible by definition.

It is often suggested that control in professions rests on social power and commitments, that it lies in the hands of the professional community (as an informal net of control) and the professional associations (as a formal net of control).[25] Both are frequently seen as analogous to the peer-group control which the jury system originally provided for members of the aristocracy. Even the reference group of professionals, as Gouldner and Wilensky have pointed out, tends to be "horizontal," consisting of other professionals and not of

25. The following studies cast considerable light on various aspects of professional control. The standard book on professionals, their codes, and modes of control is still Carr-Saunders and Wilson (1933). A major study of professionals in the United States is that of Goode and Cornish (in progress). An empirical study of doctors' social relations and their effects on professional communication and control is reported by Menzel and Katz (1955) and by Coleman, Katz, and Menzel (1957). The formal aspects of the control structure in the medical profession, e.g. that of the American Medical Association, are studied by Garceau (1941). The informal structure is the subject of two papers by Hall (1946, 1948). Studies by Brown (1954, pp. 263-65) and by Ben-David (1958) deal with both formal and informal controls. Comparisons of professionals in private practice and in bureaucracy are supplied by Lee (1944) and by Gerver and Bensman (1954, p. 233-34).

persons superior in organizational rank.[26] In particular, peers are "significant others" much more frequently than superiors.

Social power in its pure form is rarely an organizational power. If an organization is to use it to support its norms and directives, the net of social relations in which social power rests must be linked to the organizational control system, for example by means of formal leaders and downward expressive communication. This means that if we are to examine the role played by professional controls in organizations employing professionals, we must explore the ways in which peer or social control is related to vertical controls.

DIFFERENTIAL PEER CONTROL—The common image of professional control is that peers, actors equal in rank, control each other. Actually, professional control, in organizations at least, is greatly affected by the fact that professionals hold different ranks in the organization.[27] The higher the rank of a professional, in general, the larger his controlling power. The lower the rank of a professional, the lower his controlling power and the greater his subjection to control.

There are three major ranks of professionals: professionals in training, pre-tenure professionals, and professionals with tenure. There are several differentiations within each group and important differences among various types of professional organizations; we discuss both kinds of differentiation briefly in order to illustrate our major point: Although professionals are peers, some have considerably more power than others, and the control of professionals is based to a great degree on this power differentiation.

26. This point has been made by Gouldner (1957) in a study of university professors: "The expert's skills are continually being refined and developed by professional peers outside of his employing organization. Moreover, his continued standing as a competent professional often cannot be validated by members of his own organization, since they are not knowledgeable enough about it. For these reasons, the expert is more likely than others to esteem the good opinion of professional peers elsewhere; he is disposed to seek recognition and acceptance from 'outsiders'. We can say that he is more likely to be oriented to a reference group composed of others not a part of his employing organization, that is, an 'outer reference group'." (p. 288) Wilensky (1956) found the same professional, "outer," reference group among some of the types of experts he studied in labor unions. "The Professional Service expert is oriented in his job role toward an outside colleague group; his primary job identification is with his profession." (p. 129; see also pp. 138, 155-57) Reissman (1949) distinguishes among four types of professionals according to varying degrees of identification with the organization versus identification with the profession. See also Campbell and Pettigrew (1959, p. 87) and Davis (1960).

27. Eaton (1951, p. 711) refers to the performances controlled as "hierarchical teamwork."

Students are the privates and the N.C.O.'s of the professional organization. To disregard them would be to overlook a major part of the organizational hierarchy. To view them as clients would be to overlook the fact that research assistants and interns carry important work loads in universities, research organizations, and hospitals. It is obvious that their income, promotion, prestige, privileges, and facilities are controlled to a considerable degree by higher-ranking professionals. More formally, according to our three criteria for determining the lower organizational boundaries as discussed in Chapter I, students fall high to medium on all three criteria: performance obligation, subordination, and involvement.

The pre-tenure ranks—instructors and assistant professors in most universities, interns and residents in hospitals, and most researchers in research organizations—share control over the students with the tenure staff, although in cases of actual or potential differences of opinion over such issues as granting a Ph.D., or allocating a fellowship or a job, the tenure members generally have the decisive say. Pre-tenure staff have only limited control over each other, and very little control over their superiors. In many university departments this practice is formalized. Pre-tenure members have no vote on issues affecting the rewards and powers of senior members, with the exception of electing the departmental chairman, in which frequently all full-time department members participate.

The tenure ranks control the two lower ranks. The holders of the power positions, the department chairmen in universities and division heads in hospitals, are as a rule recruited from these ranks. They control access to the administration and the allocation of major rewards and facilities in the organization. Mutual control among the highest-ranking members of the tenure staff is the only place in professional organizations where control approximates pure peer control.[28]

It is often said that informal controls play an important part in

28. The hierarchical organization of physicians in hospitals and the scope of the power of those higher in rank over those lower in rank are reported and analyzed in several studies. Rose Coser (1958) showed differences in power structure between the medical ward and the surgical ward. The first is organized in a more hierarchical manner, the second in a relatively more horizontal manner. These differences are related to differences in tasks performed and self-images of the two groups of professionals involved. See also Wilson's analysis of "teamwork" in the operating room (1954; 1959-60, pp. 182-83). Hall (1948, pp. 329-32) analyzes both the central role of hospital—professional relations in the medical community and the hierarchical nature of these relations.

professional behavior. Since informal controls—gossip, slighting remarks, expressions of esteem—tend to be horizontal, they suggest that true peer control is relatively frequent. But the significance of these controls may be exaggerated if other control mechanisms are overlooked. Informal controls are affected by attitudes of superiors, and are effective in part because they are known to be reinforced by superiors through their reward allocations. Finally, as a result of this relatively equalitarian community and peer-ideology, there are comparatively few communication blocks among the ranks. This makes the transmission of information about peers to higher ranks comparatively common.

The term *differential peer control,* used here to refer to the professional control structure, serves to remind us that although the professional group has some characteristics of peer groups—all are members of a profession, have one vote in the association, and have had similar training—there are also some systematic differentiations in power within each professional group which affect the control processes.

INTERLOCKING CONTROLS—The study of interlocking control of professions and of organizations examines another aspect of the relationship between horizontal and vertical controls in R-Structures. As professional ideology and some standard discussions of professional occupations would have it, controls rest chiefly with the professional associations and community. Actually, as Goode has pointed out, contemporary trends make this view less and less correct.

The professional who is also a bureaucrat becomes less *directly* dependent on the professional community. . . . Nevertheless, the bureaucracy usually hires, fires, or advances him upon the advice of peer or superior professionals, who in turn may feel themselves to be part of the professional community. Correlatively, the bureaucracy makes and enforces rules for the professional. . . . In turn, of course, the professional community is responsible to the bureaucracy for proper staffing. (1957, p. 197)

Goode focuses on the interlocking control between professionals and lay officials in a nonprofessional organization such as a government agency. He suggests that bureaucrats exert more control over professionals, and the professional community exerts less, than is often supposed. This also applies to professional organizations, where lay administrators and higher-ranking professionals exert considerable control over professional participants in the organization. In one way or another, *a large amount of control over professional performances has been transferred from the professional community to the professional organization.* Lay administrators in many colleges and state universities exercise considerable control over professors (Lazarsfeld and Thielens, 1958, pp. 37-43). Lay control over professionals also appears in public schools, many mental hospitals, some general hospitals, and numerous research organizations. But of greater interest is the fact that even those "substantive" or goal activities left to professional self-control are *often controlled by colleagues in the same organization, and not by extra-organizational or inter-organizational professional bodies.*

In almost all universities, promotions are made largely on the recommendation of local members of the profession, often in the same organizational department. If additional controls are desired, it is much more common to grant power [29] to a committee composed of members of *other* professions than to call for judgments from off-campus professionals in the same discipline.[30] In hospitals, decisions about attending privileges and promotion are of course made by the professional staff of the hospital concerned. Many violations of the professional code of ethics, especially minor ones, are handled in a similar manner.

Control by professions and organizations is interlocking because sanctions are initiated in both directions, from the organization to the profession and vice versa. For example, in the medical profession both the association and the hospital are represented in the early selection and socialization processes—on admissions boards and on boards of trustees of medical schools. In deciding about a major promotion, the organization may seek opinions from professionals outside the organization. The organization also refers to the professional association the more severe violations of the code of ethics. On the other hand, the locus of professional power and activity is often the local hospital (if there is one in the town), or the better local hospitals, if there are several. Board members of professional associa-

29. The points made in this section refer to the locus of real power in the control processes. This fact has to be emphasized, since the ideology of peer and professional control sometimes leads to formal procedures which suggest, but do not really represent, profession-wide control.

30. This is particularly likely to be true in the case of "semi-professions." Power differentials among professions come into sharp relief both in mental hospitals and in inter-disciplinary research. Power differentials among psychoanalysts, psychologists, and social workers were studied by Zander, Cohen, and Stotland (1957, 1959). See also Russell Sage Foundation Annual Report (1958-1959, pp. 1-15).

tions are more likely to come from these hospitals, and these hospitals are used by the profession's elites to reinforce—through granting attending privileges and promotion, for example—the norms and judgments of the professional community. As there are interlocking directorates in business, so there are professionals who link the control structures of profession and organization. Thus it is not suggested that the professional community and association have no power. But this power is only in part invested in "peer" relationships. It lies to a large degree in the controls institutionalized in professional organizations. These organizations, in turn, use the professional community and associations to control their professional staff.

The same pattern is found in universities, where the local professional group, together with the profession as a whole, plays a major role in controlling organizational personnel. The "profession as a whole," however, is often the weaker partner. Many academic professions do not even have professional associations to formalize and implement professional codes.[31]

One important way the profession serves as an informal control system is by supplying information about the relative quality of a professional (his national reputation). This source of control is limited because it has no clear, institutionalized power centers. Such power rests to some degree with leading professionals who have national and international *influence;* but even they make few *decisions* concerning matters of control.

Our discussion has focused on hospitals and universities, but the points made hold also for schools. Here the interlocking control system is one of superintendents', principals', and teachers' associations. But the control which superiors have over teachers is so extensive that schools become a boundary case between R and L organizations,[32] and teachers' associations devote their efforts primarily to defending the teacher against these controls, instead of controlling their members.

No discussion of research organizations has been included here

31. Professional "societies" have other functions. On the dynamics of professional associations (or "guildism") in some academic professions, see Goode (1960).

32. The school has a power center occupied by a head who is charismatic not only for the lower participants, the students, but often for the lower elites, the teachers, as well. On the other hand, it does not have much of a line organization, and it leaves relatively many ends-decisions to the middle-ranking teachers. In short, it falls between typical L- and typical R-Structures.

because there is little systematic information about them; they are considerably smaller in number than the other organizations; and there is considerable variation among them.

As we have seen, then, control in R organizations is relatively more horizontal (or social) than in L organizations, but this point should not be overemphasized. Professionals differ in rank, and consequently in power and in exposure to control. Moreover, control over professionals is increasingly vested in the local organization— either in its administrators or in its professionals—and not in the professional association or professional community. The control systems of the professional community and the professional organization interlock through both formal and informal mechanisms, one of which occurs when the power elites of the two systems have some members in common.

Control of deviance, charismatic or not, in organizations is not simply a matter of social compliance; social compliance, if the organization is to make use of it, must be woven into hierarchical (often pure normative) relationships.

SUMMARY

Organizations which employ charismatics below the top elite level must develop mechanisms to prevent deviant exploitation of this charisma and to control deviance should it occur. In L organizations the central problem is to keep charismatics from deflecting the commitments of loyal participants to other values and organizations; in R organizations the central problem is to assure the association of charisma with adequate professional competence.

Both L and R organizations employ similar preventive mechanisms. Through selection, socialization, extended practice training, and various other means, potential deviants are screened out and deviant tendencies in those remaining are modified.

Because potential deviance is a greater threat to L organizations, these have developed post-factum control mechanisms more elaborate than those found in R-structures. The deviant may be warned, suspended, exiled, expelled, or assassinated; or, if he is too powerful for these measures, his movement may be directed into protest-absorbing units where it can spend its energy in ways useful to the organization.

Control in R organizations is relatively more horizontal than in L organizations, but social compliance must be woven into hierarchical (often pure normative) relationships if the organization is to make effective use of it. Increasingly, control over professionals is vested in the local organization and not in the professional association or the professional community.

XIV

OTHER CORRELATES REVISITED

This and the following chapter review new findings on the relationships between compliance structure and other organizational variables, a task we started earlier, when we introduced new data regarding the relationship between goals and elite structures, on the one hand, and different compliance contexts, on the other. Here, other compliance "correlates" are "revisited," including communication, consensus, cohesion, scope, pervasiveness, socialization, and selectivity. We thus continue to test the validity of the compliance theory (which is a theory, not only a hypothesis, in that it ties a whole web of significant variables to each other) to demonstrate the fruitfulness of the basic typology in terms of understanding other organizational factors than those included in the basic typology; and, finally, we continue to flesh out the emerging organizational profiles. Once we understand how consensus, socialization, selectivity, and so on differ in different compliance structures, we gain a better overall picture of the organizational types involved: of the caste system characteristic of coercive bodies, the exchange-dominated system typical of utilitarian corporations, and the mobilization characterizing effective normative organizations.

Only a few of the studies conducted since the compliance theory was published deal with one correlate at a time; most encompass two or more, although usually each covers a different set. Hence, in the following pages, we review the new data in whatever order the individual study presented them. As the majority of studies were conducted in normative organizations, these are covered first.

IN NORMATIVE ORGANIZATIONS

Recruitment, Socialization, and Selectivity in a College

The compliance theory suggests that effective normative organizations will have to rely on intensive socialization or on high selectivity of the lower participants, or, still better, on both. Zelda Gamson's (1966, 1967) study of a newly founded, small experimental college casts interesting light on what happens when a faculty aims at normative socialization in the face of initially low selectivity.[1] The "adaptation" process and its consequences, as we shall see, are varied and complex, but quite in line with the theory.

At Hawthorn, the degree of selectivity in initial recruitment was very low. Although the college was attempting to offer a more demanding, higher-quality education than its state university parent body, the students were not chosen according to academic ability; rather, any student admitted to the parent institution was allowed to attend Hawthorn. In the first years at least, Hawthorn's students were fairly representative of the larger student group (1967, p. 280). However, both natural science and social science faculty soon concluded that only certain kinds of students were likely to benefit from Hawthorn's special program. Those who could profit most from Hawthorn were not necessarily the most intelligent or the best high school students, but rather those who were somewhat offbeat, intellectual, and tolerant of ambiguity or who were highly motivated to excel academically (1966, pp. 67-68). The initial selection process ensured neither.

The lack of selectivity proved to be a problem for socialization on the part of both the social and the natural scientists. The prime effort of the natural scientists was to maintain high intellectual standards by subjecting students to a demanding curriculum and eliciting from them maximum performance as measured by "objectively" determined exam and paper grades. However, the low level of selectivity in recruitment meant that large numbers of students simply did not

1. For a more detailed introduction of Gamson's study see Ch. VIII, p. 205.

possess the preparation or the motivation to achieve high or even average grades in the face of demanding course work.

Post-admission selectivity, in the form of higher dropout or flunk-out rates, might have allowed the natural scientists to maintain both the demanding curriculum and the stringent grading standards. Such practice, however, was unacceptable to the college administrators, who viewed a high dropout rate as symptomatic of faculty failure; to the students, who were putting a great deal of pressure on the natural scientists to relax standards; and to the scientists themselves, who were proud of being able to teach "the ordinary mass of students" (1967, pp. 284-298).

Intensive socialization efforts, however, were not an effective compensatory measure. Many courses which the professors considered important and basic, such as mathematics and logic, were either too abstract for the students or did not interest them. As a result, high failure and dropout rates did occur (1967, pp. 294-297). Perhaps if the natural scientists had been willing to take a more personalistic approach to the students, stimulating their interest through personal contacts and introducing more flexible grading patterns, they might have succeeded in carrying most of the students through the more difficult courses (1967, p. 298). However, as the natural scientists were unwilling to adopt a more expressive orientation and the administration would not permit greater selectivity, the only alternative was to lower standards, i.e., to lower the college's effectiveness.

This consequence indeed followed. For a while the natural scientists held out against the pressure from administration and students until, in the spring of 1962, the third year of the college, 20% of the students failed the modern physics course (1967, p. 296). At this point much of the curriculum material on the theory of numbers, logic, and Daltonian atomics was eliminated, and the more popular courses on astronomy and evolution were expanded. This lowering of standards in response to administration and student pressure probably explains why, when the natural scientists were asked what impact Hawthorn had on its students, 6 out of 11 reported that there were no effects, while the remaining 5 mentioned only moderate intellectual achievements (1966, p. 68). In short, despite efforts at instrumental (in class) socialization that were intensive, if not sufficiently expressive, the combination of low initial selectivity and low secondary, intra-organizational selectivity resulted in low effectiveness of the instruction in the natural sciences.

For the social scientist, the lack of initial recruitment selectivity meant that most of Hawthorn's students were not the "intellectual" students, tolerant of ambiguity, who would be receptive to the social scientists' liberal arts focus, their critical political and personal values, and their emphasis on personalism. Actually, most of Hawthorn's students were vocationally oriented (1967, p. 280). Some 70% had outside jobs, giving them little time to invest in the extra-classroom campus activities the social scientists regarded as an important part of the socialization into the values they were attempting to instill. Resistance to their methods by the majority of the students and the inherent difficulty of achieving personal contact in a mass situation virtually forced the social scientists to introduce a form of selectivity into their educational strategy. (The only alternative would have been to forego their expressive orientation, lower their aims, and adopt a narrower, more instrumental approach). And, indeed, the social scientists soon introduced selectivity, not by failing students whose performance did not measure up (the social scientists in fact were able to keep their demanding curriculum only because their grading standards were flexible and lenient), but by concentrating their intensive socialization efforts on a small select group of students who became identified as their "clientele," while, if not ignoring the rest, fulfilling only minimal duties toward the majority of students. Out of 16 social scientists interviewed, 11 stated explicitly that either they or their department as a whole had out-of-class contact with only a select group of students (1967, p. 290).

This selective attention paid to a small group of students, who were more responsive to the expressive approach, probably accounts for the greater perceptions of effectiveness among the social scientists. The social scientists tended to judge their effectiveness on the basis of the responses of their clientele, not their whole student body (1966, p. 293). Thus, the problem was solved in a manner of speaking: Intensive socialization of a select minority resulted in a high level of effectiveness for a few; for the majority, there was neither selectivity nor intensive socialization, and needless to say, little effect.

The analysis could well end here. It is worth noting additionally that intensive normativeness is hard to sustain (see p. 268; and Ch. XV, p. 396). Consider what eventually happened at Hawthorn, as it moved from its initial, founding, charismatic community era to a degree of routinization: The effects of the social scientists' personalistic teaching had a boomerang effect on its proponents. Some students, primarily members of the "beat group," accepted the values of the faculty and pushed their ideology to its ultimate implications. These students questioned all authority and structure, wanted to do away with all stratification boundaries between students and faculty, and wanted more attention and intimacy than the faculty was willing or able to give. Having been encouraged by their professors to be critical and to question the world around them, these students turned their critical sights on the university, Hawthorn College, and the social science faculty as well, confronting the professors on their own hypocrisy, as these students saw it. The students demanded a voice in curriculum planning—regarded by the social science professors as the last bastion of faculty prerogative—and called into question certain elements such as grading reluctantly accepted by the social scientists as a condition of their existence at the college. In reaction, the faculty asserted that these students mistook the means for the ends, specifically taking personalism as a goal ("turning the college into a non-directive mental clinic," in one faculty member's words) rather than the means through which intellectual and normative goals were to be attained (the training of "academic guerilla fighters," according to the same professor (1967, p. 299).

Over the years, what Gamson calls the "dilemma of personalism versus performance," as faced by the Hawthorn social science faculty, contributed to a gradual weakening of the norm of personalism (a mode of expressive leadership). The confrontation between the social scientists and the group of students who demanded a voice in curriculum planning forced an awareness on both sides of the implicit limits of egalitarianism and intimacy between students and faculty. The social scientists discovered that their early emphasis on normative goals and personalism had subverted the performance standards of the College. In order to meet performance demands, the faculty were required to exercise some authority over students, yet close personal relations with students eroded faculty authority. The department's disenchantment with personalism was reflected in the departure of many of the faculty members who felt most strongly about the need for intimate student-faculty relations and in a reduced emphasis on personalism among those who remained (1967, p. 300). The change was also reflected in reports submitted by the faculty to the university indicating how the faculty spent their time. Table XIV-1 shows that the norms of the natural scientists and the social scientists about how much time should be spent in the performance of formal teach-

Table XIV-1—Mean Percentage of Faculty Time Spent on Teaching Duties, Curriculum Planning, and Counseling Students, Spring 1961–Spring 1963*

	SPRING 1961		FALL 1961		SPRING 1962		FALL 1962		SPRING 1963	
	NS	SS	NS	SS	NS	SS	NS	SS	NS	SS
Teaching duties† (Classes, grading, preparation)	83%	68%	74%	60%	79%	68%	65%	65%	71%	72%
Curriculum planning	6	8	9	9	6	4	11	6	9	8
Counseling (Individual students or organizations)	3%	12%	7%	14%	5%	11%	7%	9%	8%	5%
N	9	12	10	13	10	14	12	11	11	10

* Does not include research.
† p of differences between NS and SS in spring 1961 and fall 1961 <.05. After 1961, differences are not statistically significant.
Source: Gamson (1966), p. 66. Reprinted with the permission of the American Sociological Association.

ing duties such as giving classes, grading, preparing the lessons, and counseling of individual students and groups began to converge. Although in 1961 the social scientists were spending less time on teaching duties and more time in counseling than the natural scientists, by 1963 the two faculties were spending roughly equal amounts of time on teaching duties and the natural scientists were actually giving a somewhat larger amount of time to counseling.

To sum up, Gamson provides an excellent account of how two sub-organizations reacted to an externally imposed low degree of recruitment selectivity. Three steps, leading to gradual adaptation to their external condition, can be distinguished. At the beginning, the two departments made extensive efforts at socialization to compensate for missing selectivity—the social scientists relying on a more normative approach, the natural scientists on a more utilitarian one. Neither strategy was successful; in fact, instead of achieving socialization, both personalism and "academic standards" increasingly began to function as internal surrogates or equivalents of recruitment selectivity—leading to a high drop-out rate in the natural science department and to the selection of a few special "clients" by the social scientists. This condition was highly unstable, as it violated the organization's goals and deviated from the norms of almost all those involved; in fact, it turned out to be nothing more than a transitory stage.

In the third and final stage, the natural scientists as well as the social scientists adapted their goals and ambitions to the organization's condition of low recruitment selectivity. By lowering the standards of academic work by reducing the original resocializing goals and by reemphasizing traditional structures and values, the two departments recognized that, under the given compliance conditions, their original goals could not be successfully pursued. Selectivity, the study strongly suggests, is an important determinant of effectiveness for both highly normative or high-standard utilitarian socialization.

Scope and Pervasiveness in the Same College

The hypothesis that scope will be narrow and pervasiveness low in utilitarian organizations but that scope will be broader and pervasiveness high in normative ones also gains support from Gamson's study (1966, 1967). Her data reveal differences in the amount of extra-classroom contact with students, between the normatively oriented social scientists and the more utilitarianly oriented natural scientists. As a group, the social scientists reported a greater amount of contact and more informal contact with the students than the natural scientists (see Table XIV-2). The natural scientists tended to

Table XIV-2—Amount and Settings of Student–Faculty Contacts Outside Class (Faculty Reports)

	Natural Scientists	Social Scientists
Amount of Contact		
A lot*	3	12
A little, none	5	3
No answer	3	1
Settings of Contact		
Office	7	6
On Campus* (between classes, Student Union, campus hangouts)	5	13
Off campus† (students' apartments, faculty homes)	2	8
No answer	1	2
N‡	11	16

* p of difference between NS and SS <.05.
† p of difference between NS and SS <.10.
‡ Number of answers total to more than number of informants because multiple answers were possible.

Source: Gamson (1967), p. 288. Reprinted with the permission of the American Sociological Association.

confine their interactions with students to the campus—in particular, to the office. They felt overall that student–faculty contacts should take place within the formal curricular structure. The social scientists held that student–faculty relations should proceed not only within the formal curricular structure but within the extracurricular structure of the college as well (especially through the activities of the Student Union). Many social scientists also felt that students and faculty should socialize together outside the formal structure of the college, for example, in student apartments or faculty homes. These different patterns of student–faculty contact are also borne out in the students' reports (see Gamson, 1967, p. 289).

The high pervasiveness characteristic of the normative orientation and the low pervasiveness characteristic of the utilitarian orientation are illustrated by the answers of the social and natural scientists to questions about their educational goals. As we have already seen, the natural scientists were almost exclusively concerned with obtaining high intellectual performance from their students, while the social scientists were concerned with affecting students' social, political, and personal values as well. While the natural scientists were interested in students as students, throughout their college careers, the social scientists were concerned with inducting new recruits into the "intellectual community" and with molding "people" who, on their own in the wider world, would be different from the majority in their critical outlooks and their uncompromising life styles vis-à-vis a mass, alienating society (1966, pp. 54-59).

Even in the narrow area of intellectual performance, however, where the goals of the two faculty groups overlapped somewhat, the natural scientists placed primary reliance on the students' calculative self-interest to elicit behavioral compliance to the norms of academic scholarship, while the social scientists, viewing students as intellectuals in embryo, endeavored to socialize students into an internalization of the academic community's norms and values. This difference is aptly illustrated by Gamson's data on the typical attitudes of the natural and social science faculties toward student plagiarism. Although neither group condoned plagiarism, the natural scientists defined it far more narrowly and took a more matter-of-fact approach to it. The natural scientists punished individual instances of plagiarism in an instrumental fashion by giving E grades to those papers, but they did not regard such behavior as "cheating" nor as reflecting an overall lack of integrity on the part of the students involved. In general, they felt that students, whom they did not regard as members of the intellectual community, should not be subjected to moral judgments based on that community's norms.

The social scientists, in marked contrast, reacted to instances of plagiarism with hurt and anger, for they expected students to have absorbed from them the norms of scholarship. They further expected that the closeness, trust, and diffuseness of relationships between students and faculty should automatically preclude "cheating." In speaking of examples of plagiarism the social scientists used such morally charged words as "breach of faith," "immoral," and "disregard for a sense of propriety in the intellectual life." Finally, as social science students found plagiarizing were regarded by their professors as having shown themselves to be "untrustworthy" and undeserving of receiving a B.A., they were expelled (1966, pp. 61-63). Clearly, the more normatively oriented social scientists' relations with students were broader in scope and more pervasive in their norm setting than those of the more utiliarian natural scientists.

The Gamson work is reviewed here in detail not because of the statistical power of her study; actually the numbers of those interviewed were very small. The importance of Gamson's work lies in the insightful operationalization of the compliance correlates she worked with, in the subtle analysis of their dynamic relationships, and in the judicious combination of qualitative and quantitative data. Here, the compliance relationships and dynamics come alive.

Selectivity and Socialization in Another College

We return now to Taber's study of a college, which deals with several of the relationships Gamson explored, on a relatively more quantitative basis. One of the major conclusions Taber (1969) reaches in his study of 174 students (see p. 210), is that pedagogic obligation, i.e., the commitment of students that they are morally bound to comply with the teacher's instructions, is a pre-existing attitude acquired by the student before entering college. (Taber measures pedagogic obligation by the responses to the question of how great an obligation the student feels to do all the reading assignments given to him by a teacher). This conclusion is based on the fact that pedagogic obligation was found to be highly independent of students' experience within the college itself. For example, Taber shows that neither "attributed concern" (the students' feeling that the faculty cares about them) nor "relevant competence" (the students' assumptions about the professional competence of the faculty) significantly affect pedagogic obligation (Table XIV-3). If we keep in mind the basic distribution of pedagogic obligation—high: 15%,

Table XIV-3—The Independence of Felt Pedagogic Obligation:
Pedagogic Obligation Is Not a Function of
Perceived Faculty Competence and
Attributed Concern

PERCEIVED FACULTY COMPETENCE	PEDAGOGIC OBLIGATION UNDER CONCERN			PEDAGOGIC OBLIGATION UNDER NON-CONCERN		
	Prescriptive	Preferential	Expedient and Alienated	Prescriptive	Preferential	Expedient and Alienated
Full	21	62 N = 42	17	9	68 N = 53	23
Limited or doubtful	17	50 N = 6*	33	20	59 N = 41	22
Denied	50	50 N = 2*	0	0	64 N = 14	36

* Number of cases is too small to be useful.
Source: Taber (1969), p. 264.

medium: 63%, low: 22% (*ibid.,* p. 254)—it becomes evident from the table that neither variable studied makes much of a difference. It is for this reason that Taber concludes that "pedagogic obligation" is a resource the organization cannot produce by itself but has to acquire from its environment, in the sense that students bring it with them when they join the campus. Hence, the level of pedagogic obligation found in a college's student body can be assumed to depend highly on the organization's recruitment process, i.e., to be an indicator of selectivity.

Second, Taber argues that attributed concern, an attitude dependent to a large degree upon intra-organizational experience, is a measure of the amount of socialization received within the organization. The distribution of this variable is presented on p. 210).

Having established the validity of his indicators of selectivity and socialization, Taber then proceeds to discuss the combined effect of both variables upon organizational effectiveness. As a measure of effectiveness, Taber draws upon students' actual compliance (see Table VIII-8). Taber refers to this variable quite often as "pedagogic compliance motivation." In the context discussed in Chapter VIII, pedagogic compliance motivation was used to measure student involvement, but in the present context Taber sees it as an indicator of organizational effectiveness, on the grounds that high normative involvement on the part of the students can be considered as the immediate operative goal of educational organizations.

The next step is to test the relationships between selectivity and socialization, on the one hand, and effectiveness, on the other (on the basis of the data cited in Table VIII-9). Summarizing the pattern found in the table, Taber states that

pedagogic obligation and attributed concern are the major attitudinal assets to the behavioral dimension of faculty authority: their combined presence ensures that nearly four-fifths of the students will attain high levels of compliance motivation. The absence of either one of them drops compliance drastically, and each seems to affect the functions of the other upon compliance in a way that is analogous to the action of a catalyst upon the reaction between two other substances. A deficiency of either catalyst slows down or prevents the other's contribution to student compliance (*ibid.*, p. 329).

This finding is related by Taber to our discussion of the relative substitutability of selectivity and socialization. Taber argues that his data show that unless there is a certain level of recruitment selectivity, no educational organization can be very effective, no matter how extensive are the attempts at socialization being made (*ibid.*, p. 332). If this is so, Taber concludes, socialization is not able to substitute for recruitment selectivity—contradicting our assumption that it is. The same holds the other way around: Even a high potential of pedagogic obligation—or, in other words, high selectivity—must remain ineffective unless there is a certain amount of effective socialization (*ibid.*, p. 333). Taber sees a "requisite combination" between selectivity and socialization, instead of mutual substitutability (*ibid.*, p. 334).

Discussing his results, Taber suggests that the principle of substitutability may be more applicable to certain types of attitudes than to other, more "resistant" ones, and more to normative than to coercive organizations (*ibid.*, pp. 337ff.). In coercive organizations, Taber suggests, compliance goals are so minimal in character that socialization can easily substitute for selectivity—and has to, as selectivity of coercive organizations is typically low. However, in normative organizations where more than behavioral conformity is required, substitution of socialization for selectivity is much more difficult to accomplish and would presumably put too heavy a burden upon the socializing mechanisms. The success of educational processes, Taber writes, is ultimately measurable only "in terms of the degree to which they motivate their participants to an *attitudinal* as well as to a behavioral and doctrinal conformity to the values and norms of the organization. These goals are far more difficult to attain than is the maintenance of order or the performance of routine tasks . . ." (*ibid.,* p. 341).

But are Taber's findings really in conflict with our proposition that "all other things being equal, socialization and selectivity can frequently substitute for each other" (p. 158)? First, this statement is made under the provision that "all other things are equal" (*ibid.*). Among these "other things" is, of course, the level of effectiveness the organization as a whole is realizing. Substitutability applies to a given level of effectiveness and amount of resources; we explicitly recognized that if both factors are higher, effectiveness will increase. But given a set amount of resources, the question is one of "marginal utilities," in terms of effectiveness. Would greater allotment of resources to socialization or to selectivity yield relatively greater increases in effectiveness?

Note also that while in Taber's college both selectivity and socialization were "necessary," there are numerous normative organizations which rely only on one of the two factors; this does often cause a low level of effectiveness, but not the undoing of normative compliance. Many contemporary churches are utterly unselective; and many democratic parties provide at most minimal socialization. Taber shows that his college cannot normatively educate its students without both selection and expressive socialization, which seems quite plausible, but this only suggests that this particular organization has relatively demanding goals. See other colleges.

Selectivity in a Normative Organization

Roy J. Ingham (1968) in a brief article pointed out that compliance theory could be usefully applied to the analysis of adult education programs as they are carried out by various types of organizations that differ in their compliance structure. These include churches, colleges, schools, government agencies, community organizations, business corporations, and the Armed Forces. Ingham made the first step by briefly comparing adult education programs in colleges and in public schools. (The data is nationwide and covers the period of June 1961 to June 1962). He found the first clearly more normative and less utilitarian in content than the latter: General education was the subject of 66% of the adult education courses given in universities versus 13% of such programs in public schools. At the same time, vocational courses outnumbered general education courses in schools by a margin of greater than three to one (1968, p. 64).

As expected, normative programs were found to be more involving: the dropout rate was 18% for university programs versus 23% for those in the public schools. Also, in line with the theory, the higher retention rate of university programs was achieved at least in part through greater selectivity. University adult education programs drew three times as many students with some college education than the public schools programs, i.e., they took in "select" students closer to the desired output.

IN DUAL STRUCTURES

Cross-Rank Communicationn in Normative and Dual Structures

Julian's (1966, 1968, 1969) study of five hospitals, referred to earlier, established that three hospitals had the power and involvement characteristics of predominantly normative organizations, while the other two had a dual, normative–coercive structure. In his 1966 paper, Julian related their characteristics to his findings on intraorganizational communication flows (1966). The compliance theory predicts that "communication gaps are least frequent in normative organizations, where elites are less differentiated, alienation is lowest, and consensus among lower participants and organizational representatives is high" (p. 245). As Julian applied it to his cases: "the flow of communication in a normative organization is predicted to be smoother than in normative–coercive organizations" (1966, p. 387).

Table XIV-4 represents Julian's main relevant finding. The first section of the table reports the proportion of patients who mentioned one or another of six "communication blocks." The second segment provides the rank of the hospital with regard to the frequency of each particular communication block. (The lower the rank, the lower the frequency of the block.) The data indicate that, of the six possible blocks, few blocks of any kind occur, except 6, which is in line with the general normative character of these hospitals.

Table XIV-4—Percentage of Patients Experiencing Six Types of Communication Blocks in Five Hospitals*

TYPE OF COMMUNICATION BLOCK	PERCENTAGE					RANK				
	A	B	C	D	E	A	B	C	D	E
1. Not told enough about personal illness and progress	18	10	18	39	23	2.5	1	2.5	5	4
2. Staff holds back information on case	0	10	24	26	11	1	2	4	5	3
3. Doctor makes the rounds too fast	8	7	24	31	6	3	2	4	5	1
4. New treatment, etc., not explained ahead of time	20	13	20	24	26	2.5	1	2.5	4	5
5. Hesitate to speak up, to ask questions	15	10	15	14	23	3.5	1	3.5	2	5
6. Staff does not spend good deal of time talking with patients	40	50	36	44	43	2	5	1	4	3

* Hospitals A, B, and C are normative organizations; Hospitals D and E are normative–coercive organizations. Low ranks indicate a low frequency of communication blocks.
    Source: Julian (1966), p. 387. Reprinted with the permission of the American Sociological Association.

Furthermore, differences in the frequency of blocks among hospitals on the various items were found to be correlated with the compliance structure of the hospitals. Julian writes:

When the overall rankings of hospitals on each of the six indicators are considered, it will be observed that Hospital A (normative organization) ranks low or middle on all six items; Hospital B (normative organization) ranks low on five of the six items; Hospital D (normative-coercive organization) ranks high or middle on five of the six items; Hospital E (normative-coercive organization) ranks high or middle on five of the six items; but Hospital C (normative organization) ranks low or middle on only three of the six items. Apart from Hospital C, which is a mixed case, it is concluded that normative hospitals have fewer communication blocks than normative-coercive hospitals (1966, p. 388).

Consensus and Socialization in a Dual-Compliance Structure

In a later publication, Julian (1969) concentrated on one of the five hospitals he had previously studied: the TB sanatorium (*D*). This hospital had exhibited a relatively high reliance on both normative and coercive compliance (although it remained still a predominantly normative organization). Following the compliance theory, Julian predicted that the less the organization relied on normative means, the less consensus there would be, as well as less acceptance of its values and role descriptions (pp. 231ff.). Also, the extent of socialization was expected to correlate with the level of acceptance, that is, with consensus.

Julian's study draws on data on four kinds of members of the hospital organization, differing in hierarchical rank and required time of socialization for their particular role: M.D.s (6 subjects), registered nurses (14), practical nurses (19), and patients (20). Through an ingenious method involving a pegboard and cards, resistance to survey questionnaires was overcome (Julian, 1969, p. 181). Each group's conception of its own role and of the other three was obtained.

Julian found (Table XIV-5) that dissensus regarding one's own role was highest among the patients, with the least amount of socialization; second highest among the practical nurses, with relatively

Table XIV-5—Amount of Dissensus among Incumbents of the Same Position on Incumbents' Own Role Prescriptions*

	Percentage	Rank
M.D.s	36.8	3
Registered Nurses	30.2	4
Practical Nurses	37.3	2
Patients	40.4	1

* The higher the percentage, the more the dissensus. As rank descends, from 1 to 4, dissensus decreases.

Source: Julian (1969), p. 184. Reprinted with the permission of *Sociological Quarterly*.

more role-socialization; third among the M.D.s, with the longest preparation; and fourth among the registered nurses. Thus, the registered nurses were where M.D.s were "expected" to be and the M.D.s where the nurses "ought" to have been. Julian suggests that this may be due to the fact that the organizational specifications of the role of registered nurses are particularly high (*ibid.*, p. 184).

Julian's data allow for an indirect test of the influence of socialization on consensus. Julian shows that the general rank order in terms of dissensus—that is, on all organizational positions taken together—was almost completely the opposite of the rank order in terms of role incumbents' self-assessment. General dissensus was highest among doctors, second among registered nurses, third among practical nurses, and fourth among patients (*ibid.*, p. 185). These relationships among the groups are almost completely reversed when a group's own role is concerned. When this is the case, the effect of socialization—creating consensus among the incumbents of a particular role about their role definition—is much stronger than the effect of other factors that account for general dissensus. Needless to say, the number of respondents is small, but the data, as far as they allow one to go, accord with the expectations derived from the theory.[2]

IN UTILITARIAN ORGANIZATIONS

Hierarchical Cohesion and Its Correlates

Hierarchical cohesion is different from peer cohesion; while the latter refers to an expressive bond among participants on the same hierarchical level, the former relates to such a bond between superiors and subordinates. Unlike peer cohesion, hierarchical cohesion is expected to correlate with positive involvement with the organization (see pp. 281, 292).

The relationship between hierarchical cohesion and involvement in an industrial organization was studied by Edward W. Lehman (Lehman, 1967; n.d.). Lehman made a distinction between formal and informal hierarchical cohesion, the first concept characterizing how well a participant got along with his immediate superior (measured in terms of whether he liked or disliked him); the second being based on how many of a man's three best friends were higher-in-ranks in the same company. Job satisfaction and satisfaction with promotions were used to measure involvement. The sample was composed of 312 men, all chosen from one "organizational generation" of long-time employees in a major corporation and representing all levels from nonmanagement (level 0) to upper management (levels 3 and over).

As expected, Lehman found a positive correlation between formal hierarchical cohesion and job satisfaction. 53.2% of the men said that their relations with their superiors were "excellent." Of these, 59.6% were satisfied with their jobs. Among those whose hierarchical relationships were less than excellent, 39.7%—about 20% less—responded that they were satisfied. Thus, a lower degree of upward cohesion was found to be associated with a lower degree of involvement.

The strength of the relationship between hierarchical cohesion and involvement varies considerably by organizational levels (see Table XIV-6). While there is no relationship at all on the lowest level

2. For a brief discussion, see Harrison and Weightman (1974).

(Level 0), and one of but 13% on the next highest, at the two uppermost levels the difference that hierarchical cohesion makes for job satisfaction increases to 29.3% and 29.7%, respectively. Promotion satisfaction, the second indicator of involvement, shows a similar pattern.

The second type of hierarchical cohesion, "informal cohesion," was found to be related to involvement in a different manner than formal cohesion. Those who had two or more higher-level friends were the most satisfied with their jobs: 63.9% were satisfied, as compared to 43.3% of those with one friend in the higher ranks,

Table XIV-6—Relationship of Description of Relationship with Immediate Superior and (a) Job Satisfaction and (b) Promotion Satisfaction by Organizational Level

Level and Relationship with Superior	Per Cent Satisfied with		N
	(a) Job	(b) Promotions	
All men			
Excellent	59.6	60.8	166
Not excellent	39.7	43.2	146
Level 0			
Excellent	43.8	28.1	32
Not excellent	45.1	37.3	51
Level 1			
Excellent	63.0	66.7	27
Not excellent	50.0	60.0	20
Level 2			
Excellent	54.9	58.8	51
Not excellent	25.6	25.6	39
Level 3+			
Excellent	71.4	82.1	56
Not excellent	41.7	61.1	36

Source: Lehman (n.d.), Table 1.

and 49.4% of those with no such friend. However, the data on promotion satisfaction, although not strong, tend to go in the opposite direction; as the table shows, the more friends a respondent has in the higher ranks, the less satisfied is he with his own hierarchical standing.

As Lehman points out, the latter finding is compatible with reference group theory. "Friendship groups like other group affiliations may provide a basis for self-evaluations. If a man finds himself in a friendship group made up of those of higher rank, he is more likely to feel himself deprived as far as his own rank and advancement is concerned" (n.d., pp. 4ff.). However, this leaves open the question of why informal cohesion, at the same time, tends to increase with job satisfaction. Lehman argues that this fact, too, can be accounted for in terms of reference group theory:

Those with extensive informal hierarchic ties may adopt a more positive regard toward the formal aspects of organizational life precisely because their primary expressive bonds are with persons whose ranks are likely to make them representatives of official organizational norms. . . . In the domain of job satisfaction, higher ranking friends appear to be referential because they provide a means of positive identification with the organization. On the other hand, the same men are referential in the area of promotion satisfaction insofar as they become comparative bases for self-evaluation. (*ibid.*, p. 5)

Lehman's analysis does not stop at this point. The most significant hierarchical distinction in the organization under study is that between upper and lower management. This "intra-organizational boundary" is located between levels 2 and 3. From the viewpoint of the analysis of hierarchical cohesion, this makes the men at the second level especially interesting. In fact, Table XIV-7 shows that, at this level, the influence of informal hierarchical cohesion on job satisfaction is far stronger than for the rest of the men and that those at level 2 "account for the bulk of the variability in the inverse relationship between extent of informal hierarchic cohesive ties and promotion

Table XIV-7—Relationship of Extent of Informal Hierarchic Cohesive Bonds and (a) Job Satisfaction and (b) Promotion Satisfaction for Second Level Men Versus All Others

| | Per Cent Satisfied with | | N |
	(a) Job	(b) Promotions	
Level 2			
0 Friends higher	43.2	56.8	37
1 Friend higher	21.9	35.5	32
2–3 Friends higher	71.4	38.1	21
All Other Men			
0 Friends higher	51.3	56.4	117
1 Friend higher	53.8	60.0	65
2–3 Friends higher	60.0	52.5	40

Source: Lehman (n.d.), Table 3.

satisfaction" (*ibid.*, pp. 5ff.). This finding, together with the fact that the relationship between formal hierarchical cohesion (relationship to supervisor) and job satisfaction as well as promotion satisfaction is quite strong at this level, supports Lehman's suggestion that "affective ties which cross this 'great divide' take on added significance compared to other hierarchic links" (*ibid.*, p. 6).

In toto, these findings all are in line with the compliance theory's expectations and constitute an additional elaboration by taking into account differences in the kinds of hierarchical cohesions and in the ranks it bridges.

The Role of Scope

Lehman (1967) used the same industrial setting to explore the relationship between involvement and scope. Scope is defined as the number of activities in which participants are jointly involved (see p. 264). Lehman used two indicators to measure scope: whether on-the-job friendship extended beyond "organizational space and time" and the extent of participation in work-related clubs and social affairs. Based on these two indicators, the 312 men were divided into three groups composed of 30.1% whose scope score was low, 31.7% whose score was medium, and 38.1% whose score was high (*ibid.*, p. 6).

Using the two indicators of involvement just described, Lehman found no relationship between scope and promotion satisfaction. However, job satisfaction turned out to be related to scope (Table XIV-8): Those whose organizational scope was low were slightly more often satisfied with their job than those with medium or high scope. Lehman explains this negative correlation by referring to a possible "safety-valve" function of involvement in the "occupational community;" participation in off-the-job activities may be seen as a way of coping with "work-engendered tensions" although it does not really compensate for the men's relatively low level of satisfaction (*ibid.*, p. 7).

A more interesting picture emerged when Lehman introduced another variable, the men's organizational success, measured in terms of the relationship between their initial opportunity (measured by the men's level of education) and organizational mobility (rank reached during their career). Basically, the correlation between scope and job satisfaction remained the same as for the sample as a whole for all combinations of initial opportunity and mobility except one: Where opportunity was high and mobility was low, the pattern was reversed. Here, those with high scope were considerably more satisfied than those with low scope (Table XIV-8). This finding is inter-

Table XIV-8—Relationship of Scope and Job Satisfaction

Scope	Percent Satisfied with Job	N
A) *Entire Sample*		
Low scope	56.4	94
Medium-high scope	47.7	218
B) *By Initial Opportunity*		
and Mobility		
High opportunity–low mobility		
Low scope	15.4	13
Medium-high scope	41.9	31
All except high-low		
Low scope	63.0	81
Medium-high scope	48.6	187

Source: Lehman (1967) (edited).

esting as the high opportunity–low mobility men were all college-educated second-level managers, belonging to the "critical" stratum mentioned previously.

Lehman points out that in this group both low-scope and medium-high-scope men are less satisfied than the men in all other categories, so that broader scope does not produce more satisfaction. Rather, it seems that in this group, where dissatisfaction is most intense, the "safety-valve" is no longer participation in the occupational community but, to the contrary, withdrawal from it. "Severing as many non-obligatory ties as possible," Lehman writes, appears to be a "major means of handling this sentiment" of frustration and deprivation. This suggests that "scope" can handle dissatisfaction only as long as it does not exceed a certain level; if dissatisfaction becomes intense, the compensatory mechanism built into broad positive relationships fails, and withdrawal is the consequence.

THE NON-ROLE OF PEER COHESION

One segment of the compliance theory which was particularly at variance with treatment of the subject in previous publications is that on cohesion. Previous studies reported that the level of cohesion among organizational participants (defined as a positive, encompassing interpersonal relationship) is related to numerous other attributes, from the level of satisfaction with work in a factory to willingness to fight in a war. Cohesion was widely held to affect involvement.

However, for reasons spelled out above (see Ch. XI), we suggested that cohesion could not have such an effect.

Most compliance studies ignored this point, maybe because it was based on a logical exercise and hence not subject to empirical study; one either sees the logic, or one does not concur.[3] Two studies, though, did explore the role of cohesion and its non-relationship to compliance. As both variables can be operationalized, they can be, technically speaking, correlated, although the result, we suggest, could not be meaningful. What did the studies show?

Peer Cohesion and Involvement in a Coercive-Normative Setting: Basic Training

Smith's (1973) secondary analysis of peer cohesion and its relationship to involvement (see Ch. IV, p. 78) directly tests the thesis that the two variables are basically unrelated. Smith used two indicators of peer cohesion. Men in basic training were asked whether or not they had been involved in fights with others. 73% said they had not; 27% reported one or more fights. Second, the men were asked whether or not they participated in sports, not part of the basic training. While 43% said they had participated in one or more hours (since training started), 57% had spent less than one hour in such activities. Out of these two items Smith formed a peer cohesion index: the 30% who had no fights and did participate in sports were scored as "high" peer cohesion, the 13% who did neither were scored as "low," and the 57% who did one or the other were scored as "moderate."

A simple cross-tabulation of peer cohesion and involvement shows that there seems to exist a positive relationship between the two variables: the higher the peer cohesion, the higher the percentage of those highly involved (Table XIV-9). However, this distribution has to be seen in the context of the other variables affecting involvement. Using multivariate analysis, Smith has undertaken to assess the relative influence on involvement of the type of power used by the men's superiors, leadership climate (see p. 80), peer cohesion, and extraneous variables not included in the model. Table XIV-10 shows the result. Both power mix and leadership climate were found to contribute much more to involvement than peer cohesion. In fact, the contribution of the type of power used—one of the central variables

---

3. This is, of course, questionable. We do not know for sure whether the company really is the men's meaningful peer group; individual departments or platoons, or even cross-company groups might be much more significant.

Table XIV-9—The Relationship Between Peer Cohesion and Involvement

Peer Cohesion	Percentage Highly Involved
High	63
Medium	49
Low	39

Source: Smith (1973), Ch. 6, p. 6 (table edited).

of the compliance theory—was found to be more than four times as great as that of peer cohesion. Leadership climate was also more powerful than peer cohesion. The same holds for the extraneous variables (i.e. random effects).

Table XIV-10

Independent Variable	Proportion of Variation in Involvement Accounted for
Power mix (Degree of normativeness)	.52
Leadership climate (Weak vs. persuasive)	.16
Peer cohesion	.12
Random effects	.20
	1.00

Source: Smith (1973), Ch. 6, p. 22.

Although this result lends considerable plausibility to the theory, it is not yet fully conclusive. The fact that there was, after all, some positive relationship between cohesion and involvement—albeit a small one—might be taken as evidence that peer cohesion does act as a causal factor producing high involvement. This would not be compatible with the theory; the latter states that peer cohesion merely accentuates whatever kind of involvement there is. This includes the pattern observed by Smith, but it also includes that where the "group norm" is unfavorable to the organization, high cohesion should decrease rather than increase involvement. In other words, in order to test the theory we would have to control for a third variable which is assumed to determine the direction or at least the extent of the effect peer cohesion exerts on involvement—the dominant "group norm." Where the group norm is favorable to the organization, group cohesion and involvement should be positively related; but where the group norm is unfavorable, the relationship should be an adverse one.

Unfortunately, Selvin's study does not contain data on "group norms," because he classifies the members of his sample not in terms of platoons, but only in terms of five companies, which limits the possible number of aggregate units to be used for secondary analysis so severely that a test of the hypothesis is not possible.

Stanley S. Guterman (1970) briefly tied his study to that of peer cohesion and hierarchical cohesion. The research site is a hotel chain in the eastern part of the United States in 1963 and 1964. Scales were used to measure a number of attitudes of management and non-management employees, primarily their "Machiavellianism," a person's disposition to adopt an exploitative behavior towards others.

The main finding pertinent to our present discussion is that management's orientation not only affects hierarchical cohesion, which one would expect, but also peer cohesion of the lower participants. Thus, in hotels in which management, on the average, ranked higher on the "Machiavellism scale" than nonmanagement employees, 62% of the rank and file reported no recent quarrels among nonmanagerial personnel (high peer cohesion). This figure dropped to 51% in cases where the rank and file displayed a higher degree of "Machiavellism" than the management.

Lack of conflict between management and nonmanagement (high hierarchical cohesion), was reported by 58% of the rank and file in either type of hotel, independent from which group was more "Machiavellian" than the other. Where there was only a small difference between the "Mach scores" of the two groups, 78% reported high hierarchical cohesion; the same percentage reported high peer cohesion (1970, p. 115).

Similar results were found for management dominance (average score on six items of the need dominance scale of the Edwards Personal Preference Schedule) and management sympathy (seven items from the need intraception scale). The tau-beta correlation coefficient of dominance with hierarchical cohesion was found to be .09, while the same correlation with peer cohesion was .16. Sympathy was related at −.26 to hierarchical cohesion; the relationship of the same variable to peer cohesion, at .25, was almost of the same strength (*ibid.*, p. 116). Guterman concludes: "The manner in which the leadership of an organization relates to rank-and-file members is not confined, in its effects, to social relations between the two strata. These effects filter down until they affect social relations among the lower-level members. In this way the personality characteristics of the leadership eventually leave their mark on the whole work milieu" (*ibid.*, p. 116).[4]

IN COERCIVE ORGANIZATIONS

Scope and Pervasiveness in a Mildly Coercive Organization

In his study of Finnish draftees, Randell (1968) inquired into the effect of membership in a broad-scope organization on the uniformity of occupational role stereotypes. One would expect that, where scope is broad, uniformity increases because the organization more effectively embraces its participants (see pp. 267, 269). Randell points out that aside from the consequences of broad scope that Etzioni (1961) and Goffman, in his study of total institutions (1962), have emphasized, the military organization makes special efforts "to maximize uniformity of behavior" (Randell, 1966, p. 61).

To measure the uniformity effect Randell used the Semantic Differential Method developed by Charles Osgood (Osgood *et al.*, 1961). Two groups of respondents, high school seniors and newly graduated draftees, were asked to describe four occupational roles using 27 bipolar scales consisting of opposite adjectives.

Randell hypothesized that the theory according to "the standard deviations of the scales should be smaller in the experimental group (draftees) as compared with deviations in the control group (seniors). The table [Table XIV-13 here] shows this is true, but the null hypothesis can be rejected only with respect to the first three mentioned concepts. As far as the concept of the typical officer is concerned the research hypothesis is not statistically supported" (*ibid.*, p. 69). Randell suggests the reason may be that the draftees' frustrations and subject condition have activated their defense mechanisms, leading them to suppress their alienation toward this particular target, the one which most directly towers over them, but not to the others (*ibid.*, p. 72). Whether or not one accepts Randell's explanation of the "deviant case," the draftees scored three out of the four scales as one would have expected from the theory.

4. See also Ateson (1973).

Table XIV-11—Differences between Draftees and High School Seniors on a Semantic Differential Test

Becoming Uniform

EVALUATED	THE NUMBER OF INSTANCES THAT STANDARD DEVIATIONS OF SCALES WERE SMALLER IN		NULL HYPOTHESIS REJECTED
	Experimental Group (Draftees)	Control Group (Seniors)	
Typical engineer	25	2	Yes
Typical minister	24	2*	Yes
Typical elementary school teacher	24	3	Yes
Typical officer	16	11	No

* With respect to one scale the standard deviations were equal.
Source: Randell (1968), p. 69 (table slightly edited). Reprinted with the permission of Munksgaards Forlag.

Scope and Pervasiveness in an American Slave Plantation

Ray Simon Bryce-Laporte's meticulous analysis (1968) of the Southern plantation as a total institution draws on the categories of scope and pervasiveness.[5] Bryce-Laporte, in his exposition of his approach, argues that Goffman's concept of total institution is basically dichotomous (an organization is or is not total) and therefore not applicable where matters of degree are to be studied. Furthermore, the concept fails to distinguish between the physical confines of members' action space and the "reach" of the organization's norm-setting mechanisms. For these reasons, Bryce-Laporte resorts to Etzioni's twin concept of scope and pervasiveness. Both are conceived as continuous variables; pervasiveness relates to the norm-setting power of an organization for activities beyond its immediate boundaries, and scope can be seen as indicating the degree to which a member's actions are confined to an action space prescribed and controlled by the organization (*ibid.*, pp. 50-54).

The scope of the plantation, Bryce-Laporte reports, "was quite broad. At least by the 1800's, it seemingly influenced if not controlled the slaves' action from life through death. It seemingly governed not only their work activities but also their recreative and procreative activities" (*ibid.*, p. 136).

5. For published articles based on this study, see Bryce-Laporte 1969, 1971, and 1972.

More surprising, Bryce-Laporte shows that the plantation was also highly pervasive:

Slaves from the larger plantations were permitted to visit other plantations, to visit relatives at times outside the city, to go to town on specified days for business, pleasure, worship, or to transport goods and supplies. Slaves from smaller plantations and farms and those in cities were rented out and had more reason to go beyond the physical confines of their masters' properties. It must be recalled, however, that there were codes which determined the propriety and legality of slave behavior and movement, and that patrols were organized to challenge slaves found off the plantation, and were permitted to prosecute and punish those found without permits or passes (*ibid.,* p. 39).

He concludes:

These facts would seem to suggest that the slave plantation was broad in scope and high in pervasiveness, and its pervasiveness was not so much a question of reliance on other agencies, but of the control, influence, and power which it had over other agencies (*ibid.,* p. 40).

Bryce-Laporte also analyzes the goals of the plantation and shows that they were partly directed at production and partly at maintaining the social order their elites favored (*ibid.,* pp. 211ff.). The result of combining broad scope and pervasiveness with these goals was a high level of tension among the lower participants, expressed in a variety of ways, chiefly in attempted escapes and less frequently but more threateningly in revolts such as those of Turner, Vesey, and Prosser. This relationship, between scope and pervasiveness on the one hand and tension on the other, is in line with the theory (see p. 266). Furthermore, the theory suggests that organizations that are broad in scope and high in pervasiveness will either have to find outlets for these tensions or find their stability and continuity seriously damaged. Bryce-Laporte's study shows that the Southern plantation did, in fact, develop such mechanisms of tension management.

In order to reduce the strains imposed by plantation life, slave owners relied on a variety of "tension release and removal activities" such as: the granting of privileges of different sorts to slaves for good performance and good deportment; the promotion of stratification and instillation of feelings of status difference among the slaves; and the sponsoring of various holidays and celebrations that reduced the distance between staff and slaves (*ibid.,* p. 124). In addition, "Permission for trips to the cities and visits to relatives, and bonuses and gifts, reduced the impact of the normal deprivations, regimentation and enclosure of the slave plantation" (*ibid.,* p. 127).

Finally, "secondary adjustments," chiefly in the form of religious practices and Christianization of the slaves, were introduced with the support of the plantation staff. Religious services among the slaves—and among their masters as well—tended to be emotional and evangelical. As Bryce-Laporte notes, "they were characterized by fiery sermons and testimonies, collective ecstasy, physical gyrations, hectic shouting and singing, psychic trances, spiritual transformations and other means of temporary tension release . . . they represented one of the few levels of social cohesion and collective action which was permitted among the slaves, and between them and their staff" (*ibid.,* p. 129).

XV

OTHER CORRELATES
REVISITED
A Causal Analysis

The most extensive cumulative effort to test the compliance theory is a series of papers referred to here as the Iowa State Compliance Studies (see p. 142). As well as encompassing more correlates than other studies, the Iowa authors, led by Mulford, Klonglan, and Warren, applied causal analysis to the compliance correlates and compared these variables in a normative organization to a utilitarian one. This chapter is dedicated to a review of their efforts.

METHODOLOGICAL PRELIMINARIES

The Research Sites

The various Iowa State Compliance Studies draw upon three sets of data. The first was collected within the U.S. Civil Defense system, whose mission it is to provide the citizenry with protection and help local governments learn how to function effectively in disasters of all types. The study focuses on the local Civil Defense Director. The first set of studies (up to 1971) discussed hereafter are based on a representative sample of 240 local directors from Minnesota, Georgia, and Massachusetts. The survey, using questionnaires and Likert-type scales, was carried out in 1965. Studies carried out after 1971 are based on a nationwide sample of civil defense directors.

The Iowa State authors classified the civil defense system as a normative organization, even though one third of the local directors received a low payment on a part-time basis. As the authors emphasize, there seemed to be no visible differences between paid and unpaid local directors on any of the theoretically significant variables (Mulford, Klonglan, Beal, Bohlen, 1968, p. 75).

Another major data set used by the Iowa State Compliance Studies were collected in 1966 and 1971. The samples included 82 and 153 managers, respectively, of local farm supply and grain co-operatives in Iowa. The data is based on personal interviews with the managers as well as on self-administered questionnaires, containing 161 statements on Likert-type scales.

A classificatory problem raised by this data is similar to the one related to the civil defense. Farm co-ops are not typical utilitarian organizations; as Sampson points out, "profit making for the organization is not the primary reason for the existence of farm cooperatives . . . In a sense, farm cooperatives may be classified as rural voluntary associations in which the membership is based on economic motivation . . . Not only are economic needs met by farm cooperatives, but they also perform important communicational, educational and bargaining functions for their member-patrons" (1973, p. 14). In the same context, Sampson mentions the existence of a "cooperative philosophy" into which managers and employers are socialized by the organization (*ibid.*). On the other hand, the high pressures to cooperate efficiently and economically under which farm co-ops are placed make them utilitarian in character, and suggest the "secondary" status of their normative features.

The Iowa State group research design permitted not only the application of compliance theory but also assured comparability of the results of analyses of the several data sets. The same basic questions were asked about both organizations and, we shall see, comparable indicators were evolved wherever possible.

Furthermore, special pains were taken to focus away from persons toward collectivities, deliberately shifting the analysis from the civil defense directors and the farm co-op managers to the organizational systems to which they belong. This is achieved in two steps: First, the organizational units of which the two groups of respondents are members are defined as subsystems of two more encompassing organizations. Thus, the local director is viewed not as a participant, but rather as a subsystem of the national civil defense system, a suborganization, although it contains only one member. Similarly, the local farm cooperative is characterized as being "affiliated with a regional cooperative association," thus being comparable to the local civil defense unit. Second, the researchers, although drawing largely on information obtained from the defense directors and co-op managers, developed "subsystem measures" which characterize the organizational unit as a whole rather than merely the individual leader.

Causality as a Hypothesis

Before discussing the Iowa State Compliance reports in detail, a general remark about the relation of compliance theory to causal analysis may be appropriate. Originally, the compliance theory was not formulated in terms of causal relationships. Variables such as scope, communication, and salience were treated as "correlates," not as dependent variables of compliance—meaning that questions as to which variable "causes" the other has been deliberately left open. Interactive and "functional" "system" relations were assumed.

This, of course, does not rule out using the framework of compliance theory for causal analysis. Some of the variables, such as initial involvement and recruitment selectivity, obviously precede others; incongruence between involvement and power, for instance, in this sense, can be said to be temporally late, and in this sense, causally dependent. Also, one can derive a hypothesis on causal relations from the general concept of organization. Thus, the Iowa State Compliance Studies make use of the concept that organizations are, by definition, oriented towards effective realization of their goals. Hence, analyzing all other features of an organization in terms of their causal contribution to effectiveness qualifies as an intrinsically meaningful approach. Finally, causal relations are treated as an hypothesis, subject to empirical test: Does the sequence explain and how great is its explanatory power, the ultimate test of any theorizing?

In principle, causal analysis should preferably be based on longitudinal rather than lateral data, that is, on observations of organizational processes over time rather than on comparisons of data from different organizations, collected at the same point in time. The Iowa State group, which is quite aware of the theoretical and methodological problems involved in their approach (see, for instance, the concluding remarks in Mulford, Klonglan, and Warren, 1972, p. 79), themselves make the point that longitudinal data are urgently needed because they "will permit more appropriate applications of multivariate causal techniques." But, even without such data, the causal analysis "worked," that is, it yielded theoretically significant results.

CORRELATES RELATED IN A NORMATIVE SETTING

Selectivity, Socialization, and Effectiveness

The first of the studies to be discussed, carried out by Charles L. Mulford, Gerald E. Klonglan, George M. Beal, and Joe M. Bohlen, was published in 1968. The study concerns itself with the relationship of compliance to selectivity and socialization and their combined effects on organizational effectiveness. Specifically it explores the question, to what degree, given a particular compliance structure and level of selectivity, does socialization enhance effectiveness, as measured in terms of individual role performance?

Compliance theory contains a series of propositions concerning the relationships among the three variables. It is suggested, first, that higher socialization and higher selectivity will be positively associated with the lower participants' having organizationally desired attributes, from religious devotion to working hard (see pp. 262-3). Although both selectivity and socialization can jack up performance, it was furthermore suggested that the two factors could substitute for each other, such that an increase in one could make unnecessary a greater input of the other. Furthermore, it was hypothesized that higher performance, often believed to be the result of effective socialization efforts, is often actually due at least in part to higher selectivity. Normative organizations are expected to vary all the way from highly selective and highly socializing ones (religious sects, the Communist party) to structures highly "open" and quite low in socialization ("mass" churches and democratic parties). Mulford and his co-authors hypothesized that the typical normative organization enforces only an intermediate amount of recruitment selectivity and that socialization might have to be "considerable" to insure attainment of organizational goals.

The measurements used by the Iowa State authors are generally quite intricate. Hence, a detailed description is beyond the scope of this review, and those interested must turn to the research reports cited. In this case, socialization was measured by assessing the amount and the quality of job orientation the local director had received from other local directors, from local government officials, and from state civil defense personnel right after accepting his job. Two other questions were asked determining how well he understood his responsibilities and how much additional training he felt he needed to successfully perform his tasks. Selectivity was determined by asking the local director for the number of people who were interested in his position (perceived number of applicants) and for the degree of selectivity used by others when choosing him for this position.[1]

Testing the above mentioned hypotheses regarding "typical" normative organizations, the authors were able to support the basic compliance hypothesis. For example, only 31.0% of those local directors experiencing low socialization and low recruitment selectivity were above average in effectiveness, while 75% of those ranking high on both variables were also highly effective. Table XV-1 shows the data in detail.

Next, the authors inquired into the specific nature of the relationship between socialization and selectivity in producing effectiveness. Basically the table shows that the impact on effectiveness of the one variable decreases to the degree that the value of the other variable increases. Thus, at a low level of socialization, the difference in terms of above-average effectiveness between civil defense officials with low selectivity and those with high selectivity is 32.6%. This figure declines at a medium level of socialization, reaching no more than 20.9%. Finally, when socialization is high, the difference made by selectivity becomes minimal (3.6%). The same holds the other way around, although at a medium level of selectivity socialization seems to affect effectiveness more than at a low level of selectivity—the figures being 40.4%, 53.4%, and 11.4%. However, this deviation is not so much due to a particularly high amount of effectiveness at this level of selectivity, but rather to the low level of effectiveness of those directors with medium selectivity and low socialization.

In summary, the "marginal productivity" of each of the two factors seems to depend on how much of the other factor the organization is employing. When selectivity is very high, even the most intensive efforts at increasing effectiveness through more socialization

1. The technique of measuring effectiveness employed by the Iowa State Compliance Study has already been reported (see p. ***).

will yield only minimal returns, and vice versa. Holding the level of effectiveness constant, it follows that increasing either socialization

Table XV-1—Percentage of Above-Average Role Performers (Effectiveness) by Degree of Recruitment Selectivity and Socialization

	Selectivity						
	LOW		MEDIUM		HIGH		
SOCIALIZATION	Number in Cell	Percentage Above Average	Number in Cell	Percentage Above Average	Number in Cell	Percentage Above Average	N
Low	29	31.0	20	15.0	11	63.6	60
Medium	32	46.8	48	56.2	31	67.7	111
High	14	71.4	19	68.4	36	75.0	69
N	75		87		78		240

Source: Mulford, Klonglan, Beal, and Bohlen (1968), p. 72 (table slightly edited).

or selectivity makes possible a reduction of the amount of the second factor used to achieve a given level of effectiveness. However, as the increase in the first factor diminishes the marginal—and thus, the average—returns of the second one, this relationship of mutual substitutability must not be conceived of as linear. Rather, the higher the proportion of the first factor in the organization's "factor mix," the less the amount of the second factor for which a given increase in the first one is able to compensate, and the less the savings possible in terms of the second factor. This relationship of nonlinear substitutability between selectivity and socialization has been predicted by the theory (see pp. 262ff.).

The Role of Communication

In a later re-analysis of the same data, Mulford, Klonglan, and Warren (1972) introduced communication as a further variable relevant to role performance. Compliance theory had predicted that in normative organizations the level of downward expressive communication would be higher than in either utilitarian or coercive ones (see p. 244). A lack of such communication, it was hypothesized, would be detrimental to organizational effectiveness (ibid.).

In operational terms, the researchers focused on communication between the local civil defense directors and civil defense personnel at the state level, as measured by its frequency and by the medium of communication utilized.[2] The data, as reported in the study, are shown in Table XV-2. The table reveals (a) that communication is meaningfully related to effectiveness (.423); (b) that communication and socialization together account for 25% of the total variance in effectiveness ($R^2 = .501$); (c) that while communication and socialization are correlated with each other at .393, their impacts on effectiveness, as witnessed by their partial correlations, are independent from each other (.315 and .339, respectively).

The latter finding, of course, is the more important one. Whatever the level of socialization, the data suggest, there will be a positive relationship between communication and effectiveness. Even if socialization is very intensive, communication will continue to modify the level of effectiveness.

Table XV-2—Relationship Between Effectiveness and Socialization, Communication

	Zero-Order Correlation	Partial Correlation Controlled for Communication (Socialization)	Partial Correlation Controlled for Selectivity
Socialization	.401	.339	.343
Communication	.423	.315	.376

$R^2 = .501$. All coefficients significant at the .01 level.
Adapted from Mulford, Klonglan, Warren (1972).

The same holds for the opposite direction: there is no level of communication at which increased socialization does not improve on the organization's overall effectiveness. However, the data do not allow one to determine whether the size of the impact of socialization, and of communication, on effectiveness remains the same, declines, or increases when either communication or socialization efforts are stepped up.

Finally, the table reveals that selectivity does not render spurious the impact of either socialization or communication. When selectivity is held constant, the relationships of both communication and sociali-

---

2. One might ask whether this measurement of communication measures expressive communication or communication in general, including both expressive and instrumental transmissions. Although the answer to this question is not essential at this point, instrumental communication may well also be expected to be high in normative organizations, although of less significance than expressive communication; this point is of importance when the effect of communication on effectiveness in normative organizations is compared to the same effect in utilitarian organizations (see p. 400).

zation to effectiveness remain considerable. As to the problem of the mutual substitutability of socialization and recruitment selectivity, this finding once more underlines that whatever level the one of the two variables reaches, there will be a linear relationship between the other one and effectiveness, so that neither one of the variables will ever be entirely replaced or rendered meaningless by the other. However, as we are dealing with correlation rather than regression coefficients, the size of the contribution to effectiveness made by each variable at any level of the other cannot be derived from the present data.

Socialization, Communication, Consensus

The Klonglan, Mulford, and Tweed (1974) paper, based on data from the national sample, adds one more variable to the analysis, that of consensus. The authors point out that consensus is a key variable of compliance theory because it occupies the status of an intervening variable between communication and socialization, on the one hand, and effectiveness, on the other (see pp. 231-234). This is interpreted by the authors as an "implied causal relationship," according to which socialization and communication exercise their influence on effectiveness not directly but rather by building up consensus (Klonglan, Mulford, and Tweed, 1974, p. 4).

In operationalizing consensus, the study draws upon the six "consensus spheres" defined by Etzioni (see p. 232). These six spheres include consensus on general values, on organizational goals, on means, policy, or tactics, on participation in the organization, on performance obligations, and on cognitive perspectives. However, not all of them were measured: "Consensus on general values and consensus on participation are assumed to be fairly high due to the normative nature of the organization. Furthermore, no attempt was made to measure consensus on cognitive perspectives because of the sheer difficulty of ascertaining what 'facts' are relevant and up-to-date within the civil defense system" (ibid., p. 18). Moreover, the authors decided to focus their operational definition of consensus on "vertical consensus" (across the ranks), the degree of consensus between the local directors and state civil defense personnel. In particular, the study measured the degree of understanding of and agreement with state-set goal priorities, state-defined methods for goal attainment, and state-defined performance obligations for the local directors.

Using path-analytical techniques, the authors found both socialization and communication significantly related to consensus (path coefficients of .133 and .373). Taken together, the two independent variables accounted for 18.5% of the variance in consensus (*ibid.*, p. 15). However, although the relationship between consensus and effectiveness was significant (.05), consensus was found to explain only 5.3% of the effectiveness variance (*ibid.*, p. 13).

The authors suggest three explanations for the weakness of the relationship. First, the relatively low influence of communication and socialization on consensus may be due to "the normative nature of the civil defense organizations. Where there is already a high general commitment to the purpose of the organization, the socialization and communication strategies may play minor roles" (*ibid.*, p. 15). This implies that the key variable to explain consensus might be selectivity, a direction of inquiry the authors do not pursue. Second, the low influence of consensus on effectiveness might suggest "that consensus within the consensus spheres is only a necessary, but not a sufficient condition for effective role performance" (*ibid.*, p. 16). Third, the authors point to a deficiency in their approach, namely their failure to "specify the status groups among which consensus is measured" (see p. 234). "The effect may be to obscure the real effects of the consensus spheres upon effectiveness by focusing only upon vertical socialization, communication and consensus." In particular, it is noted that "a combination of vertical and horizontal effects may produce more meaningful causal models" (Klonglan, Mulford, and Tweed, 1974, p. 16).[3]

Table XV-3—The Effects of Socialization, Communication, and Consensus on Effectiveness in Two Normative Organizations

| | CIVIL DEFENSE SYSTEM | | FRATERNITIES | |
	Zero-Order Correlation	Beta Weight	Zero-Order Correlation	Beta Weight
Socialization	.118	.024	.123	.007
Communication	.275	.212	.377	.292
Consensus	.229	.136	.315	.175
Variance explained		9.2%		16.6%

Source: Klonglan, Mulford, and Tweed (1974); Mulford, Woodman, and Warren (1973).

To obtain more satisfactory results, the authors supplemented

3. The limitation of the analysis to vertical relationships is due, at least in considerable measure, to the nature of the organization studied. As there is almost no interaction among the local directors, horizontal interaction plays a very little role, if any.

their path model by adding to it the direct relations between effectiveness and communication and between effectiveness and socialization. However, this did not decisively improve the model. Although communication proved to have a low but significant impact, as documented by a standardized regression coefficient of .212, the impact of socialization was not significant at the .05 level. The data, included in Table XV-3, show that the overall variance accounted for by the revised model does not exceed, in this particular organization, 9.2%.[4]

In another study carried out in 1973, Mulford, Woodman, and Warren returned to the question of how socialization, communication, and consensus are related to organizational effectiveness. This time the data were collected from campus fraternities, a normative organization.[5,6] Comparing the results with those previously reported presents some problems because, by necessity, the indicators differ from those used in the study of the other organizations. In the fraternity study, socialization was measured by members' self-assessment and self-ranking, on a 1 to 5 continuum, as to how much socialization they had received from the organization's members and officers. Communication was assessed in a similar manner, by asking how much the respondent had communicated within the organization.

The measurement of consensus is more complex. The authors developed five scales related to five of the six "consensus spheres" outlined by Etzioni (see pp. 231ff.): scales of consensus about goals, about means, of degrees of symbolic participation, of performance obligations, and of common symbolic standards (consensus on cognitive standards). No attempt was made to determine the degree of consensus on general values.

4. A comparison between Tables XV-1 and XV-2 reveals that the zero-order correlation coefficients with effectiveness of socialization and communication differ considerably (socialization: .401 and .118; communication: .423 and .275). This may be due to two reasons. First, the studies draw on different data sets—the first one on a three-state sample, the second one on a national sample. Second, and more importantly, the measurements used for socialization and communication differ. For instance, the second study (Klonglan, Mulford, and Tweed, 1974)—and all those to be reviewed—focuses exclusively on "vertical" socialization, relating to interactions with state level civil defense personnel only. On the other hand, the first one (Mulford, Klonglan, and Warren, 1972), in line with Mulford, Klonglan, Beal, and Bohlen (1968), includes interactions with other local directors and local government personnel. Details should be looked up in the research reports themselves.

5. The study specified more than the three independent variables indicated. The additional variables, however, are not pertinent to the compliance theory. Multiple regression was carried out for groups of independent variables as well as for all variables together. One of these groups was composed of the three variables presently under discussion (see the following).

6. For further discussion of the fraternities study, see Woodman, Mulford, and Warren (n.d.), and Mulford, Woodman, Warren, and Kopachevsky (n.d.).

Effectiveness was expressed in terms of individual role performance, operationalized as a member's overall contribution to the house of membership, again as self-assessed. As there were only 12 such houses on the campus under study, the authors "choose not to aggregate the data so as to produce variables indicative of effectiveness at the macro level. Rather, each subject was asked to indicate on a 1-5 continuum ranging from some contribution to much contribution, to objectively evaluate the contribution he had made to the house" (Mulford, Woodman, and Warren, 1973, p. 5).

Table XV-3 provides the results of the fraternity study and a comparison to the Civil Defense System study discussed previously in terms of the zero-order correlation coefficients between the three independent variables and effectiveness as well as in terms of the multiple regression coefficients (beta weights). Considering the differences between the two organizations (civil defense and fraternity) and between the measurements used in the two studies, the similarity of the patterns of results is quite striking.[7]

In both cases, for the zero-order correlations as well as for the beta weights, communication is most strongly related to effectiveness, with consensus holding the second place. Furthermore, in both studies the zero-order correlation of socialization with effectiveness is smaller than that of the two other independent variables, and in both cases multiple regression makes the relationship vanish. That means that, controlling for communication and consensus, there is no impact of socialization on effectiveness. Although the three variables explain almost twice as much of the variance in effectiveness in the fraternity study as they do in the civil defense study, the pattern itself remains constant.

In addition to providing data which allows for systematic comparison of the compliance variables in two normative organizations, the fraternity study explored the role of a variable not covered previously in the Iowa State studies, namely, social rank.

Rank was determined by the length of time an individual had spent in the system (Mulford, Woodman, Warren, and Kopachesky, 1974, p. 8). Thus, seniors and juniors were assumed to be organizational elites, while freshmen and sophomores were counted as lower participants. As we see from Table XV-4, the three independent

---

7. On the measurements used in the civil defense study, see p. 143. Note that no self-ranking is used for the independent variables and that the effectiveness measure has an objective base.

variables predict role performance much better the higher the rank of the participants. A significant exception is represented by the sophomore class. For seniors, the percentage of variance explained is almost twice as high as for all subjects together.

Having established the significance of rank (or, the elite/lower participant division) the authors proposed two specific hypotheses. First, based on the compliance theory, the authors suggested that "elites in any organization are more likely to be controlled with normative power than with coercive or utilitarian power" (*ibid.*, p. 4). Therefore, "consensus formation should be more strongly related to role performance of elites than of other members."

Table XV-4 shows that this is indeed the case: The partial re-

Table XV-4—The Effect of Socialization, Communication, and Consensus on Effectiveness by Social Rank: Partial Regression Slopes

	Freshmen (N = 119)	Sophomores (N = 121)	Juniors (N = 94)	Seniors (N = 69)
Socialization	−.024	−.003	.035	−.050
Communication	.180	.095	.127	.148
Consensus	.023	.049	.054	.086
Variance explained	18.6%	13.4%	25.8%	29.6%

Source: Mulford, Woodman, Warren, and Kopachesky (1974) (table edited).

gression slopes of consensus formation increase steadily as social rank increases (although the absolute values are not impressive, and the differences are statistically not significant) (*ibid.*, p. 10).

Second, it was hypothesized that "communication would seemingly be required regardless of the type of power used to control members," so that "the direct effects of communication on role performance will be equally strong for upper and lower classmen" (*ibid.*, p. 5). Indeed when freshmen and sophomores, on the one hand, and juniors and seniors, on the other, were taken together, no significant difference existed between the two groups. This finding supports the second hypothesis.

After what should be viewed as a side-trip to visit with another normative organization, the fraternities, we return to the normative organization which is at the center of the Iowa State Compliance Studies, the civil defense service.

A COMPREHENSIVE PATH MODEL

Mulford, Klonglan, Warren, and Schmitz (1972) tested the inter-relations of eight compliance correlates. In addition to four of the variables already reviewed (effectiveness, socialization, communication, and selectivity; consensus is not included in this analysis), they introduced four others: scope, salience, role tension, and pervasiveness.

Scope is defined as the number of activities in which an organization's participants are jointly involved, operationalized as "the extent to which activities of the participants of an organization are limited to other participants of the same organization, as against the degree to which activities of participants involve nonparticipants as well" (see p. 264). *Salience* "refers to the emotional significance of participation in one collectivity compared to that in others" (see p. 265). *Role tension* is defined as the emotional strain arising for the average lower participant from his being a member of the organization. Salience and tension are assumed to be directly influenced by scope: The more a participant is involved in an organization, the greater the organization's emotional significance for him, and the more strain will be experienced in connection with his involvement.

Finally, pervasiveness is different from scope in that it refers to "the number of activities in or outside the organization for which the organization sets norms," that is, the breadth of the organization's claim to regulating its members' behavior (p. 267). Scope may be viewed as the "action boundary" of an organization, and pervasiveness can be seen as its "normative boundary."

The Iowa State group measured scope using a scale of five items assessing the degree to which a local coordinator said he interacted with other organizational personnel. Pervasiveness was assessed by the degree to which participation in the civil defense organization had influenced the local coordinators' attitude toward the importance of civil defense. Level of personal role tension was measured by a single item assessing the degree to which the local coordinator was preoccupied with thoughts of his job after he left the office.

Starting from our hypotheses about the relationship of scope and pervasiveness to compliance (p. 268) the Iowa State authors, in line with their general approach, developed a hypothetical model of causal relationships among the eight variables under consideration (see Figure XV-1). Arrows indicate a sequence of cause and effect.

Uninterrupted lines are causal relationships the authors derived from the theory, and the dotted lines mark causality assumptions supplied by the authors themselves.

The hypothesized path model is based on a series of decisions. The authors' first, and probably most important decision was to de-

Figure XV-1 — *Theoretical Causal Model of Variables Affecting Local Coordina-tor's Role Performance*

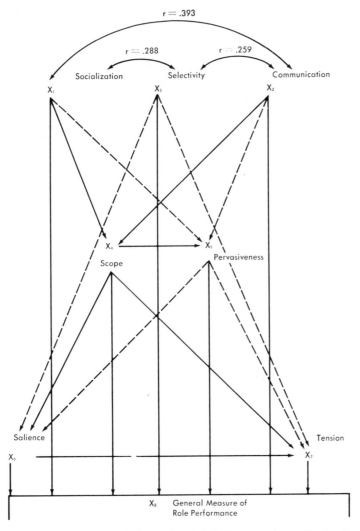

Dashed lines indicate inferred causal relations where Etzioni did not suggest proposition hypotheses.

Source: Mulford, Klonglan, Warren, and Schmitz (1972), p. 65. Reprinted with the permission of *Social Science Research.*

fine communication, socialization, and selectivity as "exogenous variables," making them the model's points of departure. The curved lines between them, then, "indicate that no theoretical explanation is given to explain their correlations" (*ibid.*, p. 12). The choice of these variables as primary concepts makes sense as they all contribute to the initial involvement of new participants and in this sense "antecede" the others logically and in time. (This is especially true of selectivity; it is somewhat less so for socialization, which occurs throughout one's participation, although often much more intensively initially, and least true for communication).

While this decision is quite justified, it does illustrate some of the general problems of causal analysis. Causal analysis demands that some variables be assumed to be "more independent" than others, while the functional and system approach would stress their interrelationships and their mutual effect on each other, avoiding the need to assume such a ranking. This is evident in the model before us. For instance, according to the compliance theory, there is no reason for ruling out that, in addition to communication affecting scope, scope in turn might affect communication. While, by increasing communication, an organization may be able to broaden the realm of its members' joint activities, by the same token an organization which manages to increase its scope by some other means, e.g., a college introducing residence requirements, may subsequently find its amount of internal communication to have increased significantly.

The same problem arises with reference to the relationship between socialization and scope and between the other "exogenous" and the intermediary variables. The authors assigned scope and pervasiveness an intermediary status, hypothesizing that they in turn, affect salience and role tension. Furthermore, it was assumed that a causal relationship existed with scope influencing pervasiveness, rather than the other way around or both affecting each other.

Finally, the model hypothesizes direct independent and positive contributions of salience and role tension to organizational effectiveness. Although saliency may well relate in this way to effectiveness in normative organizations—the more significant its activities are to the members, the more they will involve themselves and hence mobilize themselves to its "work"—the status of tension is less evident. Effective normative organizations may often create a broad-scope action space and especially establish a high level of pervasiveness, and the resulting high tension is often a "problem" the organization has to deal with, as any one who has lived on a commune, a *kibbutz,* or in the army will be quick to recognize (see pp. 266, 268). Thus, high tension might possibly cancel out part of the positive impact broad scope and high pervasiveness have on effectiveness, rather than contribute to it.

All this is not to take away from the great significance of the Iowa State Compliance Studies. Although I would not have been inclined to assume causality—and if I had, I might have arranged the factors somewhat differently—certainly there is ample room for hypothesizing sequences and, above all, for testing them.

As a first step in the process of testing the path model, the authors computed the zero-order correlations for all the variables included. All the relationships were found to be positive, and all but one were significant at the .05 level (see Table XV-5). The correlation coefficients between role performance (effectiveness) and the seven other variables ranged from .290 (selectivity) to .569 (scope), thus supporting the proposition that the included variables are significant for organizational effectiveness (Mulford, Klonglan, Warren, and Schmitz, 1972, p. 12).

Table XV-5—Zero-Order Correlation Coefficients for Variables in Model

	Variables	X_1	X_2	X_3	X_4	X_5	X_6	X_7	X_8
X_1	Socialization	—							
X_2	Communication	.393	—						
X_3	Selectivity	.288	.259	—					
X_4	Scope	.529	.557	.305	—				
X_5	Pervasiveness	.230	.219	.156	.365	—			
X_6	Salience	.136	.207	.172	.347	.269	—		
X_7	Tension	.198	.205	.268	.364	.071*	.268	—	
X_8	Effectiveness	.401	.423	.290	.569	.375	.335	.248	—

* Coefficient not significant at 5% level; $N = 240$.
Source: Mulford, Klonglan, Warren, and Schmitz (1972), p. 70. Reprinted with the permission of *Social Science Research.*

The next step was to move beyond checking for the relationship between pairs of variables to the relationships among all the independent and dependent variables of the total model. Standard partial regression coefficients were computed and tested for significance at the .05 level. By eliminating all nonsignificant or particularly weak relationships and by adding measures for unexplained variance

Figure XV-2 — *Model II: Statistically Significant Causal Model of Variables Affecting Local Coordinator's Role Performance*

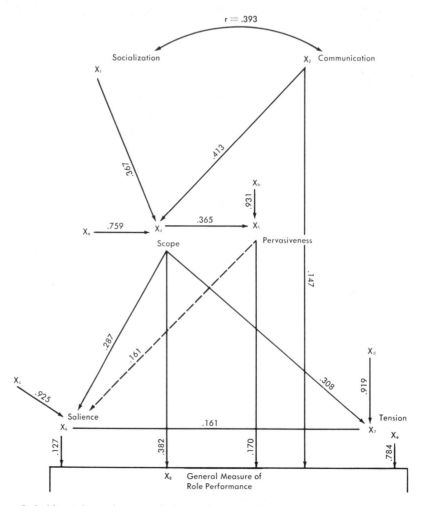

Dashed lines indicate inferred causal relations where Etzioni did not suggest proposition.

Source: Mulford, Klonglan, Warren, and Schmitz (1972), p. 73. Reprinted with the permission of *Social Science Research.*

$(x_a - x_e)$, the final path model, as shown in Figure XV-2, was arrived at.

Examining the model, the authors first found that selectivity, one of the three former "exogenous" variables, no longer appears. Furthermore, Figure XV-2 shows that 10 of the 13 causal relations indicated by uninterrupted lines (derived from the compliance thesis) withstood the test, while only one of the six causality hypotheses that were added by the Iowa State group proved significant. In the first category, socialization as well as selectivity proved to have no direct influence on effectiveness, although they had appeared to have such an effect before the introduction of the other variables. Here the value of multivariate analysis stands out. In addition, the level of tension showed no effect on role performance, its zero-order correlation having already been quite low (.248). In the second category, only the assumed relationship between pervasiveness and salience held up. The partial regression coefficients ranged from .127 (salience–effectiveness) to .413 (communication–scope). Of the eleven path coefficients, five are .17 or below, while five others are .308 or above.

The total explanatory power of the model is measured in terms of the percentage of variance accounted for by the variables contained in the model. Table XV-6 shows that while scope and effectiveness are relatively well explained, pervasiveness, salience, and tension are much less so.

An assessment of the overall strength of the causal model must take into account that although pervasiveness, salience, and tension are hardly explained at all—the contributions of "error" are, respectively, .931, .975, and .919—scope and, perhaps most importantly, effectiveness are rather well covered.

Interpreting their results, the authors point to the dominant role of scope. The six direct relationships in which scope is involved are at the same time those with the highest path coefficients; while the lowest of these is .287, the next-highest ranking coefficient—the first one without scope—is only .170. Moreover, scope contributes to or is affected by each of the remaining variables in the model, and it is at the same time best explained and contributes most to the explanation of the other variables. Taking everything together, it seems

Table XV-6—Explanatory Power of the Model for Five Factors

"Criterion" ("effects")	Predictors ("Causes")	% of Variance Accounted for
Scope	Socialization, Communication	42%
Pervasiveness	Scope	13%
Salience	Scope, Pervasiveness	14%
Tension	Scope, Saliency	15%
Effectiveness	Communication, Scope, Pervasiveness, Saliency	39%

Adapted from Table 3, Mulford, Klonglan, Warren, and Schmitz (1972), p. 74.

that the model, insofar as it is concerned with explaining effectiveness for this particular organization, would not lose much of its explanatory power if pervasiveness, salience, and tension were omitted. The basic structure of the underlying relationship seems to approximate the simplified model presented in Figure XV-3. Socialization and communication are found to affect effectiveness through scope, with communication exercising additional direct influence on effectiveness.

Figure XV-3 — *Effectiveness in Normative Organizations: Simplified, Hypothetical Path Model*

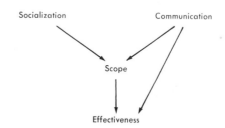

Our discussion of the Iowa State Compliance Studies seems to suggest a possible reordering of the causal sequence of the compliance variables. One could plausibly argue that the scope (and perhaps the pervasiveness) of an organization determines the amount of intra-organizational socialization and communication, rather than the other way around. And although selectivity seems not to have been of great consequence in this case, it might be advisable in further research to include it as a second (or third) exogenous variable in addition to scope and, perhaps, pervasiveness. After all, selectivity describes one of the fundamental conditions of organizational life: the degree to which an organization can make a choice between possible members. To include it would be of interest if only to provide a basis for comparison with other types of organizations, in which, as we shall see, selectivity did prove to be a potent factor.

UTILITARIAN AND NORMATIVE ORGANIZATIONS COMPARED

The last layer in the Iowa State group pyramid of analyses, reviewed here, is provided by Warren, Mulford, and Yetley (1973). In this paper the analytic approach developed with regard to a normative organization is applied to a utilitarian one, the farm co-ops.

As far as the variables covered by the Iowa State Compliance studies are concerned, compliance theory predicts four major differences between normative and utilitarian organizations. First, in a utilitarian organization, communication tends to be primarily vertical (upward as well as downward), and instrumental rather than expressive. Second, "utilitarian organizations tend to rely on autonomous external units for both instrumental . . . and . . . expressive socialization" see p. 253). Consequently such organizations are expected to be more selective than normatives ones in order to assure adequate skills and motivation on the part of their members by means of high recruitment selectivity (see p. 277). Third, while normative organizations can be either broad or narrow in scope, their pervasiveness needs to be high if they are to be effective. However, typical utilitarian organizations are narrow in scope and low in pervasiveness (see p. 269), although "the more normative utilitarian organizations are, the higher their pervasiveness is expected to be." Fourth, because scope—in utilitarian organizations—is expected to be narrow, we can assume that salience and tension (from this source) will be low, too (see p. 266). However, salience as well as tension, similar to pervasiveness, may grow to the degree that the organization assumes some normative features.

Summing up, while the selectivity of utilitarian organizations is expected to be higher, all other variables are expected to assume lower values than in normative organizations. This, however, is not a proposition about the relative contribution of the variables to overall organizational effectiveness. What is compared, in the theory, are the values of certain variables expected to be found in different types of compliance structures, not their relative contribution to effectiveness. For instance, that scope is low in utilitarian organizations—as compared to normative ones—suggests only that scope, in order to be in a congruent condition and to contribute to the organization's successful operation, will have to be low, not that it will contribute more or less than, say, selectivity. Of course, hypotheses as to relative significance may be added; for instance, concerning the relative significance of selectivity and communication. This is in effect what emerges from the Iowa State Compliance Studies.

The analysis of the intra-organizational factors influencing the degree of effectiveness in local farm cooperatives, a utilitarian organization, starts from almost the same path model that served as a point of departure for the study of the more normative civil defense organization. (Figure XV-1). The only difference is that an additional causal hypothesis is supplied by the authors: In the slightly revised model, a relationship is hypothesized between selectivity on the one hand and scope and pervasiveness on the other. This addition is justified by the larger role selectivity plays in utilitarian organizations.

Our discussion of the results will first turn to the findings re-

Figure XV-4 — *Statistically Significant Causal Model of Variables Affecting Net Operating Revenue, as a Measure of Organizational Effectiveness.*

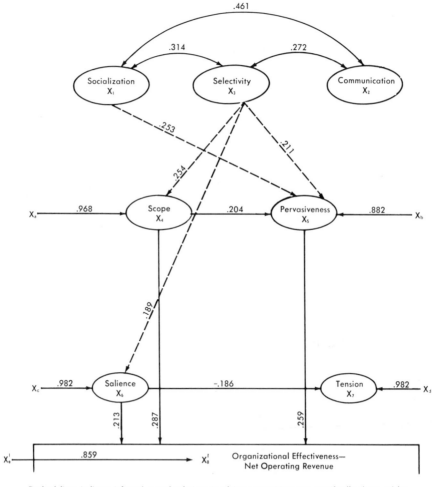

Dashed lines indicate inferred causal relations involving propositions not specifically discussed by Etzioni.

Source: Warren, Mulford, and Yetley (1973), p. 33.

garding the relationship of the two different measures of effectiveness (see p. 148) in utilitarian organizations to the seven other variables. After this, we will take a new look at the path model of normative organizations introduced previously and draw some comparative conclusions.

Figures XV-4 and XV-5 show the final path models of the farm

Figure XV-5 — *Statistically Significant Causal Model of Variables Affecting Adaptation, as a Measure of Organizational Effectiveness.*

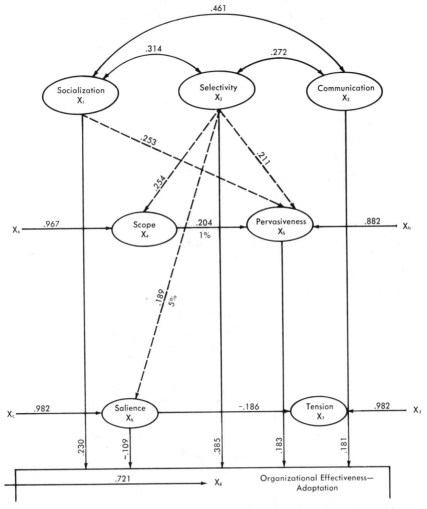

Dashed lines indicate inferred causal relations involving propositions not specifically discussed by Etzioni.

Source: Warren, Mulford, and Yetley (1973), p. 31.

co-op study, including the values for the "error" factors and for the "sociological" and "economic" effectiveness measures, respectively. Three points should be emphasized:

1. Of the 13 causal hypotheses indicated by uninterrupted lines, seven proved significant in the adaptation model and four held when related to the economic concept of effectiveness. In both models, four of the eight hypotheses supplied survived the tests of statistical significance.

A comparison of the sociological (see p. 150) and economic (see p. 149) versions of the path model for utilitarian organizations reveals that compliance variables are almost twice as powerful in explaining "adaptation" (in the sociological model, 48% of the variance of effectiveness is accounted for, while only 26% is explained in the economic model). This is not surprising. In the words of the authors "the measure of adaptation is largely based upon the presence of and extent to which certain resource acquisition activities are undertaken by participants . . . Net operating revenue is not, however, a variable as directly affected by the activities of the participants as is adaptation . . ." (*ibid.,* p. 19). Rather, economic success depends on a host of external variables which are beyond the control of even the most adaptive organization. This is why an "internally efficient" organization may be economically unsuccessful, while much less adaptive organizations may, under favorable circumstances, realize large profits. In other words, the different degrees of explanation achieved by the two versions of the model point to the fundamental distinction between external and internal factors of organizational effectiveness, a distinction which has been introduced previously (p. 149). As one might have expected, the compliance variables, although not unrelated to measures of successful operation in the environment, are much more capable of accounting for the conditions of internal adaptiveness.

2. Comparing the two versions in detail, one notes that the number of variables affecting the dependent variable directly is five in the sociological version and three in the economic one. The differences are considerable. While socialization, selectivity, and communication are significantly related to adaptation (the partial regression coefficients are .230, .385, and .181), these relationships do not appear in the economic version.

Furthermore, the values of the two relationships which both

versions have in common vary considerably. The effect of pervasiveness is .183 for the sociological measure of effectiveness versus .259 for the economic one. Even more importantly, salience, being negatively related to adaptiveness (−.109), enters into a comparatively high positive relationship with the amount of net operating revenue realized, the partial regression coefficient being .213. Finally, the economic version contains a new association, of .287, between scope and effectiveness.

These findings deserve some comments. An explanation of the unrelatedness of socialization, selectivity, and communication to the net operating revenue indicator of effectiveness has already been provided in our discussion. To reiterate, these internal organizational factors are not closely tied to an effectiveness measure significantly affected by environmental forces. However, it is far less obvious why salience is negatively related to adaptiveness and positively to economic effectiveness. The authors point to the fact that "the manner in which salience was measured included some aspects of the concepts of cohesion and job satisfaction" (*ibid.*, p. 21). The authors then argue that cohesion can be dysfunctional for sociological effectiveness and functional for economic effectiveness: functional, because group cohesion increases productivity, dysfunctional as "it is more difficult to change an individual's behavior if he belongs to a highly cohesive group than if he belongs to a less cohesive group" (p. 299). This point is in line with the thesis that cohesion by itself is basically neutral (see p. 283).

Table XV-7—Comparison of Civil Defense and Coop Data

| | | Iowa Farm Coop Study | |
INDEPENDENT VARIABLE	CIVIL DEFENSE SYSTEM	ADAPTIVENESS MODEL	NET OPERATING REVENUE
	Zero-order Correlation with Effectiveness*		
Socialization	.401	.497	.100**
Selectivity	.290	.548	.247
Communication	.423	.426	.075
Scope	.569	.266	.385
Pervasiveness	.375	.432	.365
Salience	.335	.006**	.266
Tension	.248	.154	−.032**

* Other than the partial correlation coefficient, the zero-order correlation coefficient is not affected by assumptions about causality or constellations of factors within the path model. That is why the table draws on the latter rather than the former.
** Not significant at .05 level.
Based on Warren, Mulford, Yetley (1973).

Finally, there is a need to explain why scope affects effectiveness only in the net economic revenue version of the model, but not when the adaptiveness criterion is used. The authors argue that this

may be partly explained by the items used in the composite measure of scope. This measure is heavily influenced by the extent of involvement of employees in operational decisions that affect their work. Meaningful involvement of workers in decisions of this nature, the cornerstone of the human relations approach to management, is thought to increase worker morale and productivity. . . . Scope, as measured, has a direct influence on net operating revenue, but not necessarily on the adaptive activities of management when considered in the total causal model. (*ibid.,* p. 20)

3. In both versions of the utilitarian model, selectivity has the status of a key variable. This is especially so in the sociological version, where selectivity is by far the strongest factor affecting effectiveness directly, being at the same time significantly related to scope, pervasiveness, and salience, all of which in turn affect the dependent variable. In the economic model, although there is no direct relationship between selectivity and effectiveness, selectivity affects all three variables that are significantly related to effectiveness. This finding supports strongly the over-arching hypothesis outlined earlier, that while all other variables are expected to be less powerful as causal factors related to effectiveness in utilitarian organizations as compared to normative ones, selectivity is expected to dominate the intra-organizational constellation of factors in utilitarian organizations.

FURTHER COMPARISON OF UTILITARIAN AND NORMATIVE ORGANIZATIONS

Selectivity plays no role as far as the effectiveness of the normative organization studied is concerned; instead, scope has the greatest explanatory power. The authors remark that this may be due to the differential ability of different types of organizations to select their membership. "The number of normative organizations that can be highly selective of potential members is not very large. The converse would be expected of utilitarian organizations" (*ibid.,* p. 24). I would have avoided a suggestion as to the ratio of selective, highly pervasive normative organizations versus selective, less pervasive ones, because the universe is ill-defined, although my impression is similar to that of the authors. It seems to me more promising to focus on two subtypes of normative organizations, the "sect" versus "church," and see the type under discussion as a case of the "church" subcategory, in which relatively low selectivity increases the demands directed at the other variables, e.g., socialization and communication, if effectiveness is to be achieved.

Drawing on this general approach, one can also explain why, in utilitarian organizations, selectivity, in its relationship to scope, assumes the very place communication and socialization occupied jointly in at least this subtype of normative organizations (see p. 395). The lesser role of scope in utilitarian organizations may be due to the low number of factors under its influence, as compared to normative organizations. In the utilitarian model, scope affects neither tension nor salience; significantly, in its relationship to salience, scope has been replaced by selectivity. Furthermore, the value of the path coefficient of scope to pervasiveness is considerably lower.

The fact that salience is, in normative organizations, affected by both scope and pervasiveness, while in utilitarian organizations only selectivity has a significant effect on it, lends additional support to the theory. "The combination of scope and pervasiveness seems to approximate 'established involvement' as used by Etzioni in his flow model (see p. 261). In normative organizations, this 'established involvement' is moral commitment, which would be expected to result in increased salience. In utilitarian organizations, however, this established involvement is more likely to be calculative, and this would not necessarily be expected to increase saliency" (Warren, Mulford, and Yetley, 1973, p. 25). Rather, in utilitarian organizations, the degree to which participants experience the organization as emotionally significant depends on how carefully they have been selected.

Finally, as indicated, the contrast here is not between two pure types. The utilitarian organization studied has a normative element in the cooperative ideology, and the normative one has a utilitarian element in the paid employee status of some of the civil defense directors. That despite these "impurities" the types differentiate is an additional indication of both the great value of the studies before us (if impure and "closer" units differentiate systematically, surely more distant, purer types also would) and of the validity of the compliance theory. All said and done, no other group of studies did more to advance the study of compliance than the Iowa State Compliance Studies.

PART FOUR

COMPLIANCE IN A DYNAMIC PERSPECTIVE

XVI

CONCOMITANT AND
SUCCESSIVE DIVISION
OF COMPLIANCE

Chapters XVI and XVII introduce two dynamic perspectives into the study of compliance. Chapter XVI compares organizations which systematically change their compliance structure with those which maintain a more stable form of compliance. Chapter XVII, pages 453-505, examines the study of compliance, rather than compliance itself, from a dynamic viewpoint.

Organizations are often compared to tools; they serve a goal. The goal, at least initially, is often set by a social unit other than the organization itself. This external goal-setting collectivity—a community, a society, a religious group—frequently assigns more than one goal to an organization. Universities are expected to be centers of teaching and research; many hospitals are expected to cure patients, teach medical students, and conduct research; newspapers are expected to serve culture goals but also to show a profit. Moreover, organizations which are committed to one paramount goal must often pursue quite different subgoals or tasks in order to achieve it. A drug manufacturer has to conduct research in order to produce at a profit; prison authorities often conduct some workshops as a custodial measure to keep inmates busy; and advertising agencies have both "creative" and production tasks.

Goals and tasks frequently differ in their compliance requirements. Different types of goals require different types of compliance structure. Different goals of the same general type (e.g., teaching and research, both culture goals) tend to require different emphases on the various components making up the particular type of compliance structure. Both teaching and research require a basically normative compliance structure. But teaching requires a stronger emphasis on normative compliance than research does, which can rely more on remunerative compliance. Rarely are there two goals which can be served with optimal effectiveness by compliance structures which are precisely the same in both the predominant element and the weight given it.

It is because of this association between goals and compliance that multi-goal or multi-task "organizations" face a dilemma. If they consistently emphasize one pattern of compliance, they lose in effectiveness, because this pattern is congruent with only one task. If they give equal stress to two or more patterns of compliance, effectiveness is lost through neutralization. Segregation, as we saw in Chapter III, allows organizations to combine various compliance structures without losing in effectiveness, and hence this is the form division of compliance takes in multi-task organizations.

Segregation takes two major forms. In one, different compliance structures are deployed in different subunits of the organization, where they operate at the same time but independently of each other. We refer to this as *concomitant division* of compliance. In the second form, different compliance structures are utilized by the same organizational unit or subunit at different time periods; but at any given time the unit is employing only one compliance structure. We refer to this as *successive division* of compliance. The first division of compilance is static, the second is dynamic.

DIVISION OF LABOR VERSUS DIVISION OF COMPLIANCE

Before we can proceed to study these two forms of compliance segregation, the difference between the present approach and that which is common in the literature on administration must be mentioned. This literature usually focuses on the division of labor in terms of different concrete tasks or activities, though in some cases the difference between ranks who control activities and ranks who perform them is treated as a form of division of labor. Our focus is

1. In the rest of this chapter *tasks* stand for tasks and/or goals.

on the *control* relationship between the two levels, on the kinds of power applied and the kinds of involvement recruited, not on the substance of the work carried out. We find that the division and specialization of compliance, though influenced by the division and specialization of labor, can be analyzed independently to great advantage.

Several positions have been taken in the literature on the division of labor at the control level (Meyer, 1957, pp. 26-49). One approach is represented by Simon (1957), who emphasized that the role of the executive or administrator differs from that of those lower in rank by virtue of its focus on decision making; lower ranks are primarily performance-oriented. This comes close to what might be called the *vertical* division of compliance—that is, the division between those who apply power and those who obey and respond to it. We focus, in this chapter, on the *horizontal* division of compliance, since differences within the levels, rather than between them, are stressed.

A second group of writers, who do concern themselves with horizontal comparisons, take two opposing positions; ours, as we will see, falls between them. Some of these writers hold that each control relationship is a distinctive specialty, defined in terms of the performances which are controlled. The nature of the control relationship is dictated by the executive's intimate knowledge of the tasks and performances he supervises.

The opposite position is taken by those who suggest that the control function is universal and abstract. Control always means the ability to attain performances through other people. The main skill required is a kind of "political" skill, the ability to evoke cooperation. A manager is often defined as "someone who directs the work of others and who, as a slogan puts it, 'does his work by getting other people to do theirs.' " (Drucker, 1954, p. 6) Specialized knowledge comes from experts or staff positions, and not from the executive. Thus, one position maintains that control is a highly specialized function, the other that it is highly general.

We support a third viewpoint. The control function is less specialized than the performance function, but it is not universal in the sense that a person who is an effective control agent in one structure will be equally effective in others. There seems to be a limited number of forms which control relationships can take. More important, *control differentiation is not based directly on the kind of perform-ances which are supervised, but on the kind of compliance effective performance requires.* In terms more often used in the literature on the subject, styles of leadership (we prefer *modes of control*) should be differentiated according to the kind of discipline the leader must attain, and not according to the nature of work supervised, though the two are of course related to some degree.

CONCOMITANT DIVISION OF COMPLIANCE

Concomitant division of compliance occurs when tasks which differ in their compliance requirements are carried out by different subunits of the same unit at the same time. Concomitant compliance division may take several forms. It is most extreme when the various types of task are delegated by a collectivity to separate control struc-tures—that is, to distinct organizations. It is less extreme when they are delegated to subunits of the same organization.

Division of Compliance Among Organizations

The same collectivity may assign two tasks to two distinct organi-zations, thus allowing for maximum compliance specialization. A typical example is the tendency of labor movements in Western European countries to develop both labor unions and political parties. Both organizations often share the same general task: to attain power in order to realize ideological and economic values. As a rule the parties are relatively more oriented to the ideological tasks and the unions more to the economic ones (though the dividing line is by no means sharp). There are parallel differences in the compliance structure of the two organizations. Unions often have a *relatively* more utilitarian structure than the parties with which they are affiliated or which they support. The contemporary British labor movement supplies a typical example. The majority of the labor unions appeal to their members in terms of economic goals, while the Labor party is the center of political (and, to a large degree, ideological) activity.

Applying the "sacred-profane" dichotomy to this example, we may say that the compliance division between party and union allows the labor movement as a whole to maintain the commitments of three types of members: those who are more oriented to the "sacred" (or normative) side will be more attracted to the party (e.g., non-working population groups such as teenagers; the aged; intellectuals); [2] those who are more "profane" (or calculative) in their orientation will be more attracted to the unions (e.g., the majority of blue-collar workers); and those who wish to fulfill both psychological needs in the labor movement but do not wish to mix the sacred with the profane can also be satisfied, through membership in both organizations. A comparative study of the membership involvement in a union local and in a party branch, politically affiliated with each other, in the same town, suburb, or city, would allow a test of these hypotheses.

Comparison of a labor movement which has two organizational branches with a similar movement which has only one (if possible, in the same socio-cultural environment) would enable us to examine the hypothesis asserting the effectiveness of segregated compliance structures for different tasks. We expect that the dual structure will be considerably more effective both in its recruitment (as measured by the proportion of the potential population which is actually recruited) and in the nature and intensity of involvement it achieves (cf. Goldstein, 1952, pp. 122-27).

Since different labor movements, even in the same society, differ in the substance of their ideology, which in turn affects the involvement of members, such a study would probably have to compare the same labor movement at two time periods: when it has one organizational branch, and when it has two. A study of the British labor movement in the first decades of the twentieth century would supply an interesting case in point.

The history of Soviet "labor unions" supplies another illustration of compliance segregation. According to the original Communist ideology, there could be no industrial conflict in Soviet society once ownership of the means of production had been transferred from private to public hands. [3] It was expected that administration of production and recruitment of moral involvement in production goals could be carried out in one control structure, namely the factory. [4]

2. These groups are obviously less likely to be union members. But we suggest that they will also have less positive attitudes toward the union than to the party, and be less inclined to accept the union's subideology.

3. On the development of Soviet ideology concerning "trade unions" in Russia, see Galenson (1954). See also Lazovsky (1920, pp. 4-19).

4. Unlike most material cited in this book, this illustration is taken from a nondemocratic society. In Soviet Russia, it should be emphasized, factories are not typical utilitarian organizations. Considerable emphasis is put on normative compliance (e.g., pure prestige symbols, agitation) and the goals are in part political and not strictly production goals (see e.g., Vucinich, 1950).

Control of the factories by workers was considered a major mechanism assuring the effectiveness of such a combination (B. Moore, 1951, pp. 159-60). Two years after the Revolution, this was more than mere ideology. Moore states: "By about 1919 the prevailing practice in management consisted of collegiums or boards composed of two-thirds workers and one-third engineers or technicians approved by the trade union." (*Ibid.*, p. 164)

From 1919 on, however, there has been increasing specialization and segregation of control. Management concentrates on administrative duties and remunerative controls, and the "labor unions" (directed by the party) concentrate on recruitment of moral commitments.[5] The labor unions are expected to solicit "mass participation," to communicate suggestions to management, to criticize it, and to represent the workers' interests and grievances within the limits of the system (Gordon, 1941, p. 81; Berliner, 1957, pp. 271-72). Typically, they engage in a great deal of agitation and educational work (Granick, 1954, p. 153). The fact that the labor unions, *relative* to the factory, are a channel of upward communication and the upward exercise of power enables them to be more effective in recruiting moral commitment than the factory, with its downward and utilitarian structure, could be. This division of labor is therefore more effective than a dual utilitarian-normative structure, attempting to serve both administrative and leadership functions.[6]

Division of Compliance Among Organizational Units

Concomitant division of compliance does not require completely separate control structures. Often control segregation occurs in the middle or lower levels of a single structure.

A typical example of such compliance specialization is the staff-and-line division in factories. Line personnel can rely primarily on remunerative controls, such as overtime pay, fines, incentive plans,

---

5. On the function of trade unions and their relation to the party and to management, see Berliner (1957, pp. 264-78). On the new functions of trade unions, see B. Moore (1951, pp. 167, 106 ff.).

6. This point is discussed and widely documented by Bendix (1956, pp. 387-400). Granick (1954) reports that when organization of participation is left to management through "production conferences," it is limited to technical and administrative counseling and ". . . often enough, the plant administrators have cut themselves off from the rank and file of the employees and have tried to function without their supervision." (p. 242)

recommendations for promotion, and the allocation of various privileges—for example, permission to leave the plant half an hour early. Staff personnel, especially when they occupy strictly advisory positions, must obtain cooperation and compliance mainly through the authority conferred by their superior knowledge—that is, through normative power. Dalton (1959, pp. 104-6) showed that if a staff man does not succeed in convincing a "subordinated" foreman that he is an expert and that his suggestions are worth trying out, the staff man's ability to operate and to exert control is often quite limited.

The following are additional examples of compliance differentiation within the same organization: Control in production shops require a more utilitarian and a less normative compliance structure than does the control of professionals working in laboratories of the same factory; control of service units and office staff in hospitals is considerably more utilitarian than the control of interns (Lentz, 1950; 1957, p. 458). Similar differences exist between units engaged in routine work and units engaged in innovating work—for example, between service units and planning units of a government agency; between "administrative" (including clerical) and "creative" subunits in advertising or research organizations; and between production and personnel departments (Dunlop and Myers, 1955; Myers and Turnbull, 1956).[7] There also seem to be differences in the way various library departments, such as "reference" and bindery, are run (Naegele, forthcoming, p. 61).[8]

Compliance Specialization and Executive Mobility

To underscore further the significance of the differences in compliance which distinguish organizations from one another and separate subunits within organizations, we examine the effect of shifting from

7. A report of significant differences among engineers' interests on four dimensions (ideas, things, people, and economic affairs) in seven departments of the same organization (research, development, technical services, nonsupervisory administration, supervisory administration, and sales) suggests that there are also some differences in involvement and in power applied (*Human Factors in Research Administration*, 1955, p. 12). The emphasis on normative and social over instrumental elements in the role of managers of research and development units is documented by H. C. White (1960).

8. For another study of libraries which casts light on departmental differences see Fiske (1959). The organizational implications of this study were spelled out by Parsons (in Danton, 1959).

one compliance type to another on a central organizational process, namely that of executive mobility.

EXECUTIVES AS COMPLIANCE SPECIALISTS—We began this chapter with a review of three approaches to the study of control specialization. Applied to the study of intra-organizational and inter-organizational mobility of executives, the following three *alternative* propositions can be formulated:

(*a*) An executive will be most effective if he holds positions in which the same or similar types of performance are supervised, and the same basic knowledge and skills are required. Division of labor and technology are believed to determine the scope of effective horizontal mobility.

Drucker is explicit on the subject and does not limit himself to the lower levels of management. He states:

It means in the first place that the skills, the competence, the experience of management cannot, as such, be transferred and applied to the organization and running of other institutions. In particular a man's success in management [of a business] carries by itself no promise—let alone a guarantee—of his being successful in government. A career in management is, by itself, not a preparation for major political office—or for leadership in the Armed Forces, the Church or a university. (1954, pp. 8-9)[9]

(*b*) An executive controls people, and since this is the basis of all organizational control, effective horizontal mobility is virtually unlimited. Dubin represents this alternative position. He asserts:

Note one thing. I have *not* said that the education of an executive, as *executive,* includes learning to be management-minded, government-minded, union-minded, or organization-minded in terms of the special value system of the organization that employs him. Inevitably, every executive and administrator gets 'minded' in accordance with the values of the organization for which he works. I submit, however, that the *educated executive is one who can operate effectively in different kinds of organizations having different values and objectives.* Barnard, himself, is an outstanding example of this. . . . Here is a man who wrote the classic, *Functions of the Executive,* and pursued successive or concurrent careers in a business organization, as a government official, as director of a vast social service

9. The significance of technology in shaping the managerial roles has been pointed out in a comparative study of a mining enterprise, a factory, a hospital, and a university (Thompson and Bates, 1957). The impact of automatic machinery on managerial positions has been explored by Harbison, Kochling, Cassell, and Ruebmann (1955). See also Martin and Strauss (1959, p. 88).

organization, and now, as top executive of a philanthropic institution. (1951, pp. 3-4).

The "universal" approach to the functions and characteristics of executives is clearly dominant in the literature. Barnard studies the functions of *the* executive, just as students of organization, we saw earlier, study *the* bureaucracy, not particular types. Lists of qualities of executives are typically lists of qualities every person should be blessed with (such as capacity, knowledge, courage, "quality") and those required of every officer (effective use of time, perspective and judgment, self-control) or leader (personal power, sensitivity).[10] A study of 3,000 executives by Randle (1956, pp. 122-34) is one of the few which supplement a list of "universal" characteristics with some specific traits which distinguish subgroups of executives.

Some exponents of the universal approach imply that profit-making organizations supply a model for the administration of all types of organizations. Business methods and business personnel are seen as best fitted to run any organization, whether a school, a hospital, or a community chest. Churches have been criticized for not adopting business methods. Harrison states:

The American Institute of Management, which conducted the survey, was generally critical of religious groups in this country because "viewed against the background of modern business corporations, the management practices of religious organizations are appallingly archaic." (1959, p. 5)

A similar study of the Catholic Church, sometimes referred to by members of the clergy as the "G. M. study of the Church," recommended that the Pope delegate more authority to his subordinates (decentralization is good for business), and that the Church create reserve funds and keep its budget in the black.[11] Students of hospitals have similarly claimed that "industrial techniques can be transferred" (Andrew, 1955; Greenblatt, York, and Brown, 1955, p. 21).

Ministers frequently complain about the lack of insight into the

10. For such lists, see Gebb (1948, pp. 267-84); Dimock (1959, pp. 194-95). Leadership is almost always characterized without reference to the context in which it develops. Cf. Stogdill (1948, pp. 35-71). See also Ginzberg (1955).

11. We would suggest that it is frequently desirable for the finances of a normative organization to be in the "red," and all its reserve committed, since the ensuing crisis motivates contributors to increase their donations. Whatever the value of a balanced budget in private business or a national economy, it is dysfunctional for recruiting resources to normative organizations.

differences between a church and a business which businessmen reveal when they assume that every organization can be run in basically the same way—their way.

We aren't able to get enough of the upper-class members; they won't spend time and aren't interested. We also find that they aren't able to adjust their outlook to church work, that is, they are accustomed to giving orders and having them followed out. You have to depend much more on persuasion in the church; these people treat the church as just a part of their business life, that it's like the bank and all you do is say what is to be done and then you forget it. They don't have a view of what the position of the church is.[12]

The high representation of business leaders and the low representation of labor leaders on the boards of hospitals, schools, colleges, universities, voluntary associations, and other nonutilitarian organizations in the United States reflects in part the political reality of the communities in which these organizations operate and which they serve.[13] But to some degree it also reflects the assumption that every organization can be run like a business.

(c) Our position is that the effectiveness of the mobile executive is limited to compliance areas rather than administrative or technological boundaries.[14] As long as mobility takes place between positions in organizational units or organizations which have a similar compliance structure, we would expect comparatively little loss of effectiveness. If, on the other hand, mobility requires transfer from one kind of compliance structure to another, considerable changes in behavior, orientation, or effectiveness of the executive are to be expected. An executive who was highly effective in running a steel mill may be quite ineffective in running a professional organization,

12. Interview with the head minister of a wealthy Congregational Church in New England. From a study of Protestant denominations currently in progress at the Bureau of Applied Social Research, Columbia University, under the direction of Robert E. Mitchell.

13. For analysis of the role of business in the control of hospitals, universities, social agencies, social clubs, schools, and other organizations, as well as some statistics, see E. C. Hughes (1937); Rose (1952); and Form (1959). Control of universities from this viewpoint is studied by McGrath (1936) and by Beck (1947, pp. 60-61).

14. None of the well-known studies of business leaders supplies data directly relevant to the problem at hand. Most studies focus on inter-generational mobility, which has no relevance to our problem. Susanne Keller (1953) supplies some data on inter-company and inter-industry mobility, but industies are not classified according to the kind of control typically used.

such as an engineering firm, and an executive who was quite ineffective in running a steel mill may prove to be just the man for the engineering position. Many officers who are quite effective in running production will do much less well in running a public relations department.[15]

Since we did not find any data directly bearing upon our proposition, we attempted to collect some of it.[16] The names of thirty-two members of organizational elites who had *previously* held positions in military organizations, were picked at random from daily newspapers. Their military positions were classified as "combat" or "desk" positions. Their subsequent civil positions were classified as "externalists" or "instrumentalists." "Externalist" positions require handling external relations of the organization, such as public relations, labor relations, and serving as contact man in Washington; they also include the top positions in universities and voluntary associations provided the main task is external (e.g., raising funds). "Instrumentalist" positions include only direct administration of production and expert staff positions in production, finance, marketing, and the like.

Combat posts, we suggest, require more normative power than desk posts, and externalist roles require more normative-power than instrumental roles. Hence we expected that military commanders who had made their career and gained their reputation mainly as combat leaders would be more likely to become externalists than instrumentalists, and that military leaders who had mainly desk posts would be more likely to become instrumentalists than externalists.[17] Note

15. A study of 470 navy officers by Stodgill, Shartle, Wherry and Jaynes (1955) indirectly supports our point. The study shows that certain command roles, in *different* types of organizations, are rather similar in the composition of aptitudes and skills they require. Positions are characterized by the relative weight various analytical components, such as decision making, task supervision, coordination, and personal administration, have. Assuming that these differences are related to differences in compliance, one could interpret this study as suggesting that certain forms of mobility among positions in different types of organization lead to a more effective allocation of personnel than mechanical rotation among different positions in the same organization, since a person effective in carrying out one kind of role will be more effective in carrying out other roles of the same kind than other kinds of roles.

16. A study of 222 retired generals by Reissman (1956) supplies much information about their military background and present positions. The material presented, however, does not allow a test of the association between military and civilian positions with similar and different compliance patterns.

17. Ginzberg (1957, pp. 16-17) pointed out the difficulties of using combat officers for jobs in Washington or industry.

that unlike most studies of inter-organizational mobility from one type of organization to another, we examined mobility from one type of *sub*organization to the *same* analytical subunit in *another type* of organization. This enables us to control for compliance differences in each organizational type.

Table XVI-1—Mobility from Military to Civilian Positions

PAST MILITARY POSTS	PRESENT CIVILIAN POSTS	
	Externalists (High Normative)	Instrumentalists (Low Normative)
Combat (High Normative)	11	1
Desk (Low Normative)	4	8

Of the 32 persons, 24 were classified as either externalists or instrumentalists in their present position, and as either combat leaders or predominantly desk men in terms of their military career and source of reputation. As Table XVI-1 shows, those who held combat positions were much more likely to hold externalist rather than instrumental civilian positions. This finding is in line with our hypothesis, since combat and externalist positions have similar compliance requirements; both require more normative power than desk and instrumentalist positions, which give comparatively less weight to normative controls and greater weight to utilitarian controls. As we would expect, then, those who had a desk position in their military career were twice as likely as combat officers to hold a less normative, more utilitarian position in their civilian career. Five had such a mixed military career that they were classified as "compound" types. All of these five also had a compound civilian career—that is, they moved back and forth between instrumentalist and externalist positions in civilian life. These cases also support our hypothesis concerning the relationship between compliance specialization and mobility: Less specialized actors are better able, both in the military and the civilian domain, to move from one compliance structure to another. For three cases the post-military career could not be determined with sufficient precision to allow classification. This limited material seems to illustrate our hypothesis and to lend to it some support (the significance level of Table XVI-1, computed by Fisher's Exact Test, is .0046).[18]

In sum, the first approach we have described sees executives as "specialists," the second as "generalists" in knowledge about a particular type of organizational output. We suggest that most top executives are generalists in the performances they can supervise, but specialists in the type of compliance they utilize in doing so. In other words, it seems to us that *most executives are more effective in one type of compliance structure than in the other two*. It may be true that all executive positions require the ability to work "through" people, but there are different ways of doing that—differences in the appeals which can be made to lower participants, and in the sanctions which can be applied to them.

Compliance specialization of executives is less apparent than performance specialization, in part because there are only three common types of compliance structure while there are many hundreds of performance specializations. An executive can move among positions and cross many administrative boundaries without changing to a different *type* of compliance structure. In this sense the specialization of control agents, of executives, is broader—permits more horizontal mobility without loss of effectiveness—than does the performance specialization of skilled workers and experts.

EXECUTIVE SPECIALIZATION: POSITIONS AND PERSONALITIES— Our discussion of compliance specialization rests on the following assumption: that in addition to positions requiring different types of compliance, there are actors who differ in the type of compliance they can effectively achieve and sustain, and that these individuals tend to be recruited into positions requiring the compliance pattern for which they are suited. We expect most individuals to be more effective in controlling lower participants in one way than in the other two ways, since each type of compliance seems to require a distinctive set of personality characteristics, aptitudes, and inclinations. One actor is unlikely to have the characteristics required for more than one type of compliance position.

The two distributions, of actors and positions, are related in such a way that effectiveness is supported, though never maximized, because the mechanisms which distribute persons to positions—self-

18. A full test of the hypothesis would require evidence concerning differences in efficiency among the various executives.

selection and organizational selection—are imperfect. One problem lies in the difficulty of determining precisely the compliance aptitudes of actors and the compliance requirements of positions, even when these are perceived as important criteria for selection. Other barriers to effective allocation result from the interference of particularistic criteria, such as internal political factors (e.g., *X* would be effective in position *Y*, but this would endanger the hold of the present elite over the organization), external political considerations (e.g., party affiliation), ethnic and racial factors, friendships, and the like.[18a] Nevertheless, although actors do have compliance preferences and aptitudes, they are to some degree flexible. That is, some role adaptation takes place. (By *role adaptation* we mean changes in a person which occur after he is assigned for long periods to a role which initially did not match his need-dispositions. It refers to adaptation *to* the role, not *of* the role.)

The relationship between personality types and vocations is fairly well established. Goode and Cornish (forthcoming) review a large number of studies which show personality differences among people attracted to various professions.[19] MacKinnon and Centers (1956, p. 617) showed marked differences in authoritarianism among various occupational strata. The percentage of authoritarians varied as follows: 50 per cent for large business; 23 per cent for professionals; 33 per cent for small business; 59 per cent for white-collar workers; 51-86 per cent for blue-collar workers. Applying these findings to an organization, for example a business corporation, one would expect to find authoritarianism high among the lower ranks; comparatively low in the middle ranks, where professionals are concentrated; and high among the top ranks.[20]

Other studies point directly to differences in personality structure between actors holding different organizational ranks. Argyris (1953,

18a. Dalton (1951) analyzes the careers of 226 managers and shows the effect of "background" factors such as ethnic origin, religious and political affiliation, and participation in voluntary associations on their career patterns.

19. Some insight into personality differences among the personnel of schools, universities, and churches can be gained from a study which compares students of theology, physics, and teacher-trainees (Stern, Stein, and Bloom, 1956, esp. pp. 139-60). See also Coates and Pellegrin (1957).

20. Levinson, Gilbert, Pine, Carstairs, and Heron found systematic differences of this kind among aides in mental hospitals. No rank differences were studied. See reports of their studies in Greenblatt, Levinson, and Williams (1957, pp. 197-230). On the concept of authoritarianism see Adorno, Frenkel-Brunswik, Levinson, and Sanford (1950).

pp. 50-55), for example, found that personnel lower in rank tended to be more submissive, passive, dependent, and subordinate than those higher in rank.[21] Warner and Abegglen have also related personality characteristics, such as single-mindedness and tension level, to rank (1955, pp. 72-82).

But there is very little systematic evidence that would allow us to relate differences in personality structure to different control positions in various types of compliance structure. We would expect, for example, that individuals who have leadership qualities, such as persuasive power, vision, ability to verbalize, and the like, would be more inclined to seek a career in normative than in utilitarian organizations, and to prefer a utilitarian organization to a coercive one, since these organizations differ in the opportunities they offer for satisfaction of the need-dispositions associated with leadership qualities.

A study which illustrates the kind of evidence needed is that by Pine and Levinson (1957). They show that the more authoritarian the personality of an aide in a mental hospital (as measured by an F-scale), the more custodial (i.e., coercive) and the less "humanistic" (i.e., normative) his orientation to patients and their control is likely to be (ibid., pp. 209-17).

We would expect to find officers or formal leaders of the three types of organization to score differently on a scale measuring authoritarianism. For example, authoritarian predispositions among prison guards and wardens are probably quite high, lower among foremen and corporation executives, and lowest for leaders of democratic parties, teachers, professionals, and some other elites of typical normative organizations. Again, there seems to be no evidence relevant to this proposition.[22]

There are probably many other systematic differences in the personalities of actors recruited to power positions in various compliance structures, but these remain to be established. Similarly, actors in different types of organization seem to differ systematically

21. See also Henry (1949, pp. 286-91); and De Coster (1951). Cohen and Cohen (1951, p. 53) show that top executives, unlike others, lack the ability to manipulate, depend on, and please superiors. Frank (1946) showed that sergeants are more "sociable" than lower-ranking enlisted men.
22. The relation between "democratic" leadership and moral involvement has been shown in the well-known study of different styles of leadership (Lewin, Lippitt, and White, 1939, pp. 271-99). The author (1958b, pp. 35-39) has pointed out the cultural limitations of the findings and conclusions of these leadership studies and cited some evidence from various studies to this effect.

in status characteristics such as education, socioeconomic status, age when entering the position, and the like.[23] We would, for example, expect the average education and socioeconomic status of prison elites to be lower than that of elites in industry.[24] But the very existence of such differences, and their import for the study of compliance if they exist, are yet to be established. The central point for us is that because of various processes, such as self- and organizational selection, there is an association between compliance positions and personality types. This, except for the flexibility due to role adaptation, defines the limits of effective mobility.

Compliance Specialization, Control Combinations, and "Broadening"

In addition to inter- and intra-organizational mobility of executives, compliance specialization affects two other central aspects of elite functioning. It influences the ways in which control positions are effectively combined, and the ways in which executives are socialized to top positions—a process referred to in the literature as "broadening."

CONTROL COMBINATION—It is quite frequent for one member of an elite to hold more than one control position at the same time, often in more than one organization. But these combinations are not random. Some administrators are under pressure to diversify their positions—for example, business leaders are expected by their company, and often by their occupational subculture, to hold some position in church or voluntary associations; but when there are no such pressures, actors tend to combine positions which are similar in their compliance requirements.

Teachers, for example, who tend to have a normative compliance personality, tend to be officers in other normative organizations much more often than in non-normative ones. A study of the community activities in which 2870 teachers are officers or sponsors shows that although only 0.2 per cent have such a role in economic activities or organizations, more than 50 per cent are officers or sponsors of

23. Differences among higher and lower ranks are much more often studied than differences among the controlling ranks in various types of organization. For differences in social origin and socio-cultural status among ranks in industry see Coates and Pellegrin (1956, pp. 121-26; 1957); Lipset and Bendix (1959, p. 185).

24. Three fifths of the executives studied by Keller (1953, p. 97) graduated from college. 76 per cent went to college and 57 per cent graduated in the sample studied by Warner and Abegglen (1955, p. 35). Comparable information about prison elites is required.

religious, fraternal, professional organizations, or other normative organizations (Greenhoe, 1941, p. 65).[24a]

COMPLIANCE SPECIALIZATION AND "BROADENING"—"Broadening" is a process of anticipatory socialization in which executives are prepared for top positions by rotation among various control positions. It is common both in business corporations and in military organizations (Newman, 1951, pp. 353-55). The purpose of this process is to reduce the specialization of the executive in order to prepare him for the top, highly generalized, command position. Rotation breaks up his narrow outlook and commitment to one subunit; it extends his experience, insight, and information about subunits other than the one from which he is recruited; and it develops in him a broader perspective.[25]

The process of broadening is usually analyzed as an educational one in which the executive expands his knowledge about performances and gains experience with the work conducted in various departments. No less important, we suggest, is the role of rotation in reducing compliance specialization, by increasing the executive's ability to employ different kinds of power or "leadership styles" in different situations. Such broadening is necessary since the top positions, unlike other elite positions, do not require specialization in sustaining one mode of control or another. Since the top executive is in command of all the organizational subunits, whatever their compliance structure, his position often requires flexibility in shifting from one leadership style to another. He must be able to "get along" with both research people and labor representatives; with both line and staff; with both creative people and bureaucratic-submissive personalities.

Still, following our earlier argument, we would expect complete broadening to be very rare. It is also unnecessary, since for most types of organization (except dual structures) there is one dominant form of compliance, which means that there is one form of compliance the top executive is most frequently called upon to maintain (cf. Metcalf and Urwick, 1940, pp. 260-66).

Two conclusions follow from this discussion of the broadening

24a. Other items include: 5.6 per cent, leisure pursuits; 13.6 per cent, professional associations; 9.8 per cent, youth groups; and "other organizations."

25. The need for systematic broadening has been well demonstrated. The large majority of executives tested in a situation in which a reward was supplied for taking the company-wide perspective, nevertheless took a departmental view (Dearborn and Simon, 1958).

process. First, rotating among departments is not enough. Rotation among those which differ in their compliance structure is required. Thus, little is accomplished when a personnel man is moved to a public relations department whose compliance structure is similar to that of the personnel department. Movement between production and personnel, between marketing and research and development, or between labor relations and finance, are more effective for the broadening of compliance skills.

Second, those positions which share the compliance pattern predominating in the organization are more likely to be sources of recruitment for top executives.[26] This would suggest that effective broadening requires more time to be spent in positions whose compliance structure is the same as or similar to that which predominates in the particular organization. Of course, inclusion of some positions which differ in their compliance structure is essential.

To sum up: Organizations may have multiple tasks, and tasks tend to differ in their compliance requirements; hence the need for compliance specialization. One major form of compliance specialization is the concomitant division of compliance, in which tasks requiring different compliance structures are delegated to distinct organizations, or to subunits of one organization. Compliance specialization is required not only in organizational positions but also among personnel recruited to these positions. Therefore we expect that in effective organizations, inter- and intra-organizational mobility of elites will tend to be limited to positions having a similar compliance structure. Compliance specialization provides a basis for the study of elite mobility, for the analysis of combined control positions, and for the understanding of such processes as the training and education of organizational elites in general, and of broadening in particular.

SUCCESSIVE DIVISION OF COMPLIANCE

Concomitant division of labor and compliance is by far the more common method of controlling tasks which differ in their compliance

26. Newcomer (1955) reports that out of 383 executives who reached top positions, 175 came from operations and production; 72 from finance; 58 from sales and advertising, but only one from personnel. None is listed as having been recruited from research and development (*ibid.*, p. 107; see also p. 92). W. H. Scott *et al.* (1956) report that of the 12 department managers in the factory they studied in 1935, only 2 came from the laboratory or office. By 1954 the factory had 21 department managers, but still only 2 were recruited from the laboratory or office. Other department managers rose through the line or were recruited to management positions from outside the factory (*ibid.*, pp. 75 and 85).

requirements. A second solution of this dilemma, less frequently encountered but of much theoretical interest, is the successive division of tasks and compliance. The whole organizational unit focuses on one task at a time, and emphasizes one form of compliance at a time, but changes its tasks and compliance structure after relatively short periods.[27] Specialization during each period allows the unit to avoid the neutralizing effects of competing modes of compliance, though obviously the shift from one time period to the next has a price in resources. In terms of personnel, for example, this procedure requires either a high turnover or frequent resocialization. We shall see, however, that there are mechanisms which reduce this price and that for some organizational goals a successive structure is the most effective type.

There are three major forms which successive changes of tasks and compliance may take: seasonal, shifting, and intermittent. The three types differ in the *number of activities* which are added or omitted; the activities affected may vary from very few to almost all the organization undertakes. In addition, the *pace of activities* tends to change at the same time. Changes in both range and pace are, we suggest, associated with changes in the *compliance structure.* These changes may range from a shift in emphasis from one compliance pattern to another, to the substitution of a completely different compliance structure.

The extent of change in organizational activities is related to the extent of change in the compliance structure. On both counts changes are smallest in seasonal succession; larger in shifting succession; and largest in intermittent succession.

Seasonal Succession

Seasonal changes in amount and pace of activity and in compliance orientation are required by most organizations. The changes in amount and pace are often comparatively small, and the expansion of activities as a rule takes place in one limited period, which is followed by a considerably longer period when activites are normal. Typical examples are department stores in the period preceding

27. Barnard (1938) points out that time as a basis for division of labor and specialization has not gained sufficient attention. He states: "Specialization of organizations with respect to time is one of the most obvious bases of division of labor in continuous-service enterprises . . . it has been much overlooked in the general consideration of specialization. . . ." (*Ibid.,* pp. 130-31).

Christmas; the Bureau of Internal Revenue around the first ot April; school administrations during registration and commencement exercises; the staffs of some political parties before elections and during conventions; and single-crop farms in the harvest season. All are periods of increased and accelerated output.

The change in amount and pace of activity is, as a rule, accompanied by some change in compliance. Its nature depends to a large extent on the quality of lower participants' involvement when the period of expansion and acceleration begins. If lower participants are positively involved, we would expect an increased emphasis on normative compliance. If they are alienated, this period will require stronger emphasis on non-normative controls.

There are several reasons why increases in amount and pace of activity tend to increase normative compliance when lower participants are already committed to the organization. During the hectic period employees feel that the significance of their performance has increased, and that their superiors treat them with more consideration; tasks become less routinized, either because employees are temporarily assigned to new jobs or because their regular jobs are "enlarged"; an atmosphere of excitement prevails, which makes individuals more susceptible to normative appeals; even the increased work pace may avoid dull idleness and contribute to the atmosphere of urgent and significant activity; participants who are lowest in rank are put into control positions, in charge of temporary employees. This assignment increases their sense of the significance of their work and of themselves, and enables them to delegate the less rewarding parts of their tasks to others. The general effect of all these factors is to increase commitment to the organization and hence permits the organization to rely more on normative powers.

When lower participants are alienated, the same factors have the opposite effect. The increased work load and pace are perceived as increased deprivations, and therefore alienation increases. The period is considered one of "emergency" for the organization or its management, but not for the employees. On the contrary, it is considered an opportune time to put pressure on management, for instance to obtain wage improvements through threat of a strike. New assignments and changes in routinized tasks are considered a source of annoyance, which disrupt the less demanding routine. Increased pressure to accelerate performance further increases alienation. The general effect of all these factors is that remunerative, not normative, sanctions have to be especially emphasized.[28]

Once the occasion for the seasonal increase in activity is over, the compliance structure tends to return to its "normal" state. Here two periods have to be distinguished, one of transition and one of normality. First, a period of transition takes place. These are the first days or weeks after the high-activity period has been terminated. The special conditions affecting involvement disappear. Work becomes routinized again, the pace is slowed down, the power of lower participants is reduced because temporary workers leave, and so on. This is also a period of high fatigue following the increased effort of the earlier period, and a period when awareness of fatigue increases.

Assuming that the days of high activity were days of higher commitment, then these are the days in which work seems most meaningless and frustrating, since the disenchantment of returning to routine and to more pronounced utilitarian compliance increases alienation. With time, this heightened feeling of frustration disappears; a wave of vacations, absenteeism, and slow work reduces the fatigue; and employees again get used to their routine jobs. Then the "normal" period sets in. This period lasts until preparation for the next high-activity period starts.

The nature of compliance during the transition period is determined in part by differences in compliance between the high-activity and the "normal" periods. If the high-activity period was one of strong emphasis on normative compliance, the transition period will be relatively less normative. If, on the other hand, the period of high activity was one of increased alienation, the transition period will tend to be one of gradual relief and of return to the "normal" level of alienation and control. It is difficult to predict whether the transition period will be more or less normative than the normal period.

Shifting Structures

Some organizational goals require the performance of two quite different tasks at different time periods and in different situations. Unlike the seasonal changes discussed above, serving two such different tasks requires a much more encompassing change in the

---

28. Assuming that one can control for the effects of the tighter employment market in these seasons.

amount, pace, and even substance of activity as well as the nature of compliance.[29] Often these changes are less predictable and less institutionalized than seasonal ones.

Military organizations supply a typical example. Their tasks and compliance structures in peace and war are so different that for many purposes, especially static comparison, it is more convenient to regard them as two distinct types of organization. This, of course, will not do when we examine changes in compliance and the division of labor in a military organization over time. The tasks of military organizations in peace and war differ enormously in scope. The United States Army, for example, had 267,767 men in uniform in 1940, compared with 8,266,373 in 1945 (Uyeki, 1958, p. 17). In peacetime, the military task is maintenance of preparedness over a long period. This task requires highly routinized activities, such as watching radar screens, guarding borders, patrolling seas or skies; the constant repainting of ships and barracks; training and retraining, polish and drill. Compliance in this period tends to be quite coercive for draftees and highly utilitarian for the permanent staff. Combat situations, on the other hand, require comparatively few routine activities, but they demand highly depriving and dramatic efforts. The fact that these two kinds of tasks require different compliance structures has been pointed out above (Chapter IV). Once the war is over and no new one is anticipated in the "practical future," [30] the task and compliance structures shift again to the routine, non-normative, state. Thus, one organization has two task-compliance structures which exist successively, one at a time.

A similar pattern of change exists in many labor unions. The goals of labor unions, particularly business unions, require performance of routine activities, such as processing minor grievances and collecting dues, most of the time. For most members the performances required by these tasks are few and far between. Utilitarian

---

29. Simmel (1955) discussed shifting structures of various organizations: "Take, for instance, the well-known differences between the peacetime organization and the wartime organization of the North American Indians. Or take the London tailors who in the first quarter of the nineteenth century had a very different organization, one for peace and one for war with their employers." (p. 88) Note that Simmel was interested in a different aspect of shifting structure than the one focused on the present discussion. He was not interested in changing compliance structures, but in the change in political representation. He points out, for example, that in "peace-time," a tailors' organization was democratic; in time of strife with employers, it was autocratic (*ibid.*).

30. The part of the future the organization considers it rational to provide for in its planning and maintenance activities.

compliance, coupled with some normative powers and concomitants, is quite satisfactory for this period.

All this changes once a strike takes place or is anticipated. More participation at union meetings is required; the meetings become much less routinized; members are expected to picket the factory, to share in decisions, to vote frequently, and so on (Hiller, 1928; Karsh, 1958). Since loyalty to the union and its goals becomes an important issue, union leaders increase the amount and pace of normative activities to build up members' loyalty, their moral involvement in the union, their committment to its general goals and to its specific goals in the particular strike. This is the period in which the latent commitments of many inactive members are activated.[31] Once the strike is over, the union tends to shift back to its routine, relatively utilitarian, task-compliance structure.

The war or strike period is often followed by a short period of considerable normative activity in which the strife and its consequences for the organization are assessed.[32] Some activity of this kind takes place also at the end of the peak period in seasonal structures, but they seem to be fewer and their impact less.

It is of interest to note that shifting structures often require changes in command, which supports our earlier point that most members of the elite are highly effective in only one type of compliance structure. On the other hand, organizational continuity and the morale of elite members who served the organization during the less rewarding routine period make simple replacement of elites with each shift in structure dysfunctional. The strains between the old-time professional officer, and the officer who joined the military only during the war, are in part a reflection of this dilemma. Organizations develop various mechanisms to accommodate to compliance changes without a complete change in elites. In the case of unions, for example, high-ranking elites come to help in organizing a major strike, and thus supply the additional leadership needed without removing the local leaders from their positions (Knowles, 1952, p. 40). In combat organizations, a large increase in activity mitigates the strain; there are enough positions for both old-timers

31. For a characterization of this type of union member, referred to as "crisis activists," see Tagliacozza and Seidman (1956, pp. 549-50). See also Miller and Young (1955).

32. In terms of phase-movement theory, this is the latency phase in which the "quality" or pattern of the system is changed (Parsons and Smelser, 1956, pp. 44-51).

and new leaders. Positions can be allocated so that at least some of the old-timers who cannot adjust to the new structure will be side-tracked until the end of the war. Assignment to a training base is a typical solution. Finally, one would expect organizations with shifting structures to seek for their power positions persons who, relatively speaking, are more flexible in their compliance style than the average elite member, thus reducing the need for replacement.[33]

In some shifting structures, in addition to changes in tasks, compliance, and elites, we find changes in other organizational patterns as well. Simmel pointed out the shift from democratic to authoritarian political procedures in wartime (1955, p. 88). The author observed *kibbutzim* on the frontiers of Israel shifting from a work organization to a defense system within minutes when attacked. Not only tasks and compliance changed radically, but elites also changed; branch managers (*kibbutz* "foremen") became privates, and their subordinated workers became commanding officers. Moreover, the loose, quite uncoordinated, work-by-branch structure shifted to a highly centralized, military combat organization. A short while after the military clash was over, the old work structure was reactivated.

Intermittent Structures

Seasonal changes in activities and compliance are limited; shifting structures entail considerable changes; but the most extensive changes take place in organizations whose tasks require intermittent activity only. These are organizations or organizational units which are deployed and then "folded up" till their period of activity arrives again. This technique enables the organization not only to save the resources that would be required to maintain continuous operation, but also to rely relatively heavily on normative compliance. This is true because, although the organization "exists" for a long period of time, compliance is required only sporadically, for relatively short periods, and for the control of comparatively unroutinized activities. These, we have seen, are conditions that enhance the creation and maintenance of highly normative compliance; they are one set of conditions which allow organizations to be charismatic in the long run.

Intermittent structures are maintained by organizations which are activated only once a year, such as the March of Dimes (Sills, 1957, 158ff.) and organizations which arrange events such as festivals,

33. On elite-shifts in unions as analogous to changes in military command, see Steuben (1950). See also Tannenbaum and Georgopoulos (1957, pp. 49-50).

exhibitions, and conventions. Summer camps which are reopened each year are another typical example.[34] While some organizations are more or less completely disbanded, others have intermittent subunits, the rest of the organization maintaining a quite continuous flow of activities. Summer schools in universities, and reserve units of military organizations, are examples of intermittent subunits.

Some political parties seem to have at least a partial intermittent structure, with high activity in election years and almost complete quiescence in off-years, though parties differ considerably in this respect. Many are highly intermittent, but some—especially radical parties—are so active in nonelection years that they might better be considered seasonal structures which expand when political harvest time approaches. Factors other than the program of the party (e.g., its radicalism) can affect its place on the continuum of seasonal-intermittent structures (the underlying dimension is the ratio of activities terminated to those continuously maintained). These factors include the frequency with which elections take place; the number of elections (local, state, national) in which the same party organization participates; and the way the elections are scheduled and their relative significance for the party.

A vivid description of an intermittent structure, the dispersal of a unit and its reactivation, is supplied by Berkman's report, "Life Aboard an Armed Coast Guard Ship" (1946). When the boat arrives at the home base and the sailors take shore leave, the unit as a functioning collectivity disappears. The sailors leave the boat as individuals, joining other collectivities such as their families and neighborhoods. A small subunit is left behind to guard the ship, but it has no power center of its own; it is a part of the harbor defense. All this does not mean that the unit has completely disappeared. It is merely dormant. When the leave is over, or, if necessary, when the sailors are recalled, the unit is rapidly reactivated. Dormant role expectations, informal ties, and traditions are all activated rapidly and relied upon for the operation of the ship. Such a unit is quite different from one which is acting as a unit for the first time.

CHARACTERISTICS OF INTERMITTENT STRUCTURES—Intermittent structures have the following characteristics in common:

1. Their tasks require a *very considerable change in amount and*

34. A vivid description of such a camp's organizational and control problems is included in Herman Wouk's *Marjorie Morningstar*. Moss Hart, *Act One*, supplies another account of such a camp.

pace of activity. Most intermittent structures require almost no activity over long periods of time and a high level of performance over short time intervals.

2. In terms of *compliance,* intermittent structures do not move from a coercive or a utilitarian to a normative structure, as shifting structures do, but must make the transition from a dormant state (with little compliance) to an active state with (in most cases) a primarily normative compliance structure.

3. Intermittent structures apply *various reinforcing structures and processes to maintain the commitment of their lower participants in the dormant period.* Their function resembles that of anticipatory socialization. When the organization is reactivated, expectations are already internalized and the unit can be brought to operation in a short period of time with a minimum of effort and secondary controls.

REINFORCING STRUCTURES. The most significant and most frequently used reinforcing structure is the maintenance of an *active subunit* in the dormant period. This unit includes at least the following roles:

1. *Elite roles.* Elites plan the activation period and the activity period, initiate activation and control it until the full elite takes over, and review basic policy decisions during the inactive period. These elites include the top officers, such as commanders of reserve units, heads of summer camps, and directors of summer schools.

2. *Clerical roles.* Clerks carry out the paper work, which is part of the communication system (see below) and which permits analysis of the unit's performance during the active period as well as reassignment of personnel. They also maintain the documents in which the "formal structure" of the unit is recorded, including its formal allocation of tasks, power, lines of communication, rules, and regulations.

3. *Maintenance roles.* Some care of the unit's facilities and tools must usually be maintained while the unit itself is dispersed.

4. *Communication roles.* These roles are required for reinforcement of the dormant social structure and for the activation process. For example, students have to be attracted to the summer school; soldiers must be called to the flag.

It should be pointed out that although these positions are most clearly developed and segregated in military organizations, essentially the same roles are fulfilled in universities when summer schools are organized, by enterprises or associations which have an annual summer camp, and, for that matter, by any intermittent structure. This is not to say that each organization has a different set of persons for each set of roles. Often the activities required for all roles occupy only one person part-time. Reserve units are often "represented" in the dormant period by one part-time officer and one clerk (and the vital filing cabinet). Summer camps in the winter are often the part-time job of one person.

The relationship between the intermittent unit and the larger (parent) organization to which it belongs is of interest since some or all of the intermittent unit's minimum roles can be delegated to some nonintermittent subunit of the parent organization. Thus, for example, summer schools in universities disappear almost completely during the fall semester. Their facilities are maintained by the university and their communications are handled by the ordinary offices. Still, a short period after the university itself awakens from its summer dormancy and overcomes the peak activity of registration and initiation of the new academic year, the director of the summer school and the departmental representatives prepare the summer school catalogue, communicate with prospective teachers, schedule classes, and so on. These activities in the dormant period, together with the university regulations and traditions concerning summer schools, determine to a considerable degree the performance of the summer school in the active period. Similarly, reserve units draw on regular military units for maintenance and communication functions. The March of Dimes is reactivated and helped by its parent organization, the Foundation for Infantile Paralysis. The Society for Ethical Culture performs the same functions for the Encampment for Citizenship.[35] Only a few intermittent structures rely completely on a subunit of their own which remains active while the other subunits are dormant. Whether the subunit which maintains the intermittent organization during dormant periods is part of the parent organization or autonomous determines whether an organizational unit is completely or only partially intermittent.

REINFORCING PROCESSES. The active subunit in the dormant period controls several processes which reinforce the expectation structure and culture of the intermittent unit. These processes give inter-

35. A full analysis of the impact of the Encampment for Citizenship on its members long after they leave the camp, including measures of the effect of various reinforcing activities, is included in Hyman, Wright, and Hopkins (forthcoming).

mittent units their unique social characteristics. Without them, each reactivation of an intermittent social unit would be very much like initiating a new social unit.

The reinforcing processes which operate in the dormant period include the following:

1. *Communications* from the active subunit to the dispersed participants. These communications are directed either at maintaining integration (e.g., a newsletter) or at preparing the reactivation.

2. *Short periods of activation* during the dormant period. Training days for reserve units are a typical example. According to the Israeli law, for example, citizens are called for one day's training a month.[36] Military personnel tend to see these training periods as instrumental situations, in which the use of weapons, tactics, and other elements of military training are introduced or rehearsed. Actually, these periods are often too short to accomplish much from this viewpoint, and they serve mainly an expressive function. The unit is reintegrated and expectations are reinforced by the activation. It is much like a collective tribal ceremony in which the various segments of the tribe meet each other and the leaders in ritual activity. This is not to suggest that instrumental orientations and skills need no reinforcement in long dormancy periods, or that technological and organizational innovations cannot be introduced in these periods. But these instrumental goals require longer periods of activation than do the expressive ones. In the Israeli reserves, for example, in addition to the monthly meeting of the reserve for one day, which is mainly expressive, there is an annual training period of about a month (*ibid*).

The expressive function of short activation periods is best illustrated by the fact that other intermittent organizations, which have little need to train and retrain, also activate their units for short times during the dormant period. There are winter parties for summer camp participants and personnel, and summer parties for winter resort participants and personnel. The following opening item of a summer camp winter newsletter reveals a considerable awareness of the sociological functions of these events:

There can be no better way to greet you after more than several months of squaring away at a new school term, following our happy farewells at the close of camp last August, than to summon all and sundry of you to our 10th Annual REUNION. . . . The date is set—December 20, at 2

36. *Laws of the State of Israel,* Vol. 3, p. 115.

o'clock. The Place—The beautiful North Ballroom of the Hotel New Yorker, 34th Street and 8th Avenue.

There will be some songs, some music, maybe dancing, not too many speeches, some movies of last summer's doings, some refreshments—but above all else, there will be the sheer delight of being together once more to chat, reminisce and laugh together again. Because thinking for a moment in retrospect of our glad and sad farewells at the buses and the train last August—was there ever a nicer bunch of gals and guys than the SASKATCHEWANITES of last summer? . . . We have heard from quite a few of you and there can be no doubt of it—we are all looking forward to the grand 10th ANNUAL REUNION. (*Camp Saskatchewan Tidings,* p. 1, n.d.)

The rest of the newsletter, like many others, is taken up with personal news about the various participants. The equivalent of village gossip, it has the function of sustaining the "we" feeling of the dispersed group. It also transforms memories of past summers to expectations about future ones.

3. Much of the reinforcement process is carried by the *regular flow of interaction* in the social units in which the participants are dispersed during the dormancy period, without the organization's initiating or directing them. Such reinforcement takes place as long as participants in intermittent units are recognized as such in the dormancy period, both by members of the units and by others. Thus, for example, when a ball player who spends the winter as a bartender is asked to discuss his experience as a player and thus wins the respect of his listeners, his commitment to the team, its culture and traditions, is reinforced. When two counselors of a summer camp meet in the winter, either accidentally or because social relations developed during the active period have been extended to the dormancy period, and discuss—often in a romantic light—last summer's experience and the forthcoming summer, their involvements and expectations are reinforced. It is for this reason that status symbols and social activities related to the intermittent unit are so significant for smooth activation of the unit after a dormancy period.

INTERMITTENT STRUCTURES AND COMPLIANCE—Intermittent activities have one obvious function. They save resources. What is less obvious is that intermittent structures are especially suited to one type of compliance structure. Coercive organizations never exhibit intermittent structures; utilitarian organizations occasionally do; whereas normative organizations are frequently intermittent in structure.

The reason coercive organizations are unlikely to develop an intermittent structure is obvious. It lies in the negative character of their goal: They must prevent certain activities from occurring. Since the assumption is that their lower participants have not, as a rule, internalized commitments to order goals, suspending control activities for any time interval would undermine the goal. Inmates would escape from prisons and correctional institutions, concentration camps, and camps for prisoners of war.

Normative compliance is relatively easy to maintain for short periods of time and for unroutinized activities; it is difficult to maintain for continuous and long-run activities. Weber made this point when he discussed the instability of pure charismatic relationships. Routinization of charisma means an increase in utilitarian controls (salary and established career-avenues are the two new rewards most emphasized by Weber). Therefore, there is a basic contradiction between the functional requirements of highly normative structures and those of organizations. Many of the most normatively oriented social units, such as social, political, religious, and youth movements, family and peer groups, are not organizations. Still, some organizations succeed in developing and maintaining a highly normative compliance structure, often by means of an intermittent structure.

Many normatively controlled activities do not require continuous performance. Inmates have to be kept in a prison twenty-four hours a day, every day of the week; workers have to be controlled five or six days a week, eight hours a day; but parishioners come to church only once a week, for a few hours, or less often. The same holds for members of most political organizations, such as parties and normative unions, and for members of voluntary associations and social movements.[37] It appears, then, that there is a close association

37. The distribution of participation over time poses some interesting and largely unexplored questions for the comparative study of normative organizations. Holding constant the various determinants of participation often studied, such as class-status, education, sex, and age, it would be of interest to see which organizations draw more participation ("attendance"). There may well be a limited number of established participation patterns. An obvious pattern in the one followed by *loyal* participants, who come to almost every event. Another is that of *intermittent* participants, who come once in three or four times, "to keep in touch." Then there are the *big-event* participants, and probably some other types.

Participation patterns of this kind are of interest for the study of many other aspects of normative organizations, such as power over members, leadership, apathy, the functions of the high holidays, annual conventions, and charity campaigns. For two of the best discussions of the analytical and methodological problems involved, including a typology of participants and a discussion of the various dimensions of participation, see Merton (1957a, pp. 288 ff.) and Fichter (1954, Pt. I). Renate Mayntz (forthcoming) has pointed to the striking similarity in the distribution of participants and nonparticipants in the United States, Western Germany, France, and Sweden.

between normative compliance and intermittent activities: many normative organizations have an intermittent structure; and intermittent activities tend to be normative ones.

The material examined suggests that the study of intermittent structures must take a number of dimensions into account: the extent to which an organization is intermittent (the entire organization becomes dormant; all but a "maintenance" subunit becomes dormant; only some subunits become dormant); the ranks for which it is intermittent (all ranks; lower participants only; higher participants only);[38] and the duration of active and inactive periods (both in absolute terms, e.g., a day; and in relative terms, i.e., the length of the inactive period relative to the active period).

SUMMARY

In this chapter we have described two ways in which different compliance patterns may be stressed in a single organization without loss of effectiveness: through concomitant division of compliance and through successive division of compliance.

We began by outlining two alternative approaches to the exercise of authority and supervision in the literature on administration. One approach holds that the exercise of executive authority is a highly general activity, based on skills in managing people and in eliciting performances from them. The other asserts that managerial ability is limited to activities which require similar skills and knowledge for their performance. Our own position is that control positions should not be classified according to the types of performance supervised but rather according to the types of compliance they utilize. According to this approach, the executive role should be seen as more specialized than the advocate of universal executive skills would suggest, but much more general than it appears to those who emphasize the specific tasks the executive must direct.

We suggested that just as organizations differ in the types of compliance appropriate to them, so individuals differ in their talent for utilizing one or another kind of compliance. Mechanisms of self-selection and organizational selection, however imperfect they may be, act to recruit personnel to positions for which they are suited.

It follows from this approach to executive activity that effective

38. Churches are intermittent structures only from the viewpoint of lower participants; hospitals are intermittent for higher participants, especially doctors; reserve units are intermittent for all ranks.

mobility from company to company, or from job to job, depends upon staying within the same compliance speciality, rather than with the same type of manufacturing techniques. Furthermore, it is clear that personnel and methods of supervision and control which are appropriate to one type of organization (e.g., a business corporation) cannot usefully be transferred in their entirety to another type (e.g., hospitals).

It frequently happens that organizations which are primarily of one type contain affiliates or divisions of another type in order to fulfill one or another of their varied tasks. These affiliates or divisions are, however, segregated from the main compliance structure of the organization; their executives are rarely recruited into top elite positions in the main structure. Just because these units differ in their compliance structure, however, we suggested that it is particularly important for them to be included in the sequence of positions through which executives move in the "broadening" process.

Successive, rather than concomitant, division of compliance is less frequently discussed but no less interesting. The succession or alternation of compliance types, associated with an expansion or contraction of organizational activity, may take a number of different forms, from *seasonal* changes, which are comparatively limited, to the more extensive *shifting* structures, to *intermittent* structures, which are the most extensive.

XVII | NEW DIRECTIONS

Science may thrive on verification (or rejection) of previously formulated hypotheses and the linkage of variables in new, unexpected ways, but excitement is rarely experienced in dwelling on yet another example that reveals that relationships are indeed as predicted. Excitement is more likely to be kindled by a theoretical extension, when a theory is applied to areas previously not encompassed by it or modified in ways that strengthen its explanatory power. Compliance theory has benefitted from significant developments of both types, when:

1. new correlates were added; i.e., organizational attributes whose relationship to the compliance variables had not previously been examined or "hypothesized" were studied;
2. the relationship between intra-organizational compliance and environmental pressures was explored;
3. bridges were built to other theories: distributive justice, exchange, and basic human needs;
4. the compliance concepts were applied to total societies;
5. the theory was rendered more dynamic; and
6. the theory was applied to inter-unit systems.

These developments are reviewed in this chapter. It should be noted, however, that the introduction of a causal path-analysis model is at least as innovative as the extensions about to be treated. The discussion of the Iowa State group's efforts along these lines was placed separately in Chapter XV only because the studies dealt with the variables of the immediately preceding chapter. A full list of new directions of compliance research, theory, and methodology would also include this advance.

NEW CORRELATES

Six New Organizational Variables

Hall, Haas, and Johnson (1967) analyzed data on 75 organizations, correlating compliance scores with numerous organizational attributes not explored by the original theory. The major new variables covered are complexity, formalization, goal specificity (discussed on p. 150), primary mission or "activity," interdependence, status and power structure, external relations, and change. As we shall report shortly in greater detail, Hall, Haas, and Johnson found the compliance typology strongly related to some of these variables and only weakly related to others. It must be noted from the onset, however, that the findings of this study are greatly affected by the particular manner in which organizations were classified into compliance types. (Actually, in a future publication we hope to report the results of a reclassification of these organizations and the subsequent recomputation of the strength of relationships.) The assignment of organizations to compliance types is of course highly consequential because misclassifications will tend to weaken the relationships between compliance patterns and their correlates by diluting the differences among the types. In classifying the 75 organizations in their sample, the authors report that they used the "collective judgment" of their staff rather than an independent panel of judges or, much better, empirical evidence as to the nature of the actual compliance relationships. Professor Richard Hall, in a private communication, informed me that the author had detailed information, based on interviews for "all levels of the organization" for some of the cases and some data about all of them. How these data were coded and used is still not clear, especially as our classification is based on the compliance structure of the lower participants. At least this sociologist wonders why and how a state school was classified as coercive; a medical association as utilitarian, and a "military supply command" and "state psychiatric hospital" as normative (*ibid.,* p. 121).

The authors do discuss what they refer to as "unanticipated placements," e.g., the classification of the military command in a normative category, and explain that this was arrived at on the basis of the positive orientation of lower-level and upper-level participants toward their duties. The authors add: "From the experience gained in these classificatory efforts, it is evident that detailed knowledge about the organization is necessary for adequate placement in a classification system" (*ibid.,* p. 122). We quite agree.

Finally, the authors justify their selection of these particular 75 organizations (which, as they correctly state, cannot be thought of as a representative sample because no clearly defined universe of organizations exists) on the grounds of a need for heterogeneity. This aim, however, does not seem to have been completely achieved. The study includes 6 or 8 organizations of the same kind (e.g., state penal institutions, manufacturing plants) and only one of a kind of many others.

Keeping these reservations in mind, what did the study establish?

COMPLEXITY—Theoretically one would expect utilitarian organizations to have the most elaborate division of labor and therefore to be the most organizationally complex. Pure coercive organizations, especially prisons, one would expect to be relatively simple. Normative organizations should be bimodally distributed among those very simple in their internal structure (e.g., communes) and those highly ritualized and complex (e.g., churches) but, nevertheless, be simpler than many utilitarian organizations (e.g., business corporations).

Hall, Haas, and Johnson found a statistically significant overall correlation between compliance types and complexity. Normative organizations were found, on the average, to be less complex and more "polarized," albeit unevenly, than the other two. Normative organizations tended to score either high or low with very few, compared to the other two types, scoring "medium" (see Table XVII-1). Second, significantly more normative organizations scored "low" on the measure of complexity (62%) than either the utilitarian (37%) or the coercive ones (27%). Also in line with our expectations, utilitarian organizations proved to be the most complex, as Table XVII-1 shows.

One would expect coercive organizations to be much simpler than

Table XVII-1—Compliance and Complexity

Overall Complexity	Coercive %	Utilitarian %	Normative %
Low	27	37	62
Medium	73	40	10
High	0	23	28
	N = 11	N = 35	N = 29

The difference is statistically significant at better than 0.05 points. $\chi^2 = 11.96$, df = 4.
Source: Haas, Hall, and Johnson (1967), p. 126, table edited. Reprinted with the permission of Administrative Science Quarterly.

the other two. It is likely that the differences shown in the table would have been greater if more purely coercive organizations had been included among the organizations studied.

Complexity then can be added to the list of compliance correlates. Coercive organizations are the least complex. Force is a great simplifier; a high degree of differentiation in the division of labor cannot be sustained by relying on force. Utilitarian organizations are the most complex; because of the emphasis on efficiency, division of labor is at its highest. Finally, normative organizations may be either as simple in their structure as a social movement or as complex as, say, the Roman Catholic Church.

Of the five indicators of complexity correlated with compliance types, one showed a degree of association much stronger than the others and hence deserves to be reproduced here (Table XVII-2).

Table XVII-2—Subdivisions

In Whole Organization	Coercive	Utilitarian	Normative
1–2	27	37	41
3	9	23	35
4 or more	64	40	24

Significant at better than 0.01 level. $\chi^2 = 16.20$, df = 4.
Source: Hall, Haas and Johnson (1967), p. 126. Reprinted with the permission of Administrative Science Quarterly.

The other four indicators used by the authors to measure complexity included number of major activities, number of major divisions (horizontal complexity), mean number of hierarchical levels, and number of levels "in most specialized single department."

FORMALIZATION—A relatively high degree of formalization, as

exemplified by written job specifications, explicit instructions, and detailed record keeping, as Weber has stressed, is integral to the concept of organization, but where is formalization most pronounced: in the modern factory? in the rigid prison? in the church?

To study this question the authors used 10 indicators but computed no summary measurement. Among those indicators correlating most strongly with the compliance typology are the prevalence of written job descriptions, the extent to which the authority structure is outlined in a formal organizational chart, and the extent to which penalties for violating the rules are clearly stipulated, again in writing. According to all three of these indicators, as well as on six of the other seven, coercive organizations rank as the most formalized. Second on seven indicators in degree of formalization are utilitarian organizations; normative organizations are second on two, coercive, on one.

The overall order that emerges is thus—moving from the most to the least formalized—coercive, utilitarian, normative. This stands to reason, as informal normative organizations would pull down the average score of formalization for this type and, once explicit and written penalties are added to the picture, one might well expect utilitarian organizations, in this age of human relations, to be relatively less formalized than coercive organizations.

MAIN MISSION OR "ACTIVITIES"—Here six different indicators were used to see if organizations differing in compliance profile also differ in the kinds of activities they engage in. Again, no overall summary index is provided.

Some of the findings under this heading are self-evident. For instance, it is hardly surprising that no coercive and no normative organizations are engaged in production as their major activity. An interesting finding, though, which the authors correctly flag, is that utilitarian organizations have many more "support" departments than other organizations; this might reflect both a higher degree of division of labor and functional rationality, which in turn would go well with their less emotive involvement and more quantifiable means of control. Other indicators are an odd mixture rendering this into a clearly residual category; none of these are indicators of variables widely used in either sociological or administrative theory.

INTERDEPENDENCE—The degree to which various organizational segments hang together was measured by two indicators, interdependency of departments and ratio of the number of committees to number of paid employees (see Hall, Haas, and Johnson, 1967, p. 133).

No explanation is given as to how the first indicator variable was measured. It is not at all self-evident why all the coercive organizations would find their departments highly interdependent, while quite a few utilitarian ones score only "medium" or "low" interdependence. This may explain why the relationship formed is not significant at .05 or even .10.

The second indicator is very clearly operationalized. Number of committees divided by number of paid employees, established a statistically significant link (better than .02) between this ratio and the compliance typology. Normative organizations' reliance on volunteers and their greater need to mobilize members' involvement is reflected in a high reliance on committees. The score obtained for coercive organizations would certainly be much lower if inmates rather than employees had been considered by the authors to be the lower participants, as they are in the compliance typology. Hence, the score given is simply in error. The similarity in low overall scores between utilitarian and coercive organizations reflects not necessarily an infrequent use of committees by utilitarian organizations, but simply that their committee members tend also to be paid. If this were disregarded, I would expect utilitarian organizations in line with their greater need for rationality to score higher than coercive ones, although the normative organizations, with their low ability to pay and great need to mobilize, would still retain the lead.

STATUS AND POWER—While the preceding correlates bridge the theory of administrative and compliance studies, the two indicators discussed next are more intimately sociological (see Hall, Haas, Johnson, 1967, p. 133).

The data about status (in effect, emphasis on status symbols) was derived from questionnaire items rather than observation. Normative organizations are reported as having more participants who see "high" status differences than either coercive or utilitarian organizations. It is difficult to accept the respondents' answers; scores of studies of prisons, other correctional institutions, and armies indicate very high concern with status in these organizations. It appears that in normative organizations status differences are more legitimate and hence more openly acknowledged. (This is indirectly supported by the fact that while there are 11% fewer "highs" in coercive than in normative organizations, there are 29% more "medium" and 18%

fewer "low".) The finding of less visible status symbols in utilitarian organizations makes sense, as does the relatively greater polarization (between high and low) which characterizes the distribution of the normative organizations (smallest "medium" category of the three). Using the data as given, the correlation is not significant at the .10 level.

In contrast, the loci of power are highly correlated (significant at 0.01) with the compliance typology. Coercive organizations are completely dependent on higher control by other agencies, a finding which is consistent with their license to use force. That 40% of the utilitarian organizations studied are owned by "another" organization reflects the high number of holding companies and conglomerates. Normative organizations are more often run by their own boards than are the other two types, presumably because they must be either more responsive to their members than to "another organization" or cease to be normative.

EXTERNAL RELATIONS—Seven indicators were used to measure the links between organizations of the different compliance types and the external world. Competition was found to exist for all three types, but to be much higher (or to be experienced as much higher) among utilitarian organizations than among normative ones (who compete over memberships and contributions) and least among coercive organizations (who compete over budgets). (The finding is significant at .001, $\chi^2 = 62.65$, df $= 4$.) At the same time government regulations are strongest for coercive organizations, intermediate for utilitarian ones, and mildest for normative organizations (significant at .001, $\chi^2 = 52.82$; df $= 4$). Other indicators correlate less strongly but in the expected direction.

CHANGE—Four indicators were used to measure the relative flexibility, adaptability, and innovativeness of organizations differing in their compliance structure. Shifts in activities, emphasis on activities, personnel, and budget were studied. No significant differences were found on the first two indicators. On the last two, coercive organizations were found to be the most "changeable," normative next so, with utilitarian organizations clearly taking the third place. Whether this finding reflects particular historical conditions or a deeper logic remains to be explored (Table XVII-3).

In conclusion, the Hall, Haas and Johnson study suggests several indicators and relationships. Their implications for the understanding of compliance patterns are practically endless. It must be noted,

Table XVII-3—Compliance and Change

	COERCIVE		UTILITARIAN		NORMATIVE			
	%	N	%	N	%	N	χ^2	df
Patterns of growth								
(personnel)		4		28		21		
							7.21*	2
Decline	0		61		33			
Growth	100		39		67			
Pattern of growth								
(budget)		5		26		23		
							7.54**	2
Decline	0		58		30			
Growth	100		42		70			

Source: Hall, Haas, and Johnson (1967), p. 137. Reprinted with the permission of *Administrative Science Quarterly*.
* significant at .10
** significant at .05

however, that I interpret the findings somewhat differently than the authors do. They report "strong relationships" between compliance and indicators of goal specificity, power structure, internal interdependence, and relations with external environment; "weaker relationships" with indicators of complexity, formalization, major activities, and change. Frequently, they complain that the links found are not surprising and otherwise deprecate their own findings. The authors see their own typology as more effective, although it is not submitted to empirical test as that of Blau-Scott and Etzioni (see Haas, Hall, Johnson, 1966). As I see it, a considerable number of statistically significant and theoretically meaningful linkages were uncovered, extending substantially the study of compliance correlates.

New Hypotheses about Small Groups and Cliques

Noel Tichy (1973) explored the factors which shape informal groupings within formal organizations, especially small groups and cliques, and the differential effect of compliance patterns on these relationships. The significance of informal groupings for solidifying the orientations of participants towards their organization have often been discussed (see Ch. XI; see also our discussion of group cohesion, p. 384). Tichy takes as his starting point our observation that "normative systems tend to develop informal structures that are integrated and that overlap with the formal structure; coercive systems tend to develop segregated informal structures that control a large sphere of activities; and utilitarian organizations tend to fall between the normative and coercive, with informal structures emerging to fulfill expressive needs" (1973, p. 195). He then "crosses" these compliance types with two other variables: organizational size (small versus large) and mobility (high, "seniority," and low). Some of the combinations are held to be non-plausible (e.g., a coupling of high mobility with coercion). Next he analyzes the clique structure for each compliance type based on theoretical considerations (to be subject later to empirical test), although several qualitative reports are cited supporting the hypotheses.

Tichy predicted that cliques among lower participants in coercive organizations, all of whom are of the "no mobility" type (inmates are not promoted to become guards), would tend to oppose the organization's values, and will themselves utilize coercion internally over their inmate members. Their goal is typically to gain power. Tichy expected to find high clique "density" in coercive organizations because membership in a clique is almost a prerequisite for survival. Typically, these cliques are expected to be limited exclusively to "lower participants." The inmates' work statuses (kitchen, garden) should have little effect on their clique status. Finally, Tichy expected high intra-clique hierarchization as a result of the group's defensive orientation to the organization-at-large. For the same basic reason, ability to apply pressure, larger cliques were expected to be preferred over smaller ones.

In normative organizations Tichy foresaw there to be little impetus toward clique formation, with formal relations tending to absorb informal ones. Work (instrumental) and friendship (expressive) relations tend to overlap. Inter-rank links are likely to be common. Density of cliques is expected to be low, because they serve chiefly intimate friendship needs. For the same reason, little internal hierarchization is expected. Among utilitarian organizations, significant differences are expected to show up according to the degree of intra-organizational mobility, and status of the clique. Here, rather than repeat the details of Tichy's arguments, the reader is referred to Tichy's summary table (1973, p. 200).

Tichy's extension of the theory to cover the specifics of informal organization in the three compliance types is linked to a major methodological breakthrough. To test his hypothesis on differences in informal structure from one compliance type to another, large numbers of sociometric relations have to be studied. Tichy reports, however, that Kadushin's (1971) review of the literature points out that using traditional sociograms becomes increasingly inaccurate as the groups under study grow larger than fifty members. This would make it practically impossible to test Tichy's propositions in most organizations. Fortunately, Kadushin and his associates have developed a computer program called SOCK (a sociometric analysis system) which allows large-scale mapping of sociometric relations among up to as many as 19,000 members. The next step, which needs to be undertaken, is to combine Tichy's new propositions with Kadushin *et al.*'s new methodology.

A RELATIONSHIP TO ORGANIZATIONAL ENVIRONMENT

Definition, Boundaries Revisited

How to draw the lines separating organizations from nonorganizations, and organizations from their environments, as well as what term to use to refer to the unit under study, are problems which have generated a surprising amount of dialogue. My preference for the term "complex organization" over "formal organization" and "bureaucracy," and the related definition of organizations as goal-oriented social systems (see p. xi; and 1964, p. 4) have been supported by a multivariate analysis conducted by Pugh, Hickson, Hinings and Turner (1968, especially p. 86). They pointed out that Etzioni defines complex organizations as planned, deliberately structured entities, and that, in fact, "structuring" turned up as the "most highly loaded" factor of their analysis. (See also Albrow, 1970, p. 101; Price, 1972, p. 11; and Merrill, 1970, p. 128.)

Certainly not everybody has agreed. MacKenzie finds that both the designations "formal organization" used by March and Simon and "complex organization" used by Etzioni are "hard to construe" (1967, p. 245). He does not detail what the difficulty is.

Whereas I pointed out that "formal organization refers to only one segment of organization activities . . ." (p. xi), thereby explaining my preference for the term complex organization, Blau and Scott have stressed that formality is in their view the essence of the phenomenon under study and that a "formal organization" need not be either complex or large-scale (Blau-Scott, 1962, pp. 1-7; see also

Waldo et al., 1966, pp. 21-22; Hall, 1972, pp. 7-8; Haas and Drabek, 1973, p. 183; and Weissenberg, 1971, pp. 63-64, 75). While indeed an organization need not be large-scale (nor is that part of my definition), once a formally separate subsystem is introduced, even in so small a unit as a family small business, the unit becomes sociologically complex. Matters of definition, to be sure, are not very consequential; but as long as we are defining, it seems desirable to use a more encompassing term and one relatively free from undesirable connotations. "Complex organizations" still strikes me to be the most suitable.

As to the question of boundaries of organizations, who is "in" and who is "out," the definition suggested (pp. 20-21) has served rather well empirically, as many of the new studies reported here seem to me to indicate. And Scott (1964, p. 515) has pointed out another reason why the suggested definition is effective: it defines which persons are linked to the organization in routine, patterned exchanges of rewards for contributions. That is, transient contacts which do not make for organizational membership, by our definition, also do not provide for a routinized exchange relationship, and conversely, patterned exchanges qualify as organizations according to our criteria.

Aldrich (1973, pp. 387ff.) suggested that the way boundaries are drawn and membership is defined in compliance theory also leads to a set of hypotheses concerning *inter*-organizational relations, conflict in particular. The more persons are defined (or define themselves) as belonging to a given organization, and the more active their participation, all other things being equal, the greater will be the organization's chances of success. (For more on the mobilization thesis implied, see Etzioni, 1968, Ch. 15). Aldrich next suggests that organizations in conflict will seek to expand their own definitions of their boundaries and heighten the demands they put on their participants. This is a well-taken point, but it refers to the subjects' definition of the boundaries; the observers' variables for characterizing the world need not change. Thus, the subjects may feel the organization is more important to them, in this sense "bigger." The observers may only note a higher score of the saliency variable, no new "definition."

Finally, Aldrich ties the definition of boundaries to the compliance typology, suggesting that participation in normative organizations is highly voluntary, much less so in utilitarian organizations, and least of all in coercive ones (1973, p. 389). This holds probably for most, but not all, normative organizations. For instance, the pressure to participate in state-required religious or ideological activities in some societies and in the Colonial period of America was quite high. Nevertheless, Aldrich's thesis may hold when across-the-board, statistical comparisons are made. Furthermore, it might be argued that once membership in normative organizations is not voluntary but subject to pressure, even if the pressure is itself normative, these organizations lose some of their involving quality.

Questions concerning the definition of the "upper" limits of an organization, e.g., is a board of trustees "in" or not, attracted less attention both from us and other students of organization, a point flagged by Price (1972, p. 40) and Brager (1969, p. 483). This deficiency should be corrected, as interest in the guidance of organizations and their articulation into more encompassing and higher-level units, especially total societies, increases. As a starting point, I suggest that three criteria of participation similar to those used to define lower participants be adopted. That is, persons will be "in" as higher participants if they are linked to other participants and the organization as a whole by involvement and performance (pp. 17-21) and superordination (rather than subordination). Hence, a person who reports low saliency in his or her feelings about an organization, has few performance links (e.g., attends board meetings once every three months), and/or has little power over the organization (he is only one of many trustees) may be a participant in a formal sense but not in the sociological sense here intended.

Compliance in a Crisis

Brager's study (1969) strikes out in a major new direction by examining the relationship between an organization's internal compliance make-up and the conditions of its social environment. The case he studied concerns the attack Mobilization For Youth came under in 1964 when it was accused, in the press and in Congress, of harboring communists and using its facilities for subversive purposes. In the face of this hostility, the organization's executive directors decided to follow a "survival" rather than a "value" strategy and ended up by dismissing the "subversive" members and otherwise choosing to "compromise" rather than to fight (*ibid.*, p. 484).

The reaction of the organization's participants to this defensive organizational posture, Brager shows, was based on its compliance structure: The more involved members were, the more negative was their reaction to the crisis strategy. Specifically, "54.1% of MFY's most committed participants were negative reactors, as compared to 13.1% who reacted positively. Among the least committed mobilization participants, the figures are reversed" (*ibid.*, p. 488). (See also Table VI-7.)

The new line of investigation Brager has opened up rests on the sociological insight that organizations are, at least to some degree, integrated units whose members respond to external challenges—from the social or ecological environment—not individually but in line with their collective relations. As the compliance make-up of an organization, as we have shown, affects so significantly the organization's internal processes, it could not help but significantly affect the organization's response to external challenges. This logical "derivation" or conclusion is given empirical back-up by the Brager study. We also gain from him several hypotheses concerning the specific ways an organization can be expected to respond to external threats. His case study suggests that organizations, when endangered, will choose a "survival" response (concentrating on sheer maintenance) over a value-oriented response (goal advancement). This, in turn, can be expected to increase internal disaffection, dissensus, and discord among the previously most committed members. To further advance this line of research, we would need to set forth a typology of possible external challenges and study how organizations differing in compliance structure respond to them.

NEW THEORETICAL BRIDGES: LINKS TO THE THEORY OF DISTRIBUTIVE JUSTICE AND EXCHANGE THEORY

Exchange and Involvement

The largest concentration of compliance studies carried out thus far, that of the Iowa State group, has recently resulted in a publication which builds upon the same data base but takes a rather different analytical direction. An article by Robert Schafer and Gerald Klonglan (1974) explored the applicability of the notion of distributive justice and social exchange in normative as well as utilitarian organizations.

The concept of distributive justice addresses issues such as what share of the total rewards a social entity commands are allocated internally to its various individual participants, ranks, and subgroups; how close is the prevailing pattern of distribution to a pattern defined as just; and in what ways do "just" versus "unjust" distributions affect the conduct of participants, most notably, their degree of involvement, i.e., commitment versus alienation.

Exchange theory postulates that participants in exchange relationships are cognizant of the relative justice of various investment-reward ratios and will adjust their behavior so as to create or maintain justice in relations between themselves and other individuals and between themselves and the organization as a collectivity (*ibid.*, pp. 1-2).

It appeared clear to Schafer and Klonglan that such processes of distributive justice and exchange do occur in utilitarian organizations as exchange of investments (labor) for rewards (wages), are highly visible and the units exchanged are specific, tangible and readily comparable (*ibid.*, p. 3). But, they asked, are the concepts and theorems of "exchange" and "distributive justice" equally applicable to coercive and normative organizational types?

In the case of coercive relations, the authors quote Peter Blau's dictum that such behavior cannot be defined as an exchange pattern (however, a closer examination of this matter is perhaps in order since most power wielders in effect bargain a measure of moderation in the use of force they command in exchange for a lower inclination to rebel by those subject to coercion).

As for normative relations, in what sense can exchange be said to occur when participants are committed to and have internalized the values of the organization, or the organization is authentically committed to realize their values? How does exchange proceed when rewards are symbolic and personal, and participants less conscious or unconscious of them, hence unable or disinclined to make constant comparisons with other participants in the exchange system (*ibid.*, p. 5)? Will actors under these circumstances still seek a proportionality between their investments and perceived rewards?

To test the hypothesis that participants in normative organizations do strive for proportionality, Schafer and Klonglan analyzed the conduct of the Civil Defense directors, familiar to us from previous discussions of the Iowa State studies. The authors carefully separated what they termed "ascribed" investments, seen as being beyond the participants' manipulative control (e.g., years of formal education), from the "achieved" investments within their control (e.g., time volunteered). While the former have been found to be significant in previous studies of utilitarian exchange, only the latter investments were thought relevant to the maintenance of justice in a normative exchange relationship. Rewards, following Etzioni, were considered to be based on the manipulation of social and prestige symbols (p. 36), as falling into two broad categories: (1) community approval of the role in terms of prestige and social rank, and (2) approval accruing to the individual by significant others (spouse and other participants), and personal satisfaction, akin to self-esteem (*ibid.*, p. 8).

Schafer and Klonglan found that in the normative organizations they studied, "ascribed" inputs had almost no correlation with rewards. However, out of six possible correlations between "achieved" inputs and community approval of the role, three proved significant. Hours per week on the job correlated .23 with prestige (significant at .001 level) and .17 with social rank (significant at .05 level). "Actual role performance" correlated .21 with prestige (at .01 level), but the .04 correlation with social rank was not significant. Training did not correlate significantly with either prestige or social rank.

Significant correlations were found in 5 out of 6 possible relationships between achieved inputs and symbolic rewards to the self. Correlations between investments and approval of significant others were weaker than those between investments and personal satisfaction. Personal satisfaction correlated .34 with role performance, .24 with hours volunteered (both at .001 level), and .19 with training (.01 level). Approval of significant others correlated .18 with training and .14 with hours per week (significant at .05), while the .12 correlation with role performance was not significant at .05 (see Table XVII-4).

Table XVII-4—Investments and Rewards: Exchange in a Normative Organization
(Pearson Correlation Coefficient)

ACHIEVED INVESTMENTS	COMMUNITY APPROVAL OF ROLE		COMMUNITY APPROVAL OF INDIVIDUAL	
	Prestige	Social Rank	Significant Others	Personal Satisfaction
Training	—	—	.14	.19
Hours per week	.23	.17	.11	.24
Role performance	.21	—	—	.34

Only correlations significant at .15 level or better.
Source: Schafer and Klonglan (1974), tables 2 and 3 (slightly edited).

Schafer and Klonglan concluded from these correlations that their hypothesis has been verified, i.e., that the participants in this normative organization did, by and large, keep their investments in time, training, and quality of performance congruent with the rewards they received from their civil defense work. The authors do note, however, that this "striving for proportionality" operates quite differently in this normative organization than in a typical utilitarian organization. In a utilitarian organization participants exchange their resources for tangible rewards such as money and, as one goes up the hierarchy, for symbolic community rewards such as prestige and social rank. In the civil defense organization, however, there were no material rewards and few community rewards related to the position. The rewards were mainly symbolic rewards to the person, esteem from relatives, friends, and fellow workers, and self-esteem, a feeling of satisfaction with oneself and one's work. And participants in the normative organization measured the acceptability of the rewards received not by comparing their rewards with those of a reference group of others of the same class or rank but by evaluating their rewards against an internal expectation of the level of symbolic reward which justifies a specific level of investment.

The authors suggest that these findings—particularly the notion of an internal standard of judgment—revalidate the concept of distributive justice and give it a new thrust. One might ask whether this interpretation does not blur the concept of distributive justice. If distributive justice is to mean anything precise, it should mean the "equitable" allocation of a group's or society's total rewards either "objectively" (according to a fixed standard such as equal distribution of "from each according to his ability, to each according to his needs") or "intersubjective" (with each person "satisfied" that he has gained what he "deserves" as he compares himself to the participants).

The authors also conclude, with some qualifications, that their findings support the applicability of exchange theory to normative organizations. While the "internal comparison standards" characteristic of "normative exchange" are declared to be inconsistent with George Homan's brand of behaviorist exchange theory, they are deemed by the authors to be in keeping with Blau's more normatively oriented exchange theory. Again, it must be pointed out that while Blau does include what he terms "indirect exchanges" in which, for example, Mr. X gives $1000 to Hospital Y in order to gain a good reputation in his community (akin to the community approval and esteem rewards for our Civil Defense workers), Blau stresses the self-interest motivated or utilitarian rather than consensual or normative aspects of these transactions. Furthermore, Blau specifically cites "autistic exchange" (all behavior in which a person's sole or chief reward for certain behaviors is his own self-esteem) as falling outside the rubric of social exchange (Blau, 1964, p. 91). In addition, such reciprocal relationships as "love," wherein, for example, John may give Mary flowers not in order to "get" the kiss she gives him in return but in order to express his feelings, also fall outside the purview of social exchange. However, as long as the level of esteem that participants "give" each other co-varies with their contributions to the organization, and their involvement in it, esteem is subject to the laws of social exchange, even if the participants are not aware of it. One would expect this association to be all the stronger, the more normative the organization.

Basic Human Needs and Compliance

There is a deep relationship between compliance, as an ordering, organizational principle of human relations, and the question of what human nature is like. Substantively, the question is, which kinds of governance in institutions as well as society at large will people tolerate, accept, and thrive on? What are the long-term consequences of relying on remunerative rewards and settling for calculative commitment on the part of participants (the basis of capitalist systems)? Can a system last which relies on "higher" sanctions and loyalties implied in the notion of "permanent revolution?" Can an organizational system survive relying on no rewards or punishments, each participant doing his or her own thing, completely voluntarily (the ideal of the *kibbutzim* and numerous communes)?

The main answer provided to these questions in the original publication of the compliance theory was limited and relativistic. It suggested that these questions could not be answered independently of historical-societal conditions as reflected in organizational missions. Each organizational type answered a societal need (not necessarily a universal one but a need of the existing society). Law and order could be enforced, despite alienated relations, in coercive organizations; production and exchange could be carried out in the relatively "cool," rational world of utilitarian organizations; only "cultural" goals (including educational, political, and religious ones) required a deep involvement, and only normative organizations could mobilize such commitment.

A clue as to what the theory was lacking, as I see it now, lies in the proposition that while it is not possible to mass produce routinely or keep order by relying on normative means—society and its organizations (at least modern civilization) has alienating elements—and while people are truly involved only in normative organizations, there are signs of a yearning, and of a secular trend, toward greater reliance on normative organizations and less on coercive and utilitarian ones.

Only in a later publication (Etzioni, 1968) did the theoretical foundation for this position evolve. The concept of basic human needs was introduced, building on the work of Abraham Maslow and others (*ibid.*, pp. 624, 657). It was suggested that all persons have the same basic needs and that those are arranged hierarchically, so that first physical and safety needs are experienced as the most urgent; next, needs for affection and respect; and last (and in this sense, at the "highest" level) a need for self-actualization is felt.

The concept of basic human needs was long considered metaphysical, empirically impossible (i.e., not subject to operationalization), and logically unnecessary (we can explain the world just as well, it had been suggested, without this concept). My effort, not to be recapitulated here, was dedicated to restoring the theoretical status of the concept and showing not only that it can be operationalized but also that it is empirically plausible and intellectually productive (Etzioni, 1968, Ch. 21).

If one works with the assumption that basic human needs are organized hierarchically, it follows that societies which have answered to varying degrees the physical and safety needs of their members should be objectively ready to satisfy demands for higher needs and to develop organizational forms suited to fulfilling these needs: objectively we should be able to enter an era of greater reliance on symbolic, normative compliance with less need for the other two types. There remains the question of the historical and societal conditions under which normative compliance could be effectively mobilized instead of inauthentically manipulated to deflect pressures toward higher satisfaction and sustain the current centrality of material production and consumption and use of force. The theoretical and practical problem, then, is to determine the conditions under which the objective possibility will be exercised rather than suppressed. (As we cannot take the space to address this issue here, see *ibid.*, Chs. 15 and 18).

William H. Weber, III (1973), also deals with the articulation of Maslow's concept of basic human needs and the compliance typology. His treatment is in the humanist intellectual rather than logical-empirical tradition. He anchors his general discussion by exploring one particular context and one relationship: the faculty leader and student follower in universities. Focusing on liberal arts colleges, Weber views the purpose of education as providing for self-actualization. He then argues that while colleges used to be normative organizations (*ibid.*, p. 29), under the impact of developments such as faculty unionization and stress on research output they have turned into utilitarian organizations. Faculty are treated as "hired hands," deans as "foremen," students behave like "consumers," and the university has become a "knowledge factory" (*ibid.*, p. 29, quotation marks in original).

Can "true" education take place in such a context? Weber answers that "organizations which depend primarily upon coercive power to obtain compliance will stunt any development [on the Maslow hierarchy] beyond the level of safety needs" (*ibid.*, p. 40). "Remunerative power, with the interpersonal competition which it often promotes, will frequently block the satisfaction of belongingness and love needs" (*ibid*). Finally, "normative power facilitates the satisfaction of the belongingness and love needs, but places strict limits on the free use of cognitive capacities and is, therefore, inconsistent with satisfaction of the self-actualization needs" (*ibid*). Weber sees the need for a fourth type of power and hence argues against the "return" of colleges to a normative type, favoring instead their becoming centers of his new "social exchange power" (*ibid.*, p. 51ff.). This is defined as "power growing out of face-to-face relations where those relations are frequent, where there is mutual personal involvement" (*ibid*).

I shall now both characterize what seems to me to be at issue and deal with Weber's arguments. The issue must be faced both on an individual level and on a collective, organizational level. For the student, to be self-actualizing requires autonomous action. Yet, only completely voluntary "submission" to an intellectual leader whose superior standing is recognized strictly on substantive, merit grounds —like that of a guru—is compatible with pure self-actualization as Weber has it (see *ibid.*, p. 44), and even this fit is not a comfortable one. To submit is to accept someone else's preferences, and as we deal with ideals and concepts and values, such submission is, by definition, nonrational. It, hence, involves processes of identification, emotional involvement with the other, not compatible with a high level of autonomy of the self. Also, it often will not serve as a source of instruments for self-actualization (e.g., acquisition of a new painting technique, to express one's own artistic predisposition), but instead is more likely to set patterns of belief and cognition, which limit self-actualization (leading, for example, to counter-culture conformism). In short, there is at least a residue of contradiction in any leader–follower relationship, between following and self-actualization.

Once such a relationship is institutionalized as, for instance, in a college, the problems multiply. The faculty becomes a source of rewards and punishment, which tends to introduce a utilitarian element (Weber, p. 49), although not necessarily utilitarian dominance (see Gamson, 1966, pp. 69ff.). Steps can be taken to reduce this utilitarian aspect, by abolishing grades, "credits," and exams and automatically granting a degree to anyone who remains registered in college for a given number of years. Some European universities approximate this condition. In such circumstances either there is negligible faculty–student contact or it acquires a relative pure normative character (students attend only those classes which they find stimulating, etc.). Nevertheless, even here, there is no normative following without a measure of submission because, to repeat, following entails a constriction of the submitting self, however voluntary the act.

The ultimate solution, self-actualization without submission, is hence in a peer situation, without any hierarchical relations. However, such a step, by definition, removes us from the organizational world to that of egalitarian communes (and not all communes, by far, are egalitarian) and student dialogues in coffee houses and beer joints (a situation whose sociological significance is restricted by the triviality of the situation). Thus, although various degrees of self-actualization can be maintained in highly normative organizations, especially in R (rank) structures, in which there are strong peer elements (p. 327), self-actualization can be maximized, as I see it, only where there is no compliance.

Now Weber seeks to overcome this dilemma and to define an organizational self-actualizing compliance relationship in terms of exchange theory. Weber sees the solution in a situation where "the degree of reciprocity is unusually high" (*ibid.,* p. 52) and the basis of the exchange is that the master is "good and wise," and on this basis the apprentice (or student) accords him "deep respect, deference" (p. 52).

As I see it, exchange theory is not particularly well suited for this purpose because it tends to assume actors who, often self-consciously and calculatively, pursue their own interests, in a situation in which, as a rule, advantages to one decrease the assets of the other, and vice versa. Exchange theory best suits utilitarian conditions; next best, coercive ones; but not nearly as well normative, especially not pure normative relations. Here persons act chiefly on the basis of nonrational considerations, not aware, and not in pursuit of self-interest, and become richer either by giving of themselves or by working toward shared goals, in ways which allow all to gain and none to be shortchanged (e.g., as in collective prayer). True, notions of reciprocity have been applied to normative relations (Homans, 1958), but these are often either not true normative conditions (some people are rather calculative in their gift-giving) or grasp at the margin but not the essence of the relationship.

Finally, even if exchange theory is applied to the issue at hand, one reaches the same conclusion the preceding discussion came to. In order to see why this must be, the place of power needs to be indicated. As I see it (1968, pp. 333ff.), power is best conceived, in exchange theory, as an exchange *rate*. The more powerful A is over B, the more asymmetrical is the exchange rate. Thus, when the goods an imperial power exports to a colony are compared to those the colony exports to the imperial power, using an independent measurement (e.g., "real" work time invested in each export unit, calculated in terms of a third country currency), we see that for each unit the colony gains, it must return several units. In contrast, exchanges between two major powers are more symmetrical.

Now, organizations are power structures, in which the higher ranks command more power than the lower participants. While organizations may differ in nature and amount of hierarchization, even those with the fewest ranks and the highest degree of peer relations have some hierarchy, for coordination by organization (in contrast to that of the marketplace) requires some kind of a pyramiding of decision points based on authority differentials. This is not a rejection of the possibility of a truly egalitarian relationship but only a recognition that it cannot be made compatible with organizational structure. Hence, either self-actualizing reciprocity is to be found in social units other than colleges, which are the organizational structures of higher education, or it will have to be balanced, to some extent, by their organizational needs. The comparative study of normative organizations points to the conditions under which self-actualizating education can be maximized within an organizational structure. Weber, in his essay on "hippie" society, deals in effect with the limits of self-actualization within organizations and the role of non-organizational association in making possible greater self-actualization.

Compliance, Esteem, and Prestige

Mitzner's (1968) dissertation explores the links between compliance patterns, prestige, and esteem. Esteem was defined as the degree to which an individual's performance was perceived to fulfill the requirements of his position or office. Six components of esteem were studied: self-evaluation, group evaluation, subject's estimate of group evaluation, superior's evaluation, subject's estimate of superior's evaluation, and subject's evaluation of superior. Esteem was deemed to be a highly significant organizational variable: to the degree that individuals in a formal organization do the work required from them, and to the extent that superiors perceive this and back up their approvals and disapprovals with rewards and punishments, this will function to motivate these individuals to conform to group-shared expectations, that is, to the systems of roles and rules pertaining to the various positions in the particular organization. Thus, esteem is important to the organization's motivation system.

Mitzner's study shows, first, that esteem and prestige (the importance of an individual's position or office to the goal of the organization) were nearly always related, whatever the organization's compliance structure. This indicates that an individual is more likely to be perceived, by himself and by others, as doing an "excellent" or "good" job when he occupies a high prestige position (*ibid.*, p. 109).

Second, Mitzner found that three of the six dimensions of esteem—self-evaluation, group evaluation of subject, and subject's evaluation of superior—were significantly, but not very strongly, related to the compliance pattern prevailing in each particular organization. The strength of these overall relationships, measured in terms of Cramer's V, was .11, .12, and .12, respectively (*ibid.*, p. 112). Unfortunately, Mitzner says nothing about the direction of these relationships.

Third, Mitzner found that the relationship between compliance patterns and various dimensions of esteem increases only for some of the prestige levels studied. In particular, the relationship between compliance patterns and subject's self-evaluation for high prestige subjects is .25, as opposed to .11 for the entire sample. Although the association is not strong, the data suggest that there is a tendency for high-ranking members of coercive organizations to evaluate themselves lower than do members of utilitarian or normative organizations (Table XVII-5).

Table XVII-5—Compliance Patterns and Self-Evaluation in Esteem: High Prestige Subjects

COMPLIANCE PATTERNS	SELF-EVALUATION IN ESTEEM (IN PERCENT)			
	Average	Above Average	High	Total
Coercive	36.6%	33.3%	30.1%	100
Utilitarian	13.5	73.0	13.5	100
Normative	13.3	66.7	20.0	100

Source: Mitzner (1968), p. 349.

Generally speaking, Mitzner's data lend support to the proposition that the compliance type of an organization makes much less of a difference for the higher ranks than it does for the lower ones. "Superior's evaluation of subject" was unrelated to the compliance types even when controlled for different ranks (*ibid.*, p. 213). "Subject's estimate of superior's evaluation," in addition, was related to compliance only for low prestige subjects (V = .23; Table XVII-6), not

Table XVII-6—Compliance Patterns and Subject's Estimate of Superior's Evaluation: Low and Average Prestige Subjects

COMPLIANCE PATTERNS	SUBJECT'S ESTIMATE OF SUPERIOR'S EVALUATION (IN PERCENT)				
	Low	Average	Above Average	High	Total
Coercive	0.0	42.1	52.6	5.3	100
Utilitarian	9.1	33.3	42.7	14.9	100
Normative	1.4	55.2	44.8	2.8	100

Source: Mitzner (1968), p. 354 (slightly edited).

where prestige was high. Finally, for "subject's evaluation of superior" the correlation increased from .12 to .21 when only those low or average in prestige were considered (Table XVII-7). Mitzner sum-

Table XVII-7—Compliance Patterns and Subject's Evaluation of Superior: Low and Average Prestige Subjects

COMPLIANCE PATTERNS	SUBJECT'S EVALUATION OF SUPERIOR IN ESTEEM (PERCENT)				
	Low	Average	Above Average	High	Total
Coercive	0.0%	31.6%	10.5%	57.9%	100
Utilitarian	3.0	24.2	45.5	27.3	100
Normative	1.5	21.7	52.2	24.6	100

Source: Mitzner (1968), p. 328 (slightly edited).

marizes the pattern emerging in the data by pointing out that "as far as Average and Above Average Esteem evaluations are concerned, the table supports Etzioni's assumption that subjects in coercive organizations are more alienated from persons who are in power positions. However, a larger proportion of the lower ranks in coercive groups also rate their superiors high in esteem. This phenomenon merits further investigation" (*ibid.*, p. 216).

TOTAL SOCIETIES

Compliance theory dealt with intra-organizational relationships, but the analytic elements, the typology of power, the modes of involvement, the correlates, are not inherently limited to this level of analysis. Indeed, several efforts have been undertaken to apply the theory to total societies, societal change, and international systems.

Political Compliance

William Gamson (1968) has traced the implications of the basic compliance thesis for relations between a political elite and the members of a polity. Here the "lower participants" are no longer individuals but politically mobilized collectivities (e.g., black ghetto rioters) or more formally constituted "interest groups" (such as the National Association of Manufacturers). In addition, Gamson attempts to integrate Lane's (1964) observations about political alienation and allegiance, Easton's (1965) about political support, and Almond and Verba's (1965) concerning positive, neutral, and negative affective orientations toward the government, with the attitudes of commitment, neutrality, and alienation distinguished in compliance theory.

He assimilates these into the concept of "political trust." According to Gamson, "Trust in the government is a political attitude. The term political attitude usually connotes opinions on specific public issues or, if something more general, a syndrome of attitudes which can be characterized on a left–right dimension" (pp. 39-40).

Though not neglecting how differential use of power toward different constituencies on the part of government may be differentially productive of commitment, neutrality, and alienation, Gamson emphasizes the role of affective orientations toward government in a group's choice of strategies in attempting to influence the government. Gamson distinguishes three levels of "political trust" or affective orientation toward political institutions and authorities: confidence, neutrality, and alienation. A "confident solidary group" which identifies its interests with those of right and the community or nation as a whole and which expects responsiveness from the government will tend to employ moral suasion as its chief means of influence.

A confident group presupposes that under most circumstances the authorities will of their own accord take the course of action favored by the group. Failure to do so signifies merely an informational error—insufficient information, oversight, incorrect interpretation—all minor problems which can be easily rectified through persuasion.

Neutral solidary groups, who have goals which neither conflict with nor compliment those of the authorities, will tend to rely on inducements (i.e. utilitarian power) as a means of influence. A neutral group assumes that the authorities have no particular stake, pro or con, in the outcome desired by the group. The conditions for a *quid pro quo* transaction exist when a group of authorities has control of something (a binding choice) that is unimportant to them but is important to a solidary group and the latter has something (inducement resources) that is important to the authorities.

Alienated groups, who believe that the authorities are actively hostile or at least predisposed against their cause, will tend to use constraints (i.e., coercive power). An alienated group believes that the authorities have a vested interest in not responding to their demands and therefore must be shown through force that the disadvantages of noncompliance outweigh the advantages.

Just as compliance theory predicts that use of normative power by an organization is typically coupled with commitment on the part of the lower participants, utilitarian power with calculative involvement, and coercion with alienation, so Gamson expects to find confidence in and commitment to the government on the part of interest groups to be associated with persuasion as an influence technique, affective neutrality to be associated with the use of inducements, and alienation from or distrust in the government to be associated with the use of constraints. These three hypothesized combinations of political "trust" and means of inducing political compliance are congruent ones. Moreover, the use of one type of influence typically agitates against the use of one of the other two; that is, just as coercive prisons cannot easily rehabilitate their inmates, so partisan groups cannot easily use both constraints and persuasion to influence the government. (For a related exploration in the context of urban communities, see Fainstein and Fainstein, 1974, pp. 259-260.)

In support of his position, Gamson correlated data on the percentage of citizens in five countries who are alienated in their expectations about government outputs reported by Almond and Verba (1965) and the level of internal violence in different countries measured by Rummel (1965) and Tanter (1965). Table XVII-8 repre-

Table XVII-8—Degree of Alienation and Frequency of Constraints for Five Countries

Country	Percentage Alienated*	Constraint Scores**
United States	12	414
Great Britain	26	327
West Germany	26	60
Italy	42	604
Mexico	71	701
$r = 0.69$		

* These figures are from Almond and Verba (1965, Table II.10). They are contaminated somewhat for our purposes by the inclusion in them of "parochials" (individuals who are unaware of the impact of the government on their lives) in addition to "alienates" (individuals who have negative expectations about the impact of government).
** These figures are from Tanter (1965). They are the scores on "turmoil," a general factor with high loadings on demonstrations, riots, general strikes, and assassinations.
Source: Gamson (1968), p. 172

sents a correlation of the Almond Verba alienation scores with Tanter's "turmoil" factor, one of two factors he obtained from a factor analysis of nine measures of conflict within nations and the one which loads most highly on demonstrations, riots, assassinations, and general strikes. The correlation is a high one: .69.

Development Strategies

The first step in applying the compliance typology to strategies of development was undertaken by Mohammad Niaz (1963) in his Ph.D. thesis, sponsored by Professor Garth N. Jones. They published a joint paper on the subject in 1963 (Jones and Niaz, 1963), followed by an additional elaboration by Jones (1965). By far the most extensive discussion of the basic approach and presentation of relevant data is that included in Jones' 1969 book. The discussion here starts with Niaz's early work and then focuses on Jones' book.[1]

Niaz's sample takes in 100 descriptions of cases of "a conscious, deliberate and collaborative effort to improve the operation and performance of organizational systems . . ." (1963, p. 17). The strategies employed were classified as *coercive* when the emphasis was placed on generating pressure on subordinates, inducement of stress, and reliance on hierarchy or when strategies were characterized by "non-mutual goal setting, imbalanced power relationships and one-sided deliberativeness" (*ibid.*, pp. 74-75) as well as by the application or threat of application of physical sanctions and restrictions.

Classified as *normative* strategies were those which achieved compliance through internalization of directives seen to be legitimate, and in which control is exercised through symbolic rewards and sanctions, loyalty toward leaders, manipulation of mass media, prestige symbols and rituals. Strategies include: participation; involvement-commitment; feedback evaluation and follow-up; displacement of values; social awareness; education.

Utilitarian strategies involved "control over material resources and rewards through allocation of increased contributions, benefits and services. The rewards are only available to the client system when it does what it is required to do by the change agent" (*ibid.*).

Next, Niaz classified the goals the strategies were seeking to advance. He correlated the goals with the compliance development strategies for 78 cases for which sufficient data were available. No clear relationship emerged. Most of the strategies reviewed here fall either under normative or "others;" only a total of 16 are classified as either coercive or utilitarian, and of these two are classified as

1. For another interesting work, not sufficiently tied to compliance analysis to be reviewed here, see Morse (1969), pp. 276-279, 299.

dealing with the nonspecific goal of "organizational change." The data base is too small for most statistical operations.

Niaz goes on to discuss the relative success of the 3 types of strategies in advancing the different goals and to correlate them with various attributes of "change agents." As the same attributes are discussed, however, using a larger body of data and more variables, in a much more accessible source (Jones, 1969), the remainder of the discussion draws on Jones' book.

Jones' definition of the strategies in terms of compliance is the same as the one used by Niaz (*ibid.,* pp. 116-118). He covers 190 cases of "planned organizational change," including communities, societies, and corporations, lifted from journal articles and monographs.

Jones found that in 52 cases the strategy was highly normative (27%); 15 largely utilitarian (8%); 3 coercive (1.59%); 51 normative–utilitarian (27%); 21 coercive–normative (11%); 21 utilitarian–normative (11%); and few in the remaining combinations (*ibid.,* pp. 121-122). One might be tempted to conclude from this data that reliance on normative strategies is most common, utilitarian second, and coercive least; but in view of the fact that the universe of strategies has not been defined (i.e., there is no exhaustive list of all the strategies used by all the countries and communities and corporations) and in view of the fact that a single strategy (e.g., nationalization in USSR) may carry more weight than scores of others (e.g., advertising campaigns against smoking), one best sees in this distribution a picture of the sample analyzed by Jones, rather than a world picture.

Jones' most significant contribution is not in characterizing development strategies but in tracing relations found within the sizeable body of data analyzed. The first step was to study the relationships between a compliance strategy used and the tactics applied in the same situation. While *strategies* are viewed as "the planning and directing of operations," *tactics* are defined as "the maneuvering of forces and factors into positions of advantage" (*ibid.,* p. 115). Tactics were also classified in compliance categories. An average of 4.43 different tactics were identified per case, a total of 839. The pattern of association between tactics and strategies which emerged from the research is given in Table XVII-9.

The table shows a very high association between application of coercive strategies and reliance on coercive tactics, which is hardly surprising. More interesting is that actors who employed normative strategies, while relying predominantly on normative tactics (61%),

Table XVII-9—Percentage Relationships Between Strategies and Tactics

| CLASS OF STRATEGY | CASES | | Categories of Tactics | | | | | | | | | Total | Average Number of Tactics |
| | Number | Percent of Total | COERCIVE-LIKE | | NORMATIVE-LIKE | | UTILITARIAN-LIKE | | NEUTRAL-LIKE | | | | |
			Number	Percent of Total	Number	Percent of Total	Number	Percent of Total	Number	Percent of Total			
Coercive	3	1.57	6	66.66	1	11.11	1	11.11	1	11.12	9	3.00
Normative	52	27.41	27	11.68	141	61.03	17	7.35	46	19.96	231	4.63
Utilitarian	15	7.80	9	14.28	25	39.70	20	31.74	9	14.28	63	4.20
Coercive and Normative	21	11.05	44	45.36	34	35.05	7	1.21	12	12.38	97	4.62
Utilitarian and Coercive	9	4.73	13	38.23	6	17.64	5	14.70	10	29.43	34	3.77
Normative and Utilitarian	51	26.84	31	13.47	125	54.34	32	13.93	42	18.28	230	4.51
Normative and Coercive	11	5.78	15	29.41	29	56.86	4	7.85	3	5.88	51	4.64
Coercive and Utilitarian	7	3.68	11	31.42	12	34.30	6	7.14	6	17.14	35	5.00
Utilitarian and Normative	21	11.05	13	14.60	37	41.57	14	15.73	25	28.08	89	4.24
Total	190		169		410		106		154		839	4.42

Source: Jones (1969), p. 119. Reprinted with permission of Praeger Publishers, copyright 1969.

also drew to some extent on utilitarian and even on coercive measures. Though this may seem paradoxical, on second thought it makes sense. Consider a highway safety campaign which relies chiefly on persuasion, driver education in schools, commercials, and billboards, but incorporates in addition steeper fines and harsher jail sentences for violators. Thus, on this level, too, the compliance patterns are not monolithic, but one compliance type does tend to dominate (p. 7).

Even less predictable is the finding that utilitarian strategies have no dominant tactics, and the actors using them are reported to rely somewhat more on normative than utilitarian means (39.7% versus 31.7%). However, some of the tactics classified as "neutral" (14.3%), e.g., "technical modification," "timing," and "marginality" may well belong in the utilitarian category.

Most of the other "dual" compliance relationships, which combine two elements, also employ tactics which are more or less compatible (*ibid.,* p. 121). A detailed breakdown of the tactics used (e.g., legitimation versus social awareness) is also provided. "Participation" stands out among the normative ones; "elite involvement" among the coercive ones; there is no similarly favored utilitarian one.

Jones next asked if strategies which differ in their compliance content differ also in the effectiveness of the change agent. Interestingly, he found no correlation (*ibid.,* p. 123).

Jones suggests that the telling factor is how well the strategy was used, rather than which one, but this also implies that despite the various conditions there were no systematic differences in the "suitability" of strategies employed or that, if an unsuitable one was tried, the strategy was transformed, under the pressure of events, into a more compatible one in line with the congruence hypothesis of the compliance theory. (Otherwise, even if all strategies are employed with the same or similar distribution of skills, there should be differences in effectiveness).

Jones also examined the relationship among compliance strategies used, client's receptivity to the goals being advanced, and procedures through which these goals were set (were they set by the elites, the clients, or jointly?). Here he found only weak associations, indicating a very mild tendency for more participatory "change agents" to be more selective in their means than less receptive ones. This, Jones explains, is due to the fact that less participatory elites are more akin to persons shooting in the dark, while the more open ones are better informed *a priori* about what will work. This is a significant point

Table XVII-10—Goal Achievement and Use of Strategies

GOAL ACHIEVEMENT

CLASSES OF STRATEGIES

GOAL ACHIEVEMENT	Number	Coercive	Normative	Utilitarian	Coercive & Normative	Utilitarian & Coercive	Normative & Utilitarian	Normative & Coercive	Coercive & Utilitarian	Utilitarian & Normative
Not achieved	31	1	8	2	4	2	6	3	3	2
Partially achieved	79	—	20	5	8	4	28	4	3	7
Achieved	80	2	24	8	9	3	17	4	1	12
Total	190	3	52	15	21	9	51	11	7	21

Source: Jones (1969), p. 128. Reprinted with permission of Praeger Publishers, copyright 1969.

indicative of the virtues of upward communication, representing viewpoints rather than mere information (the latter being available, say, through domestic intelligence gathering), and of the superiority of open elites to closed ones.

Jones also found a close correlation between the strategy used and the level of goal achievement. "For example, in the normative class of strategies, 8 or 26 percent was found in the category of goals not achieved, 20 or 25 percent for goals partially achieved, and 24 or 30 percent for goals achieved" (*ibid.*, p. 125). For the rest of the data see Table XVII-10.

This is by far Jones' most interesting finding, which he modestly does not tout. Viewed together with the previous one, on the "indifference" of the performance of change agents and the relevance of client's involvement, this last finding clearly suggests that overall success is much more significantly affected by differences in the extent to which clients are involved than by elites' performance. Few findings will have more implications than this one. It suggests reliance on normative compliance or, when this is not practical, on a normative–utilitarian combination, rather than on coercive measures or coercive–utilitarian strategies, because the former are far more compatible with client participation.

Jones' data and analysis extend far beyond that reported here. However, the main point, it seems, has been sufficiently illustrated: that the compliance approach can be applied fruitfully to organized efforts at the societal as well as on the corporate level, and to characterize the efforts of governments, of major social movements, and organizations of society rather than only processes within organizations.

Total Change

G. William Skinner and Edwin A. Winckler (1969) explore, both theoretically and empirically, the implications of the compliance theory for social change in entire societies.[2] The authors identified a sequence of compliance states, which has recurred in rural Communist China and analyze this in terms of the interaction over time of

2. See also Skinner (1971), pp. 278ff., and Winckler (1973), pp. 560-566. Another important work, which deals with total change and states is Peter Nettle's study of mobilization and modernization (1967). Though he states his work is deeply influenced by the compliance theory and related work (*ibid.*, p. 15), we do not review it here because no specific findings or conceptual elaborations directly related to the theory are included. Nettle was a highly independent thinker.

recurring sequences in each of the components of the rural compliance system. The study includes both relationships among goals, power, and involvement and associated changes in the correlates of compliance. Virtually none of the theorems included in the original text are left unconsidered.

As we shall see in the following pages, Skinner and Winckler's greatest achievement is in elaborating the original theory of intra-system dynamics—the striving of noncongruent types toward congruent ones —into a fully dynamic theory by developing the transformation rules, which explain the transition from one compliance state to another.[3] They demonstrate how incompatibilities among goals, power, and involvement propel systems from one state to the next. A more significant extension of the theory is hard to conceive.

Perhaps the central premise of Skinner and Winckler's argument is that ". . . the search behavior of the Chinese communist political system in exploring after a compliance state which offers satisfactory returns on order, economic, and ideological goals is a symptom of significant contradictions among the compliance requirements of these three goals, given the structure of Chinese society and the particular forms of the Communist leaders' ambitions" (*ibid.*, p. 414). The authors contend that it is these "contradictions" that have kept the Chinese compliance system in motion. Such contradictions are "the basic cause of the compliance cycling we shall observe" (*ibid.*).

Skinner and Winckler construct a "compliance cycle," which they define as "a recurring sequence of compliance arrangements and performance outcomes within a compliance system" (1969, p. 411). The three basic components of the compliance theory are discussed: goals, power, and involvement. Following Etzioni, each of these components is viewed as composed of three pure ingredients. Goals, for example, can be economic goals, ideological goals, order goals, or some combination of these.

Skinner and Winckler arrange the three compliance types as points along a continuous cycle. They observe that in Communist China, goals, power, and involvement progressed recurrently through each of their successive forms. Goals, for example, pass from an emphasis on economic goals to one stressing ideological objectives, finally moving to a state where order goals are given primacy. Similar cyclical patterns are observed for involvement patterns and organizational power.

3. On these rules, see p. 490.

To formalize these interpretations, the authors present separate models depicting the goal, power, and involvement cycles. The *goal cycle* behaves "as though when it achieved a satisfactory level of order, it tried to maximize economic and ideological goals, favoring the latter whenever minimal attainment of the former permitted" (*ibid.,* pp. 414-415). The *power cycle* is set in motion by a shift in the relative influence of leaders who favor different compliance arrangements. Advocates of normative power are basically the preeminent force in the Communist government, yet they are focused to relinquish their primary role to supporters of remunerative and coercive power when economic performance and social order goals are not attained. The *involvement cycle* is seen primarily as a response to the application of power: "it is in the Chinese case typically precipitated by an increase in normative power, applied in order to communicate and instill a new set of goals and to elicit performance in service of these goals" (*ibid.,* p. 418).

Skinner and Winckler see their data as supporting the core thesis that goals, power, and involvement tend toward congruence and that certain patterns of compliance are intrinsically more stable and successful than others. Skinner and Winckler do observe a tendency for Chinese compliance to seek congruence, as hypothesized. In the Chinese case, empirically such congruence among goals, power, and involvement has been difficult to reach and even more difficult to maintain over time. Nevertheless, the theory correctly predicts the constraints on compliance policy. When the situation is incongruent— as here it almost always is, albeit to different degrees—eventually changes are attempted to make goals, power, and involvement more congruent until satisfactory performance is reached. When the next "contradiction" arises, incongruency again increases and forces the compliance system forward to a new phase.

To clarify this complex process Skinner and Winckler consider the interaction of goals, power, and involvement two at a time. The result is two composite cycles: the *compliance cycle,* relating power to involvement, and the *policy cycle,* relating power to goals.

The compliance cycle is attained by superimposing the involvement cycle on the power cycle (Figure XVII-1). In its ideal form, the compliance hypothesis dictates that the following relationships are to be expected: remunerative power is associated with indifferent involvement of the lower participants, normative power with com-

mitted involvement, and coercive power with alienated involvement
(p. 13). Skinner and Winckler find in their historical study that only

Figure XVII-1 — *The Compliance Cycle: Interaction between Power and Involvement and the Sequence of Compliance Phases*

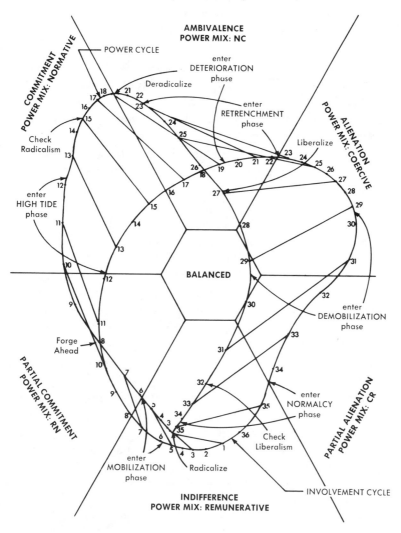

The entire span of the power cycle has been subdivided into 36 equal time segments, defined and
numbered so that Segment 1 begins when the R component of the power mix is at a minimum. The
36 segments into which the involvement and goal cycles have also been subdivided are synchronized
with those of the power cycle.

Source: Skinner and Winckler (1969), p. 419.

at a few points along the compliance cycle is a congruent power–
involvement relationship reached. Rather, one component often seems
to "lead" the other toward a new state of congruency, only fleetingly
achieved.

More specifically, during the first third of the cycle (see Figure
XVII-1) normative power is exerted in hopes of moving an indifferent Chinese peasantry toward states of higher commitment. Yet
during the second third of the cycle, the peasants' involvement reaches
this level of high commitment, only to move on rapidly to a state of
increasing alienation. The result of this "unforeseen" reaction of the
peasants is for the organization (i.e., the Communist Chinese rural
administrative structure) to initiate a power mix giving greater emphasis to coercion. During the final phases of the cycle, power once
again "leads" involvement, an increasing proportion of remunerative
power reducing alienation and mollifying the peasantry back to calculative indifference.

The second cycle derived by Skinner and Winckler is labeled the
policy cycle and results from the superimposition of the power cycle
on the goal cycle. What emerges is roughly the same "cat-chasing-
tail" pattern just discussed. According to the compliance theory three
situations would be expected with greatest frequency: Remunerative
power would be expected to be most effective when economic goals
are sought, normative power for ideological goals, and coercive power
for order goals. Yet in observing twenty years of rural Chinese society, Skinner and Winckler conclude that "for the greater part of
the compliance cycle the effective power mix does not match the
goals being pursued very exactly" (*ibid.,* p. 420). (This conclusion
is illustrated in Figure XVII-2.) For the brunt of the cycle, power is
consistently more "radical" (i.e., more normatively oriented) than the
desired goals. The authors attribute this to a strong ideological commitment to the view that normative power is, and should be, the most
effective means to attain economic and ideological goals. In its strict
adherence to this "theory of success," "the regime propagates policies
and encourages procedures which are unrealistically related to goals"
(1969, p. 422). Thus, as with the power–involvement cycle, Chinese
society can be depicted as a never-ending attempt to reach a power–
goal congruency. Only for fleeting moments is a state of congruency
reached, and the greater part of the twenty years under investigation
sees a choice of power mix that is inappropriate to the desired goals.

Attempting to summarize the interaction of these various cycles, Skinner and Winckler divide up the compliance cycle into six distinct phases, each characterized by its own unique combination of power, involvement, and goals. Phase I, "Normalcy" for precommunist Chinese peasant society, is characterized by a fairly high level of goal–

Figure XVII-2 — *The Policy Cycle: Interaction between Goals and Power and the Sequence of Policy Decisions*

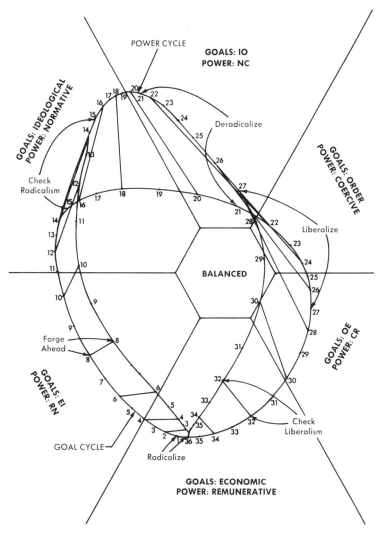

Source: Skinner and Winckler (1969), p. 421.

power–involvement congruency. Remunerative power is employed to attain goals that are primarily economic in emphasis and the involvement of the power participants, as predicted by the central compliance hypothesis, is calculative and of low intensity. In the later stages of Phase I, however, government leaders favoring a more normative power mix seize control and initiate attempts to mobilize the peasants to a higher degree of commitment. As these efforts intensify during the Mobilization Phase (Phase II), there results an ever-widening gap between the normative power exerted and the still relatively calculative involvement of the lower participants. However, as the objectives of the campaign are widely discussed and internalized, the level of involvement becomes more intense, moving the relationship between power and involvement more toward a state of congruency.

With the advent of Phase III (High Tide), involvement reaches full commitment, and congruency between power (normative) and involvement (commitment) is briefly attained. However, power (by now predominately normative) remains considerably more "radical" than the intended goals (economical as well as ideological). However, toward the end of Phase III, as rural peasants become increasingly disillusioned with the actual results produced by the government's "normative push," involvement begins to move toward alienation. An incongruency between power (still normative) and involvement results. A state of Deterioration (Phase IV) sets in as involvement moves very rapidly toward negative involvement. Power, in response, shifts slowly toward a normative–coercive mix.

By the beginning of Phase V (Retrenchment), order goals become crucial. A fleeting moment of power–involvement congruency occurs as the regime resorts to coercion to restore order and maintain production. In the final phase, described as "Demobilization," progressive substitution of remunerative for coercive power successfully reduces alienation. Normalcy is then attained, and the cycle is ready to repeat itself anew.

The authors take special note of three key points along the compliance cycle where crucial political policy decisions are made. During the Normalcy phase a "Decision to Radicalize" is made, and normative power is exerted in hopes of increasing the involvement of the lower participants. The "Decision to Check Radicalism" is made sometime during the High Tide phase, when it appears that this normative power is producing greater degrees of alienated involvement. Finally, a "Decision to Liberalize" is made during the Retrenchment phase, which relaxes the coercive power and reinstates a greater emphasis on economic goals. This last decision reflects the passing of the "order crisis" that reached its peak during the Deterioration phase.

With this theoretical model in hand, Skinner and Winckler attempt to explain the successive attempts of the Communist government to revolutionize rural Chinese society during the years 1949 to 1968. They observe a series of eight complete cycles of radicalization (i.e., a move toward a more normative power mix, and more ideological goals), crisis (i.e., the sudden salience of order goals and resort to coercion), and deradicalization (i.e., return to an increasingly remunerative power mix in hopes of reattaining economic goals).

During the first decade of this revolutionary period, five complete turns of the compliance cycle were needed to dissolve the class-based rural society and replace it with a communistic system emphasizing the role of "People's Communes." The authors are careful to point out (cf. 426-427) that in the early years in different parts of the country different stages of socialism are being achieved in the same compliance cycle. Although the discussions of historical events are brief, they suffice to indicate that the actual occurrences during the twenty-year period do conform quite uniformly to the authors' compliance cycle.

Why compliance cycling in the Chinese case? The answer, it is implied, is not due to a permanent element of organizational or societal nature but lies in the peculiarities of the situation. There is an unwavering commitment among a majority of Chinese political leaders to the exercise of normative power in pursuit of both ideological and economic goals. Thus when moments of congruency are attained, the leadership has repeatedly upset this congruency by introducing an excessive degree of normative power. It is this faith in normative power that separates the Chinese political organization from most Western formal organizations. Such organizations, according to the compliance hypothesis, might well be expected to cease making major alterations of their power-mix once a congruent compliance structure has been found. Their societal engineering is less optimistic and ambitious, more pragmatic, which makes both for less total change and more likelihood of the system to "settle" until contradictions stemming from sources other than of the elite ideologizing unsettle it. Unbalancing factors here are more external (technological, environmental) than internal contradictions in the compliance structure.

The types of changes discussed by Skinner and Winckler bear some resemblance to the concept of "ultrastability," as applied to political organizations by Kaplan (1964) and previously developed by Ashby (1952, p. 98). Kaplan writes: "Ultrastable systems may be said to 'search' for stable patterns of behavior. They are capable of recognizing the failure of existing patterns of response and of making changes in themselves that permit them to respond differently. The old patterns are rejected because they fail and new organizational means and behavior patterns are adopted" (Kaplan, 1964, p. 478).

A different model for total societal change is presented in *The Active Society* (Etzioni, 1968). Here, an attempt is made to apply the distinction between stable systems and transformable systems to macro-sociology. The *stable* system is one in which the former societal pattern must totally collapse before a new central structure can be evolved. In contrast, the *transformable* system is capable of revising its core pattern during a continuous course of activities (*ibid.,* p. 470). Whether the Communist Chinese regime is stable or ultrastable is unclear. On the one hand, the very fact that it keeps revising its congruency pattern without collapsing suggests it is ultrastable. On the other hand, whether or not such a contradiction-ridden pattern can be stabilized is open to question. Possibly, the system will grow less ideological and "settle" around one pattern or collapse.

Also, there is the question of long-run trends in compliance. The possibility that a secular trend toward ever less reliance on non-normative means is evolving, on a world-wide basis, has been raised (Etzioni, 1968, pp. 375-381), based on increases in income per capita, the spread of education, technological progress, and other developments. This possibility has also been raised with reference to China. In his study of bureaucratization and modernization in Maoist China, Martin King Whyte notes: "While coercion and material incentives remain important [he cites here Skinner and Winckler, 1969], there is a constant effort to get people to respond more to what Etzioni calls normative and social power" (1973, p. 154). In a chart summarizing his findings, Whyte describes the Maoist conception of compliance as: "Normative and social compliance should play the main role everywhere" (*ibid.,* p. 157). He makes the distinction between this Chinese conception and a second view, labeled the "Western conception," wherein "varied compliance strategies are needed, depending on the organization" (*ibid.*). See also Whyte (1974, pp.

14-15, 217, 222-223; Dallin and Breslaver (1970), p. 193; Johnson (1970), pp. 9-12; Cell (1974); and Heginbotham (1975).

Whyte seems to observe an overall trend toward an ever greater emphasis upon normative and social compliance structures. Skinner and Winckler see the normative phase as but one node on a never-ending cycle of compliance structures. The two articles would be in accord were Skinner and Winckler to indicate that the relative emphasis upon the normative compliance structures was greater during "C8," the most recent phase, than during "C1," the earliest among the eight stages they depict. However, Skinner and Winckler confine themselves in this article to cyclical aspects of the development process in agriculture, leaving to an ongoing research project "linear" and "transformative" aspects of the dynamics of compliance systems in this and other areas of development policy.

In the final section of their article, Skinner and Winckler relate cycling in goals, power, and involvement to changes in compliance theory's "organizational correlates." They give a phase-by-phase account of how each of the organizational correlates changes as the compliance arrangement is altered. Although it is impossible to summarize here each of these correlates in each of the phases, highlighting the general behavior of three groups of correlates in three contrasting phases of the compliance cycle will convey the nature of the analysis. In general, the limited data available on these organizational variables with regard to rural Communist China tend to confirm the original compliance hypotheses; that is, they show that each organizational correlate adapts to the particular compliance arrangement in the manner predicted by the compliance theory.

The first group of correlates includes the balance of instrumental and expressive functions assumed by leadership roles, the distribution of charisma within the organization, and the volume and direction of communication between organizational levels. In the "liberal" demobilization and normalcy phases, leaders tend to be positional supervisors, basing their instrumental leadership on the authority of expertise. Charisma is limited to the very top leadership of the country as a whole. Communication is task specific, adequate in volume, and well balanced between upward and downward flows. In the "radical" mobilization and high tide phases, leadership roles become increasingly expressive, diffuse, and participatory; charisma spreads down the party chain of command and across the ranks of the local leadership; and the volume of downward communication rises rapidly, overwhelming the upward flow of information about actual local conditions.

A second group of correlates concerns the number of activities organizational members perform within the organization's boundaries (scope), the number of activities for which the organization attempts to set norms for its members, within or without the organization (pervasiveness), and the level of generality of the norms on which organizational members are obliged to agree (consensus). Compliance theory hypothesized that utilitarian organizations could be characterized by narrow scope and low pervasiveness (p. 268). This combination has been observed by Skinner and Winckler during the Normalcy Phase of the compliance cycle, when the organization is in its most utilitarian guise (that is, it emphasizes economic goals, employs remunerative power, and evokes a minimal, calculative involvement). As compliance theory predicts, scope broadens and pervasiveness increases during the normative phases of the compliance cycle, as the government mobilizes increasing numbers of peasants for increasingly diverse organization objectives. In coercive organizations, the compliance hypothesis expects scope to be broad, but pervasiveness to be low. Although the data here is extremely thin, such a situation seems likely to occur during the Retrenchment phase, when scope has declined only partially while pervasiveness has dropped precipitately.

A third group of correlates concerns the inverse relationship between selectivity of recruitment and type of socialization of organizational members and the bases and extent of cohesion among organizational participants. Recruitment is low, selective, and voluntary in liberal phases, increasingly rapid and inclusive during radical phases. During crisis phases less enthusiastic members selectively withdraw. In the course of the compliance cycle the emphasis in socialization changes from informal and instrumental to formal and expressive and back again, rising in intensity as recruitment becomes less selective. The bases and extent of cohesion within work groups vary from segmentation along lines of traditional local social structure to an attempt at absolute solidarity within the framework of large-scale socialist formal organization.

In conclusion, it can be safely stated that no other compliance study has contributed more per published page to the compliance theory than this article by Skinner and Winckler, which itself is based on years of historical and sociological research.

Historical Trends

Societal changes are a combination of their own dynamics and of their historical condition, which encompasses the larger civilization. We have already suggested a general secular trend toward greater normativeness and discussed a study of China from this viewpoint. The following two studies cast additional light on historical trends in compliance structure.

John E. Rouse (1973) advances the thesis that the Catholic Church in the U.S. has shifted from a greater reliance on "calculative commitments and utilitarian compliance [which] often overshadowed specific theological and moral goals" (*ibid.,* p. 24) during the nineteenth century, toward greater reliance on normative controls in this century. The earlier utilitarian stress was caused by the context (a developing capitalist nation) and the need to provide material services to a mass of immigrants. Rouse underlined the point that these pressures stemmed from the "dominant culture and were not the product of the ideological commitments of the Catholic minority itself" (*ibid.,* p. 10).

With the increased assimilation of the immigrants into American life after World War I, with accumulation of wealth, growing cultural pluralism, and the ecumenical movement, normative elements within the Church began to predominate (*ibid.,* pp. 17-21).

Pirages (1966) departed from the general observation that "the political compliance structure [i.e., of total societies] differs somewhat from organizational compliance structure in that the former is usually characterized by use of a greater mixture of the three types of power than the latter" (*ibid.,* p. 19). He then predicts the following compliance trend: As countries become more developed, more individuals make more "participatory" demands. These demands tend to be met, entailing increased normativeness on the part of elites and the system as a whole. The only alternative, Pirages suggests, is greater reliance on coercive compliance. However, he argues, the costs of this alternative become "prohibitive in terms of resources which must be devoted to maintaining coercive establishments as well as the loss of innovative human resources due to alienation from the political system" (*ibid.,* p. 20).

Pirages tests his prediction by correlating, for 35 countries, the level of socioeconomic development, measured in terms of GNP per capita, with the coerciveness of its political compliance structure and with the political system's responsiveness (or openness to participation).[4] Coercion is measured by four indicators of equal weight. Responsiveness is determined using a similar procedure, drawing on openness and representativeness of the country's elites, the competitiveness of the electoral system, and the status of the legislature. Based on Pirages' data, we found a rank-order correlation coefficient (Spearman's rho) of $-.736$ between economic development and coercion and of $.809$ between economic development and responsiveness.

INTER-UNIT SYSTEMS

A core question inevitably arises when one deals with more than one organization, community, or nation: How broadly and deeply are the units interrelated, and is the relationship an egalitarian one or characterized by one or another form of domination? The question has a logical origin. If there is more than one unit and we are to make statements about the next level, the inter-unit level, we must know to what degree we are dealing with an aggregate or an integrated entity. Linked to the answer are significant substantive issues such as the capacity to act in unison (which is low for aggregates; higher for communities), the extent to which market or government forces are at work (the former are more significant for aggregates; the latter relatively more for integrated systems), the extent to which they are prone to internecine price wars or violence (more common among aggregates), the degree to which outsiders are jointly faced (more common among more integrated systems), and the degree to which units are inclined to rebellion (rebellion is common when the community's internal power structure is unrepresentative and unbalanced). Actually, there are few domestic or international issues which are not affected by the specific attributes of inter-unit relations.

But what has all this to do with compliance theory? The link is the suggestion that the compliance tripology encompasses not only the kinds of power employed and involvement elicited, but is *also relevant to the bonds which link units and the assets they command.* To illustrate this point, and to bring some data to bear on it, I shall refer to a study of four attempts to forge political communities out of groups of nations which heretofore had not been members of such a binding system.

4. See also Pirages (1968, pp. 4ff.).

Political Unification, a study by Etzioni (1965), covers the six original members of the European Economic Community, in the years from 1958 to 1964; the relations among the Nordic countries, chiefly Sweden, Norway, and Denmark (1953 to 1964); an attempt by Egypt and Syria to form a United Arab Republic (1958 to 1961); and successive attempts to unite ten Carribean islands into a Federation of the West Indies (1958 to 1962).

The study started from the premise that "a community is established only when it has self-sufficient integrative mechanisms; that is, when the maintenance of its existence and form is provided for by its own processes and is not dependent upon those of external systems or member-units" (*ibid.,* p. 4). The three integrative mechanisms are directly based on the compliance tripology: "(a) the system has an effective monopoly over the use of the means of violence . . .; (b) it has a decision-making center capable of significantly affecting the allocation of resources and rewards throughout the community; and (c) it is the dominant focus of political identification for the large majority of politically aware citizens" (*ibid.*). A community is "thus a state, an administration-economic unit, and a focal point of identification" (*ibid.*). (On this point, see also Stein and Carreau, 1968, p. 579 and p. 638; Clark, 1968, pp. 48-49; Gitelman, 1970, pp. 239-244; and Brickman, 1974, p. 17.)

When the level of integration in all three spheres is low but not nil, we have a system, because the units have enough integration to interact in a closed feedback loop. Nevertheless, this is not sufficient to autonomously secure the level and form of the system, i.e., not enough to form a political community which requires high levels of integration on all three fronts.

It was further suggested that unbalanced integrations make for recognizable types of inter-unit systems. Thus, when coercive integration is high and the other two forms low, we have an empire. When normative integration is high and the other two low, we see before us a commonwealth. Similarly, when integration is chiefly utilitarian and also relatively egalitarian, we have a common market. The dynamics and stability of the various types, it was hypothesized, can, in part, be predicted from the level and kind of integration as specified by compliance variables.

Before the relevant data can be introduced, an additional point must be made. The question of the loci of power, traced in the compliance publication in terms of T, R, and L structures (pp. 310ff.)

and by those concerned with slope of control and the relationship *between* elites (pp. 93-94), is of central importance here. No inter-unit system is "born" a full-fledged community; it has to evolve, and in the process internal elites (either the elites of one or more of the member units or a "neutral" system elite) take over the guidance of the system from external elites, or fashion new, previously nonexistent, guidance centers. This is a corollary of the system's growing capacity to act in unison.

What did the study of four attempts at political unification show? The Federation of the West Indies fell apart, as one would expect, in view of the fact that (a) there was little utilitarian integration (the ten islands traded more with other nations than with each other) and few shared administrative links were created; (b) identification with the new nation initially was weak, and later declined, as islanders identified chiefly with their individual island societies; (c) there were no federation-wide coercive links to speak of, neither a shared army nor a police. Guidance was "internalized" in a manner directly in conflict with the internal power realities, because of outside (British) pressures. The smaller islands (especially Barbados) were given proportionally more representation than the two bigger ones (Jamaica and Trinidad). The federation lasted less than four years, with the secession of the bigger islands marking its demise.

The UAR lasted an even shorter time than the Federation of the West Indies. Although the Egyptian and Syrian elites and mobilized publics in the two nations were committed to the idea of unity in principle, it soon became clear that there was little agreement with reference to specific content. Egypt, in those days, wanted a much more leftist, radical union than Syria, as well as a much greater degree of amalgamation, i.e., the normative bond was shallow. The two economies were not complementary but competitive in their main crops (cotton, sugar) and industries (textile). The discontiguous territories, also a factor in the West Indies, made economic and administrative integration difficult. In short, utilitarian links were very weak. Coercion was relied upon, briefly, toward the end, but this was too little and too late to save the union.

The unification of the Nordic countries which shared several organizational structures (chiefly the Nordic Council), was much more stable. Though it did not fall apart in the period studied, neither did it evolve into a stronger union. Though Denmark, Sweden, and Norway are contiguous and traded with each other more than either the West Indies or Syria and Egypt, they each had strong economic links to other countries, especially West Germany and the United Kingdom. Also, two of the countries were NATO members, while Sweden was not. In short, utilitarian links were stronger than in the other two cases studied, but not really strong or expanding. There was a fairly long tradition of commitment to a Scandinavian or Nordic community; many cultural values and traditions were shared; so were the Lutheran Church and numerous informal bonds among the leaders of the three core nations. But these normative links were not particularly conducive to the evolution of formal institutions of cooperation which hence did not progress in effectiveness, as a comparison of the Nordic Council to a parliament quickly shows. Finally, there were no coercive links.

Last, the EEC, which included in the period studied six countries, was found to be the most effectively bound; it was more integrated, and integrating, than the other three unions. In those days, the idea of a United States of Europe or *Europa* carried much more appeal than it has in recent times. Economic integration of the six contiguous countries was much more extensive than in the other three unions studied, including not just removal of trade barriers and a fair measure of standardization of various economic measures (from certain taxes to size of truck axles), but also the formulation of an integrated economic policy, in Brussels, which gave EEC an administrative and, to a lesser degree, a political capital. Finally, the community developed at least some right to levy sanctions directly against firms in the six countries, i.e., the beginning of coercive integration.

This very brief description of the development of the four international unification systems studied is meant only to provide clues as to how the compliance tripology can be employed on a higher level of generality. For details of the measurements and dynamics involved, the interested reader must turn to the original report (Etzioni, 1965). Here we merely wish to record the suggestion that bonds among nations (and other supra-organizational units) can be fruitfully analyzed in terms of the compliance tripology.

Similarly, the concept of *scope* also transfers well. It was measured, on the international level, in terms of the number of shared social sectors *of the member-units* that an evolving system encompasses (e.g., only military versus both military and economic) as well as the significance of these sectors for the survival of the units and realization of their interests (e.g., postal services versus defense alliance).[5] The main finding was that the broader and more salient the scope of the evolving international system, the higher the level of integration. Monofunctional international organizations tend to be low on both counts; communities, high on both. In terms of the cases studied, the scope and saliency of the EEC and Nordic community bonds greatly exceeded those of the UAR and West Indies federations, although the latter unions were nominally defined as much more encompassing. Again, the purpose of this brief discussion is not to repeat data or analysis provided elsewhere, but to provide a brief illustration of how various compliance "correlates" can be applied to the analysis of inter-unit systems.

Simulation of Alliances

Dennis P. Forcese (1973) has applied the compliance theory to the cohesion of military alliances. In his paper, which is based on the author's Ph.D. thesis at Washington University, Forcese assumes that in each such alliance (or organization) there exists power differentials among the members. These differentials expressed in a rank order with one nation assuming the leading position and forming the center of intra-alliance control. Forcese argues, however, that since in an ideal military alliance all members are considered equally sovereign and independent, these power differentials cannot be transformed into legitimate authority. Hence, one would expect a relative inability on the part of the leader nation to rely on normative power and a consequent greater reliance on the other two types.

Forcese chose as a setting for his study a situation in which the three power hierarchies are congruent, i.e., in which the militarily strongest nation is also the richest as well as the ideological leader.

The independent variable of Forcese's study is the alliance's internal cohesion. Cohesion is seen as the degree to which the weaker members of the alliance comply with the policy and strategy of the most powerful nation (this diverges from the use of the concept in the compliance theory and in other studies, and hence from here on we use willingness to follow instead). Willingness to follow, in turn, is seen as dependent upon the alliance leader's use of power. The subject of the study, then, is the question of what kind of power the most powerful nation of a military alliance uses in order to produce an optimum degree of obedience to its leadership.

5. For an application of the concept of consensus on the societal level, see Greer and Orleans (1964), p. 817.

Forcese used a complex composite measurement to assess the attitudes of the alliance members toward the policies of the alliance in general and toward the leading power in particular. First, a base score of 8 was coded to represent the continuing formal existence of the alliance after each "run" of the simulation game used to test the study's proposition. This score was then increased on the basis of a content analysis of the communications of the alliance's rank-and-file member units, directed either to their fellow members or to members of the opposing alliance. The more these messages expressed support of the alliance and preparedness for coordinated action, the more points were added to the base score. In addition, Forcese used reports by "players" acting on behalf of the leading power on the alliance's internal discussions in order to assess the degree of solidarity within the alliance.

As to the operationalization of the three types of power, coercive power was measured in terms of the relative military superiority the alliance leader commands over the rest of the alliance's membership *and* of its relative military strength as compared to the leading nation of a second, inimical military alliance. What Forcese analyses is not whether an alliance can be kept together by making use of such power in order to control its members but, rather, whether military strength and external threats alone can induce weaker nations to join a stronger one in a military alliance and to abide by its decisions.

Utilitarian power is seen as the amount of economic advantages, especially in the form of favorable trade agreements and economic aid, the richer nation can afford to grant the poorer ones. Similarly, normative power is defined as the degree to which a nation is able to assume, by effectively manipulating shared symbolic or ideological sentiments, the ideological leadership of the alliance.

In order to find out how the three kinds of power effect cohesion, Forcese relies, rather than on "real world" data, on a simulation game experiment with the Inter-Nation Simulation (INS) model.[6] It would carry us too far to describe in detail the intricate set-up used in Forcese's study. Suffice it to say that the model includes two military alliances, each of which consists of four nations, and two neutrals. One of the alliances is the "experimental" one; the "power

6. In a follow-up paper (1973a), Forcese has tried to establish the validity of the INS for experimental research. He argues that in several cases, the model has validated theoretically derived hypotheses on international relations, thus demonstrating its own "homomorphism to the referent system" (p. 1). Furthermore, Forcese reports that preliminary research, done by himself, on NATO tends to show a similar pattern as the simulation experiment (p. 7).

output" of its leading nation is manipulated by researchers. Tensions between the two blocs are kept alive by guerilla attacks on both sides. Ideological differences are introduced by giving each side a different version of a simulated "world history," thus creating diverging historical perspectives. The nations, each being assigned a certain amount of power and a certain policy to start with, are "played" by social science students.

Data was collected on 13 simulation runs. "Players" were changed for each new run. For each of the independent variables, four runs were carried out in which the two other independent variables (i.e. two of the powers used) were held constant and on a low level and only the test variable (the third kind of power) was permitted to change its values. In the one remaining run, all three kinds of power were varied simultaneously. The results of the first 12 runs are summarized in Table XVII-11.

Table XVII-11—Simulation Tests for Three Power Variables

	Mean Cohesion*	Correlations of Power and Followship—4 Runs			
Utilitarian power	12.67	.911	.969	.911	.994
Identive power	11.18	.885	.932	.963	.994
Coercive power	9.67	.819	.789	.820	.828

Based on Forcese (1973). Correlations are given for each run separately.

Utilitarian power turned out to have the most significant impact on willingness to follow. The more utilitarian power the leading nation used vis-à-vis its fellow members, the stronger were the bonds within the alliance. Moreover, the effect of economic support was longer-lasting than with any other kind of power. Even when the amount of power exercised was decreased, the emerging manifestations of "rank-and-file independence . . . did not extend to major deviations from a monolithic alliance organization policy" (1973a, p. 41). At all times, "extra-alliance communications were infrequent, as were extra-bloc economic exchanges" (ibid., p. 40).

Although normative power was somewhat weaker in its effect, it nevertheless contributed to alliance "cohesion," although in three of the four high normative runs some inter-bloc economic exchanges took place. This leads Forcese to conclude that "inter-bloc barriers might be more readily broken down in alliances oriented about an identive [normative] or an ideological base rather than a utilitarian base. The demands of national economies gradually overcome the polemic of national ideologies, unless the economic needs of the nations in alliance are fully satisfied within the alliance" (*ibid.,* p. 45). Furthermore, as willingness to follow seemed to drop off faster when normative power was decreased, faster, that is, than with utilitarian power, Forcese concludes that the effect of normative power might be more short run in nature, while utilitarian power seems to have a stronger long-run effect.

However, the picture changes considerably when the leading nation relies exclusively on coercive power. In two of the four runs, the alliance "failed to survive in its initial form, with the second strongest member . . . leaving (towards the end of the experiment), and other departures apparently imminent" (*ibid.,* p. 49). In one case, war broke out among former alliance members. Economic exchanges between the two blocs were common, even where there was no doubt about the uncertain, threatening military situation or the superiority of the leading nation (*ibid.,* p. 50). Forcese draws the conclusion that "there is a very real possibility that the employment of coercive power has the effect of not inducing cooperation and solidarity, . . . but rather, of *alienating the alliance organization rank-and-file*" (*ibid.,* p. 51).

In the final run, in which the leading nation was allowed to use all three kinds of power at the same time, the results, displayed in Table XVII-12, largely sustained the earlier findings. In this run, the mean "cohesion" measure of the alliance was considerably higher than in the other runs. Furthermore, in line with the previous experiments, multiple regression analysis established that coercive power is almost meaningless for eliciting willingness to follow. However, run #13 deviates from the other experiments in that the beta of normative

Table XVII-12—Compliance and Alliance Cohesion: Experiment Thirteen

Period	Alliance Cohesion	Coercive Power	Utilitarian Power	Identive Power
1	24	36	30	16
2	25	55	33	17
3	16	35	21	13
4	15	57	20	13
5	19	36	27	14
6	21	44	32	14
	$\bar{X} = 20.00$	$\bar{X} = 43.83$	$\bar{X} = 27.17$	$\bar{X} = 14.50$
	$s = 4.0988$	$s = 9.988$	$s = 5.565$	$s = 1.643$
		$r = .010$	$r = .929$	$r = .950$
		$R^2 = .993$		

Source: Forcese (1973), Table XIII.

power is somewhat higher than that of utilitarian power. This, in Forcese's words, makes the relative importance of the two somewhat "ambiguous." However, this difficulty does not impair Forcese's main finding: that "the military superiority of the dominant nation, or coercive power, in and of itself, was inadequate to increase alliance cohesion, even in a situation of international tension and extra-alliance threat" (*ibid.*, p. 51).

Forcese's findings are, of course, very consistent with findings of other compliance studies. It remains to be established whether simulation runs of nations are valid for predicting the behavior of actual nations.[7] On an impressionistic basis, the findings seem to hold.

GUIDABILITY

Compliance theory most needs further development along more "active" lines. The initial theory was one of relationships and, to a lesser degree, of dynamics, but not of guided, deliberate change. Later work (Etzioni, 1968) made this the focus of a theory of society; the concepts of guidability developed, though, are at least as well suited to organized analysis. Although societies have a measure of deliberateness, governing overlay, and citizen mobilization (not just modern societies but also such "primitive" societies as the Zulu, mobilized for war, and ancient Egypt, for pyramid building), even the most mobilized and organized societies are still quite "natural" and unorganized. In contrast, organizations, which also have elements of natural relations, ongoing processes, and "community," are the most guided of all social units. Moreover, to the extent other social units are guided, they often rely on organizations, especially government agencies.

The variables of guidability are chiefly of two kinds—those which characterize the attributes of the controlling overlayer and those of the consensus-building, power-based, mobilization underlayer. In organizational terms, the rough parallels are elites and lower participants. The question is basically how powerful, well-informed, solidaric, and strategic the lower participants are as compared to the elites.

7. Amitai Etzioni, "Social-Psychological Aspects of International Relations," in Gardner Lindzey and Elliot Aronson (eds.), *The Handbook of Social Psychology* (Reading, Massachusetts: Addison-Wesley Publishing Co., 1973), Vol. V, pp. 538-601.

Quite a few of the core compliance hypotheses have simply found here a new theoretical home, without any or with very little modification. A case in point is the theorem that coercive organizations, dominated by elites, lack the support of their lower participants, and hence are capable of only limited collective, guided actions. The high degree of cross-rank integration in normative organizations allows for a much greater amount of collective action, albeit maybe not as much guidability because of the expressive, nonrational focus of the relationship; utilitarian organizations have a greater capacity for collective action than coercive organizations but less collective capacity than normative ones, though they are possibly the most guidable of all three types.

At the same time, guidance analysis highlights several new issues raised by the core concepts of knowledge, decision-making, power, mobilization, and consensus:

1. How aware are the organizational elites of the prevailing compliance relations? To what extent are they trying to defy them? These are "knowledge" and decision-making variables, respectively.

2. Guidance theory highlights the importance of the relative power of the elites as compared to the lower participants. While all organizations have both, there are great differences in the degrees (as well as the kind) of the power differential.

3. Change may occur, it follows, not only because there is a natural "striving" toward congruency, propelled by the quest for goal realization or for an effectiveness which the less congruent types cannot attain, but also as a result of deliberate elite policies and various degrees of organizational consensus and mobilization of the lower participants. Here, for instance, the role of labor unions finds a theoretical base. (On the link between guidance theory and organizational compliance analysis, see Heydebrand (1973), p. 28. See also Capener and Brown (1971), pp. 176ff.; Coward, Beal, and Powers (1970), pp. 281ff.; and Helsabeck (1973). On this point with special reference to business corporations, see Werner Kirsch (1972), pp. 27-31.)

The purpose here is neither to summarize the guidance theory nor to work out the details of its application to organizational analysis in general or to compliance theory in particular, but to indicate a direction in which, I suggest, fruitful theoretical as well as empirical explorations of compliance may develop.

LIST OF NEW COMPLIANCE
STUDIES CITED

AMENDOLA, SUSAN. A study of compliance division at a mental health clinic. Unpublished study, no date.

ANDES, J. A conceptualization of university compliance systems. Doctoral dissertation, University of Florida, 1968.

ANFOSSI, ANNA. Funzioni della parrocchia e partecipazione dei parrocchiani alla vita religiousa in comuni agricoli della Sardegna. Estratto dai *Quaderni di Sociologia,* 1967, XVI: 190-216.

ASHBROOK, J. The relationship of church members to church organization. *Journal for the Scientific Study of Religion,* 1966, 5: 397-419.

ASHBROOK, J. Ministerial leadership in church organization. *Ministry Studies,* 1967, 1: 5-32.

BIGELOW, D. A. & DRISCOLL, R. H. Effect of minimizing coercion on the rehabilitation of prisoners. *J. of Appl. Psychol.,* 1973, 57: 10-14.

BRAGER, G. Commitment and conflict in a normative organization. *Amer. sociol. Rev.,* 1969, 34: 482-491.

BRYCE-LAPORTE, R. S. The conceptualization of the American slave plantation as a total institution. Doctoral dissertation, University of California, Los Angeles, 1968.

DUTTON, J. M. & DUNBAR, R. L. M. Competence and change in a college faculty: A field study. 1973a.

DUTTON, J. M. & DUNBAR, R. L. M. Change and the control of charisma in a university department. 1973b.

ETZIONI, A. & LEHMAN, ETHNA. Dual leadership in a therapeutic organization. *International Review of Applied Psychology,* 1968, 17: 51-67.

EVERS, F., WARREN, R. & ROGERS, D. Organizational goals of farm supply cooperatives in Iowa. Sociology Report No. 108, Department of Sociology and Anthropology, Iowa State University, 1973.

FORCESE, D. P. Simulation experiments in alliance organization cohesion. Unpublished paper, 1973*a*.

FORCESE, D. P. The validity of the inter-nation simulation: A research note. Unpublished paper, 1973*b*.

FRANKLIN, J. L. Power, commitment, and task performance: A test of Etzioni's compliance theory. Paper presented at midwest Sociological Society meetings, Kansas City, Missouri, 1972*a*.

FRANKLIN, J. L. The normative organization: An empirical test of Etzioni's compliance classification. Paper presented at the American Sociological Association, New Orleans, Louisiana, 1972*b*.

FRANKLIN, J. L. The normative organization: An empirical test of Etzioni's compliance theory. Revision of papers read at 1972 meetings of Midwest Sociological Society and the American Sociological Association, 1972*c*.

FRANKLIN, J. L., KITTREDGE, L. D. & THRASHER, J. H. The geographic unit system: Success or failure? Evaluation Monograph No. 17, Evaluation Services, Division of Mental Health Services, State of North Carolina Department of Human Resources, 1973.

GAMSON, W. Means of influence, political trust, and social control. Chapter 8 in *Power and discontent*. Homewood, Ill.: Dorsey Press, 1968.

GAMSON, ZELDA. Performance and personalism in student–faculty relations. *Sociology of Education*, 1967, 40: 279-301.

GAMSON, ZELDA. Utilitarian and normative orientations toward education. *Sociology of Education*, 1966, 39: 46-73.

GREENE, C. N. & ORGAN, D. W. An evaluation of causal models linking the received role with job satisfaction. *Admin. Sci. Q.*, 1973, 18: 95-103.

HAAS, J. E., HALL, R. H. & JOHNSON, N. J. Toward an empirically derived taxonomy of organizations. In R. V. Bowers, ed., *Studies on behavior in organizations: A research symposium*. Athens: University of Georgia Press, 1966. Pp. 157-180.

HALL, R. H., HAAS, J. E. & JOHNSON, N. J. An examination of the Blau-Scott and Etzioni typologies. *Admin. Sci. Q.*, 1967, 12: 118-139.

HODGKINS, B. J. & HERRIOTT, R. E. Age-grade structure, goals, and compliance in the school: An organizational analysis. *Sociology of Education*, 1970, 43: 90-105.

HUDSON, W. W. Commitment and alienation in a public welfare agency. Doctoral dissertation, The University of Chicago, 1973.

INGHAM, G. K. Organizational size, orientation to work and industrial behavior. *Sociology*, 1967, I: 239-258.

INGHAM, R. A comparative study of administrative principles and practices in adult education units. *Adult Education*, 1968, XIX: 52-68.

JONES, G. N. Strategies and tactics of planned organizational change: Case examples in the modernization process of traditional societies. *Human Organization*, 1965, 24: 192-200.

JONES, G. N. *Planned organizational change*. New York: Praeger, 1969.

JONES, G. N. & NIAZ, A. Strategies and tactics of planned organizational change: A scheme of working concepts. *Philippine Journal of Public Administration*, 1963, 7: 275-285.

JULIAN, J. Compliance patterns and communication blocks in complex organizations. *Am. sociol. Rev.,* 1966, 31: 382-389.

JULIAN, J. Organizational involvement and social control. *Social Forces,* 1968, 47: 12-16.

JULIAN, J. Some determinants of dissensus on role prescriptions within and between four organizational positions. *Sociological Quarterly,* 1969: 177-189.

JULIAN, J. & ETZIONI, A. Continuities in social research: The compliance theory. (Forthcoming)

KAPLAN, M. A. Essential roles and rules of transformation. In Eva Etzioni-Halevi & A. Etzioni, eds., *Social change: Sources, patterns and consequences.* New York: Basic Books, 1964.

KIRSCH, W. *Betriebswirtschaftspolitik und geplanter Wandel betriebswirtschaftlicher Systeme.* Wiesbaden, Germany: Betriebswirtschaflicher Verlag, 1972.

KLONGLAN, G., BEAL, G., BOHLEN, J. & MULFORD, C. Prediction of local civil defense directors' role performance: Minnesota, Georgia and Massachusetts. Rural Sociology Report No. 52, Department of Sociology and Anthropology, Iowa State University, 1969.

KLONGLAN, G., MULFORD, C. & TWEED, D. A causal model of consensus formation and effectiveness. Paper presented at the Midwest Sociological Society meetings, Omaha, Nebraska, April 6, 1974.

KNUTSSON, K. E. *Authority and change: A study of the Kallu Institution among the Macha Galla of Ethiopia.* Goteborg, Sweden: Ethnografiska Musett, 1967.

LANE, R. *Political ideology.* New York: The Free Press, 1962.

LANG, K. Military organizations. In J. G. March, ed., *Handbook of organizations.* Chicago: Rand McNally, 1965. Pp. 838–878.

LEEDS, RUTH. The absorption of protest: A working paper. In W. W. Cooper, H. J. Leavitt & M. W. Shelly, eds., *New perspectives in organization research.* New York: Wiley, 1964. Pp. 115-135.

LEHMAN, E. W. Hierarchic cohesive bonds and organizational satisfactions. Unpublished paper, no date.

LEHMAN, E. W. Scope, mobility and satisfaction within an industrial organization. Paper read at annual meeting of the Eastern Sociological Society, New York City, April 14–16, 1967.

LEHMAN, E. W. Opportunity, mobility and satisfaction within an industrial organization. *Social Forces,* 1968, 46: 492-501.

LEHMAN, E. Toward a macrosociology of power. *Am. sociol. Rev.,* 1969, 34: 453-465.

LEHMAN, E. W. & ETZIONI, A. Some dangers in "valid" social measurement: Preliminary notes. *The Annals of the American Academy of Political and Social Science,* 1967, 373: 1-15.

LEONARD, P. Social workers and bureaucracy. *New Society,* 1966, 2: 12-13.

LEVINSON, P. Chronic dependency: A conceptual analysis. *Social Service Review,* 1964, 38: 371-381.

LEVINSON, P. & SCHILLER, J. Role analysis of the indigenous nonprofessional. *Social Work,* 1966, 11: 95-101.

Love, Ruth Leeds. The absorption of protest. In H. Leavitt & L. Pondy, eds., *Readings in managerial psychology*. 2d ed. Chicago: University of Chicago Press, 1973.

Macha, J. *Ecclesiastical unification*. Rome: Pont. Institutum Orientalium Studiorum, 1974.

Miller, G. Professional in bureaucracy: Alienation among industrial scientists and engineers. *Am. sociol. Rev.*, 1967, 32: 755-768.

Mitzner, M. An investigation of the relationship of prestige, compliance patterns and dogmatism to interpersonal perception of esteem in the chain of command of formal organization. Doctoral dissertation, Emory University, 1968.

Mulford, C., Klonglan, G., Beal, G. & Bohlen, J. Selectivity, socialization, and role performance. *Sociology and Social Research*, 1968, 53: 68-77.

Mulford, C., Klonglan, G. & Schmitz, P. Causal model analysis of local civil defense director/coordinator's building roles in horizontal-vertical community systems. Sociology report No. 93, Department of Sociology, Iowa State University, 1971.

Mulford, C., Klonglan, G. & Warren, R. Socialization, communication and role performance. *Sociological Quarterly*, 1972, 13: 74-80.

Mulford, C., Klonglan, G., Warren, R. & Schmitz, P. A causal model of effectiveness in organizations. *Social Science Research*, 1972, 1: 61-78.

Mulford, C., Klonglan, G., Warren, R. & Padgitt, Janet. A system evaluation of individual effectiveness in a non-economic organization. Scientific Paper Series, Department of Sociology, Iowa State University, 1973.

Mulford, C., Woodman, W. & Warren, R. Content and non-content aspects of consensus in normative organizations. Paper presented at the Midwest Sociological Society meeting, Omaha, Nebraska, April 6, 1974.

Mulford, C., Woodman, W., Warren, R. & Kopachesky, J. The mediating role of social rank on consensus and role performance in the normative organization. Scientific Paper Series, Department of Sociology, Iowa State University, 1974.

Niaz, M. A. Strategies of planned organizational change. Doctoral dissertation, University of Southern California, 1963.

Pirages, D. Socio-economic development and political change in the Communist system. Research paper no. 9, Stanford Studies of the Communist System, 1966.

Randell, S. On some social influences of the military organization. In Torben Agersnap, ed., *Contributions to the theory of organizations I*. Copenhagen, Denmark: Scandinavian University Books, 1968. Pp. 58-74.

Rossel, R. The ideology of administration. Doctoral dissertation, Yale University, 1966.

Rossel, R. Instrumental and expressive leadership in complex organizations. *Admin. Sci. Q.*, 1970, 15: 306-316.

Rossel, R. Required labor commitment, organizational adaptation, and leadership orientation. *Admin. Sci. Q.*, 1971, 16: 316-320.

ROUSE, J. E. An organizational analysis of American Catholicism. Paper presented at the Spring Conference, National Capital Area Political Science Association, College Park, Md., 1973.

SAMPSON, O., JR. A social system analysis of the effectiveness of an economic organization. Doctoral dissertation, Iowa State University, 1973.

SCHMITZ, P. Causal model analysis of local coordinators building roles in community and complex organizational systems. Doctoral dissertation, Iowa State University, 1971.

SKINNER, G. W. & WINCKLER, E. Compliance succession in rural Communist China: A cyclical theory. In A. Etzioni, *A sociological reader on complex organizations*. 2d ed. New York: Holt, 1969. Pp. 410-438.

SMITH, C. G. & BROWN, M. E. A comparative analysis of factors in organization control. Unpublished paper, no date.

SMITH, R. *Why soldiers fight: Causes of fighter spirit*. Draft of Monograph 1, Social and Policy Research, Santa Barbara, 1973.

SPREHE, J. T. Latent protest movements and the second Vatican council: Some implications for sociological theory. Draft of paper presented at meeting of the Eastern Sociological Society, Philadelphia, Pa., 1966.

TABER, W. Normative authority of college faculty: Bases, manifestations, and limitations. Doctoral dissertation, Columbia University, 1969.

THOMAS, C. & MILLER, M. Goal conflict and organizational effectiveness in change-oriented total institutions. Unpublished paper, no date, *a*.

THOMAS, C. & MILLER, M. Adult resocialization in coercive organizations. Unpublished paper, no date, *b*.

TICHY, N. An analysis of clique formation and structure in organizations. *Admin. Sci. Q.*, 1973: 194-208.

WARREN, R., KLONGLAN, G. & SABRI, M. The certainty method: Its application and usefulness in developing empirical measures in social sciences. Rural Sociology report No. 82, Iowa State University, 1969.

WARREN, R., ROGERS, D. & EVERS, F. Interrelationships among goals in farmer cooperatives. Paper presented at the Rural Sociological Society Meeting, College Park, Md., August 25, 1973.

WEBER, W. H., III. *The dialogic college: Leadership power, and involvement in higher education*. Unpublished book, 1973.

YETLEY, M. Sociological and economic factors related to managerial success. Doctoral dissertation, Iowa State University, 1973.

As we were going to press, several additional studies were sent to us. It was not possible to integrate a discussion of these in the present edition. These include, in alphabetical order, Curtis and Zurcher, Jr. (1974); Dunn (1974); Franklin, Kittredge, Thrasher (n.d.); Heidt (1975); Langdale (1974); Shichor and Empey (1974); Shinnick (1974); and Smith (1974).

SELECTED BIBLIOGRAPHY

AAGE, H. L'égalité dans les communautés utopiques. *Cahiers Internationaux de Sociologie*, 1974, LVI: 127-138.

ABEGGLEN, J. C. Subordination and autonomy attitudes of Japanese workers. *Am. J. Soc.*, 1957, 63: 181-189.

ABEGGLEN, J. C. *The Japanese factory: Aspects of its social organization* Glencoe, Ill.: The Free Press, 1958.

ABEL, T. The sociology of concentration camps. *Soc. Forc.*, 1951, 30: 150-155.

ABERLE, D. F. Introducing preventive psychiatry into a community. *Hum. Org.*, 1950, 9: 5-9.

ABRAMSON, E., CUTLER, H. A., KAUTZ, R. W. & MENDELSON, M. Social power and commitment: A theoretical statement. *Am. sociol. Rev.*, 1958, 23: 15-22.

ADAMS, S. Social climate and productivity in small military groups. *Am. sociol. Rev.*, 1954, 19: 421-425.

ADLER, H. G. Ideas toward a sociology of the concentration camp. *Am. J. Soc.*, 1958, 63: 513-522.

ADORNO, T. W., FRENKEL-BRUNSWIK, ELSE, LEVINSON, D. J., & SANFORD, R. N. *The authoritarian personality*. New York: Harper, 1950.

AHMAD, J. *The expert and the administrator*. Pittsburgh: University of Pittsburgh, 1959.

ALBERT, R. Comments on the scientific function of the concept of cohesiveness. *Am. J. Soc.*, 1953, 59: 231-234.

ALBROW, M. *Bureaucracy*. New York: Praeger, 1970.

ALLEN, V. L. *Power in trade unions*. London: Longmans, Green, 1954.

ALLISON, G. T. *Essence of decision: Explaining the Cuban missile crisis*. Boston: Little, Brown, 1971.

ALMOND, G. & VERBA, S. *The Civic Culture*. Boston: Little, Brown, 1965.

ALMOND, R. *The Healing Community*. New York: Jason Aronson, 1974.

American Association of University Professors. The place and function of faculties in college and university government. *A.A.U.P. Bull.*, 1955, 41: 62-81.

ANDREW, C. K. Industrial techniques *can* be used. *Modern Hospital*, 1955, 84: 67-72.

ANDRZEJEWSKI, S. *Military organization and society*. London: Routledge & Kegan Paul, 1954.

ARCHIBALD, KATHERINE. *Wartime shipyards*. Berkeley and Los Angeles: University of California Press, 1947.

ARENSBERG, C. M. Industry and the community. In S. C. Hoslett, *Human factors in management*. New York: Harper, 1947.

ARENSBERG, C. M. Behavior and organization: Industrial studies. In Rohrer & Sherif (1951). Pp. 324-352.

ARENSBERG, C. M. & MACGREGOR, D. Determination of morale in an industrial company. *Appl. Anthr.*, 1942, 1: 12-34.

ARGYRIS, C. *Executive leadership*. New York: Harper, 1953.

ARGYRIS, C. Some characteristics of successful executives. *Pers. J.*, 1953a, 32: 50-63.

ARGYRIS, C. *Organization of a bank*. New Haven: Labor and Management Center, Yale Univ., 1954.

ARGYRIS, C. Top management dilemma: Company needs vs. individual development. *Personnel*, 1955, 32: 123-134.

ARGYRIS, C. *Personality and organization*. New York: Harper, 1957.

ARGYRIS, C. Understanding human behavior in organizations: One viewpoint. In Haire (1959). Pp. 115-154.

ARNOLD, M. *Schools and universities on the continent*. London: McMillan, 1868.

ARNOLD, M. *Higher schools and universities in Germany*. London: McMillan, 1892.

ARON, R. Problems and methods of contemporary sociology. In *German Sociology*. Glencoe, Ill.: The Free Press, 1957.

ASCH, S. E. Effects of group pressure upon the modification and distortion of judgments. In Guetzkow (1951). Pp. 177-190.

ASHBY, W. R. *An introduction to cybernetics*. New York: Wiley, 1956.

ASHDOWN, R. A sociological study of a trade union. Unpublished, no date.

ATELSON, J. Work group behavior and wildcat strikes: The causes and functions of industrial civil disobedience. *Ohio State Law Journal*, 1973, 34: 750-815.

AVERY, R. Enculturation in industrial research. *IRE Transactions on Engineering Management*, 1960, EM-7, 20-24.

AXELROD, M. A study of formal and informal group participation in a larger urban community. Unpublished doctoral dissertation, University of Michigan, 1953.

BACK, K. W. Influence through social communication. *J. abnorm. soc. Psychol.*, 1951, 46: 9-23.

BAKER, A. W. & DAVIS, R. C. *Ratios of staff and line employees and stages of differentiation of staff functions*. Bur. Bus. Res., No. 72. Columbus: Ohio State University, 1954.

BAKER, F. *Organizational systems: General systems approaches to complex organizations*. Homewood, Ill.: Richard D. Irwin, Inc., 1973.

BAKKE, W. E. *Bonds of organizations.* New York: Harper, 1950.

BALDWIN, MONICA. *I leap over the wall.* New York: Signet, 1957.

BALES, R. F. The equilibrium problem in small groups. In T. Parsons, R. F. Bales & E. A. Shils, *Working papers in the theory of action.* Glencoe, Ill.: The Free Press, 1953. Pp. 111-161.

BALES, R. F. In conference. *Harv. Bus. Rev.,* 1954, 32: 44-50.

BALES, R. F. Task status and likeability as a function of talking and listening in decision-making groups. In L. D. White, ed., *The state of the social sciences.* Chicago: The University of Chicago Press, 1956. Pp. 148-61.

BALES, R. F. Task roles and social roles in problem solving-groups. In Maccoby, Newcomb & Hartley (1958). Pp. 437-447.

BALES, R. F. & SLATER, P. E. Role differentiation in small decision-making groups. In Parsons & Bales (1955). Pp. 259-306.

BALOG, A. Die Justiz und ihre Klienten. *Österreichische Zeitschrift für Politikwissenschaft,* 1973, 3: 161-179.

BANFIELD, E. *The moral basis of a backward society.* Glencoe, Ill.: The Free Press, 1958.

BARBASH, J. *Labor unions in action.* New York: Harper, 1948.

BARBASH, J. *The practice of unionism.* New York: Harper, 1956.

BARBASH, J., ed. *Unions and union leadership.* New York: Harper, 1959.

BARBER, B. Mass apathy and voluntary social participation in the United States. Unpublished doctoral dissertation, Harvard University, 1948.

BARBER, B. Participation and mass apathy in associations. In A. W. Gouldner (1950). Pp. 477-504.

BARBER, B. *Social stratification.* New York: Harcourt, Brace, 1957.

BARNARD, C. I. *The functions of the executive.* Cambridge: Harvard University Press, 1938.

BARNES, H. E. Some leading phases of evolution of modern penology. *Poli. Sci. Q.,* 1922, 37: 256.

BARNES, H. E. *The evolution of penology in Pennsylvania.* Indianapolis: Bobbs-Merrill, 1927.

BARNES, L. B. *Organizational systems and engineering groups.* Boston: Harvard Business School, 1960.

BARTON, A. H. The concept of property space in social research. In Lazarsfeld & Rosenberg (1955). Pp. 40-53.

BARTON, A. H. Legitimacy, power, and compromise within formal authority structures—a formal model. Bur. Appl. Soc. Res., Columbia University, 1958. Mimeo.

BARTON, A. H. & ANDERSON, B. Change in an organizational system: Formalization of a qualitative study. In Etzioni (1961). Pp. 400-418.

BARZUN, J. *Teacher in America.* New York: Little, Brown, 1946.

BASS, B. M. *Leadership, psychology, and organizational behavior.* New York: Harper, 1960.

BATES, S. *Prisons and beyond.* New York: Macmillan, 1938.

BAUMGARTEL, H. Leadership, motivation and attitudes in twenty research laboratories. Unpublished doctoral dissertation, University of Michigan, 1955.

BAUR, E. J. Public opinion and the primary group. *Am. sociol. Rev.,* 1960, 25: 208-219.

BAVELAS, A. Communication patterns in task-oriented groups. *J. acoust. Soc. Amer.,* 1950, 22: 725-730.

BAVELAS, A. Leadership: Man and function. *Admin. Sci. Q.*, 1960, 4: 491-498.

BAYNE-POWELL, ROSAMUND. *The English child in the eighteenth century.* New York: Dutton, 1939.

BECK, H. P. *Men who control our universities.* New York: King's Crown Press, 1947.

BECKER, H. *Systematic sociology on the basis of the Beziehungslehre and Gebildelehre of Leopold von Wiese.* New York: Wiley, 1932.

BECKER, H. S. The career of the Chicago public schoolteacher. *Am. J. Soc.*, 1952, 57: 470-477.

BECKER, H. S. The teacher in the authority system of the public school. *J. educ. Soc.*, 1953, 27: 128-141.

BECKER, H. S. Notes on the concept of commitment. *Am. J. Soc.*, 1960, 66: 32-40.

BECKER, H. S. & CARPER, J. W. The development of identification with an occupation. *Am. J. Soc.*, 1956, 61: 289-298.

BECKER, H. S. & GEER, BLANCH. The fate of idealism in medical school. *Am. sociol. Rev.*, 1958, 23: 50-56.

BECKER, H. S. & STRAUSS, A. L. Careers, personality and adult socialization. *Am. J. Soc.*, 1956, 62: 253-263.

BELKNAP, I. *Human problems of a state mental hospital.* New York: McGraw-Hill, 1956.

BELL, D. Some aspects of the New York longshoremen situation. *Proceedings of the Seventh Annual Meeting of Industrial Relations Research Association*, Detroit, Mich., December, 1954.

BELL, D. The power elite—reconsidered. *Amer. J. Soc.*, 1958, 64: 238-250.

BELL, D. The "rediscovery" of alienation. *J. Phil.*, 1959, 56: 933-952.

BELL, D. *The end of ideology.* Glencoe, Ill.: The Free Press, 1960.

BELL, D. The racket-ridden longshoremen. In Bell (1960). Pp. 159-190.

BELL, N. W. & VOGEL, E. F., eds. *A modern introduction to the family.* Glencoe, Ill.: The Free Press, 1960.

BEN-DAVID, Y. Report of the research project on youth movements in Israel. *Transactions of the Second World Congress of Sociology*, 1954, 1: 90-95.

BEN-DAVID, Y. The professional role of the physician in bureaucratized medicine: A study in role conflict. *Hum. Rel.*, 1958, 11: 255-274.

BENDIX, R. Bureaucracy: The problem and its setting. *Am. sociol. Rev.*, 1947, 12: 493-507.

BENDIX, R. Compliant behavior and individual personality. *Am. J. Soc.*, 1952, 58: 292-303.

BENDIX, R. *Work and authority in industry.* New York: Wiley, 1956.

BENDIX, R. Industrialization, ideologies, and social structure. *Am. sociol. Rev.*, 1959, 24: 613-623.

BENDIX, R. *Max Weber: An intellectual portrait.* Garden City, N. Y.: Doubleday, 1960.

BENDIX, R. & BERGER, B. Images of society and problems of concept formation in sociology. In Gross (1959). Pp. 92-118.

BENNIS, W. G. Leadership theory and administrative behavior. *Admin. Sci. Q.*, 1959, 4: 259-301.

BERELSON, B. *Graduate education in the United States.* New York: McGraw-Hill, 1960.

BERELSON, B., LAZARSFELD, P. F. & MCPHEE, W. *Voting: A study of opinion formation in a presidential campaign.* Chicago: The University of Chicago Press, 1954.

BERGER, M. Law and custom in the Army. *Soc. Forc.*, 1946, 25: 82-87.

BERGER, M. *Bureaucracy and society in modern Egypt.* Princeton, N. J.: Princeton University Press, 1957.

BERKMAN, P. L. Life aboard an armed Coast Guard ship. *Am. J. Soc.,* 1946, 51: 380-387.

BERKOWITZ, L. Group standards, cohesiveness, and productivity. *Hum. Rel.,* 1954, 7: 509-519.

BERLINER, J. S. *Factory and manager in the USSR.* Cambridge, Mass.: Harvard University Press, 1957.

BETTELHEIM, B. Individual and mass behavior in extreme situations. *J. abnorm. soc. Psychol.,* 1943, 38: 417-452.

BEVAN, D. & TRZINSKI, E. *Stalag 17.* New York: Dramatists Play Service, 1951.

BIERSTEDT, R. An analysis of social power. *Am. sociol. Rev.,* 1950, 15: 730-738.

BIERSTEDT, R. The problem of authority. In M. Berber, T. Abel & C. Page, eds., *Freedom and control in modern society.* New York: Van Nostrand, 1954. Pp. 67-81.

BIERSTEDT, R. *Social order.* New York: McGraw-Hill, 1957.

BIRNBAUM, N. Friends and enemies. *Twentieth Century,* 1960, 167: 460-470.

BLAKELOCK, E. A new look at the new leisure. *Admin. Sci. Q.,* 1960, 4: 446-467.

BLAU, P. M. Cooperation and competition in a bureaucracy. *Am. J. Soc.,* 1954, 59: 530-535.

BLAU, P. M. *The dynamics of bureaucracy.* Chicago: The University of Chicago Press, 1955.

BLAU, P. M. *Exchange and power in social life.* New York: Wiley, 1964.

BLAU, P. M. Formal organization: Dimensions of analysis. *Am. J. Soc.,* 1957, 63: 58-69.

BLAU, P. M. Structural effects. *Am. sociol. Rev.,* 1960, 25: 178-193.

BLAU, P. M. & SCOTT, W. R. *Formal organizations: A comparative approach.* San Francisco: Chandler Publishing Co., 1962.

BLAUNER, R. Alienation in work: Industrial variations and industrial trends. Mimeo., 1960.

BLAUNER, R. Work satisfaction and industrial trends in modern society. In Galenson & Lipset (1960). Pp. 339-360.

BLOCH, H. A. The personality of inmates of concentration camps. *Am. J. Soc.,* 1947, 52: 335-341.

BLOCK, L. Ready reference of hospital facts. *Hospital Facts,* 1956, 34.

BLUM, F. H. *Toward a democratic work process.* New York: Harper, 1953.

BLUM, J. N. *Landowners and agriculture in Austria, 1815-1848.* Baltimore: Johns Hopkins University Press, 1948.

BONDY, C. Problems of internment camps. *J. abnorm. soc. Psychol.,* 1943, 38: 453-475.

BORGATTA, E. F., BALES, R. F. & COUCH, A. S. Some findings revelant to the great man theory of leadership. *Am. sociol. Rev.,* 1954, 19: 755-759.

BOSSARD, J. H. S. *The sociology of child development.* Rev. ed. New York: Harper, 1954.

BOSSE, R., O'FLANNERY, ETHNA & MACISCO, J. J. The monsignors of the New York archdiocese. New York: Fordham Sociol. Lab. Working Papers. Mimeo.

BOTTOMORE, T. Social stratification in voluntary associations. In Glass (1954). Pp. 349-382.

BOULDING, K. E. *The organizational revolution.* New York: Harper, 1953.

BREED, W. The newspaperman, news and society. Unpublished doctoral dissertation, Columbia University, 1952.

BREED, W. Social control in the newsroom: A functional analysis. *Soc. Forc.,* 1955, 33: 326-335.

BRETON, R. Reward structures and participation in an organization. Paper presented to the Eastern Sociological Society, April 1960.

BRICKMAN, P. *Social conflict: Readings in rule structures and conflict relationships.* Lexington, Mass.: Heath, 1974, 1-33.

BRIM, O. G. JR. *Sociology and the field of education.* New York: Russell Sage Foundation, 1958.

BRINTON, C. *The anatomy of revolution.* New York: Prentice-Hall, 1938.

BRISSENDEN, P. F. *The I. W. W.: A study of American syndicalism.* New York: Columbia University Studies in History, Economics and Public Law, 83, 1919.

British Broadcasting Corporation. *Annual Reports.* London: H. M. Stationery Off., 1928.

BROGAN, D. W. *Politics in America.* Garden City, N. Y.: Doubleday, 1960.

BROOKS, G. W., DARBER, M., McCABE, D. A. & TAFT, P., eds. *Interpreting the labor movement.* Madison, Wisc.: Industrial Relations Research Association, 1952.

BROOM, L. & SELZNICK, P. *Sociology.* 2nd ed. Evanston, Ill.: Row, Peterson, 1958.

BROTZ, H. & WILSON, E. Characteristics of military society. *Soc. Forc.,* 1946, 51: 371-375.

BROWN, D. V. & MYERS, C. A. The changing industrial relations philosophy. *Proceedings of the Industrial Relations Research Association,* December 1956, pp. 1-16.

BROWN, PAULA. Bureaucracy in a government laboratory. *Soc. Forc.,* 1954, 32: 259-268.

BRYCE-LAPORTE, R. S. The American slave plantation and our heritage of communal deprivation. *American Behavioral Scientist,* 1969, XII: 2-8.

BRYCE-LAPORTE, R. S. Slaves as inmates, slaves as men: A sociological discussion of Elkin's thesis. In Ann Lane, ed., *The debate over slavery.* Urbana, Ill.: University Press, 1971.

BRYCE-LAPORTE, R. S. The slave plantation: Background to present conditions of urban blacks. In P. Orleans & W. R. Ellis, Jr., eds., *Race, change and urban society,* Vol. 5, Urban Affairs Annual Reviews. Beverly Hills, Calif.: Sage Publications, 1972.

BUBER, M. *Path to Utopia.* Boston: Beacon Hill, 1949.

BUCHANAN, B., II. Building organizational commitment: The socialization of managers in work organizations. *Admin. Sci. Q.,* 1972, 19: 533-546.

BUCKLEY, W. Social stratification and the functional theory of social differentiation. *Am. sociol. Rev.,* 1958, 23: 369-375.

BURLING, T., LENTZ, EDITH M. & WILSON, R. N. *The give and take in hospitals.* New York: Putnam, 1956.

BURNS, T. The comparative study of organizations. In V. H. Vroom, ed., *Methods of organizational research.* Pittsburgh: University of Pittsburgh Press, 1967.

BURTON, M. K. *Destiny for Congregationalism.* Oklahoma City: Modern Publishers, 1953.

CALDWELL, M. G. Group dynamics in the prison community. *J. crim. Law, Criminol. & Police Sci.,* 1956, 46: 648-657.

CAMPBELL, A. GURIN, G. & MILLER, W. E. *The voter decides.* Evanston, Ill.: Row, Peterson, 1954.

CAMPBELL, E. Q. & PETTIGREW, T. F. *Christians in racial crisis.* Washington, D. C.: Public Affairs Press, 1959.

CAMPBELL, NELLIE M. *The elementary school teacher's treatment of classroom behavior problems.* New York: Teachers' College, Columbia University, 1935.

CAMPBELL, R. F. & GREGG, R. T. *Administrative behavior in education.* New York: Harper, 1957.

CANTRIL, H. *The psychology of social movements.* New York: Wiley, 1941.

CAPENDER, H. R. & BROWN, E. J. Strategies for implementing development. In G. M. Beal, R. C. Powers & E. W. Coward, Jr., eds., *Sociological perspectives of domestic development.* Ames, Iowa: Iowa State University Press, 1971. Pp. 166-183.

CAPLOVITZ, D. Student-faculty relations in a medical school: a study of professional socialization. Unpublished doctoral dissertation, Columbia University, 1960.

CAPLOW, T. The criteria of organizational success. *Soc. Forc.,* 1953, 32: 1-9.

CAPLOW, T. *The sociology of work.* Minneapolis: University of Minnesota, 1954.

CAPLOW, T. & McGEE, R. J. *The academic market place.* New York: Basic Books, 1958.

CARAN, RUTH S. *Criminology.* New York: Crowell, 1948.

CARR-SAUNDERS, A. M. & WILSON, P. A. *The professions.* Oxford: Clarendon, 1933.

CARTWRIGHT, D. A field theoretical conception of power. In Cartwright (1959). Pp. 183-220.

CARTWRIGHT, D., ed. *Studies in social power.* Ann Arbor: University of Michigan, 1959.

CARTWRIGHT, D. & ZANDER, A., eds. *Group dynamics.* Evanston, Ill.: Row, Peterson, 1953.

CASH, W. J. *The mind of the South.* Garden City, N. Y.: Doubleday, 1954.

CAUDILL, W. A. Perspectives on administration in psychiatric hospitals. *Admin. Sci. Q.,* 1956, 1: 155-170.

CAUDILL, W. A. Problems of leadership in the overt and covert social structure of psychiatric hospitals. In *Symposium on preventive and social psychiatry.* Washington: Walter Reed Army Medical Center, 1958. Pp. 345-363.

CAUDILL, W. A. Similarities and differences in psychiatric illness and its treatment in the United States and Japan. *Mental Hygiene,* 1959, 61-2: 15-26.

CAVALCANTE, CAETANA MYRIAM PARENTE. *O comportamento do individuo na organizacao.* Secao de Publicaceos, 1966.

CELL, C. Making the revolution work: Mass mobilization campaigns in the Peoples' Republic of China. Unpublished doctoral dissertation, University of Michigan, 1973.

CHALMERS, W. E., CHANDLER, MARGARET K., McQUITTY, L. L., STAGNER, R., WRAY, D. E. & DERBER, M. *Labor-management relations in illini city.* Champaign: University of Illinois, 1954.

CHAMBERLAIN, D. B. Communication in the parish ministry. Unpublished doctoral dissertation, Boston University, 1958.

CHAMBERS, ROSALIND C. A study of three voluntary organizations. In Glass (1954). Pp. 383-406.

CHAPMAN, S. H. The minister: Professional man of the church. *Soc. Forc.,* 1944, 23: 202-206.

CHAPPLE, E. D. & COON, C. S. *Principles of anthropology.* New York: Holt, 1941.

CHAPPLE, E. D. & HARDING, C. F. Simultaneous measure of human relations and emotional activity. *Nat. Acad. Sci. Proc.,* 1940, 26: 319-326.

CHAPPLE, E. D. & SAYLES, L. R. *The measure of management.* New York: Macmillan. 1961.

CHARQUES, DOROTHY. *The nunnery.* New York: Coward-McCann, 1960.

CHARTERS, W. W., JR. A study of role conflict among foremen in a heavy industry. Unpublished doctoral dissertation, University of Michigan, 1952.

CHERKAOUI, M. & LINDSEY, J. K. Le poids du nombre dans la réussite scolaire. *Révue Française de Sociologie,* 1974, XV: 201-215.

CHESLER, D. J., VAN STEENBER, N. J. & BRUECKEL, JOYCE E. Effect on morale of infantry team replacement and individual replacement systems. *Sociometry,* 1955, 18: 587-597.

CHESSMAN, C. *Cell 2455, death row.* New York: Permabooks, 1956.

CHILL, E. S. The Company of the Holy Sacrament: 1630-1666. Unpublished doctoral dissertation, Columbia University, 1960.

CHINOY, E. *Autmobile workers and the American dream.* New York: Doubleday, 1955.

CHRISTENSEN, A. N. *The evolution of Latin American government.* New York: Holt, 1951.

CHRISTIE, L. S., LUCE, R. D. & MACY, J., JR. *Communication and learning in task-oriented groups.* Cambridge, Mass.: M. I. T. Research Laboratory of Electronics, Technical Report 231, 1952.

CHURCHILL, A. *The improper bohemians.* New York, Dutton, 1959.

CICOUREL, A. V. The front and back of organizational leadership: A case study. *Pacific sociol. Rev.,* 1948, 1: 54-58.

CLARK, B. R. The influence of organizational image on student selection. Paper presented to the Conference on Selection and Educational Differentiation, Berkeley, Calif., May 1959.

CLARK, B. R. The "cooling-out" function in higher education. *Am. J. Soc.,* 1960, 65: 569-576.

CLARK, B. R. *The open door college: A case study.* New York: McGraw-Hill, 1960a.

CLARK, H. F. & SLOAN, H. S. *Classrooms in the factories.* Rutherford, N. J.: Institute of Research, Fairleigh Dickinson University, 1958.

CLARK, T. N. *Community structure and decision-making: Comparative analyses.* San Francisco: Chandler Publishing Co., 1968.

CLARKSON, J. F., EDWARDS, J. H., KELLY, W. J. & WELCH, J. J., tr. *The church teaches.* St. Louis, Mo.: B. Herder, 1955.

CLEMMER, D. Leadership phenomena in a prison community. *J. crim. Law & Criminol.,* 1938, 28: 681-872.

CLEMMER, D. *The prison community.* New York: Holt, Rinehart, Winston, 1958.

CLOWARD, R. A. Social control and anomie: A study of a prison community. Unpublished doctoral dissertation, Columbia University, 1959.

COATES, C. H. & PELLEGRIN, R. J. Executives and supervisors: A situational theory of differential occupational mobility. *Soc. Forc.,* 1956, 35: 121-126.

COATES, C. H. & PELLEGRIN, R. J. Executives and supervisors: Contrasting self-conceptions and conceptions of each other. *Am. sociol. Rev.,* 1957, 22: 217-222.

COATES, C. H. & PELLEGRIN, R. J. Executives and supervisors: Informal factors in differential bureaucratic promotion. *Admin. Sci. Q.,* 1957a, 2: 200-215.

COCH, L. & FRENCH, J. R. P., JR. Overcoming resistance to change. In Swanson, Newcomb & Hartley (1952). Pp. 474-490.

COHEN, E. A. *Human endeavor in the concentration camp.* New York: Norton, 1953.

COHEN, I. *The Ruhleben prison camp.* London: Methuen, 1917.

COHEN, MABLE B. & COHEN, R. A. Personality as a factor in administrative decisions. *Psychiatry,* 1951, 14: 47-53.

COKER, R. E., MILLER, N., BACK, K. W. & DONNELLY, T. The medical student, specialization and general practice. *N. C. Med. J.,* 1960, 21: 96-101.

COLADARCI, A. P., ed. *Educational psychology.* New York: The Dryden Press, 1955.

COLB, L. The mental hospitalization of the aged: Is it being overdone? *Am. J. Psych.,* 1956, 112: 627-635.

COLEMAN, J. S. Multidimensional scale analysis. *Am. J. Soc.,* 1957, 63: 253-263.

COLEMAN, J. S. The adolescent subculture and academic achievement. *Am. J. Soc.,* 1960, 65: 337-347.

COLEMAN, J. S. Relational analysis: The study of social organizations with survey methods. In Etzioni (1961). Pp. 441-453.

COLEMAN, J. S. *The Adolescent Society,* Glencoe: The Free Press, 1961.

COLEMAN, J. S., KATZ, E. & MENZEL, H. Diffusion of an innovation among physicians. *Sociometry,* 1957, 20: 253-270.

COMFORT, G. O. *Professional politicians: A study of British party agents.* Washington, D. C.: Public Affairs Press, 1958.

COMMONS, J. R. American shoemakers, 1648-1895: A sketch of industrial evolution. *Q. J. Econ.,* 1909, 24: 39-98.

COMMONS, J. R. Labor movement. *Encyclopedia of the Social Sciences.* New York: Macmillan, 1932. Pp. 682-696.

COMMONS, J. R. *Legal foundations of capitalism.* Madison: University of Wisconsin, 1957.

CONSTAS, HELEN. Max Weber's two conceptions of bureaucracy. *Am. J. Soc.,* 1958, 63: 400-409.

CONSTAS, HELEN. The Soviet Union as a charismatic bureaucracy—viewed comparatively. Paper presented to American Sociological Society, Seattle, Wash. August 1958a.

COOK, F. J. & CLEASON, G. The shame of New York. *The Nation* (special issue), Oct. 31, 1959.

COOLEY, C. H. *Social organization.* New York: Scribner, 1915.

COPELAND, M. T. *The executive at work.* Cambridge, Mass.: Harvard University Press, 1952.

CORNISH, MARY JEAN. Participation in voluntary associations. Unpublished report, Bur. appl. soc. Res., Columbia University, 1960.

COSER, L. A. *The functions of social conflict.* Glencoe, Ill.: The Free Press, 1956.

COSER, L. ROSE. Authority and decision-making in a hospital: A comparative analysis. *Am. sociol. Rev.,* 1958, 23: 56-63.

COWARD, E. W., JR., BEAL, G. M. & POWERS, R. C. Domestic development: Becoming a postindustrial society. In G. M. Beal, R. C. Powers & E. W. Coward, Jr., eds., *Sociological perspectives of domestic development.* Ames, Iowa: Iowa State University Press, 1971. Pp. 262-302.

CRESSEY, D. R. Achievement of an unstated organizational goal: An observation on prisons. *Pac. sociol. Rev.*, 1958, 1: 43-49.

CRESSEY, D. R. Prison organizations. In J. March, ed., *Handbook of organizations*. Chicago: Rand McNally, 1965. Pp. 1023-1070.

CRESSEY, D. R. with BROOM, L. & SELZNICK, P. Criminal and delinquent behavior. In Broom & Selznick (1958). Pp. 600-642.

CROZIER, M. & PRADIER, B. Groupes et chefs: *Les relations hierarchiques dans 6 companies d'assurances Parisiennes*. Paris: Groupe de Recherches de Sociologie Administrative, 1959.

CUMMING, ELAINE, CLANCEY, I. L. W. & CUMMING, J. Improving patient care through organizational changes in the mental hospital. *Psychiatry*, 1956, 19: 249-261.

CUMMING, ELAINE & CUMMING, J. The locus of power in a large mental hospital. *Psychiatry*, 1956, 19: 361-369.

CUMMING, ELAINE & CUMMING, J. *Closed ranks—an experiment in mental health education*. Cambridge, Mass.: Harvard University Press, 1957.

CURLE, A. Transitional communities and social re-connection. *Hum. Rel.*, 1947, 1: 42-68.

CURRAN, F. J. Organization of a ward for adolescents in Bellevue psychiatric hospital. *Am. J. Psych.*, 1939, 95: 1365-1386.

CURTIS, R. & ZURCHER, L. Social movements: An analytical exploration of organizational forms. *Social Problems*, 1974, 21: 356-370.

CUTTS, NORMA E. & MOSELEY, N. *Teaching the disorderly pupil in elementary and secondary schools*. New York: Longmans, Green, 1957.

DAHL, R. A. The concept of power. *Behav. Sci.*, 1957, 2: 201-215.

DAHLKE, O. H. Values and group behavior in two camps for conscientious objectors. *Soc. Forc.*, 1945, 51: 22-33.

DAHLSTROM, E. Exchange, influence and power. *Acta Sociologica*, 1966, 19: 237-284.

DAHRENDORF, R. *Class and class conflict in industrial society*. Stanford, Calif.: Stanford University Press, 1959.

DALLIN, A. & BRESLAUER, G. *Political terror in Communist systems*. Stanford, Calif.: Stanford University Press, 1970.

DALTON, M. Worker response and social background. *J. Poli. Econ.*, 1947, 55: 323-332.

DALTON, M. Informal factors in career achievement. *Soc. Forc.*, 1951, 56: 407-415.

DALTON, M. The role of supervision. In Kornhauser, Dubin & Ross (1954). Pp. 176-185.

DALTON, M. *Men who manage*. New York: Wiley, 1959.

DANIELSON, L. E. Management's relations with engineers and scientists. *Proceedings of the Industrial Relations Research Association*, December 1957, pp. 315-321.

DANTON, J. P., ed. *Climate of book selection: Social influences on school and public libraries*. Berkeley: University of California Press, 1959.

DAVID, H. *The history of the Haymarket affair*. New York: Rinehart, 1936.

DAVIES, D. R. & IANNACCONE, L. Ferment in the study of organization. *Teachers Coll. Rec.*, 1956, 60: 61-72.

DAVIS, A. K. Bureaucratic patterns in the Navy officer corps. *Soc. Forc.*, 1948, 27: 143-153.

DAVIS, F. J. Conceptions of official leader roles in the Air Force. *Soc. Forc.*, 1954. 32: 253-258.

DAVIS, J. A. Teachers versus researchers: Locals and cosmopolitans in graduate school. Paper presented to the American Sociological Association, New York, August 1960.

DAVIS, K. The sociology of prostitution. *Am. sociol. Rev.*, 1937, 2: 744-755.

DAVIS, K. A conceptual analysis of stratification. *Am. sociol. Rev.*, 1942, 7: 309-321.

DAVIS, K. Reply. *Am. sociol. Rev.*, 1953, 18: 394-397.

DAVIS, K. & MOORE, W. E. Some principles of stratification. *Am. sociol. Rev.*, 1945, 10: 242-249.

DEAN, D. G. Alienation and political apathy. *Soc. Forc.*, 1960, 38: 185-189.

DEAN, L. R. Union activity and dual loyalty. *Ind. labor Rel. Rev.*, 1954, 7: 526-536.

DEARBORN, D. C. & SIMON, H. A. Selective perception: A note on the departmental identification of executives. *Sociometry*, 1958, 21: 140-143.

DE COSTER, S. L'exercise de l'autorité, problème de psychologie sociale. *Revue d'Institut Sociologie*, 1951, 1: 35-65.

DEMERATH, N. J. Social solidarity and the mental hospital. *Soc. Forc.*, 1942, 21: 66-71.

DEUTSCH, K. W. *Nationalism and social communication*. New York: Wiley, 1953.

DEUTSCH, K. W. et. al. *Political community and the North Atlantic area*. Princeton, N. J.: Princeton University Press, 1957.

DEUTSCHER, I. Toward avoiding the goal-trap in evaluation research. Paper read at the annual meetings of the American Sociological Association, Montreal, Canada, August 1974.

DEVIS, J. A. A partial coefficient for Goodman and Kruskal's gamma. *Journal of the American Statistical Association*, 1967, 62: 189-193.

DIAMOND, S. From organization to society: Virginia in the seventeenth century. *Am. J. Soc.*, 1958, 63: 457-475.

DILL, W. Environment as an influence in managerial autonomy. *Admin. Sci. Q.*, 1958, 2: 409-443.

DIMOCK, M. *Administrative vitality*. New York: Harper, 1959.

DODGE, EMILY P. Evolution of a city law office, I: Office organization. *Wisc. Law Rev.*, 1955, 180-207.

DOLL, E. E. Social and economic organization in two Pennsylvania German religious communities. *Am. J. Soc.*, 1951, 57: 168-177.

DONALD, G. A study of a consumer's cooperative. *Appl. Anthr.*, 1942, 2: 22-28.

DONOVAN, FRANCES R. *The saleslady*. Chicago: The University of Chicago Press, 1929.

DORNBUSCH, S. M. The military academy as an assimilating institution. *Soc. Forc.*, 1955, 33: 316-321.

DOUGLASS, H. P. *1000 city churches*. New York: Doran, 1926.

DOUGLASS, H. R. *Organization and administration of secondary schools*. Rev. ed. Boston: Ginn, 1945.

DRAKE, J. T. *The aged in American society*. New York: Ronald Press, 1958.

DRUCKER, P. F. Management and the professional employee. *Harv. Bus. Rev.*, 1952, 30: 84-90.

DRUCKER, P. F. *The practice of management*. New York: Harper, 1954.

DUBIN, R. *Human relations in administration*. Englewood Cliffs, N. J.: Prentice-Hall, 1951.

DUBIN, R. Industrial workers' worlds: A study of the "central life interests" of industrial workers. *Soc. Prob.*, 1956, 4: 131-142.

DUBIN, R. Industrial conflict and social welfare. *Conflict Resolution*, 1957, 1: 179-199.

DUBIN, R. Power and union-management relations. *Admin. Sci. Q.*, 1957a, 2: 60-81.

DUBIN, R. *Working union-management relations.* Englewood Cliffs, N. J.: Prentice-Hall, 1958.

DULCHIN, JOAN. Congregationalism: A case study in centralization. Unpublished, based on paper presented to a seminar conducted by R. K. Merton, Columbia University, 1960.

DUNLOP, J. T. & MYERS, C. A. The industrial relations function in management. *Personnel*, 1955, 6: 3-10.

DUNN, W. The economics of organizational ideology. *Journal of Comparative Administration*, 1974, 5: 395-435.

DURKHEIM, E. *Division of labor in society.* 2d ed. Glencoe, Ill.: The Free Press, 1947.

DUVERGER, M. *Political parties.* London: Methuen, 1954.

EASTON, D. *The political system.* New York: Knopf, 1952.

EASTON, D. *A systems analysis of political life.* New York: Wiley, 1965.

EATON, J. W. Social processes of professional teamwork. *Am. sociol. Rev.*, 1951, 16: 707-713.

ECKSTEIN, A. Economic fluctuations in Communist China's domestic development. In Ping-ti Ho & Tang Tsou, eds., *China in crisis.* Vol. I. Chicago: University of Chicago Press, 1968. Pp. 691-729.

EISENSTADT, S. N. Conditions of communicative receptivity. *Pub. Opin. Q.*, 1953, 17: 363-374.

EISENSTADT, S. N. The process of communication among immigrants in Israel. *Pub. Opin. Q.*, 1953a, 16: 42-58.

EISENSTADT, S. N. *The absorption of immigrants.* London: Routledge & Kegan Paul, 1954.

EISENSTADT, S. N. Communication systems and social structure: An exploratory comparative study. *Pub. Opin. Q.*, 1955, 19: 153-167.

EISENSTADT, S. N. *From generation to generation.* Glencoe, Ill.: The Free Press, 1956.

EISENSTADT, S. N. Bureaucracy and bureaucratization. *Current Sociol.*, 1958, 7: 99-124.

EISENSTADT, S. N. Toward a sociological theory of communication. Mimeo., n.d.

ELLING, R. J. The hospital-support game in urban center. In E. Freidson, ed., *The hospital in modern society.* Glencoe, Ill.: The Free Press, 1963. Pp. 73-111.

ELLSWORTH, J. S., JR. *Factory folkways.* New Haven, Conn.: Yale University Press, 1952.

EPAGNEUL, M. A functional diaconate. *Theol. Dig.*, 1959, 7: 73-76.

ERIKSON, T. Postwar prison reform in Sweden. *Annals Am. Acad. poli. soc. Sci.*, 1954, 293: 152-162.

ESTES, W. K. An experimental study of punishment. *Psychol. Monogr.*, 1944, 57, No. 3.

ETTISCH, W. The selection of candidates for the ministry among American theological seminaries. Columbia University, 1960. Mimeo.

ETZIONI, A. *Befrotz haportzim* (A diary of a commando soldier). Jerusalem: Achiasaf, 1952.

ETZIONI, A. The organizational structure of "closed" educational institutions in Israel. *Harv. educ. Rev.*, 1957, 27 (2): 107-125.

ETZIONI, A. Solidaric work-groups in collective settlements. *Hum. Org.*, 1957a, 16: 2-6.

ETZIONI, A. Administration and the consumer. *Admin. Sci. Q.*, 1958, 3: 251-264.

ETZIONI, A. Human relations and the foreman. *Pac. sociol. Rev.*, 1958b, 1: 33-38.

ETZIONI, A. Industrial sociology: The study of economic organizations. *Soc. Res.*, 1958c, 25: 303-324.

ETZIONI, A. Alternative ways to democracy: The example of Israel. *Poli. Sci. Q.*, 1959, 74: 196-214.

ETZIONI, A. Authority structure and organizational effectiveness. *Admin. Sci. Q.*, 1959a, 4: 43-67.

ETZIONI, A. Lower levels of industrial leadership. *Sociol. & soc. Res.*, 1959b, 43 (3): 209-212.

ETZIONI, A. Interpersonal and structural factors in the study of mental hospitals. *Psychiatry*, 1960, 23: 13-22.

ETZIONI, A. The functional differentiation of elites in the *kibbutz*. *Am. J. Soc.*, 1959c, 64: 476-487.

ETZIONI, A. New directions in the study of organizations and society. *Soc. Res.*, 1960a, 27: 223-228.

ETZIONI, A. Two approaches to organizational analysis: A critique and a suggestion. *Admin. Sci. Q.*, 1960b, 5: 257-278.

ETZIONI, A. *Complex organizations: A sociological reader.* New York: Holt, Rinehart, and Winston, 1961.

ETZIONI, A. *Modern organizations.* Englewood Cliffs, N.J.: Prentice-Hall, 1964.

ETZIONI, A. Dual leadership in complex organizations. *Amer. sociol. Rev.*, 1965, 30: 688-698.

ETZIONI, A. Organizational control and structure. In J. March, ed., *Handbook of organizations.* Chicago: Rand McNally, 1965.

ETZIONI, A. Social control: Organizational aspects. *International Encyclopedia of Social Science.* Vol. 14. New York: Macmillan, 1967. Pp. 369-402.

ETZIONI, A. *The active society: A theory of societal and political processes.* New York: The Free Press, 1968.

ETZIONI, A. Organizational dimensions and their interrelationships: A theory of compliance. In B. P. Indik & F. K. Berrien, eds., *People, groups and organizations.* New York: Teachers College Press, 1969.

ETZIONI, A. Indicators for the capacities for societal guidance. *The Annals of the American Academy of Political and Social Science,* 1970, 338: 25-34.

ETZIONI, A. Policy research. *American Sociologist,* 1971, 6, Supplementary issue (June): 8-12.

EVAN, W. M. Indices of the hierarchical structure of industrial organizations. Paper presented to Fourth World Congress of Sociology, Stresa, Italy, 1959.

FAINSOD, M. *How Russia is ruled.* Cambridge, Mass.: Harvard University Press, 1954.

FAINSTEIN, N. I. & FAINSTEIN, SUSAN S. *Urban political movements.* Englewood Cliffs, N.J.: Prentice-Hall, 1974.

FALK, H. A. *Corporal punishment.* New York: Bureau of Publications, Teachers College, Columbia University, 1941.

FALLERS, L. A. *Bantu bureaucracy.* Cambridge, England: W. Heffer, 1956.

FARAGO, L., ed. *German psychological warfare.* New York: Committee for National Morale, 1941.

FARNER, F. M. The public high school principalship. *Bull. nat. Assoc. sec. School Principals,* 1948, 32: 82-91.

FAUNCE, W. A. Automation in the automobile industry: Some consequences for in-plant social structure. *Am. sociol. Rev.,* 1958, 23: 401-407.

FAUNCE, W. A. The automobile industry: A case study in automation. In H. B. Jacobson & J. B. Roucek, eds., *Automation and society.* New York: Philosophical Library, 1959. Pp. 44-53.

FELD, M. D. Information and authority: The structure of military organization. *Am. sociol. Rev.,* 1959, 24: 15-22.

FELDMAN, A. S. The interpenetration of firm and society. Paper presented at International Social Science Council Round Table on Social Implications of Technical Change, Paris, March 1959.

FERENCE, T., GOLDNER, F. & RITTI, R. Priests and church: The professionalization of an organization. In E. Freidson, ed., *The professions and their prospects.* Beverly Hills, Calif.: Sage Publications, 1973.

FESTINGER, L. The role of group belongingness in a voting situation. *Hum. Rel.,* 1947, 1: 154-180.

FESTINGER, L., SCHACHTER, S. & BACK, K. *Social pressures in informal groups.* New York: Harper, 1950.

FICHTER, J. H. *Social relations in the urban parish.* Chicago: The University of Chicago Press, 1954.

FICHTER, J. H. *Parochial school: A sociological study.* Notre Dame, Ind.: University of Notre Dame, 1958.

FIEDLER, F. E. Assumed similarity measures as predictors of team effectiveness. *J. abnorm. soc. Psychol.,* 1954, 49: 381-388.

FIEDLER, F. E. The influence of leader-key man relations on combat crew effectiveness. *J. abnorm. soc. Psychol.,* 1955, 51: 227-235.

FIELD, M. G. The academy of the social sciences of the Communist party of the Soviet Union. *Soc. Forc.,* 1950, 56: 137-141.

FISCHER, J., KALNOKY, H. & LENARD, L. *Forced labor and confinement without trial in Hungary.* Washington, D. C.: Mid-European Studies Center, 1952.

FISKE, MARJORIE. *Book selection and censorship: A study of school and public libraries in California.* Berkeley: University of California Press, 1959.

FLEISHMAN, E. A. A study of the leadership role of the foreman in an industrial situation. Columbus: Ohio State University, 1951. Mimeo.

FLEISHMAN, E. A. The description of supervisory behavior. *J. appl. Psychol.,* 1953, 37: 1-6.

FLEISHMAN, E. A., HARRIS, E. F. & BURTT, H. E. *Leadership and supervision in industry.* Bur. educ. Res. Monogr. No. 33. Columbus: Ohio State University, 1955.

FORD, C. *Cross-cultural approaches: Readings in comparative research.* New York: Taplinger Publishing Co., 1967.

FORM, W. H. Organized labor's place in the community power structure. *Ina. Labor Rel. Rev.,* 1959, 12: 526-539.

FOSTER, W. Z. *Misleaders of Labor.* Chicago: Trade Union Educational League, 1927.

Fox, J. B. & Scott, J. F. *Absenteeism: Management's problem.* Boston: Grad. School Bus. Admin., Harvard University, 1943.

Fox, Renee. Training for uncertainty. In Merton, Reader & Kendall (1957). Pp. 207-241.

Fox, S. D. Voluntary association and social structure. Unpublished doctoral dissertation, Harvard University, 1953.

Fox, V. The effect of counselling on adjustment in prison. *Soc. Forc.,* 1954, 32: 285-289.

Frank, A. G. Conflicting standards and selective enforcement. Paper presented to American Sociological Society, Seattle, Wash., September 1958.

Frank, A. G. Goal ambiguity and conflicting standards: An approach to the study of organization. *Hum. Org.,* 1958-59, 17: 8-13.

Frank, J. D. Personal problems related to Army rank. *Am. J. Psych.,* 1946, 103: 97-104.

Franklin, J. L. Power, commitment, and task performance: A test of Etzioni's compliance theory. Paper presented at Midwest Sociological Society meetings, Kansas City, Missouri, April 20, 1972a. (*Human Relations,* forthcoming.)

Franklin, J., Kittredge, L. & Thrasher, Jean. Normative power structures and staff-patient involvement and integration in a state mental hospital. Unpublished paper, no date.

Franklyn, G. J. Alienation and achievement among Indian-Metis and non-Indians in the Mackenzie District of the Northwest Territories. *Alberta Journal of Educational Research,* 1974, XX: 157-169.

Freeman, F. D. The Army as a social structure. *Soc. Forc.,* 1948, 27: 78-83.

French, J. R. P., Jr. & Raven, B. The bases of social power. In Cartwright (1959). Pp. 150-167.

Friedrich, C. J., ed. *Authority.* Cambridge, Mass.: Harvard University Press, 1958.

Friedsman, H. J. Bureaucrats as heroes. *Soc. Forc.,* 1954, 32: 269-274.

Fry, L. C. *Diagnosing the rural church.* New York: Doran, 1924.

Galenson, W. Soviet Russia. In Kornhauser, Dubin & Ross (1954). Pp. 478-486.

Galenson, W. & Lipset, S. M., eds. *Labor and trade unionism.* New York: Wiley, 1960.

Galtung, J. The social functions of a prison. *Soc. Prob.,* 1958, 6: 127-140.

Garceau, O. *The political life of the American Medical Association.* Cambridge, Mass.: Harvard University Press, 1941.

Gardner, B. B. & Whyte, W. F. The man in the middle: Position and problems of the foreman. *Appl. Anthr.,* 1945, 4: 1-28.

Gardner, E. F. & Thompson, G. C. *Social relations and morale in small groups.* New York: Appleton-Century-Crofts, 1956.

Garfinkel, H. Conditions of successful degradation ceremonies. *Am. J. Soc.,* 1956, 61: 420-424.

Garinger, E. H. *The administration of discipline in the high school.* New York: Teachers College, Columbia University, 1936.

Gebb, C. A. The principles and traits of leadership. *J. abnorm. soc. Psychol.,* 1948, 3: 267-284.

Georgion, P. The goal paradigm and notes towards a counter paradigm. *Admin. Sci. Q.,* 1973, 18: 291-310.

GEORGOPOULOS, B. S. & TANNENBAUM, A. S. A study of organizational effectiveness. *Am. sociol. Rev.,* 1957, 22: 534-540.

GERARD, H. B. The anchorage of opinions in face-to-face groups. *Hum. Rel.,* 1954, 7: 313-325.

GERTH, H. H. The Nazi party: Its leadership and composition. *Am. J. Soc.,* 1940, 45: 517-541.

GERTH, H. H. & MILLS, C. W. *From Max Weber: Essays in sociology.* New York: Oxford University Press, 1946.

GERVER, I. & BENSMAN, J. Toward a sociology of expertness. *Soc. Forc.,* 1954, 32: 226-235.

GIBB, C. A. Leadership. In Lindzey (1954). Pp. 887-920.

GILBERT, DORIS C. & LEVINSON, D. J. "Custodialism" and "humanism" in staff ideology. In Greenblatt, Levinson & Williams (1957). Pp. 20-35.

GINZBERG, E., ed. *What makes an executive?* New York: Columbia University Press, 1955.

GINZBERG, E. & REILLEY, E. W. *Effecting change in large organizations.* New York: Columbia University Press, 1957.

GLASER, B. G. & STRAUSS, A. L. *The discovery of grounded theory: Strategies for qualitative research.* Chicago: Aldine Publishing Co., 1967.

GLASER, W. A. American and foreign hospitals. In E. Freidson, ed., *The hospital in modern society.* Glencoe, Ill.: The Free Press, 1963. Pp. 37-72.

GLASS, D. V., ed. *Social mobility in Britain.* Glencoe, Ill.: The Free Press, 1954.

GLAZER, N. The rise of social research in Europe. In D. Lerner, ed., *The human meaning of the social sciences.* New York: Meridian, 1959. Pp. 43-72.

GLOCK, C. Y. & RINGER, B. B. Church policy and the attitudes of ministers and parishioners on social issues. *Am. sociol. Rev.,* 1956, 21: 148-156.

GOFFMAN, E. On cooling the mark out. *Psychiatry,* 1952, 15: 451-463.

GOFFMAN, E. The characteristics of total institutions. In *Symposium on preventive and social psychiatry.* Washington, D. C.: Walter Reed Army Institute of Research, 1957. Pp. 43-84.

GOFFMAN, E. The moral career of the mental patient. *Psychiatry,* 1959, 22: 123-142.

GOLD, M. Power in the classroom. *Sociometry,* 1958, 21: 50-60.

GOLDHAMER, H. & SHILS, E. A. Types of power and status. *Am. J. Soc.,* 1939, 45: 171-182.

GOLDSCHMIDT, W. *Comparative functionalism.* Berkeley: University of California Press, 1966.

GOLDSEN, ROSE K., ROSENBERG, M., WILLIAMS, R. M., JR. & SUCHMAN, E. A. *What college students think.* New York: Van Nostrand, 1960.

GOLDSMER, H. Some factors affecting participation in voluntary associations. Unpublished doctoral dissertation, University of Chicago, 1943.

GOLDSTEIN, J. *The government of a British trade union.* Glencoe, Ill.: The Free Press, 1952.

GOODACRE, D. M. The use of a sociometric test as a predictor of combat unit effectiveness. *Sociometry,* 1951, 14: 148-152.

GOODE, W. J. Community within a community: The professions. *Am. Sociol. Rev.,* 1957, 22: 194-200.

GOODE, W. J. Encroachment, charlatanism, and the emerging profession: Psychology, sociology, and medicine. *Amer. sociol. Rev.,* 1960, 25: 902-914.

GOODE, W. J. A theory of role strain. *Am. sociol. Rev.*, 1960a, 25: 483-496.

GOODE, W. J. & FOWLER, I. Incentive factors in a low-morale plant. *Am. sociol. Rev.*, 1949, 14: 618-624.

GORDON, MANYA. *Workers before and after Lenin.* New York: Dutton, 1941.

GORDON, R. A. *Business leadership in the large corporation.* Washington, D. C.: The Brookings Institution, 1945.

GORDON, T. Group-centered leadership and administration. In C. Rogers (1951). Pp. 320-383.

GORDON, C. W. *The social system of the high school.* Glencoe, Ill.: The Free Press, 1957.

GORDON, C. W. & BABCHUK, N. A typology of voluntary associations. *Am. sociol. Rev.,* 1959, 24: 22-29.

GOSS, MARY E. W. Physicians in bureaucracy: A case study of professional pressures on organizational roles. Unpublished doctoral dissertation, Columbia University, 1959.

GOSS, MARY E. Patterns of bureaucracy among hospital staff physicians. In E. Freidson, ed., *The hospital in modern society.* Glencoe, Ill.: The Free Press, 1963. Pp. 170-194.

GOULD, J. The Komsomol and the Hitler Jugend. *Br. J. Soc.,* 1951, 2: 305-314.

GOULDNER, A. W., ed. *Studies in leadership.* New York: Harper, 1950.

GOULDNER, A. W. *Patterns of industrial bureaucracy.* Glencoe, Ill.: The Free Press, 1954.

GOULDNER, A. W. *Wildcat strike.* Yellow Springs, Ohio: Antioch Press, 1954a.

GOULDNER, A. W. Cosmopolitans and locals: Toward an analysis of latent social roles. *Admin. Sci. Q.,* 1957, 2: 281-306.

GOULDNER, A. W. Reciprocity and autonomy in functional theory. In L. Gross (1959). Pp. 241-270.

GOULDNER, A. W. Organizational analysis. In R. K. Merton, L. Broom & L. S. Cottrell, Jr., eds., *Sociology today.* New York: Harper, 1959.

GOULDNER, HELEN P. Dimensions of organizational commitment. *Admin. Sci. Q.,* 1960, 4: 468-490.

GRANICK, D. *Management of the industrial firm in the U.S.S.R.* New York: Columbia University Press, 1954.

GRANICK, D. *The Red executive: A study of the organization man in Russian industry.* Garden City, N. Y.: Doubleday, 1960.

GRANICK, RUTH. The effect of social isolation on learning of norms in a home for the aged. Unpublished doctoral dissertation, Columbia University, 1962.

GRANICK, RUTH & NAHEMOW, LUCILLE D. Preadmission isolation as a factor in adjustment to an old age home. Paper presented to American Psychopathological Association, New York, February 1960.

GREENBLATT, M., LEVINSON, D. J. & WILLIAMS, R. H., eds. *The patient and the mental hospital.* Glencoe, Ill.: The Free Press, 1957.

GREENBLATT, M., YORK, R. H. & BROWN, ESTHER L., with HYDE, R. W. *From custodial to therapeutic patient care in mental hospitals.* New York: Russell Sage Foundation, 1955.

GREENE, C. N. & ORGAN, D. W. An evaluation of causal modes linking the received role with job satisfaction. *Admin. Sci. Q.,* 1973, 18: 95-103.

GREENHOE, FLORENCE. *Community contacts and participation of teachers.* Washington, D. C.: Council on Public Affairs, 1941.

GREER, S. A. *Social organization.* Garden City, N. Y.: Doubleday, 1955.

GREER, S. & ORLEANS, P. Political sociology. In R. E. L. Faris, ed., *Handbook of modern sociology.* Chicago: Rand McNally, 1964. Pp. 808-851.

GRIFFITHS, D. E. *Administrative theory.* New York: Appleton-Century-Crofts, 1959.

GRINKER, R. R. & SPIEGEL, J. P. *Men under stress.* Philadelphia: Blakiston, 1945.

GROSS, E. Primary functions of the small group. *Am. J. Soc.,* 1954, 60: 24-29.

GROSS, E. Industrial relations. In R. E. L. Faris, ed., *Handbook of modern sociology.* Chicago: Rand McNally, 1964. Pp. 619-679.

GROSS, E. Universities as organizations: A research approach. In *Am. sociol. Rev.,* 1968, 33: 519-544.

GROSS, E. & GRAMBSCH, P. *Changes in university organization 1964–1971.* New York: McGraw-Hill, 1974.

GROSS, L. ed. *Symposium on social theory.* Evanston, Ill.: Row, Peterson, 1959.

GROSS, N. & MARTIN, W. E. On group cohesiveness. *Am. J. Soc.,* 1952, 57: 546-554.

GROSS, N., MASON, W. S. & MCEACHERN, A. W. *Explorations in role analysis.* New York: Wiley, 1958.

GRUSKY, O. Role conflict in organization: A study of prison camp officials. *Admin. Sci. Q.,* 1959, 3: 452-472.

GUEST, R. H. Organizational change and the successful leader. Unpublished doctoral dissertation, Columbia University, 1960.

GUEST, R. H. Managerial succession. Paper read at the annual meeting of the American Sociological Association, August 1960.

GUETZKOW, H., ed. *Groups, leadership, and men.* Pittsburgh, Pa.: Carnegie Press, 1951.

GUETZKOW, H. & DILL, W. R. Factors in the organizational development of task-oriented groups. *Sociometry,* 1957, 20: 175-204.

GUSFIELD, J. R. Social structure and moral reform: A study of the Woman's Christian Temperance Union. *Am. J. Soc.,* 1955, 61: 221-232.

GUSTAFSON, J. M. An analysis of the problem of the role of the minister. *J. Relig.,* 1954, 34: 187-191.

GUTERMAN, S. S. *The Machiavellians.* Lincoln, Neb.: University of Nebraska Press, 1970.

GUTTMACHER, M. S. & WEIHOFEN, H. *Psychiatry and the law.* New York: Norton, 1952.

GUTTMAN, L. The Cornell technique for scale and intensity analysis. *Educ. & psychol. Measurement,* 1947, 7: 247-279.

GUTTMAN, L. The principal components of scale analysis. In Stouffer *et al.* (1950). Pp. 312-361.

GUTTMAN, L. The principal components of scalable attitudes. In Lazarsfeld (1954). Pp. 216-257.

GYR, J. Analysis of committee member behavior in four cultures. *Hum. Rel.,* 1951, 4: 193-202.

HAAS, J. E. & DRABEK, T. *Complex organizations: A Sociological perspective.* New York: Macmillan, 1973.

HAGSTROM, W. The Protestant clergy as a profession: Status and prospects. *Berkeley Publ. Society & Institutions,* 1957, 3: 54-69.

HAIRE, M. *Psychology in management.* New York: McGraw-Hill, 1956.

HAIRE, M. Biological models and empirical histories of the growth of organizations. In Haire (1959). Pp. 272-306.

HAIRE, M., ed. *Modern organizational theory*. New York: Wiley, 1959.

HALL, O. The informal organization of the medical profession. *Canad. J. Econ. & poli. Sci.*, 1946, 12: 30-44.

HALL, O. The stages of a medical career. *Am. J. Soc.*, 1948, 52: 327-336.

HALL, R. H. *Organizations: Structure and process*. Englewood Cliffs, N.J.: Prentice-Hall, 1972.

HALPIN, A. W. The leadership behavior and combat performance of airplane commanders. *J. abnorm. soc. Psychol.*, 1954, 49: 19-22.

HALPIN, A. W. *Administrative theory in education*. Chicago: Midwest Admin. Center, University of Chicago, 1958.

HAMBLIN, R. L. Leadership and crises. *Sociometry*, 1958, 21: 322-335.

HAMMOND, P. The role of religious ideology in church participation. Unpublished doctoral dissertation, Columbia University (1960).

HANSON, M. Organizational bureaucracy in Latin America and the legacy of Spanish colonialism. *Journal of Interamerican Studies and World Affairs*, 1974, 16: 199-219.

HARBISON, F. H. & BURGESS, E. W. Modern management in western Europe. *Am. J. Soc.*, 1954, 60: 15-23.

HARBISON, F. H. & COLEMAN, J. R. *Goals and strategy in collective bargaining*. New York: Harper, 1951.

HARBISON, F. H., KOCHLING, E., CASSELL, F. H. & RUEBMANN, H. C. Steel management on two continents. *Management Sci.*, 1955, 2: 31-39.

HARDMAN, J. B. S. *The house of labor*. New York: Prentice-Hall, 1951.

HARNQUIST, K. *Adjustment, leadership and group relations*. Stockholm: Almqvist & Wiksell, 1956.

HARPER, IDA. The role of the "fringer" in a state prison for women. *Soc. Forc.*, 1952, 31: 53-60.

HARRINGTON, M. & JACOBS, P. *Labor in a free society*. Berkeley: University of California Press, 1959.

HARRIS, P. E. *Changing conceptions of school discipline*. New York: Macmillan, 1928.

HARRISON, M. J. & WEIGHTMAN, K. Academic freedom and higher education in England. *Br. J. Soc.*, 1974, 25: 32-35.

HARRISON, P. M. *Authority and power in the free church tradition: A social case study of the American Baptist Convention*. Princeton, N. J.: Princeton University Press, 1959.

HART, C. W. Some factors affecting the organization and prosecution of given research projects. *Am. sociol. Rev.*, 1947, 12: 514-519.

HART, M. *Act one*. New York: Random House, 1959.

HARTSHORNE, H. & FROYD, M. C. *Theological education in the Northern Baptist Convention (A survey)*. Philadelphia, Pa.: Board of Education, Northern Baptist Convention, 1945.

HARTUNG, F. E. & FLOCH, M. A social-psychological analysis of prison riots. *J. crim. Law, Criminol. & Police Sci.*, 1956, 47: 51-57.

HAYNER, N. S. & ASH, E. The prisoner community as a social group. *Am. sociol. Rev.*, 1939, 4: 362-369.

HAYNER, N. S. & ASH, E. The prison as a community. *Am. sociol. Rev.*, 1940, 5: 577-583.

HEADY, F. Recent literature on comparative public administration. *Admin. Sci. Q.*, 1960, 5: 134-135.

HEATH, P. The medical administrator in the National Health Service. *Community Health,* 1974, 5: 178-182.

HEBERLE, R. *Social movements.* New York: Appleton-Century-Crofts, 1951.

HEGINBOTHAM, S. *Cultures in conflict: The four faces of Indian bureaucracy.* New York: Columbia University Press, 1975.

HEIDT, S. *Community crime control.* New York: Praeger, 1975.

HEINICKE, C. M. & BALES, R. F. Developmental trends in the structure of small groups. *Sociometry,* 1953, 16: 7-38.

HEISKANEN, IKKO. *Theoretical approaches and scientific strategies in administrative and organizational research: A methodological study,* 1967, 39, No. 2. Helsinki: Commentationes Humanarum Litterarum, Societas Scientiarum Fennica.

HELSABECK, R. *The compound system: A conceptual framework for effective decisionmaking in colleges.* Berkeley: Center for Research and Development in Higher Education, University of California, 1973.

HEMPHILL, J. K. Situational factors in leadership. *Bur. educ. Res. Monogr.,* No. 32. Columbus: Ohio State University, 1950.

HEMPHILL, J. K. & COONS, A. E. *Leader behavior description.* Columbus: Ohio State University, 1950.

HEMPHILL, J. K. & WESTIE, C. M. The measurement of group dimensions. *J. Psychol.,* 1950, 29: 325-342.

HENDERSON, C. R. The place and functions of voluntary associations. *Am. J. Soc.,* 1895, 1: 327-334.

HENRY, J. The formal structure of a psychiatric hospital. *Psychiatry,* 1954, 17: 139-151.

HENRY, J. Types of institutional structure. In Greenblatt, Levinson, & Williams (1957). Pp. 73-90.

HENRY, W. E. The business executive: The psychodynamics of a social role. *Am. J. Soc.,* 1949, 54: 286-291.

HERBST, P. G. Task differentiation of husband and wife activities. In Bell & Vogel (1960). Pp. 339-346.

HERO, A. *Voluntary organizations in world affairs communication.* Boston: World Peace Foundation, 1960.

HERZ, K. G. & ZELDITCH, M., eds. *Administration of homes for the aged: Selected papers on management and program planning.* New York: Council of Jewish Federation of Welfare Funds. 1952.

HERZBERG, F., MAUSNER, B., PETERSON, R. & CAPWELL, D. *Job attitudes: Review of research and opinion.* Pittsburgh, Pa.: Psychological Service, 1957.

HERZBERG, F., MAUSNER, B., SNYDERMAN, BARBARA, E. *The motivation to work.* New York: Wiley, 1959.

HESSE, K. *Wandlung des Soldaten.* Berlin: Mittler, 1930.

HEVDEBRAND, W. V. *Hospital bureaucracy.* New York: Dunellen Publishing Co., 1973.

HILL, J. M. M. & TRIST, E. L. Changes in accidents and other absences with length of service. *Hum. Rel.,* 1955, 8: 121-150.

HILLER, E. T. *The strike.* Chicago: The University of Chicago Press, 1928.

HILTON, J. *Good-bye, Mr. Chips.* Boston: Little, Brown, 1934.

HOESS, R. *Commandant of Auschwitz.* New York: World, 1960.

HOFFER, E. *The true believer.* New York: Harper, 1951.

HOLLINGSHEAD, A. B. Adjustment to military life. *Soc. Forc.,* 1946, 51: 439-447.

HOLLINGSHEAD, A. B. *Elmtown's youth.* New York: Wiley, 1949.

HOMANS, G. C. The small warship. *Am. sociol. Rev.,* 1946, 2: 294-300.

HOMANS, G. C. *The human group.* New York: Harcourt, Brace, 1950.

HOMANS, G. C. Group factors in worker productivity. In Swanson, Newcomb & Hartley (1952). Pp. 637-649.

HOMANS, G. C. Status among clerical workers. *Hum. Org.,* 1953, 12: 5-10.

HOMANS, G. C. Social behavior as exchange. *Amer. J. Sociol.,* 1958, 63: 597-606.

HOMANS, G. C. & SCHNEIDER, D. M. *Marriage, authority, and final causes.* Glencoe, Ill.: The Free Press, 1955.

HOPKINS, T. K. Rank, influence, and leadership. Paper presented to Eastern Sociological Society, Philadelphia, April 1958.

HOPKINS, T. K. Innovation and authority structure. Paper presented to Fourth World Congress of Sociology, Stresa, Italy, 1959.

HORSFALL, A. B. & ARENSBERG, C. M. Teamwork and productivity in a shoe factory. *Hum. Org.,* 1949, 8: 13-25.

HOSELITZ, B. F., ed. *The progress of underdeveloped areas.* Chicago: The University of Chicago Press, 1952.

HOULT, T. F. *The sociology of religion.* New York: The Dryden Press, 1958.

HOXIE, R. F. *Trade unionism in the United States.* New York: Appleton, 1917, 2nd ed., 1923.

HOURIET, R. *Getting back together.* New York: Coward, McCanns, Geoghegan, Inc., 1971.

HOY, W. & REES, R. Subordinate loyalty to immediate superior: A neglected concept in the study of educational administration. *Sociology of Education,* 1974, 47: 268-286.

HUGHES, E. C. The institutional office and the person. *Am. J. Soc.,* 1937, 43: 404-413.

HUGHES, E. C. The study of institutions. *Soc. Forc.,* 1942, 20: 307-310.

HUGHES, E. C. *Men and their work.* Glencoe, Ill.: The Free Press, 1958.

HUGHES, HELEN M. The compleat anti-vivisectionist. *Sci. Monthly,* 1947, 65: 503-507.

HUGHES, T. *Tom Brown's school-days, by an old boy.* New York: Harper, 1911.

HULME, KATHRYN. *The nun's story.* Boston: Little, Brown, 1956.

Human factors in research administration. Ann Arbor: Foundation for Research on Human Behavior, 1955.

HUNTER, E. *The blackboard jungle.* New York: Simon & Schuster, 1954.

HUNTINGTON, S. P. *The soldier and the state: The theory and politics of civil-military relations.* Cambridge, Mass.: Harvard University Press, 1957.

HYMAN, H. H. *Survey design and analysis.* Glencoe, Ill.: The Free Press, 1955.

HYMAN, H. H., WRIGHT, C. R. & HOPKINS, T. K. Applications of methods of evaluation. Berkeley: University of California Press, 1962.

ISRAEL, J. *Self-evaluation and rejection in groups.* Stockholm: Almqvist & Wiksell, 1956.

JACKMAN, N. Survival in the concentration camp. *Hum. Org.,* 1958, 17: 23-26.

JACOB, P. *Changing values in college.* New York: Harper, 1957.

JACOBSON, E. Foreman and steward, representatives of management and the union. In Guetzkow (1951). Pp. 90-95.

JANOWITZ, M. *Sociology and the military establishment.* New York: Russell Sage Foundation, 1959.

JANOWITZ, M. *The professional soldier.* Glencoe, Ill.: The Free Press, 1960.

JENKINS, D. *The Protestant ministry.* Garden City, N. Y.: Doubleday, 1958.

JENNINGS, E. E. Improving supervisory behavior. *Wisc. Comm. Stud.,* 1954, 2 (1): 1-35.

JENNINGS, HELEN. *Leadership and isolation.* New York: Longmans, Green, 1943.

JOHN, GABRIEL (Sister). *Through the patient's eyes: Hospitals, doctors, nurses.* Philadelphia. Lippincott, 1935.

JOHANSSON, S. Om forandring i totala institutioner. *Sartryck Sociologisk Forskning,* 1965: 154-168.

JOHNSON, C. A., ed. *Change in Communist systems.* Stanford, Calif.: Stanford University Press, 1970.

JOHNSON, N. Toward a taxonomy of organizations. Unpublished doctoral dissertation, Ohio State University, 1963.

JONES, M. *The therapeutic community.* New York: Basic Books, 1953.

JONES, W. H. M. In defense of apathy. *Poli. Stud.,* 1954, 2: 25-37.

JONES, W. H. S. *The Story of St. Catherine's College, Cambridge.* Cambridge, England: W. Heffer, 1951.

JOSEPHSON, E. Irrational leadership in formal organizations. *Soc. Forc.,* 1952, 31: 109-117.

JOYNER, NANCY & JOYNER, C. Prescriptive administrative proposal: An international machinery for control of the high seas. *International Lawyer,* 1974, 8: 57-73.

KADUSHIN, C. G. Individual decisions to undertake psychotherapy. *Admin. Sci. Q.,* 1958, 13: 379-411.

KADUSHIN, C. G. Decisions to undertake psychotherapy. Unpublished doctoral dissertation, Columbia University, 1960.

KAHN, R. L. & KATZ, D. Leadership practices in relation to productivity and morale. In Cartwright & Zander (1953). Pp. 612-628.

KAHN, R. L., MANN, F. C. & SEASHORE, S. Introduction. *J. soc. Issues,* 1956, 12: 2-4.

KARSH, B. *Diary of a strike.* Urbana: University of Illinois, 1958.

KARSH, B., SEIDMAN, J. & LILIENTHAL, DAISY M. The union organizer and his tactics: A case study. *Amer. J. Soc.,* 1953, 59: 113-122.

KATZ, D. & KAHN, R. L. Some recent findings in human relations research in industry. In Swanson, Newcomb & Hartley (1952). Pp. 650-665.

KATZ, D., MACCOBY, N., GURIN, G. & FLOOR, LUCRETIA G. *Productivity, supervision and morale among railroad workers.* Ann Arbor: Survey Research Center, Michigan University, 1951.

KATZ, D., MACCOBY N., & MORSE, NANCY C. *Productivity, supervision and morale in an office situation.* Ann Arbor: Survey Research Center, University of Michigan, 1950.

KATZ, E. The two-step flow of communication: An up-to-date report on an hypothesis. *Publ. Opin. Q.,* 1957, 21: 61-78.

KATZ, E., BLAU, P., BROWN, M. L. & STRODTBECK, F. L. Leadership stability and social change: An experiment with small groups. *Sociometry,* 1957, 20: 36-50.

KATZ, E. & EISENSTADT, S. N. Some sociological observations on the response of Israeli organizations to new immigrants. *Admin. Sci. Q.,* 1960, 5: 113-133.

KATZ, E. & LAZARSFELD, P. F. *Personal influence.* Glencoe, Ill.: The Free Press, 1955.

KAUFMAN, R. The patron-client concept and macro-politics: Prospects and problems. *Comparative Studies in Society and History,* 1974, 16: 284-308.

KEEDY, E. R. Irresistible impulse as a defense in criminal law. *Univ. Penn. Law Rev.,* 1952, 100: 933-956.

KELLER, F. E. *Geschichte der Preussischen Volksschulenwesens.* Berlin: Oppenheim, 1873.

KELLER, SUSANNE I. The social origins and career lines of three generations of American business leaders. Unpublished doctoral dissertation, Columbia University, 1953.

KELLEY, FLORENCE. Aims and principles of the Consumers' League. *Amer. J. Soc.,* 1899, 5: 289-304.

KENDALL, PATRICIA L. Medical education as social process. Paper presented to American Sociology Association, New York, August 1960.

KENDALL, PATRICIA L. & LAZARSFELD, P. F. Problems of survey analysis. In Merton & Lazarsfeld (1950). Pp. 133-197.

KENDALL, PATRICIA L. & SELVIN H. C. Tendencies toward specialization in medical training. In Merton, Reader, & Kendall (1957). Pp. 153-174.

KERN, ALICE & BAHR, H. Some factors affecting leadership climate in a state parole agency. *Pacific Sociological Review,* 1974, 17: 108-118.

KERR, C. Trade unionism and distributive shares. *Am. Econ. Rev.,* 1954, 44: 279-292.

KERR, C., HARBISON, F. H., DUNLOP, J. T. & MYERS, C. A. The labor problem in economic development: A framework for a reappraisal. *Int. Labor Rev.,* 1955, 71:3-15.

KERR, C. & SIEGEL, A. The inter-industry propensity to strike—an international comparison. In Kornhauser, Dubin & Ross (1954). Pp. 189-212.

Kerschensteiner, G. *Grundfragen der Schulorganization.* Leipzig: Teubner, 1909.

KILLIAN, L. M. The significance of multiple-group membership in disaster. In Cartwright & Zander (1953). Pp. 249-256.

KING, M. L., JR. *Stride toward freedom.* New York: Harper, 1958.

KING, W. *Social movements in the United States.* New York: Random House, 1956.

KINKEAD, E. The study of something new in history. *The New Yorker,* Oct. 26, 1957. Pp. 114-169.

KINKEAD, E. *In every war but one.* New York: Norton, 1959.

KNELLER, G. F. *Higher learning in Britain.* Berkeley & Los Angeles: University of California Press, 1955.

KNOWLES, K. G. J. C. *Strikes—a study in industrial conflict.* Oxford: Blackwell, 1952.

KOGON, E. *The theory and practice of hell: The German concentration camps and the system behind them.* New York: Farrar, Strauss, 1950.

KOHN, R. L., TANNENBAUM, A., WEISS, R. *et al.* A study of the League of Women Voters of the United States. Ann Arbor: University of Michigan, 1956. Mimeo.

KOMAROVSKY, MIRRA. Patterns of voluntary association among urban working-class families. *Am. sociol. Rev.,* 1946, 2: 686-698.

KORNHAUSER, A., DUBIN, R. & ROSS, A. M., eds. *Industrial conflict.* New York: McGraw-Hill, 1954.

KORNHAUSER, A., SHEPPARD, H. L. & MAYER, A. J. *When labor votes.* New York: University Books, 1956.

KORNHAUSER, W. *The politics of mass society.* Glencoe, Ill.: The Free Press, 1959.

KRAUSE, K. Authoritarianism, dogmatism and coercion in child caring institutions: A study of staff attitudes. *Child Welfare*, 1974, 53: 23-30.

KRECH, D. & CRUTCHFIELD, R. S. *Theory and problems of social psychology.* New York: McGraw-Hill, 1948.

KREPS, T. J. The newspaper industry. In W. Adams, ed., *The structure of Amercian industry.* New York: Macmillan, 1954. Pp. 485-504.

LAMMERS, C. J. The Royal Institute of the Navy: Socialisation of Dutch naval cadets. Unpublished doctoral dissertation, Netherlands Institute of Preventive Medicine, Leiden.

LANGDALE, J. Toward a contingency/congruency theory for designing work organizations. Unpublished doctoral dissertation, no date.

LARKIN, E. J. Three models of evaluation. *Canadian Psychologist*, 1974, 15: 89-94.

LARRABEE, E. & RIESMAN, D. The role of business in "Executive Suite." In B. Rosenberg & D. M. White, eds., *Mass culture.* Glencoe, Ill.: The Free Press, 1957. Pp. 325-340.

LASSWELL, H. D. & KAPLAN, A. *Power and Society.* New Haven: Yale University Press, 1950.

LAVIOLETTE, F. E. *The Canadian Japanese and world war II: A sociological and psychological account.* Toronto: University Press, 1948.

Laws of the State of Israel. Jerusalem: Government Printer, 1949.

LAZARSFELD, P. F. A conceptual introduction to latent structure analysis. In Lazarsfeld (1954). Pp. 349-387.

LAZARSFELD, P. F., ed. *Mathematical thinking in the social sciences.* Glencoe, Ill.: The Free Press, 1954.

LAZARSFELD, P. F. Problems in methodology. In Merton, Broom & Cottrell (1959). Pp. 39-78.

LAZARSFELD, P. F., BERELSON, B. & GAUDET, HAZEL. *The people's choice.* 2d ed. New York: Columbia University Press, 1948.

LAZARSFELD, P. F. & MENZEL, H. On the relation between individual and collective properties. In Etzioni (1961). Pp. 422-440.

LAZARSFELD, P. F. & ROSENBERG, M., eds. *The language of social research.* Glencoe, Ill.: Free Press, 1955.

LAZARSFELD, P. F. & THIELENS, W., JR. *The academic mind.* Glencoe, Ill.: The Free Press, 1958.

LAZOVSKY, A. *The trade unions in Soviet Russia.* Moscow: All-Russia Central Council of Trade Unions, 1920.

Leadership and supervision: a survey of research findings. Washington, D.C.: U.S. Civil Service Commission, 1955.

LEARNED, W. S. & WOOD, B. D. *The student and his knowledge.* Bull. No. 29. New York: Carnegie Foundation, 1938.

LEAVITT, H. J. Some effects of certain communiction patterns on group performance. *J. abnorm. soc. Psychol.*, 1951, 46: 38-50.

LEE, A. M. The social dynamics of the physician's status. *Psychiatry*, 1944, 7: 371-377.

LEFTON, M., DINITZ, S. & PASAMANICK, B. Decision-making in a mental hospital: Real, perceived, and ideal. *Amer. sociol. Rev.*, 1959, 24: 822-829.

LEIFFER, M. H. *The layman looks at the minister.* New York: Abingdon-Cokesbury, 1947.

Leighton, A. H. *The governing of men: General principles and recommendations based on experience at a Japanese relocation camp.* Princeton, N.J.: Princeton University Press, 1945.

Lenin, V. I. *What is to be done?* Moscow: Foreign Languages Publishing House, 1952.

Lentz, Edith M. Morale in a hospital business office. *Hum. Org.,* 1950, 9: 17-21.

Lentz, Edith M. Hospital administration—one of a species. *Admin. Sci. Q.,* 1957, 1: 444-463.

Levenson, B. Bureaucratic succession. In Etzioni (1961). Pp. 362-375.

Levine, S. & White, P. E. Exchange as a conceptual framework for the study of inter-organizational relationships. Mimeo.

Lewin, H. S. Hitler youth and the Boy Scouts of America. *Hum. Rel.,* 1947, 1: 206-227.

Lewin, K., Lippitt, R. & White, R. K. Patterns of aggressive behavior in experimentally created "social climates." *J. soc. Psychol.,* 1939, 10: 271-299.

Libo, L. M. *Measuring group cohesiveness.* Ann Arbor: University of Michigan, 1953.

Likert, R. Implication of organizational research. *First management work conference in developing human resources.* Washington, D.C.: National Training Laboratories, 1956.

Likert, R. Measuring organizational performance. *Harv. Bus. Rev.,* 1958, 36: 41-50.

Lindesmith, A. R. Teachers in the Army Air Forces. *Soc. Forc.,* 1946, 51: 404-407.

Lindsay, A. D. *The democratic state.* London: Oxford University Press, 1947.

Lindzey, G., ed. *Handbook of social psychology.* Reading, Mass.: Addison-Wesley, 1954.

Linton, R. *The study of man.* New York: Appleton-Century-Crofts, 1936.

Lippitt, R. & White, R. K. An experimental study of leadership and group life. In Swanson, Newcomb & Hartley (1952). Pp. 340-355.

Lipset, S. M. American intellectuals: Their politics and status. *Daedalus,* 1959, 88: 460-486.

Lipset, S. M. *Political man.* Garden Cty, N. Y.: Doubleday, 1960.

Lipset, S. M. & Bendix, R. *Social mobility in industrial society.* Berkeley: University of California Press, 1959.

Lipset, S. M. & Linz, J. The social bases of political diversity in western democracies. Unpublished, 1956.

Lipset, S. M., Trow, M. A. & Coleman, J. S. *Union democracy.* Glencoe, Ill.: The Free Press, 1956.

Litchfield, E. H. Notes on a general theory of administration. *Admin. Sci. Q.,* 1956, 1: 3-29.

Lockwood, D. *The Blackcoated Worker.* London: George Allen & Unwin, 1956.

Loftus, J. A. Labor racketeers at work: Six examples. In Barbash (1959). Pp. 320-323.

Lombard, G. F. F. *Behavior in a selling group.* Boston: Grad. School Bus. Admin., Harvard University, 1955.

Lowenthal, R. Development vs. utopian Communist policy. In C. Johnson, ed., *Change in Communist systems.* Stanford, Calif.: Stanford University Press, 1970.

Lubin, R., ed. *Human relations in administration.* Englewood Cliffs, N. J.: Prentice-Hall, 1951.

LUCCI, Y. *The campus YMCA: Highlights from a national study.* New York: Bur. appl. soc. Res., Columbia University, 1960.

LUFT, GERDA. The party that shapes policy. *The Jerusalem Post,* July 11, 1958. Cited by M. H. Bernstein, *The politics of Israel.* Princeton, N. J.: Princeton University Press, 1957.

LYND, R. S. & LYND, H. M. *Middletown in transition.* New York: Harcourt, Brace, 1937.

McCAY, J. T. *The management of time.* Englewood Cliffs, N. J.: Prentice-Hall, 1959.

McCLEERY, R. H. Institutional change: A case study of prison management in transition, 1945-1955. Unpublished doctoral dissertation, University of North Carolina, 1956.

McCLEERY, R. H. *Policy change in prison management.* East Lansing: Michigan State University, 1957.

McCLOSKY, H. Issue conflict and consensus among party leaders and followers. *Am. poli. Sci. Rev.,* 1960, 54: 406-427.

MACCOBY, ELEANOR E., NEWCOMB, T. M. & HARTLEY, E. L., eds. *Readings in social psychology.* New York: Holt, 1958.

McCORKLE, L. W. and KORN, R. Resocialization within walls. *Annals Am. Acad. poli. soc. Sci.,* 1954, 293: 88-98.

McDILL, E. L. A comparison of three measures of attitude intensity. *Soc. Forc.,* 1959, 38: 95-99.

MACDONALD, LOIS. *Southern mill hills.* New York: Hillman, 1928.

McELROY, J. *This was Andersonville.* New York: McDowell, 1957.

McEWEN, W. J. Position conflict and professional orientation in a research organization. *Admin. Sci. Q.,* 1956, 1: 208-224.

McGRATH, E. The control of higher education in America. *Educ. Rec.,* 1936, 17: 259-272.

MacIVER, R. M. & PAGE, C. *Society.* New York: Rinehart, 1949.

McKENZIE, R. T. *British political parties.* London: Heinemann, 1955.

MACKENZIE, W. J. M. *Politics and social science.* Baltimore: Penguin Books, 1967.

MacKINNON, W. J. & CENTERS, R. Authoritarianism and urban stratification. *Am. J. Soc.,* 1956, 61: 610-620.

MACLEAN, ANNIE M. Two weeks in department stories. *Am. J. Soc.,* 1899, 4: 721-741.

MAIER, N. R. F., READ, W. & HOOVER, J. Breakdowns in boss-subordinate communication. In *Communication in organizations.* Ann Arbor: Foundation for Research on Human Behavior, 1959. Pp. 19-25.

Management Audit. The Roman Catholic Church. Special Audit No. 137, Vol. V, No. 15 (February, 1956).

MANN, F. & BAUMGARTEL, H. *Absences and employee attitudes in an electric power company.* Ann Arbor: Institute for Social Research, University of Michigan, 1953.

MANN, F. & DENT, J. *Appraisals of supervisors.* Ann Arbor: Survey Research Center, University of Michigan, 1954.

MARCH, J. G., ed. *Handbook of organizations.* Chicago: Rand McNally, 1965.

MARCH, J. G. & SIMON, H. *Organizations.* New York: Wiley, 1958.

MARCUS, P. M. Expressive and instrumental groups: Toward a theory of group structure. *Am. sociol. Rev.,* 1960, 66: 54-59.

MARENCO, C. *Employés de banque.* Paris: Groupe de Recherches de Sociologie Administrative, 1959.

MARINE, G. "Think factory" deluxe—the Air Force's project RAND. *Nation,* 1959, 188: 131-135.

MARSHALL, S. L. A. *Men against fire.* New York: Morrow, 1947.

MARTIN, H. W. & KATZ, F. E. The professional school as a model of motivation. Paper presented to the American Sociological Association, Chicago, September, 1959.

MARTIN, N. H. & STRAUSS, A. L. Patterns of mobility within industrial organizations. In W. L. Warner & N. H. Martin, *Industrial man.* New York: Harper, 1959. Pp. 85-101.

MARVICK, D. *Career perspectives in a bureaucratic setting.* Ann Arbor: University of Michigan Press, Govt. Stud. No. 28, 1959.

MATTHEWSON, S. B. *Restriction of output among unorganized workers.* New York: Viking, 1931.

MAYER, M. *Madison Avenue, U.S.A.* New York: Harper, 1958.

MAYNTZ, R. Leisure, social participation, and political activity. Mimeo.

MAYO, E. & LOMBARD, G. F. F. *Teamwork and labor turnover in the aircraft industry of Southern California.* Boston, Mass.: Grad School of Bus. Admin., Harvard University, 1944.

MECHANIC, D. *Politics, medicine, and social science.* New York: Wiley, 1974.

MELMAN, S. *Decision making and productivity.* Oxford: Blackwell, 1958.

MELTZER, L. Scientific productivity in organizational settings. *J. soc. Issues,* 1956, 12: 32-40.

MENZEL, H. & KATZ, E. Social relations and innovation in the medical profession. *Pub. Opin. Q.,* 1955, 19: 337-352.

MERTON, R. K. *Mass persuasion: The social psychology of a war bond drive.* New York: Harper, 1946.

MERTON, R. K. The role set: Problems in sociological theory. *Br. J. Sociol.,* 1957, 8: 106-120.

MERTON, R. K. Socialization: A terminological note. In Merton, Reader & Kendall (1957). Pp. 287-293.

MERTON, R. K. *Social theory and social structure.* Rev. ed. Glencoe, Ill.: The Free Press, 1957*a.*

MERTON, R. K. Some preliminaries to a sociology of medical education. In Merton, Reader & Kendall (1957). Pp. 3-79.

MERTON, R. K. Notes on problem finding in sociology. In Merton, Broom & Cottrell (1959). Pp. ix-xxxiv.

MERTON, R. K. Social conflict over styles of sociological work. Paper presented to the Fourth World Congress of Sociology, Stresa, Italy, September 1959.

MERTON, R. K., BROOM, L. & COTTRELL, L. S., JR., eds. *Sociology today.* New York: Basic Books, 1959.

MERTON, R. K., GRAY, AILSA P., HOCKEY, BARBARA & SELVIN, H. C., eds. *Reader in bureaucracy.* Glencoe, Ill.: The Free Press, 1952.

MERTON, R. K., & LAZARSFELD, P. F., eds. *Continuities in social research.* Glencoe, Ill.: The Free Press, 1950.

MERTON, R. K., READER, G. G. & KENDALL, PATRICIA L., eds. *The student-physician.* Cambridge, Mass.: Harvard University Press, 1957.

MESSINGER, S. L. Organizational transformation: A case study of a declining social movement. *Amer. sociol. Rev.,* 1955, 20: 3-10.

METCALF, H. C. & URWICK, L., eds. *Dynamic administration: The collected papers of Mary Parker Follett.* New York: Harper, 1940.

MEYER, P. *Administrative organization.* Copenhagen: Nordisk Forlag Busck, 1957.

MICAUD, C. A. Organization and leadership of the French Communist party. *World Politics,* 1952, 4: 318-355.

MICHELS, R. *Political parties.* New York: Dover, 1959.

Mid-European Law Project. *Forced labor and confinement without trial.* Washington, D. C.: National Committee for a Free Europe, Inc., 1952.

MILLER, D. R. & SWANSON, G. E. Family, personality, and bureaucracy: A speculative account. In *The changing American parent.* New York: Wiley, 1958. Pp. 196-213.

MILLER, E. J. *Workmen's representation in industrial government.* Urbana: University of Illinois, 1922.

MILLER, G. W. & YOUNG, J. E. Member participation in the trade union local. *Am. J. Econ. & Sociol.,* 1955, 15: 31-47.

MILLER, J. P. & FRY, L. J. Social relations in organizations: Further evidence for the Weberian model. *Social Forces,* 1973, 51: 305-319.

MILLS, C. W. The middle-sized cities. *Am. sociol. Rev.,* 1945, 10: 242-249.

MILLS, C. W. *White collar.* New York: Oxford University Press, 1951.

MILLS, C. W. *The power elite.* New York: Oxford University Press, 1956. (Galaxy Book Edition, 1959.)

MISHLER, E. G. The commitment of individuals to organizational goals. No. 5, Organization Behavior Section, Princeton University, 1953. Mimeo.

MISHLER, E. G. Personality and social structure: A conceptual framework with implication for research on the psychological consequences of organizational membership. Princeton University, 1954. Mimeo.

MISHLER, E. G. & TROPP, A. Status and interaction in a psychiatric hospital. *Hum. Rel.,* 1956, 9: 187-205.

MOORE, B., JR. *Soviet politics—the dilemma of power.* Cambridge, Mass.: Harvard University Press, 1951.

MOORE, D. G. & RENCK, R. The professional employee in industry. *J. Bus.,* 1955, 28: 58-66.

MOORE, W. E. *Industrialization and labor: Social aspects of economic development.* Ithaca, N. Y.: Cornell University Press, 1951.

MOORE, W. E. Comment. *Am. sociol. Rev.,* 1953, 18: 397.

MOORE, W. E. Management and union organizations: An analytical comparison. In C. M. Arensberg *et al., Research in industrial human relations.* New York: Harper, 1957. Pp. 119-130.

MORENO, J. L. *Who shall survive?* Washington, D. C.: Nervous & Mental Disease Publishing Co., 1934.

MORSE, C. et al. *Modernization by design.* Ithaca, N.Y.: Cornell University Press, 1969.

MORSE, NANCY C. An experimental study in an industrial organization. In Guetzkow (1951). Pp. 96-99.

MORSE, NANCY C. *Satisfactions in the white-collar job.* Survey Research Center, University of Michigan, 1953.

MORSE, NANCY C. & REIMER, E. The experimental change of a major organizational variable. *J. abnorm. & soc. Psychol.,* 1956, 52: 120-129.

MORSE, NANCY C. & WEISS, R. S. The function and meaning of work and the job. *Am. sociol. Rev.,* 1955, 20: 191-198.

MULFORD, C., WOODMAN, W., WARREN, R. & KOPACHESKY, J. The mediating role of social rank on two competing compliance models. Scientific Paper Series, Department of Sociology, Iowa State University, no date.

MUMFORD, ENID M. Social behaviour in small work groups. *Sociol. Rev.,* 1959, 7: 137-157.

MYERS, C. A. & TURNBULL, J. G. Line and staff in industrial relations. *Harv. Bus. Rev.,* 1956, 34: 113-124.

MYERS, R. R. Interpersonal relations in the building industry. *Hum. Org.,* 1946, 5: 1-7.

MYERS, R. R. Myth and status systems in industry. *Soc. Forc.,* 1948, 26: 331-337.

MYRDAL, G. with the assistance of STERNER, R. and ROSE, A. *An American dilemma.* New York: Harper, 1944.

NAEGELE, K. D. Clergymen, teachers, and psychiatrists: A study in roles and socialization. Revised version, paper presented to Canadian Political Science Association, Toronto, June 1955.

NAEGELE, K. D. Librarians, observations on their work and their careers in the Pacific Northwest. Mimeo.

NAGEL, E. A formalization of functionalism. In Nagel (1957). Pp. 247-283.

NAGEL, E. *Logic without metaphysics.* Glencoe, Ill.: The Free Press, 1957.

NEGANDHI, A. R., ed. *Modern organizational theory.* Kent, Ohio: Kent State University Press, 1973.

NELSON, R. & JOHNSEN, L. The role of evaluation in community mental health programmes. *Community Development Journal,* 1974, 9: 145-149.

NETTL, J. P. *Political mobilization.* London: Faber and Faber, 1967.

NETTLER, G. A measure of alienation. *Am. sociol. Rev.,* 1957, 22: 670-677.

NEUMAN, F. L. Approaches to the study of political power. *Poli. Sci. Q.,* 1950, 65: 161-180.

NEWCOMB, T. M. *Personality and social change.* New York: The Dryden Press, 1943.

NEWCOMER, MABEL. *The big business executive.* New York: Columbia University Press, 1955.

NEWMAN, W. H. *Administrative action: The techniques of organization and management.* New York: Prentice-Hall, 1951.

NICHOLLS, W., II. Social relations among medical students and attitudinal learning. Unpublished doctoral dissertation, Columbia University (in progress).

NIGG, W. *Warriors of God.* London: Secker & Warburg, 1959.

NISBET, R. A. Conservatism and sociology. *Am. J. Soc.,* 1952, 58: 167-175.

NORFLEET, B. Interpersonal relations and group productivity. *J. soc. Issues,* 1948, 4: 66-69.

O'DEA, T. F. Catholic ideology and secular pressures. Unpublished baccalaureate thesis, Harvard University, 1949.

O'DEA, T. F. The saints withdraw from secular society. In his *The Mormons.* Chicago: The University of Chicago Press, 1957. Pp. 41-52.

OHLIN, L. E. *Sociology and the field of corrections.* New York: Russell Sage Foundation, 1956.

OHLIN, L. E. The reduction of role conflict in institutional staff. *Children,* 1958, 5: 65-69.

OHLIN, L. E. When is punishment effective? *J. Assoc. Psych. Treatment of Offenders,* 1959, 3: 2.

OHLIN, L. E. Conflicting interests in correctional objectives. In *Theoretical studies in social organization of the prison.* New York: Social Science Research Council, 1960. Pp. 111-129.

OHLIN, L. E. & LAWRENCE, W. C. Social interaction among clients as a treatment problem. *Social Work*, 1959, 4: 3-13.

OHLIN, L. E., PIVEN, H. & PAPPENFORT, D. M. Major dilemmas of the social worker in probation and parole. *Natl. Probation & Parole Assoc. J.*, 1956, 2: 211-225.

OSBORN, R. & HUNT, J. Environment and organizational effectiveness. *Admin. Sci. Q.*, 1974, 19: 231-246.

OSTROGORSKI, M. *Democracy and the organization of political parties.* New York: Haskell, 1902.

ORZACK, L. H. Work as a "central life interest" of professionals. *Soc. Prob,* 1959, 7: 125-132.

PAGE, C. H. Bureaucracy's other face. *Soc. Forc.*, 1946, 25: 88-94.

PAHLEY, B. W. Pastoral support for university students—in loco parentis or functional necessity? *Universities Quarterly*, 1974, 28: 178-196.

PALISI, B. A critical analysis of the voluntary association concept. In D. H. Smith, R. D. Reddy & D. R. Baldwin, eds., *Voluntary action research.* Lexington, Mass.: Heath, 1972.

PALUMBO, D. & STYSKAL, R. Professionalism and receptivity to change. *American Journal of Political Science*, 1974, XVIII: 385-394.

PARETO, A. Elites, force, and governments. In C. Wright Mills, ed., *Images of Man.* New York: George Braziller, 1960. Pp. 262-291.

PARKER, S. Changes in the administration of psychotherapy during a collective upset. *Hum. Org.*, 1958, 16: 32-37.

PARODY, O. F. *The high school principal and staff deal with discipline.* New York: Teachers College, Columbia University, 1958.

PARSONS, ANNE. Some comparative observations on ward social structure: Southern Italy, England and the United States. *L'Ospedale Psichiatrico,* 1959, 2: 3-23.

PARSONS, T. *The structure of social action.* New York: McGraw-Hill, 1937.

PARSONS, T., ed. Introduction. In Weber (1947). Pp. 1-77.

PARSONS, T. *The social system.* Glencoe, Ill.: The Free Press, 1951.

PARSONS, T. The organization of personality as a system of action. In Parsons & Bales (1955). Pp. 133-186.

PARSONS, T. Suggestions for a sociological approach to the theory of organizations. *Admin. Sci. Q.*, 1956, 1: 63-85, 225-239.

PARSONS, T. The distribution of power in American society. *World Politics,* 1957, 10: 123-143.

PARSONS, T. The mental hospital as a type of organization. In Greenblatt, Levinson & Williams (1957). Pp. 108-129.

PARSONS, T. General theory in sociology. In Merton, Broom & Cottrell (1959). Pp. 3-38.

PARSONS, T. The implications of the study. In Danton (1959). Pp. 77-96.

PARSONS, T. *Structure and process in modern societies.* Glencoe, Ill.: The Free Press, 1960.

PARSONS, T., BALES, R. F. et al., eds. *Family, socialization, and interaction process.* Glencoe, Ill.: The Free Press, 1955.

PARSONS, T., BALES, R. F. & SHILS, E. A. Phase movement in relation to motivation, symbol formation, and role structure. In Parsons, Bales, & Shils (1953). Pp. 163-269.

PARSONS, T., BALES, R. F. & SHILS, E. A. *Working papers in the theory of action.* Glencoe, Ill.: The Free Press, 1953.

PARSONS, T., SHILS, E. A. *et al. Toward a general theory of action.* Cambridge, Mass.: Harvard University Press, 1952.

PARSONS, T. & SMELSER, N. J. *Economy and society.* Glencoe, Ill.: The Free Press, 1956.

PARVILAHTI, U. *Beria's gardens: A slave laborer's experience in the Soviet Utopia.* Tr. by A. Blair. New York: Dutton, 1960.

PAYNE, R. An approach to the study of relative prestige of formal organizations. *Soc. Forc.,* 1954, 32: 244-247.

PECK, S. M. Role strain for the union steward. Paper presented to the American Sociological Association, New York, August 1960.

PELZ, D. C. Influence: A key to effective leadership in the first-line supervisor. *Personnel,* 1952, 3: 209-217.

PELZ, D. C., MELLINGER, G. D. & DAVIS, R. C. *Human relations in research organizations.* Ann Arbor: Institute for Social Research, University of Michigan, 1953.

PERROW, C. Organizational prestige: The case of a general hospital. Paper presented to American Sociological Association, Chicago, September 1959.

PERROW, C. Authority, goals and prestige in a general hospital. Unpublished doctoral dissertation, University of California, 1960.

PERROW, C. Hospitals, technology, structure and goals. In J. G. March, ed., *Handbook of organizations.* Chicago: Rand McNally, 1965. Pp. 910-971.

PERROW, C. *Complex organizations: A critical essay.* Glenview, Ill.: Scott, Foresman and Company, 1972.

PETERSON, O. L., ANDREWS, L. P., SPAIN, R. S. & GREENBERG, B. G. An analytical study of North Carolina general practice, 1953-54. *J. Med. Educ.,* 1956, 31.

PHELAN, J. L. Authority and flexibility in the Spanish imperial bureaucracy. *Admin. Sci. Q.,* 1960, 5: 47-65.

PIGORS, P. & FAITH. *Human aspects of multiple shift operations.* Cambridge, Mass.: M. I. T. Ser. 2, No. 13, 1944.

PINE, F. & LEVINSON, D. J. Two patterns of ideology, role conception, and personality among hospital aides. In Greenblatt, Levinson & Williams (1957). Pp. 209-217.

PINNER, F. A., JACOBS, P. & SELZNICK, P. *Old age and political behavior.* Berkeley: University of California, 1959.

PIRAGES, D. C. Modernization and political organization: Pressures for new decisional models in socialist society. Paper presented at Conference on Leadership in the USSR and Eastern Europe, Northwestern University, Nov. 8–10, 1968.

PLASEK, W. Marxist and American sociological conceptions of alienation: Implications for social problems theory. *Social Problems,* 1974, 21: 316-328.

POINSETT, A. Farewell to Daddy Grace. *Ebony,* 1960, 15: 25-34.

POLANYI, K. Our obsolete market mentality. In L. Wilson & W. L. Kolb, eds., *Sociological analysis.* New York: Harcourt, Brace, 1949. Pp. 557-567.

PONTING, J. R. Rumor control centers: Their emergence and operations. *American Behavioral Scientist,* 1973, 16, No. 3.

POPE, L. *Millhands and preachers.* New Haven: Yale University Press, 1942.

PORTER, L. W. Self-perceptions of first-level supervisors compared with upper-management personnel and with operative line workers. *J. Appl. Psychol.,* 1959, 43: 183-186.

PORTER, L. W. & GHISELLI, E. E. The self-perceptions of top and middle management personnel. *Pers. Psychol.,* 1957, 10: 397-406.

PREFFER, R. M. Revolution and rule: Where do we go from here? *Bulletin of Concerned Asian Scholars,* 1970, 2, 3 (April–July): 88-95.

PRESSEY, S. L. & HANNA, D. C. The class as a psycho-sociological unit. In Coladarci (1955). Pp. 246-253.

PRESTHUS, R. V. Behavior and bureaucracy in many cultures. *Publ. Admin. Rev.,* 1959, 19: 25-35.

PRESTHUS, R. V. Social bases of bureaucratic organization. *Soc. Forc.,* 1959a, 38: 103-109.

PRICE, J. L. Design of proof in organizational research. *Admin. Sci. Q.,* 1968, 13: 121-134.

PRICE, J. L. *Organizational effectiveness: An inventory of propositions.* Homewood, Ill.: Richard D. Irwin, Inc., 1968.

PRICE, J. L. *Handbook of organizational measurement.* Lexington, Mass.: Heath, 1972.

PRINGLE, R. W. *The psychology of high school discipline.* Boston: Heath, 1931.

PUGH, D. S., HICKSON, D. J. HININGS, C. R. & TURNER, C. Dimensions of organization structure. *Admin. Sci. Q.,* 1968, 13: 64-105.

PUGH, D. S., HICKSON, D. J. & HININGS, C. R. *Writers on organizations.* 2d ed. Baltimore: Penguin Books, 1971.

PURCELL, T. V. *The worker speaks his mind on company and union.* Cambridge, Mass.: Harvard University Press, 1953.

QUARANTELLI, E. L. The community general hospital, its immediate problems in disaster. *American Behavioral Scientist,* 1970, 13, No. 3.

RADELET, L. A. Police-community relations. *Social Order,* 1960, 10: 219-225.

RANDLE, C. W. How to identify promotable executives. *Harv. Bus. Rev.,* 1956, 34: 122-134.

RAPOPORT, R. N. & RAPOPORT, RHONA S. "Democratization" and authority in a therapeutic community. *Behav. Sci.,* 1957, 2: 128-133.

RASKIN, A. H. The Dubinsky concept of unionism. In Barbash (1959). Pp. 77-82.

RAWLS, J. *A theory of justice.* Cambridge, Mass.: Harvard University Press, 1971.

READ, W. H. Upward communication in industrial hierarchies. Unpublished doctoral dissertation, University of Michigan, 1959.

REAVINS, W. C. & WOELLNER, R. C. *Office practices in secondary schools.* New York: Laidlaw, 1930.

REDL, F. Groups, emotions, and leadership. *Psychiatry,* 1942, 5: 573-596.

REDL, F. Discipline and teacher personality. In G. V. Sheriakov & F. Redl, *Discipline for today's children and youth.* Washington, D.C.: Association for Supervision and Curriculum Development, 1944.

REID, E. *Mafia.* New York: Random House, 1952.

REIMER, H. Socialization in the prison society. *Proceedings of the Sixty-Seventh Annual Conference of the American Prison Association,* 1937.

REISS, D. Assimilating the patient stranger. *Psychiatry,* 1974, 37: 267-282.

REISSMAN, L. A study in role conceptions in bureaucracy. *Soc. Forc.,* 1949, 27: 305-310.

REISSMAN, L. Life careers, power and the professions: The retired army general. *Am. sociol. Rev.,* 1956, 21: 215-221.

RETTIG, S. S., JACOBSON, F. N. & PASAMANICK, B. Status overestimation, objective status, and job satisfaction among professions. *Am. sociol. Rev.*, 1958, 23: 75-81.

RHENMAN, E. *Organization theory for long-range planning.* London: Wiley, 1973.

RHYNE, J. *Some southern cotton mill workers and their villages.* Chapel Hill: University of North Carolina, 1930.

RICE, A. K. The experimental reorganization of non-automatic weaving in an Indian mill. *Hum. Rel.*, 1955, 3: 199-249.

RICE, A. K. Productivity and social organization in an Indian weaving mill II: A follow-up study of experimental reorganization of non-automatic weaving. *Hum. Rel.*, 1955a, 3: 399-428.

RICHARDSON, S. A. Organizational contrasts on British and American ships. *Admin. Sci. Q.*, 1956, 1: 189-207.

RICHARDSON, S. A. The social organization of British and United States merchant ships. N. Y. State School for Industrial and Labor Relations, Cornell University. Mimeo.

RIECKEN, H. W. Primary groups and political party choice. In E. Burdick & A. J. Brodbeck, eds., *American voting behavior.* Glencoe, Ill.: The Free Press, 1959. Pp. 162-183.

RIEFF, P. *Freud: The mind of the moralist.* New York: Viking, 1959.

RIEGEL, J. W. *Employee interest in company success.* Ann Arbor: University of Michigan. Mimeo.

RIESMAN, D. The college student in an age of organization. *Sequoia*, 1958, 3 (2): 1-13.

RIESMAN, D., GLAZER, N. & DENNEY, R. *The lonely crowd.* Garden City, N. Y.: Doubleday, 1955.

RIGGS, F. W. Notes on literature available for the study of comparative public administration. *Am. poli. Sci. Rev.*, 1954, 48: 515-537.

RIGGS, F. W. Prismatic society and financial administration. *Admin. Sci. Q.*, 1960, 5: 1-46.

RILEY, J. W., JR. & RILEY, MATHILDA W. Sociological perspectives on the use of new educational media. Mimeo.

RILEY, MATHILDA, RILEY, J. W. & MOORE, M. E. Adolescent values and the Riesman typology. In S. M. Lipset & L. Lowenthal, eds., *Culture and social character.* Glencoe, Ill.: The Free Press, 1961.

RINDER, I. D. Polarities in Jewish identification. In M. Sklare, ed., *The Jews.* Glencoe, Ill.: The Free Press, 1958. Pp. 493-502.

ROACH, ALVA C. *The prisoner of war and how treated.* Indianapolis: Railroad City Publishers, 1865.

RODEHAVER, M. W. & SMITH, L. M. Migration and occupational structure: The clergy. *Soc. Forc.*, 1951, 29: 416-427.

ROE, ANN. *The making of a scientist.* New York: Dodd, 1953.

ROETHLISBERGER, F. J. & DICKSON, W. J. *Management and the worker.* Cambridge, Mass.: Harvard University Press, 1939.

ROGERS, C. *Client-centered therapy.* Boston: Houghton, 1951.

ROHRER, J. H. & SHERIF, M., eds. *Social psychology at the crossroads.* New York: Harper, 1951.

ROMER, S. Underworld labor tactics in Minneapolis. In Barbash (1959). Pp. 324-326.

ROSADA, S. & GWOZDZ, J. *Forced labor and confinement without trial in Poland.* Washington, D. C.: Mid-European Studies Center, 1952.

ROSE, A. M. *Theory and method in the social sciences.* Minneapolis: University of Minnesota, 1954.

ROSE, A. M. Voluntary associations under conditions of competition and conflict. *Soc. Forc.,* 1955, 34: 159-163.

ROSENFELD, EVA. Social stratification in a "classless" society. *Am. sociol. Rev.,* 1951, 16: 766-774.

ROSOW, I. *Authority in natural disasters.* Columbus: Ohio State University, Disaster Research Center, 1975 (in press).

ROSS, A. M. *Trade union wage policy.* Berkeley: University of California Press, 1948.

ROSS, AILEEN D. Organized philanthropy in an urban community. *Canad. J. Econ. & poli. Sci.,* 1952, 18: 474-486.

ROSSEL, R. Dual leadership in complex organizations: An empirical study. Southern Illinois University. No date.

ROSSITER, C. *The American presidency.* New York: Signet, 1956.

ROUCEK, J. S. Attitudes of the prison guard. *Sociol. & soc. Res.,* 1936, 20: 170-174.

ROURKE, F. E. *Bureaucracy, politics, and public policy.* Boston: Little, Brown, 1969.

ROWLAND, H. Interaction in the state mental hospital. *Psychiatry,* 1938, 1: 323-337.

RUBIN, H. Modes of bureaucratic communications: Examples from Thai local administration. *Sociological Quarterly,* 1974, 15: 212-230.

RUDGE, P. F. *Ministry and management.* London: Tavistock Publications, 1968.

RUMMEL, R. J. The dimensions of conflict behavior within and between nations. *General Systems Yearbook,* 1963, 8: 1-50.

RUSHING, W. Differences in profit and nonprofit organizations: A study of effectiveness and efficiency in general short-stay hospitals. *Admin. Sci. Q.,* 1974, 19: 474-484.

RUSHING, W. Organizational rules and surveillance: Propositions in comparative organizational analysis. *Admin. Sci. Q.,* 1966, 10: 423-443.

SAMUELS, GERTRUDE. Visit to a 600 school. *New York Times Magazine,* March 2, 1958, pp. 12-15.

SAPOSS, D. J. *Left-wing unionism.* New York: International Publ., 1926.

SAYLES, L. R. Wildcat strikers. *Harv. Bus. Rev.,* 1954, 32: 42-52.

SAYLES, L. R. & STRAUSS, G. *The local union.* New York: Harper, 1953.

SAYRE, W. S. Additional observations on the study of administration. *Teachers Coll. Rec.,* 1958, 60: 73-76.

SCALF, J. H., JR., MILLER, M. J. & THOMAS, C. W. Goal specificity, organizational structure, and participant commitment in churches. Paper presented to the Southern Sociological Association Convention, April 1972.

SCHACHTER, S. Comment. *Am. sociol. Rev.,* 1952, 57: 554-562.

SCHACHTER, S., ELLERTSON, N., McBRIDE, DOROTHY & GREGORY, DORIS. An experimental study of cohesiveness and productivity. In Cartwright & Zander (1953). Pp. 401-411.

SCHAFER, R. & KLONGLAN, G. Application of the rule of distributive justice in a normative organization. *Pacific Sociological Review,* 1974, 17: 199-213.

SCHANK, R. L. A study of a community and its groups and institutions conceived of as behavior of individuals. *Psychol. Monogr.*, 1932, 32: 1-133.

SCHEIN, E. H. *Organizational psychology.* Englewood Cliffs, N.J.: Prentice-Hall, 1965.

SCHERER, R. P. The church as a formal voluntary organization. In D. H. Smith, R. D. Reddy & B. R. Baldwin, eds., *Voluntary action research.* Lexington, Mass.: Heath, 1972.

SCHNEIDER, E. V. *Industrial sociology.* New York: McGraw-Hill, 1957.

SCHRUPP, M. H. & GJERDE, C. M. Teacher growth in attitudes toward behavior problems of children. In Coladarci (1955). Pp. 173-183.

SCHULMAN, J. *Remaking an organization.* Albany: State University of New York Press, 1969.

SCHUMPETER, J. A. *Capitalism, socialism and democracy.* New York: Harper, 1950.

SCHURMANN, F. *Ideology and organization in Communist China*, 2d ed. Berkeley: University of California Press, 1968.

SCHWARTZ, R. D. Functional alternatives to inequality. *Am. sociol. Rev.*, 1955, 20: 424-430.

SCOTT, E. L. *Leadership and perceptions of organization.* Columbus: Bur. Bus. Res., Ohio University, 1958.

SCOTT, FRANCES G. Action theory and research in social organization. *Am. J. Soc.*, 1959, 64: 386-395.

SCOTT, J. C., JR. Membership and participation in voluntary associations. *Am. sociol. Rev.*, 1957, 22: 315-26.

SCOTT, J. F. & LYNTON, R. P. *The community factor in modern technology.* Paris: UNESCO, 1952.

SCOTT, R. L., JR. *Flying Tigers: Chennault of China.* Garden City, N. Y.: Doubleday, 1959.

SCOTT, W. H., HALSEY, A. H., BANKS, J. A. & LUPTON, T. *Technical change and industrial relations.* Liverpool: Liverpool University, 1956.

SCOTT, W. R. Theory of organizations. In R. L. Faris, ed., *Handbook of modern sociology.* Chicago: Rand McNally, 1964. Pp. 485-529

SCOTT, W. R. Reactions to supervision in a heteronomous professional organization. *Admin. Sci. Q.*, 1965, 10: 51-81.

SCOTT, W. R. Professional employees in a bureaucratic structure: Social work. In A. Etzioni, ed., *The semi-professions and their organization.* New York: The Free Press, 1969. Pp. 82-140.

SCUDDER, K. J. The Open institution. *Annals Am. Acad. poli. soc. Sci.*, 1954, 293: 79-87.

SEASHORE, S. E. *Group cohesiveness in the industrial work group.* Ann Arbor: Survey Research Center, University of Michigan, 1954.

SEASHORE, S. E. & YUCHTMAN, E. Factoral analysis of organizational performance. *Admin. Sci. Q.*, 1967, 12: 377-395.

SEASHORE, S. E. & YUCHTMAN, E. A system resource approach to organizational effectiveness. *Am. sociol. Rev.*, 1972, 32: 891-903.

SEELEY, J. R., JUNKERS, B. H., WALLACE, J. R., JR. *et al. Community chest.* Toronto: University of Toronto, 1957.

SEEMAN, M. & MORRIS, R. T. The problem of leadership: An interdisciplinary approach. *Soc. Forc.*, 1950, 56: 149-155.

SEGAL, M. Organization and environment: A typology of adaptability and structure. *Public Administration Review*, 1974, 34: 212-220.

SEIDMAN, J., LONDON, J. & KARSH, B. Why workers join unions. *Annals Am. Acad. poli. soc. Sci.*, 1951, 274: 75-87.

SEIDMAN, J., LONDON, J., KARSH, B. & TAGLIACOZZO, DAISY L. *The worker views his union.* Chicago: The University of Chicago Press, 1958.

SELIGMAN, L. G. Development in the presidency and the conception of political leadership. *Am. sociol. Rev.*, 1955, 20: 706-712.

SELLIN, T. *Recent penal legislation in Sweden.* Stockholm: Strafflag-Beredningen, 1947.

SELLIN, T. The treatment of offenders in Sweden. *Fed. Prob.*, 1948, 12: 14-18.

SELVIN, H. C. The effects of leadership climate on the nonduty behavior of Army trainees. Unpublished doctoral dissertation, Columbia University, 1956.

SELVIN, H. C. *The effects of leadership.* Glencoe, Ill.: The Free Press, 1960.

SELVIN, H. C. & HAGSTROM, W. O. Methodology and theory in the study of organizational behavior. Berkeley, Calif.: Survey Research Center, 1960. Mimeo.

SELZNICK, P. Foundations of the theory of organization. *Am. Sociol. Rev.*, 1948, 13: 25-35.

SELZNICK, P. *The organizational weapon.* New York: McGraw-Hill, 1952.

SELZNICK, P. *TVA and the grass roots.* Berkeley: University of California, 1953.

SELZNICK, P. & SELZNICK, GERTRUDE J. The idea of a social system. Paper presented to American Sociological Society, Chicago, September 1959.

SHEPARD, H. A. Democratic control in a labor union. *Am. J. Soc.*, 1949, 54: 311-316.

SHEPARD, H. A. The value system of a university research group. *Am. sociol. Rev.*, 1954, 19: 456-462.

SHEPARD, H. A. Some studies of laboratory management. *Armed Forces Management,* October 1955.

SHEPARD, H. A. Superiors and subordinates in research. *J. Bus. Univ. Chicago,* 1956, 29: 261-267.

SHERIF, M. A study of some social factors in perception. *Arch. Psychol.*, 1935, 187: 1-60.

SHICHOR, D. & EMPEY, L. T. A typological analysis of correctional organizations. *Sociology and Social Research,* 1974, 58: 318-334.

SHIH, K. *China enters the machine age.* Cambridge, Mass.: Harvard University Press, 1944.

SHILS, E. A. Primary groups in the American Army. In Merton & Lazarsfeld (1950). Pp. 16-39.

SHILS, E. A. & JANOWITZ, M. Cohesion and disintegration in the Wehrmacht in world war II. *Publ. Opin. Q.*, 1948, 12 (2): 280-315.

SHINNICK, P. A comparative analysis of traditional athletic organizations in higher education. Unpublished manuscript, 1974.

SHOR, E. L. The Thai bureaucracy. *Admin. Sci. Q.*, 1960, 5: 66-86.

SIGELMAN, L. Reporting the news: An organizational analysis. *Am. J. Soc.*, 1973, 79: 132-151.

SILLS, D. L. *The volunteers.* Glencoe, Ill.: The Free Press, 1957.

SILVERMAN, D. *The theory of organizations.* New York: Basic Books, 1971.

SIMMEL, G. Superiority and subordination as subject-matter of sociology. *Am. J. Soc.*, 1896, 2: 167-189, 392-415.

SIMMEL, G. *The sociology of Georg Simmel.* Tr. by K. H. Wolff. Glencoe, Ill.: The Free Press, 1950.

SIMMEL, G. *Conflict.* Tr. by K. H. Wolff. Glencoe, Ill.: The Free Press, 1955.

SIMON, H. A. *Administrative Behavior.* 2d ed. New York: Macmillan, 1957.

SIMON, H. A. & GUETZKOW, H. Mechanisms involved in group pressures on deviate members. *Br. J. Stat. Psychol.*, 1955, 8: 93-100.

SIMON, H. A., SMITHBURG, D. W. & THOMPSON, V. A. *Public administration.* New York: Knopf, 1959.

SIMPSON, R. L. A modification of the functional theory of social stratification. *Soc. Forc.*, 1956, 35: 132-137.

SIMPSON, R. L. Vertical and horizontal communication in formal organizations. *Admin. Sci. Q.*, 1959, 4: 188-196.

SIMPSON, R. L. & SIMPSON, IDA H. The psychiatric attendant: Development of an occupational self-image in a low-status occupation. *Am. Sociol. Rev.*, 1959, 24: 389-392.

SIMPSON, R. L. & SIMPSON, IDA HARPER. Women and bureaucracy in the semi-professions. In A. Etzioni, ed., *The semi-professions and their organization.* New York: The Free Press, 1969. Pp. 196-265.

SKINNER, G. W. Chinese peasants and the closed community: An open and shut case. *Comparative Studies in Society and History*, 1971, 13: 270-281.

SLATER, P. E. Role differentiation in small groups. *Am. Sociol. Rev.*, 1959, 20: 300-310.

SLESINGER, J. A. A model for the comparative study of public bureaucracies. Ann Arbor: University of Michigan, 1957. Mimeo.

SLICHTER, S. H. The position of trade unions in the American economy. In Harrington & Jacobs (1959). Pp. 17-44.

SLICHTER, S. H. *et al.* The changing position of the foreman in American industry. *Adv. Management*, 1945, 10: 155-161.

SMIGEL, E. O. The impact of recruitment on the organization of the large law firm. *Am. sociol. Rev.*, 1960, 25: 56-67.

SMITH, A. E. Bureaucratic organization: selective or saturative. *Admin. Sci. Q.*, 1957, 2: 361-375.

SMITH, C. G. A comparative analysis of some conditions and consequences of intra-organizational conflict. *Admin. Sci. Q.*, 1966, 10: 504-529.

SMITH, C. & BROWN, M. Communication structure and control structure in a voluntary association. *Sociometry*, 1964, 27, December.

SMITH, D. H., REDDY, R. D. & BALDWIN, B. R. Types of voluntary action: A definitional essay. In Smith, Reddy & Baldwin, eds., *Voluntary action research: 1972.* Lexington, Mass.: Heath, 1972.

SMITH, H. L. The sociological study of hospitals. Unpublished doctoral dissertation, University of Chicago, 1949.

SMITH, H. L. Two lines of authority are one too much. *Modern Hospital*, 1955, 84: 54-64.

SMITH, H. L. Two lines of authority: The hospital's dilemma. In E. Gartly Jaco, *Physicians, patients and illness.* Glencoe, Ill.: The Free Press, 1958. Pp. 469-477.

SMITH, H. L. & LEVINSON, D. J. The major aims and organizational characteristics of mental hospitals. In Greenblatt, Levinson & Williams (1957). Pp. 3-8.

SMITH, R. Some consequences of military authority. Paper presented at American Sociological Association Annual Meetings, Montreal, August 26, 1974.

SMITH, W. R. *Constructive school discipline.* New York: American Book Co., 1936.

SNOOK, J. An alternative to church-sect. *Journal for the Scientific Study of Religion*, 1974, 13: 191-204.

SOEMERDJAN, S. Bureaucratic organization in time of revolution. *Adm. Sci. Q.*, 1957, 2: 182-199.

Sommer, R. & Hall, R. Alienation and mental illness. *Am. sociol. Rev.*, 1958, 23: 418-420.

Sondern, R., Jr. *Brotherhood of evil: The Mafia.* New York: Bantam, 1960.

Speier, H. "The American Soldier" and the sociology of military organizations. In Merton & Lazarsfeld (1950). Pp. 125-127.

Spinrad, W. Correlates of trade union participation: A summary of the literature. *Am. sociol. Rev.*, 1960, 25: 237-244.

Stancato, F. A. The administration of teaching personnel: Implications for a theory of role conflict resolution. *Contemporary Education*, 1974, XLV: 108-111.

Stanton, A. H. & Schwartz, M. S. *The mental hospital.* New York: Basic Books, 1954.

Star, Shirley, Williams, R. M., Jr. & Stouffer, S. A. Negro infantry platoons in white companies. In Maccoby, Newcomb & Hartley (1958). Pp. 596-601.

Steffens, L. *The shame of the cities.* New York: Sagamore Press, 1957.

Stein, E. & Carreau, D. Law and peaceful change in a subsystem: "Withdrawal" of France from the North Atlantic Treaty Organization. *American Journal of International Law*, 1968, 62: 577-640.

Stein, H. D. Organization theory—implications for administrative research. In L. Kogan, ed., *Social science theory and social work research.* New York: National Association of Social Workers, 1960.

Stein, H. D. The study of organizational effectiveness. In D. Fanshel, ed., *Research in social welfare administration.* New York: National Association of Social Workers, 1962. Pp. 22-32.

Stephansky, B. The structure of the American labor movement. In Brooks, Darber, McCabe & Taft (1952). Pp. 39-69.

Stern, G. G., Stein, M. I. & Bloom, B. S. *Methods in personality assessment: Human behavior in complex situations.* Glencoe, Ill.: The Free Press, 1956.

Steuben, J. *Strike strategy.* New York: Gaer, 1950.

Steward, D. D. Local board: A study of the place of volunteer participation in bureaucratic organization. Unpublished doctoral dissertation, Columbia University, 1950.

Stinchcombe, A. L. Bureaucratic and craft administration of production: A comparative study. *Admin. Sci. Q.*, 1959, 4: 168-187.

Stinchcombe, A. L. Social sources of rebellion in a high school. Unpublished doctoral dissertation, University of California, 1960.

Stogdill, R. M. Personal factors associated with leadership: A study of the literature. *J. Psychol.*, 1948, 25: 35-71.

Stogdill, R. M. Interlocking methods of organizational study. In Merton *et al.* (1952). Pp. 445-450.

Stogdill, R. M. Interaction among superiors and subordinates. *Sociometry*, 1955, 18: 552-557.

Stogdill, R. M. & Coons, A. E., eds. *Leadership behavior: its description and measurement.* Columbus: Ohio State University, 1957.

Stogdill, R. M., Shartle, C. L., Wherry, R. J. & Jaynes, W. E. A factorial study of administrative behavior. *Personnel Psychol.*, 1955, 8: 157-164.

Stotland, E. & Kobler, A. L. *Life and death of a mental hospital.* Seattle: University of Washington Press, 1965.

STOUFFER, S. A. *Communism, conformity, and civil liberties.* Garden City, N. Y.: Doubleday, 1955.

STOUFFER, S. A. *et. al. The American soldier.* Princeton, N. J.: Princeton University Press, 1949.

STOUFFER, S. A., GUTTMAN, L., SUCHMAN, E. A., LAZARSFELD, P. F., STAR, SHIRLEY A. & CLAUSEN, J. A. *Measurement and prediction.* Princeton, N. J.: Princeton University Press, 1950.

STRAUSS, G. Control by the membership in building trades unions. *Am. sociol. Rev.,* 1956, 61: 527-535.

STRAUSS, G. & SAYLES, L. R. Some problems of communication in the local union. *Proceedings of the Fifth Annual Meeting of the Industrial Research Association,* Chicago, December, 1952. Pp. 143-149.

STREET, D., VINTER, R. D. & PERROW, C. *Organization for treatment.* New York: The Free Press, 1966.

SUCHMAN, E. A. The intensity component in attitude and opinion research. In Stouffer *et al.* (1950). Pp. 213-276.

SULLIVAN, R. H. Administrative-faculty relationship in colleges and universities. *J. higher Educ.,* 1956, 27: 308-326, 349.

SUTHERLAND, E. *White collar crime.* New York: The Dryden Press, 1949.

SUTTON, F. X. *et al. The American business creed.* Cambridge, Mass.: Harvard University Press, 1956.

SUTTON, R. L. Cultural context and change-agent organizations. *Admin. Sci. Q.,* 1974, 19: 547-562.

SWANSON, G. E., NEWCOMB, T. M. & HARTLEY, E. L., eds. *Readings in social psychology.* New York: Holt, 1952.

SYKES, G. M. The corruption of authority and rehabilitation. *Soc. Forc.,* 1956, 34: 257-262.

SYKES, G. M. *Crime and society.* New York: Random House, 1956*a.*

SYKES, G. M. Men, merchants, and toughs: A study of reaction to imprisonment. *Soc. Prob.,* 1956*b,* 4: 130-138.

SYKES, G. M. *The society of captives.* Princeton, N. J.: Princeton University Press, 1958.

SYKES, G. M. & MATZA, D. Techniques of neutralization. *Am. sociol. Rev.,* 1957, 22: 664-670.

SYKES, G. M. & MESSINGER, S. L. The inmate social system. *Theoretical Studies in Social Organizations.* New York: Social Science Research Council, 1960. Pp. 5-19.

TAGLIACOZZO, DAISY L. & SEIDMAN, J. A typology of rank-and-file union members. *Am. J. Soc.,* 1956, 61: 546-553.

TAKAYAMA, K. P. Administrative structures and political processes in Protestant denominations. *Publius: The Journal of Federalism,* 1974, 4: 5-37.

TALMON-GARBER, Y. Social differentiation in cooperative communities. *Br. J. Sociol.,* 1952, 3: 339-357.

TANNENBAUM, A. Control in organizations: Individual adjustment and organizational performance. *Admin. Sci. Q.,* 1962, 7: 236-257.

TANNENBAUM, A. S. Control structure and union functions. *Am. J. Soc.,* 1956, 61: 536-545.

TANNENBAUM, A. S. & GEORGOPOULOS, B. S. The distribution of control in formal organizations. *Soc. Forc.,* 1957, 36: 44-50.

TANNENBAUM, F. *A philosophy of labor*. New York: Knopf, 1951.

TANTER, R. Dimensions of conflict behavior within nations, 1955–1960: Turmoil and internal war. *Papers*, 1965, 111. Peace Research Society, Philadelphia; University of Pennsylvania, Department of Regional Science.

TEC, N. & GRANICK, R. Social isolation and difficulties in social interaction of residents of a home for aged. *Soc. Prob.*, 1959-60, 7: 226-232.

THIELENS, W., JR. Some comparisons of entrants to medical and law school. *J. Legal Educ.*, 1958, 2: 153-170.

THOMAS, C. & POOLE, E. The consequences of incompatible goal structures in correctional settings. Revision of paper presented to the Pacific Sociological Association, San Jose, California, March 1974.

THOMAS, C. & ZINGRAFF, M. Organizational structure as a determinant of prisonization. Revision of paper presented at North Central Sociological Association Convention, Cincinnati, Ohio, 1974.

THOMAS, E. J. Role conceptions and organizational size. *Am. sociol. Rev.*, 1959, 24: 30-37.

THOMPSON, J. D. Leadership and administration: Competing or complimentary concepts? Paper presented to the American Political Science Association, St. Louis, September, 1958.

THOMPSON, J. D. Organizational management of conflict. *Admin. Sci. Q.*, 1960, 4: 389-409.

THOMPSON, J. D. & BATES, F. L. Technology, organization, and administration. *Admin. Sci. Q.*, 1957, 2: 325-343.

THOMPSON, J. D., HAMMOND, P. B., HAWKES, R. W., JUNKER, B. H. & TUDEN, A., eds. *Comparative studies in administration*. Pittsburgh, Pa.: University of Pittsburgh, 1959.

THOMPSON, J. D. & McEWEN, W. J. Organizational goals and environment. *Am. sociol. Rev.*, 1958, 23: 23-31.

THOMSON, D. *The democratic ideal in France and England*. Cambridge, England: Cambridge University Press, 1944.

THOMSON, D. *England in the nineteenth century*. Harmondsworth, England: Penguin Books, 1950.

TINTO, V. University productivity and the organization of higher education in Turkey. *Higher Education*, 1974, 3: 285-302.

TOREN, N. *Social work: The case of a semi-profession*. Beverly Hills, Calif.: Sage Publications, 1972.

TROW, D. B. Membership turnover and team performance. Paper presented to the American Sociological Society, Chicago, September 1959.

TROW, W. C., ZANDER, A. E., MORSE, W. C. & JENKINS, D. H. Psychology of group behavior: The class as a group. In Coladarci (1955). Pp. 229-245.

TUMA, A. H. & OZARIN, LUCY D. Patient "privileges" in mental hospitals. *Am. J. Psych.*, 1958, 114: 1104-1110.

TUMIN, M. W. Some principles of stratification: A critical analysis. *Am. sociol. Rev.*, 1953, 18: 387-394.

TURNER, A. N. Foreman, job, and company. *Hum. Rel.*, 1957, 10: 99-112.

TURNER, R. H. The Navy disbursing officer as a bureaucrat. *Am. sociol. Rev.*, 1947, 12: 342-348.

UDY, S. H., JR. "Bureaucracy" and "rationality" in Weber's organization theory: An empirical study. *Am. sociol. Rev.*, 1959, 24: 791-795.

UDY, S. H., JR. *Organization of work: A comparative analysis of production among nonindustrial peoples*. New Haven: HRAF, 1959a.

UDY, S. H., JR. The structure of authority in non-industrial production organizations. *Am. J. Soc.,* 1959*b,* 64, 582-584.

UDY, S. H., JR. The comparative analysis of organizations. In J. G. March, ed., *Handbook of organizations.* Chicago: Rand McNally, 1965. Pp. 678-709.

UNDERWOOD, K. W. *Protestant and Catholic.* Boston: Beacon, 1957.

U. S. Dept. of Commerce. *Statistical Abstract of the United States.* Washington, D. C.: U.S. Govt. Printing Office, 1959.

U. S. Dept. of Health, Education and Welfare. *Patients in mental institutions.* Washington, D. C.: Public Health Service, 1956.

University of Liverpool, Dept. of Social Science. *The dock worker.* Liverpool: Author, 1954.

UPHOFF, W. H. & DUNETTE, M. D., with AYLWARD, M., KIRCHNER, W. K. & PERRY, D. K. *Understanding the union members.* Minneapolis: University of Minnesota, 1956.

UYEKI, E. S. Sociology of the cold-war army. Paper presented to the Amer. Sociological Society, Seattle, Wash., August 1958.

VALLIER, I. A. Production imperatives in communal systems: A comparative study with special reference to the *kibbutz* crises. Unpublished doctoral dissertation, Harvard University, 1959.

VAN DER ZANDERN, J. W. The theory of social movements. *Sociol. & soc. Res.,* 1958, 44: 3-8.

VAN ZELST, R. H. Worker popularity and job satisfaction. *Personnel Psychol.,* 1951, 4: 405-412.

VAUGHAN, ELIZABETH M. *Community under stress.* Princeton, N. J.: Princeton University Press, 1949.

VIANELLO, M. A comparative analysis of complex organizations: On power, involvement and their correlates. *La Scienza e la Tecnica della Organizzazione Nella Pubblica Amministrazione,* 1964, XI: 351-356.

VINCENT, M. J. & MAYERS, J. *New foundations for industrial sociology.* New York: Van Nostrand, 1959.

VITELES, M. S. *Motivation and morale in industry.* New York: Norton, 1953.

VOLLMER, H. M. *Employee rights and the employment relationship.* Berkeley & Los Angeles: University of California Press, 1960.

VOLLMER, H. M. & KINNEY, J. A. *Identifying potential supervisors.* Bur. Labor & Management Ser., No. 12. Iowa City: State University of Iowa, 1956.

VOLLMER, H. M. & KINNEY, J. A. Informal requirements for supervisory positions. *Personnel,* 1957, 33: 431-441.

VREDEVOE, L. E. A study of practices in school discipline. Mimeo.

VUCINICH, A. The structure of factory control in the Soviet Union. *Am. sociol. Rev.,* 1950, 15: 179-186.

WACH, H. *Sociology of religion.* Chicago: The University of Chicago Press, 1958.

WALDO, D., LANDAU, M., JECHT, H. H. & PAIGE, G. D. *The study of organizational behavior: Status, problems and trends.* Washington, D.C.: The American Society for Public Administration, 1966.

WALKER, C. R. & GUEST, R. H. *The man on the assembly line.* Cambridge, Mass.: Harvard University Press, 1952.

WALKER, C. R., GUEST, R. H. & TURNER, A. N. *The foreman on the assembly line.* Cambridge, Mass.: Harvard University Press, 1956.

WALKER, J. Organizational change, citizen participation, and voluntary action. Paper presented before the Association of Voluntary Action Scholars, Denver, Colorado, September 24, 1974.

WALLER, W. *The sociology of teaching.* New York: Wiley, 1932.

WALLERSTEIN, I. The search for national identity in West Africa: The new history. Paper presented to the American Sociological Association, New York, 1960.

WARIS, H. Workers' participation in management in Scandinavian industry. Paper presented to the Fourth World Congress of Sociology, Milan, Italy, 1959.

WARNECKE, R. Non-intellectual factors related attrition from a collegiate nursing program. *Journal of Health and Social Behavior,* 1973, 14: 153-166.

WARNER, W. K. Major conceptual elements of voluntary associations. In D. H. Smith, R. D. Reddy & B. R. Baldwin, eds., *Voluntary action research: 1972.* Lexington, Mass.: Heath, 1972.

WARNER, W. L. *American life.* Chicago, The University of Chicago Press, 1953.

WARNER, W. L. & ABEGGLEN, J. *Big business leaders in America.* New York: Harper, 1955.

WARNER, W. L. & HAVIGHURST, R. J. & LOEB, M. B. *Who shall be educated?* New York: Harper, 1944.

WARNER, W. L. & LOW, J. O. *The social system of the modern factory.* New Haven, Conn.: Yale University Press, 1947.

WARNOTTE, D. Bureaucratie et fonctionnarisme. *Revue d'Institut Sociologie,* 1937, 2: 219-260.

WARREN, D. Social power, visibility, and conformity in formal organizations. *Am. sociol. Rev.,* 1968, 33: 951-970.

WARREN, R., MULFORD, C. & YETLEY, M. A test of Etzioni's model by using data from utilitarian organizations. Scientific Paper Series, Department of Sociology, Iowa State University, 1973.

WARRINER, C. K. The problem of organizational purpose. *Sociological Quarterly,* 1965, 6: 139-146.

WEBB, R. C. *The real Mormonism.* New York: Sturgis & Walton, 1916.

WEBER, M. *The theory of social and economic organization.* London: Wm. Hodge, 1947.

WEBER, S. & POLM, D. Participatory management in public welfare. *Social Casework,* 1974, 55: 299-306.

WEINBERG, K. S. Aspects of the prison's social structure. *Am. J. Soc.,* 1942, 47: 717-726.

WEISS, R. S. *Processes of organization.* Ann Arbor: Survey Research Center, University of Michigan, 1956.

WEISS, R. S. & JACOBSON, E. A method for the analysis of the structure of complex organizations. *Am. sociol. Rev.,* 1955, 20: 661-668.

WESSEN, A. F. The social structure of a modern hospital. Unpublished doctoral dissertation, Yale University, 1951.

WEISSENBERG, P. *Introduction to organizational behavior.* Scranton, Pa.: Intext Educational Publishers, 1971.

WESTLEY, W. A. Secrecy and the police. *Soc. Forc.,* 1956, 34: 254-257.

WHEELER, S. Aspects of socialization in correctional communities. Paper presented to the annual meeting of the American Sociological Association, Chicago, 1954.

WHITE, H. C. A case study in R & D as a pattern in industrial management. Mimeo.

WHITE, W. L. *The captives of Korea: Our treatment of theirs; their treatment of ours.* New York: Scribner, 1957.

WHYTE, M. K. Bureaucracy and modernization in China: The Maoist critique. *Am. sociol. Rev.,* 1973, 38: 149-163.

WHYTE, M. K. *Small groups and political rituals in China.* Berkeley: University of California Press, 1974.

WHYTE, W. F. *Human relations in the restaurant industry.* New York: McGraw-Hill, 1948.

WHYTE, W. F. The changing nature of political leadership. In Gouldner (1950). Pp. 104-117.

WHYTE, W. F. *Patterns for industrial peace.* New York: Harper, 1951.

WHYTE, W. F. *et al. Money and motivation.* New York: Harper, 1955.

WHYTE, W. F. Human relations theory: a progress report. *Harv. Bus. Rev.,* 1956, 34: 125-132.

WHYTE, W. F. & GARDNER, B. The man in the middle. *Appl. Anthr.,* 1945, 4: 1-28.

WHYTE, W. H., JR. Business influence on education. In *The organization man.* Garden City, N. Y.: Doubleday, 1957. Pp. 111-120.

WICKMAN, E. K. *Children's behavior and teachers' attitudes.* New York: Commonwealth Fund, 1928.

WIESE, VON L. & BECKER, H. *Systematic Sociology.* New York: Wiley, 1932.

WIGGINS, BELLE. Dynamics of public support of volunteer health and welfare associations. Unpublished report, Bur. appl. soc. Res., Columbia University, 1960.

WILENSKY, H. L. *Syllabus of industrial relations.* Chicago: The University of Chicago Press, 1954.

WILENSKY, H. L. *Intellectuals in labor unions.* Glencoe, Ill.: The Free Press, 1956.

WILENSKY, H. L. The labor vote: A local union's impact on the political conduct of its members. *Soc. Forc.,* 1956a, 35: 11-120.

WILENSKY, H. L. & LEBEAUX, C. N. *Industrial society and social welfare: The impact of industrialization on the supply and organization of social welfare services in the United States.* New York: Russell Sage Foundation, 1958.

WILLERMAN, B. Overlapping group identification in an industrial setting. Paper presented to the American Psychological Association, Denver, September, 1949.

WILMER, H. A. *Social psychiatry in action: A therapeutic community.* Springfield, Ill.: Charles C. Thomas, 1958.

WILSON, D. P. *My six convicts.* New York: Pocket Books, 1953.

WILSON, J. Q. *Political organizations.* New York: Basic Books, 1973.

WILSON, L. *The academic man.* New York: Oxford University Press, 1942.

WILSON, L. Academic administration: its abuses and uses. *A. A. U. P. Bull.,* 1955, 52: 684-692.

WILSON, R. N. Teamwork in the operating room. *Hum. Org.,* 1954, 12: 9-14.

WINCKLER, E. A review article: Political management of the development process: Assessing the Chinese development experience. *China Quarterly,* 1973, 55: 560-566.

WISPE, LAUREN G. A sciometric analysis of conflicting role-expectations. *Am. J. Soc.*, 1955, 61: 134-137.

WOLPERT, J. Toward a sociology of authority. In Gouldner (1950). Pp. 679-701.

WOOD, A. *Deviant behavior and control strategies: Essays in sociology.* Lexington, Mass.: Heath, 1974.

WOODMAN, W., MULFORD, C. & WARREN, R. Consensus formation and social rank in the normative group. Draft paper, no date.

WORTHY, J. C. Organizational structure and employee morale. *Am. sociol. Rev.*, 1950, 15: 169-179.

WRAY, D. E. Marginal man of industry: The foreman. *Am. J. Soc.*, 1949, 49: 298-301.

WRIGHT, C. R. & HYMAN, H. H. Voluntary association memberships of American adults: Evidence from national sample surveys. *Am. sociol. Rev.*, 1958, 23: 284-294.

WRIGHT, D. On the bases of social order: Indoctrinated control vs. voluntary cooperation. Paper presented at the Annual Meeting of the American Sociological Association, Montreal, August 1974.

ZABLOCKI, B. *The joyful community.* Baltimore: Penguin Books, 1971.

ZALD, M. N. Notes on methodological problems in the comparative study of large-scale organizations. Paper presented to the American Sociological Association, New York, August 1960.

ZALEZNIK, A., CHRISTENSEN, C. R. & ROETHLISBERGER, F. J., with the assistance and collaboration of HOMANS, G. C. *The motivation, productivity, and satisfaction of workers.* Boston: Grad. School Bus. Admin., Harvard University, 1958.

ZANDER, A., COHEN, A. R. & STOTLAND, E. *Role relations in mental health professions.* Ann Arbor: University of Michigan, 1957.

ZANDER, A., COHEN, A. R. & STOTLAND, E. Power and the relations among professions. In Cartwright (1959). Pp. 15-34.

ZELDITCH, M., JR. Role differentiation in the nuclear family: A comparative study. In Parsons and Bales (1955). Pp. 307-351.

ZELDITCH, M., JR. & HOPKINS, T. K. Laboratory experiments with organizations. In Etzioni (1961). Pp. 464-478.

ZETTERBERG, H. L. *On theory and verification in sociology.* Stockholm: Almqvist & Wiksell, 1954.

ZETTERBERG, H. L. Compliant actions. *Acta Sociologica*, 1957, 2: 179-201.

ZEWE, D. The functioning of three types of church structure in the school integration crisis. 1959. Unpublished.

INDEXES

Name Index

Aage, H., 91, 511
Abegglen, J. C., 435, 436, 511, 552
Abel, T., 28, 511
Aberle, D. F., 118, 511
Abramson, E., 9, 511
Adams, S., 285, 511
Adler, H. G., 28, 511
Adorno, T. W., 434, 511
Ahmad, J., 315, 511
Albert, R., 281, 511
Albrow, M., 462, 511
Allen, V. L., 62, 511
Almond, G., 476, 478, 511
Almond, R., 79, 511
Amendola, S., 217, 218, 506
Anderson, B., 243, 513
Andes, J., 90, 506
Andrew, C. K., 429, 512
Andrews, L. P., 321, 541
Andrezejewski, S., 512
Anfossi, A., 223, 506
Archibald, K., 512

Arensberg, C. M., 52, 284, 512, 531
Argyris, C., 9, 35, 181, 184, 292, 304, 319, 434, 512
Arnold, M., 115, 512
Aron, R., 512
Aronson, E., 504
Asch, S. E., 163, 293, 512
Ash, E., 160, 161, 162, 529
Ashbrook, J. B., 197–204, 506
Ashby, W. R., 492, 512
Ashdown, R., 91, 512
Atelson, J., 338, 512
Axelrod, M., 43, 512
Aylward, M., 551

Babchuk, N., 26, 43, 527
Back, K. W., 250, 280, 293, 512, 524
Bahr, H., 79, 533
Baker, A. W., 524
Baker, F., 139, 140, 524

Bakke, W. E., 513
Baldwin, B. R., 91, 547
Baldwin, M., 41, 513
Bales, R. F., 6, 141, 155, 156, 183, 206, 266, 513, 530
Balog, A., 91, 513
Banfield, E., 10, 513
Banks, J. A., 272, 545
Barbara, E., 530
Barbash, J., 62, 63, 267, 513
Barber, B., 34, 44, 111, 513
Barnard, C., 110, 111, 137, 140, 155, 341, 429, 439, 513
Barnes, H. E., 513
Barnes, L. B., 52, 512
Barton, A. H., 7, 14, 52, 243, 513
Barzun, J., 353, 513
Bass, B. M., 154, 180, 513
Bates, S., 26, 428, 513, 550
Baumgartel, H., 51, 53, 513, 536
Baur, E. J., 293, 513
Bavelas, A., 154, 241, 513
Beal, G. M., 142, 147, 393, 395, 397, 505, 508, 509, 519
Beck, H. P., 430, 513
Becker, H., 260, 262, 553
Becker, H. S., 9, 329, 513
Belknap, I., 29, 134, 513
Bell, D., xvi, 9, 513
Bell, N. W., 513
Ben-David, Y., 54, 357, 513
Bendix, R., 3, 180, 185, 246, 270, 306, 309, 436, 513, 535
Bennis, W. G., 154, 513
Bensman, J., 315, 357, 526
Berelson, B., 58, 264, 293, 513, 534
Berkman, P. L., 445, 515
Berkowitz, L., 283, 515
Berliner, J. S., 426, 515
Bettleheim, B., 28, 515
Bevan, D., 163, 515
Bierstedt, R., xvi, 180, 357, 515

Bigelow, D. A., 75, 76, 127, 213, 214, 506
Birnbaum, N., xvi, 515
Blau, P. M., 96–99, 186–188, 281, 284, 285, 291, 292, 460, 462, 466, 468, 469, 515, 532
Blauner, R., 33, 38, 515
Blizzard, S. W., 171
Bloch, H. A., 29, 515
Block, L., 329, 515
Bloom, B. S., 548
Blum, F. H., 515
Blum, J. N., 113, 168, 515
Bohlen, J. M., 142, 147, 393, 395, 397, 401, 508, 509
Bondy, C., 28, 515
Borgatta, E. F., 183, 515
Bossard, J. H. S., 515
Bosse, R., 339, 515
Bottomore, T., 515
Boulding, K. E., 5, 515
Brager, G., 83, 130–132, 149, 217, 464, 465, 506
Breed, W., 52, 516
Breslaver, G., 493, 520
Breton, R., 12, 516
Brickman, P., 497, 516
Brim, O. G., Jr., 48, 173, 516
Brinton, C., 108, 109, 516
Brissenden, P. F., 62, 516
Brogan, D. W., 516
Brooks, G. W., 59, 516
Broom, L., xvii, 516, 520, 537
Brotz, H., 273, 537
Brown, D. V., 516
Brown, E. J., 505, 517
Brown, E. L., 49, 429
Brown, M. E., 91–94, 510, 547
Brown, M. L., 186, 532
Brown, P., 357, 516
Brueckel, J. E., 297, 518
Bryce-Laporte, R. S., 389–391, 506, 516

Buber, M., 348, 516
Buchanan, B., II, 516
Buckley, W., 111, 516
Burgess, E. W., 331, 529
Burling, T., 43, 516
Burns, T., 96, 516
Burton, M. K., 333, 516
Burtt, H. E., 185, 186, 236

Caldwell, M. G., 161, 162, 163, 516
Campbell, A., 9, 517
Campbell, E. Q., 42, 358, 517
Campbell, N. M., 45, 517
Campbell, R. F., 49, 517
Cantril, H., 53, 517
Capender, H. R., 505, 517
Caplovitz, D., 251, 264, 517
Caplow, T., xiii, 111, 137, 233, 256, 353, 517
Capwell, D., 38, 530
Caran, R. S., 163, 517
Carlin, J. E., 52
Carreau, D., 497, 549
Carr-Saunders, A. M., 357
Carstairs, G. M., 434
Cartwright, D., 4, 282, 292, 517
Cash, W. J., 55, 517
Cassell, F. H., 428, 529
Caudill, W. A., 156, 168, 174, 517
Cavalcante, C., xxiv, 517
Cell, C., 493, 517
Centers, R., 434, 536
Chalmers, E. W., 236, 517
Chamberlain, D. B., 171, 244, 517
Chambers, R. C., 43, 517
Chandler, M. K., 236, 517
Chapman, S. H., 340, 517
Chapple, E. D., 43, 517
Charques, D., 41, 518
Charters, W. W., Jr., 185, 518
Cherkaoui, M., 91, 518
Chesler, D. J., 297, 518

Chessman, C., 247, 518
Chill, E. S., 348, 518
Chinoy, E., 35, 518
Christensen, A. N., 108, 301, 518, 554
Christie, L. S., 241, 518
Churchill, A., 172, 307, 518
Cicourel, A. V., 104, 518
Clancey, I. L., 119, 519
Clark, B. R., 48, 259, 519
Clark, H. F., 248, 519
Clark, T. N., 497, 519
Clarkson, J. F., 341, 518
Clausen, J. A., 109, 519
Cleason, G., 109, 519
Clemmer, D., 10, 263, 269, 518
Cloward, R. A., 161, 162, 518
Coates, C. H., 434, 436, 518
Coch, L., 292, 299, 519
Cohen, A. R., 361, 554
Cohen, E. A., 28, 30, 105, 519
Cohen, I., 28, 519
Cohen, M. B., 435, 519
Cohen, R. A., 435, 519
Coker, R. E., 250, 519
Colb, L., 106, 519
Coleman, J. R., 168, 176, 274, 290, 357, 519
Coleman, J. S., 6, 45, 63, 519, 528, 535
Commons, J. R., 5, 64, 519
Contas, H., 309, 312, 519
Cook, F. J., 109, 519
Cooley, C. H., xi, 519
Coon, C. S., 43, 234, 518
Coons, A. E., 197, 536, 548
Copeland, M. T., 304, 519
Cornish, M. J., 44, 251, 357, 434, 519
Coser, L. A., xvi, 519
Coser, R. L., 359, 519
Cottrell, L. S., xvii, 537
Couch, A. S., 183, 515

Coward, E. W., 505, 519
Cressey, D. R., 91, 140, 163, 519
Crozier, M., 520
Crutchfield, R. S., 154, 534
Cumming, E., 118, 119, 174, 520
Cumming, J., 118, 119, 174, 520
Curle, A., 520
Curran, F. J., 50, 520
Curtis, R., 520
Cutler, H. A., 9, 511
Cutts, N. E., 520

Dahl, R. A., 4, 520
Dahlke, O. H., 106, 520
Dahlstrom, E., 68, 520
Dahrendorf, R., xvi, 4, 520
Dallin, A., 493, 520
Dalton, M., 185, 287, 288, 427, 434, 520
Danielson, L. E., 315, 520
Danton, J. P., 520
Darber, M., 59, 516
David, H., 520
Davies, D. R., 49, 520
Davis, A. K., 304, 520
Davis, F. J., 234, 520
Davis, J. A., 358, 521
Davis, K., 10, 111, 137, 521
Davis, R. C., 51, 541
Dean, D. G., 9, 521
Dean, L. R., 13, 44, 521
Dearborn, D. C., 437, 521
DeCoster, S., 435, 521
Demerath, N. J., 105, 521
Denney, R., 543
Dent, J., 34, 186, 536
Derber, M., 236, 517
Deutsch, K. W., 5, 327, 521
Deutscher, I., 140, 521
Devis, J. A., 521
Diamond, S., 271, 521
Dickson, W. J., 178, 187, 188
Dill, W. R., 241, 521, 528

Dimock, M., 429, 521
Dinitz, S., 534
Dodge, E. P., 52, 521
Doll, E. E., 41, 521
Donald, G. A., 64, 521
Donnelly, T., 250, 519
Donovan, F. R., 38, 521
Dornbusch, S. M., 337, 521
Douglass, H. P., 521
Douglass, H. R., 47, 274, 521
Drabek, T., 463, 528
Drake, J. T., 106, 521
Driscoll, P. F., 75, 76, 127, 212, 213, 214, 506
Drucker, P. F., 423, 521
Dubin, R., 53, 270, 282, 315, 428, 521, 533
Dulchin, J., 333, 522
Dunbar, R. L. M., 226, 227, 506
Dunlop, J. T., 427, 522, 533
Dunnette, M. D., 182, 522, 551
Durkheim, E., xvi, xxi, 240, 288, 522
Dutton, J. M., 226, 227, 506
Duverger, M., 109, 522

Easton, D., 4, 476, 522
Eaton, J. W., 358, 522
Eckstein, A., 522
Edwards, N. H., 518
Eisenstadt, S. N., 26, 54, 104, 241, 242, 308, 522, 532
Ellertson, N., 283, 545
Elling, R. J., 121, 522
Ellsworth, J. S., xi, 522
Empey, L. T., 546
Epagneul, M., 522
Erikson, T., 50, 522
Estes, W. K., 522
Ettisch, W., 337, 522
Etzioni, A., 24, 26, 62, 64, 68, 73, 88, 92, 97, 99, 111, 120, 122, 133, 136, 138, 139, 141, 156,

157, 158, 175, 177, 191, 192,
214, 215, 222, 223, 225, 256,
322, 323, 330, 347, 388, 399,
401, 405, 460, 462, 463, 467,
470, 492, 497, 504, 506, 508,
522, 523
Evan, W. M., 51, 522
Evers, F. T., 142, 145, 146, 147,
506

Fainsod, M., 343, 523
Fainstein, N. I., 478, 523
Fainstein, S. S., 478, 523
Falaguerra, T., 251
Fallers, L. A., xiii, 524
Farago, L., 524
Farner, F. M., 524
Faunce, W. A., 35, 524
Feld, M. D., 175, 524
Feldman, A. S., 17, 524
Ference, T., 91, 524
Festinger, L., 280, 293, 524
Fichter, J. H., 17, 41, 167, 171,
319, 450, 524
Fiedler, F. E., 524
Field, M. G., 337, 524
Fischer, J., 107, 524
Fiske, M., 427, 524
Fleishman, E. A., 185, 186, 236,
524
Floch, M. A., 161, 529
Floor, L. G., 179, 532
Forcese, D. P., 500–504, 507
Ford, C., 524
Form, W. H., 430, 524
Foster, W. Z., 134, 524
Fox, R., 251, 525
Fox, S. D., 43, 525
Fox, V., 162, 525
Frank, A. G., 104, 525
Frank, J. D., 525
Franklin, J. L., 72–75, 122, 123,
150, 507, 525

Franklyn, G. J., 91, 525
Freeman, F. D., 273, 525
French, J. R. P., Jr., 14, 292, 299,
519, 525
Frenkel-Brunswik, E., 434, 511
Freud, S., 322, 351
Friedrich, C. J., 14, 525
Friedsman, H. J., 319, 525
Froyd, M. C., 238, 249, 529
Fry, L. C., 91, 238, 525
Fry, L. J., 538

Galenson, W., 425, 525
Galtung, J., 247, 525
Gamson, W., 476, 477, 478, 507
Gamson, Z., 205–208, 366, 369,
370, 371–73, 472, 507
Garceau, O., 525
Gardner, B., 185, 525, 553
Gardner, F, F., 284, 525
Garfinkel, H., 304, 525
Garinger, E. H., 46, 47, 525
Gaudet, H., 58, 293, 534
Gebb, C. A., 429, 525
Georgiou, P., 140, 525
Georgopoulos, B. S., 111, 140,
444, 525, 549
Gerard, H. B., 293, 525
Gerth, H. H., xvii, 10, 259, 305,
306, 525, 526
Gerver, I., 315, 357, 526
Ghiselli, E. E., 130, 341, 541
Gibb, C. A., 180, 526
Gilbert, D. C., 13, 434, 526
Ginzberg, E., 429, 431, 526
Gjerde, C. M., 545
Glaser, B. G., 526
Glaser, W. A., 91, 100, 350, 526
Glass, D. V., 526
Glazer, N., 526, 543
Glock, C. Y., 237, 526
Goffman, E., ix, 265, 304, 350,
526

Gold, M., 174, 526
Goldhamer, H., 4, 526
Goldner, F., 91, 524
Goldsen, R. K., 237, 526
Goldsmer, H., 43, 526
Goldstein, J., 425, 526
Goodacre, D. M., 285, 526
Goode, W. J., 185, 357, 360,
   362, 434, 527
Gordon, C. W., 26, 43, 45, 527
Gordon, M., 304, 527
Gordon, R., 426, 527
Goss, M. E. W., 226, 251, 527
Gould, J., 54, 527
Gouldner, A. W., 71, 135, 168,
   284, 292, 314, 357, 358, 527
Gouldner, H. P., 9, 527
Grambsch, P., 528
Granick, D., xiii, 106, 426, 527
Granick, R., 550
Gray, A. P., 537
Greenberg, B. G., 321, 541
Greenblatt, M., 49, 429, 434, 527
Greene, C. N., 87, 88, 89, 507, 527
Greenhoe, F., 235, 251, 437, 527
Greer, S. A., xi, 185, 500, 528
Gregg, R. T., 49, 517
Gregory, D., 283, 545
Griffiths, D. E., 49, 528
Grinker, R. R., 59, 282, 528
Gross, E., 121, 528
Gross, L., 226, 528
Gross, N., 235, 281, 282, 528
Grusky, O., 117, 528
Guest, R. H., 34, 71, 147, 270,
   528, 551
Guetzkow, H., 241, 293, 528, 547
Gurin, G., 9, 179, 517, 532
Gusfield, J. R., 54, 528
Gustafson, J. M., 172, 528
Guterman, S. S., 387, 528
Guttmacher, M., 528
Guttman, L., 9, 528, 549

Gwazdz, J., 113, 544
Gyr, J., 528

Haas, J. E., 95–97, 150, 151,
   454–56, 458–60, 463, 507,
   528
Hagstrom, W. O., 331, 528, 546
Haire, M., 186, 529
Hall, O., 507, 529
Hall, R. H., xxiv, 91, 95–97,
   150, 151, 191, 454–56, 458–
   60, 529, 548
Halpin, A. W., 184, 234, 529
Halsey, A. H., 545
Hamblin, R. L., 155, 529
Hammond, P. B., 529, 550
Hanna, D. C., 543
Hanson, H., 91, 529
Harbison, F. H., 168, 428, 529,
   533
Harding, C. F., 307, 518
Hardman, J. B. S., 63, 529
Härnqvist, K., 115, 250, 529
Harper, I., 330, 529
Harrington, M., 529
Harris, E. F., 185, 186, 236, 524
Harris, P. E., 529
Harrison, M. J., 380, 429, 529
Harrison, P. M., 306, 332, 529
Hart, C. M., 529
Hart, M., 529
Hartley, E. L., 293, 536, 549
Hartshorne, H., 238, 249, 529
Hartung, F. E., 161, 529
Havighurst, R. J., 552
Hawkes, R. W., 550
Hayner, N. S., 160–63, 529
Heady, F., 529
Heath, P., 226, 530
Heberle, R., 53, 530
Heginbothan, S., 493, 530
Heidt, S., 530
Heinicke, C. M., 156, 530

Heiskanen, I., 98, 99, 530
Helsabeck, R., 505, 530
Hemphill, J. K., 155, 234, 530
Henderson, C. R., 43, 530
Henry, J., 327, 530
Herbst, P. G., 156, 530
Hero, A., 44, 530
Heron, A., 434
Herriott, R. E., 127–30, 507
Herz, K. G., 106, 530
Herzberg, F., 530
Hesse, K., 530
Heydebrand, W. V., 91, 530
Hickson, D. J., xxiv, 462, 542
Hill, J. M., 530
Hiller, E. T., 443, 530
Hilton, J., 115, 530
Hinings, C. R., xxiv, 462, 542
Hockey, B., 537
Hodgkins, B. J., 127–30, 507
Hoess, R., 28, 530
Hoffer, E., 54, 530
Hollingshead, A. B., 250, 530
Homans, G. C., 37, 52, 158, 178,
    184, 290, 293, 314, 468, 473,
    531
Hoover, J., 235, 536
Hopkins, T. K., 154, 177, 294,
    447, 531, 554
Horsfall, A. B., 284, 531
Hoselitz, B. F., 531
Hoult, T. F., 239, 531
Houriet, R., 134, 531
Hoxie, R. F., 61, 531
Hoy, W., 531
Hudson, W. W., 84, 85, 86, 507
Hughes, E. C., xi, 430, 531
Hughes, H. M., 54, 531
Hughes, T., 531
Hulme, K., 41, 178, 531
Hunt, J., 140, 540
Hunter, E., 48, 134, 170, 531
Huntington, S. P., 175, 531

Hyman, H. H., 44, 286, 447, 531,
    554

Iannaccone, L., 49, 520
Ingham, G. K., 90, 507
Ingham, R. A., 376, 507
Israel, J., 531

Jackman, N., 531
Jacob, P., 98, 531
Jacobs, P., 338, 529, 541
Jacobson, E., 13, 531, 542, 552
Jacobson, S. S., 53, 183, 275, 543
Janowitz, M., xiii, 5, 9, 56–59,
    114, 282, 292, 297, 337, 339,
    531, 532, 546
Jaynes, W. E., 431, 548
Jecht, H. H., 551
Jenkins, D. H., 172, 532, 550
Jennings, H., 164, 185, 532
Johannsson, S., xxiv, 532
John, G., 42, 532
Johnsen, L., 140, 539
Johnson, C. A., 493, 532
Johnson, N. J., 95–97, 150, 151,
    454, 456, 458, 460, 507
Jones, G. N., 124, 125, 479, 484,
    507
Jones, M., 49, 532
Jones, W. H. M., 25, 322, 532
Jones, W. H. S., 532
Josephson, E., 180, 532
Joyner, C., 140, 532
Joyner, N., 140, 532
Julian, J., 68–72, 92, 377–79, 508
Junkers, B. H., 44, 545, 550

Kadushin, C. G., 462, 532
Kahn, D., 38, 111, 181, 532
Kahn, R. L., 180, 532
Kalnoky, H., 107, 524
Kaplan, A., 4, 534
Kaplan, M. A., 492, 508

Karsh, B., 60, 64, 115, 443, 532, 546

Katz, D., 38, 179, 180, 532

Katz, E., 58, 168, 181, 186, 252, 305, 308, 519, 532, 533

Katz, F. E., 537

Katz, J. S., 357

Kaufman, R., 226, 533

Keating, B., 60

Keedy, E. R., 533

Keller, F. E., 115, 533

Keller, S. I., 430, 436, 533

Kelley, F., 64, 533

Kelly, W. J., 518

Kendall, P. L., 250, 251, 286, 533, 537

Kern, A., 79, 533

Kerr, C., 62, 274, 533

Kerschensteiner, G., 115, 533

Killian, L. M., 317, 533

King, M. L., Jr., 54, 533

King, W., 53, 533

Kinkead, E., 30, 533

Kinney, J. A., 236, 551

Kirsch, W., 505, 508

Kirschner, W. K., 551

Kittredge, L. D., 122, 123, 507

Klonglan, G. E., 142–45, 147, 148, 392, 393, 395, 397–400, 404–405, 407–409, 465–68, 508, 509

Kneller, G. F., 272, 533

Knowles, K. G. J. C., 443, 533

Knutsson, K. E., 219, 508

Kobler, A. L., 91, 548

Kochling, E., 428, 529

Kogon, E., 28, 533

Kohn, R. L., 44, 533

Komarovsky, M., 44, 533

Kopachevsky, J., 401, 403, 509, 538

Kopald, S., 134, 508

Korn, R., 113, 160, 161, 536

Kornhauser, A., 9, 289, 317, 338, 533, 534

Krader, L., 309

Krause, K., 91, 534

Krech, D., 154, 534

Kreps, T. J., 24, 534

Lammers, C. J., 250, 534

Landau, M., 551

Lane, R., 476, 508

Lang, K., 91, 508

Langdale, J., 534

Larkin, E. J., 140, 534

Larrabee, E., 319, 534

Lasswell, H. D., 534

La Violette, F. E., 27, 534

Lawrence, W. C., 162, 540

Lazarsfeld, P. F., xxi, 58, 168, 172, 256, 281, 286, 293, 294, 305, 328, 330, 361, 532, 534, 537, 549

Lazovsky, A., 425, 534

Learned, W. S., 330, 534

Leavitt, H. J., 241, 534

Lebeaux, C. N., 553

Lee, A. M., 357, 534

Leeds, R., 508, 534

Lefton, M., 534

Lehman, E., 214, 215, 506, 508

Lehman, E. W., 68, 339, 380–84, 508

Leiffer, M. H., 236, 237, 534

Leighton, A. H., 27, 29, 113, 164, 180, 535

Le Nard, L., 107, 524

Lenin, V. I., 109, 535

Lentz, E. M., 43, 427, 535

Leonard, P., 91, 508

Levenson, B., 186, 309, 526, 535

Levine, S., 535

Levinson, D. J., 13, 91, 105, 434, 435, 541, 547

Levinson, P., 508

Lewin, H. S., 54, 393, 546
Lewin, K., 535
Lewis, J. L., 350
Likert, R., 131, 181, 202, 271, 392, 393, 535
Lilienthal, D. M., 115, 532
Lindesmith, A. R., 535
Lindsay, A. D., 117, 535
Lindsay, J. K., 91, 518
Lindzey, G., 504, 535
Linton, R., xxi, 535
Linz, J., 38, 535
Lippitt, R., 292, 435, 535
Lipset, S. M., xxi, 38, 64, 108, 274, 290, 436, 509, 535
Litchfield, E. H., xii, 535
Loeb, M. B., 552
Loftus, J. A., 61, 535
Lombard, G. F. F., 37, 284, 535 537
London, J., 60, 64, 546
Love, R. L., 219, 221, 222, 225
Low, J. O., 32, 264, 552
Lowenthal, L., xxi
Lowenthal, R., 535, 536
Lubin, R., 535
Lucci, Y., 111, 536
Luce, R. D., 241, 518
Luft, C., 535
Lund, A., 35
Lupton, T., 545
Lynd, H. M., 56, 172, 536
Lynd, R. S., 56, 172, 536
Lynton, R. P., 271, 545

Maccoby, E. E., 179, 536
Maccoby, N., 532
MacDonald, L., 270, 526
Macgregor, D., 52, 512
Macha, J., 509
Macisco, J. J., 339, 515
MacIver, R. M., xvi, 536

MacKenzie, W. J. M., xxiv, 462, 536
MacKinnon, W. J., 434, 536
Maclean, A. M., 536
Macy, J., Jr., 241, 518
Maier, N. R. F., 235, 536
Mailer, N., 10
Mann, F. C., 34, 111, 186, 532, 536
March, J. G., xii, 20, 111, 234, 462, 536
Marcus, P. M., 158, 536
Marenco, C., 535
Marine, G., 51, 537
Marshall, S. L. A., 57, 537
Martin, H. W., 252, 537
Martin, N. H., 428, 537
Martin, W. E., 428, 528
Marvick, D., 53, 537
Marx, K., 9, 15
Maslow, A., 470, 471
Mason, W. S., 183, 235, 528
Matthewson, S. B., 282, 537
Matza, D., 247, 549
Mausner, B., 38, 530
Mayer, M., 9, 52, 537
Mayers, J., 271, 551
Mayntz, R., 450, 537
Mayo, E., 284, 537
McBride, D., 283, 544
McCabe, D. A., 59, 516
McCay, J. T., 274, 536
McCleery, R. H., 161, 168, 243, 244, 247, 536
McClosky, H., 536
McCorkle, H., 113, 160, 161, 536
McDill, E. L., 9, 536
McEachern, A. W., 183, 235, 528
McElroy, J., 30, 536
McEwin, W. J., 158, 536
McGee, R. J., 256, 353, 517
McGrath, E., 252, 430, 536
McKay, J. T., 536

McKenzie, R. T., 348, 536
McPhee, W., 293, 514
McQuilty, L. I., 236, 517
Mechanic, D., 536
Mellinger, G. D., 51, 541
Melman, S., 51, 537
Meltzer, L., 51, 53, 537
Mendelson, M., 9, 511
Menzel, H., 294, 357, 519, 534, 537
Merton, R. K., xvii, xxi, 7, 16, 58, 90, 105, 110, 135, 137, 246, 250, 251, 264, 314, 321, 450, 537
Messinger, S. L., 54, 160, 537, 549
Metcalf, H. C., 437, 537
Meyer, P., 423, 537
Micaud, C. A., 338, 538
Michels, R., 107, 134, 167, 349, 538
Miller, D. R., 538
Miller, E. S., 168, 538
Miller, G. A., 82–84
Miller, G. W., 443, 509, 538
Miller, J. P., 91, 538
Miller, M., 76, 126, 127, 151, 510
Miller, W. E., 9, 517
Mills, C. W., xvi, xvii, 10, 32, 39, 185, 259, 305, 306, 325, 526, 538
Mishler, E. G., 9, 275, 538
Mitchell, R. E., 430
Mitzner, M., 80, 81, 82, 474, 475, 476, 509
Monck, E., 118
Moore, B., Jr., 339, 426, 538
Moore, D. G., 538
Moore, M. E., 543
Moore, W. E., 26, 33, 111, 137, 282, 538
Moreno, J. L., 164, 538
Morris, R. T., 154, 545
Morse, C., 479, 538

Morse, N. C., 9, 33, 37, 179, 538
Morse, W. C., 550
Moseley, N., 47, 520
Mulford, C. L., 142, 143, 145, 147–50, 392, 395, 397–99, 400–405, 407–10, 412, 413, 415, 417, 508, 509, 538, 554
Mumford, E. M., 292, 538
Myers, C. A., 427, 516, 533, 539
Myers, R. R., 36, 539
Myrdal, G., 111, 539

Naegele, K. D., 351, 427, 539
Nagel, E., 110, 314, 539
Nahemow, L. D., 106, 527
Nasatir, E. D., 251
Negandhi, A. E., 539
Nelson, R., 140, 539
Nettl, J. P., 539
Nettler, G., 9, 539
Neuman, F. L., 5, 539
Newcomb, T. M., 169, 293, 536, 539, 549
Newcomer, M., 304, 438, 539
Newman, W. H., 437, 539
Niaz, M., 479, 480, 509
Nicholls, W., II, 250, 251, 539
Niebuhr, R., 5
Nigg, W., 344, 346, 539
Nisbet, R. A., xvi, 180, 539
Norfleet, B., 156, 539

O'Dea, T. F., 347, 539
O'Flannery, E., 399, 515
Ohlin, L. E., 28, 104, 162, 168, 247, 539, 541
Organ, D. W., 87–89, 507
Orleans, P., 500, 528
Orzack, L. H., 53, 540
Osborn, R., 140, 540
Osgood, C., 77, 388
Ostrogorski, M., 134, 540
Ozarin, L. D., 49, 50, 550

Padgitt, J. B., 142, 143, 509
Page, C. H., xvi, 536, 540
Pahley, B. W., 540
Palisi, B., 90, 540
Palumbo, D., 226, 540
Pappenfort, D. M., 540
Pareto, A., xv, 540
Parker, S., 50, 540
Parody, O. F., 45, 540
Parsons, T. xi, xvi, 4, 6, 10, 26,
    41, 90, 98, 103, 105, 139,
    141, 155, 156, 174, 183, 206,
    231, 238, 245, 265, 266, 305,
    309, 427, 443, 540
Parvilahti, U., 27, 113, 541
Pasamanick, B., 53, 534, 543
Payne, R., 541
Peck, S. M., 182, 541
Pellegrin, R. J., 434, 436, 518, 519
Pelz, D. C., 51, 184, 541
Perrow, C., 73, 104, 541
Perry, D. K., 551
Peterson, O. L., 38, 321, 541
Peterson, R., 530
Pettigrew, T. F., 42, 358, 517
Phelen, J. L., 541
Pigors, F., 274
Pigors, P., 274
Pine, F., 434, 435, 541
Pinner, F. A., 338, 541
Pirages, D. C., 495, 496, 509, 541
Piven, H., 540
Poinsett, A., 54, 541
Polm, D., 91, 552
Polyani, K., 541
Ponting, J. R., 541
Poole, E., 126, 550
Pope, L., 541
Porter, L. W., 234, 541
Powers, R. C., 505, 519
Pradier, B., 519
Preffer, R. M., 542
Pressey, S. L., 542

Presthus, R. V., 90, 542
Price, J. L., 122, 140, 462, 464,
    542
Pringle, R., 542
Pugh, D. S., xxiv, 462, 542
Purcell, T. V., 13, 542

Quarentelli, E. L., 91, 542

Radelet, L. A., 542
Randell, S., 76, 77, 388, 509
Randle, C. W., 429, 542
Rapoport, R. N., 50, 542
Rapoport, R. S., 50, 542
Raskin, A. H., 63, 542
Raven, B., 14, 525
Read, W. H., 235, 245, 542, 536
Reader, G., 250, 251, 537
Reavins, W. C., 47, 542
Reddy, R. D., 91, 547
Redl, F., 45, 154, 542
Reid, E., 542
Reilley, E. W., 526
Reimer, H., 247, 538, 542
Reiss, D., 226, 542
Reissman, L. A., 358, 431, 542
Remarque, E. M., 10
Renck, R., 538
Rettig, S. S., 53, 543
Rhyne, J., 270, 543
Rice, A. K., 543
Richardson, S., 543
Riecken, H. W., 293, 543
Rieff, P., 351, 543
Riesman, D., xxi, 11, 319, 543
Riggs, F. W., 543
Riley, J. W., Jr., 282, 543
Riley, M., 282, 543
Ringer, B. B., 237, 526
Ritti, R., 91, 524
Roach, A. C., 30, 543
Rodehaver, M. W., 340, 543
Roe, A., 53, 543

Roethlisberger, F. J., 178, 187, 188, 301, 543, 554
Rogers, C., 34, 543
Rogers, D., 145–47, 506
Rohere, J. H., 543
Romer, S., 61, 543
Rosada, S., 113, 544
Rose, A. M., 43, 44, 539, 544
Rosenberg, M., 110, 237, 526, 534
Rosenfeld, E., 111, 544
Ross, A. M., 62, 533, 544
Rossel, R., 95, 192–97, 509, 544
Rossiter, C., 307, 544
Roucek, J. S., 161, 544
Rourke, F. E., 90, 544
Rouse, J. E., 495, 510
Rowland, H., 165, 288, 544
Rudge, P. F., 91, 544
Ruebmann, H. C., 428, 529
Rummel, R. J., 478, 544
Rushing, W., 549

Sampson, O. F., 142, 144, 145, 393, 510
Samuels, G., 48, 544
Sanford, R. M., 434, 511
Saposs, D. J., 62, 544
Sartre, J. P., 339
Sayles, L. R., 62, 63, 168, 170, 182, 518, 544, 549
Scalf, J. H., Jr., 151, 544
Schacter, S., 280–82, 524, 544
Schafer, R., 143, 465–68, 544
Schank, R. L., 104, 545
Schein, E. H., xxiv, 545
Scherer, R. P., 90, 545
Schmitz, P. F., 142, 404, 407, 408, 409, 509, 510
Schneider, D. M., 531
Schneider, E. V., 314, 545
Schrupp, M. H., 545
Schulberg, H. C., 140
Schulman, J., 545

Schumpeter, J. A., 244, 545
Schurman, F., 191, 545
Schwartz, M. S., 273, 340, 341, 548
Schwartz, R. D., 111, 137, 545
Scott, J. C., Jr., 44, 545
Scott, J. F., 271, 349, 463, 545
Scott, W. R., 96–99, 545
Scudder, K. J., 50, 259, 545
Seashore, S. E., 111, 139, 270, 284, 295, 296, 297, 532, 545
Seeley, J. R., 44, 134, 545
Seeman, M., 154, 545
Segal, M., 545
Seidman, J. A., 60, 61, 64, 115, 443, 532, 546, 549
Seligman, L. G., 332, 546
Sellin, T., 50, 546
Selvin, H. C., 180, 250, 267, 387, 533, 536, 537
Selznick, P., 25, 108, 167, 338, 516, 520, 541
Shartle, C. L., 431, 548
Shepard, H. A., 51, 241, 546
Sheppard, H. L., 9, 534
Sherif, M., 543
Shichor, D., 546
Shih, K., 546
Shils, E. A., 4, 6, 9, 10, 57, 58, 59, 115, 141, 156, 266, 292, 526, 540, 541, 546
Shinnick, P., 546
Shor, E. L., 546
Siegel, A., 274, 533
Sills, D. L., 44, 172, 332, 444, 546
Silverman, D., 121, 139, 546
Simmel, G., 3, 442, 444, 546
Simon, H. A., xii, 15, 20, 98, 111, 137, 234, 242, 293, 306, 313, 437, 462, 521, 536, 546, 547
Simpson, I. H., 32, 547
Simpson, R. L., 32, 91, 111, 187, 242, 547

Skinner, G. W., 228, 484–89, 491–94, 510, 547
Slater, P. E., 156, 547
Slichter, S. H., 60, 185, 547
Sloan, H. S., 248, 518
Smelser, N. J., 443, 541
Smigel, E. O., 52, 547
Smith, C. G., 71, 91–94, 510, 547
Smith, D. H., 90, 547
Smith, H. L., 42, 547
Smith, L. M., 340, 543
Smith, R. B., 78–80, 212, 213, 385, 386, 510, 547
Smithburg, D. W., 15, 547
Snook, J., 91, 547
Snyderman, B. E., 38, 530
Soemerdjan, S., 546
Sommer, R., 548
Sondern, R., Jr., 61, 548
Spain, R. S., 321, 541
Speier, H., 233, 548
Spiegel, J. P., 59, 282, 528
Spinrad, W., 548
Sprehe, J. T., 222–26, 510
Stagner, R., 236, 517
Stancato, F. A., 226, 548
Stanton, A. H., 273, 340, 341, 548
Star, S., 297, 548, 549
Steffens, L., 109, 548
Stein, E., 497, 548
Stein, H. D., 139, 548
Stein, M. I., 548
Stephansky, B., 59, 548
Stern, G. G., 548
Sterner, R., 539
Steuben, J., 444, 548
Steward, D. D., 111, 548
Stinchcombe, A. L., 26, 47, 51, 278, 548
Stogdill, R. M., 197, 429, 431, 548
Stotland, E., 91, 361, 548, 554
Stouffer, S. A., xxi, 238, 250, 293, 297, 548, 549

Strauss, A. L., 100, 428, 526, 537
Strauss, G., 62, 63, 170, 182, 549
Street, D., 548
Strodtbeck, F. L., 186, 532
Styskal, R., 226, 540
Suchman, E. A., 9, 238, 549, 526
Sullivan, R. H., 172, 549
Sutherland, E., 56, 549
Sutton, R. L., 548
Swanson, G. E., 293, 538, 549
Sykes, G. M., 10, 117, 160, 161, 163, 188, 247, 547

Taber, W. R., 208–12, 374–76, 510
Taft, P., 59, 516
Tagliacozzo, D. L., 61, 64, 443, 546, 549
Takayama, K. P., 91, 549
Talmon, Y., 111, 549
Tannenbaum, A. S., 44, 71, 92, 111, 444, 526, 533, 549
Tanter, R., 478, 550
Tec, N., 106, 550
Thielens, W., Jr., 172, 251, 353, 361, 534, 550
Thomas, C. W., 76, 126, 127, 151, 510, 550
Thomas, E. J., 237, 550
Thompson, G. C., 284, 525
Thompson, J. D., 26, 258, 180, 428, 550
Thompson, V. A., 15, 547
Thomson, D., 308, 550
Thrasher, J. H., 122, 123, 507, 525
Tichy, N., 460, 462, 510
Tinto, V., 226, 550
Toren, N., 91, 550
Trist, E. L., 534
Tropp, A., 275, 538
Trow, W. C., 63, 257, 274, 290, 535, 550

Trzinski, E., 163, 515
Tuden, A., 550
Tuma, A. H., 49, 50, 550
Tumin, M. W., 111, 137, 550
Turnbull, J. G., 427, 539
Turner, A. N., 63, 187, 550, 551
Turner, C., 462, 542
Tweed, D. L., 142, 148, 399, 400, 401, 508

Udy, S. J., Jr., 99, 551
Underwood, K. W., 172, 551
Uphoff, W. H., 182, 551
Uris, L., 175
Urwick, L., 437, 537
Uyeki, E. S., 56, 442, 551

Vallier, I. A., 41, 551
Van Der Zandern, J. W., 551
Van Steenber, N. J., 297, 518
Van Zelst, R., 551
Vaughan, E. M., 551
Verba, S., 476, 478, 511
Vianello, M., xxiv, 551
Vincent, M. J., 271, 551
Viteles, M. S., 551
Vogel, E. F., 156, 551
Vollmer, H. M., 236, 270, 551
Vredevoe, L. E., 47, 551
Vucinich, A., 425, 551

Wach, H., 310, 551
Waldo, D., 463, 551
Walker, C. R., 34, 187, 192, 270, 551
Wallace, J. R., Jr., 44, 545
Waller, W., 49, 552
Wallerstein, I., 318, 552
Waris, H., 168, 552
Warnecke, R., 226, 552
Warner, W. L., 32, 43–90, 264, 435, 436, 537, 552
Warnotte, D., 552

Warren, D., 68, 552
Warren, R. R., 142, 143, 145–47, 149, 150, 392, 395, 397, 398, 401–405, 407–10, 412, 413, 415, 417, 509, 510, 538, 552, 554
Warriner, C. K., 121, 552
Webb, R. C., 41, 552
Weber, M., xi, xvi, xvii, 14, 91, 98, 113, 259, 260, 305, 306, 307, 308, 310, 312, 334, 450, 457, 552
Weber, S., 552
Weber, W. H., III, 471, 472, 550
Weightman. K., 380, 529
Weihofen, H., 528
Weinberg, K. S., 117, 552
Weiss, R. S., 33, 44, 53, 275, 552
Weissenberg, P., 463, 552
Welch, J. J., 518
Wessen, A. F., 42, 552
Westley, W. A., 552
Wheeler, S., 235, 552
Wherry, R. J., 431
White, H. C., 427, 553
White, R. K., 535
White, W. L., 28, 30, 292, 330, 435, 553
Whyte, M. K., 492, 493, 553
Whyte, W. F., 13, 24, 36, 182, 185, 287, 553
Whyte, W. H., 248, 287, 553
Wiggens, B., 44, 553
Wilensky, H. L., 59, 170, 267, 320, 333, 337, 357, 358, 553
Willerman, B., 13, 553
Williams, R. H., 105, 434
Williams, R. M., Jr., 237, 297, 526, 548
Wilmer, H. A., 50, 553
Wilson, D. P., 247, 553
Wilson, E., 273, 516

Wilson, J. Q., 91, 138, 553
Wilson, L., 172, 329, 553
Wilson, P., 357, 517
Wilson, R. N., 43, 351, 359, 516
Wing, J., 118
Winkler, E. A., 484–89, 491–94, 510, 553
Wispe, L. G., 156, 554
Woellner, R. C., 47, 542
Wolpert, J., 554
Wood, A., 554
Wood, B. D., 330, 534
Woodman, W., 401–403, 538, 554
Worthy, J. C., 554
Wouk, H., 155, 445
Wray, D. E., 185, 236, 554
Wright, C. R., 44, 447, 531, 554
Wright, D., 91, 554

Yetley, M. J., 142, 148, 149, 150, 410, 412, 413, 415, 417, 510, 552
York, R. H., 49, 429
Young, J. E., 443, 538
Yuchtman, E., 139, 545

Zablocki, B., 134, 554
Zald, M. N., 554
Zaleznik, A., 301, 554
Zander, A., 282, 292, 361, 550, 554
Zelditch, M., Jr., 106, 156, 294, 530, 554
Zetterberg, H. L., 3, 280, 554
Zewe, D., 42, 554
Zingraff, M., 126, 550
Zurcher, L., 520

Subject Index

accelerated promotion, 341
achieved charisma, 307
actual goals, 122 ff., 132
adaptation, defined, 143–44
adaptive structures, 339
AFL-CIO, 350
Ahdut Ha-Avodah, 347
aides, mental hospitals, 435
alienation, defined, 9
alienative involvement, defined, 9, 10, 477–78
All-India Trade Unions Federation, 62
allocation as a system need, 155
American Baptist Convention, 332–33
American Institute of Management, 429
American Medical Association, 357
anchorage effect, 298, 300
Andersonville, 30
antagonism vs. cooperation, 158
apathy (utter indifference), 25, 28

ascribed charisma, 307
assassination, 344, 356
"attributed concern," 209–10, 373
    as measure of socialization, 374
authoritarianism by ranks, 434
authority and compliance, 14–16
    defined, 14
    types of, 15

Bank Wiring Observation Room, 178
basic human needs, defined, 470
bishops "without authority," 340
Blau-Scott typology, 96–97, 99
"blue collar industries," 31, 32, 33–36, 75
blue collar workers, commitment, 75
    frequency of primary relations, 165–66, 171, 269–70, 275
"Broadening," 280–82
built-in mechanisms, defined, 336, 343, 354

Bullock's Job Satisfaction Scale, 88
business representation in community, 430
business schools, 259
business unions, 62–63, 118

calculative involvement, defined, 10
California Institution for Men, 259
camps for conscientious objectors, 106
campus fraternities, 401 ff.
canonization, 345, 356
captive audience, 334, 355
cardinals "without authority," 340
caste structure, 278
Catholic church, 223–26, 310, 340, 341, 344–45, 346–47, 348, 419, 456, 495
Catholic parish, 171–72
Catholic Youth Center, 347–48
causal analysis, in compliance theory, 394, 406
change, as a compliance variable, 454, 459
character assassination, 344–45
character-formation, 272
charisma, defined, 305
    distribution, 309 ff.
    familial, 306
    Pope John XXIII, 222–26
    pure in organizational positions, 307–308
    role in university, 227, 330–31
    routinization of, 221, 368–69, 450
    routinized, 306–307
    shamanism, 309
    training, 338
    types of, 305–306, 309 ff.
    Victoria, 308
charismatic position, defined, 313

church, administration, 332–33, 429–30
    consensus in, 237
    orders, 260
    selectivity, 260
    scope and pervasiveness, 267, 268, 272
churches, egalitarian, 172
    elites, 167, 168, 171, 172, 223
    as an intermittent structure, 450
civil defense agency, 143, 148, 392 ff., 466 ff.
clients, 17
    of professionals, 352
closed-shop, 62
coercive compliance, defined, 14
coercive power, defined, 5, 471
coercive unions, 60–61
cohesion and combat discipline, 279
    compliance, 279, 385
    defined, 280
    formal vs. informal, defined, 380, 460
    hierarchical, 291–93, 380
    power, 279, 500–504
    productivity, 279
    of ranks, 293–95
    variability of involvement, 279
collaboration, 168, 169
collectivities, boundaries, 267
    integrated vs. segregated, 159
colleges, classified, 48
    control of, 252
    elites, 169, 170
    leadership patterns in, 205–208
    pervasiveness and scope, 272, 371–72
    recruitment, 258, 366
    selectivity, 260, 366, 373, 375–76
combat organizations, 56–59
    cohesion in, 57–58

combat organizations (*cont.*)
  elites, 175
  honor, 57–58
  scope and pervasiveness, 268
  See also military organizations
combat unit, 310
  recruitment, 277
commitment, defined, 9
  other usages of, 9
communication, and role per-
      formance, 397–98
  downward vs. upward, 242, 411
  functional and structural analy-
      sis, 241
  gap in, 243, 377
  instrumental and expressive, 242
communication, in intermittent
      structures, 446, 448
communication industries, 51
Communist China, 484–94
Communist party, 108, 344–45
Company of the Holy Sacrament,
      348
comparisons, "across-the-board,"
      328–30
comparisons, dynamic, 330–33
compartmentalization, 346
competence, of faculty, 210, 373–
      74
competent noncharismatic, 352
complexity as a compliance vari-
      able, 454–56
compliance, and guidance analysis,
      504–505
  congruent types, 12–13
  cycles, 485–94
  incongruent types, 13–14
  status, in Communist China,
      484–94
  sub-systems, 90
  tripology, 496–99
  typology, 12
compliance trends, 470, 484, 495

concentration camps, classified,
      28 ff.
concomitant, division of com-
      pliance, defined, 422
Confédération Générale du Travail,
      62
Congregationalists, 333
congruent types, 119–20, 485
  of compliance, 12–13
consensus, 232 ff.
  as an intervening variable, 399
  and pervasiveness, 289
  in religious organizations, 238–
      39
  and socialization, 379
consensus spheres, 232–34, 238–
      39
  in church, 237
  in factory, 236
  other organizations, 238–39,
      399 ff.
  in prison, 235
  and status-groups, 234
Consideration, 184–85
control, amount of and involve-
      ment, 71–72
  differential peer, 358–60
  horizontal vs. vertical, 357 ff.
  interlocking, 360
  prediction of amount, 92–95
control combinations, 436–37
control-segregation, 155–56
  scope of, 17
  "tight" vs. remote, 17
co-optation, 167, 168
"core" organizations (of social
      movements), 53–54
correctional institutions, 276
  classified, 28 ff.
"corruption of authority," 188
counter-elites, 160, 214
cross-pressures, 265
cultural goal, 124–25

achievement of, 174, 212
defined, 105
and scope and pervasiveness, 272
culture, defined, 105
See also cultural goal
curates, 340
custodial mental hospitals, classified, 29 ff.
goals and effectiveness, 117
customers, 17, 18, 20

decisions, ends and means, 313, 350–51
defiance, conspicuous, 199
ritual, 199
deviance, and charisma, 325 ff.
differential peer control, 361–63
differential rank structure, 278
Discalced Carmelites, 219 ff.
dismissal, 343
dissensus and role socialization, 379
distributive justice, defined, 465, 469
divisions, compliance in, 31–32
types of, 422, 423, 439
divisions, of hospitals, 359
of organizations, 426 ff.
of professional organizations, 52
doctor's personality, 353
domination as a compliance variable, 78–79
Donatist heresy, 341, 356
dual compliance structures, defined, 55
types of, 55 ff.
dynamic hypothesis, 14, 119–20, 330–33, 485 ff.

ecological segregation, 274
economic effectiveness, measure of, 149–50

economic goals, defined, 73, 105, 124–25
educational organizations, adult, 376–77
classified, 45–49
units, subordinated, 337
Edwards Personal Preference Schedule, 307
effectiveness, compared to survival defined, 110, 133, 144
and involvement, 201–205, 213
mode, 110–11, 137–38
related to leadership behavior, 200–201, 213
role of recruitment and selectivity, 258–63, 366–70, 375
role of socialization in, 396–97
types of, 147–49
elite, dual-structure, 183
goals, 107
elite hierarchy, 157, 170–76, 189, 194, 216–17
as related to goal-means hierarchy, 157–58
elites, and cultural integration, 27
defined, 5, 153
differentiated vs. amalgamated, 159
higher and lower, 153, 303–304
interrelations, 157–58
role in intermittent sturcture, 448
and subcollectivities, 158–59
types of, 154
employees, 17, 20
Essenes, 402
esteem as a source of compliance, 36, 474–76
European Economic Community, 497–99, 500
exchange theory, 465–69, 472–73
excommunication, 343, 344
execution, 344, 356

executive, 329, 423 ff.
  and business, 319
  as compliance specialists, 428–33
  lists of qualities, 429
  mobility, 427–38
expert, charismatic, 317
expressive activities, 155 ff. 202–204
  communication, 358
  involvement, in three types of organizations, 313
expressive leaders, professionals as, 174, 192 ff.
expressive leadership behavior, 162, 192, 197, 205, 209, 369
expulsion, 343, 356
external factors of effectiveness, 140, 196, 370, 414, 464–65
external relations as a compliance variable, 59, 454

factions, 347, 349
factories, absenteeism, 284
  consensus in, 236
  educational programs, 248–49
  primary groups, 270
  recreational activities, 271
  reducing scope, 271
  relations among elites, 157–58
  scope and pervasiveness, 268
  socialization in, 248
  in Soviet Russia, 425
  as a total organization, 270
  in Tsarist Russia, 270
"faculties," 346
farm cooperatives, 144 ff., 393 ff.
Father Feeney, 347–48
"federal" organizations, 331
Federation of the West Indies, 497–98, 500
field assignments, 339
flow model, 261–63

Flying Tigers, 219, 349
force, 5, 27
forced labor camps, 27, 106, 113
foreman as a leader, 177 ff.
formal leaders, 357
formalization as a compliance variable, 454, 456–57
formed organization (*see* organization)
foundations, 350
Franciscan order, 343–44
functional alternatives, 314, 406
  vs. equivalents, 110, 137
functional prerequisites, defined, 141
  operationalized, 142 ff.
functionalism, 110–11, 137 ff., 314

General Confederation of Italian Labor, 62
general hospitals, classified, 42–43
  scope and pervasiveness, 269, 275
generalists, defined, 314, 315, 325
goal attainment, defined, 143–44
goal model, 133
  compared to system model, 138–41
goal specificity as a compliance variable, 150–51
goals (*see* organizational goals)
goals, organizational, classified, 104 ff.
  congruence of, 122–23
  defined, 103–104
  as a front, 104
  as incongruence grows, 130
  as part of a continuous cycle, 485
  specificity of, 150–51
"great men," 156, 183
guidability theory, variables of, 504–505

halo effect, 267

Harvard, 347, 348

Hawthorne, 187

heretics, 337

hiererchical-cohesion, defined, 281, 380

"hierarchical teamwork," 358

homes for aged, 31, 106

horizontal control, 357 ff.

horizontal division of compliance, 423

hospitals, 362, 429

    communication flows, 377–78

    compliance structure of, 68 ff.

    goals, 421

    heads, 329

human relations, 185–87

Hyde Park, 339

ideal types, 309, 311, 328

ideological unions, 61

I.L.G.W.U. (International Ladies' Garment Workers Union), 63, 64

incompatible role orientations, 155

incompetent charismatic, 352

incongruence, as a dynamic situation, 130–31

incongruent types, 119–20

    of compliance, 13–14

    mental hospitals as, 119

    of organizational structures, 125–26

Index of Required Labor Commitment, 196

individual role performance, 395, 402–403

Industrial Workers of the World, 62

industries, classified, 31 ff.

    goals and compliance, 107

    types of, 24, 25

influence typology, 85

informal group structure, 380–84, 460–62

Initiating structure, 184, 185

inmates, 17 ff.

instrumental activities, 155 ff.

instrumental leadership, 215, 217

integration, cultural, 231

    defined, 143, 144

    and elites, 231

    social, normative, 155, 162, 176

integrative mechanisms among units, 497–98

interdependence as a compliance variable, 454, 457–58

interlocking controls, 360 ff.

intermittent division of compliance, 439, 449–51

internal factors of effectiveness, 140, 196, 414

Inter-Nation Simulation model, 501

International Alliance of Theatrical and Stage Employees and Moving Picture Machine Operators, 64

International Brotherhood of Electrical Workers, 63

International Typographical Union, 62–63

interns, 355

inter-unit links, 496–500

involvement, defined, 8, 69

    continuum of, 11

    cycle, 486–87

    and effectiveness, 203–205

    "established," 256–57, 417

    and hierarchical cohesion, 390

    "initial," 256, 261

    kinds of, 9–11

    in the organization, defined, 11

    and power, 68 ff., 80

involvement, intensification of, 298
involvement, legitimation, and
    need-dispositions, 15–16
isolation, 345

Janizaries, 256
Jesuit order, 260, 349
    elite hierarchy, 171
job satisfaction, 34, 53
    and cohesion, 289–90, 301–302,
        380–81
    and role accuracy, 87–89
    and scope, 383–84

kibbutzim, shifting structure, 407,
    444, 469

labor market, 355
labor unions, 7–8, 320, 338, 358,
    424–26, 428–29
    in Britain, 424–25
    classified, 59–65
    coercion in, 60
    elites, 170
    goals, 118
    influence on members' voting,
        267
    participation, 18
    role of ideology, 61–62
    scope of pervasiveness, 274
    shifting compliance, 424–43
    in Soviet Russia, 425–26
    types of, 24
Latin America, juntas, 108
Leader Behavior Description
    Questionnaire, 197
leaders, expressive and instru-
    mental, 157
    formal, informal, defined, 154–
        55
    informal, foreman vs. workers,
        182–83

in business organizations, 192–
    94
in churches, 197 ff., 226 ff.
in educational institutions,
    205 ff.
in a military organization, 213,
    385
in a mental patient rehabilitation
    program, 214
in prison, 162 ff.
leadership, as a compliance pre-
    dictor, 92
    definitions, 179–80
    strategies and labor commit-
        ment, 195–97
    styles, 437
leadership-absorption, 167
leadership climate, 80, 385–86
library, 427
Likert Scale, 131, 393–93
lower participants, defined, 5, 17
    and commitment, 74, 195–96
    types of, 17–20, 199
L (line)-structure, 310, 319–20,
    326, 330 ff., 355, 357, 362
Luther, 350

Machiavellianism, 387–88
Mapai, 347
March of Dimes, 24, 114, 444, 447
medical profession, 457
    ward, 359
medicine, practice and income, 323
    aides, 123–24, 435
    custodial, 29 ff.
    goal of, 105
    leaves, 269, 273
    members, 17, 19, 20
    mental hospitals, 119, 175–76
    participation, 18
    scope and pervasiveness, 269
mental hospitals, and correctional
    institutions, compared, 29–30

mental hospitals, elites, 174–76
  goals, 122–23
  therapeutic, 49–51
Michigan studies in leadership,
  156, 180
military, and civilian career of
  generals, 431, 433
military alliances, cohesion of, 500
military organizations, 343 ff.
  and charisma, 308–309
  and cohesion, 283, 292, 297
  draftees, 76–78, 213, 388
  intermittent compliance, 445
  reserves, 448
  shifting compliance, 442, 443–
    44
  socialization, 250
  types of, 24, 25
  use of power in, 78
military schools, 337
ministers as elites, 197
  evaluated by lay church mem-
    bers, 197–98
mobility, executives, 427–38
  in organizations, 341, 339, 325–
    26
Mobilization for Youth, 130–31,
  217, 464–65
mobilized system model, 136
monasteries, 268, 274
moral involvement, defined, 9–10
  two kinds of, 10–11
Mormons, 320

natural scientists, 205–207
  selection of students by, 366–67
  socialization by, 366–67
natural system model, 135
neophyte, 337
newspapers, 52, 72–73, 347
nonconformist enclave, 219 ff.
normative compliance, defined, 14

compared to normative authority,
  15
normative integration, 157
normative organizations, and expressive socialization, 272
  scope and pervasiveness, 268,
    272–76
  stratification in, 278
normative power and charisma,
  305–306
  defined, 5, 471
normative unions, 61–62, 63–64
novice, 338–39
nunneries, 268, 274
nurses, 275, 379

observation, 337, 355
occupational communities, 275
"officers," defined, 154
Ohio leadership studies, 343–44,
  349
orders, 106, 268, 340, 341, 343–
  44, 349
  discipline, 346–47
  functional requimements of,
    116 ff.
  goals, defined, 104, 124–25
organization, definition, 111
organizational boundaries, 20–21,
  257, 359, 382, 404, 462–64
organizational correlates, 493–94
organizational decision-making,
  145 ff.
organizational divisions, compliance in, 426–27
organizational effectiveness, measures of, 81
organizational environment, 148–
  50
organizational goals compared to
  elite goals, 107
  and compliance, 421–22
  development strategies, 479–80

organizational goals compared to
elite goals (*cont.*)
  goal-setting collectivity, 421
  multi-goal structures, 107, 118
  as related to elite hierarchy, 157–58
organizational quality, defined, 262
  related to selectivity and socialization, 262–64
organizational representatives, 5
organizational state, 330–31
  normal, transition, and high
    activity period, 440–41
organizational structures, incongruent types, 126–27
other-directed, 11
"Outer-Mongolia" device, 345, 346

pace of activities and compliance,
  439 ff.
parishioners, 20
participants, types of, 5, 17–20
  loyal, intermittent, "big event,"
    450
participation, 256 ff.
  church attendance, 239
  dimensions of, 17, 20
  effect of external membership,
    13–14
  in parties and unions, 424–25
  in various types of organizations,
    18–19
path model of causal relationships,
  404, 414, 453
patients, 355
  compliance of, 42–43, 379
  discipline of, 321–22
  involvement, 68
  mental, 49–50
patronage, 109
peacetime armies, scope and pervasiveness, 268

See also military organizations,
  combat organizations
pedagogic compliance motivation,
  dependent on organizational
  recruitment, 373–74
  as indicator of selectivity, 374
  as measure of student involvement, 211
peer-cohesion, defined, 281, 380
Perceived Closeness of Supervision
  Scale, 72
performance, as a participation-dimension, 17, 20
  and personalism, 369–70
personality and compliance, 269,
  314–15, 433–36
pervasiveness, defined, 268, 404
  compared to consensus, 268
  as a continuous variable, 389
  range of, 268, 372
planned organizational change,
  479–84
policy cycle, described, 487–90
political goals, 107–109
political officers, 57
political organizations, 108–109,
  331, 339, 343 ff.
  classified, 42
  compartmentalization, 347
  discipline, 341
  scope and pervasiveness, 274
  socialization, 252
political parties, 108, 347
  intermittent compliance in, 445
  and labor unions, 424–25
  and seasonal compliance, 440
  selectivity, 260
  types of, 24
political schools, 249, 337, 338,
  349
political unification, 497–500
Pope, 333, 429

Pope John XXIII, 222–26
Popular Front, 341
post-factum mechanisms, 337, 343, 350, 356–57
defined, 336
power, accumulation, 346
power, combinations of, 6–8
cycle, 486–87
defined, 4
in exchange theory, 473, 500–504
and involvement, 68 ff., 80, 385
kinds of, 5–6
positions, 5
power, political, 107–108
"power-mix" score, 72
and involvement, 80
power of jurisdiction, 346
power of orders, 346
practice and test assignments, 338
president, of universities, 330–31
of USA, 332
prestige as a source of compliance, 36, 37–38, 304, 474–76
pre-tenure professionals, 358
preventive mechanisms, 337, 343, 350, 354–56
defined, 336
primary activity as a compliance variable, 454, 457
primary groups, frequency, 269–70, 275
principal, 329
prisoner-of-war camps, classified, 28 ff.
prisoners, involvement and amount of coercion, 76
prisoners, caste system, 161
classified, 28 ff.
communication structure, 243
consensus, 131, 235
elites, 160

goals and compliance, 107, 126–27
goals and effectiveness, 116–17
as a non-intermittent structure, 450
primary groups, 269
scope and pervasiveness, 267, 268, 269
socialization, 247–48
production, functional requirements, 112 ff.
professional organizations, 31, 33, 252, 320–23, 327–30, 350–53
classified, 51 ff.
defined, 51 ff.
frequency of primary relations in, 275
recruitment to, 256
scope and pervasiveness of, 275
socialization, 250
two types of, 51
professional schools, 251–52
expressive socialization in, 272–73
professional socialization, 251–52
professional staff, 122–23, 269
professionals, 323, 329, 350–63
and administrators, 329–30
as charismatic, 311, 321–23
protest-absorbing units, 225, 348–49, 350
protest absorption, defined, 219
punishments, compared, 29–30
pure moral involvement, defined, 10–11
pure normative power, 354 ff., 357 ff.
defined, 6

radicalization, 298–99
rank-cohesion, 293–95
rational model of effectiveness, 135

recidivism, 259
recruitment and socialization as substitutes, 263–64, 375–76, 395 ff., 399
recruitment as a factor of effectiveness, 258–61, 366–70, 411
  criteria of, 257 ff.
recruitment means, 255
Red Army, 345
reference group, 381–82
 of professionals, 53, 357–58
rehabilitation, 30, 273
rehabilitation centers (open prisons), 50, 106, 259
reinforcing processes, 447–49
  structures, 446–57
religious organizations, 343 ff.
  classified, 41–42
  communication, 252
  movement from R to L structure, 331–32
  scope and pervasiveness, 274
relocation camps, 164–65
remunerative power, defined, 5
  role in industry, 33 ff.
  role in political entities, 490
replacement, 283
research organizations, 51–52, 88–89, 329–30, 352–63 362–63
reserves, military, as intermittent structures, 448
Retreat Houses, 339
retreat-line, 342
"reverse selectivity," 260
revolutionary organizations, 108, 109
role accuracy and satisfaction, 87–89
role-adaptation, defined, 380
role-conflict, 184
role-expectations, as participation-dimension, 17

role-set, 264
role-socialization and dissensus, 379
role-strain, 185, 186
role tension, 404
Rome, 340
rotation, 437
routinization of charisma, 330, 368–69
R (rank)-structure, 310, 311, 320–23, 325, 326 ff., 330 ff., 350 ff.

sacred-profane, 424–25
sainthood and deviants, 345
salesgirls, 37–38
saliance, of goals, 124–25
saliency, defined, 265, 404
  distinct from intensity, 265
Saliency of Labor Commitment, 195–96
Salvation Army, 350
sanction-rounds (reward ladder), 50
schools, cohesion, 282
  for charismatics, 338
  communication, 244
  elites, 173–74
  pervasiveness and scope, 269, 274–75
  primary, 45
  seasonal compliance in, 438
  secondary, 46
  special, 48
  for typing, 106
  vocational, 47
scope, as continuous variable, 389
  defined, 264, 383, 404
  of faculty relations to students, 372–74
seasonal division of compliance, 439–41

Secretariat for Promoting Christian Unity, 225
sects, scope and pervasiveness, 274
segmentalists, defined, 314, 315
segregated mechanisms, defined, 336
segregation, ecological, 274
temporal, 274
selection, 354
selectivity, degree of, defined, 258
and effectiveness, 366–68
Semantic Differential Method, 77, 388
semi-professionals, 33, 322
servile labor, 113
shamanism, 309
shifting division of compliance, 439, 441–44
ships, 346
compliance on, 56
sidetracking, 339–40, 355–56
significant other, 358
Sisters of Charity, 324
slope, as a compliance variable, 92–95
social exchange power, defined, 471
social goals, defined, 105
social integration, 155
social involvement, defined, 10–11
social license, 340
social movements, classified, 53–54
social power, 354 ff., 357 ff.
defined, 6
social rank, 402–403
social scientists, 205–207
socialization by, 366–67
selection of students by, 366–67
social structure as a compliance predictor, 92
social unions, 62–63, 64–65
social work agency, 234

socialization, 354–55
and consensus, 379
defined, 245
formal vs. informal, 245
instrumental and expressive, 245, 272–73
measured by attributed concern, 374
specific vs. charismatic, 245
socialization, military, 273
socialization, professional, 251–52
sociological effectiveness, 149–50
SOCK (sociometric analysis system), 462
soldiers, 19
solidarity relations, workers, 269–75
Southern plantations, 389–91
Soviet Encyclopedia, 344
Soviet Union, 343
specialists, 315, 323
defined, 314
specialization, 423 ff.
squealing, in various types of organizations, 178
staff, 225, 427
staff-and-line, 426–27
stated ("public") goals, 104, 151
compared to actual goals, 122–23
status and power structure as a compliance variable, 454, 458–59
strike, 118
and compliance, 443
students, 359
evaluations of, 206–208
self-actualization by, 471–72
subordination, a participation-dimension, 17, 20
succession, 309
successive division of compliance, defined, 422, 439

summer camp as intermittent structure, 448–49
supervision, 34
  styles of, 194–95
surgical ward, 359
survival model, compared to effectiveness model, 110–11, 136 ff.
  defined, 110
suspension, 356
system model, 135
  compared to goal model, 138–41
  two types of, 136 ff.
system-needs, 155

tasks, 421 ff.
teachers, 322, 328, 353, 436–37
  control combination of, 436–37
temporal segregation, 274
tension-level, scope and pervasiveness, 266, 390–91
tension-management, 268, 390
tenure, 340, 358
testing grounds, 338
theological seminaries, 249, 251
therapeutic community, 49, 259
  milieu, 273
  orientation, 259
therapeutic mental hospitals, 49–51
therapy, 30
Tito, 350
  as a charismatic leader, 317–18
top position, compliance required, 437–38
total organizations, 265, 337, 348
  and character-formation, 272–73
  two kinds, 268
transfers, 355
transformation rules, 485–94
T (top)-structure, 310, 316–19, 325, 326 ff.
turnover, 255, 273–74

United Arab Republic, 497, 498, 500
United Automobile Workers, 63
United Mine Workers, 64
United Rubber Workers, 63
United States Congress, 350
United Steel Workers, 63
Universalists, 340
universities, 362
  classified, 48
  goals of, 421, 471
  presidents, 320, 330–31
  scope and pervasiveness, 275
utilitarian compliance, defined, 14

Vatican II, 223–26
vertical control, 411 ff.
vertical division of compliance, 423
Victoria, 308
visibility, 349
vocational schools, control of, 252
voluntary associations, classified, 43–44
  elite-hierarchy, 172–73
  participation, 19, 450
  selectivity, 261
  types of, 24–25
Volunteers of America, 350

"wash-out" effect, 185–86
Weber's model of bureaucracy, 113, 255, 256, 259, 260, 288, 312, 330, 334, 450
Western Federation of Miners, 62
"white colar industries," 31, 32–33, 36–39
  scope and pervasiveness, 275
white collar workers, frequency of primary relations, 270

zone of indifference, 155